Handbook of Research on Information Security and Assurance

Jatinder N.D. Gupta
The University of Alabama in Huntsville, USA

Sushil K. Sharma
Ball State University, USA

INFORMATION SCIENCE REFERENCE

Hershey · New York

Director of Editorial Content: Kristin Klinger
Managing Development Editor: Kristin M. Roth
Assistant Development Editor: Deborah Yahnke
Editorial Assistant: Heather A. Probst
Senior Managing Editor: Jennifer Neidig
Managing Editor: Jamie Snavely
Assistant Managing Editor: Carole Coulson
Copy Editors: Laura Kochanowski, Jennifer Young
Typesetter: Carole Coulson
Cover Design: Lisa Tosheff
Printed at: Yurchak Printing Inc.

Published in the United States of America by
Information Science Reference (an imprint of IGI Global)
701 E. Chocolate Avenue, Suite 200
Hershey PA 17033
Tel: 717-533-8845
Fax: 717-533-8661
E-mail: cust@igi-global.com
Web site: http://www.igi-global.com

and in the United Kingdom by
Information Science Reference (an imprint of IGI Global)
3 Henrietta Street
Covent Garden
London WC2E 8LU
Tel: 44 20 7240 0856
Fax: 44 20 7379 0609
Web site: http://www.eurospanbookstore.com

Library of Congress Cataloging-in-Publication Data

Handbook of research on information security and assurance / Jatinder N.D. Gupta and Sushil K. Sharma, editors.

    p. cm.

  Summary: "This book offers comprehensive explanations of topics in computer system security in order to combat the growing risk associated with technology"--Provided by publisher.

  Includes bibliographical references and index.

  ISBN 978-1-59904-855-0 (hardcover) -- ISBN 978-1-59904-856-7 (ebook)

  1. Computer networks--Security measures--Handbooks, manuals, etc. 2. Electronic information resources--Access control--Handbooks, manuals, etc. 3. Computer crimes--Prevention--Handbooks, manuals, etc. I. Gupta, Jatinder N. D. II. Sharma, Sushil K.

  TK5105.59.H353 2008

  005.8--dc22

                    2008008472

British Cataloguing in Publication Data
A Cataloguing in Publication record for this book is available from the British Library.

All work contributed to this book set is original material. The views expressed in this book are those of the authors, but not necessarily of the publisher.

Editorial Advisory Board

List of Contributors

Table of Contents

Section I
Enterprise Security

Section III
Security Policies and Procedures

Section IV
Mitigating Security Risks

Detailed Table of Contents

Section I
Enterprise Security

As new technologies emerge, organizations recognize the need for enterprise security solutions. Enterprise security is important to almost all organizations. Seven chapters in Section I discuss various kinds of security threats that enterprises face today. This section also dwelves upon the risk management, audit and control approaches that could be used for security assurances in a variety of business environemnt, including e-commerce. The synopsis of each chapter is outlined below:

Chapter I

    Xin Luo, The University of New Mexico, USA
    Qinyu Liao, The University of Texas at Brownsville, USA

The first chapter, titled *"Ransomware: A New Cyber Hijacking Threat to Enterprise"* by Xin Luo and Qinyu Liao, attempts to discover the surreptitious features of ransomware in information systems security research. This chapter proposes a ransomware extortion scheme, compares ransomware with other malware, and discusses future trends and research directions.

Chapter II

    Joon S. Park, Syracuse University, USA
    Jillian K. Lando, Syracuse University, USA

The second chapter deals with the benefits, security risks, and countermeasures of e-commerce. In this chapter, Jillian K. Lando and Joon S. Park not only describe the benefits of e-commerce, but also the security threats and risks that it presents, along with the main problems organizations and individuals face as a result. These authors then discuss the proposals that have been established that have the goal of making e-commerce more secure.

Pamela Ajoku, in her chapter, "*Information Warfare: Survival of the Fittest*", presents a basic understanding of the concept of Information Warfare (IW) and the need for relevant strategies to aid its successful implementation. Based on the adaptive nature of IW, she discusses a Survival of the Fittest IW (SFIW) conceptual framework and uses a case study is for its validation.

In their chapter on "*Evolution of Enterprise Security Federation*", Gaeil An and Joon S. Park discuss the evolution of enterprise security federation, including why the framework should be evolved and how it has been developed and applied to real systems. They analyze the vulnerabilities and weaknesses in current security approaches. This leads them to propose the Policy-based Security Management (PSM) architecture for an integrated security framework and the Packet-Marking (PM) architecture for a cooperative security framework. The simulation result shows that the PSM architecture can automatically detect and respond against network attacks and the PM architecture can effectively handle suspicious traffic such as DDoS traffics.

The chapter, "*A Holistic Approach to Information Security Assurance and Risk Management in an Enterprise*", by Roy Ng discusses a holistic approach to information security assurance and risk management in an enterprise. The "information life cycle" with its stage value and the underlying security operatives (gate-points) is designed to protect the information. The "information assurance" framework and its functions are designed to audit the information security implemented in an enterprise. The author suggests that an organization must assess the value and the business impact of the information so that optimal and effective security and assurance systems can be designed.

The chapter, "*An Integrative Framework for the Study of Information Security Management Research*", by John D'Arcy, and Anat Hovav review the current state of information security management (ISM) research and propose an integrative framework for future studies. Using the proposed framework as a guide, they identify areas of depth within current ISM literature and areas where research is underdeveloped. Finally, they call for a more comprehensive approach to ISM research that considers multiple dimensions of our framework and their interrelationships.

Aditya Ponnam, Britta Harrison, and Ed Watson, in their chapter on "*Information Systems Risk Management: An Audit and Control Control Approach*", review the most common risks and threat agents for a typical organization's information technology infrastructure. They discuss the manner in which systematic risk management procedures and controls can manage and minimize these risks

Section II
Security Approaches, Frameworks, Tools, and Technologies

As attacks on computer systems are becoming much more sophisticated—and potentially devastating—than they ever were in the past, new and effective tools and technologies are needed to prevent, detect, and correct the security breeches in organizations. Sixteen chapters in Section II of this handbook describe the development, implementation, and application of various approaches, tools, technologies, and frameworks for effective information assurance and security protection in various types of enterprises. The synopsis of each chapter is outlined below:

Udaya Kiran Tupakula and Vijay Varadharajan in their chapter "*Distributed Denial of Service Attacks in Networks*" explain how DDoS attacks are performed and what best could be done for defending against the DDoS attacks in the Internet. They thoroughly analyse some of the important techniques that have been recently proposed. They also outline some best practices that the users are urged to follow to minimize the DoS attacks in the Internet.

This chapter is designed as an introductory tutorial to the underlying concepts of firewall technologies. In this chapter, Andy Luse, Anthony Townsend, and Kevin Scheibe describe various firewall conventions and how these technologies operate when deployed on a corporate network. Highly neglected internal security mechanisms utilizing firewall technologies are presented including host-based firewalls and the more novel distributed firewall implementations.

The chapter on "*An Immune-Inspired Approach to Anomaly Detection*", by Jamie Twycross and Uwe Aickelin show that, through realistic testing and validation, second generation artificial immune systems are capable of anomaly detection beyond generic system policies. The chapter also outlines the next steps in this exciting area of computer security.

The chapter by Wasim A. Al-Hamdani on "*Cryptography for Information Security*", discusses cryptography from an information security perspective including their practical applications. This chapter introduces classical cryptography, block, stream cipher, and public key family. The chapter concludes with a discussion of the most advanced systems such as elliptic curve, digital signature, cryptography key managements, and the cryptography application in protocols, communications, and e-mails.

Chapter XII

Carlo Bellettini, Università degli Studi di Milano, Italy
Julian L. Rrushi, Università degli Studi di Milano, Italy

Carlo Bellettini and Julian L. Rrushi, in their chapter "*Memory Corruption Attacks, Defenses, and Evasions*", describe representative defense mechanisms to protect from both basic and advanced exploitation of low-level coding vulnerabilities. These authors argue that most of the defensive techniques protect only from a limited set of attack techniques, thus a defense employment requires multiple complementary mitigation techniques. In response to these limitations, these authors propose better defensive mechanisms such as pointer taintedness detection and attack data burning capable of countering any kind of control-data or pure-data attack.

Chapter XIII

Dalila Boughaci, LRIA – USTHB, Algeria
Brahim Oubeka, LRIA – USTHB, Algeria
Abdelkader Aissioui, LRIA – USTHB, Algeria
Habiba Drias, LRIA – USTHB, Algeria
Belaïd Benhamou Technopôle de Château-Gombert, France

Dalila Boughaci, Brahim Oubeka, Abdelkader Aissioui, and Habiba Drias, in their chapter "*Design and Implementation of a Distributed Firewall*", discuss the design and implementation of a decentralized firewall. The proposed framework includes a set of controllers' agents that ensure the packets filtering services, a proxy agent that plays a role of a proxy server, and an identifier agent which is responsible for user authentication.

Chapter XIV

Tom Coffey, University of Limerick, Ireland
Reiner Dojen, University of Limerick, Ireland

This chapter on "*A Formal Verification Centered Development Process for Security Protocols*", by Tom Coffey and Reiner Dojen discusses the importance of formal verification of security protocols prior to their release. A discussion on logic-based verification of security protocols and its automation provides the reader with an overview of the current state-of-the-art of formal verification of security protocols. The authors propose a formal verification centered development process for security protocols. This process provides strong confidence in the correctness and reliability of the designed protocols.

Chapter XV

Ahsan Habib, Siemens TTB Center, Berkeley, USA

This chapter, "*Edge-to-Edge Network Monitoring to Detect Service Violations and DoS Attacks*", by Ahsan Habib, proposes a distributed monitoring scheme that uses edge-to-edge measurements to identify congested links. The proposed scheme captures the misbehaving flows that violate service-level-agreements and inject excessive traffic that leads into denial of service (DoS) attacks. The author introduces a new way to measure communication and computation overhead among monitoring schemes. Results in this chapter show that, compared to edge-to-edge network monitoring scheme, core-assisted network monitoring has higher communication and computation overhead.

Doug White and Alan Rea, in their chapter "*A 'One-Pass' Methodology for Sensitive Data Disk Wipes,*" argue that hard disk wipes are a crucial component of computing security. These authors argue that when an organization does not follow a standard disk wipe procedure, the opportunity to expose sensitive data occurs. The chapter proposes the one-pass methodology, verified with a zero checksum, which is more than adequate for organizations wishing to protect against the loss of sensitive hard drive data.

This chapter, "*Securing E-mail Communication with XML Technology*", by Lijun Liao, Mark Manulis, and Jörg Schwenk, discusses the most popular security mechanisms and standards related to the e-mail communication and identify potential threats and vulnerabilities. Authors suggest a new approach, called XMaiL, which can be considered as an advanced e-mail security mechanism based on the popular XML technologies. The proposed XMaiL supersedes all currently available e-mail security standards in the sense of the higher flexibility and security.

The chapter by Li Yang, Raimund K. Ege, and Lin Luo, "*Aspect-Oriented Analysis of Security in Object-Oriented Distributed Virtual Environments*", describes an approach to handle security in a complex Distributed Virtual Environment (DVE). This chapter illustrates an aspect-oriented approach to the impact analysis of security concerns upon the functionalities of DVEs. A design-level security model for DVEs is provided to show how to weave security concerns into the models of DVE designs seamlessly.

Deepak Khazanchi and Andrew P. Martin in their chapter, "*Information Availability*", discuss the notion of information availability as it relates to information security and identify key first and second order factors that impact information availability. Based on an analysis of the *a priori* academic and practitioner literature, they discuss the implications of information availability for research and practice.

The next chapter, *"Formal Analysis and Design of Authentication Protocols"*, by Siraj Ahmed Shaikh, discusses the concept of formal analysis of authentication protocols. It briefly introduces the basic notions of cryptography and its use in authentication protocols. The chapter looks at the Needham-Schroeder (1978) protocol as an example of an authentication protocol and examine the history of the protocol as a stimulus to the formal analysis of such protocols.

This chapter, *"Access Control Framework for Distributed System"*, by Rajeev R. Raje, Alex Crespi, Omkar J. Tilak, Andrew M. Olson, and Carol C. Burt, focuses on access control properties of a distributed system. It provides a framework that addresses the issues such as specifying access control properties for individual components, identifying components with required access control properties, and formulating compositional models for predicting the access control properties of a composed system from those of its individual components.

This chapter, *"An Implications of FFIEC Guidance on Authentication in Electronic Banking"*, by Manish Gupta, JinKyu Lee, and H.R. Rao, discusses the Federal Financial Institutions Examination Council (FFIEC) recommendations for reliably authentication methods for financial institutions to deploy security measures. The chapter will allow Information Technology managers to understand information assurance issues in e-banking in a holistic manner and will help them make recommendations and actions to ensure security of e-banking components.

Sue Conger and Brett Landry start their chapter, *"Disruptive Technology Impacts on Security"*, with emerging technologies such as RIFD tags, GPS, and smart notes and proceed on to discuss the disruptive effects caused by these technologies on network security. This chapter also discusses the methods to mitigate risks which emerge due to use of modern technologies.

Section III
Security Policies and Procedures

Security Policy is a foundational element in any Security Program. The purpose of a general security policy is to outline the legal, privacy, and security-related responsibilities that members of the institution have. Because probing a network for vulnerabilities can disrupt systems and expose private data, organizations need a policy in place to address Acceptable Use Policies. There is also a need for policies and ethical guidelines for making employees understand the appropriate action when illegal materials are found on their systems during a vulnerability scan. Eight chapters in this Section III discuss all those security policy related concerns and issues. The synopsis of each chapter is outlined below.

Chapter XXIV

This chapter, "*Internal Auditing for Information Assurance*", by Sushma Mishra and Amita Goyal Chin, discusses how auditing helps organizations in internal control assessment, change management, and better governance preparedness, thus enhancing information assurance. Various facets of internal auditing are discussed in this chapter and the role of internal auditing in information assurance is analyzed.

Chapter XXV

William Friedman in his chapter "*IT Continuity in the Face of Mishaps*", proposes a general theoretical context for IT disasters within the wider class of all types of disasters to which a business is subject—whether caused by natural or human action. He suggests numerous practical and proactive prevention methods that can be applied both before and after an IT disaster.

Chapter XXVI

This chapter, "*Business Continuity and Disaster Recovery Plans*", by Yvette Ghormley, describes the tools that businesses can use to create a business continuity and disaster recovery plan. Author argues that business continuity and disaster recovery plan are much more likely to survive than businesses that do not have such a plan.

Chapter XXVII

Yvette Ghormley in her chapter on "*Security Policies and Procedures*", discusses the manner in which organizations can save more by having effective security policy and procedures. Author argues that since attacks are becoming increasingly more sophisticated and while the human element is often the weakest link in security, much can be done to mitigate this problem provided security policies are kept focused and properly disseminated, and training and enforcement are applied.

Chapter XXVIII

Arjmand Samuel, Purdue University, USA
Ammar Masood, Purdue University, USA
Arif Ghafoor, Purdue University, USA
Aditya Mathur, Purdue University, USA

This chapter, "*Enterprise Access Control Policy Engineering Framework*", by Arjmand Samuel, Ammar Masood, Arif Ghafoor, and Aditya Mathur, outlines the overall access control policy engineering framework in general and discusses the subject of validation of access control mechanisms in particular. Requirements of an access control policy language are introduced and their underlying organizational philosophy is discussed.

Chapter XXIX

Sushil K. Sharma, Ball State University, USA
Jatinder N.D. Gupta, The University of Alabama at Huntsville, USA

Sushil Sharma and Jatinder Gupta, in their chapter "*Examining IS Security Policies for Organizations: Precepts and Practices*", review the IS security framework and examine few security policies of few organizations.

Chapter XXX

Paul D. Witman, California Lutheran University, USA
Kapp L. Johnson, California Lutheran University, USA

Paul Witman and Kapp Johnson, in their chapter "*Guide to Non-Disclosure Agreements for Researchers*", describe a set of guidelines to assist information assurance and security researchers in creating, negotiating, and reviewing non-disclosure agreements, in consultation with appropriate legal counsel. It also reviews the use of non-disclosure agreements in academic research environments from multiple points of view.

Chapter XXXI

Omkar J. Tilak, Indiana University-Purdue University Indianapolis, USA
Rajeev R. Raje, Indiana University-Purdue University Indianapolis, USA
Andrew M. Olson , Indiana University-Purdue University Indianapolis, USA

This chapter, "*Assurance for Temporal Compatibility Using Contracts*", by Omkar Tilak, Rajeev Raje, and Andrew Olson, depicts a formal method to specify component interactions involving temporal constraints. Using the component interactions, various types of temporal interaction compatibility classes are defined. A simple case study is presented that indicates the benefits of the component interaction specifications are discussed.

Chapter XXXII

Arjan Durresi, Indiana University-Purdue University Indianapolis, USA

In his chapter "*Spatial Authentication Using Cell Phones*", Arjan Durresi proposes a scheme to use the omnipresent cell phones and the secure cellular network for access and location control. Arjan argues that his scheme also provides spatial control of the entity seeking authentication.

Section IV
Mitigating Security Risks

While the new regulations and statutes are sure to get some attention, the pressure to mitigate data security risks certainly increases. It is becoming increasingly obvious then that inadequate data policies and data security measures can have very costly consequences. Organizations for mitigating security risks invest substantial resources developing complicated solutions that are critical to daily operations and long term success. Therefore, the 15 chapters in this section discuss ways and means to mitigate the security risks. The synopsis of each chapter is outlined below:

This chapter, "*Plugging Security Holes in Online Environment*", by Sushil Sharma, Jatinder Gupta, and Ajay Gupta, points out the various security holes in online environments and suggests a comprehensive framework to defend against these security holes.

Erik Graham and Paul John Steinbart in their chapter "*Six Keys to Improving Wireless Security*", discuss a step-by-step approach to improve the security of wireless networks. It describes the basic threats to achieving the security objectives of confidentiality, integrity, and availability when using wireless networking. It also explains various countermeasures that can be used to reduce the risks associated with wireless networks.

This chapter, "*Human Factors in Information Security and Privacy*", by Robert Proctor, Eugene Schultz, and Kim-Phuong Vu, reviews basic components of information security and privacy with an emphasis on human factors issues. The authors conclude by discussing how human factors analyses can lead to the design of usable systems for information security and privacy assurance.

This chapter, "*Threat Modeling and Secure Software Engineering Process*", by Wm. Arthur Conklin, introduces the concept of threat modeling to include security in the process of developing software. The author argues that adding threat modeling to the software development process will improve the quality of the process.

Christopher Botelho and Joseph Cazier, in their chapter *"Guarding Corporate Data from Social Engineering Attacks"*, discuss the results of a social engineering attack based on a survey conducted in the downtown area of a large financial center in the United States. The authors suggest that corporate policies should include ways to protect their employees and systems from intrusions based on social engineering attacks.

This chapter, *"Data Security for Storage Area Networks"*, by Tom Clark, provides an overview of storage networking technology and the security mechanisms that have been developed to provide data integrity for data center storage infrastructures. The authors argue that data storage is playing an increasingly visible role in securing application data in the data center. He suggests that the established and emerging Fibre Channel and IP standards are required to secure the storage infrastructure and protect data assets from corruption or misappropriation.

This chapter, *"Security Awareness: Virtual Environments and E-Learning"*, by Edgar Weippi, outlines advanced options for security training. The author lists various examples that characterize successful programs. The author cooperated with ENISA (http://www.enisa.eu.int/) to create a new multi-language awareness training program that uses virtual environments to allow users to train on real systems without any danger.

This chapter, titled *"Security-Efficient Identity Management Using Service Provisioning (Markup Language)"*, by Manish Gupta and Raj Sharman, outlines how imminent technologies such as Provisioning and Identity Management, leverage information security and productivity in an organization. This chapter also discusses SPML architecture and benefits of using SPML in detail.

Dwayne Stevens and David Green, in their chapter *"A Strategy for Enterprise VoIP Security"*, describe how Voice over Internet Protocol (VoIP) networks can be protected against various kinds of attacks such as: DOS attacks, crash attacks, packet spoofing, buffer overflow attacks, spam over Internet telephony (SPIT), and word injection.

This chapter, "*Critical Success Factors and Indicators to Improve Information Systems Security Management Actions*", by Jose Torres, Jose Sarriegi, and Javier Santos, presents an Information Systems Security Management Framework (ISSMF) which encapsulates 11 Critical Success Factors (CSFs) along with a set of 62 indicators to properly manage and track the evolution of security management models. These CSFs have been identified as the most cited key factors published in the current information security literature.

Rebecca Rutherfoord, in her chapter "*Privacy, Societal, and Ethical Concerns in Security*", discusses issues of privacy, societal, and ethical concerns in enterprise security. She argues that privacy of individual's data must be considered both internally and externally and laws protecting corporations and individuals need to be understood to keep a company from being liable for infringements of unprotected data.

This chapter, "*An MDA Compliant Approach for Designing Secure Data Warehouse*", by Rodolfo Villarroel, Eduardo Fernández-Medina, Mario Piattini, and Juan Trujillo, presents an approach for designing secure data warehouses (DWs) that accomplish the conceptual modeling of secure DWs independently from the target platform where the DW has to be implemented. Authors claim that their complete approach follows the model driven architecture (MDA) and the model driven security (MDS).

In their chapter "*Survivability Evaluation Modeling Techniqes and Measures*", Hai Wang and Peng Liu introduce the concept of survivability evaluation, especially on the corresponding evaluation criteria and modeling techniques. Their chapter provides an overview of the literature of computer system dependability or security evaluation techniques and their limitation. This chapter will help information security professionals to learn the methods of measuring information security and survivability.

In his chapter "*The Last Line of Defense: A Comparison of Windows and Linux Authentication and Authorization Features*", Art Taylor states that, although much attention has been focused on the role of the network in security attacks, evidence suggests that the computer server and its operating system deserve closer examination since it is ultimately the operating system and its core defense mechanisms of authentication and authorization which are compromised in an attack. This chapter provides an exploratory and evaluative discussion of the authentication and authorization features of two widely used server operating systems: Windows and Linux.

This chapter, "*Bioterrorism and Biosecurity*", by M. Pradhan and Y. Xia, gives a picture how information technology can be used to combat bio-terrorism. Also, this chapter gives an understanding of different Bioinformatics techniques and tools that are widely used for biosecurity measures.

Preface

Information Systems and Technology have evolved to a level that its use is becoming a common occurrence. While the academic profession is still debating the utility or value of Information Systems and Technology, its use in organizations all over the globe is rising at an increasing rate. However, this widespread use of information systems and technology is not without its associated problems. While several emerging information and internet ubiquitous technologies provide tremendous positive opportunities, there are still a number of vulnerabilities and risks associated with technology systems. Organizations invest heavily in the latest firewalls, intrusion detection systems and other advanced security technologies, yet losses from security incidents continue to grow each year. According to the Computer Emergency Response Team at Carnegie Mellon University, during 2003 and 2004, approximately 42,000 cyber incidents were reported. As technologies advance, hackers also advance their tools, techniques, and methods to break-ins. Up until a few years ago, phishing attacks (phony e-mails designed to entice users to give up personal information) were unheard of. Now they are relatively common and pharming (creating phony Web sites designed to extract personal information) has become one of the latest strategies employed by identity thieves. Security experts noted that the legions of infected computers are adding to the number of bot networks controlled by hackers. Symantec observed an average of 10,352 active bot network computers per day, an increase of more than 140 percent from the previous reporting period's 4,348 bot computers. According to Symantec, denial-of-service attacks grew from an average of 119 per day to 927 per day since January 2005, a 680 percent increase over the previous six months.

As a result of the above risks associated with the deployment of Information Systems and Technology, information assurance and security has become an important research issue in networked and distributed information sharing environments. Finding effective ways to protect information systems, networks, and sensitive data within the critical information infrastructure is challenging even with the most advanced technology and trained professionals. Information assurance and security has become an important research issue in networked and distributed information sharing environments. In today's companies, information systems not only support business functions but are also an integral part of business operations. For example, ERP systems (Enterprise Resource Planning) are now essential for organizations and their supply chains. Incorrect information in ERP systems can have serious consequences for the inter-networked companies. Information security means protecting information from malicious threats and damage due to external or internal sources. Assurance in computer security is a measure of confidence that the security features and architecture of an automated information system accurately mediate and enforce the security policy.

Information assurance combines the requirements of information security, integrity, and significance. Assuring information means having a safe information system, which guarantees that information is secure and at the same time keeps its integrity and its significance during its lifetime. The goal of information assurance is to provide trustworthy and significant information to users in operational, service systems that rely on the information for the fulfillment of their objectives. However, despite an organization's best efforts at protection, there have been and will continue to be breaches, even as IT security improves. The difference now is that companies are required to report on more of their financial information than ever before. Sarbanes Oxley, Gramm-Leach-Bliley, PCI standards, and HIPAA regulations, each in different ways, mandate that companies and executives be accountable for the integrity of their customers' data as well as the company's bottom line.

The security breeches with more advanced tools necessitate enterprises to reexamine their security frameworks, tools, methods, policies, and procedures to protect their enterprise data and systems. The purpose of this handbook is to make readers understand the need for enterprise security strategies, current security tools, procedures and processes, techniques, and tools that are required to protect data and systems. An enterprise security handbook that includes methodologies, techniques, and methods to protect data and systems would be a great contribution to practitioners as well as academicians.

To create such a handbook of research on information assurance and security, we decided to launch this handbook project where researchers from all over the world were invited to contribute. The primary objective of this project was to assemble as much research coverage as possible related to the information security and assurance. As you would agree that information security and assurance subject is not only challenging but also continuously changing. The idea behind this project was to gather latest information from researchers worldwide on information security and assurance. Therefore, in order to provide the best balanced coverage of concepts and issues related to the selected topics of this handbook, researchers from around the world were asked to submit proposals describing their proposed coverage and the contribution of such coverage to the handbook. All proposals were carefully reviewed by the editors in light of their suitability as well as the researchers' record of similar work in the area of the proposed topics.

The goal was to assemble the best minds in the information security and assurance field from all over the world to contribute to the handbook. Upon the receipt of full chapter submissions, each submission was forwarded to expert external reviewers on a double-blind, peer review basis. Only submissions with strong and favorable reviews were chosen as chapters for this handbook. In many cases, submissions were sent back for several revisions prior to final acceptance. As a result, this handbook includes 47 chapters highlighting current concepts, issues, and emerging technologies. All entries are written by knowledgeable, distinguished scholars from many prominent research institutions around the world. The authors who have contributed to this book are well known security experts who have been doing research on various aspects of information assurance and security for several years and have tried to present their technical work in most lucid and simple words. It is hoped that readers will find it easy to understand and implement some of suggested approached to protect their organizations from various kind of security attacks and breaches.

This handbook or organized into four broad sections to cover a variety of topics related to the identification, specification, correction, and mitigation of the security threats in varying conditions. In each case, the role of information assurance and security are clearly identified. Brief description of each section and the coverage of various chapters in each section is provided below.

Section I, titled *Enterprise Security*, starts the discussion of informaion assurance and security issues. As enterprises are becoming increasingly dependent on their information systems, Information assurance and security has become an important aspect for safety of their data, information, and systems. Finding effective ways to protect information systems, networks, and sensitive data within the critical information infrastructure is challenging even with the most advanced technology and trained professionals. Information systems security and assurance is a complicated subject, and historically only tackled by well-trained and experienced experts. However, as more and more companies are networked and have started using pervasive computing technologies, an increasing number of people need to understand the basics of security in a networked world. Enterprise security is important to almost all organizations. As new technologies emerge, organizations must recognize the need for enterprise security solutions. The seven chapters in Section 1 discuss various kinds of security threats that enterprises face today. Various chapters in this section also dwelves upon the risk management, audit, and control approaches that could be used for security assurances in a variety of business environment, including e-commerce.

Section II, called *Security Approaches, Frameworks, Tools, and Technologies,* deals with the approaches, frameworks, methods, tools, and technologies that have been developed and are available for use for information assurance and security in organizations. Attacks on computer systems are becoming much more sophisticated—and potentially devastating—than they ever were in the past. As such, organizations need to stay abreast of the latest protective measures and services to prevent cyber attacks. It is becoming imperative that networks must have self-defending capabilities to mitigate security threats before they affect operational continuity. Despite the increased awareness, the recent frequency of security breaches seems to indicate that many companies have not adequately responded to the issue of data security within their organizations. Therefore, new and effective tools and technologies are needed to prevent, detect, and correct the security breaches in organizations. Sixteen chapters in Section 2 of this handbook describe the development, implementation, and application of various approaches, tools, technologies, and frameworks for effective information assurance and security protection in various types of organizations in centralized and decentralized modes of operations.

Section III, titled **Security Policies and Procedures,** is devoted to the important topic of Information security polices and procedures. Security Policy is a foundational element in any Security Program. The purpose of a general security policy is to outline the legal, privacy, and security-related responsibilities that members of the institution have. Because probing a network for vulnerabilities can disrupt systems and expose private data, organizations need a policy in place to address Acceptable Use Policies. There is also a need for policies and ethical guidelines for making employees understand the appropriate action when illegal materials are found on their systems during a vulnerability scan. Eight chapters in Section 3 discuss those various security policy related concerns and issues and offer suggestions for the information assurance and security researchers and practitioners. The discussion in these chapters also discusses the need for effective business continuity and disaster recovery plans and the means to develop, implement, and use these plans to minimize the disruptions in business continuity.

Section IV of this handbook deals with is the topic of **Mitigating Security Risks.** While the new regulations and statutes are sure to get some attention, the pressure to mitigate data security risks certainly increases. It is becoming increasingly obvious then that inadequate data policies and data security measures can have very costly consequences. Regardless of the solutions employed to reduce the risk of data security breaches, a balance of prevention strategies and mitigation efforts is likely the best possible protection. In fact, given how dependent modern business is on electronic data transmissions, it may no longer be an option to develop a data protection strategy. In order to mitigate security risks, organizations invest substantial resources in developing complicated solutions that are critical to daily operations and long term success. Fifteen chapters in this final section of the handbook describe various developments in identifying and mitigating information assurance and security risks in various types of organizations. The authors of these various chapters also suggest some guidelines to effectively implement risk mitigating solutions including the use of biosecurity measures to understand and mitigate the bioterrorism threats.

This handbook is written with the basic computer user and information systems manager in mind, explaining the concepts needed to read through the hype in the marketplace and understand risks and how to deal with them. Companies need not only to invest in more sophisticated security tools and technologies but also to educate their employees about security and assurances. The market is challenged with an increased need for security and assurance to present security in terms the audience can understand and hopefully this book will do an excellent job of meeting that challenge. Therefore, this handbook is also written for the academic and professional researcher interested in developing appropriate and state-of-the-art tools, techniques, and approaches to deals with various issues arising in information assurance and security.

It is hoped that the diverse and comprehensive coverage of information security and assurance in this authoritative handbook will contribute to a better understanding all topics, research, and discoveries in this evolving, significant field of study. Furthermore, we hope that the contributions included in this handbook will be instrumental in the expansion of the body of knowledge in this vast field. The coverage of this handbook of research on information assurance and security provides a reference resource for both information science and technology researchers and also decision makers in obtaining a greater understanding of the concepts, issues, problems, trends, challenges, and opportunities related to this field of study. It is our sincere hope that this publication and its great amount of information and research will assist our research colleagues, faculty members, students, and organizational decision makers in enhancing their understanding of the current and emerging issues in information assurance and security. Perhaps this publication will even inspire its readers to contribute to the current and future discoveries in this immense field, tapping possibilities to assist humankind in making the world a better place to live for all its inhabitants.

Jatinder N. D. Gupta
The University of Alabama in Huntsville

Sushil K. Sharma
Ball State University

Acknowledgment

This book would not have been possible without the cooperation and assistance of many people: the authors, reviewers, our colleagues, and the staff at IGI Global. The editors would like to thank Mehdi Khosrow-Pour for inviting us to produce this book, Jan Travers for managing this project, and Jessica Thompson and Heather Probst as assistant managing development editors for answering our questions and keeping us on schedule. Many of the authors of chapters in this book also served as reviewers of other chapters, and so we are doubly appreciative of their contributions. We also acknowledge our respective universities for supporting us for this project. Finally, the editors wish to acknowledge their families for their support throughout the project.

Jatinder N. D. Gupta, The University of Alabama in Huntsville
Sushil K. Sharma, Ball State University

Section I
Enterprise Security

Chapter I
Ransomware:
A New Cyber Hijacking Threat to Enterprises

Xin Luo
The Univeristy of New Mexico, USA

Qinyu Liao
The University of Texas at Brownsville, USA

ABSTRACT

In computer virology, advanced encryption algorithms, on the bright side, can be utilized to effectively protect valuable information assets of enterprises. Yet, on the dark side, they can also be of use for malicious attackers to conduct pernicious activities. This article attempts to discover the surreptitious features of ransomware and to address it in information systems security research. It intends to elicit attention from enterprises with regard to ransomware—a newly emerged cyber hackjacing threat using such encryption technology as RSA—and to help both academic researchers and IT practitioners understand the technological characteristics of ransomware, along with its severity analysis. As ransomware infections continue to rise, and attacks employing refined algorithm become increasingly sophisticated, data protection faces serious challenges. This chapter draws a ransomware extortion scheme, compares ransomware with other malware, and discusses future trends and research directions in an effort to cater to both practitioners and researchers.

INTRODUCTION

Today's enterprises confront not only keen peer competitions in business society, but also increasingly sophisticated information security threats in cyberworld, as online presence and business transaction are considered as a possible profit-driven avenue and a necessary means for global competence. In computer virology, as technologies continue to evolve, advanced encryption algorithms, on the bright side, can be utilized to effectively protect valuable information assets of enterprises. On the dark side, however, they can also be employed by malicious attackers to conduct pernicious activities in search of profits or benefits. Past informa-

tion systems security research has investigated such malware programs as Trojan horse, worms, and spyware from a plethora of scientific perspectives (Warkentin, Luo, & Templeton, 2005), and relevant strategies and tactics have been proposed to alleviate and eradicate the cyber threats (Luo, 2006).

Young and Yung (2004) indicated that future attacks will result from combining strong cryptography with malware to attack information systems. Very recently, the emergence of a new form of malware in the cyberspace, known as ransomware or cryptovirus, starts to draw attention among information systems security practitioners and researchers. Imposing serious threats to information assets protection, ransomware victimizes Internet users by hijacking user files, encrypting them, and then demanding payment in exchange for the decryption key. Seeking system vulnerabilities, ransomware invariably tries to seize control over the victim's files or computer until the victim agrees to the attacker's demands, usually by transferring funds to the designated online currency accounts such as eGold or Webmoney or by purchasing a certain amount of pharmaceutical drugs from the attacker's designated online pharmacy stores.

This chapter attempts to discover the surreptitious features of ransomware, and to address it in information systems security research. In an effort to cater to both security practitioners and researchers, the rest of this chapter is organized in four parts. Part 1 will address ransomware's underpinning structures (recent statistics and attack methodologies of ransomware infection are also offered); Part 2 will compare the technological differences between ransomware and Trojan horse, worm, and spyware (a sample attack scheme will be listed to address the attacking process); Part 3 will discuss the future trend of ransomware in terms of technological sophistication level; and Part 4 will propose the recommendations for antiransomware.

IN-DEPTH ANALYSIS: HOW RANSOMWARE WORKS

In the cyber world, computer users have faced certain types of threat such as worms, spyware, phishing, viruses, and other malware. Ransomware is an extortion scheme whereby attackers hijack and encrypt the victim's computer files, and then demand a ransom from the victim for these files in original condition. Kaspersky, one of the global leading antivirus companies, warned that ransomware is a serious threat, because there is no way to recover the effected data.

We thereby define ransomware as a piece of pernicious software that exploits a user's computer vulnerabilities to sneak into the victim's computer and encrypt all his/her files; then the attacker keeps the files locked unless the victim agrees to pay a ransom. In a typical ransomware attack, the attacker reaches into a compromised computer by seeking the exposed system vulnerabilities. If this system was victimized earlier by a worm or Trojan, the attacker can easily enter the weakly configured system. He then searches for various types of important files with such extension names as *.txt, .doc, .rft, .ppt, .chm, .cpp, .asm, .db, .db1, .dbx, .cgi, .dsw, .gzip, .zip, .jpg, .key, .mdb, .pgp .pdf.*

Knowing these files are of possible crucial importance to the victims, he then encrypts these files, making them impossible for the victim or owner to access. Later, the attacker sends the victim an e-mail ransom or pop-up window demanding for the encryption key that unlocks the frozen files.

Once the attacker locates these files, there are several processing strategies that he might implement. First, he can compress all the located files into a password-protected zip package, then he removes the entire original files; second, he can individually encrypt each located file, and then remove the original files. For example, if the original file is *"DissertationFinalVersion.doc,"* ransomware will create a file such as *"Encrypted_DissertationFinalVersion.doc"* in order to label the original file; third, the attacker might create a hidden folder and move all the located files to this folder, producing a pseudophase to deceive the victim. The third strategy, of course, carries the slightest damage, and is comparatively feasible for the victim to retrieve all the "lost" files.

Furthermore, when ransomware attacks successfully take control of an enterprise's data, the attacker encrypts the data using a sophisticated algorithm. The password to the encryption is only released if ransom is paid to the attackers carrying out the attack. The attacker usually notifies the victim by means of a striking message, which carries specific instructions as to how the victim reacts to retrieve the lost files. A text file or a pop-up window message is generally created in the same folder where files are encrypted. The text file or message box clearly indicates that all the important files are already encrypted and informs the victim of specific money remittance methods. Table 1 lists all the methodologies used by recent ransomware attacks and ransom methodologies as to what the attacker demands for.

MALWARE COMPARISONS

Despite the fact that the infection record is still comparatively limited, ransomware has become a serious security concern for both businesses and individual computer users. It's a new form of Internet crime that extorts computer files. Ransomwares are induced through the Internet like other computer viruses such as the Trojan horse, worms, and spyware. This part compares ransomware with other types of malware from a technological perspective.

Table 1. Typical ransomware attack and function methodologies

Name	Time	Attack Methodologies	Ransom Methodologies
Trojan.Pluder.a	6-14-2006	Copy different types of file to hidden folders	Remit $10 to designated Chinese Industrial and Commercial Bank
Arhiveus	5-5-2006	Link all the files in folder "My Documents" to a single file named EncryptedFiles.als, and delete all the original files. Create a text file named "INSTRUCTIONS HOW TO GET YOUR FILES BACK.txt" in the folder, directing how users can receive the decrypt key, which exists in the malicious code	Ask victims to purchase $75 pharmaceutical products from certain Russian websites. Once victims make the purchase and e-mail the order ID to the attacker, the ID will be confirmed by the attacker, who will e-mail the decryption key back to the victims if the ID is validated.
Trojan.Randsom.A	5-1-2006	A notification window always shows above other windows to distract victims. This bluffs that a file is deleted every 30 minutes, but no files are indeed deleted	Remit $10.99 through Western Union
Trojan.Cryzip	3-11-2006	Compress document files (txt, doc, rft, etc.), data base files, and multimedia files into a password-protected ZIP file. The decryption key used for the ZIP file is stored in file Cryzip.	Notify victims to remit $300 to a designated E-Gold account. Specific instructions are given.
Trojan.Cryzip Variant	3-22-2006	The decryption key can be dynamically downloaded for Cryzip's new version	
Trojan.PGPCode	5-23-2005	Encrypts all files using RSA algorithm	Notify victims to remit $200 to a designated E-Gold account.

Unlike other viruses, the Trojan horse virus is a type of virus that does not replicate itself. They get into a computer by hiding inside other software, such as an e-mail attachment or download. They are destructive programs that masquerade as benign applications. One of the most insidious types of Trojan horse is a program that claims to rid the user's computer of viruses, but instead introduces viruses onto his/her computer.

Worms, on the other hand, are the most prevalent type of virus that can spread themselves, not just from file to file, but from computer to computer via e-mail and other Internet traffic. They find the e-mail address book of the intruded computer, help themselves to the addresses, and send themselves to all the contacts, using the victim's e-mail address as the return address.

Spyware, defined as a client-side software component that monitors the use of client activity and sends the collected data to a remote machine, surreptitiously comes hidden in free downloadable software and tracks, or uses movements, mines the information stored on the victims' computer, or uses the computer's CPU and storage for some tasks the victims know nothing about. The information collection by the spyware can be going on when the victims are not even on the Web, and can stay on victims' computer long after they have uninstalled the original software.

Unlike worms, ransomware is not able to actively propagate for wide infections. Therefore, security professionals could obtain a sample infection code and further analyze it for possible solutions. Similar to Trojan horses, most ransomware infections stem from the victim's lack of attention on unknown e-mail attachments, careless browsing, and downloading from malware-embedded Web pages that exploit security flaws in the browser. Thus, we believe that ransomware is the second generation malicious software that deploys attacking strategies seeking system vulnerabilities potentially caused by its precedents. As previously mentioned, a typical ransomware attack seeks targets that are victimized earlier by a worm or Trojan, and then grabs a slew of files. The attacker employs a cryptosystem to encrypt those files, and then sends the victim a notification which normally emphasizes that:

1. The files are encrypted, and other decryption or antivirus software won't work;
2. Following the instruction in the notification is the only solution;
3. Reporting to law enforcement or relevant bureaus cannot resolve this problem;
4. Timely remittance is required, otherwise files will be removed.

Ransom viruses can be spread in several ways, including through spam or a so-called drive-by download that exploits a browser's vulnerability when a user visits a malicious Web site. Figure 1 lists a ransomware extortion schema, which indicates the process where ransomware penetrates the system, encrypts important user files, and demands a ransom. The earliest ransomware simply stored the kidnapped files in compressed archives, then password-protected those archives. In 2006, however, attackers turned to asymmetric encryption, like RSA, to lock hijacked data.

FUTURE TRENDS

It is argued that we will probably get to the point where we are not able to reverse the encryption, as the length of ransomware encryption keys are pushing the boundaries of modern cryptography—for example, if we add a rootkit to hide the installer of the ransomware so that if we break its password, it then randomly encrypts the files again; or after, say, five failed logins, it scrambles everything. In this way, it can hold us to total ransom. But so far, no fancy rootkits like this have been reported. Overall, Trojans which archive data tend to present a threat to Western users; Russian virus writers are more likely to use data encryption for blackmail purposes.

Despite the keen efforts that enterprises have contributed towards information security hardening, we, however, deem that the occurrences of ransomware will continue to rise. More importantly, the encryption algorithms used by ransomware writers will become increasingly complicated. As more technologically sophisticated encryption technologies are employed for cybercrime, an encryption war between the malicious perpetrators and the security professionals seems inevitable and increasingly intense. This scenario, again, mirrors what we have witnessed in a cat-and-mouse battle between virus producers and antivirus companies

in computer virology. As such, security professionals endeavor to crack the encrypted code, and attackers, in turn, promptly respond back with more complex methodologies. By the same token, simple encryption codes being cracked by security professionals will trigger the birth of further complicated encryption seeking ransom. Very recently, complex incarnations of RSA encryption embarks and ransomware writers will continue to seek out increasingly sophisticated methods of password-protecting and hiding corrupted files.

Social engineering is now also involved in the spreading of ransomware, as the attackers tend to exploit such popular Web sites as online recruitment to victimize unwary users. Furthermore, the RSA algorithm—or any other similar algorithm which uses a public key—will continue to generate far more complicated digital keys in terms of bit unit. The initial 50-bit key which did not pose any difficulties for security professionals has enabled attackers to rethink the attacking approach and to birth a 260-bit key, which has been extended to a 330-bit key. In addition, the recent emergence of Gpcode ransom virus featured a 660-bit key, which could take security professionals about 30 years to break using a 2.2 GHz computer.

Based on Kaspersky's research, it is argued that the encryption methods are reaching the limits of modern cryptography. As such, future incarnations could be theoretically unbreakable, thereby forcing the IT community to face a dilemma, in that those infected may have no choice but unwillingly to pay the ransoms in order to unlock their important files. Even though the documented ransomware attacks have been fair, the use of asymmetric encryption in malicious programs may continue to evolve to exploit computer users for the gain of profit. According to Alexander Gostev, a senior virus analyst, it is only a matter of time before ransomware hackers have the upper hand. As the criminals turn to ever-more-elaborate encryption, they may be able to outpace and outwit antivirus vendor researchers. With a longer key appearing at any time in a new creation, IT security businesses may fail to win the war, even if maximum computing power were to be applied to decrypting the key. Ransomware will undoubtedly remain a major headache for the security industry. Figure 2 categorizes different types of ransomware, based on the degree to which threat severity varies.

Figure 1. Ransomwares extortion scheme adapted from Brant (2006)

An unsuspecting user accidentally visits a rigged web site, and the ransomware Trojan horse slithers into the PC.	The ransomware zips up **the entire contents of the** My Documents folder into a password-**protected file.**	The user gets a ransom note demanding money, or a purchase at a particular online store, in return for the password.

Figure 2. Ransomware categorization on threat severity

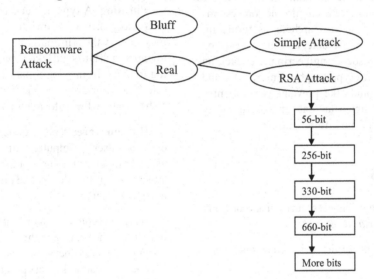

RECOMMENDATIONS FOR ANTIRANSOMWARE

Ransomware started off in the business community, and has now extended more into the consumer space, because while businesses regularly back up data and follow set security policies, at-home and small business users usually neglect both. It will undoubtedly remain a major headache for the antivirus industry, at least in the near future (Oswald, 2006).

Ransomware is currently a PC problem, rather than a Mac problem. Currently, there is no panacea to the eradication of ransomware. We recommend, at this moment, that enterprises, as well as individual users, should take preventative measures to ensure that all important user documents, data, and e-mails are backed up on a regular basis. The multiple layers of security that the typical corporation already has in place will most likely stop the ransonware before it infects the network, because ransomware needs to first seek system vulnerabilities prior to its breach (Fontana, 2005). If people are effectively to protect against these kinds of attacks, they should deploy up-to-date antivirus software, update operating systems, have a firewall that controls what information people can access on your computer, keep up-to-date with the security patches, and using a pop-up blocker can also help, because a lot of ransomware is delivered via pop-ups to keep the computer from being compromised in the first place.

In addition to the system hardening recommended above, we suggest that if people find themselves being blackmailed, they should contact their local law enforcement instead of simply remitting money to the attacker. They should also contact their network security management and software security vendor who might be able to provide possible technical support by recovering their work. This would provide security professionals with attacking traces for possible solutions. At the same time, antivirus companies have to continue working on proactive protection which will make it impossible for malicious users to encrypt or archive users' data.

CONCLUSION

With occurrences of ransomware on the rise, the encryption algorithms employed are becoming increasingly sophisticated. Ransomware will undoubtedly continue to be a serious challenge for both information systems security professionals and researchers, as future incarnations could be unbreakable, and the encryption methods, powered by social engineering, are reaching the limits of modern cryptography. Enterprises and individual users should take preventative measures to regularly back up important data and continuously harden their systems from different layers.

REFERENCES

Brant, A. (2006). The 10 biggest security risks you don't know about. *PC World*, 76-88.

Fontana, J. (2005). The service-oriented business app. *Buzz Issues*, 96-97.

Luo, X. (2006, May-June). A holistic approach for managing spyware. *Information Systems Security, 15*(2).

Oswald, E. (2006). Ransomware becoming a serious problem. *BetaNews*.

Warkentin, M., Luo, X., & Templeton, G.F. (2005). A framework for spyware assessment. *Communications of the ACM, 48*(8), 79-84.

Young, A. & Yung, M. (2004). *Malicious cryptography: Exposing cryptovirology*, (pp. 416). Wiley Publication.

KEY TERMS

Cyber Extortion: The webjacking activity that infects a computer with malicious code that encrypts user-based documents, then demands ransoms for a key that can be used to decipher them.

Cryptosystem: Used as shorthand for "cryptographic system". A cryptographic system is any computer system that involves cryptography. Such systems include, for instance, a system for secure electronic mail which might include methods for digital signatures, cryptographic hash functions, key management techniques, and so on.

Cryptovirus: A malware that contains and uses the public key of its author.

Phishing: A type of fraud whereby a criminal attempts to trick their victim into accepting a false identity presented by the criminal. The common application of this approach is to send fake e-mails to a victim purporting to come from a legitimate source and requesting information or directing the victim to a fake Internet website where this information can be captured.

Ransomware: A piece of pernicious software that exploits a user's computer vulnerabilities to enter the user's computer and encrypt all his/her files, and the attacker keeps the files locked unless the victim agrees to pay a ransom.

RSA: A cryptology algorithm for public-key encryption. It was the first algorithm known to be suitable for signing as well as encryption, and one of the first great advances in public key cryptography. RSA is widely used in electronic commerce protocols, and is believed to be secure, given sufficiently long keys and the use of up-to-date implementations.

Spyware: A client-side software component that monitors the use of client activity and sends the collected data to a remote machine.

Chapter II
E–Commerce:
The Benefits, Security Risks, and Countermeasures

Joon S. Park
Syracuse University, USA

Jillian K. Lando
Syracuse University, USA

ABSTRACT

E-commerce has grown immensely with the increase in activity on the Internet, and this increase in activity, while immeasurable, has also presented several different security risks. As with any other means of business, it cannot be assumed that all players will abide by a code of moral conduct. This essentially means that all users of e-commerce, whether they are on the consumer or supplier side, must be wary of the problems that this technology can present. Both the legal and illegal services present a unique set of security risks that can present immense problems to anyone who is affected by them. In order to combat these problems, the user must first understand them. Only then will they be able to take proper action, so as to protect themselves from the risks presented by online music files. To build this foundation of understanding, this chapter is going to first focus on not only the benefits of e-commerce, but also the security threats and risks that it presents, along with the main problems organizations and individuals face as a result. Lastly, the discussion will go on to argue some of the proposals that have been established that have the goal of making e-commerce more secure.

INTRODUCTION: WHY E-COMMERCE?

E-commerce is a very useful and convenient technology, but it is something that must not be taken lightly, and until its security risks are worked out and lessened, it will not be able to reach its full potential (Ghosh, 1998). The technology is a necessary asset for any business that wants to be successful in today's high tech world. Customers expect that they will be able to purchase items online and that their personal and financial information will be secure and not given to other companies without their consent.

For customers, e-commerce can be used in new commercial ways to do such things as file and pay taxes and attend to other personal matters (Scheer, 2005). Also, e-commerce makes it convenient for customers, because it enables them to directly make payments for purchases made online. A bill can be sent electronically to a customer, who then can authorize the bank by electronic check to transfer funds from the customer's account to the vendor's account. The customer's monthly electronic bank statement then lists the payments.

Technically, e-commerce is a new channel for doing common, everyday actions via the Internet. The Internet's main feature is that it improves productivity, streamlines some operations, and achieves cost savings. Companies that want to affect measures for cost control should use e-commerce as a gateway to more customers, as well as to save on overhead. E-commerce reduces operating costs by improving coordination and communication in manufacturing, sales, and distribution. Research has shown that further cost reductions enhance competitive position, and may also ensure better operating efficiency, but can also lead to downsizing (Mazon, 2001). Using the Internet can also reduce or lower costs by eliminating paper use for certain information—for instance, issuing and filling purchase orders in electronic form, rather than the traditional paper form. Depending on the type of items the company is selling, the company can actually deliver over the Internet, eliminating the need for packaging and printed documentation (Ghosh, 1998). Product upgrades may be automatically transmitted to the customer by computer, instead of subject to the will and memory of an employee to upgrade a product. Furthermore, online electronic catalogs save time and eliminate the costs of printing and mailing. All of these examples make it apparent that e-commerce can be a very cost-effective way of doing business for both the consumer and supplier.

Another positive reason to move toward e-commerce as a business method is the competitive advantage an e-commerce business may have over physical businesses. A "digitalized" company can gain this advantage by adding special features, more options, adapting to variability in customer demand, providing more and better products and services, shortening the product life cycle, and eliminating geographic boundaries (Kuzic, 2005). To have a successful site, the company should offer automated suggestions for accessories, add-ons, or other compatible products throughout the product selection process. The company must also offer substitutions for items that are out of stock. These features are necessary, since digitalized companies do not have the advantage of a live employee to suggest these factors to customers. Furthermore, companies should offer customers the ability to pick up the item in the store that is located nearest to them. This allows for the cost of shipping and packaging to be low, compared to if the company would have to send the package to the customer. This

can also serve as a mechanism to ensure that the proper product is going home with the customer.

Some other key reasons that a company would want to participate in e-commerce are related to distribution control, inventory management, better management of supplier relationships, making payment management more efficient, and channeling management (Ghosh, 1998). Distribution control is improved by using e-commerce to progress how shipping is done, and improve how purchase orders, shipping notices, bills of lading, and claims are transmitted. E-commerce also enhances the timeliness and accuracy of the data transmitted in these documents. When it comes to inventory management, e-commerce is beneficial because it takes less time between order and shipment. Inventory information is transmitted instantly, which is important for inventory management, as stock is always up to date. Also, with e-commerce, there is better tracking than with physical stores, because it is done electronically. This allows for things such as better documentation for audits. As a result, inventory can be reduced, inventory turns over faster, and stocking of merchandise is better. E-commerce also makes it easier for companies to reduce the number of suppliers and the cost of using these suppliers. A result, an e-commerce company would need fewer staff members to process purchase orders, which will further reduce cycle time between a placement order and product shipment (Kuzic, 2005). Payment management is also better achieved electronically, because when electronically linking businesses with suppliers and distributors, e-commerce enables electronic transmission of payments. This inevitably leads to more accurate computation of invoices, faster invoice processing, and lower transaction costs. Also, in e-commerce, electronic linking of manufacturing information with global distributors and resellers lowers man-hours and facilitates the sharing of more reliable data.

SECURITY RISKS IN CURRENT E-COMMERCE

Despite the potential rewards of conducting business via the Internet, there are several major organizations that have been unenthusiastic to embrace e-commerce. Research has shown that there are critical reasons for this concern that we discuss in this section.

Privacy Breach

Contrary to the past, when it was believed that the government was the biggest threat to ones' privacy, businesses represent the largest threat to consumers today. For example, in 1999, U.S. Bankcorp had litigations brought against them for deceptive practices (Marchany & Tront, 2002). They supplied Member-Works, a telemarketing organization, with customer information such as name, phone number, bank account and credit card numbers, and social security numbers. From this information, MemberWorks contacted individuals to attempt to sell dental plans, videogames, and other various services. While this case was settled out of court, it shows how much of a threat e-commerce can present to an individual. The average person would not think twice to question the validity of a bank, but this information shows that any organization can potentially distribute ones' personal information without their consent, which may ultimately lead people away from using e-commerce.

It is claimed that the selling of consumer data without their knowledge or permission is the major internal threat to e-commerce privacy. Clearly, issues arise if a site fails to secure the customer data at either the server or on the client side. It is just as easy to modify customer data, as it is to publish it. This ability to instantly rewrite a consumer's history with a particular business is quite possible and extremely easy to do with the various Trojan horse programs that are installed on an unsuspecting client's machine. An example of the way in which this information is collected and used is with the Internet advertising organization DoubleClick (Araujo & Araujo, 2003). This firm collects customer information and then routes it to other firms for use in creating customer profiles. The receiving firm will then use this information to cater to the perceived needs and wants of the customers. While some may see this as harmless, many consumers feel that it is no ones business but their own as to where they shop online and what they like.

A critical issue that is current is the issue of identity theft, which is the unlawful gain of another person's individual data, and using it in a way that involves fraud or deception (Marchany & Tront, 2002). Examples of identity theft include the stealing of credit card information, home addresses, telephone numbers, and other types of personal data, and since consumers are required to enter most, if not all of this information when using e-commerce, it puts them at risk. Concerns about identity are that it is not only

an inconvenience if someone steals another's credit card number and makes fraudulent charges, but it also can instill fear in people. The thought of another person being able to gain access to ones home address or telephone number may simply turn people off to the areas where this information is highly available, such as e-commerce sites. From a July 2005 poll in Britain, surveying 1,000 consumers, it was found that 17% of them had moved away from online banking and another 13% had discontinued retail shopping online. These numbers are significant, because they show that more and more consumers are moving away from using e-commerce, due to the fear of having their identity stolen.

Solutions for overcoming this problem revolve around the fact that consumers must have the opportunity to know what is going on and be aware of all risks at all times. This includes having clearly defined privacy statements on a company's site, along with easy-to-find contact information, should any questions about privacy matters arise. Further, sites must gain the consent of customers to send out any type of promotional material. At any time, if a customer no longer wants to receive this promotional material, they should have the ability to opt out. Other options include companies purchasing things such as identity theft insurance or early notification if a breach of one's privacy has occurred.

Responsibility

When it comes to protecting consumers, it is difficult to determine who holds most of the responsibility. Does all of it lie with the e-commerce site, or is the consumer responsible for some, due to the large amount of information that is available?

E-commerce site's responsibility: E-commerce sites need to do everything in their power to format their security settings so that the demands of ensuring customer privacy and company resources are not at risk or used to attack other Internet sites. Further, it must be made clear that the many risks that e-commerce sites face need to be attended to in an efficient manner, or the organization risks facing even greater problems. If an organization unintentionally has their network attacked, and the problem is corrected quickly and efficiently, without much hype, they can survive, because none of the sites' customers are likely to be directly affected or get wind of the vulnerability. On the other hand, they will not survive if publicity is generated about customer credit, purchase, or personal data being stolen without the customer's knowledge or permission. For example, a hacker broke through the site of CD Universe, and published 300,000 customer credit card numbers when the store refused to meet his extortion demands (Araujo & Araujo, 2003). This shows that CD Universe was not only vulnerable in the technological sense but also that they were more concerned with their own well being than they were with protecting customer information. This turned out to be a very big mistake, and both CD Universe and the entire e-commerce industry felt the negative affects. Another setback for the industry and CD Universe was when it was discovered during a security investigation that the security weakness in the system was easy to fix and that a vendor patch was available to correct it. Again, this shows that CD Universe was not on top of the situation and made it apparent to customers that their security was not a priority. If, in fact it were, this situation would likely not have occurred at all.

Consumer responsibility: There are a variety of ways that consumers can connect to the Internet, including cable modems, DSL connections, and broadband. Each one of these connections presents an entirely different set of security issues, including confidentiality, privacy, or integrity compromises. It is the responsibility of the Internet Service Provider (ISP) to uphold network integrity and create a model for containing any attack with their domain. The client's main responsibility deals with requiring e-commerce sites to acknowledge the right of the customer to examine their credit history and to be provided with information about who gets that information. It is up to e-commerce businesses to increase a point of reference for their customers that will teach them about some basic security practices. Doing so will help to make certain confidence in the business' ability to secure and protect the customer information.

The main problem here is that it is difficult to determine who should be blamed in a particular situation. There is a fine line, and often times, customers would rather not deal with that line, and consequently stay away from e-commerce all together.

Lack of Trust

In e-commerce, there are a number of different entities, such as buyers, sellers, and third parties. The main problem is for all of these entities to work together and establish a cohesive and trustworthy environment. In the e-commerce arena, trust may be regarded as a judgment made by the user, based on general experience learned from being a consumer and from the perception of a particular merchant (Araujo & Araujo, 2003; Mc-Cusker, 2001; Renaud & van Dyk, 2001). Because it is difficult for people to trust others without first meeting them fact to face, this could have a negative impact on the future of e-commerce businesses. Further, trust encompasses all of the vulnerable areas that have to do with e-commerce, including security, privacy, and communication. It is often a very big challenge for the end user to put his or her trust in all of these areas, so often times, this lack of trust will lead them away from using e-commerce altogether.

Because it is highly unlikely that a customer will ever come face to face with a vendor, there is often a high degree of uncertainty when it comes to initially buying a product. How does the customer know that the product is exactly what it says to be and that it is of the same value? The answer to that is that they do not know, they simply have to trust the vendor's site, which can present a challenge for many individuals. Although features such as e-mail support, Frequently Asked Questions (FAQ), and online chat may attempt to bridge the gap, this is an area that e-commerce will never be able to match when compared with brick and mortar stores.

The solution for businesses that are serious about E-commerce is to implement a reliable e-commerce trust infrastructure. This means that to succeed in the fiercely competitive e-commerce marketplace, businesses must become fully aware of Internet security threats, take advantage of the technology that overcomes them, and win customers' trust. The process of addressing general security questions about e-commerce determines the fundamental goals of establishing an e-commerce trust infrastructure, which should provide user/merchant authentication, confidentiality, data integrity, and nonrepudiation.

The Spyware Debate

There are two sides to the Spyware debate. One is that Spyware is only a bad thing that can negatively affect users, and the other is that there are some positives and benefits that can actually result from Spyware. This statement is widely supported by Merrill Warkentin's Spyware Assessment Model (Warkentin, Luo, & Templeton, 2005). Warkentin's model is based on two key considerations: user consent and user consequences. Giving consent means that a user has agreed to a given software component to be installed and executed on their machine. Consequences are the affects, both positive and negative, that this consent places on the users. The model also proposes four distinct characterizations of Spyware and how it can be classified. The first category is the overt provider. This is a situation in which user's consent to having Spyware installed, and the consequences because of it are positive. An example of one of the positive things that overt providers of Spyware is the use of globally unique identifiers (GUID) to collect customer information that is shared within a network of inter-linked Web sites to better serve the user. This can increase efficiency for the user, as it expedites the use of passwords and personalized information updates. Double agents are a category of Spyware that fall into the negative realm. While it has the user's consent, it is damaging to the user. Components such as these can place damaging information, such as viruses, and then advertise services to the user to manage the problem or remove the offending components, which then results in negative consequences, similar to a Trojan. The covert supporter is a category of Spyware that has a low consent level for users, but results in positive consequences for them. One of the most useful instances of covert supports is that of browser cookies. Cookies personalize interfaces for users, based on their previous behavior. For example, after a user initially enters their user ID and password into an online shopping Web site, that information is saved for all of their subsequent visits. However, we should understand that cookies are insecure. Unless the user deletes his or her cookies, they will not have to re-enter their information, which can often be an inconvenience. In other words, there is neither owner authentication nor content protection in the cookie mechanism (Park & Sandhu, 2000). The last type of Spyware category that is going to be discussed is that of the parasite. This Spyware does not have the user's consent, and places negative consequences on them. "Drive-by downloading" is a big thing this Spyware does. It is when a user is forced to download software after they visit certain URLs. Programs such as these can degrade performance and are set up to make removal as difficult as possible (Warkentin et al., 2005).

In regards to e-commerce, it poses serious privacy and security issues (Awad & Fitzgerald, 2005; Shukla & Nah, 2005; Thompson, 2005). For that reason, it is without doubt an issue that any e-commerce site must be prepared to deal with well into the future. To be specific, in this category, Spyware is the term for a group of threatening software that affects privacy and confidentiality. It is software that, among other things, monitors user's behavior and spreads information about it over the Web. Further, while viruses, spam, and other types of malicious software may receive more notice, Spyware is actually more of a threat.

Although removal of Spyware is mainly a positive act, it can result in more problems. As the Spyware is being removed, there is the chance that valuable components of freeware are also removed. Although freeware is not likely to be of vital importance, the removal of it may result in business interruption while searching for alternative non-Spyware software that achieves the same result. This business interruption will not only result in a decrease in revenue, but it can also lead to a loss of customer base.

One of the challenges to fully receiving the benefits of positive Spyware is that many programs that users use to protect their computers often classify all Spyware as bad, and consequently disable it. For example, Lavasoft Ad-Aware is a product that many people have on their machines. This product identifies all applications as negative Spyware if they remember what the user's most recent files were or where they preferred to save their work. Another example is the fact that cookies, which were developed by Netscape, had the initial purpose of facilitating shopping cart applications and personalization. This is still their primary use today, and it brings millions of Internet users. It would be a severe negative consequence for users if cookies were disabled and they were forced to enter new information every time they visited an online shopping site. Further, if legislation continues to enact laws against any and all types of Spyware, it may be the case that could make valid corporate network monitoring illegal. This shows how extreme the situation could possibly become. Any corporation has the ability and right to know what their employees are doing on the corporate network, and the fact that this might become illegal is a clear contradiction of how technology should be used and the best practices that go along with it.

TECHNICAL COUNTERMEASURES

In order to fight against the threats and risks that e-commerce applications pose, there are several technologies that have been implemented into current practices today. Basically, we classify them into the protection mechanisms of data transmission and commerce servers. In this section, we highlight major countermeasures, but technical details in each countermeasure are not covered here because of the space limitations.

Securing Data Transmission

There are two fundamentally different types of data transactions used for e-commerce: stored-account and stored-value payment systems. Stored-account payment systems are modeled after existing electronic payment systems such as credit and debit card transactions in which a corresponding account of credit is maintained. In contrast, stored-value payments systems use bearer certificates that are similar to physical cash.

Secure channels: The Internet is naturally an insecure channel for sending messages. When a message is sent from one Internet site to another, it is routed through a number of transitional sites before reaching its destination. Unlike voice circuits that transmit conversations, a fixed path is not established for all messages passed between the message originator, also known as the source, and its recipient, also known as the sink. Dynamic routing algorithms can alter the flow of the packet through the Internet, depending on the traffic conditions between the various links that direct the message to its destination. The intermediaries that transfer packets from link to link are generally unknown to the source and sink in a transmission, and any furtive intermediary can intercept, read, destroy, or modify an Internet packet that is passed through its interface. Secure Sockets Layer (SSL) (ISO/IEC9594-8, 1993; Wagner & Schneier, 1996) provides a type of secure channel between Web clients and Web servers that choose to use the protocol for Web sessions. SSL serves two main functions: authenticating the Web server and/or client, and encrypting the communication channel. To accomplish these two functions, both public key and secret key cryptographic technologies are used. Unlike the Internet protocols such as TCP/IP, SSL must be selectively employed by the Web client and server in order to use the protocol. SSL is a layered approach to providing a secure channel. This means that it is simply another protocol in the network protocol stack that is on top of the TCP/IP stack. Because SSL is located on top of the TCP/IP layers, it can ultimately secure the communications of any application-level protocols that communicate via the Internet.

Stored-account payment systems: Stored-account payment systems are modeled after existing electronic payment systems, such as credit and debit card transactions, in which a corresponding account of credit is maintained. In regards to E-commerce, these systems represent new ways of accessing traditional banking services to transfer funds electronically via the Web. In order to support these transactions, there are a number of protocols that have been created specifically for e-commerce. An example of one is the application implemented by First Virtual (FV). In October of 1994, FV deployed one of the first Internet commercial payment systems, called First Virtual Internet Payment System (FV, 1996). The payment system is based on an exchange of e-mail messages and the honesty of customers. There is a very straightforward process for buying a product over the Internet using FV. Once a consumer is interested in a product, they request it by e-mail or attempt to download it over the Internet. Before the product is received by the customer, they must answer the request of verification from FV in one of three ways: yes, no, or fraud. Once the customer receives the product, they have a few days to review it before deciding whether or not to keep it. If the consumer decides to keep the item, their credit card is charged by FV. FV then waits 90 days before paying the merchant. The most attractive feature of this protocol is that it is very simple. For example, there is no special software that is required for consumers to purchase FV products via the Web. Also, FV never asks for credit card information. All transactions use VirtualPIN, which works like an ID that relates the customer with his or her credit card number, issued by the FV company. The credit card number is stored offline, on secured computers not connected to the Internet, and the card is not charged until the FV company receives a reply to confirm the sale. As a result, the security mechanism for the FV protocol is very minimal, because there is no involvement of credit card numbers inside the messages sent over the Internet.

Stored-value payment systems: Stored-value payment systems use bearer certificates that are very similar to hard cash. The bearer certificate is located within a device such as a personal computer or smart card, and is transferred between parties, much like when cash changes hands. Stored-value systems use e-cash as their means of value. These systems are able to instantaneously transfer value with no approval of a bank required. Also, during this instantaneous transaction, bank accounts are neither credited nor debited.

Because of issues such as undetectable counterfeiting, and the ability to have instantaneous transactions, stored-value payment systems are much more secure than stored-account systems are. For example, some stored-value smart cards have secret keys fixed in them that are used to make e-cash (Chaum, 1992; Cox, Tygar, & Sirbu, 1995; Kawatsura, 2003;). A protocol that is currently being used that can support the use of stored-value payment systems and e-cash is CyberCoin (Ghosh, 1998). CyberCoin is CyberCash's payment system for online commerce. Its main purpose, when designed, was for small value payment for online commodities such as Web content. An example of when it would be a good idea to use CyberCoin is when collecting fees for articles, papers, and images downloaded from a company's Web site. The smallest transaction that can be used for CyerCoin is $.025.

E-cash: E-cash, also known as Digicash, is an E-commerce protocol that attempts to preserve the anonymity and untraceability associated with cash transactions. At the focal point of the anonymous transaction scheme is the idea of blind signatures. The Digicash protocol requires two new components: A representative is a smart-card sized computer containing memory and a microprocessor. It can communicate with the outside world via card readers or terminals, and is enclosed in a tamper-resistant package. A certified authority that certifies the behavior of the representative in which it is embedded issues an observer. The Digicash protocol is based on the interaction of the observer and representatives. For example, suppose Customer A wants to pay for some goods bought from B. Customer A withdraws money from a bank by connecting his representative to the bank's terminal. The observer witnesses this transaction and records which notes were withdrawn. To spend the money, A sends the bank notes and his pseudonyms to B. The bank notes are signed by A's observer using a secret key which states that these notes will only be spent at B's shop at a particular time and date. This prevents A from double spending, because the observer is programmed to sign any given note only once. In addition to being used for financial transactions, observers and representatives can also be used for user authentication proof of credentials, and other purposes (Aslam, 1998).

Securing Commerce Servers

If the server side security is not strong, it will most definitely be one of the first targets for Internet hackers.

There are several potential losses that may occur if the server is not secure. For example, information that is located in back-end databases such as enterprise-critical data can be compromised if it is accessed by hackers. If this happens, it can result in the loss of customer confidence, and a potential lawsuit.

Web server: The three main components that make up the Web server are the front-end server software, the back-end databases, and the interface of software. Vulnerabilities in any one of these components can allow not-permitted users to gain access to files and information, which could lead to a very dangerous situation. The best defense against Web-based attacks is to know where the most vulnerable areas of a system are. Once they are known, it is much easier to secure them. Testing is the best way to detect errors in configuration and to determine where vulnerabilities are. Because of the ever-changing nature of the Web, the complexity of the Web server software has grown along with it. This growth in software complexity has resulted in security flaws. One of the problems that can arise is that it is very expensive and time consuming to test for these errors beforehand. The immense majority of security errors with the Web server, result from simple errors that occur when the Web server is initially configured.

Databases: Databases must be access-controlled to prevent unauthorized insiders or outsiders from accessing sensitive data, such as client account information or company proprietary data. An example of database usage with e-commerce is how databases can be used to aid in the implementation of shopping cart systems for online shopping Web sites. Much like a database, a shopping cart feature holds a large amount of data, which can be frequently updated. Databases are very important for Web commerce related applications and are often used for authenticating users before access to certain Web pages is permitted. They are also used for issues such as storing commercial transactions or asking the server for the status of a transaction. Also, commercial Web sites usually place their most sensitive data in the databases that are behind the corporate firewalls. One of the problems with databases is that their performance and security usage decreases as the number of users expands. To fight against this problem, many Web servers now offer a type of fast flat-file format (Kawatsura, 2003). This format is called database manage, (DBM), and it is able to store and retrieve entries from a client authentication database.

The genius of DBM is that it allows for greater access and also is able to store files in encrypted form. Access control is very important to be employed with databases. It is a security control that prevents unauthorized access to the database. Without access control mechanisms in place, it is possible for an individual, either internal or external, to access, modify, or delete any information that is stored in the database. As a response to this problem, the majority of commercial databases offer access control lists and passwords to access different areas of the database. For example, the database administrator may have access to read or write entries to a database, while all other authorized users are only granted permission to query the database. Another vulnerability with databases is that all data, no matter where it originates from, must be processed by an application or CGI program. Doing this creates temporary files, which can be a source of security vulnerability. These files are so risky, because most /tmp directories have extremely liberal access permissions that make it possible for any user to access the temporary directories. The best thing to do with temporary files is to delete them as soon as they have served their purpose.

Server-side scripts: The interface software is made up of programs known as Common Gateway Interface (CGI) scripts. CGI scripts are used fairly often for accessing information from forms on other Web sites and performing online Web site searches, as well as updating the back-end databases. CGI scripts make the Web much more interactive and entertaining to use and view. One of the vulnerabilities with CGI scripts is that they are often used with scripting languages. These languages are a risk, because they can allow the input decisions of system commands to be at the discretion of the user instead of the programmer. If a user decides to change scripts, they can create errors that are detrimental to the whole system. A flaw like this exploits the vulnerabilities in CGI scripts. CGI scripts allow for the interactive nature of Web Pages and give rise to commercial functions. These scripts also play a very important role with assisting in the various business transactions of E-commerce. One of the risks that CGI scripts present is that they can act maliciously on behalf of remote Web client requests (Lerner, 1997). CGI scripts present various problems to the Web server. These risks include the ability for remote Web clients to execute system commands that may do some of the following activities: read, replace, modify or remove files, mail files back over the Inter-

net, execute programs downloaded on the server such as a password sniffer or a network daemon that will provide unauthorized telnet access to the server, and launch a denial of service attack by overloading the server CPU with a computation-intensive task such as file system searches. The problems that CGI scripts present must be able to be worked around, because due to the growth of the Internet, it is not possible to bar CGI scripts from running on the Web server. In order to defend against CGI vulnerabilities, the best thing to do is to create CGI programs that have strong security practices from the start. Another defense strategy is to configure the directories from which CGI programs run. Doing so will limit the amount of risk that CGI scripts are able to place upon the server.

Software programs: Most programming languages used for software applications are not written so that they can prevent server side/software programs from performing risky actions. For example, if a software program is programmed to remove all files on the disk, it will, with no questions asked, do exactly that. This could lead to a very detrimental situation for the server. There are two main techniques for preventing the dangers of server side programs from breaching the security and confidentiality requirements for a Web site. The first one is that software programs are best if they are designed and implemented with techniques for minimizing the types of problems that can be accredited to security breaches. The other main technique is using analytical methods to detect the existence of either dangerous structures or behaviors within a certain program. One of the reasons for the security risks in software is that developers are under a great amount of pressure to create the software in a very short amount of time. This can lead to errors, which result in security risks. Also, software is not developed with security in mind. This is due to the fact that the individuals creating the software believe that security is not their concern, and that only security analysts and system administrators should be concerned with it. This is not a good attitude to have, but nonetheless, it happens, which ultimately makes software risky. In order to lessen the risks of software, the first step is that everyone who may be involved with it becomes aware of how important an issue security is today.

Software test: Testing and analyzing of software and its security is one of the ways to reduce the security vulnerabilities that software presents. This testing must be conducted with no less than two purposes in mind. The first is that the software should meet its required functionality, and the second is that the software should be tested to make sure it does not behave anomalously to unexpected inputs. There are several different analytical methods for testing software. Static analysis is a type of analysis that can be programmed to automatically search the source code for anything that appears to be unsafe. Dynamic analysis is a type of testing that involves executing the program to detect flaws. It studies the behavior of the application instead of the structure. Static analysis, by itself, can reveal the potential for vulnerabilities to exist, but when used with dynamic analysis, the existence of program flaws can be confirmed.

NON-TECHNICAL SECURITY ENHANCEMENT IN E-COMMERCE

Because of the inherent risk that e-commerce has proven to present, in addition to the technical countermeasures described in the previous section, many nontechnical countermeasures have been developed that aid in making e-commerce a more secure technology to use.

One of the most important nontechnical enhancements that can aid in the embetterment of e-commerce is that the current legislation system needs to be clarified. Presently, it is almost like a broad blanket that classifies all Spyware as bad, and it only seems that it will keep moving further in that direction in the future. Since the current legislation is so broad, it can leave many questions unanswered, such as who is responsible for correcting any problems that may be caused because of Spyware. Legislation needs to take a good look at the positives that Spyware emits, and alter the existing law so that these positive activities are officially permitted. This will force more time to be spent analyzing the various aspects of Spyware, along with the positives and negatives that result from it. While this may seem tedious, it is necessary, as the world is only going to become more and more technologically inclined.

Users must understand all of these countermeasures, and each one needs to be continuously looked at for possible improvements. A successful security plan has several important features. It is reviewed regularly, established, takes into account other factors, and sets goals for security. A successful and well developed plan is necessary for any type of business, if they want to be secure. Developing a strong access control policy is another important countermeasure. It is imperative that only the correct individuals have access to certain files and information. If confidential data ends up in the hands of the wrong person, the security of many different people can be threatened. Access can be controlled in several different ways; by only allowing authorized personnel access to certain computers and files, configuring computer operating systems with appropriate object, device, and file access controls, and by deactivating old accounts (Tronvig, Thompson, & Gonnella, 2004).

Awareness training is a very important countermeasure, because any security mechanism implemented is essentially useless if people do not know how to use it. Users should be trained and enlightened of possible scenarios that could arise. Further, usage polices should be set up, and training should be provided on these policies. It should be the goal of both users and the business, that both sides understand the security issues prevalent with e-commerce. Only then can a maximum secure e-commerce experience be had.

Finally, it needs to be said that possibly the most important point to make about countermeasures is that security should be built into the Web application at the design stage itself. In fact, one of the key activities during the design phase should be a detailed risk assessment exercise. With this, the team must identify the key information assets that the Web application will be dealing with. These could include configuration information, user transaction details, session IDs, credit card numbers, and so on. Each of these information assets needs to be classified in terms of sensitivity. Depending upon the tentative architecture chosen, the developers, along with security experts, must analyze the threats, impact, vulnerabilities, and threat probabilities for the system. Once these risks are listed out, system countermeasures must be designed, and, if necessary, the architecture itself may be modified. Countermeasures should also include strict input validation routines, a three-tier modular architecture, use of open-source cryptographic standards, and other secure coding practices (Mookhey, 2005).

CONCLUSION AND FUTURE TRENDS

One of the main problems with foreseeing the future of e-commerce is that it is always going to be changing and will always involve technology that is developing and advancing. It will be difficult for any technology or security mechanism to ever be created that will completely secure the risks of the commerce application. In a sense, e-commerce and the individuals involved with it will always be on the defensive end, having to catch up. Developers must be able to quickly react and combat security issues as they arise, so that any problems will be minimized. Never being able to fully get ahead of the game can cause problems to be compounded, which will lead to a delicate situation for everyone involved.

That being said, research has shown that there are going to be several trends, in the future, that e-commerce will likely follow, if the industry is going to continue to be successful. First, security must be enhanced greatly. Two-factor authentication is going to replace traditional password authentication (Thomson, 2005). Simply put, two-factor authentication is any authentication protocol that requires two independent ways to establish identity and privileges, while password authentication only requires one factor in order to gain access to a system. Many Internet banking sites are at the forefront of this trend, as online banking is an e-commerce avenue that relies highly on trust, to aid the fight against identity theft. One problem that shows the need for two-factor authentication is that many consumers are not educated enough and do not know the proper steps to take in order to protect themselves. For example, according to a study by Bank of America and National Cyber Security Alliance, 87% of consumers polled said that they were confident they could recognize fraudulent e-mails, but a massive 61% failed to identify a legitimate e-mail. Most respondents categorized all e-mails in the study as fake, even though one of them was real (Koprowski, 2006). Further, the study also presented images of sample Web sites and asked consumers whether they could discern whether a site was secure—and a whopping 67% could not identify a secure Web site. What's more, 6 out of 10 respondents relied on symbols, such as "padlocks" to determine whether a site was secure, while 4 in 10 consumers felt there was no real way to determine if a site was secure. Online security is a shared responsibility between the consumer and the business, and it is evident that until consumers are up to speed with what precautions to take while online, that the security of e-commerce is going to have to continue to be enhanced.

Another future trend of e-commerce are the challenges presented with usability and navigation. Many e-commerce businesses still do not know why consumers visit their sites, and while it may not be an obvious fact, being unfamiliar with usability and navigation can lead to security risks (Millard, 2003). For example, if an e-commerce company does not know the reason for which their site is being visited, they may not design the security mechanisms to their fullest ability. There are so many different security tools available, and not using the right one, or using one in the incorrect way, can lead to a very big security risk for the consumer and e-commerce company alike. It will take time and research for e-commerce companies to understand exactly how to cater their site to consumers. Only then will they be able to design it in the most secure way, which will be in the best interests of the consumer and the company.

Lastly, society must have a reasonable grasp of what technology is and where it is going. This is because technology and e-commerce will go on to affect all aspects of an individual's life, including work, school, and play. Further, legislators need to become aware of the issues surrounding technology. Since they are the people who are creating the laws, it is best and most efficient if they are reasonably trained on it.

REFERENCES

Araujo, I., & Araujo, I. (2003, October 06–09). Developing trust in Internet commerce. In *Proceedings of the 2003 Conference of the Centre For Advanced Studies on Collaborative Research* (pp. 1-15). IBM Centre for Advanced Studies Conference, Toronto, Ontario, Canada. IBM Press.

Aslam, T. (1998). Protocols for e-commerce: Paving the way for electronic business. *Dr.'s Dobb's Journal*.

Awad, N., & Fitzgerald, K. (2005, August). The deceptive behaviors that offend us most about spyware. *Communications of the ACM, 48*(8).

(2003). *Building an e-commerce trust infrastructure*. Guides and Whitepapers.

Chaum, D. (1992). Achieving electronic privacy. *Scientific American, 267*(2).

Cox, B., Tygar, J., & Sirbu, M. (1995). Netbill security and transaction protocol. In *The First USENIX Workshop on Electronic Commerce*.

First Virtual (FV). (1996). *The first virtual internet payment system*. Retrieved April 16, 2008, from http://fv.com/

Ghosh, A. (1998). *E-commerce security: Weak links, best defenses*. Wiley Computing Publishing.

ISO/IEC9594-8. (1993). *ITU-T Recommendation X.509*. Information technology - Open systems Interconnection – The Directory: Authentication Framework.

Kawatsura, Y. (2003). *Secure electronic transaction (SET)*. Supplement for the v1.0 Internet Open Trading Protocol (IOTP), RFC 3538.

Koprowski, G. (2006). *Survey: Majority of consumers can't spot fake e-mails*. Retrieved April 16, 2008, from http://www.ecommercetimes.com/story/50872.html

Kuzic, J. (2005). E-commerce benefits: Wishful thinking? *Information Technology Interfaces. 27th International Conference.*

Lerner, R. (1997). *At the forge: CGI programming*. Linux Journal.

Marchany, R., & Tront, J. (2002). E-commerce security issues. *Annual Hawaii International Conference on System Sciences. IEEE.*

Mazon, C. (2001). *Electronic commerce, consumer search, and retailing cost reduction*. Econ Papers.

McCusker, R. (2001). *E-commerce security: The birth of technology, the death of common sense. Journal of Financial Crime, 9*(1).

Millard, E. (2003). *Ghosts of e-business past, present & future*. Retrieved April 16, 2008, from http://www.ecommercetimes.com/story/trends/32373.html

Mookhey, K. (2005). *Common security vulnerabilities in e-commerce systems*. Retrieved April 16, 2008, from http://www.securityfocus.com/infocus/1775

Park, J., & Sandhu, R. (2000, July/August). Secure cookies on the Web. *IEEE Internet Computing, 4*(4), 36-44.

Renaud, K., & van Dyk, T. (2001). Tailoring e-commerce sites to ease recovery after disruptions. *Computer Software and Applications Conference, IEEE.*

Scheer, A. (2005). The power of business processes in e-commerce. *E-commerce Security. IEEE.*

Shukla, S., & Nah, F.F. (2005, August). Web browsing and spyware intrusion. *Communications of the ACM, 48*(8), 85-90.

Thompson, R. (2005, August). Why spyware poses multiple threats to security. *Communications of the ACM, 48*(8).

Thomson, I. (2005). *Microsoft to abandon passwords*. Retrieved April 16, 2008, from http://www.vnunet.com/vnunet/news/2126966/microsoft-abandon-passwords

Tronvig, M., Thompson, T., & Gonnella, C. (2004). *E-commerce security: Risks and countermeasures*. Retrieved April 16, 2008, from http://www.ac.wwu.edu/~tronvim/mis424/Countermeasures.htm

Wagner, D., & Schneier, B. (1996). Analysis of the SSL 3.0 protocol. In *Proceedings of the Second UNIX Workshop on Electronic Commerce.*

Warkentin, M., Luo, X., & Templeton, G. F. (2005, August). A framework for spyware assessment. *Communications of the ACM, 48*(8).

KEY TERMS

Confidentiality: One of the primary security properties that protects information from unauthorized disclosure.

E-Cash: An e-commerce protocol that attempts to preserve the anonymity and untraceability associated with cash transactions.

E-Commerce: All forms of business activities for buying and selling goods or services on the Internet.

Integrity: One of the primary security properties that protects information from unauthorized modification.

Spam: Unsolicited bulk e-mails that receivers are not willing to get. Today, it gradually becomes a serious problem, which results in the significant cost on e-mail receivers and ISPs (Internet Service Providers).

Spyware: In general, any software that gathers information about users or organizations without their knowledge.

Secure Socket Layer (SSL): A security protocol that provides a type of secure channel between Web clients and servers.

Chapter III
Information Warfare:
Survival of the Fittest

Pamela Ajoku
University of Pittsburgh, USA

ABSTRACT

Even though weapons and money are considered important factors for running a modern world, at the end of the day, it is all about controlling and exploiting information for political, military, economic, and commercial advantage. The objective of this chapter is to present a basic understanding of the concept of Information Warfare (IW) and the need for relevant strategies to aid its successful implementation. IW is an important topic in this electronic era and within enterprises, security strategies, tools, and processes are essential in order to maintain a competitive advantage against an adversary or group of adversaries. In this chapter, a Survival of the Fittest IW (SFIW) conceptual framework is presented based on the adaptive nature of IW, and a case study is used to discuss its validity.

INTRODUCTION

Various groups provide definitions for Information warfare (IW) based on their own contexts. For example, IW within a military context is any action to deny, exploit, corrupt, or destroy the enemy's information and its functions while exploiting internal information functions. Although it has been defined in several different ways, the term has appeared increasingly in books, articles, professional military journals, and official publications (DiNardo & Hughes, 1995). In the mid-nineties, the IW concept became popular within certain circles of the U.S. defense establishment as a result of the indisputable fact that information and information technologies (IT) are increasingly important to national security in general, and warfare specifically (Libicki, 1995). There are techniques to mastering IW, and those who do master these techniques will find themselves at an advantage over those who have not.

IW is based on the assumption that information technologies have developed to the point where they can now be employed as a weapon in their own right, and thus wars can be won or lost without shots being fired (Ryan, 1995). The driving forces behind IW include the increasing recognition of information as a strategic asset and the continuing evolution of technology. As stated in a comment by the Washington Post, Schwartau (1996) reports that information warriors could modify credit reports, bank accounts, driving records, and plane reservations. Such malicious acts could bring the stock exchange to a halt. Nothing is safe, and our vulnerabilities come through loud and clear. The possibilities are enough to induce paranoia. As a result, IW is increasingly important to the military, business, and intelligence community. However, eradicating information attacks is not a realistic expectation. A more pragmatic approach would be to protect information and other resources by thoroughly understanding IW and developing formal frameworks to ensure its successful implementation.

IW involves strategies and multilayered attacks. Most of the time, these strategies and attacks are complex. Recently, in view of an increase in terrorist activities, governments are beginning to expand computer network attack capabilities in a silent information war. The inherent vulnerability and accessibility of the Internet makes such a war very possible and easy to achieve. Advanced IW methodologies include creating huge networks of remote-controlled machines or *"botnets"* that attack corporate or government Web sites or send out false messages. News reports also confirm the significance of IW in the 21st century. For example, the Washington Post (Wolf, 2006) stated that the U.S. Airforce was setting up what would become a new four-star command to fight in cyberspace, and stated that the U.S. had already come under attack from China among others. Other recent headlines, like one from the New York Times (Markoff, 2007), confirm that botnets are secretly installing themselves on millions of personal computers and using the collective powers of the evolved network to commit Internet crimes.

The problem of cyberwarfare is not only for well-known or relatively large countries. Cyrus Farivar (2007) in a recent article described the small, wired country of Estonia, in which parking meters can be paid for via cell phone, Wi-Fi can be accessed at every gas station, and national elections can be voted for via personal computers, but is the first government to get targeted for large-scale cyberwarfare. Also, there are various levels and scopes associated with information warfare. Thus, in studying the details surrounding IW, it is important to acquire background information on the topic, and thus the following section provides a background for foundational IW-related elements. A Survival-of-the-Fittest IW framework is then presented, Followed by an analysis of the proposed framework, while the chapter concludes in with framework limitations and a summary.

BACKGROUND

Information has become a strategic and valuable resource, as predicted by Arquilla and Ronfeldt (1993). Whoever controls information flow has a tremendous advantage: "perfect information" for oneself, and imposed ignorance—through either denial or corruption—for an enemy (Meilinger, 1999). As a strategic resource, information can be managed, lost, transferred, deleted, edited, interrupted, fabricated, or enhanced. The availability of information in a digital format makes it more powerful as a weapon. Information plays critical roles in:

- The elimination of ignorance or the creation of awareness
- The creation of actual or implied safety
- The reduction of uncertainty
- The elimination, minimization, or structuring of complexity

These roles take effect on the physical domain, which in turn controls various economic, political, military, and business realms and decision-making.

As a result of the critical roles information plays, it has been employed in a modern type of warfare, now popularly termed Information Warfare (IW). Based on its growing popularity, there is a lot of debate on what IW actually is. At this time, IW may be considered a conceptual framework that enables some degree of information superiority. It uses technology and other methods such as electronic jammers and deception to achieve or promote specific objectives over a well-defined adversary or group of adversaries. Countries, organizations, and individuals engage in IW with the main objective or goal of diminishing the adversary's power, control, and/or competitive advantage. IW is either used for defensive or offensive purposes, and is practiced at a local, national, and global scale within military, political, and business contexts.

The players in IW scenarios can take on offensive, defensive, or dual roles. Offensive IW may include (and is not limited to) eavesdropping, psychological operations (PSYOPs), distortions, computer break-ins, viruses, worms, Trojan horses, hoaxes, fabrication, and harassment. On the other hand, defensive IW may focus on cryptography, codes and passwords, biometrics, access controls, filters, and firewalls. IW is also known as I-War or Cyberwar. The Internet, with its ubiquitous characteristics, has also gone a long way to promote IW. The past few years have seen governmental, military, and commercial organizations widely adopt Web-based commercial technologies because of their convenience, ease of use, and ability to take advantage of rapid advances in the commercial market (Jajodia, Ammann, & McCollum, 1999). However, with the increasing reliance on internetworked computer resources comes an increasing vulnerability to IW.

The concept of an information war may seem a bit over the top. However, the origin of the term "Information Warfare" dates back to the early and mid-nineties

(Crumm, 1998). There are many who do not believe that the so-called electronic Pearl Habor is possible, and even though there is recognition of scary-sounding stories about violated military or intelligence Web sites, many claim that these menacing scenarios have remained just that—only scenarios (Smith, 1998). Despite the skeptics, the ability of using information as a weapon is a very present reality, and it can be inferred that IW will be a significant term in the 21st century. Although the concept of IW appears vague, a number of definitions within different domains are presented below:

Air Force. *IW is any action to deny, exploit, corrupt, or destroy the enemy's information and its functions; protecting ourselves against those actions and exploring our own military information functions* (Crumm, 1998)

U.S. Department of Defense. *IW is defined as actions taken to achieve information superiority by affecting adversary information, information-based processe,s and information systems, while defending one's own* (Fredericks, 2002).

With multiple definitions and interpretations, IW has been described as elusive, an enigma, or paranoid delusions. What, indeed, is the worse case scenario in the information war? Nationwide traffic lights blinking erratically, emergency services becoming intermittent or entirely unresponsive, power blackouts occuring nationwide, national security or business or personal databases are hacked into, and vital information is lost, stolen electronic data is transposed onto physical realities and individuals, businesses and nations becoming even more vulnerable than they are now. This list could go on and on. There is also a difference between IW and information in warfare. The latter is not necessarily meant to achieve the objectives outlined by the definitions above.

Nevertheless, the essence of IW is to maintain the safety and integrity of our information, while being able to manipulate the enemy's information or decision processes that surround such information. To do this, there is a need to understand the ins and outs of IW. Unfortunately, the main problem with trying to understand IW is that actual factual knowledge of real-world examples are not properly documented. In cases where there is documentation, such data is usually not available in the public domain, because the information is usually too sensitive for disclosure.

Computer networks get hacked or broken into on a daily basis, and some of these intrusions are not even detected. Thus, IW is a silent type of warfare where no shots are fired. IW also involves a psychological and mental approach, where the objective is to create unrest and a sense of terrorism. Everything connected to IT becomes a target for information terrorism at some point. Cyberterrorism, which can be defined as terrorism occurring in cyberspace, thrives on the advancement of IT. The famous sentences or phrases from the historic book *The Art of War* written by Sun Tzu and translated by Giles (1910) appears to be echoing in the 21st century. A few phrases listed below:

- "To subdue the enemy without fighting is the acme of skill"
- "All warfare is based on deception
- "The good fighter is able to secure himself against defeat, but cannot make certain of defeating the enemy"
- "Security against defeat implies defensive tactics; Ability to defeat enemy means taking the offensive"
- "The art of war teaches us not to rely on the likelihood of the enemy not coming, but on our own readiness to receive him; Not on the chance of the enemy not attacking, but rather on the fact that we have made our position unassailable"

Networks could be used by terrorists to spread terrorism, but could also be used by government agencies to combat terror. Terrorists prevail in networks as a result of free e-mail accounts, free user groups, Internet Relay Chat (IRC), bulletin boards, and anonymous message boards, which enable faceless meetings and the spread of propaganda. Such propaganda also results in the recruitment of like-minded members or an increasingly uneasy reaction, such as fear and a change of lifestyle on the part of the intended target. Malicious instructions can also be sent over the Internet. Thus, the same tool (the Internet) can be used in favor of the enemy or adversary. However, the advantage is that legitimate Government officials can masquerade as terrorist cell members in order to bring down such cells. Following are brief examples on some other relevant information warfare elements. These include computer viruses, hackers, denial-of-service attacks, public affairs, information operations, and psychological operations (PSYOP).

Computer Viruses

The computer virus is the most famous type of malicious software. Computer viruses that do the most damage are those that are able to spread unnoticeably. Viruses are currently blamed for data loss, data corruption, and system crashes. However, it is important to thoroughly understand what effect such viruses could have in future electronic warfare. In the 21st century, malicious code is able to spread like the plague. Some time ago, a virus named the "ILOVEYOU" virus infected millions of computers with Microsoft Windows using Microsoft Outlook as an e-mail client around the globe. The presence of a script within the e-mail client, which programmers argue satisfy customer preferences, was to blame for the mishap. Also to blame was the implicit social engineering that is needed to trick users into using the code. The damage done included halting activities in the British Parliament and the United States Department of Defense. Other types of malicious software include worms, logic bombs, and Trojan horses. Worms do not affect other programs, as is the case with computer viruses. However, worms replicate themselves and end up swamping or flooding the system.

Logic bombs, on the other hand, can lie dormant within a computer, until triggered or activated by some previously programmed event, such as a date, upon which they can delete or alter data. Trojan horses masquerade or appear to be genuine, and usually accompany freeware or downloads. However, after entry into the computer system, such programs reveal their true nature and can wreck havoc as well.

Hacking

A hacker is a person who breaks into a system with no authorization, or a person who intentionally oversteps their bounds on systems for which they do have legitimate access. The effects of hackers may be described as mere nuisances in certain scenarios, while other effects could be quite catastrophic. Smith (1998) discusses the 1994 intrusion of two young British men at the Air Force's Rome Labs in Rome, New York, which became the centerpiece of a U.S. General Accounting Office (GAO) report on network intrusions at the Department of Defense (DOD) and discussed during congressional hearings on hacker break-ins that same year. Also in 1994—and as reported by Smith (1998), one of the British hackers mention earlier—logged on to the Goddard Space Center in Greenbelt, Maryland from a system in Latvia, and copied data. Based on the origin of the intrusion (n country in east Europe), officials immediately assumed the worst.

Information Denial

There are different ways to disrupt information systems using malicious attacks. A popular method is the *Denial of Service* (DOS) attack, in which electronic systems are flooded with long and repeated messages tying down valuable resources, and ultimately causing the system to shut down or crash. An Internet presence is essential for certain organizations, especially high-profile Web sites, and thus DOS is a serious attack on their information and service-rendering capabilities. If some sites are disabled even for a single hour, this can translate to huge losses in business, in millions of dollars.

Public Affairs

The public information activity directed towards the general public and organized by the media and other groups is referred to as Public Affairs (PA). The relationship between IW and PA has been debated by a number of authors, especially on the grounds of morality and ethics. Crumm (1996) proposes three options with an Air Force context regarding IW roles that could be adopted by PA:

- A Hands Off Policy, which avoids any association with IW (currently practiced)
- A Primacy of Truth Policy, acknowledging the active role PA must take in IW
- Abandon Truth Policy, which suggests that PA abandons its policy to tell the truth and actively engage in all IW activities

Information Psychological Operations

From a military point of view, Information Operations (IO) usually occur in peacetime. In wartime, IO quickly becomes IW. IO are activities that involve the protection of one's own information and information systems. Often, steps are also taken to generate some effects on a potential adversary's information and information systems.

The U.S. Department of Defense (IWS, 2006) defines Psychological Operations (PSYOP) as:

Planned operations to convey selected information and indicators to foreign audiences to influence their emotions, motives, objective reasoning and ultimately the behavior of foreign governments, organizations, groups and individuals. The purpose of PSYOP is to induce and reinforce foreign attitudes and behavior favorable to the originators objectives."

In a document issued by the Department of the Navy in 1997 (IWS, 2006), PSYOPs are also described as being an integral part of military operations, and an inherent responsibility of all military commanders with applicability across the operational continuum from peacetime to conflict.

In any country, PSYOP as an IW element can be very successful, depending on the capabilities of the originator. Military power may be exaggerated by sending off warnings, threats, and conditions for surrender, safe passage promises for deserters, or examples of an impending attack. To achieve the desired effect, the originator must have enough credibility to back up its messages. Military PSYOPs may be divided into categories including:

- **Strategic PSYOP:** Such PSYOPs may be conducted outside the country and outside military arenas; strategic PSYOPs most likely occur in peacetime.
- **Operational PSYOP:** These are conducted prior to or during war or conflict; Sometimes, it is also necessary to conduct operational PSYOPs at the end of the conflict to maintain control or reinforce strategies.
- **Tactical PSYOP:** Tactical leaders conduct tactical PSYOPs; thus, these may be considered a subset of the operational PSYOP.
- **Consolidation PSYOP:** Such operations occur where cohabitation occurs in foreign areas

Despite a lot of effort in trying to understand IW, a number of problems and difficulties have been identified including the absence of a coherent IW architecture (Fredericks, 2002). Thus, Section 3 presents a conceptual IW framework based on the notion of an adaptive environment as is characterized by the 21st century.

SURVIVAL OF THE FITTEST

In this section, it is argued that a Survival of the Fittest IW (SFIW) framework is necessary to become or

remain on top in a sustainable information ecosystem, and the basic tools and strategies that accompany the framework are presented. The necessity of SFIW is attributed to the constant adaptation of IW participants, even though all adaptations are not always successful. It is still essential to remain one step ahead. The development of this framework was motivated by the need to formally document IW issues, models, and strategies, because this is the first step to continuous improvement and suitable baselines for points of reference. The basic principles of the framework are based on the requirements of a robust information infrastructure to support the ever-increasing vulnerabilities and threats associated with information systems. SFIW operates as a closed loop control system, and is made up of seven elements and one base.

The seven elements are *Defense, Status, Vermin, Decision-Making, Report and Baseline, Reactor, and Offense.* Even for a single scenario, these elements and base are nontrivial. The environment becomes even more complicated with thousands of variant threats and vulnerabilities. For the sake of clarity, within the context of this chapter, the *opponent* (or *enemy* or *target*) is defined as the party or individual that is the offender, or that is on the offensive, or just the intended target. Within the same perspective, the *defender* is defined as the party or individual on the defensive side, and/or is about to initiate an IW offensive. Depending on the session of play, both opponent and defender can be described as the *attacker*. A *victim* is the party or individual under attack and within this text, focus will be on the point of view of the party that needs to defend its information systems.

One Base and Seven Elements

Figure 1 depicts an overview of the SFIW framework. The base of SFIW is *Adaptation*. The truly successful enemy (or attacker) is one that can adapt or overcome the unexpected to achieve its objective. Since the information environment has previously been compared to an ecosystem, a biological analogy will also be used to describe the process of SFIW adaptation. According to Hoffman and Frodsham (1993), a successful natural enemy should have a high reproductive rate, good searching ability, host specificity, be adaptable to different environmental conditions, and be synchronized with its host.

Viruses and other threats to the information ecosystem are able to adapt and evolve. Other elements of IW, such as hackers, are also becoming more sophisticated. Hence, the only way for organizations to survive is to adapt their IW strategies and methodologies. If the defensive environment is not prepared for an attack, it falls. The only means of escape for a doomed system is an adaptation. Thus, all seven elements must possess this ability, and remain at least one step ahead of the offending environment's status. This chapter will focus on defining the overview of the proposed framework and their relationships, but will not go into the detailed complexities surrounding their functionalities. IW is an expensive game involving a number of factors, including intelligence, power, challenge, control, psychology, and various resources. Adaptation can take the form of advanced software that can detect potential hacking, rebuild data files, or modify its code appropriately. The issue with the adaptive process is in the time it may take. This is critical time that the defender may not have. Hence, the quicker critical intelligence is acquired, the sooner the system can adapt. Such a system, in perfect working order, will decrease the defending environment's vulnerability amongst other advantages. In a less-than-perfect environment, the same virus or threat that the defending environment is trying to eliminate may reprogram the defending environment's system in favor of the offending environment. The seven SFIW elements are briefly described below:

Element 1: *Defense: Protecting the Home-Front*
The root concept of IW is intended as an offensive stance. However, in view of possible retaliation—and to protect one's own information systems and other resources—a defensive stance is also a necessity. The defense module adjusts its output, based on the current status of the framework.

Element 2: *Status: Current State of Affairs*
The current state of affairs (status) directly controls the other six elements. There is flexibility in the number of status levels that may be configured within the system. For example, a range of Level 0 (meaning no threat) to Level 5 (meaning the highest threat or vulnerability) could be configured, and the system adjusts itself based on the six elements and adaptive capabilities of the base.

Element 3: *Vermin*
This is the collective name for mechanisms that implement IW strategies and processes, including viruses, deliberate hacking efforts, Trojan horses, worms, and targeted denial-of-service attacks. The term "vermin" is used in the context of IW weapons that

are offensive, extremely unpleasant, or undesirable. The categorization stems from the comparison of the IW stage to a biological ecosystem. Vermin, within a biological context are sometimes difficult to control, and for some reason or the other, keep coming back. So do IW vermin, without an adaptable defense.

Element 4: *Decision-Making: The Fast but Right Decision*
It is essential to make the right decision in the shortest amount of time possible. Getting information for warfare in a reliable and timely manner is key in winning the battle. There are many decision-making methodologies that can be applied and managed effectively. It is beyond the scope of this chapter to provide details on such methods. However, using artificial intelligence, multiple criteria decision-making techniques, data mining, and so on can establish automated decision modules.

Element 5: *Report and Baseline: Documentation and Reference Point*
The Report and Baseline is necessary in an adaptive system to ensure that updated system status remains better than previous instances.

Element 6: *Reactor: Enemy's Anticipated Reaction*
Within the SFIW framework, the engine that analyzes, infers, and presents the enemy's anticipated reaction is called the Reactor. The entire information infrastructure of the opponent is of interest to the IW practitioner. Understanding the history and temperament of decision-making entities within the offending environment is also important. For example, military strategists must be aware that they are dealing with an enemy who is part rational and part irrational, and who is motivated by reasons of both policy and passion (Meilinger, 1999).

Element 7: *Offense: Attack!*
This is a partial or full-fledged offensive attack on the specified target.

Information Warfare Strategies

From a military perspective, developing a strategy of information warfare starts with serious, creative and "color-outside-the-lines" thinking about current information technologies and ways in which these might be turned to strategic purpose to serve the national command authorities and military use, but will involve

Figure 1. SFIW framework overview

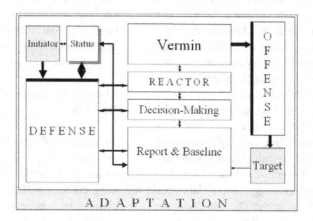

thinking about information in new ways (Stein, 1995). This thinking approach has been labeled "command and control warfare" (CCW) (Hutcherson, 1994). Orr (1993) discusses a series of questions to ask regarding new information thought processes, including:

- What information is needed?
- What organizational changes will occur in the way that information is gathered, processed, distributed, and used?
- What information-based operational changes can happen?

IW is typically applied in a defensive and/or offensive manner using somewhat-complicated strategies and, in some cases, multilayered procedures. Strategies include perception management and deception techniques such as tactical or strategic deception. Borden (1999) and Kopp (2000, 2003) state that all strategies used in IW are combinations or forms of four canonical strategies, each of which involves a specific mode of attack on an information channel or system, and these strategies are defined as:

- **Degradation, Destruction, or Denial of Information:** This is the concealment of information where there is so much noise in a signal so that the receiver cannot discern its presence from that of the noise in the channel.
- **Corruption, Deception, or Mimicry:** This is the insertion if intentionally misleading information such that the fabricated signal appears to successfully mimic a known signal, and the

receiver cannot distinguish the phony signal from the real one.

- **Disruption:** This is the insertion of information producing a dysfunctional environment inside the opponent's system; denial can also exist via disruption amounting to the introduction of a lot of noise into the channel such that the receiver cannot understand the signal.
- **Subversion or Denial:** This is the insertion of information into the channel to trigger a self-destructive process in the opponent's target system.

Opponents must determine whether information accumulated is deceptive, or whether there are multiple layers to particular IW attacks as depicted in Figure 2. It is also important to determine what the goal of a validated deception may be. Thus, there are four important questions to ask and answer:

1. What does the opponent want the defender to think?
2. Why does the opponent desire this train of thought, or what goal does the opponent hope to achieve?
3. What techniques can the defender use to counter the opponent's deceptive perception management strategy?
4. After threats have been countered, what measure can be taken to ensure a superior stance against future attacks?5.

Employed offensively, IW emphasizes the manipulation of electronic information systems using tools like computer viruses and electromagnetic pulse devices to influence an adversary's perceptions and behavior (Ryan, 1995). Many deceptions involve the intentional omission of information by the opponent. Multilayer deceptive strategies can be dependent on previous events, and require in-depth analysis and backtracking to uncover essential details.

Case Study

Schwartau (1996) reports that IW costs the United States an estimated $100 to $300 billion per year, and also states that like all wars, IW needs a stage. In this section, the SFIW is compared to the software development industry. This case study deals with the similarity between the industry, which is still successful today, and the main base of the SFIW framework, which is adaptation.

The Case of Software Development

Software development and the SFIW framework presented in this chapter have a common denominator: their adaptable base. Validating an IW methodology is no easy task. Sometimes, the only way to fully test a strategy in warfare is to just implement it. In-house testing could be done to thoroughly analyze the methodology or strategy. However, based on the response from actual implementation, there may still be need for a revision—which is called an adaptation in the SFIW framework. This is similar with software development. Most software today is tested for security (assurance testing) by the penetrate-and-patch approach—when someone finds an exploitable security "hole," the

software manufacturer issues a patch (Reiter, 1999). Thus, the method of software development has proved successful, simply because there is no other way of achieving the perfect software than to simple let the users test it. The trick is in being able to handle the need for an update in a timely manner. Hence, as in the SFIW framework, subtle codes as embedded within the current status software base (which may also be a beta version, meant for extensive testing), and intelligence is collected to enable the system adapt its current status to overcome established or potential threats. Such adaptation may occur manually, but in the future, artificial intelligence can be built into the framework to achieve a more automated response. An automated response is feasible, using existing and proven methods like data mining to reduce data dimensionality, and association rules to manipulate data dependence. Also, Bayesian networks, which can provide statistical probabilities in a hierarchical format, can also be applied with caution to predict future behavior or responses from the enemy, and prepare the homefront against such an attack.

Another point of similarity and case for validity between the SFIW and software development is the intrinsic intellectual complexity associated with both models. Even the case of nonoffensive hacking carried out by teenagers, simply for the purpose of the thrill of the ride, requires a significant amount of intellectual merit to carry out a successful intrusion. In the same vein, IW carried out for the purpose of actual offence or defense can be multichanneled, multilayered, and intellectually complex. The complexity of IW naturally calls for a framework like SFIW that can adapt positively to handle any loopholes within the system. The need for adaptation is also essential,

Figure 2. Single and multi-layer information warfare attacks

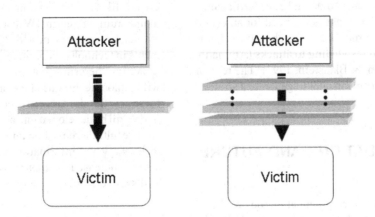

given the fact that various opponents or adversaries may have dissimilar attributes. Thus, it is not the case of *"one system fits all."* According to Yurcik (2000), the intellectual complexity associated with software design, coding, and virtual testing ensures the presence of "bugs" in software that can be exploited by attackers. Contrary to the software industry's possible desire to leave bugs in the product, an effective SFIW model should deploy a bug-free plan to start with, if maximum effect is to be achieved. However, in preparedness for Murphy's law, *which broadly states that things will go wrong, if given the chance*, an adaptive protocol is necessary to remain the strongest party in the game at all times.

Nevertheless, even with the best security patches for software, there is always going to be a need for adaptation as a result of the ever-increasing advances in IT and the determination of the adversary. The natural escalation of offensive threats vs. defensive countermeasures has demonstrated time and again that no practical systems can be built that is invulnerable to attack, and despite the software industry's effort (or in spite of them), there can be no assurance that any system will not be compromised (Yurcik, 2000). Hence, there is a need for survivable systems. Such systems can only exist with adaptation as employed by the SFIW framework. One way to prevent IW attacks from succeeding is to have an IW defense. However, this is also the problem with any existing strategies. The best way to prevent IW attacks from succeeding is to have an adaptable IW defense. Although ultimately preventing malicious attacks from succeeding is key, not all attacks can be averted at the outset, and the goal, therefore, should be to develop an adaptable system that maintains maximum availability, even when under attack (Jajodia et al., 1999). The term IW-D (defensive Information Warfare) is used to describe all actions taken to defend resources against information attacks. It certainly makes sense to defend one's self against attacks. Also with defense is the need for an offensive module. There must be comprehensive support for identifying and responding to attacks (Ammann, Jajodia, McCollum, & Blaustein, 1997). The reactor works with the vermin arsenal to generate a strategy for offense.

RECOMMENDATIONS AND FUTURE TRENDS

This section provides recommendations on IW-D, and future trends of IW. The goal is to deter IW attacks

by providing adequate protection. In this era, most organizations have already taken certain measures to ensure that some form of protection is available for information and other significant resources. Hence, the question is—What else can be done from a defensive perspective? Depending of what level of functional protection is already in play, the following are standard recommendations on IW-D:

- Where possible, physically isolate the resource or provide strategic access control; strategic thinking is important to ensure that the mechanisms used are implemented properly and regularly maintained.
- Continually gather timely intelligence information on potential threats to the information or resources.
- Develop an infrastructure that is useable, repairable, and resilient; there should be adequate warning of an attack, the effect that the attack would have (if successful), and the subsequent course of action in the case of a successful attack.
- Education. There is the assumption that employees and other nonsecurity staff within organizations know enough to keep data safe; people are valuable resources, and need to be continuously educated and updated on what to do, how to do it, and when to do it, in terms of IW.
- Keep up with evolving technology!

Today, IW relates to a wide range of processes including, but not limited to, information piracy, intelligence collection, PSYOP, deception, perception management, military espionage, corporate espionage, attacks on (public and private) communication systems, and consumer fraud. In the future, these areas are not likely to change, but will most likely gather momentum. The entire IW discussion is just gathering momentum, and will most likely evolve as the advancements in technology continue. There will also be new trends in cybercrime. Future research in the area of IW will explore techniques that can successfully engage these new trends in record time. The conceptual phase of IW will be developed into a more operational phase. As a result, there will be an increase in information technology and information superiority careers, and also an increase in companies and organizations that will seek to employ such individuals.

CONCLUSION

The explosion of IT has set in motion a virtual tidal wave of change that is in the process of profoundly affecting organizations and individuals in multiple dimensions (Alberts, 1996). On a national level, the importance of IW cannot be overemphasized. According to Toffler and Toffler (1993), if the world is really moving into a third-wave, information-based era, failure to develop a strategy for both defensive and offensive information warfare could put the United States and the U.S. military into the situation of being on the receiving end of an "Electronic Pearl Harbor." Physical wars can be lost if the control of information is lost. Thus, IW is a very important topic in the 21st century. This chapter presented a Survival of the Fittest Information Warfare (SFIW) conceptual framework based on the constant need for adaptability within information-based wars. The validity of the framework was discussed using a case study, showing that it has logical grounds for robustness, implementation, and for use as a baseline. However, it should also be noted that the framework is only as efficient as the adaptive tools, such as timely intelligence and advanced software, which are essential to its successful functionality.

REFERENCES

Ammann, P., Jajodia, S., McCollum, C.D., & Blaustein, B.T. (1997). Surviving information warfare attacks on databases. In *Proceedings of the IEEE Symposium on security and Privacy.*

Arquilla, J., & Ronfeldt. (1993, Spring). Cyberware is coming! *Comparative Strategy, 12*(2), 141-165.

Alberts, D.S. (1996, April). The unintended consequences of information age technologies. *Advanced Concepts, Technologies and Information Strategies (ACTIS).*

Borden, A. (1999, November). *What is information warfare?* Aerospace Power Chronicles. United States Airforce, Air University. Maxwell AFB. Air & Space Power Journal, Contributor's Corner. Retrieved April 21, 2008 from http://www.airpower.maxwell.af.mil/airchronicles/cc/borden.html

Crumm, R. (1996, June). Information warfare: An air force policy for the role of public affairs. *IWS – The Information Warfare Site.* Retrieved April 21, 2008 from http://www.iwar.org.uk/psyops/

DiNardo, R.L., & Hughes, D.J. (1995, Winter). Some cautionary thoughts on information warfare. *Airpower Journal.*

Fredericks, B. (2002, October). Information warfare: The organizational dimension. *Sun Tzu Art of War in Information Warfare.* Retrieved April 21, 2008 from http://www.ndu.edu/inss/siws/ch4.html

Hoffmann, M.P., & Frodsham, A.C. (1993). Natural enemies of vegetable insect pests. *Cooperative Extension* (pp. 63). Cornell University, Ithaca, NY.

Hutcherson, N.B. (1994, September). *Command and control warfare: Putting another tool in the war-fighters database.* Maxwell AFB: Air University Press.

IWS—The Information Warfare Site. (2006, November). Retrieved April 21, 2008 from http://www.iwar.org.uk/psyops/

Jajodia, S., Ammann, P., & McCollum, D.C. (1999, April). Surviving information warfare attacks. *IEEE Computer Society, Innovative Technology for Computing Professionals, 32*(4), 57-63.

Kopp, C., Shannon. (2003). Hypergames and information warfare. *Journal of Information Warfare, 2*(2), 108-118.

Kopp, C. (2000, February). Information warfare: A fundamental paradigm of infowar. *Systems: Enterprise Computing Monthly* (pp. 46-55). Sydney, Australia: Auscom Publishing Pty Ltd.

Libicki, M.C. (1995, August). *What is information warfare?* National Defense University, Institute for National Strategic Studies. The Center for Advanced Concepts and Technology.

Markoff, J. (2007, January 7). Attack of the zombie computers is growing threat. *The New York Times.*

Meilinger, S.P. (1999, Winter). Air strategy: Targeting for effect. *Aerospace Power Journal.* Retrieved April 21, 2008 from http://www.airpower.maxwell.af.mil/airchronicles/apj/apj99/win99/meilinger.htm

Reiter, M. (1999, November/December). Staying connected. *IEEE Internet Computing,* 52-54.

Ryan, D. (1995). Implications of information-based warfare. *Joint Forces Quaterly,* 114.

Schwartau, W. (1996). *Information warfare: Cyberterrorism: Protecting your personal security in the electronic age (Second Edition)*. Thunder's Mouth Press. ISBN: 1560251328.

Smith, G. (1998, Fall). An electronic pearl habor? Not likely. *Issues in Science and Technology Online, 15.1*. Retrieved April 21, 2008 from http://issues.org/15.1/index.html

Stein, G.J. (1995, Spring). Information warfare. *Air-power Journal*.

Toffler, A., & Toffler, H. (1993). *War and anti-war: Survival at the dawn of the 21st century*. Boston, MA: Little, Brown and Company.

Tzu, S. (1910). *The art of war: The oldest military treatise in the world* (L. Giles, Trans.). eBook Release. Retrieved April 21, 2008 from www.gutenberg.org

Wolf, J. (2006, November 2). U.S. air force prepares to fight in cyberspace. *The Washington Post*.

Yurcik, W. (2000, July). Information warfare survivability: Is the best defense a good offense? In *Proceedings of the 5th Annual Ethics and Technology Conference*.

KEY TERMS

Botnets: Huge network of remote-controlled machines or computers.

Control and Command Warfare (C2W): A subset of IW and a military strategy that implements IW on the battlefield. C2W aims at victory on the battlefield. It is the integrated use of operations security, PSYOP, electronic warfare, military deception, and physical destruction.

Command, Control, Communications, Computer and Intelligence (C4I): An interoperable linking network that focuses on harnessing information storage and exchange.

Cyberspace: The global network of interconnected computers and communication systems.

Cyberwar: A synonym for information warfare.

Hacker: A person who breaks into a system with no authorization, or a person who intentionally oversteps his/her bounds on systems for which they do have legitimate access.

Information Warfare (IW): This is the exploitation of the enemy's (adversary's) information and information systems, while protecting one's own information and information systems for political, economic, or other purposes.

PSYOP: Planned operations to convey selected information and indicators to foreign audiences to influence their emotions, motives, objective reasoning, and ultimately the behavior of foreign governments, organizations, groups, and individuals.

Survival of the Fittest Information Warfare (SFIW): This is a conceptual framework proposed in this chapter and based on the need for information warfare environments to continually adapt to achieve success.

Virus: A self-replicating program that is hidden in another piece of computer Code.

Worm: A self-replicating destructive program that stands alone and spreads itself through computer networks.

Chapter IV
Evolution of Enterprise Security Federation

Gaeil An
Electronics and Telecommunications Research Institute, Korea

Joon S. Park
Syracuse University, USA

ABSTRACT

In this chapter, we discuss the evolution of the enterprise security federation, including why the framework should be evolved and how it has been developed and applied to real systems. Furthermore, we analyze the remaining vulnerabilities and weaknesses in current approaches and propose new approaches to resolve those problems. Then, to overcome those weaknesses and vulnerabilities, we propose the PSM (Policy-based Security Management) architecture for an integrated security framework, and the PM (Packet-Marking) architecture for a cooperative security framework. The PSM architecture is able to efficiently realize the security purposes of an organization by controlling, operating, and managing various kinds of security systems consistently based on security policies. The PM architecture is able to effectively deal with suspicious network traffic without requiring new protocol, while reducing the false-positive problem and perfectly protecting QoS for innocent traffic from attacks. We simulated the PSM and PM architectures to evaluate their performance. The simulation result shows that the PSM architecture can automatically detect and respond against network attacks, and the PM architecture can effectively handle suspicious traffic, such as DDoS traffics.

INTRODUCTION

As Internet service is developed and used by various organizations and applications, the threats of cyber attacks become more critical issues, especially in sensitive applications that may span multiple organizations or systems. In order to protect enterprise systems from cyber attacks, researchers and vendors have introduced new technologies such as the Intrusion Detection System (IDS), Intrusion Prevention System (IPS), firewall, antivirus, and so on (Debar, Dacier, & Wespi, 1999; Malik, 2002). The enterprise

security federation for managing and controlling security systems has evolved since its first generation to handle new threats and policy conflicts more effectively and efficiently.

The enterprise security federation can be classified as three frameworks: a simple security framework, an integrated security framework, and a cooperative security framework. The enterprise security federation has developed from an initially simple security framework into a cooperative security framework via an integrated security framework. A simple security framework has difficulty integrating heterogeneous security systems made by different multivendors into single management architecture. This problem is addressed by using an integrated security framework, whose purpose is to consistently control and manage various kinds of security systems based on a security policy, while providing for automation of both threat response service and security configuration service (Ahn, Yoon, & Nah, 2005). The key benefit of the cooperative security framework is a better view of global network attack activity (Locasto, Parekh, Keromytis, & Stolfo, 2005).

To address the integrated security framework, we introduce two security management technologies: Enterprise Security Management (ESM) (Check Point, 2000) and Policy-based Security Management (PSM) (Dinesh, 2000; Kim, Kim, & Na, 2005; Tishkov, Kotenko, & Sidelnikova, 2005; Westerinen, Schnizlein, Strassner, Scherling, Quinn, Herzog, Huynh, Carlson, Perry, & Waldbusser, 2001). We focus, in this chapter, on PSM and propose policy-based security management architecture. The PSM architecture is able to efficiently realize the security purpose of an organization by controlling, operating, and managing various kinds of security systems consistently based on security policies.

We also introduce and analyze several cooperative security frameworks, such as Cisco's architecture (Turk, 2004), Intel's architecture (Durham, Govindarajan, Larson, Rajagopal, & Sahita, 2002), and pushback architecture (Mahajan, Bellovin, Floyd, Ioannidis, Paxson, & Shenker, 2002). Even though these cooperative security architectures are effective at mitigating network attacks, they have weak points. Cisco's architecture has the problem that not only attack traffic, but also innocent traffic, is blocked. Intel's architecture may experience communication overhead and have difficulty handling false-positive problems, because it has no mechanism for effectively dealing with suspicious traffic. Finally, pushback architecture has demerits in determining precise rate-limit values and in requiring new protocol between routers. To address those problems, we propose a Packet-Marking (PM) architecture as a cooperative security framework that is able to effectively deal with suspicious network traffic without requiring new protocol, while reducing the false-positive problem, and protecting perfectly the Quality of Service (QoS) for innocent traffic from attacks.

BACKGROUND AND MOTIVATION

In the early stage of the Internet, security framework was not greatly addressed, because the destructive power and effects of cyber attackers against computer and network systems were not so high. Simple security framework typically consists of several security systems such as IDS or Firewall, and simple security management system for displaying attack information detected by security systems (Debar et al., 1999; Malik, 2002). A firewall accepts or denies incoming traffic according to a set of predefined rules called an access control list (ACL). An IDS detects suspicious traffic based on a predefined attack signature or behavior. A security administrator identifies the source of attack by manually analyzing alert information received from an IDS, and then blocks the attack traffic by directly inserting new ACL into Firewalls.

With the appearance of new types of attacks and an increase of security threat against enterprise networks, the importance of security has more increased. To deal with the security threat, various kinds of advanced security systems have been developed, and the scope of the network to protect has been enlarged. However, a simple security framework has difficulty integrating heterogeneous security systems made by different multivendors into single management architecture, because there is no standard protocol between a security system and a security management system. The simple security framework needs to evolve into a new security framework that is able to consistently control and manage various kinds of security systems, while providing for automation of both threat response service and security configuration service. We will call the new security frame all "integrated security frame."

Another problem of a simple security framework is that there is no mechanism to provide cooperation between security systems or between security management systems. Cooperation is very important when security systems defeat network attacks that exercise a bad effect on entire networks. One such network attack is the Distributed Denial of Service (DDoS) (Geng & Whinston, 2000; Mirkovic & Reiher, 2004). The first DDoS attack was seen in 1999. In 2003, there was a cyber incident by the DDoS attack executed by a Worm called Slammer (Moore, Paxson, Savage, Shannon, Staniford, & Weaver, 2003). The attack paralyzed Internet for many hours, so that network users could not access the Internet. A DDoS attack is very difficult to detect exactly, because the DDoS attack traffic is very similar to normal selfish traffic such as P2P (Point-to-Point) traffic (Risson & Moors, 2006) and flush crowd (Jung, Krishnamurthy, & Rabinovich, 2002). And also, a DDoS attack is capable of resulting in not only congestion of an enterprise system, but also congestion of entire networks.

Figure 1 shows the destructive power of a DDoS attack, which was obtained using a Network Simulator (NS) (Fall & Varadhan, 2007). The experiment uses four kinds of traffic, innocent UDP and TCP traffic getting service from a server node, DDoS traffic attacking the server node, and third-party traffic getting services of other servers. When many attacking nodes generates DDoS traffic toward a server node at the same time, it results in severely degrading the QoS not only for innocent traffic going toward the victim server, but also for third-party traffic going toward other servers, as shown in Figure 1. Moreover, DDoS attackers commonly employ source IP spoofing skill to hide their location, which makes it more difficult to identify DDoS attackers. So, it is more effective to block attacks by using the security systems located close to sources of the attack. And also, defense mechanisms against DDoS should be applied not only to enterprise networks, but also to whole networks. This is why network security nodes should cooperate with each other to detect and mitigate DDoS traffic effectively.

INTEGRATED SECURITY FRAMEWORK

In this section, we will discuss architectures for providing an integrated security framework. The ultimate purpose of an integrated security framework is to integrate heterogeneous security systems made by different multivendors into single management architecture.

Related Work

The integrated security framework has been proposed in order to efficiently realize the security purposes of an organization by controlling, operating, and managing various kinds of security systems consistently based on a security policy. There are two kinds of management architectures—an Enterprise Security Management (ESM) (Check Point, 2000) and a Policy-based Security Management (PSM) (Dinesh, 2000; Kim et al., 2005; Tishkov et al., 2005; Westerinen et al., 2001)—for providing an integrated security framework.

ESM especially addresses an integrated security management system that is able not only to collect, coordinate, and analyze heterogeneous logs and alerts from various kinds of security systems, but also to provide an automated threat response service. As an example of ESM, Open Platform for Secure Enterprise Connectivity (OPSEC) has been proposed by Check Point (Check Point, 2000). OPSEC provides a client/server-based integrated network frame called a security virtual framework to integrate third-party security systems. OPSEC defines three ways to support integration of security systems: application programming interfaces (APIs), industry-standard protocols, and a high-level scripting language. First, the API of OPSEC is used to integrate third-party security applications such as virus scanning software and access control into the security virtual framework. OPSEC supports many open industry standard protocols such as RADIUS, SNMP, and LDAP to allow interoperability with a third-party security system that uses such standard protocol. Finally, OPSEC defines a high-level scripting language called INSPECT for new security applications. Once a rule-based security

Figure 1. DDoS attack

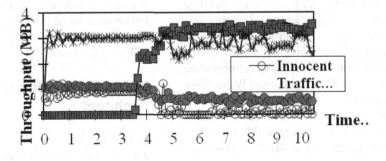

Figure 2. Policy architecture in policy-based network management

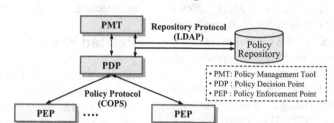

policy is defined by INSPECT, an INSPECT script is generated from the rule base for each security system being managed. The INSPECT scripts are then compiled and sent to the corresponding security system which contains an INSPECT virtual machine to deal with any action the INSPECT script requests.

PSM is an extended framework of the Policy-Based Network Management (PBNM) (Dinesh, 2000; Westerinen et al., 2001) that has been proposed by the Internet Engineering Task Force (IETF). Although PBNM was originally planned for the purpose of providing policy-based control over the ReSerVation Protocol (RSVP) and integrated services, it has been recognized as a useful model for other technologies that need policy support, such as security system management technology (Durham, Boyle, Cohen, Herzog, Rajan, & Sastry, 2000). In PBNM, a security policy consists of one or more rules that describe an action to occur when a specific condition exists. The greatest merit of PBNM is providing automation of network configurations.

Figure 2 shows the policy architecture of PBNM proposed by IETF. This architecture is composed of Policy Management Tool (PMT), Policy Decision Point (PDP), and Policy Enforcement Point (PEP). PMT is a policy editor that provides a user interface to input policy. PDP is the point at which policy decisions are made, and PEP is the point at which the policy decisions are actually enforced.

The automation of network configuration in the policy architecture is accomplished by using the concept of roles. Role is an administratively specified characteristic of a managed element. It is used as a selector for policy rules to determine the applicability of a rule to a particular managed element. As the object-oriented information model for representing policy information, IETF has proposed Policy Core Information Model (PCIM), which describes the basic concepts of policy groups, rules, conditions, actions, repositories, and their relationships (Moore, Ellesson, Strassner, & Westerinen, 2001). IETF considers

Lightweight Directory Access Protocol (LDAP) (Wahl, Howes, & Kille, 1997) as a repository protocol that can be used to access policy stored in a policy repository. It also defines Common Open Policy Service (COPS) protocol as a policy protocol that can be used to exchange policy information between PDP and PEP (Durham et al., 2000; Chan, Seligson, Durham, Gai, McCloghrie, Herzog, Reichmeyer, Yavatkar, & Smith, 2001).

COPS protocol is a simple query-and-response protocol that employs a client/server model and uses Transmission Control Protocol (TCP) as its transport protocol for reliable exchanges of messages. COPS protocol defines two kinds of models: outsourcing model and provisioning model (Durham et al., 2000). Under an outsourcing model, a PEP turns its policy decision over to a PDP, using a COPS Request message. If the PDP receives the policy decision request from the PEP, it performs a policy decision for the PEP, and then returns the result to PEP using a COPS Decision message. The outsourcing model has been used for RSVP. Under the Provisioning (also known as Configuration) model, PDP can trigger policy decision for itself without a request from PEP. The Provisioning model is used to configure network systems. PSM follows the provisioning model, because it focuses on the configuration of security systems. In the provisioning model, the operation between PDP and PEP is as follows: When a PEP boots, it opens a COPS connection to its PDP and sends the PDP information about the capability of the PEP. In response, the PDP performs policy decisions based on the capability information about the PEP, and transfers to the PEP the policy that it needs. On receiving the policies, the PEP installs them.

Policy-Based Security Management Architecture

In this section, we propose policy-based security management architecture as an integrated enterprise framework that is able to efficiently realize the security purpose of an organization by controlling, operating, and managing various kinds of security systems consistently based on security policies and a standard protocol called COPS.

Defining Security Policy

Policy-based security management architecture consists of a security policy server (SPS) and security policy clients (SPCs). SPS and SPC correspond to the PDP and PEP shown in Figure 2, respectively. SPS is a central management system that manages security systems based on security policy. It has a responsibility to manage security policy, decide security policy rules to apply to SPC, provision them to SPC using COPS protocol, and analyze attack alert information received from SPC. SPC is a security system (e.g., IDS, IPS, and firewall) in which security policy is enforced. Once SPC detects an attack based on security policy, it reports alert information about the attack to SPS.

In policy-based security management, all information for detecting and responding to attacks is represented as policy, so there may be various kinds of policies, such as packet filtering, intrusion-detection, and intrusion-response. Policy consists of one or more rules that basically describe the action to occur when a specific condition is true.

According to the PCIM proposed by IETF, a policy rule is represented as a *PolicyRule* class, as shown in Figure 3. *PolicyRule* class contains *PolicyCondition, PolicyAction,* and *PolicyTimerPeriodCondition* classes. The *PolicyTimerPeriodCondition* is used to express time information for the rule. The *PolicyRule* has several attributes, such as *PolicyKeywords, Enabled,* and *PolicyRoles.* The *PolicyKeywords* attribute is used to characterize or categorize policy rules, so the characteristic of each security policy is described by using *PolicyKeywords.* The *Enabled* attribute is used to indicate whether a policy rule is activated or inactivated. A policy rule has a life cycle: it is created, updated, and finally extinguished. A policy rule becomes either an enabled (activated) or disabled (inactivated) state for its lifetime by the administrator's request or the policy server's request. *PolicyRoles* indicates an administratively specified characteristic of policy rules. In the policy-based security management architecture, the concept of role is very important, because it is a key for providing for automation of a security configuration. Role is used as a selector for policy rules to determine the applicability of a rule to a particular managed element.

Security networks consist of heterogeneous security systems such as an IDS or Firewall. Communication protocols are standardized in standard bodies like IETF. COPS protocol is one such protocol. COPS protocol is used to exchange policy information between a SPS and its SPC. COPS protocol uses Policy Information Base (PIB) as a named structure for identifying policy information that is sent to a managed system. So, PCIM and PIB each need to be extended in order to model security policy and to define a named structure for it. SPS takes the responsibility of translating a PCIM-based policy rule into a PIB object. Figure 4 shows a representation of both a PCIM-based policy rule and a PIB object for "smurf DoS attack."

Strategy for Autoconfiguration of Security Systems

For automatic management of security systems, SPS provides the following four capabilities with respect to security policy rule: self-creation, self-activation, self-selection, and custom-made-provisioning.

Self-creation means the capability that SPS can automatically create/extinguish intrusion response policy rules on the basis of security status, such as intrusion alerts received from SPC. When SPS receives intrusion alert information from SPCs, SPS correlates and analyzes it. If SPS regards it as a real attack, it automatically generates an intrusion response rule and transfers it to an SPC to defeat the attack.

Self-activation refers to a capability that SPS can automatically activate/inactivate security policy rules on the basis of current security status or a timer. A security administrator may want to establish security policy that denies personal Internet traffic such as P2P during working hours and accepts it after working hours. And also, a security administrator may want to establish various levels of traffic-blocking policies according to the severity of the current security state. To provide for self-activation, the policy-based security management architecture allows specifying not only security policy rules with timer, but also a high level of policy rules that describe when security policy rules should be activated or inactivated.

Self-selection means a capability that SPS can automatically select target security systems to apply a rule on the basis of the content of a rule and the topology of security networks. The real merit of self-selection appears when SPS wants to find the security systems that are able to most effectively defeat a detected at-

Figure 3. Structure of policyrule class in PCIM

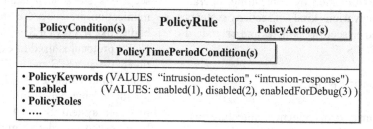

Figure 4. Translation of a PCIM-based policy rule into a PIB object

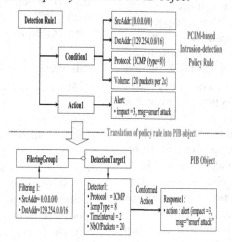

tack. For example, if SPS simply broadcasts attack response rules to all SPCs, then SPCs may experience poor resource utilization, because their memory for storing rules is limited. Similarly, if security administrators manually determine to which SPC attack response rules are applied, it will take long time while annoying them.

In support of self-selection, we propose five kinds of roles, as follow: *ingress, egress, both, all,* and *spc_address*. All security policy rules are associated with one of those roles. The *ingress* role is used to select the SPC nearest the detected attacker. The *egress* role is used to select the SPC nearest the victim system. The *both* role is one that satisfies both *ingress* and *egress* roles. The *all* role is used to select all SPCs that the SPS manages. Finally, the *spc_address* role indicates the IP address of the SPC specified explicitly by an administrator. The *ingress* role can be set to security policy rules that detect attacks, such as IP spoofing and DoS attacks. The *egress* role is a default one to be set to all the rules. The *both* role can be effectively used when mitigating crafty attacks like DDoS ac-

companied with IP spoofing attacks (e.g., Rule B to apply to the ingress SPCs: drop the packets of which the destination IP is the IP of the victim system, Rule C to apply to the egress SPC: drop flows with traffic volume beyond a threshold for a given time). The *all* role is very useful if set to security policy rules that detect attacks paralyzing entire networks like Internet Worm. SPS has topology information about security networks that it manages. So, if SPS identifies the source of an attack, then it can select the best suitable SPCs by using the topology and role information of the rule used to detect the attack.

Custom-made-provisioning means that SPS can automatically provide security systems with different policy rules according to their capability. Security network administrators may have different requirements in configuring their own security networks. For example, a certain administrator may want to detect only critical and explicit attacks on the network to keep the quality of network service from degrading because of a false-positive problem. Similarly, a security system may have different capability in terms of attack detection and attack response. For example, an IDS has no attack response function, whereas a Firewall has such function, even if its detection capability is less than that of an IDS. So, SPS needs to optimally provision each security system according to its capability and the requirements of the administrator.

To provide for custom-made-provisioning, we define several kinds of capabilities, such as *fine-Detection* or *coarseDetection*, *hostBasedDetection* or *networkBasedDetection*, and *packetBlock*. An SPC with *fineDetection* capability indicates that the SPC wants to have security policy rules to be able to detect not only critical, but also trivial intrusion. An SPC with *coarseDetection* capability indicates that the SPC wants to have security policy rules to be able to detect only critical intrusion. An SPC with *hostBasedDetection* capability means host-based IDS, whereas an SPC with *networkBasedDetection* capability means network-based IDS. Finally, an SPC with *packetBlock* capability indicates that the SPC has a capability that can block packets. An SPC notifies an SPS of its capability when it first connects to the SPS. Once an SPS receives the capability information from an SPC, the SPS decides security policy rules based on the capability information and provides them to the SPC.

To deal with autoconfiguration of security systems, the PSM architecture comprises the following steps, as shown in Figure 5:

1. When an SPC boots, it reports its capability and topology information (e.g., the addresses of the networks to protect) to the SPS, and requests policy to the SPS using COPS protocol.
2. If the SPS receives a policy request from the SPC, after the SPS decides security policy rules based on the capability of the SPC, it provides them to the SPC using COPS protocol.
3. The SPC executes intrusion detection function using the security policy rule, and sends an intrusion alert whenever it detects an attack.
4. If the SPS receives alerts from SPCs, the SPS analyzes them to identify the source of the attack. The SPS creates a new intrusion response rule, and then gives it to the SPCs that can defeat the attack most effectively using COPS protocol.

Figure 6 shows the simulation results of the PSM architecture detecting and blocking against "smurf DoS attack." To detect the attack, SPCs have an intrusion detection rule like the rule shown in Figure 4, which regards an incoming ICMP flow producing traffic volume beyond a threshold for a given time as a smurf attacker. If an SPS that manages SPCs receives an alert from an SPC which detects attack flows, it generates an intrusion response policy and provisions it to SPCs that can block the attack.

Figure 6-(a) and -(b) are when the *egress* role is applied to the intrusion response policy and when *ingress* role is applied to it, respectively. An intrusion response rule with the *egress* role is only applied to the SPC nearest the victim system. In Figure 6-(a), the SPCs do not detect all the attack flows. This is because the SPCs have a difficulty in exactly measuring the traffic volume of attack flows. The attack traffic in this experiment causes network congestion not only in the stub network, but also in the core networks. The congestion in core networks influences network traffic, including the attack flows. This makes it difficult for the SPCs to know the original traffic volume of the attack flows. An intrusion response rule with the *ingress* role is applied to the ingress SPC nearest the detected attacker. The security policy rule with *ingress* role blocks all the attack flows, as shown in Figure 6-(b). In Figure 6-(b), the SPCs are able to measure the attack flows exactly, because the attack flows regarded as an attack are blocked by the ingress SPCs before they result in network congestion in the core networks.

This experiment shows that the *ingress* role is more effective than the *egress* role in mitigating attacks like DoS. Even though the PSM architecture is able to provide for automatic detection and response of network attacks by using autoconfiguration, it may suffer from false-positive problem when it deals with attacks like DDoS, because it is generally so difficult to distinguish between DDoS traffic and innocent traffic exactly. This issue will be addressed in the next section.

COOPERATIVE SECURITY FRAMEWORK

In this section, we will discuss architectures that provide a cooperative security framework. The ultimate purpose of a cooperative security framework is to allow security systems to cooperate with each other so as to effectively detect and respond to attacks by DDoS and Internet Worm that can paralyze the whole networks.

Figure 5. Scenario for supporting autoconfiguration of security networks

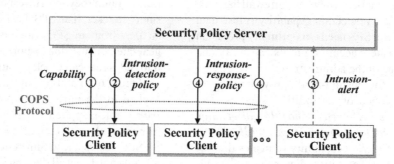

Figure 6. Blocking against smurf DDoS attack in PSM architecture

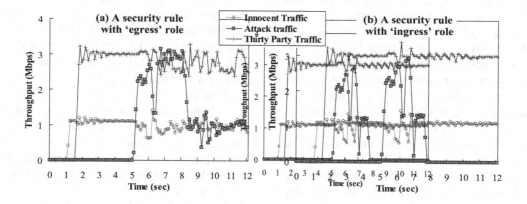

Related Work

With the appearance of network attacks like DDoS devastating enough to paralyze the entire Internet, cooperation between security networks has become more emphasized. A DDoS attack is a challenging issue for Internet service providers and content providers alike. A DDoS attack involves a large number of attacking hosts simultaneously overwhelming a victim. Under DDoS attacks, it is almost impossible for legitimate users to get their fair share of available network resources. Malicious users execute DDoS attacks by combining several well-known schemes such as TCP SYN flooding, UDP flooding, and the "ping of death" (Houle & Weaver, 2001). They typically use IP spoofing (i.e., using a faked source address in an IP packet) and generate huge volumes of traffic (Geng & Whinston, 2000).

Generally, determining whether a packet is part of a DDoS attack is difficult for three reasons. First, the criteria to determine whether a packet is part of a DDoS attack are relative. For example, we can easily imagine a scenario in which real DDoS traffic is regarded as innocent traffic, because it does not result in any congestion on a node with abundant network resources. On the contrary, innocent traffic may be regarded as attack traffic if a normal user is trying to get better network service from a node with poor network resources, and finally results in congestion on the node. Second, smart attackers may change the traffic generation pattern at will so as not to be easily detected. Also, a certain kind of innocent traffic is very similar to DDoS traffic in traffic property. For example, the property of P2P and flash crowd traffic, which is found in innocent traffic, is actually similar to that of DDoS traffic.

We introduce here several cooperative security architectures; Cisco's architecture (Turk, 2004), Intel's architecture (Durham et al., 2002) and pushback architecture (Mahajan et al., 2002).

Cisco's architecture defines two kinds of security routers—a blackhole router and a sinkhole router—to protect not only the enterprise system, but also the global network from DDoS attacks. The purpose of a blackhole router is to block attacks by cooperating with existing security systems. The sinkhole router is used to pull down and analyze all sorts of junk traffic such as attack noise, network scans, backscatters, DoS attacks, and other abnormal behavior. So the sinkhole router is thought of as a kind of "honey pot" system.

Figure 7 shows Cisco's Architecture with blackhole and sinkhole routers. When a router detects that a local system with an IP address, 10.0.2.1 is being attacked, it informs its neighboring routers directly by using Common Line Interface (CLI) or indirectly by using a Border Gateway Protocol (BGP) update. The blackhole routers that received the notification drop all the packets going toward the victim system by adding a field into their routing tables to indicate that the next hop of 10.0.2.1/32 is null0. The attacking packets going toward the victim system may be redirected to the sinkhole router instead of being dropped. For this, the sinkhole router advertises the IP addresses of victim systems and unused IP space on the network. The sinkhole router is used to analyze attack information. Through the analysis, we can obtain information on who is being attacked by analyzing backscatter traffic, and who the attacker or infected system is by analyzing attack traffic such as network scan attacks and Internet Worms.

Intel's architecture basically follows the policy-based security architecture introduced in the previous section. Intel's architecture consists of a smart link (SL) and a network health control center (NHCC). SL monitors the network and collects statistical information. SLs periodically report summarized information to NHCC. NHCC is a central management server responsible for SL management and control using COPS protocol. NHCCs communicate with each other using Simple Object Access Protocol (SOAP) and Extensible Markup Language (XML) to effectively trace and respond to attacks.

Figure 8 shows Intel's architecture that can automatically detect and defeat attacks. If an SL detects an anomalous traffic pattern on the Internet, the SL reports it to an NHCC which it belongs to. The NHCC identifies the attack by correlating and analyzing the statistical information collected at the SL in its domain, and then the NHCC traces the path of the attack by communicating information for the attack with neighboring NHCCs in different domains. Finally, if an NHCC identify the source of the attack, it blocks the attack by configuring the SLs closest to the source of the attack to stop the attack traffic.

As a cooperative architecture for alleviating the impact of DDoS attacks, pushback architecture has been proposed. Figure 9 shows the pushback architecture. In pushback architecture, the congested router asks its adjacent upstream routers to rate-limit the attacking aggregate flow. This request is sent only to the contributing neighbors that have been sending a significant fraction of the aggregate traffic. The receiving routers can recursively propagate pushback further upstream.

Even though all of the cooperative security architectures introduced in this section are able to mitigate DDoS attacks, they have weak points. Cisco's architecture has the problem that not only DDoS traffic, but also innocent traffic is blocked. Intel's architecture may experience communication overhead between NHCCs and have difficulty in handling false-positive problems, because it has no mechanism for effectively dealing with suspicious traffic which cannot be definitively categorized as malicious or as normal traffic. Finally, pushback architecture has demerits in determining precise rate-limit value and in requiring new protocol between routers. These weak points are addressed in the next section.

Packet-Marking (PM) Architecture

We propose a packet-marking (PM) architecture (An & Park, 2006) as a cooperative security framework that is able to effectively deal with suspicious network traffic without requiring new protocol, while reducing the false-positive problem and protecting perfectly the QoS for innocent traffic from attacks.

Within the framework of intrusion detection, network traffic can be divided into three kinds of traffic: innocent, attack, and suspicious. Innocent traffic is generated by a normal user. Attack traffic is generated by an attacker. Suspicious traffic cannot be definitively categorized either as malicious or as normal traffic. It is easy to deal with normal and malicious traffic. If an incoming packet is normal, it will be delivered to the destination node. On the other hand, if an incoming packet is an attack packet, it will be dropped. However, suspicious traffic does not fall neatly into either of those two scenarios and thus presents a challenge to the system. Simply dropping suspicious traffic may result in a false-positive problem.

A typical example of suspicious traffic is Distributed Denial of Service (DDoS) attack traffic. The

Figure 7. Cisco's architecture with blackhole and sinkhole routers

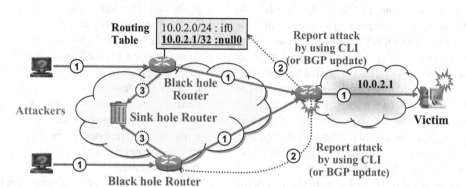

Figue 8. Intel's architecture based on policy-based security management architecture

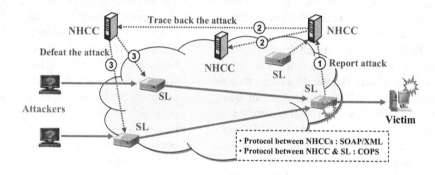

Figure 9. Pushback architecture

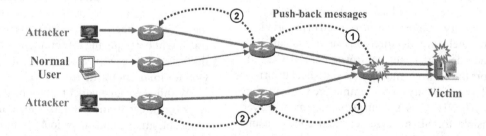

nature of a DDoS attack makes it difficult to recognize one. For example, the property of P2P and flash crowd traffic, which is found in innocent traffic, is actually similar to that of DDoS traffic.

Figure 10 shows the PM architecture that is able to effectively deal with such suspicious network traffic. The architecture consists of four modules, the Packet-dropper, Packet-marker, Threat-detector, and Packet-forwarder. The Packet-dropper and Packet-marker are used to drop attack packets and to mark suspicious packets, respectively. The Threat-detector

is a module to detect attacks. Finally, the Packet-forwarder provides packets with differentiated packet-forwarding service.

When the security node with the PM architecture receives a packet from networks, it operates as follows. The security node first inspects to find if the incoming packet is marked. If it is, the security node sends it to the worst queue to serve it using the worst quality of packet-forwarding service. If no, the Threat-detector module inspects to find out whether the incoming packet is innocent, suspicious, or an attacking packet. If

Figure 10. Packet-marking architecture

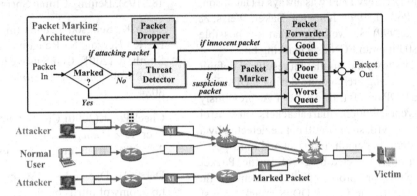

Figure 11. Performance of packet-marking architecture

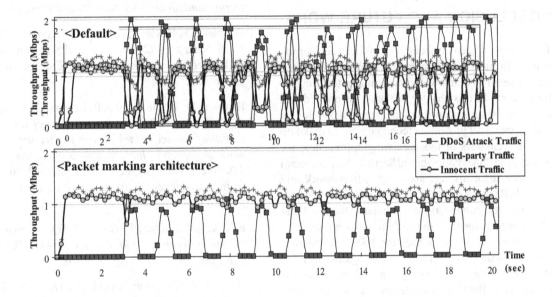

it is an attacking packet, it is sent to the Packet-dropper to be dropped. If it is a suspicious packet, it is marked and sent to the poor queue to be served using the poor quality of packet-forwarding service. Finally, if it is an innocent packet, it is sent to the good queue to be served using the good quality of packet-forwarding service. So, under the PM architecture, attack traffic is blocked, suspicious traffic experiences the poor or worst quality of packet-forwarding service, and innocent traffic receives the good quality of packet-forwarding service. Currently, one of the most difficult issues in handling DDoS traffic is the false-positive problem in which traffic judged to be malicious is

innocent traffic in reality. The PM architecture does not drop the suspicious packet, but provides it with minimum network resources (i.e., LPS). This strategy may be very helpful in weakening the false-positive problem.

To support the packet-marking concept proposed in this chapter, we need a field in the IP header. There is the Type of Service (ToS) field in IP header to show precedence and the ToS for a packet. The ToS field is now used by Differentiated Service (DiffServ) (Nichols, Blake, Baker, & Black, 1998). The six most significant bits of the ToS byte are now called the DiffServ field. The last two Currently Unused (CU) bits are now used as Explicit Congestion Notification (ECN) bits. Until now, DS0 in DiffServ Field was always 0 (Jacobson, Nichols, & Poduri, 1999; Jeinanen, Baker, Weiss, & Wroclawski, 1999). So, we believe that it is possible to use a DS0 bit or an ECN as a marking bit.

Figure 11 shows the simulation results of default and packet-marking architecture during a DDoS attack using a UDP on-off traffic pattern. As previously noted in this contribution, smart attackers can control attack traffic at will, so they will not be detected by a security system. In default, innocent and third-party traffic is seriously affected by DDoS traffic. Packet marking architecture protects both innocent traffic and third-party traffic from a DDoS attack against networks almost infallibly, as shown in Figure 11.

CONCLUSION AND FUTURE WORK

The enterprise security federation has been developing from an initially simple security framework to a cooperative security framework via an integrated security framework. In this chapter, we have introduced and analyzed existing security management technologies and cooperative protection technologies. To make up for the weakness of those existing approaches, we propose the PSM (Policy-based Security Management) architecture for an integrated security framework, and the PM (Packet-Marking) architecture for a cooperative security framework. We simulated the PSM and PM architectures to evaluate their performance. The simulation result shows that the PSM architecture can automatically detect and respond against network attack by using autoconfiguration. and the PM architecture can effectively handle suspicious traffic such as DDoS traffics.

REFERENCES

Ahn, G., Yoon, S., & Nah, J. (2005). COPS protocol-based security poicy distribution mechanism for management of security systems. *GESTS International Transactions on Computer Science and Engineering, 14*(1), 87-98.

An, G., & Park, J. (2006, November 29–December 1). Packet marking-based attack response for suspicious traffics on the Web. In H. Lipmaa, M. Yung, & D. Lin (Eds.). In *Proceedings of the Conference on Information Security and Cryptology (Inscrypt)*, volume 4318 of *Lecture Notes in Computer Science (LNCS)* (pp. 182-195). Beijing, China: Springer.

Chan, K., Seligson, J., Durham, D., Gai, S., McCloghrie, K., Herzog, S., Reichmeyer, F., Yavatkar, R., & Smith, A. (2001). COPS usage for policy provisioning (COPS-PR). *Internet Engineering Task Force.* RFC 3084.

Check Point. (2000). Check Point, into to OPSEC: SDK overview. *Homepage of Check Point.* Retrieved April 26th, 2008, from http://www.opsec.com

Debar, H., Dacier, M., & Wespi, A. (1999). Towards a taxonomy of intrusion-detection systems. *Computer Networks, 31*, 805-822.

Dinesh, V. (2000). *Policy-based networking: Architecture and algorithms.* New Riders Press.

Durham, D., Boyle, J., Cohen, R., Herzog, S., Rajan, R., & Sastry, A. (2000). The COPS (common open policy service) protocol. *Internet Engineering Task Force.* RFC 2748.

Durham, D., Govindarajan, P., Larson, D., Rajagopal, P., & Sahita, R. (2002). *Elimination of distributed denial of service attacks using programmable network processors: Intel research and development 1.0.* Intel's white paper. Retrieved April 26, 2008, from http://developer.intel.com/design/network/papers/DDoS_whitepaper.pdf

Fall, K., & Varadhan, K. (Ed.). (2007). *The ns manual (formerly ns notes and documentation).* Retrieved April 26, 2008, from http://www.isi.edu/nsnam/ns

Geng, X., & Whinston, A.B. (2000). Defeating distributed denial of service attacks. *IT Pro*, 36-41.

Houle, K., & Weaver, G. (2001). Trends in denial of service attack technology. *The Fall 2001 NANOG Meeting.* CERT Coordination Center.

Jacobson, V., Nichols, K., & Poduri, K. (1999). An expedited forwarding PHB. *Internet Engineering Task Force.* RFC 2598.

Jeinanen, J., Baker, F., Weiss, W., & Wroclawski, J. (1999). Assured forwarding PHB group. *Internet Engineering Task Force.* RFC 2597.

Jung, J., Krishnamurthy, B., & Rabinovich, M. (2002). Flash crowds and denial of service attacks: Characterization and implications for CDNs and Web sites.

The 11th International World Wide Web Conference (pp. 252-262). ACM Press.

Kim, G., Kim, J., & Na, J. (2005). Design and implementation of policy decision point in policy-based network. *ACIS International Conference on Computer and Information Science* (pp. 534-538). IEEE Press.

Locasto, M. E., Parekh, J.J., Keromytis, A.D., & Stolfo, S.J. (2005). Towards collaborative security and P2P intrusion detection. *IEEE Workshop on Information Assurance and Security* (pp. 30-36). IEEE Press.

Mahajan, R., Bellovin, S. M., Floyd, S., Ioannidis, J., Paxson, V., & Shenker, S. (2002). Controlling high bandwidth aggregates in the network. *ACM SIGCOMM Computer Communications Review, 32*(3), 62-73.

Malik, S. (2002). *Network security principles and practices*. Ind: Cisco Press.

Mirkovic, J., & Reiher, P. (2004). A taxonomy of DDoS attack and DDoS defense mechanisms. *ACM SIGCOMM Computer Communications Review, 34*(2), 39-53

Moore, B., Ellesson, E., Strassner, J., & Westerinen, A. (2001). Policy core information model—version 1 specification. *Internet Engineering Task Force.* RFC 3060.

Moore, D., Paxson, V., Savage, S., Shannon, C., Staniford, & S., Weaver, N. (2003). Inside the slammer worm. *IEEE Security & Privacy*, 33-39.

Nichols, K., Blake, S., Baker, F., & Black, D. (1998). Definition of the differentiated services field (DS Field) in the IPv4 and IPv6 headers. *Internet Engineering Task Force.* RFC 2474.

Risson, J., & Moors, T. (2006). Survey of research towards robust peer-to-peer networks: Search methods. *Computer Networks, 50*, 3485-3521.

Tishkov, A., Kotenko, I., & Sidelnikova, E. (2005). Security checker architecture for policy-based security management. *Lecture Note in Computer Science, 3685*, 460-465. Springer Press.

Turk, D. (2004). Configuring BGP to block denial-of-service attacks. *Internet Engineering Task Force.* RFC 3882.

Wahl, M., Howes, T., & Kille, S. (1997). Lightweight directory access protocol (v3). *Internet Engineering Task Force.* RFC 2251.

Westerinen, A., Schnizlein, J., Strassner, J., Scherling, M., Quinn, B., Herzog, S., Huynh, A., Carlson, M., Perry, J., & Waldbusser, S. (2001). Terminology for policy-based management. *Internet Engineering Task Force.* RFC 3198.

KEY TERMS

Cooperative Security Framework: This is a framework in which security systems cooperate with each other to increase effectiveness of responding to network attack.

DDoS Attack: This is a network attack that prevents normal users from getting network resources by letting a lot of the compromised nodes attack a victim node at the same time.

Integrated Security Framework: This is a framework that is able to provide consistent control and management of heterogeneous security systems.

Packet Marking-Based Attack Response: This deals with network attack traffic in the way that a downstream network node determines whether or not to discard packets marked as suspicious by an upstream security system.

Security Autoconfiguration: This refers to the capability that security systems are able to configure security network for themselves.

Suspicious Network Traffic: This is a traffic that cannot be definitively categorized as either malicious or innocent traffic.

Security Policy Server: This is a central management system that can realize the security purposes of an organization based on security policy.

Chapter V
A Holistic Approach to Information Security Assurance and Risk Management in an Enterprise

Roy Ng
Ryerson University, Canada

ABSTRACT

The hypergrowth of computing and communications technologies increases security vulnerabilities to organizations. The lack of resources training, the complexity of new technologies, and the slow legislation process to deter the breach of security all constitute to the trends of increasing security risk in an enterprise. Traditional approaches to risk assessment focusing on either the departmental or branch level lacks of an enterprise perspective. Many organizations assess and mitigate security risks from a technology perspective and deploy technology solutions. This approach ignores the importance of assessing security risk in policy and execution. This chapter discusses a systematic and holistic approach to managing security risk. An approach that utilizes the information life cycle and information assurance (IA) assessment points for the creation of policy, monitoring, auditing of security performance, regulate, and initiate corrective action to minimize vulnerabilities. An "information life cycle" is being proposed with its stage value and the underlying security operatives (gate-points) to protect the information. An information assurance framework and its functions to audit the information security implemented in an enterprise are proposed. Organization must assess the value and the business impact of the information, so that optimal and effective security system and security assurance can be designed.

INTRODUCTION

The exponential growth of the powerful, feature-rich computing and communications technology give rise to two contradicting influences to business. On one hand, it answers the business survival needs to hypercompetition (Burlton, 2001), which constantly shrinks the business cycles and time to market. On the other hand, it gives rise to security vulnerabilities and attack, due to the user's ignorance and company's lim-

ited resources in the management especially disasters recovery of the new and complex technology.

Enterprise is at risk in maintaining an effective level of information assurance due to the hypergrowth in technology and the lagging behind of resources training and legal ramifications in the deterrence of security hacking and cracking. From a practitioner's point of view, many organizations still treat information security as a technological issue which requires only a technology solution. Others companies mitigate security risk in a silo manner of departmental or branch-level solution. Security risk distributed across the enterprise, and the weakest security protection on one part, is the weakest link of the whole security protection system within the enterprise.

Security, by nature, requires a comprehensive and a total-system approach. Effective security implementation demands a holistic and systematic design and implementation. Information security and assurance should be a proactive process by design, rather than a reactive implementation as an after-effect patch tool. Security metrics should be used to measure the performance of the information security systems (Jaquith, 2007). A well-defined metrics will not only benchmark the security system enables a systematic and holistic approach to improve the existing system continually.

BACKGROUND

Information Assurance (IA) is a risk management tool. It reduces the probability of security vulnerability and minimizes the effects should a security incident occurs. IA provides the guiding principles and audit to the underlying information security (InfoSec) process across an enterprise. IA affirms the stakeholders' trust, confidence, and the quality of information in areas of confidentiality, integrity, and authenticity of the information being processed.

Various risk assessment models have been proposed, such as the Risk Level Matrix, Business Impact Analysis and the Annualized Loss Exposure (ALE) (Krutz & Vines, 2001; Stonebumer et al., 2002; Tipton & Krasuse, 2000). These are very useful models dealing with a specific assessment of risk within a risk scenario. On the contrary, the standard "17799 common information security architecture" from the Committee of Sponsoring Organizations of the Treadway Commission's (COSO's) enterprise risk management architecture and Zachman's information systems architecture provide an enterprise level and a comprehensive approach. These models and frameworks, when applied in the context of information assurance, increase the trust and confidence level in the performance of the information security. Security policy, procedure, and the execution of the information security process should include the assessment of security risks and the defined metrics should be evaluated to form an integrated approach in an enterprise.

BUSINESS DRIVERS THAT INCREASE SECURITY EXPOSURE

Every organization exists to fulfill its mission. A for-profit organization strives to increase revenue and shareholders' profits. A nonprofit organization endeavors to provide more services within the allocated grants and funding. In order to maximize the goals to achieve their mission, both types of organizations make every effort to increase efficiency and effectiveness with cost reduction or savings. The ability to outreach to clients or customers will enjoy a better return on investment. It also increases the "service to funding" ratio for nonprofit organization. It is believed that by providing the right information to clients helps the increase of sales or services. Information is now believed to be an asset, and helps organizations to gain a competitive advantage over other organizations. The followings are some of the many business drivers that increase the efficiency and effectiveness, but also create the propensity of increasing security vulnerabilities and attacks.

Driver 1: Competition drives efficiency and effectiveness. Three factors have made possible the increase of efficiency and perhaps effectiveness of an organization. They are (1) the continuing of lower cost of computing equipment such as desktops, laptops and handheld devices, (2) the feature-rich multimedia applications that allow for portability of "anywhere, any time, any systems" connections, (3) acceptance of the use and the growth of the Internet. Organizations take advantage of these three factors and outreach to more customers in order to increase the market share. However, information security to protect the services, process, and procedure of computing environment has been lagging behind in the research and development of solution.

Driver 2: Customer choices of a better purchase experience. As early as 2001, the awareness of hypercompetition (Burlton, 2001) has been recognized as a new business driver that shrinks business cycles. Ever since, it has been observed that over the years, customers demand a better purchase experience by expecting better product information to be available for product selection and purchase decisions, and more convenience to shop both with time (7/24) and the use of handheld or laptop devices over the Internet for purchase.

With the availability of competitive product information, the customer also expects a better price performance ratio, forcing companies to compete in price with increasing functionality. To satisfy the needs of customers, many organizations ventured into high efficiency technology solutions without the consideration of information security impacts resulting from these new technologies. This is especially true for those technologies that are still in incubation stage where the technology works, but comprehensive process and information security are not part of the built-in solution. With full knowledge of such risk, business needs power and feature-rich technology for survival, knowing that security vulnerabilities may be increased.

Driver 3: Cost reductions. Using outsource and off-shore operations internationally will fulfill the cost reduction aspects of the goods and services. These operations include outside of design and operation, offshore manufacturing, and outsourced call centre. By doing so, organizations extend their enterprise to multiple legal requirements, privacy legislation compliances, multicultural workforce, and round-the-clock operation. Thus, it will require a holistic approach design and multidimensional security requirements and protection systems.

The aforementioned drivers accelerate business growth, but also increase the gap of security vulnerability and security protection. The advance of multimedia communications with increasing wireless connectivity infrastructure has further improved the efficiency of business. Multimedia cellphones with capability of Internet access, video, and image transmission increase the security vulnerability. Nowadays, cellphones are actually small, handheld computers with processing, memory, input, and output capabilities. With the injections (illegal downloading) of malicious software (malware) from a cracker, the microphone of a cellphone can be activated, which then becomes a listening device. This technique is called "roving bugs."

A cell-phone can be sent with a maintenance code and place it on diagnostic mode, therefore, can used to listen to conversation while the phone is apparently inactive. (National Reconnaissance Organization, 1997)

Gaps of information security and information assurance to security vulnerabilities will be widened as power and feature-rich technologies proliferates the market. Hackers and crackers will also step up their level and effectiveness of their attacks using advanced technologies and communications.

Ineffective Approach to Information Security

Traditional approaches to threat, risk, and vulnerability assessment focus either at a departmental or branch level and lack an enterprise perspective. In addition, many organizations assess and mitigate security risk from a technology perspective and deploy technology solutions. This approach ignores the importance to assess security risk in policy and execution.

Organizations deploy security solutions using technology instead of a holistic comprehensive approach. The three core areas that the approach should include are:

1. Risk in policy and procedure design,
2. Risk in systems configuration (hardware, software and facilities),
3. Risk in execution of security systems including human factors, and
4. Integration of the three core areas to form an enterprise level of protection.

Before we can effectively deal with the design and deployment of security solutions, we need to understand the value of the underlying information assets that need to be protected.

Concepts of the Information Life Cycle

Very often, information vulnerabilities are detected only when it is in an online production environment. Therefore, the patching to mitigate the vulnerabilities becomes an after effect. Information protection must be enforced throughout the creation, consumption when used by users and at the disposition (archiving) of the information to prevent privacy issues.

It is suggested that the flow of a piece of information from creation to disposition is called the "Information Life Cycle." Often when information is created, it is in a data format and carries minimum value to the holder and users of this data. When raw data is collected, it is not a piece of information yet. When data is placed within a framework, or multiple data are connected together to form a framework, only then it is called information. Such information can be used for processing and action can be derived out of the interpretation of the information. For example, 45 persons in a retail store is only a piece of data. However, when the 45 persons are lining up at the cashier windows with the invoice and delivery request, it becomes information (information creation stage). At this stage, there is a value of this information. However, the replenishment of the lost information at this stage will not be great as the administrative process has not been applied to the information. A rewrite of the sales slip, invoice, and deliver request could take a few minutes to recreate.

As information is developed, interpreted, and placed in a system, it becomes consumable information. Based on this information, the company will be able to perform actions on it. These include scheduling of delivery, processing of credit card transactions and creating reports on the statistics of the rate of inventory depletion and sales volume of the day. When action is taken based on the stored consumable information, this is the stage of "consumption" in the information life cycle. Any changes or incorrect information results from a security attack on the confidentiality, integrity, or availability of this information could be costly for the company. In many cases, the loss of a customer's complete information with credit card information at the stage (the stage of consumption of information) could mean that the company cannot process the sales and delivery, resulting in a loss of revenue, reputation, goodwill, and even legal action against the company. Information at this stage has the highest value as its consumption by users realizing its immediate value. The security protection of such information should also be highest.

When the product is delivered and the customer has signed off receiving the purchase, the information is now moved to the archive or disposition stage. The information still has some residual value attached with it. However, the loss of the information at this stage will not cause major issues to the company. It is noted that many merchants have the practice of not keeping the credit card information of the customer. It will be destroyed once the goods are delivered as a separate system (credit card company's record) will be made available to the company.

The final stage of the information life cycle also concludes that as the piece of current information is replaced by newer, more relevant and higher quality information, the current information becomes less useful and will become obsolete or require archiving as in the case of storage requirement only needed for legal or operational requirement. For example, the time-based information, such as deadlines for business tender, the result of the name of the company awarded with a contract or the formula of a patented drug that is newly retired into public information.

Information life cycle suggests that at its different stages, the associated intrinsic value changes. It is important that we use the Total Cost of Protection (as described below) to optimize the appropriate security mechanism to maximize the effects of the security protection implementation of information. Figure 1 shows an information life cycle.

The Concepts of Information Assurance

What is Information Assurance

Despite the many different perspectives and definitions of information assurance, it is commonly defined as "the set of measures intended to protect and defend information and information systems by ensuring their availability, integrity, authentication, confidentiality, and nonrepudiation" (National Security Agency FAQ, #2). The goal of information assurance is to assure the quality of information which results to inspire confidence on the use of information by its stakeholders. To achieve this goal, information assurance needs to assess policies and implementations of the underlying information security (InfoSec) systems. IA should monitor and audit the various levels of information security protection. The goal and functions of information assurance is presented in Figure 2.

The information assurance framework has three major components:

1. Specifying the guiding principles to the information policy
2. Auditing and monitoring of the performance of information security operations
3. Regulating the information security (InfoSec) system to minimize vulnerability

The Practice of Information Assurance Functions

(1) Specifying the guiding principle to the information security (Infosec) policy. The purpose of Information Assurance is to assure the quality of information. This includes the confidentiality, integrity, availability, privacy protection, proper authentication, and nonrepudiation of the origin and contents of information. From a policy point of view, information assurance specifies a set of policies and guiding principles to meet established information

Figure 1. Information life cycle

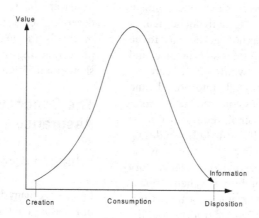

Figure 2. The goal and functions of information assurance

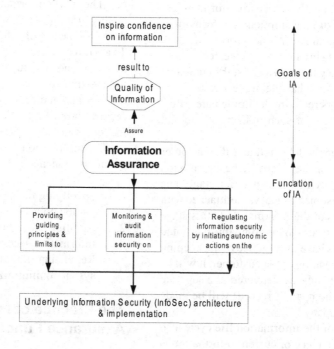

assurance standards that are carefully derived after risk management assessment are conducted on company information assets. IA should be in a form of directions, aspiration, and ultimate desired security objectives when at a policy level. In a design level, it could be a range of acceptable limits of acceptable security parameters to be used by the InfoSec system. For example, the Information Assurance design should specify the upper limit of using a firewall in the or-

ganization should be a stand-alone, hardware-based firewall with its specific and independent operating systems, whereas the lower limits could be the use of application firewalls that are installed on top of an existing desktop operating system.

Another example of a policy statement is the mandates to use a cost-based evaluation of information security vulnerability. This helps develop tools and design specification, such that the cost of security protection should never exceed the sum total of the value of the information. After implementation, the IA system can audit the Deployment Ratio (D_R) to ensure implementation follows the policy guidelines and specifications. Deployment Ratio is a ratio to ensure that company resources are justly deployed without spending more protection costs than the value of the information.

$$\text{Total Cost of protection} = \sum_{p=1}^{n} C_P$$

$C = f(P_1\ P_2\ .....P_n)$
For example,
P_1 = Process cost, P_2 = Equipment cost ,
P_3 = Human resources
P_4 = Goodwill and reputation
P_5 = Protection by designing built-in autonomic communications
V_1 to V_5 are the corresponding quantified value of the protection (it is also the value of the information under protection)

$$D_R = \frac{\sum\limits_{p=1}^{n} C_P}{\sum\limits_{x=1}^{n} V_i}$$

The value of D_R should, in most cases, be lower than or equal to one. IA should flag any D_R value that is over one as an exception, so that it can be reviewed by the policy maker of the organization. The implementation of a D_R value that is greater than one can be an example of a company's strategic decision.

(2) Auditing and monitoring of the performance of information security operations. This function should monitor the Information Security (InfoSec) function of the organization from the policy, design to implementation. This component fulfills the function of monitoring and auditing of the existing InfoSec system's performance. If vulnerabilities or attacks are detected, the IA system will proceed to the next stage of regulating the InfoSec system to achieve security assurance. The design of the level of assurance must be optimized and segregated in accordance to the cost of the impacts on the violation of the protection, such as information loss, failure of privacy protection, or illegal contents modifications. The concepts of defense in-depth should be used in the underlying information security (InfoSec). It should be matched with similar capability and capacity in the assurance level.

(3) Regulating the information security. Another function of the IA system should be the regulating of the Information Security (InfoSec) function of the organization in accordance to the policy design and implementation. If irregularities or vulnerabilities are detected, the IA system will initiate an autonomic mechanism to regulate the policy and implementation of the InfoSec policy and make changes to the InfoSec policy within the computing machines. If, however, there are no irregularities, then information flow will continue to the next stage.

The concept of this part of the checking system is depicted in Figure 3 with the implementation of a computer autonomics system. It is important to consider using autonomic machine to reduce security risk during execution, so as to avoid the reliance of human inconsistencies in the application of the security process.

The concept of this part of the regulating system is depicted in Figure 3.

Gate-Points of Information Assurance on the Information Life Cycle

To further illustrate how Information Assurance can be used to audit and to regulate security vulnerabilities, gate-points are created for decision making. When violations occur, it initiates a regulatory remediation to correct the unacceptable vulnerabilities. This correction will uphold the purposes of the IA in assuring the quality of information, and thus results to an inspiring of the confidence level of information used by stakeholders.

Information must be protected throughout its life cycle. It is also important to practice the complete IA constructs and practices across the whole enterprise. The weakest point of security protection within the enterprise system is also the weakest point of the complete security value chain (the successive additional value of security protection built upon from the previous stage of protection). Below is a figure on how an information assurance system assesses and audits information based on its stage within the life cycle. The degree of sophistication and level of intensity of audit is based on the different value of the information found in its different stage. This fulfills the cost optimization or proper cost appropriation given the value it needs to be protected. This is another very important practice as many organizations have an unbalance of cost/security protection value. Implementation in such organization are either overly

Figure 3. The autonomic information assurance system

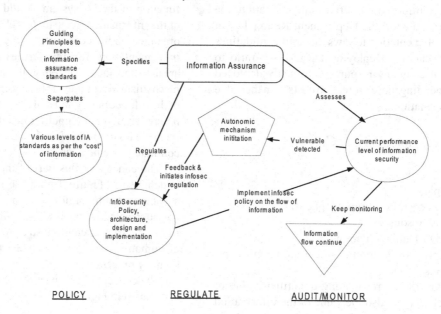

Figure 4. IA gate points with information life cycle

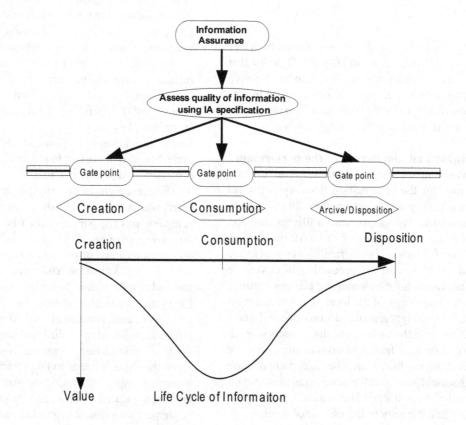

costly or under-protection, due to insufficient funding used for protection. To practice the Information Assurance concepts correctly, a correspondingly large amount of security costs can be incurred at points where information value at that life cycle stage is the highest and most critical to the organization.

The creation of information in many instances comes from recording or operation from a database of various data. The communication of information from one stage to another should be atomic. Any failure of a proper transfer of information should be backtracked to its original state before the transfer to ensure information integrity. Three different intensities of "information assurance gate-points" can be used to assure the quality of information. When information is created, the IA system is mostly concerned with the completeness and quality of information creation and the proper operations of the states within the computing systems. At the consumption stage, the information assurance system is concerned with the integrity, the confidentiality and availability of the information especially when transmitting the information over unsecured network such as Internet. In the disposition stage, information assurance concerns with the proper storage, accessibility and the integrity of the information.

Gate-points are set up to assure that the quality of the information at each stage is within the specification of the Information Assurance framework. A piece of information should be stopped from passing through the next state if the information does not meet the requirement of Information Assurance specification. This could be the result of irregularities of data being exposed or vulnerabilities causing data in an unprotected state.

Autonomic Computing Based on Triggers From Result of Audit Failure at Gate-Points

Implementation of autonomic systems can be established when information fails to pass the IA gate-point. In order to initiate the appropriate autonomic process, a specific scenario has to be created and parameters with threshold value have to be measured. Once a deficiency scenario is detected, the predefined back-out plan and correction procedure can be initiated.

Many organizations have adapted information security policies and implemented them to defend against crackers and the resulting fraudulent use

of information. However, the guiding, testing and regulating of the information security policies and implementations are greatly inadequate or deficient. This is in part because of the lack of a holistic approach to the assessment and protection of the complete enterprise. In order to understand the performance of the information security establishment, an enterprise and holistic view must be used for implementation.

CASE EXAMPLE

Let us take an example to illustrate the various models suggested in this chapter. This includes the Deployment Ratio, the process of Autonomic Information Assurance system. We will analyze how to apply the framework to address the information security breach in this case. In particular, we focus on how IA can be used to evaluate the quality of data and gate-point procedure can be used to initiate corrective procedure for autonomic communications.

Case: Police Secret Password Blunder

Case Background

On April 5, 2006, the NSW police e-mail list of 800 people with passwords was published on the Internet. While some of the passwords were used only for subscribing to the NSW Police media releases, many appeared to be the secret codes journalists use to access their e-mail accounts and other password-dependent information. The list included the password and e-mail details of two of the state's most senior counter-terrorism police officers, newly appointed Assistant Commissioner and Detective Chief Superintendent. The assistant commissioner regarded as the foremost terrorism expert among Australia's police services, said he had no idea it was available on the Internet. The database also included passwords belonging to well-known journalists at *The Sydney Morning Herald*, *The Daily Telegraph*, the ABC, and the commercial TV networks, as well as regional newspapers and radio stations.

NSW Police Media Unit was informed the password leak by its Internet host that the passwords used by subscribers are visible on the Internet. NSW Police had not contacted their media release subscribers over the apparent breach of privacy and security. Although the database appeared to have been taken offline within the past month, it could still be accessed through Google.

Accordingly to the police, the programming code behind the database had been "screwed up," causing it to show up on screen. Mr. Smith, the editor of data industry journal *Image and Data Manager,* said:

It's a cock-up rather than a conspiracy. It seems to be a serious breach of systems—it looks to be a massive breakdown of Web control systems. That database should never have been displayed on-screen; the information should just sit in the background. Publication of the information made it ripe for exploitation by hackers. People use the same passwords for a whole bunch of stuff, so from a social hacking point of view, it doesn't take a genius to work out how to use them.

A senior Channel Seven journalist, said he was "extremely pissed off" by the blunder. "I think it is an extraordinary case of incompetence from police and we expect the highest standards from police when dealing with confidential information." A Channel Nine reporter complained:

We are led to believe that NSW Police are experts in the area of security and it almost defies belief that a lapse such as this could ever occur. I'm concerned on behalf of my colleagues who may well have used the same password they use to access bank accounts and other confidential documents.

Another reporter indicated, "You would've thought if anyone was going to protect the security of information of this sort it would be the police force."

To rectify the problem, Police Media has arranged for all access to the service to be deleted. All subscribers will have to re-register and can do so without a password. The Police Media Unit is also advising those who registered using a password, one they would use for other purposes, to change that password immediately. (April 5, 2005, Sydney Morning Herald)

Analysis

Password published over the internet. The potential risk of this vulnerability is high, as the exposed data is available to hackers worldwide. The C_p for such vulnerability should be high in order to create more gate-points to block exposure of this information on the Web page.

Passwords of "power and normal users" should be categorized at different security levels. The cost of protection $C_{p\,should}$ be different from "power users" who are provider of information from the TV news media and radio. In many cases, they are the providers of information to the police database by exporting information from their source (media servers). General users who only subscribe to the police media release, on the other hand, are importer of information from the police Internet Web site into their desktop computers. The e-mail information should be categorized differently and exporter's information should be protected at a higher cost since losing this information caused more risk and damage than the general users.

No action from the provider after information security breached indicates a lack of IA monitoring and evaluation. Human factor is an integral part of information assurance. Extending from the InfoSec model, newer Information Assurance model Maconachy et al. (2001) has proposed information assurance, which includes people as part of a dimension in the model.

Deficiency of software programming quality testing. In building software, information assurance contribute its evaluation on the software by specifying the security requirement in the design of the software. In this case, it appears that the program is not implemented with any IA functions and specifications.

Suggested changes:

1. Implement IA to supervise InfoSec.
2. Setup IA Gate-point on all information delivered from database to any outputs, such as screen device and Internet Web page.
3. Classify security level of different e-mail group. For example, media and radio companies are provider of information and general users are user of information. Higher security protection should be placed on the e-mail and password information of the importer.
4. Setup autonomic procedures. This includes any e-mail and password (other than public contact e-mail address should not be contains in public access Web page in the Internet. When such irregularity occurs, the IA software will close the gate-point from database to piping the output to a Web page. Autonomic process will segregate any violated data and process. Any other legitimate data and information should

be able to pass through the gate-point and still be available to the Internet Web page.

5. IA software and autonomic process should relate message to administrator using a network communication system to page, e-mail and log the event in log file. This will prevent external report of such exposure as described in the case.

ENTERPRISE LEVEL RISK MANAGEMENT

No matter how well an IA framework and system is practiced within a protection domain, it must be implemented at an enterprise level. Many enterprise architecture frameworks and risk management models have been proposed. These include Hennings (2004) Policy Decompose System, 17799 Common Information Security Architecture by Committee of Sponsoring Organizations of the Treadway Commission and Zachman Information Systems Architecture. To assist practitioners, a brief introduction of various risk management and information architecture models are presented below. The selecting of these models should be based on a clear understanding of the needs of the enterprise, not the needs of an individual branch and division.

To create a holistic assurance policy, decomposition of the policy into various sub-policies is necessary. Hennings (2004) has taken a divide and conquer method to properly decompose a system security policy.

The concepts of "divide and conquer" by decomposition should be practiced in the architecture, design, process and procedure, and finally implementation level. As an example, to ensure an enterprise wide practice of the information assurance policy, it should be divided into different areas of concentrations. They are (1) identification and authentication of the protection domains, (2) the access control, network connections and the policy for authorization and extension of privileges from one system to another, (3) the penetration, testing, and audit of the security assurance procedure and the underlying InfoSec procedure.

Other holistic approach to risk management and security implementation include a 17799 Common Information Security structure. The model can be seen at URL: http://www.coso.org/Publications/ERM/COSO_ERM_ExecutiveSummary.pdf

We can use this model to create a blueprint appropriately to the specific organization for the security

architecture design and implement from top organizational levels down to the operational levels. Emphasis should be placed upon a holistic approach to the organization by including every branch and every division of the enterprise. Supplementary policy should be set up for intranet for employees and extranet services with business partner. By extending a coverage across the enterprise and to its trading partners, a relatively enclave security system may be created.

The Zachman framework (source: http://www.zifa.com/ Zachman Framework overview) provides a systematic approach as to how information is to be classified. One can use the same taxonomy to create the framework on information assurance process of how each of the information should be valued and protected.

As an example to a holistic approach to enterprise security, the inclusion of physical branch and division is important. It is also important to include the various business requirements on the protection of information. The architecture of a security framework for an insurance company which has an Internet Web site for an e-commerce transaction would look like the following Figure 5.

In addition to the above models, practitioners can use the model on enterprise risk management framework proposed by the Committee of Sponsoring Organizations of the Treadway Commission (Flaherty & Maki, 2004). URL http://www.coso.org/Publications/ERM/COSO_ERM_ExecutiveSummary.pdf shows a three dimensional matrix of the model. The three dimensions depict the "objectives," enterprise risk management components and what is needed to achieve the objectives.

For those who would like to use a mathematical approach to assist in the discovery of vulnerabilities. The Kolmogorov Complexity-based Vulnerability (Evans et al., 2000) techniques can be used.

New research has been generated to address the complexity and create capability of automated discovery of vulnerabilities. This can be found in Kolmogorov Complexity-based Vulnerability Analysis to

$$K_{\varphi}(x) = \left\{ \min_{\varphi(p)=x} l(p) \right\}.$$

where cp represents a universal computer, p represents a program, and x represents a string: Random strings have rather high Kolmogorov Complexity.

Figure 5. Example of security architecture

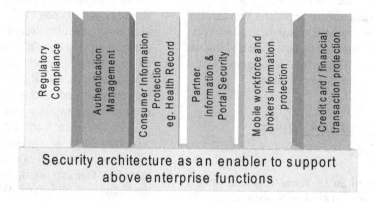

Suggested Procedure to Create an Information Assurance System in an Enterprise

1. Determine the enterprise's regional and international legal requirement for compliance especially if the enterprise operates internationally.
2. Determine what information is needed to be protected.
3. Identify potential risks based on (2) and categorize them in a quantifiable value, according to impact level (that is, the calculation of the total value of information within the Information Life Cycle).
4. Determine the information assurance protection level of the information under protection.
5. Develop a security policy in relation to the information under protection.
6. Review and benchmark the capability of the current information systems and its associated InfoSec protection system within the enterprise.
7. Perform force field analysis or strength weakness opportunity and threat (SWOT) analysis on the current InfoSec and information system based on benchmark in (6).
8. Based on identified information that need to be protected, perform an enterprise risk assessment of security vulnerability and benchmark result based on the life cycle and the process flow of the specific information within the enterprise.
9. Determine the logical location and type of gatepoints within the information assurance security system.
10. Create information architecture and design of the Information Assurance system.
11. Develop gate point decision criteria and predefine process and procedure to minimize vulnerability using autonomic computing facilities.
12. Conduct training and implement pilot test and enterprise implementation.
13. Post implementation review and ensure full documentation at each stage.
14. Evaluate performance of the Information Assurance system.
15. Perform penetration test, audit every half year or when major system changes.
16. Redesign and repeat IA system enhancement from Step 1 onwards as needed after each audit.
17.
18. IA software and autonomic process should relate message to administrator using network communication system to page, e-mail, and log the event in log file. This will prevent external report of such exposure as described in the case.19.

20. Create a periodic audit schedule (usually every six months) to confirm that policy is being practiced, and the underlying infrastructure has not been changed to the extent that vulnerability exceeds the level of protection.

FUTURE TRENDS

Giga-bit communication networks are now common in many organizations. Future trends of terra-bit multimedia network (voice-over IP, image, and data) allow for new vulnerabilities to be transmitted much faster than before. Multimedia personal digital assistants (PDA) and wireless devices constitute opportunity for more vulnerability. According to Saydnari (2006), Information Assurance in the near future will require addressing new requirements in privacy. It is also observed that multimodel biometric authentication and multiple factors authentication will be increasingly popular in the next five years.

CONCLUSION

To address the ever-changing new technology, legal requirement, the need to gain competitive advantage within an industry, and the cost reduction of outsourcing which result to the requirement of enterprise security, a comprehensive approach must be used to implement security. Various concepts and frameworks have been provided for evaluating and creating a holistic approach to an enterprise security information assurance. This chapter has shown the drivers that caused the needs for an enterprise requirement of security architecture. By using the information life cycle model and total cost of deployment calculation method, a proper assurance of cost benefits value of security protection can be measured. The use of the suggested gate-points (decision making) process, an autonomic and automatic computer initiation of the security protection mechanism can be implemented to reduce vulnerability. By employing the enterprise wide coverage and the above described tools and methodologies, autonomic protection can be created with less human intervention. This in turn will increase the protection and the quality of information and achieve an effective Information Assurance across the enterprise.

REFERENCES

Burlton, R. (2001). Business process management: Profiting from process. *SAM,* (1), 11.

Evans, et al. (2000). Information assurance through Kolmogorov complexity. *IEEE.*

Flaherty, J., & Maki, T. (2004). Enterprise d: Integrated framework, executive summary. *USA Committee of Sponsoring Organizations of the Treadway Commission.*

Gibson, J. (2006). Police secret password blunder. *Sydney Morning Herald.* Retrieved May 1, 2008, from http://www.smh.com.au/news/technology/police-secret-password-blunder/2006/04/05/1143916566038.html?page=fullpage

Hennings, R. (2004). *Use of the zachman architecture for security engineering.* Florida, USA: Harris Corporation.

Jaquith, A. (2007). *Security metrics: Replacing fear, uncertainty and doubt.* New Jersey: Addison-Wesley.

Krutz, R., & Vines, R. (2001). *The CISSP prep guide.* John Wiley & Sons, Inc.

Maconachy et al. (2001). A model for information assurance: An integrated approach. **In** *Proceedings of the 2001 IEEE Workshop on Information Assurance.* New York.

National Reconnaissance Organization. (1997). Just how secure is your cellular phone? *National Reconnaissance Organization Newsletter.* Retrieved May 1, 2008, from http://www.wasc.noaa.gov/wrso/security_guide/cellular.htm

Saydjari, O. (2006, January/February). Information assurance technology forecast. *IEEE Computer Society Journal of IEEE Security & Privacy,* 62-69.

Stoneburmer, G. et al. (2002). Risk management guide for information technology systems. *National Institute of Standards and Technology Special Publication* (pp. 800-803). Virginia, USA: Booz Allen Hamilton Inc.

Tipton, H., & Krasuse, M. (2000). *Information security management handbook 4th Ed.* New York: Auerbach.

Warkentin, M., & Vaughn, R. (2006). *Enterprise information systems assurance and system security: Managerial and technical issues.* London Idea Group Publishing.

KEY TERMS

Gate-Point: An evaluation point within an information security implementation which allows for the decision to initiate a predefined counter action to reduce the impact of a security vulnerability or attack.

Information Assurance (IA): The set of measures intended to protect and defend information and information systems by ensuring their availability, integrity, authentication, confidentiality, and nonrepudiation.

Information Life Cycle: A model whereby information is classified into a spectrum from creation, consumption to disposition within its useful life span. This allows the appropriate evaluation of the "value" of the information within each stage.

Total Cost of Protection: This is the sum total of the cost deployed in order to protect the underlying information. This total cost should include both tangible and intangible costs, such as hardware, software, administrations, goodwill, opportunity costs, and human resources.

Chapter VI
An Integrative Framework for the Study of Information Security Management Research

John D'Arcy
University of Notre Dame, USA

Anat Hovav
Korea University, Korea

ABSTRACT

A number of academic studies that focus on various aspects of information security management (ISM) have emerged in recent years. This body of work ranges from the technical, economic, and behavioral aspects of ISM to the effect of industry standards, regulations, and best practices. The purpose of this chapter is to review the current state of ISM research, while providing an integrative framework for future studies. Using the proposed framework as a guide, we identify areas of depth within current ISM literature and areas where research is underdeveloped. Finally, we call for a more comprehensive approach to ISM research that considers multiple dimensions of our framework and their interrelationships.

INTRODUCTION

As organizational reliance on information systems (IS) has increased over recent decades, so has the number of IS security breaches and their impact on organizations. This impact is evidenced in survey reports by the Computer Security Institute (Gordon, Loeb, Lucyshyn, & Richardson, 2006) and CompTIA Research (2002). Considering that only a fraction of security incidents are discovered (Whitman & Mattord, 2005), and that organizations are often reluctant to disclose such information for fear of negative publicity that could damage their image and/or stock price (Hoffer & Straub, 1989), it is likely that actual losses are significantly higher than reported. The frequency of

IS security breaches and the amount of losses associated with them has spurred increased interest among information security practitioners and researchers. "Security and privacy" was ranked as the number two most important IT management issue in a key issue survey of IT executives (Luftman, 2005). Research by Ernst and Young (Global Information Security Survey, 2004) indicates that 93% of organizations view information security as highly important to achieving their overall objectives. Among academic researchers, a number of studies that focus on various aspects of information security management (ISM) have emerged in recent years. This body of work ranges from the technical, economic, and behavioral aspects of ISM to the effect of industry standards, regulations, and best practices. The purpose of this chapter is to review the current state of ISM research, while providing an integrative framework for future studies. Using the proposed framework as a guide, we identify areas of depth within current ISM literature and areas where research is underdeveloped. Finally, we call for a more comprehensive approach to ISM research that considers multiple dimensions of our framework and their interrelationships.

DIMENSIONS OF INFORMATION SECURITY MANAGEMENT

Information security is described in terms of confidentiality, integrity, availability, privacy, identification, authentication, authorization, and accountability of information (Whitman & Mattord, 2005). This description points to the multifaceted nature of ISM and the fact that it involves far more than technical solutions. We propose that ISM can be conceptualized in terms of the five dimensions depicted in Figure 1. Three of the ISM dimensions are organizational in nature: financial/economic impact, strategy and best practices, and behavioral issues. The other two dimensions are external to the organization in the sense that managers have less control over them: standards and regulations and available information security technology. As depicted by the arrows in Figure 1, the three organizational dimensions are interrelated. In addition, both external dimensions have some affect on the organizational dimensions. For example, standards and regulations may impact organizational

strategy and best practices, or the financial impact of ISM, or the expected behavior of users. Similarly, the external dimensions are interrelated. For the sake of brevity and clarity, we do not illustrate all possible relationships between the five dimensions. However, we do acknowledge that alternative interrelationships may exist.

In the following sections, we describe the current state of ISM research and identify gaps in our knowledge. Our objective is not to provide an exhaustive review of the literature, but rather to outline existing research streams within each of the proposed dimensions. We also identify future research opportunities based on the interrelationships between the dimensions.

Information Security Technology

The focus of most technical ISM has been on the formal automated part of an information system (Dhillon & Backhouse, 2001). This literature views ISM as a technical issue that can be effectively managed by selecting appropriate hardware and software components and designing a robust architecture to protect organizational information assets. Technical ISM research is rooted in computer science, and as such, includes seminal work from this field. For example, Saltzer and Schroeder (1975) provided a comprehensive overview of the architectural structures (physical and logical) necessary to support information protection in hardware and software. Denning (1987) developed a model for an intrusion detection expert system capable of detecting internal

Figure 1. Framework for the study of information security management

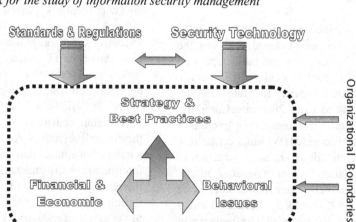

and external computer abuse incidents. The model provides a foundation for current intrusion detection technologies and is based on the premise that security violations can be detected from abnormal patterns of system usage. More recent technical ISM research has focused on technological solutions for fundamental security problems such as how to restrict information resource access to authorized individuals, how to transmit and receive information in a secure manner, and how to keep information accurate and available in the face of internal and external threats (Stanton, Stam, Mastrangelo, & Jolton, 2005). This body of work includes studies on: (1) secure identification and personal verification technologies such as passwords and personal identification numbers (e.g., Furnell, Dowland, & Papadaki, 2002), access controls (e.g., Osborn, Ravi, & Qamar, 2000), and biometric devices (Boukhonine, Krotov, & Rupert, 2005); (2) encryption and secure communications (e.g., Lou & Liu, 2002); and (3) protective devices such as firewalls (e.g., Kamara, Fahmy, Shultz, Kerschbaum, & Frantzen, 2003) and intrusion detection systems (e.g., Axelsson, 2000; Cavusoglu, Mishra, & Raghunathan, 2005).

Another topic of technical ISM research is the incorporation of security into the design of information systems. In one of the earliest studies, Conway, Maxwell, and Morgan (1972) introduced a security matrix that allowed system designers to specify the conditions under which a user could access a particular data structure and the action that a user could perform upon the data structure. Bell and LaPadula (1976) developed a model for secure operating environment based on the MULTICS operating system, using memory segmentation and rings of protection architecture. In the 1980s, the United States (U.S.) National Security Agency (NSA) produced a series of documents called The Rainbow Series that included evaluation criteria for secure computer design. The purpose of The Rainbow Series was to offer guidelines for meeting the U.S. Department of Defense's criteria for trusted computer systems. More recently, the U.S. National Institute of Standards and Technology (NIST) has produced a series of publications, called the NIST 800 series, which include current best practices in secure information system design. Academic research on secure design includes a study by Johnston, Eloff, and Labuschagne (2003) that applied usability criteria from human computer interface (HCI) research to the interface of Windows XP's Internet Connection Firewall and Payne's (2002) investigation of security issues associated with the design of open source software.

A related stream of technical ISM research has examined risk analysis methods for the design of secure information systems (e.g., Fisher, 1984; von Solms, van de Haar, von Solms, & Caelli, 1994). Risk analysis methods suggest that information systems can be made more secure if security controls are developed and implemented within the system development life cycle. Baskerville (1993), however, questioned the risk analysis approach to secure systems design, asserting that these design methods assume that a largely similar set of controls can be used effectively across a widely dissimilar population of information systems.

In addition to technical ISM research that has focused on the security of information systems themselves, there is also work that has explored the technical details of various threats to information systems. Cohen (1984) discussed the technical aspects of computer viruses and conducted a series of experiments that demonstrated the feasibility of a viral attack against unprotected systems. Spafford (1989) detailed the technical functioning of the Robert Morris worm, which is the first known viral attack against the Internet. More recent studies include technical accounts of the Slammer (Panko, 2003) and Blaster (Chen, 2003) worms.

A final area of technical ISM research is the IT industry. The IT industry (i.e., hardware and software vendors, consultants, industry consortiums) is a primary driver of security technology. However, the impact of the IT industry on ISM technology has received little attention from academic researchers. Caelli (2002) argued that decisions made by IT vendors in the early 1980s have affected the current state of security affairs. For example, lessons learned from the MULTICS project were ignored in the development of Microsoft operating systems and the Reduced Instruction Set Computer (RISC) architecture, resulting in vulnerable computer systems. Anderson (2001) asserted that the IT industry has emphasized cheap and fast development over security concerns. Hovav (2005a) discussed several issues involving the recent trustworthy computing initiative and its impact on the IT industry and information security ecosystem. Hovav and D'Arcy (2005) conducted an empirical investigation and found that the stock market does not penalize vendors for software defects, which suggests little economic incentive for vendors to produce "secure" software products. In addition, Cavusoglu, Mishra, and Raghunathan (2004) found that public security breach announcements have a positive influence on the stock prices of security technology developers.

Research Opportunities

While the preceding discussion reveals a large body of research that focuses on technical solutions to information security problems, evolving threats such as e-commerce security and identity theft underscore the need for additional technical ISM research. Research is also needed on technical security solutions for emerging technologies such as the Next Generation Internet Protocol (i.e., IP version 6), wireless networks, mobile devices, and voice-over IP telephony. There is also a need for more advanced tools for managing user authentication both on the Internet and for internal organizational computing systems. Password security systems suffer from several limitations (Irakleous et al., 2002), and therefore, research must continue on alternative access control technologies. Finally, the mixed results regarding the impact of vulnerable hardware and software on IT vendors and the interrelated nature of the information security ecosystem suggest the need for additional investigation on this topic. Future research is also needed to better understand the culture of the information security industry, and the industry factors that drive or inhibit the development and utilization of security technologies.

Standards and Regulations

A number of standards have been proposed for ISM. ISO 17799 is one of the most prominent international standards on information security (Ma & Pearson, 2005). ISO 17799 outlines 10 control areas consisting of 36 security practices, has its origins in British Standard (BS) 7799, and is mandatory in the United Kingdom (U.K.) and in certain European countries. The recently published ISO 27001 outlines the steps necessary for implementing ISO 17799 controls within an ISM program. The U.S. has not adopted a mandatory standard. Instead, organizations in the U.S. rely on a combination of security guidelines from NIST (i.e., the 800 series), ISO 17799, and industry consortiums (Whitman & Mattord, 2005). Many of these guidelines have come from U.S. government-based initiatives such as The Rainbow Series and the Federal Information Security Management Act (FISMA), whose purpose is to develop federal computer security standards. Moteff (2004) provides a summary of key U.S. laws of interest and government directives involving information security.

Considering the popularity of ISO 17799, it is not surprising that several studies have addressed this topic. Ma and Pearson (2005) constructed a set of survey items that measure the ten ISO 17799 control areas. The researchers confirmed the validity and reliability of these measures and offer them as self-assessment tools for gauging compliance with ISO 17799. Pattinson (2003) proposed a methodological approach based on goal attainment scaling (GAS) for assessing the degree of compliance with ISO 17799. Theoharidou, Kokolakis, Karyda, and Kiountouzis (2005) performed a critical analysis of ISO 17799 in terms of its effectiveness in addressing the insider threat to information systems. The analysis suggests that ISO 17799 draws heavily from general deterrence theory and could be improved by additional theoretical perspectives such as social bond theory and situational crime prevention theory. Backhouse, Hsu, and Silva (2006) used the circuits of power framework and found that politics and power played significant roles at various levels (e.g., organizational, industry, national, and international) in making ISO 17799 the dominant standard for ISM.

In addition to ISO 17799-based studies, there is research that focuses on additional ISM standards, as well as the relationships between these standards. Tulu and Chatterjee (2003) presented an ISM framework for achieving compliance with the Health Insurance Portability and Accountability Act (HIPAA). Hoxey and Shoemaker (2005) examined the relationship between ISO 17799 and ISO 15408, an international standard that deals with evaluating the security functionality embedded within IT products and systems. The authors suggest that an understanding of both standards is necessary for a comprehensive ISM program. Siponen (2003) critically analyzed the foundations of three widely used ISM standards: BS 7799, GASSP, and SSE-CMM, and concluded that these standards are naïve in that they generalize across organizations, promote reactionary security activities, and stifle security innovations. Tejay (2005) conducted an analysis of various ISM standards and cautioned that the decision as to which standards to adopt must be aligned with business objectives.

Research Opportunities

As is evident from the aforementioned review, current research on ISM standards is limited to critical analyses of these standards, prescriptive advice on standard implementation, and assessments of standard compliance. However, the postimplementation effectiveness of many of these standards remains unclear. For example: (1) what is the effect of various ISM standards in reducing the number of security breaches, and (2) are there industry, cultural, size, and/or geopolitical differences in the effectiveness of these standards? Furthermore, it is not feasible to adopt every standard or every single facet of a particular standard (Tejay, 2005). Hence, there is a need for detailed empirical analyses that assess the effectiveness of individual components of ISM standards in various organizational contexts to provide managers with more effective implementation guidelines.

In addition to mandatory and voluntary standards that promote effective ISM practices, governments have begun to enforce additional regulations (e.g., HIPAA, Sarbanes-Oxley). For example, the California Database Security Breach Act (CA SB 1386) requires organizations that do business with California residents to notify these individuals if their personal information has been compromised (or potentially compromised) due to a security breach. Similar laws are currently in the works for other U.S. states and in many other countries. Presently, there is little research that has studied the impact of such regulations on organizational security policies and practices. This is a salient issue for multinational companies, because they have to abide by regulations in various countries, adding to the complexity of their ISM programs. Finally, it should be noted that most of the aforementioned studies come from conference proceedings, so it seems that research on ISM standards and regulations has not reached mainstream status within the information security literature. Given the general trend towards "beefing up" ISM regulations both in the U.S. and worldwide, it appears that this topic is a fruitful avenue for future work.

Strategy and Best Practices

As suggested by Baskerville (1993), the "one size fits all" taken by much of the above two ISM research streams may not be appropriate. The assumption that a particular security control, standard, or regulation will work the same for all companies, every information system, or under all circumstances is quite simplistic. For example, D'Arcy and Hovav (2007) found that certain security countermeasures are more/less effective in deterring certain IS misuse types.

There is a sizable body of literature on ISM best practices that comes from the U.S. government and its affiliated organizations (e.g., NIST 800 series, The Rainbow Series, Federal Agency Security Practices).

There is also a small but growing body of academic research that looks at organizational ISM strategy and best practices. von Solms and von Solms (2004) presented guidelines on how organizations can move from security policies to a positive security culture. Doherty and Fulford (2006) argued that alignment of security policy with the strategic information systems plan is necessary for achieving ISM effectiveness. Siponen and Iivari (2006) used design theories to develop a contingency-based framework of security policies and guidelines based on type of organization and business environment. For example, conservative-deontological design theory is used as a basis for security policies in stable business environments and in rule-oriented organizations (where people are accustomed to acting by the book), while utilitarian-based security policies are suggested for organizations in more turbulent business environments. Woon (2001) developed a framework for ISM that combines security standards, user profiles, assessment heuristics, and automated tools and procedures, providing recommendations for implementing the framework and how the components can be modified to achieve an effective ISM program.

Research Opportunities

Beyond those mentioned above, there is little academic research regarding organizational ISM strategy and best practices. Moreover, existing research consists mostly of prescriptive advice on strategies for managing security with little empirical evidence to support their effectiveness. Much of the current best practice research is driven by industry standards (see "Standards and Regulations" section above). However, there is limited research that attempts to apply these standards to a particular organization or strategy. Future research should focus on ISM implementation strategies and best practices across a variety of industries and organizational contexts. This research should include empirical investigations of the effectiveness of various ISM strategies and best practices.

Financial and Economic

There is a growing body of literature on the financial and economic aspects of ISM. This literature includes a diverse set of topics such as security investment decisions, economic analyses of software piracy and intrusion detection systems, and the financial impact of security breaches. Gordon and Loeb (2002) developed an economic model to determine the optimal amount that organizations should invest in information security. Cavusoglu et al. (2004a) presented an economic model based on game theory to evaluate the return on security investments. Gopal and Saunders (1997) used an economic model to determine the effect of deterrent and preventative antipiracy efforts on software developers' profits. Anderson (2001) used economic analysis (i.e., network externalities, asymmetric information, moral hazard, adverse selection) to explain several IS security problems and argued that unsecured systems result from perverse economic incentives in which the party who is in a position to protect the system is not the party who suffers the negative results of a security failure.

Financial/economic ISM research has also focused on assessments of financial damage caused by various types of security breaches. This research is of interest to organizations trying to decide where to spend their security budgets as well as for insurance companies that provide cyber-risk policies. A popular methodological approach has been the event study. The event study, which is based on the semistrong form of the efficient market hypothesis (Brealey & Myers, 1996), examines the stock market reaction to the public announcement of a particular event. Hovav and D'Arcy (2003) studied the impact of denial-of-service (DOS) attacks on the stock prices of attacked companies and found little overall impact, except for e-commerce companies. Hovav and D'Arcy (2004) also assessed the impact of computer virus announcements on the stock prices of attacked companies and found no significant effects. Campbell, Gordon, Loeb, and Zhou (2003) found a highly significant negative market reaction for breaches involving confidential data (i.e., customer credit card numbers), but not for other types of breaches. Other studies (Anthony, Wooseok, & Grabski, 2006; Cavusoglu, Mishra, & Raghunathan, 2004b) that examined the market impact of various security breaches found only a minor effect that was limited to e-commerce companies.

Research Opportunities

Although the financial/economic impact of ISM is a growing area of research, several prolific avenues for future work remain. Trade magazines report increasing costs to repair security breaches while academic studies provide little evidence of these costs other than short-term changes in stock prices for e-commerce companies (e.g., Cavusoglu et al., 2004b; Hovav and

D'Arcy, 2003). Hence, from a bottom-line perspective, there appears to be little strategic incentive for organizations to invest in security. Research is needed to better understand the total cost of security and the underlying factors that drive security investment decisions to determine whether managers are acting rationally or are simply responding to institutional pressures. Further, as organizations shift from viewing information security as a capital investment to the insurance model of risk reduction (Gordon, Loeb, & Sohail, 2003), research is needed to better understand the costs and benefits of security investments using risk management models and theories. Finally, extraneous factors such as government regulations (see "Standards and Regulations" section above) are likely to affect security investments. Many U.S. organizations are becoming increasingly concerned with the costs of regulatory compliance, which could become prohibitive (Hovav, 2005b). Furthermore, monetary penalties for noncompliance can be substantial. For example, consumer data broker ChoicePoint was ordered to pay over $15 million in liability charges after a security breach exposed the credit information of thousands of individuals (Anonymous, 2006). Further investigation of the economic impact of government regulations on ISM programs is necessary.

Behavioral Issues

Research on behavioral issues has become an increasingly important component of the ISM literature. This research has been driven by the results of academic studies and industry statistics that indicate that technological countermeasures alone do not provide adequate security of information resources (Stanton et al., 2005).

Behavioral ISM studies have examined both positive and negative security behaviors. Thomson and von Solms (1998) argued for the use of theoretically-driven techniques from social psychology (i.e., persuasion, social learning, and attribution) as a strategy for improving security compliance among end users. Magklaras and Furnell (2005) examined the influence of end user sophistication in predicting inappropriate use of IS resources by internal users. Aytes and Connolly (2004) found that computer expertise and perceived probability of negative consequences were positively associated with regularly backing-up data, scanning unknown e-mail attachments for viruses, changing passwords, and not sharing passwords. Stanton et al. (2005) found that secure password behavior among end users was associated with training, awareness, monitoring, and motivation.

A number of studies have also examined the impact of various security countermeasures on IS misuse behaviors. This work is based on the theoretical perspective of general deterrence theory, which suggests that the existence of security countermeasures can deter illicit computing behavior by increasing the perceived certainty and severity of sanctions for such activity. Straub (1990) found that use of procedural and technical security controls was associated with lower levels of computer abuse. Similarly, Kankanhalli, Hock-Hai, Tan, and Wei (2003) found that greater organizational deterrent efforts (in the form of person-hours expended on IS security purposes) and preventative efforts (in the form of more advanced security software) were associated with higher perceived security effectiveness. Doherty and Fulford (2005), however, reported no significant relationships between the adoption of security policies and the incidence or severity of security breaches in sample of large U.K. organizations.

At the individual level of analysis, D'Arcy and Hovav (in press) examined user awareness of security policies, security awareness programs, and preventative security software and found that each was negatively associated with IS misuse intention. Gopal and Sanders (1997) found that providing users with policy statements that prohibit software piracy and discuss its legal consequences resulted in lower piracy intentions. Conversely, Foltz (2000) found that a university computer usage policy had no effect on IS misuse intentions and behaviors involving modifying, stealing, or destroying software and data. Harrington (1996) assessed the impact of general and IS-specific codes of ethics on computer abuse judgments and intentions among IS employees. Results indicated that general codes of ethics had no effect on computer abuse judgments and intentions, while IS-specific codes of ethics had a slight effect for one type of computer abuse (computer sabotage). Lee, Lee, and Yoo (2004) found that security policies and security systems had no impact on the computer abuse behaviors of a sample of Korean managers.

Behavioral ISM research has also expanded beyond traditional organizational boundaries to include topics such as hacker motivation and home user security. Seminal hacker motivation studies include Landreth (1985), Parker (1998), and Denning (1998). Denning (1998) examined the psychological profiles of hackers and identified curiosity, challenge, recognition from peers, personal satisfaction, and feelings of power as motivating factors for engaging in hacking activities. Research on home user security has become important given the rise in telecommuting and other virtual work arrangements that require remote access to organizational systems. Conklin (2006) used diffusion of innovation theory to study computer security practices among home users and found that suitability, risk awareness, perceived importance of security, communication with the security vendor, and perceptions of others were important factors in predicting this behavior. Woon, Tan, and Low (2005) tested a model of home wireless security based on protection motivation theory and found that self-efficacy, response cost, and perceived severity of threats were key variables that predict whether home users secure their wireless networks.

Research Opportunities

As is evident from the above discussion, there is a substantial amount of research on the behavioral aspects of ISM which explores the antecedents of compliant security behaviors and the impact of security countermeasures on IS misuse behavior. Further, unlike research within the other ISM dimensions, much of the behavioral ISM research has a strong theoretical underpinning. However, this body of work has produced inconclusive results. One potential explanation for the inconsistent findings is the differences among offenders (or potential offenders). Criminological research suggests that individual and situational differences moderate the impact of various countermeasures (Tittle, 1980). Future research should explore whether variables such as computer experience, risk propensity, industry, and culture have an impact on the effectiveness of security countermeasures. Additional research is also needed to understand the long term impact of security countermeasures, which may include negative consequences such as loss of trust, productivity and loyalty, increased dissatisfaction and stress, aggression, fear, and withdrawal behavior (Siponen, 2000). Behavioral ISM research should also examine the misuse behaviors of nontraditional employees such as contractors and third-party business partners. Finally, most current behavioral ISM research is concentrated in the U.S. Given the global nature of most large organizations, geographical, regulatory, and cultural differences among user populations are likely to have an impact on security-related behaviors, and therefore should be examined.

OVERALL ANALYSIS

In analyzing the current state of ISM research, it is evident that a substantial proportion focuses on technical solutions to security problems. Technical ISM research dates back to the early 1970s and its prominence within the literature is undoubtedly an outgrowth of the IS field's roots in computer science and software engineering. Our analysis also indicates that there is substantial amount of research on the financial/economic and behavioral aspects of ISM. However, there is limited theoretically-driven research in terms of ISM standards and regulations and strategy and best practices. Moreover, current ISM research also suffers from the following limitations:

1. A "one size fits all" approach to ISM solutions.
2. A lack of an integrative approach.
3. Limited geopolitical scope—most studies are limited to organizations within the U.S.
4. Limited organizational scope—most studies are limited to a single organization.
5. Extraneous factors such as regulations and the IT industry are often ignored.

The proposed framework attempts to address some of the limitations listed above. Aside from the five dimensions of ISM research depicted in Figure 1, the diagram also includes arrows connecting several of the separate dimensions to signify the need for a more integrative approach. Thus, in addition to the research opportunities discussed in the previous sections, we propose that future research include more than one of the five dimensions within a single study. Examples of such integrative ISM research include:

- Research that examines the impact of various security technologies on user behaviors. The impact of IT artifacts on the humans who directly and indirectly interact with them as one of the core properties of the IS discipline (Benbasat & Zmud, 2003). However, there is a dearth of empirical research that has explored such relationships within the domain of information security. Two exceptions are Hazari's (2005) study of end user adoption and use of personal firewall software and James, Pirim, Boswell, Reithel, and Barkhi's (2006) study of end user adoption of biometric devices.
- Research on the interaction of organizational characteristics and security best practices. Cur-

rent ISM standards and best practices assume that the same practice would work effectively for all organizations regardless of size, industry, culture, etc. Future ISM research can utilize theories from organizational strategy (e.g., institutional theory, ecological theory, contingency theory) to examine the "fit" between organizational characteristics and their ISM program, the effect of institutionalization on ISM implementation, and the environmental conditions that drive ISM in various organizations.

- Research on ISM standards and regulations and their impact on the IT industry and available security technologies. This research should examine current and future trends in the "locus of cyber-liability." Presently, cyber-liability rests with the users of information technology. However, recent regulations shift some of the liability to service organizations. New standards and regulations can cause further shifts that might impact both the organization and the IT industry. Future research should also address the impact of regulatory activities on organizational ISM best practices and security investment decisions.
- A total cost of ownership approach to budgeting information security that can provide organizations with a framework to assess the proper allocation of each security measure (i.e., guidance on how much of the security budget should be allocated to technologies, policies, user education and training, and other preventative measures, depending on organizational context).
- Research on the economics of various security breaches. Currently, there is little research on the actual cost to repair security breaches. Therefore, it is not clear if it is more cost effective to continue the current trend of implementing security fixes on an "as needed" basis or if it would be more cost effective to redesign some of the major software packages used. This is a complex issue that depends on the cost of including security in the design phase of an information system (i.e., return on security investment from the vendor perspective), the economics of the IT industry, and the costs to repair accrued by commercial and private users of information technology.
- Research on the development and evaluation of metrics for measuring the effectiveness of ISM programs. Such metrics are especially impor-

tant for information security practitioners, and should cover all five dimensions discussed in this chapter.

The above list is by no means exhaustive. However, it can serve as a starting point toward a set of potential new areas of ISM research that will complement the existing, largely isolated research streams.

CONCLUSION

As evident from the above discussion, some ISM research areas are well developed while others are lacking. While computer scientists continue to develop new technologies to support information security, the effectiveness of these solutions (from a strategic, economic, and/or behavioral perspective) within organizations remains unclear. As ISM becomes a prevailing and strategic issue for organizations, a more integrative research approach will be necessary. Using the existing research streams as a foundation, IS researchers are well positioned to tackle these challenges.

REFERENCES

Anderson, R. (2001). Why information security is hard—An economic perspective. *Seventeenth Annual Computer Security Applications Conference.* New Orleans, LA.

Anonymous. (2006). ChoicePoint pays $15 million for information mis-management. *Hearsay.com: Intellectual Property & CyberLaw Journal.* Retrieved May 1, 2008, from http://www.hearsay.com/wp-archives/2006/01/27/choicepoint-ameriprise/

Anthony, J.H., Wooseok, C., & Grabski, S. (2006). Market reaction to e-commerce impairments evidenced by Web site outages. *International Journal of Accounting Information Systems, 7,* 60-78.

Axelsson, S. (2000). The base-rate fallacy and the difficulty of intrusion detection. *ACM Transactions on Information and System Security, 3*(3), 86-205.

Aytes, K., & Connolly, T. (2004). Computer security and risky computing practices: A rational choice perspective. *Journal of Organizational and End User Computing, 16*(3), 22-40.

Backhouse, J., Hsu, C.W., & Silva, L. (2006). Circuits of power in creating de jure standards: Shaping an international information systems security standard. *MIS Quarterly, 30,* 413-438.

Baskerville, R. (1993). Information systems security design methods: Implications for information systems development. *ACM Computing Surveys, 25*(4), 375-414.

Bell, D.E., & LaPadula, L.J. (1976). *Secure computer system: Unified exposition and MULTICS interpretation.* Bedford, MA: The Mitre Corporation.

Benbasat, I., & Zmud, R.W. (2003). The identity crisis within the IS discipline: Defining and communicating the discipline's core properties. *MIS Quarterly, 27*(2), 183-194.

Boukhonine, S., Krotov, V., & Rupert, B. (2005). Future security approaches and biometrics. *Communications of the AIS, 16,* 937-966.

Brealey, R.A., & Myers, S. (1996). *Principles of corporate finance, 5th edition.* New York: McGraw-Hill.

Caelli, W.J. (2002). Trusted...or...trustworthy: The search for a new paradigm for computer and network security. *Computers & Security, 21*(5), 413-419.

Campbell, K., Gordon, L.A., Loeb, M.P., & Zhou, L. (2003). The economic cost of publicly announced information security breaches: Empirical evidence from the stock market. *Journal of Computer Security, 11*(3), 431-448.

Cavusoglu, H., Mishra, B., & Raghunathan, S. (2004a) A model for evaluating IT security investments. *Communications of the ACM, 47*(7), 97-92.

Cavusoglu, H., Mishra, B., & Raghunathan, S. (2004b). The effect of Internet security breach announcements on shareholder wealth: Capital market reactions for breached firms and internet security developers. *International Journal of Electronic Commerce, 9*(1), 69-104.

Cavusoglu, H., Mishra, B., & Raghunathan, S. (2005). The value of intrusion detection systems in information technology security architecture. *Information Systems Research, 16*(1), 28-46.

Chen, T.M. (2003). Trends in viruses and worms. *The Internet Protocol Journal, 6*(3), 23–33.

Cohen, F. (1984). Computer viruses: Theory and experiments. In J.H. Finch & E.G. Dougall (Eds.), *Computer Security: A Global Challenge.* North-Holland: Elsevier.

CompTIA Research. (2002). Committing to security: A CompTIA analysis of IT security and the workforce. *CompTIA Research*. Oakbrook Terrace, IL.

Conklin, W.A. (2006). *Computer security behaviors of home PC users: A diffusion of innovation approach.* Unpublished Doctoral Dissertation, The University of Texas at San Antonio.

Conway, R.W., Maxwell, W.L., & Morgan., H.L. (1972). On the implementation of security measures in information systems. *Communications of the ACM, 15*(4), 211-220.

D'Arcy, J., & Hovav, A. (in press) Deterring internal information systems misuse: An end user perspective. *Communications of the ACM.*

D'Arcy, J., & Hovav, A. (2007) Towards a best fit between organizational security countermeasures and information systems misuse behaviors. *Journal of Information System Security, 3*(2).

Denning, D.E. (1987). An intrusion-detection model. *IEEE Transactions on Software Engineering 13*(2), 222-232.

Denning, D. (1998). *Information warfare and security.* Reading, MA: Addison-Wesley.

Dhillon, G., & Backhouse, J. (2001). Current directions in IS security research: Towards socio-organizational perspectives. *Information Systems Journal, 11*(2), 127-153.

Doherty, N.F., & Fulford, H. (2005). Do information security policies reduce the incidence of security breaches: An exploratory analysis. *Information Resources Management Journal, 18*(4), 21-39.

Doherty, N.F., & Fulford, H. (2006). Aligning the information security policy with the strategic information systems plan. *Computers & Security, 25*, 55-63.

Ernst & Young. (2004). *Global Information Security Survey 2004.*

Fisher, R. (1984). *Information systems security.* Englewood Cliffs, CA: Prentice Hall.

Foltz, C.B. (2000). *The impact of deterrent countermeasures upon individual intent to commit misuse: A behavioral approach.* Unpublished Doctoral Dissertation, University of Arkansas.

Gopal, R.D., & Sanders, G.L. (1997). Preventative and deterrent controls for software piracy. *Journal of Management Information Systems, 13*(4), 29-47.

Gordon, L.A., & Loeb, M.P. (2002). The economics of information security investment. *ACM Transactions on Information and System Security, 5*(4), 438-457.

Gordon, L.A., Loeb, M.P., Lucyshyn, W., & Richardson, R. (2006). *2006 CSI/FBI computer crime and security survey.* San Francisco: Computer Security Institute.

Gordon, L.A., Loeb, M.P., & Sohail, T. (2003). A framework for using insurance for cyber-risk management. *Communications of the ACM, 46*(3), 81-85.

Harrington, S.J. (1996). The effect of codes of ethics and personal denial of responsibility on computer abuse judgments and intentions. *MIS Quarterly, 20*(3), 257278.

Hazari, S. (2005). Perceptions of end users on the requirements in personal firewall software: an exploratory study. *Journal of Organizational and End User Computing, 17*(3), 47-65.

Hoffer, J.A., & Straub, D.W. (1989). The 9 to 5 underground: Are you policing computer crimes? *Sloan Management Review, 30*(4), 35-43.

Hovav, A. (2005a). Critical success factors for trusted computing: The Microsoft initiative and beyond. *4th Security Conference.* Las Vegas, NV.

Hovav, A. (2005b). *A framework for the study of cyber liability.* Jeju Island, Korea: KMIS.

Hovav, A., & D'Arcy, J. (2003). The impact of denial-of-service attack announcements on the market value of firms. *Risk Management and Insurance Review, 6*(2), 97-121.

Hovav, A., & D'Arcy, J. (2004). The impact of virus attack announcements on the market value of firms. *Information Systems Security, 13*(3), 32–40.

Hovav, A., & D'Arcy, J. (2005). Capital market reaction to defective IT products: The case of computer viruses. *Computers & Security, 24*(5), 409-424.

Hoxey, C., & Shoemaker, D. (2005). Navigating the information security landscape: Mapping the relationship between ISO 15408:1999 and ISO 17799:2000. *Eleventh Americas Conference on Information Systems.* Omaha, NE.

Irakleous, I., Furnell, S.M., Dowland, P.S., & Papadaki, M. (2002). An experimental comparison of secret-based user authentication technologies. *Information Management & Computer Security, 10*(3), 100-108.

James, T., Pirim, T., Boswell, K., Reithel, B., & Barkhi, R. (2006). Determining the intention to use biometric devices: An application and extension of the technology acceptance model. *Journal of Organizational and End User Computing, 18*(3), 1-24.

Johnston, J., Eloff, J.H.P., & Labuschagne, L. (2003). Security and human computer interfaces. *Computers & Security, 22*(8), 675-684.

Kamara, S., Fahmy, S., Shultz, E.E., Kerschbaum, F., & Frantzen, M. (2003). Analysis of vulnerabilities in internet firewalls. *Computers & Security, 22*(3), 214-232.

Kankanhalli, A., Hock-Hai, T., Tan, B.C.Y., & Wei, K.K. (2003). An integrative study of information systems security effectiveness. *International Journal of Information Management, 23*(2), 139-154.

Landreth, B. (1985). *Out of the inner circle.* Redmond, WA: Microsoft Books.

Lee, S.M., Lee, S.G. & Yoo, S. (2004). An integrative model of computer abuse based on social control and general deterrence theories. *Information and Management, 41*(6), 707-718.

Lou, D., & Liu, J. (2002). Stenographic method for secure communications. *Computers & Security, 21*(5), 449-460.

Luftman, J. (2005). Key issues for IT executives. *MISQ Executive, 4*(2), 269-285.

Ma, Q., & Pearson, J.M. (2005). ISO 17799: Best practices in information security management? *Communications of the AIS, 15,* 577-591.

Magklaras, G.B., & Furnell, S.M. (2005). A preliminary model of end user sophistication for insider threat prediction in IT systems. *Computers & Security, 24*(5), 371-380.

Moteff, J. (2004). Computer security: A summary of selected federal laws, executive orders, and presidential directives. *Congressional Research Service: The Library of Congress.* Retrieved May 1, 2008, from http://www.fas.org/irp/crs/RL32357.pdf

Osborn, S., Ravi, S., & Qamar, M. (2000). Configuring role-based access control to enforce mandatory and discretionary access control policies. *ACM Transactions on Information and System Security, 3*(2), 85-106.

Panko, R.R. (2003). Slammer: The first blitz worm. *Communications of the AIS, 11*(12), 207-218.

Parker, D.B. (1998). *Fighting computer crime.* New York: John Wiley & Sons.

Pattinson, M.R. (2003). Compliance with an information security management standard: A new approach. *Ninth Americas Conference on Information Systems.* Tampa, FL.

Payne, C. (2002). On the security of open source software. *Information Systems Journal, 12*(1), 61-78.

Saltzer, J.H., & Schroeder, M.D. (1975). The protection of information in computer systems. In *Proceedings of the IEEE, 63*(9), 1278-1308.

Siponen, M.T. (2000). Critical analysis of different approaches to minimizing user-related faults in information systems security: Implications for research and practice. *Information Management & Computer Security, 8*(5), 197-209.

Siponen, M.T. (2003). Information security management standards: Problems and solutions. *Seventh Pacific Asia Conference on Information Systems.* Adelaide, Australia.

Siponen, M.T., & Iivari, J. (2006). Six design theories for IS security policies and guidelines. *Journal of the AIS, 7*(7), 445-472.

Spafford, E.H. (1989). Crisis and aftermath. *Communications of the ACM, 32*(6), 678-687.

Stanton, J.M., Stam, K.R. Mastrangelo, P.R., & Jolton, J. (2005). Analysis of end user security behaviors. *Computers & Security, 24*(2), 124-133.

Straub, D.W. (1990). Effective IS security: An empirical study. *Information Systems Research, 1*(3), 255-276.

Tejay, G. (2005). Making sense of information systems security standards. *Eleventh Americas Conference on Information Systems.* Omaha, NE.

Tittle, R. (1980). *Sanctions and social deviance: The question of deterrence.* New York: Praeger.

Theoharidou, M., Kokolakis, S., Karyda, M., & Kiountouzis, E. (2005). The insider threat to information systems and the Effectiveness of ISO 17799. *Computers & Security, 24,* 472-484.

Thomson, M.E., & von Solms, R. (1998). Information security awareness: Educating your users effectively. *Info. Mgt & Computer Security, 6*(4), 167-173.

Tulu, B., & Chatterjee, S. (2003). A new security framework for HIPAA-compliant health information systems. *Ninth Americas Conference on Information Systems*. Tampa, FL.

von Solms, R., & von Solms, B. (2004). From policies to culture. *Computers & Security, 23*(4), 275-279.

von Solms, R., van de Haar, H.H., von Solms, S.H., & Caelli, W.J. (1994). A framework for information security evaluation. *Info. and Mgt, 26*(3), 143-153.

Whitman, M. & Mattord, H. (2005). *Principles of information security, second edition*. Boston: Course Technology.

Woon, I.M.Y (2001). A framework for managing information systems security.

Pacific Conference on Information Systems. Seoul, Korea.

Woon, I.M.Y., Tan, G.W., & Low, R.T. (2005). A protection motivation theory approach to home wireless security. *Twenty-Sixth International Conference on Information Systems*. Las Vegas, NV.

KEY TERMS

Denial-of-Service (DOS) Attack: Attack that attempts to make a computer resource (e.g., Web servers, DNS servers, routers, and so on) unavailable to its intended users. Hackers run a program, such as a string of ping commands, that requires considerable amounts of the target's resources, resulting in degradation or complete loss of services.

Federal Agency Security Practices (FASP): An initiative by the U.S. National Institute of Standards and Technology (NIST) Computer Security Division to identify, evaluate, and disseminate best practices for information security. This best practice information is available on the FASP website at http://fasp.nist.gov.

Generally Accepted System Security Principles (GASSP): Developed by the International Information Security Foundation (http://www.infosectoday.com/Articles/gassp.pdf).

Health Insurance Portability and Accountability Act (HIPAA): Federal regulations establishing national standards for the confidentiality and security of health care data.

Information Security Ecosystem: The IT ecosystem is defined by Forrester Research and others as "the network of organizations that drives the creation and delivery of information technology products and services" and includes customers, suppliers, and influencers (key stakeholders). Similarly, one can define the information security ecosystem as the network of entities that drives information security products and services, and includes information security hardware and software vendors, consultants, digital forensics experts, standardization agencies, accreditation and education facilities, academic conferences and journals, books, magazines, hackers, and their paraphernalia.

Information Security Management (ISM): Administrative and managerial activities designed to implement an organizational information security program. These activities include setting the information security mission, vision, and policies, implementing technical and procedural controls, business continuity and disaster recovery planning, analyzing the economic effectiveness of implemented controls, and compliance with relevant regulations.

Multiplexed Information and Computing Service (MULTICS): A time-sharing operating system developed by MIT, General Electric, and Bell Labs in the early 1960s. MULTICS was the first operating system to be designed as a secure system from the ground up.

National Institute of Standards and Technology (NIST) 800 Series: A set of documents that describe U.S. government information security policies, procedures, and guidelines. The series was developed by the National Institute of Standards and Technology and is available for free at: http://csrc.nist.gov/publications/nistpubs/index.html.

Sarbanes-Oxley Act: A U.S. law designed to enforce accountability for the financial record keeping and reporting at publicly traded corporations. Publicly traded organizations are responsible for the security, accuracy, and reliability of the systems that manage and report their financial data.

Systems Security Engineering Capability Maturity Model (SSE-CMM): Describes the essential characteristics of an organization's security engineering process that must exist to ensure good security engineering. The model focuses on the requirements for implementing security in a system (specifically an IT system), the processes used to achieve IT security, and their level of maturity. More information available at: http://www.sse-cmm.org/docs/ssecmmv3final.pdf.

Chapter VII
Information Systems Risk Management:
An Audit and Control Approach

Aditya Ponnam
Louisiana State University, USA

Britta Harrison
Louisiana State University, USA

Ed Watson
Louisiana State University, USA

ABSTRACT

Organizations worldwide recognize the importance of a comprehensive, continuously evolving risk assessment process, built around a solid risk strategy that properly manages internal and external threats. A comprehensive enterprise risk management strategy must ideally contribute to the protection of the organizations' assets, operations, shareholder's value, and customer satisfaction while meeting imposed regulatory requirements and standards. As IT represents an integral part of the process required to achieve the aforementioned objectives, managing the risks associated with the information technology infrastructure of an organization is critical. The goal of this chapter is to review the most common risks and threat agents for a typical organizations' information technology infrastructure and to discuss how systematic risk management procedures and controls can manage and minimize these risks.

INTRODUCTION

Defining and Understanding Risk and Control

Today's business environment requires highly competent risk management functions with the capabilities to address a continuously changing risk profile.

In order to put risk in the proper context, two terms are defined (Stoneburner, Goguen, & Feringa, 2002):

vulnerability, and threat. Vulnerability is a flaw or weakness in system security procedures, internal controls, or implementation that can be exercised (either accidentally or intentionally) and that can result in loss or harm. For example, a weak disaster recovery plan of an organization located in a disaster-prone area represents a vulnerability to the organization. A threat, such as a natural disaster, is the potential for a threat-source to exercise a specific vulnerability, such as a weak disaster recovery plan.

A risk is a circumstance or event that has the potential to hinder achievement of specific objective(s) or to cause harm. With respect to the previous example, the sudden disruption of a business or the loss of critical data in the event of a natural disaster is a risk that must be addressed. Therefore, organizations located in areas prone to environmental disasters should pursue a strong off-site data backup and recovery strategy by selecting a location less vulnerable to environmental disasters. A risk always has a cost associated with it. Once the vulnerabilities, threats, and respective costs are rated, risk can be interpreted by the following equation (Akin, 2002).

Risk = Threat * Vulnerability * Cost

Cost is the total cost of the impact of a particular threat incurred by a vulnerable target. Costs are of three types: hard-dollar, semihard, and soft. Hard-dollar costs are measured in terms of "real " damages to hardware, software, or other assets, as well as quantifiable IT staff time and resources spent repairing these damages. Semihard costs might include such things as lost business or transaction time during a period of downtime. Soft costs include such things as diminished end-user productivity, damage to reputation, decreased stockholder confidence, or lost business opportunities (International Charter, 2006).

Business risks can be broadly classified into the following types (Business Link, 2006):

- Strategic (e.g., market competition, customer preferences, industry changes)
- Compliance (e.g., regulations, standards)
- Financial (e.g., foreign exchange, interest rates, credit)
- Operational (e.g., organizational culture, process risk, technology risk)
- Hazard (e.g., natural events, environment, physical employees)

These categories are not rigid, as some parts of your business may fall into more than one category. An environmental disaster threatening an organization's ability to successfully back-up and recover data could, for example, potentially reach across and impact hazard, operational, financial, and compliance business risk categories.

Risks have the potential to deter an organization from achieving its goals and objectives. Management, therefore, must implement a risk control framework in order to prevent or mitigate risks to a level deemed acceptable to the organization.

It is important to understand the nature of controls. Controls are formal activities taken by business process owners to achieve an objective set by the organization to mitigate a respective risk. A control can be defined as a process, policy, or procedure designed to provide reasonable assurance that business objectives will be achieved. Controls, when exercised effectively, reduce or eliminate the exposure of a process to certain risks and, therefore, make the process less likely to incur losses associated with the risk. Controls can be preventive, detective, or corrective, as described below.

- **Preventive:** Implemented to prevent the risk from causing any loss or harm.
- **Detective:** Implemented in situations where it is important to understand that something adverse has happened. They warn of violations or attempted violations of organizational policy.
- **Corrective:** Implemented when the objective is to fix errant situations or events as they are identified.

Controls can be further classified as automated or manual (Rajamani, 2006).

- **Automated or programmed controls:** Automated controls are embedded within an organization's application systems and work in the background by virtue of the programming logic or application configuration, without any need for manual intervention. A financial application that calculates interest rates automatically based on a hard coded logic is an example of an automated control.
- **Manual controls:** These controls require a person to manually enforce the control. For example, a review and sign off that the quality of material obtained from a supplier has been inspected is a manual control.

Informaton Technology and Risk: They Always Coexist

In today's globalized business environment, opportunities and risks go hand in hand. The more complex the business process and business model, the higher the scale and variety of risk that needs to be addressed. Risk also stems from poorly designed business processes, reliance on manual activities, use of legacy systems, and use of multiple system landscapes. As information technology advances, more and more business activities and processes are being driven by information systems. As a result, IT plays a significant role in the support of business processes today. Increased business activity associated with such things as collaboration, diversification, and geographical expansion of business units are generally found to be correlated with the risks an organization faces.

The threats to an organization, as well as their vulnerabilities, come in different shapes and forms. Emerging technologies, which may lead to specific competitive advantages, may expose organizations to serious threats that must be mitigated (Ernst & Young, 2005). Rapidly developing technologies like voice-over IP telephony, open source, server virtualization, and wireless technologies empower businesses and consumers. Advanced technologies, however, also carry their own set of risks that must be mitigated in order to enable businesses to leverage the technology most effectively. Computer network threats such as Worms, Trojans, and viruses also pose serious risks to businesses everyday. It is estimated that approximately 150 to 200 viruses, Trojans, and other threats emerge every day (Mcafee, 2007). Additional network threats are increasingly employed by cyber world criminals (e.g., phishing targeted hacking, botnets, and other techniques to steal critical private information). Poorly designed security and business process control frameworks leave open significant vulnerabilities in an information systems environment.

Social engineering in organizations is perhaps the most vexing problem facing security experts today. The employees who maliciously exploit vulnerabilities in critical applications pose a serious and significant threat to their organization. Breaches due to internal attacks are on the rise. Deloitte Consulting notes that for the first time in its 2005 Global Security Survey, the number of organizations who have experienced internal attacks is higher than the number who have experienced them externally (Deloitte Touché Tomhatsu, 2005). This report indicates that poor new-hire screening processes, lackadaisical subcontractor controls, security-ignorant employees, and deficient management processes are all examples of internal vulnerabilities that allow many of today's security breaches to occur. This puts into perspective the new information risk age that has dawned upon the business world, and the increasingly important role that managers play in risk management.

Need for a Holistic Risk Management Approach

The increasing adoption of technology and IT-enabled dynamic business models in today's global business environment have forced organizations to place greater emphasis on measures to manage security threats and risks associated with information technology. As information technology supports the business and permeates many operations in different capacities, organizations need to approach a holistic risk assessment effort and align business objectives with a strong information technology risk strategy. Efforts in this direction will make the organization proactive in managing the risks that could negatively impact business initiatives.

Compliance standards and requirements have grown to be the most pressing reason for organizations to rethink their information risk management strategies and place a greater emphasis on fostering a risk-smart environment and work culture. According to the Ernst and Young Global Information Security survey 2005, 61% of the survey respondents believe that compliance with regulations will be the most important driver that significantly impacts organization's information security practices in the next 12 months (Ernst & Young, 2005). Two other prominent drivers identified include: meeting demanding evolving business needs, and dealing with threats due to viruses and worms.

An organization's successful overall risk management plan must incorporate a continuous risk assessment process in combination with the specific strategic alignment of business process controls and information technology. Standards like COBIT (Control Objectives for Information Technology), COSO ERM (Committee of Sponsored Organizations Enterprise Risk Management), and ISO 17799 (International Organization for Standardization) facilitate best practice frameworks around risk management to assist organizations in this process.

Risk Management From an Audit and Control Viewpoint

Risks can be managed in different ways. For example, a potential risk may be prevented, detected, transferred, or accepted (Griffiths, 2006). A company can prevent the risk of potential fraud by implementing a strong security access and change control framework.

Insuring a business against potential damages from environmental hazards is an example of transferring the risk to an insurance company. Accepting a risk reflects an organization's understanding and acceptance of the respective cost associated with a risk. A risk detection mechanism can assist an organization in managing the overall implications and costs associated with a risk. Controls are set in place to prevent or detect a risk.

The risk that remains even after a control is deployed is called residual risk. An equation that relates the concepts of risk, control, and residual risk can be written as follows

Risk – control = residual risk

It is the responsibility of management to implement controls that address risk as part of a risk management strategy within an organization. The purpose of an audit is to evaluate the control framework to identify gaps within the control framework and to recommend remediation efforts as needed.

A RISK-BASED AUDIT APPROACH

The Risk and Control Universe

Risks and controls are interchangeable within an organization. Every control, by design, mitigates one or more risks. A high-level IT control framework provides a better perspective on the risk and control universe of an organization:

Figure 1 illustrates the structure of an organization's control framework. Two main control categories, IT General Controls and Business Process Controls, represent the high-level picture of an internal control environment within the organization. The business process/application controls can be further classified as followsinto three categories:

- Manual controls
- Automated controls
- IT dependent manual controls

IT General Controls

IT General Controls refer to pervasive controls that relate to the entire IT environment, as opposed to controls over an individual system. Examples of IT General Controls include:

- Controls over the physical IT environment (data center, servers)
- Process used to define software changes, test new code, and release to production
- Controls related to access (IDs / Passwords)

Business Process Controls

Business Process Controls encompass all controls implemented over a business process (for example, purchase to pay process, order to cash process, treasury process). Business process controls can be manual, automated, or IT dependent manual controls.

- Manual controls are enforced by human actions/authorizations without the assistance of an application system. Examples include supervisory controls, manually reconciling purchase orders to goods receipt statement and providing authorized sign off at completion of this task. Manual controls are subject to inherent risk of human error and, as a result, are often considered less reliable. Manual controls are dictated by company policies and procedures.
- Application controls are automated controls that apply to the processing of individual transactions within the business process. Application controls are typically preventative in nature and are embedded within the application or could be configured. They help ensure the completeness and accuracy of transaction processing, authorization, and validity. Examples include data input validity checks,edit checks, calculations, interfaces, and authorizations (e.g., roles defined in the system, authorization limits)
- IT-dependent manual controls (usually detective in nature) are manual controls that rely on the completeness and accuracy of the output of Information technology processing. An example of an IT dependent manual control is a review of a system generated report that lists unmatched invoices to ensure all invoices have a corresponding purchase order and a goods receipt.

Security refers to application access authorizations and manual authorizations. Security focuses on restricted access and sensitive transaction controls. In essence, a user should only be assigned to the specific access authorizations required to perform their job. Security may refer to application security as well as manual authorizations (e.g., manual approval of a purchase order vs. system approval)

Segregation of duties takes security one step further by evaluating combinations of access authorizations. Access to sensitive transactions and responsibilities need to be segregated among individuals to reduce the risk of potential fraud. Access should be limited to the permissions/authorization a user needs in order to carry out their responsibilities. An example of an SoD with respect to the purchasing process would be prohibiting an individual from creating and approving the same purchase order.

Understanding the risk and control framework of an organization is crucial to developing a strong risk based audit approach.

A risk based audit approach analyzes risks, defines materiality, and gathers evidence to define reportable findings. The outcomes of this approach are control recommendations that aim to mitigate the risks identified. In the following sections, this methodology is explained step by step.

PLANNING THE AUDIT

Understanding Business

A risk-based audit must begin by gaining insight into the business and related business practices including ownership, investments, products, and so on. It is also important to validate market forces and stakeholder influences, as well as management's objectives, strategies, and critical success factors. The audit team should also validate the current assessment of risks and internal controls and challenge the significance of identified risks. Gaining a general understanding of the business and the IT environment supporting the business processes will help auditors perform the audit tasks effectively and knowledgeably.

An example list of questions presented by the audit team is listed below.

The business:

- What are the company's functions and objectives?
- What is the nature of the company's business and what regulations govern the business?
- What are the current trends and future trends of the products and services of the business?
- What are the inherent risks in the business?
- What is the client base of the company, which industries do they serve, and how sensitive are the business offerings to its clients?
- Are prior audit reports available?
- Who should be interviewed?

Management culture and control environment:

- What is the organizational structure of the company?

Figure 1. IT general controls and business process/application controls framework

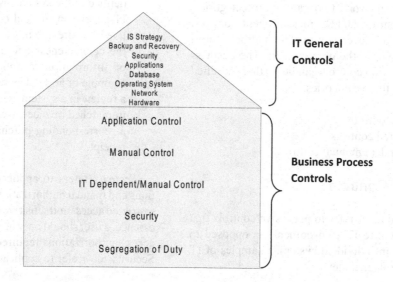

- What is the general impression that is obtained from observing management's attitude?
- What is the extent to which the organization depends on internal auditing?
- What is the impression gained from observing employee motivation and their perceptions about management?
- What is the management's attitude towards ethical dealings?
- Do any of these observations reveal any potential weaknesses or gaps that may result in any risk to the organization?
- What is the perception of the company towards Sarbanes-Oxley and other regulatory requirements?

IT environment:

- What constitutes the IT environment of the organization? An inventory of applications, databases, operating systems, and servers affecting the business process is prepared. In addition, a network diagram of the IT components can be very helpful in getting a quick understanding of the IT infrastructure supporting the business process.
- What operations within the business process are automated?
- What are the major changes or updates made to the critical applications since the last time audited or implemented?

- Are systems predominately developed in-house or packaged?
- Is there an IT steering committee or an equivalent committee within the organization?
- Who defines security policies and various security related functions?
- Are problem resolutions tracked and trends identified and analyzed?

Defining Scope and Objectives

Establishing the scope and objectives of an audit to determine the nature and extent of testing to be performed is a crucial step to the audit engagement. Determination of planning materiality and tolerable error in addition to identifying significant accounts are the key tasks within this phase. Management, together with internal and external audit entities will define the scope of the IT audit engagement. For example, if the purpose of an IT audit is to evaluate the application controls over a business process like purchase-to-pay based on the respective risk and key significant accounts associated with this process, an appropriate audit scope is specified that covers all the systems supporting the business process.

An audit scope statement must clearly define (Drake & Kerrigan, 2007):

- Personnel requirements
- Roles and responsibilities of audit personnel
- List of in-scope systems and audit objectives
- Audit procedures
- Milestone dates

In the course of the audit process, auditors may need to make note of issues that fall outside the current scope so that they can be addressed appropriately.

Identifying Scope Limitations

In an IS audit project, auditors need to identify if any restrictions have been placed upon the scope of the audit that precludes the department from accomplishing its objectives and plans. In the event of a scope limitation, auditors need to discuss the possible implications of limitation with management and the audit committee, and review the audit objectives and risk management strategy to determine whether an audit is still possible and will meet defined objectives. The audit report should explain specific restrictions and their impact on the audit.

A scope limitation may restrict the:

- Auditor's access to records, personnel, and physical properties relevant to the performance of audits
- Approved audit work schedule
- Performance of necessary auditing procedures
- Approved staffing plan and financial budget
- Ability to obtain sufficient evidence for any reason

Defining the IT Audit Universe and Auditable Domains

The next step in the planning process must be to identify the IT audit universe. Characterizing the IT audit universe in terms of functions, systems, infrastructure, processes, and people establishes the scale and capacity of the assessment and is essential to defining the risks.

Besides defining the IT audit universe, it needs to be divided into auditable domains so that the risk analysis could be carried out most productively (Hurtaud, 2006). An auditable domain is a manageable auditable activity, which may be defined in a number of ways, such as by function or activity, by organizational unit or division, or by project or program. Some examples of auditable domains are policies and procedures, business units, business functions such as purchasing, accounting, and information systems supporting business processes.

Two major risk and control frameworks have been the dominating standards in the United States: CobiT and COSO.

The CobiT model presents a solid framework to guide auditors through the risk identification processes. It can also be used as a benchmark in assessing implemented controls coverage.

The Control Objectives for Information and related Technology (COBIT) was developed by the Information Systems Audit and Control Association (ISACA) and IT Governance Institute (ITGI) in 1992. COBIT is a tool that provides a reference framework for management, users, and IS audit, control and security practitioners for evaluating security and controls over information.

COBIT, now in its fourth edition, has 34 high-level objectives that cover 215 control objectives categorized in four domains:

- Plan and organize
- Acquire and implement
- Deliver and support
- Monitor and evaluate

Figure 2 shows the CobiT model with four domains and high-level objectives in each domain.

An IT audit universe and auditable domains can be established based on the 34 CobiT processes. Not all 34 CobiT processes are required by regulatory compliance. Only risks applicable to the respective organization are included as part of the IT audit universe. For example, the risk associated with the project management process (PO 10) is that the IT projects are not classified by priority and delivered on time and within budget. Therefore, the high-level control objective for this process is to set priorities and deliver within agreed time frames, budget, and quality. Based on the control objective, control activities which assure achievements of control objectives are designed and implemented.

COSO

Committee of Sponsoring Organizations of the Treadway Commission (COSO) is a voluntary private-sector organization, formed in 1985 to sponsor the National commission on Fraudulent Financial Reporting, whose charge was to study and report factors that can lead to

Figure 2. COBIT domains (Hurtaud, 2006)

Plan and Organise	Deliver and Support
PO1 Define a strategic IT plan.	DS1 Define and manage service levels.
PO2 Define the information architecture.	DS2 Manage third-party services.
PO3 Determine technological direction.	DS3 Manage performance and capacity.
PO4 Define the IT processes, organisation and relationships.	DS4 Ensure continuous service.
PO5 Manage the IT investment.	DS5 Ensure systems security.
PO6 Communicate management aims and direction.	DS6 Identify and allocate costs.
PO7 Manage IT human resources.	DS7 Educate and train users.
PO8 Manage quality.	DS8 Manage service desk and incidents.
PO9 Assess and manage IT risks.	DS9 Manage the configuration.
PO10 Manage projects.	DS10 Manage problems.
Acquire and Implement	DS11 Manage data.
AI1 Identify automated solutions.	DS12 Manage the physical environment.
AI2 Acquire and maintain application software.	DS13 Manage operations.
AI3 Acquire and maintain technology infrastructure.	**Monitor and Evaluate**
AI4 Enable operation and use.	ME1 Monitor and evaluate IT performance.
AI5 Procure IT resources.	ME2 Monitor and evaluate internal control.
AI6 Manage changes.	ME3 Ensure regulatory compliance.
AI7 Install and accredit solutions and changes.	ME4 Provide IT governance.

fraudulent financial reporting .Since its initial under-taking, it has expanded its mission to improving the quality of financial reporting through business ethics, effective internal controls, and corporate governance. In 1992, COSO published *Internal Control-Integrated Framework,* which established a common definition of internal controls, standards, and criteria against which companies and organizations can evaluate their control systems.

COSO internal control framework has five com-ponents: control environment, risk assessment, con-trol activities, information and communication, and monitoring. In 2004 COSO published *Enterprise Risk Management—Integrated Framework*, expanding the initial COSO framework. This *Enterprise Risk Man-agement—Integrated Framework* expands on internal control, providing a more robust and extensive focus on the subject of enterprise risk management. While it is not intended to and does not replace the internal control framework (i.e., it incorporates the internal control framework within it), companies may decide to look to this enterprise risk management framework both to satisfy their internal control needs and to move toward a fuller risk management process.

The eight components of this framework are:

- Internal environment
- Objective setting
- Event identification
- Risk assessment
- Risk response
- Control activities
- Information and communication
- Monitoring

RISK ASSESSMENT

Risk assessment is the next step after identifying the audit universe and auditable domains. The objective of the risk assessment process is to proactively identify areas of significant risk within the organization and determine the impact of potential threats, in order to allocate resources and direct efforts to mitigate the risks. Risk assessment can use either a quantitative approach, which attempts to assign real dollar value to the cost of threats, cost of recovery, fraud, and so on, and determine the expected cost of loss related to a risk. A qualitative approach uses a prioritization method to analyze the seriousness and the impact of the threat against the criticality and sensitivity of the asset.

An audit risk assessment should take into account the following types of risks (Cannon, Bergmann, & Pamplin, 2006):

- **Inherent risks:** These are natural risks that exist by default, due to the nature of the business's or process's environment or activities.
- **Control risk:** These are the risks that an inter-nal control system will fail to prevent or detect material errors or fraud in a timely manner. In the evaluation of internal controls, the auditor will test organization's internal controls for compliance with control objectives. The auditor should assess the control risk as high unless rel-evant internal controls are identified, evaluated as "effective " and "adequate ", and tested and proven to be operating in compliance with the objectives.
- **Detection risks:** These are the risks that an auditor will fail to detect material errors or fraud in a timely manner.
- **Sampling risks:** These are the risks that an auditor will falsely accept or erroneously reject an audit sample (evidence).
- **Nonsampling risks:** These are risks that an auditor will fail to detect a condition because of not applying the appropriate procedure or using procedures inconsistent with the audit objective.
- **Residual risk:** The risk that remains after appro-priate controls are installed and risk mitigation efforts are performed.

The following risk assessment methodology com-prises seven steps, which are illustrated in Figure 4.

Identification of Critical Assets and Services

In this step, the boundaries of the IT system are iden-tified, along with resources and the information that constitute the system. Identifying risks related to IT systems supporting a business process needs a clear understanding of the operational infrastructure of the IT system. To characterize the operational environ-ment related to IT system requires system-related information like:

- Hardware
- Application software
- Operating Systems
- Database

- System interfaces (external and internal connectivity)
- Data and information
- People who use and support the IT system
- System objectives
- Criticality and sensitivity of the system
- Policies governing the system (security policies, organizational policies, federal requirements)
- Physical security environment, and Environmental security implemented for the IT system
- Controls pertaining to the IT system

THREAT-VULNERABILITY IDENTIFICATION

The goal of this step is to identify potential threat sources and prepare a threat statement listing potential threats applicable to the IT systems and business. The common threat sources can be human, natural, and environmental. Unauthorized access to confidential information, malicious attack on the network or database, and misuse of authority are examples of threat events that can be caused by humans. Hurricanes, floods, earthquakes, avalanches, and other natural disasters are examples of natural threats. A long-term power failure (e.g., from fire accident) is an example of an environmental threat. Information about known threats is available from websites, intelligence agencies, and organizations specializing in threat information collection. Along with threat statement vulnerability analysis is also undertaken in this step.

Vulnerabilities in IT systems result from poorly designed or insufficient security controls. For example, inadequate segregation of duties in an ERP system may result in users performing fraudulent activities via system access. Vulnerabilities in IT systems and applications can be identified based on vendor documentation or security audit/assessment reports. Information Technology can be tested manually or by using automated tools to expose vulnerabilities. The output of this step is a list of potential threats and vulnerabilities that could be exercised.

Evaluation Of Internal Controls

COSO defines internal control as: "a process, influenced by an entity's board of directors, management, and other personnel, that is designed to provide reasonable assurance in the effectiveness and efficiency of operations, reliability of financial reporting, and the compliance of applicable laws and regulations." The auditor evaluates the organization's control framework by understanding the organization's five interrelated control components. They include:

1. **Control environment:** Encompasses such factors as management's philosophy and operating style.
2. **Risk assessment:** Consists of risk identification and analysis.
3. **Control objectives and activities:** Consists of the policies and procedures that ensure employees carry out management's directions. Types of control activities an organization must implement are preventative controls (controls intended to stop an error from occurring), detective controls (controls intended to detect if an error has occurred), and corrective controls (control activities that can mitigate the risks associated with a key control not operating effectively).
4. **Information and communication:** Ensures the organization obtains pertinent information, and then communicates it throughout the organization, or as appropriate.
5. **Monitoring:** Reviewing the output generated by control activities and conducting special evaluations of their performance and effectiveness.

Test of Controls

Tests of controls are audit procedures performed to assess the design and/or operational effectiveness of an internal control. Tests of controls directed toward the design of the control focuses on evaluating whether the control is suitably designed to mitigate the respective risk. Tests of controls directed towards the operational effectiveness focuses on assessing how the control was applied, the consistency of application, and who applied it.

Likelihood-Impact Characterization

In determining the likelihood of a threat exploiting vulnerability, the following factors must be considered (Stoneburner, et al., 2002).

- Threat-source motivation and capability
- Nature and susceptibility of vulnerability
- Existence and effectiveness of internal controls

Figure 3. Flow chart of risk assessment process (Stoneburner et al., 2002)

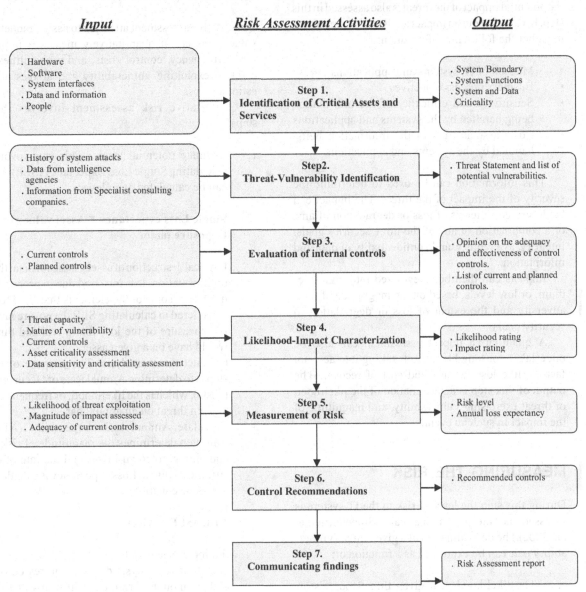

Based on the above factors a probability can be assigned to a threat that indicates the likelihood of the threat exercising vulnerability. Also, qualitatively, likelihood can be categorized into high, medium, or low. An example rating of likelihood levels is presented below.

- **High:** The threat source is highly motivated and sufficiently capable, and controls to prevent the

vulnerability from being exploited are ineffective

- **Medium:** The threat source is motivated and capable but controls in place hinder successful exploitation of the vulnerability

- **Low:** The threat source lacks motivation or capability or controls in place are sufficiently capable to prevent the threat from exploiting the vulnerability.

In addition to analyzing the likelihood of a threat, the potential impact of the threat is also assessed in this step. In carrying out an impact analysis, it is important to gather the following information:

- Mission of IT systems and applications
- Business process objectives
- Sensitivity and criticality of the information being handled by the systems and applications
- Costs associated with the information being handled by the systems and applications

This information can be used to determine the severity of the impact of the threat. The impact can be described in terms of loss or degradation of any, or a combination of any of the three security goals: integrity, availability, and confidentiality of data and information.

Impacts can then be categorized into high, medium, or low levels, based on the magnitude of their adversity and the extent of loss or degradation to security goals.

A quantitative impact assessment can also be undertaken for tangible impacts taking into account factors, like lost revenue and cost of recover. The output of this step is determination of the likelihood of threat exercising vulnerability, and magnitude of the impact in such an event.

MEASURING THE RISK

During this step the level of risk to the IT system is assessed and interpreted on a scale. (Stoneburner, et al., 2002).The determination of a given threat/vulnerability pair can be expressed as a function of:

a. The likelihood of a given threat-source's attempting to exercise a given vulnerability.
b. The magnitude of the impact should a threat source successfully exercise a given vulnerability.
c. The adequacy of planned or existing controls for mitigating or eliminating the risk.

Based on the above three parameters, a risk level can be determined quantitatively or qualitatively (Gregg, 2005).

Quantitative Risk Assessment

Quantitative assessment attempts to assign monetary value to assets. It quantitatively measures impact, threat frequency, control costs, and probabilities of a threat exploiting vulnerability and arrives at an estimated loss.

Quantitative risk assessment involves three steps:

1. Estimate potential losses: This step involves calculating Single Loss Expectancy (SLE). SLE can be calculated as follows:

Single Loss expectancy * Asset value= Exposure factor

Physical destruction of assets, losses of data, theft of information, loss incurred due to processing delays are some of the elements that need to be considered in calculating SLE. Exposure factor is a measure of the loss that a realized threat would have on a given asset.

2. Conduct threat analysis: The purpose of this step is to determine Annual Rate of Occurrence (ARO), which is the likelihood, or frequency, of a given threat on an annual basis.

3. Calculate Annual Loss Expectancy (ALE): This step determines the magnitude of risk by combining potential losses and the rate of occurrence. Annual Loss expectancy is calculated using the equation:

ALE=SLE * ARO

Example: See Box 1
Quantitative analysis of risk requires considerable amount of resources in terms of time, and personnel. Also, the results of quantitative measurement may be difficult to interpret the risk level. However, this approach provides measurement of risk's magnitude, which can be used in cost benefit analysis of recommended controls

Qualitative Risk Measurement

In some scenarios monetary values cannot be assigned to risk elements. In such cases, qualitative risk analysis can be used to rank severity of threats against sensitivity of assets and categorize risk in classes such as low,

Box 1.

Asset	Risk	Asset Value	Exposure Factor	SLE	Annual Frequency	ALE
Corporate e-commerce website	Hacked	$253,000	.65	$164450	.15	$24668

medium and high. The grading of risks is subjective. An example risk definition is presented below:

- **High**: May result in a very costly loss of tangible assets or resources and may significantly impair the organization in achieving its objectives or damage the reputation of the business. Such a risk may require immediate attention.
- **Medium**: May result in a moderate loss of tangible assets or resources and requires a moderate amount of time, money, and effort to deal with the risk.
- **Low**: May result in a manageable loss of tangible assets or resources and may not require immediate attention or a high amount of resources to deal with the risk.

The advantage of a qualitative risk analysis is that it provides a measurement of risk's magnitude and identifies areas that require immediate improvement. The disadvantage of qualitative risk analysis is that it does not provide quantifiable measurements of the magnitude of the risks, therefore making cost benefit analysis of the recommended controls difficult.

CONTROL RECOMMENDATIONS

The purpose of this step is to recommend controls that could mitigate or eliminate risks identified. At a minimum, controls should reduce the identified risks to the IT systems, and to the business processes it supports, to an acceptable level. The following factors should be considered in recommending controls (Stoneburner, et al., 2002).

- Effectiveness and suitability of recommended controls to mitigate the risks
- Compliance with standards and regulations governing the business practice
- Organizational policy
- Impact on operations
- Safety and reliability
- Feasibility of implementation

Control recommendations must be weighed in comparison to the risks and their potential impacts and also a cost benefit analysis must be performed to identify which controls are required and appropriate. This selection of controls is undertaken as a part of risk mitigation strategy.

Communicating Audit Results and Facilitating Change

The audit must provide a report in an appropriate form, upon the completion of the audit. The report should state the scope, objectives, period of coverage, and the nature, timing, and extent of the audit work performed. The report should state the findings, conclusions, and recommendations and any restrictions with respect to the scope of the audit. The content of the final audit report must be a logical extension of interim reports generated during the course of the audit. The final report must present an objective opinion on the conditions identified and lead to realistic, cost-effective, workable, and timely recommendations. The audit report must be linked or cross-referenced to supporting working papers or other resources.

Language should be carefully chosen to present factual information with appropriate emphasis on material and significant issues. Management uses the audit report as a basis for making informed decisions and therefore information presented in the audit report must be accurate, relevant, and useful to the management.

An overall opinion on the audit objectives should be presented before describing individual reportable findings. All findings considered material in the engagement must be included in the report. The auditor will have to exercise their professional judgment to identify material findings in their observations.

An audit report should contain the following (Kramer, 2003):

1. Report title (must indicate the name of area audited)
2. Recipients of the report

3. Date the report was issued and the period covered by the audit
4. Scope of the audit
5. Objectives of the audit engagement
6. Brief description of the work performed
7. Overall audit opinion
8. Findings, recommendations, and risk level assigned to the issue (from high to low)

RISK MITIGATION

Once the risks are identified, they provide the basis for identifying controls that mitigate the risks. Controls must be evaluated taking into consideration risk and respective cost/benefit of the implementation and maintenance effort involved. Also, Management must define the acceptable level of risk as they hold the accountability and responsibility around the business process environment. If the controls in place are identified to be ineffective, better alternatives to mitigate the risk need to be determined.

Methodology

The approach for control implementation must address the greatest risks first in a cost-conscious manner with minimal impact on other capabilities of the business processes or systems supporting these business processes.

The following steps illustrate a methodical approach to risk mitigation (Stoneburner, et al., 2002):

- **Step 1: Prioritize actions.** Based on the risks levels identified through risk assessment, the control implementation actions are prioritized. Highest priority is give to those risks with high ranking and need immediate attention.
- **Step 2:** Evaluate recommended control recommendations. Controls recommended in the risk assessment process are evaluated for their feasibility of implementation and effectiveness in addressing the risk.
- **Step 3:** Conduct cost benefit analysis. A cost benefit analysis of control implementation is conducted to determine whether the controls are cost effective in mitigating the risk.
- **Step 4:** Identify/develop a control. Controls are identified for implementation.
- **Step 5:** Assign responsibility. Appropriate personnel are selected and control implementation

and maintenance responsibilities/ownership are assigned.

- **Step 6: Develop a control implementation plan.** A control implementation plan is developed that documents:
  - Risks identified and risks levels assigned
  - Controls recommended
  - Prioritized actions based on the risk rankings
  - Selected planned controls
  - Required resources for implementing the selected planned controls
  - Start and target completion dates for control implementation
  - Maintenance requirements for controls
- **Step 7: Implement controls.** Selected controls are implemented to mitigate or eliminate the risk.

Cost-Benefit Analysis of the Control Implementation

Controls need to be reasonable in terms of cost-benefit in order to be considered for implementation. Organizations need to conduct a cost benefit analysis to determine whether the identified controls are feasible.

A cost-benefit analysis of implementation of proposed new controls includes the following (Stoneburner, et al., 2002):

- Analyzing the impact of implementing proposed controls vs. not
- Estimating the cost of control implementation. Some of the factors that must be included to estimate the cost are:
  - Hardware and software purchases
  - Impact on operational effectiveness of the systems due to increased security demands on systems
  - Cost of implementing additional policies and procedures
  - Cost of hiring additional personnel to implement proposed policies and new procedures, training and maintenance
  - Assessing the implementation costs against the benefits expected, the extent to which the risk is mitigated, and the value addition perceived out of implementing the control.

○ Calculating the revised annual loss of expectancy (ALE) and comparing the difference between the original ALE and revised ALE to the cost of implementing the control. This demonstrates whether it is cost effective to implement the control or not.

Leading Practices of Control Efforts

The pressure on companies in the form of regulatory compliance requirements and threats to the organization have increased in direct correlation to their costs. More than ever, companies are looking for leading practices and solutions that enable them to reduce costs, manage risk, and drive business value.

Organizations are focusing on aligning IT with the business and improving controls on the functions IT provides to the business. Utilizing already existing process controls allows organizations to become more confident in managing risk, and therefore take the opportunity to optimize their control framework. Adoption of common controls across multiple regulatory standards is sought by many companies. This exercise goes in hand with control optimization, which has been a great undertaking since 2006, as companies approached their second or third year of Sarbanes Oxley Compliance. Organizations have, over time, been able to strengthen and enhance their internal control framework. Automated controls are the most effective types of controls. As organizations undergo systems implementations and upgrades, utilizing the system capabilities to automate controls/requirements is of tremendous benefit.

To maximize compliance efforts and reduce costs, Protiviti, an independent risk consulting firm, recommends that organizations do the following (Protiviti, 2006):

Achieve the proper balance of control mechanisms between manual and automated controls and preventive and detective controls. It is important for the organization to evaluate its overall control structure to determine whether the benefits justify the time and money required to automate all manual controls and upgrade detective controls to preventive controls. Although preventive controls are more expensive to implement, they provide the highest level of assurance that company wide activities are appropriate because they are easier to audit.

Aggregate controls evidence in a central repository. Once a control is automated, monitoring can be become a continuous activity. Collecting information from continuous monitoring activities can provide important risk metrics to the organization. To begin, companies can collect control information from disparate sources, such as application logs and monitoring and management tools, and maintain this information in a central repository or location.

Continually monitor the controls information to identify actionable improvements. Once key control information is collected from significant systems, companies should restrict access to the central repository. Ideally, this information repository should be physically and electronically isolated and accessible to relevant audit personnel only, none of whom should have rights to alter the data.

Optimize the controls environment to improve business performance and address the entire data risk landscape. To optimize the controls environment, companies should create a layer of analytics on top of the repository. This layer should operate on a set of rules developed to check and cross-reference specific data, searching for known patterns. To let the organization know when a potential risk is identified, a granulated alarming scheme can be set up, such as routine e-mail notifications or real-time paging when a breach occurs.

EMERGING ISSUES AND TRENDS

Organizations have begun to see the importance of an integrated enterprise wide risk management strategy that involves devising and adopting management policies and procedures for risk management. As a result, risk management has become a dedicated function within organizations.

A global Ernst and Young survey of 1,200 information security professionals from 350 organizations in 48 countries has identified five key security priorities that are critical to business success (Finfacts, 2007). Of them the most notable priority is privacy and personal data protection. The Ponemon Institute has discovered that during the past year, more than 120 major corporate data breaches have been reported, affecting nearly 56 million individuals (Ponemon, 2006). With increasing regulatory pressure and businesses becoming sensitive to consumer confidence, organizations have become very active and begun to revise and formalize their data protection and privacy approaches, and, in the process, these issues have garnered great importance in corporate compliance and risk management.

The five priorities of organizations today identified in the survey are:

- Integrating information security into mainstream organizational strategy
- Extending the impact of compliance and fostering a risk smart environment
- Managing the risk of third party relationships
- Focusing on privacy and personal data protection
- Designing and building strong information security practices

CONCLUSION

Companies are increasingly adopting systematic risk management procedures to identify, assess, and manage risks across the entire organization, or within a particular business area. The principal objective of a risk management strategy must be to allow the organization to achieve its mission and add value to its business operations by minimizing risk and maximizing opportunities. Information technology spells both opportunities and risks for any company that relies on it to achieve its business objectives. Unless IT related risks to the business are managed properly, an organization stands to fail in accomplishing its objectives. Developing a risk-based information systems audit approach that can be implemented in conformance with the generally accepted audit standards and guidelines will facilitate deployment of adequate controls over IT and the business processes it supports and contributes towards meeting organization's business objectives. In this chapter, we have presented a risk-based audit approach and studied how risk can be identified and assessed, and appropriate control mechanisms deployed to mitigate those risks in order to achieve organizational objectives. A risk management strategy's success depends on management's commitment and ability to stress the need and benefit of a strong internal control framework across the organization, as well as provide full support to the key business and IT drivers to facilitate a successful initiative. Other factors contributing to a successful risk management strategy are an educated user environment, competent internal and external auditors, and a clear roadmap to implement a strong internal control framework.

REFERENCES

Akin, T. (2002, February). *Hardening CISCO routers, 1st edition*. O'Reilly Media, Inc.

Business Link. (2006). *Managing risk*. Retrieved May 2, 2008, from http://www.businesslink.gov.uk/bdotg/action/detail?type=RESOURCES&itemId=1074405311

Cannon, D.L., Bergmann, T.S., & Pamplin, B.(2006). *CISA: Certified information systems auditor study guide*. Indianapolis, IN: Wiley.

Deloitte Touché Tomhatsu. (2005). *2005 global security survey*. Retrieved May 2, 2008, from http://www.deloitte.com/dtt/cda/doc/content/dtt_financialservices_2005GlobalSecuritySurvey_2005-07-21.pdf

Drake, G., & Kerrigan, M. (2007). *Plan the audit process*. Retrieved May 2, 2008, from http://office.microsoft.com/en-us/workessentials/HA011377721033.aspx

Ernst & Young. (2005). Global information security survey 2005: Report on the widening gap. *Technical Report No. EYG No. DJ0001*. Retrieved May 2, 2008, from http://int.sitestat.com/ernst-and-young/international/s?Global-Information-Security-survey-2005&ns_type=pdf

Finfacts Team. (2007, January). *Global information security survey highlights concerns over privacy and personal data protection*. Retrieved May 2, 2008, from http://www.finfacts.com/irelandbusinessnews/publish/article_10008053.shtml

Gregg, M.C. (2005, October). *CISSP security-management practices exam: CISSP exam cram 2*. Retrieved May 2, 2008, from http://www.examcram2.com/articles/article.asp?p=418007&seqNum=4&rl=1:.

Griffiths, D. (2006). *Risk based internal auditing, version 2.0.3*. Retrieved May 2, 2008, from http://www.internalaudit.biz/

Hurtaud, S. (2006). How CobiT can help you to assess IT risks and to develop your IT audit plan. *Dexia BIL Group*. Retrieved May 2, 2008, from http://www.iaci.lu/archives/tr/HowtouseCOBITtodefinetheITaudituniverse_dratftversion.pdf

International Charter. (2006). *The risk equation*. Retrieved May 2, 2008, from http://www.icharter.org/articles/risk_equation.html

Kairab, S. (2004). *A practical guide to security assessments*. Florida: CRC Press.

Kramer, J.B. (2003). *The CISA prep guide*. Indianapolis, IN: Wiley.

Ponemon, L. (2006, March 16). Opinion: Ignoring data breaches means ignoring risk management. *Search Security*. Retrieved May 2, 2008, from http://searchsecurity.techtarget.com/originalContent/0,289142,sid14_gci1173214,00.html

Mcafee. (2007). *Newly discovered malware*. Retrieved May 2, 2008, from http://vil.nai.com/vil/newly_discovered_viruses.aspx

McConnel, D. Jr., & Banks, G. (2003, September). How Sarbanes-Oxley will change the audit process. *AICPA Journal of Accountancy*.

Retrieved May 2, 2008, from http://www.aicpa.org/pubs/jofa/sep2003/mcconn.htm

Protiviti Corporation. (2006, December 10). Automated and preventive controls can decrease compliance costs. *IT Audit Newsletter, The Institute of Internal Auditors (Vol. 9)*. Retrieved May 2, 2008, from http://www.theiia.org/itaudit/index.cfm?catid=28&iid=509

Rajamani, B. (2006). Certifying automated information technology controls. *Deloitte Consulting*. Retrieved May 2, 2008, from http://www.deloitte.com/dtt/article/0,1002,sid=68725&cid=96127,00.html?list=gfsi-rp

Ramos, M. (2004). *How to comply with Sarbanes-Oxley section 404: Assessing the effectiveness of internal control*. New Jersey: John Wiley and Sons.

Stoneburner, G., Goguen, A., & Feringa, A. (2002). Risk management guide for information technology systems. *National Institute of Standards and Technology*. Retrieved May 2, 2008, from http://csrc.nist.gov/publications/nistpubs/800-30/sp800-30.pdf

KEY TERMS

Application Controls: Application controls are automated controls that relate to the processing of transactions within the business process. Application controls are typically preventative in nature and are embedded within the application or could be configured. Examples of Application controls are edit checks, data input validations, calculations, interfaces, and authorizations.

Auditable Domain: An auditable domain is a manageable auditable activity, which may be defined in a number of ways, such as by function or activity, by organizational unit or division, or by project or program.

Internal Control: An internal control is processes, policies, procedures, and practices, designed to provide reasonable assurance that business objectives will be achieved, and that undesired events will be prevented or detected, and corrected or mitigated.

IT General Controls: IT General controls are controls that apply to the entire infrastructure of the organization. The most common IT General controls are logical access controls over applications, infrastructure and data, change management controls, system and data backup and recovery controls.

Residual Risk: Risk that remains after a control is implemented is called residual risk.

Risk: A risk is a circumstance or event that has the potential to hinder achievement of objectives or cause harm.

Threat: Threat is the potential for a threat-source to exercise (accidentally trigger or intentionally exploit) a specific vulnerability.

Vulnerability: Vulnerability is a flaw or weakness in system security procedures, internal controls, or implementation that could be exercised (accidentally triggered or intentionally exploited) and result in loss or harm.

Section II
Security Approaches, Frameworks, Tools, and Technologies

Chapter VIII
Distributed Denial of Service
Attacks in Networks

Udaya Kiran Tupakula
Macquarie University, Australia

Vijay Varadharajan
Macquarie University, Australia

ABSTRACT

In this chapter we discuss Distributed Denial of Service (DDoS) attacks in networks such as the Internet, which have become significantly prevalent over the recent years. We explain how DDoS attacks are performed and consider the ideal solution characteristics for defending against the DDoS attacks in the Internet. Then we present different research directions and thoroughly analyse some of the important techniques that have been recently proposed. Our analysis confirms that none of the proposed techniques can efficiently and completely counteract the DDoS attacks. Furthermore, as networks become more complex, they become even more vulnerable to DoS attacks when some of the proposed techniques are deployed in the Internet. The gap between the tools that can generate DDoS attacks and the tools that can detect or prevent DDoS attacks continues to increase. Finally, we briefly outline some best practices that the users are urged to follow to minimise the DoS attacks in the Internet.

INTRODUCTION

Today, enterprises are becoming increasingly dependent on the Internet to perform their business online. Recently there has been rapid migration of several critical applications such as health-care services to the online environment. In addition to the several advantages of the Internet, the stateless nature of the Internet and inherent weakness in the TCP/IP protocol have proven to be very lucrative for several crackers and a great entertainment tool for script kiddies. Since the current Internet architecture is mainly destination oriented, the attacker can easily generate an attack on almost any host/network in the Internet by spoofing the source address.

As organisations and critical applications are becoming increasingly dependent on the Internet to provide their services, even a minor disruption of these services can prove to be enormously expensive and cause severe damage to the organisations. A "denial-of-service" (DoS) [CERT, 2000] is an attempt by attackers to prevent access to resources by legitimate users for which they have authorisation. In the case of Distributed Denial of Service (DDoS) attack, an attacker compromises several hosts on the Internet and then uses these compromised computers to launch coordinated attacks on victim machines. There are no standards to classify DDoS attacks. Mirkovic and Reiher [2004] classified attacks based on the degree of automation of the attack tools, exploited vulnerability to deny service, source address validity, attack rate dynamics, possibility of characterisation, persistence of agent set, victim type and impact on the victim.

DDoS attacks are a fundamental challenge faced by the organizations conducting online business today over the Internet. A series of DDoS attacks crippled several major sites like Microsoft, Yahoo, Amazon, FBI in the year 2000. The recent survey by Symantec confirms that 1,000 DoS[1] attacks of one form or another occur on a daily basis over the Internet. These attacks are ranked among the top 5 security threats for the past consecutive years. Every year, these attacks account to several millions of dollars in lost revenue. Today there is an increased gap between the ease of generation of DoS attacks (with advanced tools) and techniques that are available to counter these attacks.

ATTACK MECHANISM

The DDoS architecture is shown in Figure 1. There can be several handlers in the case of DDoS and each handler is capable of controlling multiple zombies. The attacker does the major part of her/his work in identifying and creating the handlers. The attacker initiates a scan on a number of hosts in the Internet for a known vulnerability. If a vulnerable host is found, the attacker gains root access to the machine by compromising it and install attack tools on the compromised machines. The compromised machines that are controlled by an attacker are called handlers. There can be several handlers in the case of DDoS attacks. The handlers can be randomly located in the Internet and the communication between the attacker and the handlers can be encrypted. There can be several stages in the handler mechanism and the handlers do not directly conduct the attack on the victim machines. As the number of stages within the handler mechanism increases, it becomes more difficult to trace the attacker.

The attacker uses the handlers to further scan and compromise several hundreds of hosts in the Internet. The machines that are compromised and controlled by handlers are called zombies. Each handler is capable of controlling several hundred zombies. The communication between the handlers and the zombies can be encrypted. Zombies are the actual hosts that flood the victim's machine or network with attack traffic. In many cases, the owners of the zombie machines are not aware that their machines are compromised and being used to generate attack traffic on the victim's

machines. Since several hundred zombies may be involved in the case of DDoS attack, the victim can experience severe flood of traffic at its end even if each zombie contributes to a small amount of attack traffic. Technologies such as cable modems for home users have further increased the threat of DDoS attacks. This is because with the cable modems the home users are always connected to the Internet and it is easier for an attacker to compromise these systems, which often have weak security. It would be even more difficult to prevent such attacks if the compromised systems attacked with a spoofed source address and constantly changed the attack traffic pattern.

The victim can protect her/his network from the attack traffic at its end by configuring some form of security tools like firewalls or intrusion detection systems. Even if the victim can protect her/his network from the attack traffic, all the victim's network bandwidth is consumed by the attack traffic. So the victim's machines cannot have access to other networks (Internet) and other networks cannot access the victim's network. This will have a considerable impact on the sites conducting online business.

IDEAL SOLUTION CHARACTERISTICS

Before we can consider any solution to thwart DDoS attacks, it is useful to identify and examine the essential characteristics [Tupakula and Varadharajan, 2004] of a robust DDoS solution architecture. Consider Figure 1, where the attacker has already performed a substantial amount of work in creating the zombies. So it is only a matter of few keystrokes for the attacker to launch a severe DDoS attack on the victim's machine/network. An effective approach against these attacks would be to trace the attacker and prevent her/him from commanding the zombies to attack the particular host or network. However, this is not possible with the presently available technology, because often the zombies are controlled by an attack control mechanism or handlers, which is remotely controlled by the attacker. Moreover, the communication between the zombies, handlers and the attacker can be encrypted.

The victim should have a mechanism such as the one shown in Figure 2 to counter the DDoS attacks effectively. In this case, the victim identifies the attack at the point where it occurs but prevents the attack nearest to the attacking source. An ideal solution against distributed denial of service attacks should have the following characteristics:

Figure 1. DDoS architecture

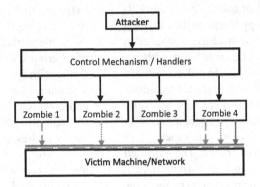

Figure 2. Ideal solution characteristics

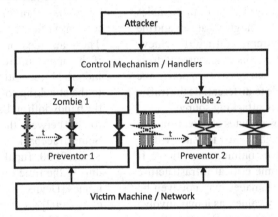

- **Economically attractive for deployment:** Even if a technique has several advantages and minimal disadvantages, it may not be deployed if it incurs huge costs to deploy the technology or if it does not prove to be economically beneficial to its deployer. The deployment cost of any proposed technique is dependent on the modifications to the existing system to support the proposed technique. The more modifications required to the existing system, the higher are the deployment costs and the fewer the chances for the technique to be deployed in practice.

- **Invoked only during the attacks:** Any proposed technique will inevitably contribute to at least some additional overhead on the existing system. Also, it is easier for an attacker to exploit a continuously working system rather than an intermittently invoked system. To minimise these disadvantages, the proposed technique should be invoked only during attack times

and at other times allow the system to function normally. There are also some disadvantages associated with this characteristic. A system that is invoked only during the times of attack will have a slow response compared to a continuously invoked technique. So the response time in this case will be dependent on i) how fast the victim can identify the attack and invoke the model; and ii) the response time of the proposed technique to prevent the attack.

- **Solution simple to implement and effective against attacks:** A system that is simple to implement and operate incurs lower deployment costs. For instance, if the system is easy to operate, its deployer need not employ highly technical staff. Furthermore, a complex system can itself lead to several DoS attacks.

- **Identify the attacks at the victim's end and prevent them nearest to the attacking source:** The victim can identify the attack traffic efficiently because only the victim can decide which traffic is good or bad for its network. If attack packets are dropped near to the attacking source, considerable bandwidth can be saved in the upstream routers. The saved bandwidth can be used to route good traffic. In order to achieve this property in practice, the proposed technique should be scalable so that it can be universally deployed. This is because the attacking sources can be randomly located in the Internet.

- **Prevent only the attack traffic:** The proposed technique should be able to differentiate a malicious traffic flow from a regular benign flow by incorporating different attack signatures for different attacking sources. Attack signature [Stone, 2000] is the pattern of traffic that enables differentiation between the good packets and the attack packets. It is extremely difficult to achieve this property in practice. Since the source address of the attack packets can be easily spoofed, the victim will not be able to differentiate the traffic originating from each attacking source.
- **Fast response:** A few minutes of downtime can result in huge financial losses for sites whose core business involves online transactions. If the attacks target some critical infrastructure like healthcare, the damages may not even be specified in monetary values, as it may involve human lives. Hence the proposed system should have a very fast response time to trace the approximate source of attack and prevent the attack nearest to the source of attack. Also, the system should provide a mechanism to detect and quickly respond if the attacking sources change the attack traffic pattern.
- **Trace the approximate source of attack with minimal packets:** Since there are several hundred attacking sources in the case of DDoS, the victim can notice a severe flood of traffic even if each attacking source contributes to a small amount of attack traffic. So the proposed technique should be capable of performing the traceback with minimal attack packets.

BACKGROUND

As already discussed, the attack traffic has to be prevented nearest to the attacking source in order to deal with the DDoS attacks efficiently. Over the past few years there has been considerable research in

different directions to deal with the DDoS problem in the Internet. Let us consider some of the important research directions.

Some authors have suggested different types of filtering techniques [Ferguson, 1998] to prevent traffic with spoofed source addresses in the Internet. The main idea is that if traffic with spoofed source addresses can be minimised in the Internet, then this can also minimise DDoS attacks with spoofed source addresses. This will only leave DDoS attacks with correct source addresses. Since the attack traffic has a correct source address, the victim can identify different attack signatures for each attacking source and filter the attack traffic at its end or nearest to the source of attack.

Some authors have suggested traceback techniques to identify the approximate spoofed source of attack. The main idea of the traceback techniques is that if the approximate spoofed source of attack can be identified, then attack traffic can be filtered nearest to the attacking source. This will result in saving of the bandwidth at the victim's end and for all upstream routers between the victim and the attacking sources. Some traceback techniques [Mahajan et al., 2002; Stone, 2000, Tupakula, 2004] can be performed only during the time of attack and some traceback techniques [Dean et al., 2002; Savage et al., 2001; Snoren et al, 2002] are capable of performing post-mortem analysis. Some authors suggested traceback through selective flooding, logging [Stone, 2000; Snoren et al., 2002], packet marking [Dean et al. 2002; Savage, 2001; Tupakula and Varadharajan, 2004] ICMP messages [Bellovin, 2000] overlay networks [Stone, 2000] and pushback technique [Mahajan et al., 2002].

Some tools such as Mazu enforcer, Peakflow SP, and Cisco NetFlow have been specifically developed to deal with the DoS attacks. Several techniques have been proposed to enhance the attack detection/prevention capabilities of the existing tools such as routers, intrusion detection systems, firewalls and network management systems to efficiently deal with the DDoS attacks. For example, the ACC router proposed by Mahajan et al. [2002] identifies DDoS attack at the congested router or from the request of the DDoS victim server and treats the traffic by punishing the aggregates that are causing congestion. The D-ward technique [Mirkovic et al., 2002] monitors the two-way communication of the sources that are connected to the edge router and limits the traffic that is found to be suspicious. Tupakula and Varadharajan [2004] have proposed an automated model that is based on the Controller-Agent model. The packet marking technique and agent design also enables the victim to track the changes in attack pattern and dynamically apply filter at the edge routers which are nearest to the source of attack.

ANALYSIS OF FEW IMPORTANT TECHNIQUES

Let us consider some of the important proposed techniques and analyze them in detail. We will focus our discussion on some of the real time issues for the techniques to be deployed in the Internet.

Ingress or Egress Filtering

The most standard approach against denial of service attacks is the use of ingress or egress filtering techniques. Ingress filtering [Ferguson, 1998] is from the point of view of the Internet. Here an Internet Service Provider (ISP) filters out packets with illegitimate source address, based on the ingress link through which the packet enters the network. In contrast, egress filtering is from the point of view of the customer network and the filtering occurs at the exit point of a customer's domain. Here a router checks whether the source addresses of packets actually belong to the customer's domain. Packets with invalid source addresses are dropped. In Figure 3, if the ISP performs filtering at router R3 to validate the source address of the traffic originating from the customer network, then it is called ingress filtering. If the customer applies a filter at router R5 to validate the source address of the traffic that is leaving its network, then it is called egress filtering.

While this is considered to be a first step to prevent DoS attacks with spoofed source addresses, it is not likely to completely eliminate the ability to spoof the source IP address. For instance, the attacker can still forge her/his machines source address with an address that is within the domain. The main disadvantages of this approach include the extra overhead and the associated reduction in the performance of the routers. It is necessary to check every packet that flows in or out of the network. Perhaps the major stumbling block is the unwillingness of many ISPs to provide this feature. This technique is not effective against attack traffic that originates from compromised machines with valid source addresses. This type of filtering will affect

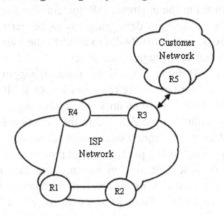

Figure 3. Ingress/Egress filtering

some forms of mobile communication. In some cases of mobile communication, if a mobile node is within the domain of the foreign agent, then all the communication to the mobile node is tunneled from the home agent to the foreign agent. The communication from the mobile node to other networks is directly through the foreign agent. If ingress filtering is deployed in this case, then all the packets from the mobile node will be dropped by the foreign agent.

Input debugging

Input debugging is a process of determining the approximate spoofed source of attack through hop-by-hop traceback. This process starts at the router which is connected to the victim's network and proceeds in the reverse direction of attack traffic until it reaches the attacking source/network or network boundary. This method is only suitable to trace continuous floods that are in progress. The DDoS victim requests her/his ISP administrator to identify the approximate source of attack. If the ISP is willing to co-operate with the victim, then the hop-by-hop traceback is initiated, starting from the router that is connected to the victim's network. The next upstream router is determined by the input link of the first router through which attacking traffic is arriving. This can be achieved by using the access control list (ACL) or debugging or logging features available on the routers. This process is recursively repeated until the traceback reaches the ingress edge router through which the attack traffic is entering the ISP domain. This will determine the approximate attacking source (other customer network of the ISP or the upstream ISP router). If the upstream ISPs are willing to co-operate then the attack can be further traced in the upstream ISP domain. For example, in Figure 4, input debugging has to be performed in the direction R0-R4-R6 to identify the ingress edge router R6 through which attack traffic A1 is entering the ISP domain. Similarly, input debugging has to be performed in the direction R0-R4-R7-R8 and/or R0-R2-R5-R8 to identify the ingress edge router R8 for attack traffic A2, and in the direction R0-R1 to identify the ingress edge router R1 for attack traffic A3. This technique is a manual process and requires a considerable amount of time and manpower to trace the attacking source. It is extremely difficult to trace the DDoS attacks, since the traceback has to be performed in several directions. Also, this technique can be used to trace the attacking source only if the attack is in progress. The attacks that last for a short time period and which occur at regular or irregular intervals cannot be traced.

CentreTrack

In Stone's [2000] approach, an overlay network is created by deploying special tracking routers which link all the edge routers to a central tracking router.

In Figure 4, assume that an overlay network is created by linking all the edge routers R0, R1, R3, R6, R8, and R9 to a CenterTrack router. During an attack, only the victim's traffic is routed through the overlay network by dynamic routing. Then, starting from the edge tracking router closer to the victim, hop-by-hop tracking (Input debugging) is used to trace back the ingress point of the attacking source. Compared to input debugging, this technique can trace the ingress edge routers of the attack traffic with minimum number of hops.

The main disadvantage of this approach is the changes required to the global routing table. A poor implementation of this approach would make it too easy for a small error to severely disturb the total network. The attack traffic originating from the backbone cannot be prevented. Even if the victim's traffic is diverted through the overlay network, the attacking source is traced through the process of input debugging which is a manual process and consumes a lot of time and manpower. It is extremely difficult to trace the DDoS attacks since the traceback has to be performed in several directions. This technique can be used to trace the attacking source only if the attack is in progress. So, intermittent attacks that last for a short time period at regular/irregular intervals cannot be traced.

Figure 4. Attack scenario

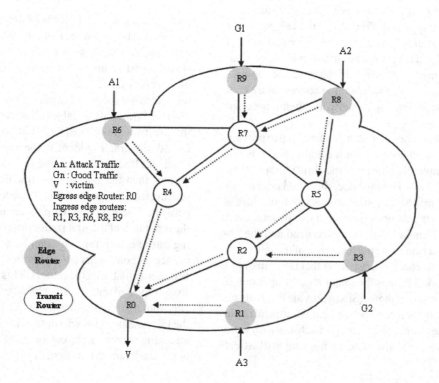

Stone [2000] also proposed another approach whereby all the edge routers (see Figure 4) maintain the database of all the traffic passing through them. The data includes the source address, destination address, adjacency and approximate number of packets. When an attack is reported, the database is searched based on the attack signatures and the ingress adjacency is determined. The main advantage of this technique is that no tracking hops are required to trace the ingress edge and the tracing is possible even after the attack is completed. Since the current routers deal with gigabits of data per second, this approach has very high overheads of storage and processing. There are also additional issues on the time period for which the database has to be maintained and the location where the database has to be maintained. If database is maintained at every router, then all the routers have to be queried to determine the ingress edge router through which the attack traffic is entering the ISP domain. If the database has to be maintained at a single location, then all the data has to be transferred to a particular location. This will increase the network traffic within the ISP domain.

Single Packet IP Traceback

Snoeren et al. [2002] proposed a Source Path Isolation Engine (SPIE) which incorporates Data Generator Agent (DGA) into all the routers (both edge routers and transit routers in Figure 4) within the ISP. While forwarding the packets, the DGA masks the varying fields (TTL, Checksum, ToS and options field in Figure 5) of the IP header [Postel, 1981] and calculates the digest of the remaining fields in the IP header and the first 8 bytes of the payload. The DGA stores the digest in a time-stamped table and periodically pages out the portion of the table to the local aggregation points. Each aggregation point monitors a group of DGAs

and generates a periodic graph of the traffic path. When the victim IDS reports the attack by sending the malicious packet and the time of receipt, the SPIE Traceback Manager (STM) queries each individual aggregation nodes for the local attack patch. The STM assembles each individual attack path received from the aggregation nodes, determines the total attack path and updates it to the victim. The novelty of this technique is the minimisation of the storage overhead using bloom filters and storing only the digest of non-varying fields in the IP header and the first 8 bytes of payload, instead of storing the complete packet.

The main advantage of this technique is the traceback of a single packet with the capability to deal with the compromised routers within the ISP domain. The main disadvantage of this technique is that the overhead on the routers is extremely high since hash of the packets has to be calculated at every router. Since the packets are stored at every hop and since the current routers carry gigabits of data per second, the proposed technique has extremely high overhead and severe limitation on the time period for which the database can be maintained. Hence the response time for the victim to identify the malicious packet and send a request to the STM should be very fast. In addition, the response time should also include the time required for the STM to authenticate the victim before the traceback can be performed. For each attack packet generated by the attacker, multiple queries have to be initiated to determine the approximate source of attack. This can result in the increase in traffic within the ISP domain.

IP Packet Marking Techniques

The first probabilistic packet marking technique and a detailed analysis of the traceback problem was proposed by Savage et al. [2001]. This technique is very

Figure 5. IP header

Ver	H.Len	ToS (8-bits)	Total Length (16-bits)		
Fragment ID (16-bit)			Flags	Fragment Offset	
TTL		Protocol	Header Checksum		
Source IP Address (32-bits)					
Destination IP Address					

novel and has attracted several researchers [Dean et al., 2002] to perform further research in this area. In general, most of the packet marking techniques mark the 32-bit IP address of the router with their own techniques by overloading the 16-bit fragment ID field (see Figure 5) of an IP packet. These techniques make the assumption that there would be a considerable amount of packets generated during an attack. They argue that a victim will be able to reconstruct the route followed by the packets by combining a modest number of marked packets, although each marked packet represents only a sample of the path it has traversed.

For example, in Figure 4, if the victim receives considerable number of marked packets, the path traversed (R0-R4-R6) by the attack traffic A1 can be calculated from the information present in the fragment ID field and the approximate spoofed source of attack can be determined. The main advantage of these techniques is that the traceback can be performed in heterogeneous networks without the co-operation of the ISPs. However, since packets are probabilistically marked, the victim would need a large number of packets to calculate the total path traversed by the attack traffic. Even if we assume that each packet is marked, it could take a considerable amount of time for the victim to calculate the path, as computation is needed to retrieve the 32-bit IP address of the marked router. In general, the time taken to reconstruct the path (RT) is dependent on the number of attacking systems, the number of parallel paths and the length of the path. The number of false positives is also dependent on the number of attacking hosts, the length of path and the number of parallel paths. Let us focus our discussion on some of the real time issues that are related to IP packet marking techniques. Unless specified, the following discussion deals with the traceback techniques in general.

Co-operation of ISPs: Some schemes claim that their technique is capable of tracking the approximate source of attack in heterogeneous networks without the co-operation of the ISPs. Even if the technique is capable of tracking the attack source in heterogeneous networks, we believe that a fair amount of co-operation is needed between the ISPs, both for the deployment and for the functioning of traceback technologies.

Problems with routes: Several routing protocols such as BGP, EIGRP, IGRP, OSPF, IS-IS and RIP are used to route the packets in the current Internet architecture. Each routing protocol uses different metrics to calculate the best path to a particular destination. The traceback techniques assume that routes between the attacking source and the victim are fairly stable. This

condition may not hold true in all the cases and it is dependent on the routing protocols. For example, the RIP protocol only chooses the route with minimum hop count as the best/shortest route for a particular destination. Even in the case of RIP, we should note that there can be equal paths for a particular destination and the packet may take any of the routes to that particular destination. The advanced routing protocols such as OSPF, EIGRP and IS-IS calculate the shortest path based on several parameters such as hop count, time delay, bandwidth, load balancing between equal paths and load balancing between unequal paths. In the case of DDoS there will be a sudden burst of traffic. This burst of data can cause the packets to be routed through different routes. Due to the advanced routing protocols, the packets can take different paths depending on parameters such as time delay and load balancing between the routes. It has been observed that BGP instabilities occur during the time of DDoS attack. So we believe that the routes may not be stable within a small time interval of time and the traceback techniques should also consider the routing protocols used in the Internet architecture.

Issue with fragments: Several schemes such as [Dean et al., 2002; Savage, 2001] propose the use of the fragment ID field in an IPv4 packet to mark the packets for traceback purpose, since fragments constitute only 0.22 % of the total Internet traffic. Once deployed, traceback is a continuous process and there is more probability for all the hosts in the Internet to receive packets that are marked in the fragment ID field. There is no procedure to differentiate between packets that are fragments and packets that are marked in the fragment ID field for traceback purposes. Added to this complication, some DoS attacks use fraudulently marked fragmented packets. So there should be a procedure for the victim to differentiate packets that are real fragments, packets that are marked for traceback purposes and packets that are malicious fragmented packets

ICMP Traceback

Bellovin [2000] suggests a similar approach to the IP traceback, but the traceback is performed through out-of-band signalling with ICMP packets. In this approach, when forwarding packets, routers send an ICMP traceback message to the destination with a low probability (say, 1/20,000). The ICMP traceback packet includes the identity of the router, the contents of the packets, and information about the adjacent routers. During the time of attack, after receiving a considerable number of traceback messages, the victim can identify the approximate source of the attack by tracing the total path traversed by attack traffic with the information received in the ICMP traceback packets. In order to trace the route, the victim should compare and find a match between the received attack traffic/packets with the ICMP traceback messages to determine the routers through which attack traffic has traversed. After receiving a considerable number of ICMP traceback packets, the victim can trace the chain of routers through which the attack traffic has traversed and find the approximate source of attack. For example, in Figure 4, since the flood of attack traffic A1 is destined to the victim, there is more probability for the routers R6, R4, and R0 to generate ICMP traceback messages to the victim. From the information received in the ICMP traceback messages, the victim can reconstruct the attack path R0-R4-R6 and determine attacking source/network. The technique also proposed to use some security protocols to authenticate the ICMP traceback messages that are received at the victim's end.

The advantages of this technique are: There will be more number of packets to the victim in the case of DDoS attacks. So there is more probability for the victim to receive a greater number of ICMP traceback messages compared to other destinations. This approach has little overhead at the routers, since ICMP packets are generated on very low probability.

The disadvantages of this technique include the following: ICMP packets are generated even if there is no attack. This technique generates additional traffic in the Internet. Some ISPs do not allow ICMP packets through their networks. So the victim may not receive the ICMP traceback messages. Since ICMP traceback messages are generated on very low probability the victim should receive large number of attack packets in order to trace the path traversed by the attack traffic. Authentication scheme for the ICMP traceback messages can be an overhead at the routers and this may lead to some form of DoS attacks on the routers. In addition to all these issues, DDoS floods can be generated with the ICMP traceback messages itself. A detail discussion on how DDoS attacks can be generated by exploiting the limitation in ICMP traceback technique is discussed in [Tupakula, 2005].

Controlling High Bandwidth Aggregates

The idea behind the approach proposed by Mahajan et al. [2002] is to identify the particular set of packets that are causing overload. These are referred to as aggregates. An aggregate is defined as a collection of packets from one or more flows that have some property in common. For instance, "packets to destination X", "TCP SYN packets" and "IP packets with a bad checksum" are examples of aggregates. The aim is to identify aggregates responsible for congestion/attacks and prevent them getting to the victim. Prevention can be carried out by the victim or at the router where there is congestion. Prevention is implemented using two mechanisms: one uses a local aggregate based congestion control (ACC) scheme in which a router deals with sustained overload by itself, and the other is referred to as a pushback scheme which extends the local ACC to other routers upstream. The ACC itself can be broken into two phases, namely detection and control. In the detection phase, the ACC agent is responsible for identifying the aggregate and calculating the rate limit for them. The rate limit in the control phase determines whether a packet is to be discarded or forwarded. The advantage is that the aggregates can be completely stopped or limited to a particular bandwidth. In a certain sense, pushback is similar to the traceroute. Once the aggregates are identified, the router can ask the upstream routers to prevent them and hence reach the source of the attacker. When pushback is applied upstream, there is more bandwidth for legitimate traffic in downstream routers. In Figure 4, if we assume that congestion occurs at the router R0 due to the attack traffic A1, A2 and A3, then the router R1 will identify the congestion signature A1, A2 and A3 and rate limits the traffic to a certain bandwidth. Attacking sources can be identified by applying pushback in the direction R0-R4-R6, R0-R4-R7-R8, R0-R2-R5-R8 and R0-R1. When pushback is applied in the reverse direction of attack traffic, there is more bandwidth for good traffic that is originating from ingress edge routers R3 and R9.

The main advantage of the ACC routers is the automatic identification of the congestion/attack signature at the congested router and dynamic placement of the filters. This approach addresses the DDoS attacks in a broad sense. We believe that further research on this approach can efficiently lead to counter some of the zero day attacks (attacks that are previously not known). The disadvantages associated with this approach are that strong authentication is required to perform a pushback; otherwise this in itself could turn out to be a DoS attack. Furthermore, even if strong authentication is implemented, if the attacker can compromise a single ACC router, then the attacker can cause severe damage. ACC routers should be capable of storing large amounts of data in order to identify the attack signatures efficiently. Since the ACC router is not the real victim and since each attack packet can have a random number as the source address, it is extremely difficult to identify the congestion/attack signatures. The identified attack signatures are very broad. Once the attack signatures are identified, each arriving packet has to be compared with a broad congestion signature to determine if the packet contributes to the congestion. This can cause considerable delays for routing the packets at the ACC routers.

Automated Model

The automated model is based on the controller-agent model. The controller is implemented on a dedicated host and the agents are implemented on all the edge routers. The victim that is under attack requests the controller in its domain to prevent the attack upstream. A session is established between the controller and the victim after proper authentication of the victim. Depending on the number of agents present within its domain, the controller generates and issues a unique ID to each of its agents and commands them to mark the victim's traffic with the issued ID. The controller updates the victim with the unique ID's. The ingress edge routers/agents filter the traffic that is destined to the victim and mark the packets with the unique ID in the fragment ID field of IP packet. If the packets are already marked, the agents drop the packets. This is because the packet could be a fragment or it could be marked by an attacker. The egress edge router/agent forwards only the packets with valid ID's to the victim.

Since agents are deployed on all the edge routers, all the traffic to the victim is marked with the ingress edge agent unique ID. Though the source address of the attack traffic is spoofed, for example in Figure 4, all the attack traffic A1 will have unique ID of ingress edge agent R6 in the fragment ID field. Since the controller has already updated the victim with valid ID's, this enables the victim to identify different attack signatures for each ingress edge agent (A1 for R6, A2 for R8 and A3 for R1). The victim updates the controller with different attack signatures based on the unique ID. The controller retrieves the 32-bit IP address of the ingress edge agent from its database based on unique ID and commands that particular agent to prevent the attack traffic from reaching the victim. Since attack signatures are identified based on the unique ID, only the ingress edge agents through which the

attack traffic is passing (R6, R8 and R1) will receive this command. Now all the agents that receive this command will start preventing the attack traffic from reaching the victim. The traffic that is matching with the attack signature will be dropped and logged at the agent. The traffic that is not matching with the attack signature is marked with the unique ID and destined to the victim. This enables the victim to easily track the changes in the attack traffic pattern. In Figure 4, since the packets are marked even if the traffic is not matching with the attack signature, the victim can easily detect and respond if the attack traffic A1 from ingress edge agent R6 changes the attack pattern from X to Y. Also, the victim can easily detect and quickly respond if the good sources connected to the ingress edge agent R4 suddenly start sending attack traffic to the victim. The agents update the controller at regular intervals on how much attack traffic the agents are still receiving. Packet marking and prevention process will be done until the agent receives a reset signal from its controller. However the victim can request the controller to continue the packet marking process for an excess amount of time. This is very useful for intermittent type of attacks where attacking systems do not flood the victim continuously but send attack traffic at regular intervals.

The main advantages of this model are: the model is invoked only during the time of attack and the victim's traffic is processed separately. Hence the model has minimal overhead. The packet marking technique and agent design enables the victim to identify the ingress edge router of the attack traffic by observing a single attack packet even if the source address of the packet is spoofed. In addition the design also enables the victim to detect the changes in attack traffic pattern and automatically configure filters. Once attack signatures are identified, prevention of attack traffic is directly near to the attacking source (ingress edge agent) instead of hop by hop upstream. Furthermore, the model can be easily integrated with the existing tools [Tupakula and Varadharajan, 2007] such as network intrusion detection systems and network management systems. The main disadvantages of this approach are: Since there are only 16 bits in the fragment ID field of IP packets, the model is only suitable for an ISP with less than 65535 routers. The dropped fragments may include some good fragmented packets to the victim. However this happens only during DDoS attack on the victim. The attacker can generate severe DDoS attacks by compromising the controller of the ISP.

FUTURE TRENDS

The current attacks are becoming so sophisticated and complex that classification of attacks itself is becoming extremely difficult. For example, due to the introduction of new legislations on spam, spammers are using DDoS techniques to send spam. The main idea is to send the spam through zombies. Now only the owners of the zombie machines will be liable for legal proceedings. Recently several worms were used to perform DDoS attacks in the Internet.

Viruses and worms have the property of self-spreading. Unlike the DDoS attacks which target single/multiple victim networks, the virus and worms attacks target the whole of the Internet [Arce, 2004]. These attacks make use of the vulnerabilities present in the operating systems or database systems. In general, these attacks spread by scanning for vulnerable machines in the Internet. For example, the SQL Slammer worm which occurred during January 2003 was spread with packets that were only 376 bytes long. Once a vulnerable system is found, the machine is infected with the malicious code and the process is repeated recursively. These attacks can spread much faster. The spam and phishing emails can be used to spread the viruses and worms in the Internet.

Today, network operators and service providers are working [Lee and Knight, 2005; Vrdoljak, 2000] on the convergence of wired, wireless and cellular networks with the aim to provide additional services with seamless and uninterrupted access to the end users. It is believed that IP protocol [Deering and Hinden, 1998; Postel, 1981] will be the predominant protocol that will be used for both data and voice communication in next generation networks. Also, end users will be extensively making use of wireless mobile devices for communication. The wireless devices have extremely limited resources and are vulnerable to several attacks. In particular, these wireless mobile devices are easily vulnerable to Denial of Service attacks. Recently there has been increasing activity of viruses and worms that can infect the mobile nodes and spread through the wireless medium. Currently voice over IP (VoIP) transmission is dominating over the traditional voice transmission. In general, VoIP traffic receives high priority compared to the data transmission. The attacker can exploit the inherent weaknesses in the IP protocol, and generate several types of DDoS attacks with the VoIP traffic.

Traditional security tools like firewalls and intrusion detection systems that can detect and prevent some forms of DoS attacks often require considerable resources such as processing power, memory, and storage space. Hence there are several challenges in detecting the DoS attacks on wireless mobile nodes. In addition, the recently proposed techniques such as IP Traceback, logging, and automated model which can deal with DoS attacks in wired networks assume that the victim node can detect the attack at its end and has considerable resources (such as processing power, memory, storage, and network bandwidth) at its end to perform the traceback. Hence these techniques cannot be directly applied to counteract DoS attacks in wireless networks.

BEST PRACTICES

From the above discussion, we can see that it is extremely difficult to deal with the DDoS attacks in the Internet. Although several tools are currently available and several techniques have been proposed, none of the existing tools and techniques can deal efficiently with the DDoS attacks. Furthermore, the gap between the ease of tools to generate DDoS attacks and the tools to defend DDoS is increasing. Also, we have seen that networks become complex and more vulnerable to DDoS with the deployment of some of the proposed techniques. For example, the security tools have become so complex that the attacker is able to generate DDoS by exploiting their limitations. Hence the best approach to minimize DoS attacks in the Internet is to make the computer users aware of the DoS problem and urge them to follow the best practices. Some of the best practices [CERT, 2003] include the following:

- Keep the machine physically secured
- Prevent unauthorised access by using strong password
- Use encryption instead of sending passwords in plain text
- Shutdown all unused ports
- Run the machine with limited privileges
- Download and install the updates regularly (use automatic updates)
- Enable firewall if supported by the operating system
- Install the antivirus software and regularly update
- Disconnect machine from the Internet if it is not going to be used for longer periods

- Make sure that all traffic that is leaving the network has the correct source address

CONCLUSION

In this chapter, we have discussed the vulnerability of the current networks to DDoS attacks. We have identified ideal solution characteristics, considered different directions and thoroughly analyzed some of the important proposed techniques. None of the existing tools and proposed techniques can deal efficiently and completely with the DDoS attacks. There is an increasing gap between ease of tools that can generate DDoS and the tools that can defend DDoS attacks. On the other hand with the introduction of new technologies, the current networks are becoming complex and even more vulnerable to DDoS attacks. Perhaps the best way to deal with the DDoS is to make the computer users aware of the DDoS problem and urge them to follow the best practices to minimize DDoS attacks in the Internet.

ACKNOWLEDGMENT

The Australian Government Departments of the Prime Minister and Cabinet (PM&C) and the Defense Signals Directorate (DSD) signals have contributed funding to the SHINE project under the Research Support for Counter-Terrorism Programme. The PM&C and DSD funding should not be taken to imply endorsement of the contents or conclusions of the SHINE project.

REFERENCES

Arce, I. (2004). More Bang for the Bug: An Account of 2003's Attack Trends. *IEEE Security & Privacy, 2*(1), pp. 66-68.

Baba, T., & Matsuda, S. (2002). Tracing Network Attacks to their sources. *IEEE Internet Computing, 6*(2), pp.20-26.

Bellovin, S. (2000). *The ICMP Traceback Message.* Retrieved March 5, 2002 from http://www.research. att.com/~smb, 2000

CERT (2000). *Denial of Service developments.* Retrieved March 4, 2002 from http://www.cert.org/advisories/CA-2000-01.html

CERT (2003). *Before you connect a new computer to the Internet.* Retrieved February 20, 2004 from http://www.cert.org/tech_tips/before_you_plug_in.html

Dean, D., Franklin, M., & Stubblefield, A. (2002). An Algebraic Approach to IP Traceback. *ACM Transactions on Information and System Security (TISSEC), 5*(2), 119-137.

Deering, S., & Hinden, R. (1998). *Internet Protocol,* Version 6 (IPv6) Specification. RFC 2460.

Ferguson, P., & Senie, D. (1998). *Network Ingress Filtering: defeating denial of service attacks which employ IP source address spoofing.* RFC 2267

Lee, C.S., & Knight, D. (2005). Realization of the Next-Generation Network. *IEEE Communications Magazine, 43*(10), pp. 34-41.

Mahajan, R., Bellovin, S.M., Floyd, S., Ioannidis, J., Paxson, V., & Shenker, S. (2002). Controlling high bandwidth aggregates in the network. *ACM SIGCOMM Computer Communication Review, 32*(3), 62-73.

Mirkovic, J., Prier, G., & Reiher, P. (2002). Attacking DDoS at the Source. In *Proceedings of 10th International Conference on Network* Protocols: IEEE.

Mirkovic, J., & Reiher, P. (2004). A taxonomy of DDoS attack and DDoS defense mechanisms. *ACM SIGCOMM Computer Communication Review, 34*(2), 39-53.

Postel, J. (1981). *Internet Protocol.* RFC 791.

Snoeren, A.C., Partridge, C., Sanchez, L.A., Jones, C.E., Tchakountio, F., Schwartz, B., Kent, S.T., & Strayer, W.T. (2002). Single-packet IP traceback. *IEEE/ACM Transactions on Networking (ToN), 10*(6), 721-734.

Stefan Savage, David Wetherall, Anna Karlin, and Tom Anderson (2001). Network support for IP traceback. *ACM/IEEE Transactions on Networking, 9*(3), 226-239.

Stone, R. (2000). CenterTrack: An IP Overlay Network for Tracking DoS Floods. In *Proceedings of 9th Usenix Security Symposium.*

Tupakula, U.K., & Varadharajan, V. (2004). Tracing DoS floods: An automated approach. *Journal of Network and Systems Management, 12*(1), 111-135.

Tupakula, U.K. (2005). *Modeling, Design and Implementation techniques for counteracting Denial of Service Attacks in Networks*, PhD Thesis, Macquarie University, Australia.

Tupakula, U.K., Varadharajan, V., Gajam, A.K., Vuppala, S.K., & Pandalaneni, N.S.R. (2007). DDoS: design, implementation and analysis of automated model. *International Journal of Wireless and Mobile Computing, 2*(1), 72-85.

Vrdoljak, M., Vrdoljak, S.I., & Skugor, G. (2000). Fixed-mobile convergence strategy: technologies and market opportunities. *IEEE Communications Magazine, 38*(2), 116-121.

KEY TERMS

Attack Signatures: pattern of traffic that enables differentiation between the good packets and the attack packets.

Denial of Service (DoS): is an attempt by attackers to prevent access to resources by legitimate users for which they have authorisation

Distributed Denial of Service (DDoS): an attacker compromises several hosts on the Internet and then uses these compromised computers to launch coordinated attacks on victim machines.

Handlers: Compromised machines which controls zombies

Input Debugging: is a process of determining the approximate spoofed source of attack through hop-by-hop traceback.

Zombies: Compromised machines that flood the victim's machine or network with attack traffic.

ENDNOTE

[1] From this point forward, unless specified, DoS refers to both DoS and DDoS.

Chapter IX
Firewalls as Continuing Solutions for Network Security

Andy Luse
Iowa State University, USA

Anthony Townsend
Iowa State University, USA

Kevin Scheibe
Iowa State University, USA

ABSTRACT

This chapter describes various firewall conventions, and how these technologies operate when deployed on a corporate network. Terms associated with firewalls, as well as related concepts, are also discussed. Highly neglected internal security mechanisms utilizing firewall technologies are presented, including host-based firewalls and the more novel distributed firewall implementation. Finally, a section on how to perform a cost-benefit analysis when deciding which firewall technologies to implement is included. The chapter is designed as an introductory tutorial to the underlying concepts of firewall technologies. This understanding should provide a starting point for both systems support specialists implementing network security and researchers who are interested in firewall technologies.

INTRODUCTION

The organizational firewall continues to be the most highly deployed information system security device by organizations. The traditional perimeter firewall provides an invaluable first line of defense against would-be attackers, malicious programs, and many other electronic nuisances which threaten the integrity of the corporate network. The key to maintaining the security protection of the firewall lies in the effective deployment and maintenance, to continually configure the firewall to balance security and usability for internal users as well as external customers, business partners, and so on.

In addition to the traditional challenges of network security, an emerging issue garnering increasing attention is that of internal network security. Scandals such as Enron, increasing governmental policies and regulations with regard to security and privacy, as well as increased anxiety regarding corporate intellectual property, have lead many corporations to implement heightened security measures on their internal network. Many falsely believe that firewalls have limited effectiveness when deployed within the internal network, and so only recently have internal firewall deployments been considered by many security professionals. Unfortunately, in spite of the increased security that secondary firewall installations can provide, many network administrators continue to fear an unmanageable security infrastructure when firewalls are brought inside the corporate network perimeter.

WHAT IS A FIREWALL

The term firewall historically gets its name from the physical concrete barriers running from the basement to the roof in buildings designed to limit the spread of fire and heat from one portion of the building to another (Whitman & Mattord, 2005). This model is mirrored with the concept of a firewall as it pertains to computer networks. Firewalls are typically thought of as devices placed between the internal corporate network and the external Internet designed to keep the "bad guys" and mischievous programs out of the internal network.

Firewalls, in their simplest construct, can be defined as a collection of components placed between two networks of differing security levels (Cheswick & Bellovin, 1994). Firewalls are designed to allow certain information into and out of a group of computers, or possibly a standalone computer, by way of a controlled point of entry (Zalenski, 2002). This controlled point must use some mechanism to keep track of which types of traffic are both allowed to enter as well as leave the network or computer.

Firewall functions. Firewall technologies come in several types which implement varying functionality for protecting internal computer(s) from external threats. These different methods all have their associated advantages and disadvantages relating both to security as well as usability, speed, and manageability. Understanding these concepts can help in the evaluation of the correct firewall technology for a specific application. While the most common application of firewall technology involves leveraging the device to protect the corporate network from the outside Internet, all the underlying functional types described in this section can be used in a large external firewall down to a host-based firewall protecting a single machine.

While the primary objective of all firewalls is the same, the methods used to accomplish these goals may vary. The following is a description of three main categories of firewalls: *Packet Filters*, *Circuit Gateways*, and *Application Gateways*.

Packet Filtering

The first generation of firewall technology involved analyzing packets entering and leaving a network for malicious traffic. This can involve inspecting just certain header values within the packet all the way up to analyzing the actual content of the message being transmitted in the packet payload (Strassberg, Gondek, & Rollie, 2002). One of the original firewall mechanisms, packet filtering is still widely used in many firewall appliances and applications today.

Packet filtering is a broad term which subsumes two separate methodologies: *static packet filtering* and *stateful packet inspection*. Although they can operate independently, these methods are traditionally not seen in isolation from each other, so a de facto third category also exists, the *hybrid packet filter*.

Static Packet Filtering

Static packet filtering involves specifying a predefined set of rules by which each packet entering and/or leaving a network is evaluated for admittance. The rules are typically defined in a list or access control list (ACL). The rules must be identified and installed before they can be used by the firewall device (Whitman & Mattord, 2005). Typically, the traditional static packet-filtering firewalls rely on existing protocols for verifying the legitimacy of a packet. This involves analyzing the header of the packet to validate source and destination IP addresses, the network protocol involved (TCP, UDP, and so on), and the port number being used (Strassberg et al., 2002).

The static packet filter offers some advantages when compared to other packet filtering technologies. First, due to its simple implementation and overhead, it usually performs quite efficiently. Second, it is relatively inexpensive to implement due to its simple approach. Third, again due to its simplistic approach, static packet filtering systems are typically easy to understand and manage (Strassberg et al., 2002).

Despite its benefits, the static packet filter does not provide the functionality needed for most corporate firewall implementations. First, the system does not allow easy updateability. For new rules to be added to the system, and administrator must first input these rules. Second, by necessity, it leaves open a number of holes in the firewall due to its lack of knowledge about existing connections from internal clients. This is especially apparent when connectionless protocols such as UDP are utilized. For example, say someone on the corporate network is involved in a video conference with another individual outside the company. If this software utilizes UDP, then there is no acknowledgement by the software on the corporate network with the external host. The firewall would therefore not be sure when the connection was over and therefore could risk leaving open a hole in the firewall well past the end of the conference. Third, the system is open to spoofing attacks. Since only the header values are typically analyzed, a malicious user can thwart the system by modifying the packet to seem as though it is coming from a trusted address (Strassberg et al., 2002).

Stateful Packet Inspection (SPI)

Stateful Packet Inspection (SPI) packet filters allow the system to dynamically update rules to correspond with varying conditions on the network. This capability was developed as a direct response to a static packet filter's inability to adequately deal with connectionless communications as noted above. A SPI packet filter takes note of IP addresses, source, and destination ports of traffic leaving the network so that the firewall can then only allow replies from the external host with the above credentials. This type of setup can also be used for connection-oriented protocols such as TCP to only allow replies to dynamically allocated rules from internal client requests (Pohlmann & Crothers, 2002). SPI packet filters typically can also analyze other values in the TCP header such as the SYN bit to verify a connection, as one example (Bragg, Phodes-Ousley, & Strassberg, 2004). This setup is analogous to having a guard at the door that keeps track of who has left the building and only allows that individual, or those tightly associated with that individual, back through when they return.

SPI packet filters improve on many of the short-comings associated with static packet filters. First, updateability is made much simpler as the SPI packet filter can make system changes depending on the traffic it sees (Zwicky, Cooper, & Chapman, 2000). Second, since the SPI packet filter inspects each packet based on whether it is part of an existing conversation, the SPI packet filter has far fewer holes left for spurious traffic (Strassberg, Gondek, & Rollie, 2002). Third, the connection table kept by the SPI packet filter greatly reduces the chances of spoofing (Bragg, Phodes-Ousley, & Strassberg, 2004).

SPI packet filters must also contend with their own unique set of disadvantages. First, due to keeping track of packet states, there is greater overhead and therefore a greater load on the firewall, as compared with a simple static packet filter operation. Also, with all this extra processing, the door is open to possible denial of service (DOS) attacks against the firewall, as its more complex operations can be significantly stalled by a relatively smaller level of attack traffic. A third problem exists with the time requirements for entries in the connection table; a proper balance must be kept between holding the connection state information long enough to properly permit legitimate connections, and opening the door to possible spurious traffic (Zwicky, Cooper, & Chapman, 2000). This is again a greater problem with connectionless protocols (see above). The firewall cannot tell when the connection has been terminated due to the lack of traffic acknowledgements between hosts. Therefore, if the hole is left open too long, an attacker can use this as an entry point to possibly exploit the internal corporate network.

Hybrid Packet Filtering

Current packet filtering systems usually implement a combination of the above mechanisms. Most corporate environments have both internal users as well as services for external clients which they wish to have access through the perimeter firewall at the same time. The company will therefore typically open static holes in their external firewall to allow external access to such services as the business Webpage for making online purchases from the company. These static holes usually have very few, if any, restrictions related to who can traverse them. Conversely, the company would not like to leave holes in their external firewall for each internal user who establishes a connection with the outside Internet. A SPI packet filter is implemented here to keep track of valid connections from current internal users.

Circuit Gateway

A circuit gateway acts as a relay agent which forwards information from internal network clients to the intended destination. The circuit gateway acts as an intermediary between the internal trusted network and the external untrusted network (Strassberg et al., 2002). It operates at the TCP layer by forwarding traffic based on port assignments. The primary advantage of circuit gateways is that the internal client is hidden from the external network by preventing direct connections between the two (Whitman & Mattord, 2005).

Although the circuit gateway offers a buffer between the internal and external networks, it still contains some flaws. First, clients must be able to use a circuit gateway. Sometimes this involves time and money to modify client software to utilize this functionality (Bragg et al., 2004). Second, the circuit gateway typically operates at only the TCP level, and therefore is not aware of any application-specific communication protocols or data. This means that the circuit gateway cannot examine packet contents at the application level, and therefore may still allow nefarious content into or out of the network (Strassberg et al., 2002).

Application Gateway

The application gateway extends the idea of the circuit gateway by adding functionality to analyze packets at the application level. The same basic functionality present in the circuit gateway for relaying information between the internal and external networks is still present in an application gateway. The primary advantage with the application gateway is that now the firewall can analyze application-specific traffic (Zwicky, Cooper, & Chapman, 2000). This provides for both added security, as specific communications within the application are now visible, and greater functionality, as the firewall can now accommodate more application-specific communication needs.

Many terms are used synonymously with application gateway, such as proxy server and bastion host. Proxy server is typically used to describe a more specialized application gateway which is specific to a certain application (Web, e-mail, and so on) or protocol (SOCKS). The bastion host is typically used to describe a single host which acts as an application gateway and which has been heavily secured against external attack (Bragg et al., 2004; Strassberg et al., 2002).

While it does offer many advantages over other firewall mechanisms, the application gateway also possess some disadvantages. First, with this greater application awareness comes greater performance needs. If a great deal of analysis is done for the traffic processed by an application gateway, then network performance may degrade (Bragg et al., 2004). Second, application gateways are not easily configurable. Most have been designed for a specific set of application protocols and it takes a significant amount of effort to update these (Whitman & Mattord, 2005). Third,

there is a lack of transparency for the end user. Many applications must be modified in order to work correctly with an application gateway (Strassberg et al., 2002). Fourth, there are always limits to the amount of application awareness which an application gateway is capable of maintaining; there is no way that the application gateway can analyze every piece of information which goes through it. Also, any information which has been encrypted, such as a VPN connection or secure Web transaction, is typically not visible to the application gateway without explicit knowledge of the encryption keys used.

Related Concepts

Many organizational applications and services are involved in a direct interaction with corporate firewalls. While these applications are not firewalls themselves, they are closely coupled with corporate firewall technologies. The following is a brief list of concepts which are typically discussed in conjunction with firewall technology.

Demilitarized Zone (DMZ)

The demilitarized zone, or DMZ, is an operational buffer zone between networks of differing security levels (Strassberg et al., 2002), which is protected from external networks by a firewall structure, and which is then isolated from the internal network by a second firewall. The DMZ includes components which are not actually part of the security divider between the differing networks, and may consist of servers with services which may require access to the external network but to which internal users also require access: Web servers, virtual private network (VPN) servers, e-mail servers, domain name system (DNS) servers, and so on. The DMZ allows these services to be reachable from the external network, but should a successful attack compromise one of these systems, another firewall still stands between the attacker and the internal corporate network (Bragg et al., 2004). Figure 1 shows a simple example of a DMZ lying between the Internet and the internal network.

Figure 1. Demilitarized zone (DMZ)

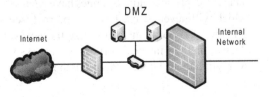

The firewalls that are typically implemented on both sides of the DMZ are configured with distinctive filtering characteristics based on their position in the topology. The first firewall from the Internet typically provides rules granting access to services desired by external users and services (Web, DNS, and so on), and therefore usually has weaker access rules. The internal firewall provides a second hurdle with greater access restrictions if an attacker happens to gain access to a machine within the DMZ (Pohlmann & Crothers, 2002). Also, by implementing two firewalls by differing manufacturers and with differing configurations, security is heightened because a vulnerability in one firewall will most likely not affect the second firewall (Goncalves, 2000). A DMZ can also be used to implement internal security measures on the corporate network (internal security will be discussed more in-depth in the next section). By placing a firewall between the DMZ and the internal network, access restrictions can also be implemented for users on the internal network attempting to access services located in the DMZ (Pohlmann & Crothers, 2002). Those without the proper access rights can also be prevented from accessing this information in the DMZ.

While DMZs have many advantages, there exist some drawbacks to their implementation. First, the primary shortcoming is maintenance. By implementing two, typically differing, firewall technologies at each end of a DMZ, administrators must configure two different appliances. Also, with some services lying within the DMZ, this may prevent some valid users gaining access to those services. More complex administrative systems must be implemented to allow these internal users access to data and services which they require for their jobs.

Network Address Translation (NAT)

Network Address Translation, or NAT, allows internal corporate IP addresses to be mapped to a specific set, or even single, public IP on the Internet. Current Internet technology utilizes Internet Protocol version 4 (IPv4) for assigning addresses to nodes for routing of traffic. While providing around four billion addresses, this has not been sufficient in recent years to match a unique address to all Internet hosts. Therefore, private address ranges have been set aside which will never be used on the Internet (see Table 1 below). Corporations can utilize these private addresses on their internal corporate networks without worrying about using a large number of public ad-

dresses. The problem then arises when these internal clients with private addresses wish to communicate with clients on the public Internet. NAT is employed to map these internal private addresses to an address which can be used to communicate on the Internet (Bragg et al., 2004).

While originally not intended for security and not specifically a security measure in and of itself, NAT offers a form of firewall-like protection for internal users. NAT provides some security by concealing the internal network hosts and overall topology from the external network. By translating between internal and external addresses, an attacker has difficulty identifying the specific internal host a transmission originated from or is destined for. NAT also helps to enforce control over outbound connections since all outbound traffic must be converted and possibly analyzed before being sent outside the internal corporate network. Moreover, NAT helps to restrict incoming traffic by only allowing traffic currently part of a transmission which is stored in its translation table (Zwicky et al., 2000).

NAT can be implemented using a varying number of methods depending on the setup of the corporate network. The following are the three primary methods for implementing NAT.

Static NAT

Static NAT provides a fixed mapping of one internal IP to that of a singe external IP. This type of approach is typically implemented for a specific host on the internal network, such as a Web server. While this type of one-to-one setup does accommodate most protocols (see below), it also opens the host to many of the security vulnerabilities which are typically hidden by NAT. Since only this one host is mapped to a specific IP, the host is not effectively hidden from an external attacker (Strassberg et al., 2002).

Dynamic NAT

Dynamic NAT uses a group of external IP addresses which a group of internal addresses are then dynamically assigned to. Each time an internal host attempts a connection with an external host, the internal host is assigned to one of these external IP addresses which have been assigned to the organization. Again, this one-to-one setup accommodates most protocols, since only a single host is assigned to a specific external address at a time.

Table 1. Private addresses—RFC 1918 (Rekhter, Moskowitz, Karrenberg, Groot, & Lear, 1996)

Address	Mask	Range
10.0.0.0	255.0.0.0	10.0.0.0 – 10.255.255.255
172.16.0.0	255.240.0.0	172.16.0.0 – 172.31.255.255
192.168.0.0	255.255.0.0	192.168.0.0 – 192.168.255.255

Dynamic NAT's primary disadvantage deals with the limitation on the number of concurrent internal users allowed. Typically, the number of external addresses for the organization is smaller than the number of internal users. If more users wish to connect to the Internet at a specific moment than there are external addresses, then some users will have to wait. While this could also be a potential problem with static NAT, historically static NAT has been used for specific machines and therefore certain addresses are reserved for these machines alone. Another disadvantage again deals with the direct mapping of users to a single address. While the external address is not always assigned to the same host, during a specific conversation the host is again open to vulnerabilities just like in static NAT (Strassberg et al., 2002).

Port Address Translation (PAT)

Port Address Translation (PAT) allows many different internal users to all use the same external address simultaneously. This allows all hosts on the internal corporate network to utilize only one external address (Strassberg et al., 2002). This is accomplished by mapping all internal hosts to the same external address and then distinguishing the host and protocol used by mapping this information to a specific port of the external address (Zwicky et al., 2000). PAT provides greater external address conservation as all internal hosts are mapped to one external address. Also, PAT provides greater security as internal hosts and programs are hidden behind port mappings of the external address (Strassberg et al., 2002).

The primary disadvantage of PAT is its difficulty handling connectionless protocols. Connection-oriented protocols can be easily mapped to specific ports of the external address. Conversely, connectionless protocols are troublesome to map to these ports. Even when mapped to a specific port, it is hard to determine when the connection has ended. Typically a timeout is set for these connections, but erring on the low side could shut a connection before it has ended and erring

on the high side could open the network to vulnerabilities within the specific application(Strassberg et al., 2002).

Logging

Most firewalls provide some method of logging of various types of events and traffic which occur on the firewall. These logs can be very important for a number of reasons:

1. Periodic scanning of logs is one of the best ways for detecting attacks against a network.
2. Logs can provide valuable reconnaissance information in the unfortunate circumstance that a network is compromised.
3. Audit data for host and application utilization can be used for system upgrades.
4. Security audits utilize logs to verify corporate security regulation compliance of both internal and external hosts.

Proper utilization of firewall logs is of utmost importance. First, always store multiple copies of logs. Be sure to store the log information on at least one other machine than the firewall is located on, as attackers typically attempt to modify the firewall logs to cover their tracks. Second, setup a corporate plan for how often firewall logs are audited, and how log backups are maintained. Third, have a specific log which contains an aggregation of multiple firewall logs into one, for greater understanding of network events. While a single firewall entry may not provide sufficient information pertaining to a specific network attack, this information in multiple logs may shed more light on the specific occurrence (Zwicky et al., 2000).

Intrusion Detection (ID) technologies can also be used in combination with firewalls and their associated logs for greater threat discovery on the network. ID systems attempt to detect network intrusions on the corporate network as immediately as possible. By analyzing firewall logs in real-time, these systems may be able to stop or mitigate an attack which is in progress. ID systems are a very large subject, and will not be covered in this chapter.

INTERNAL SECURITY

Internal security deals with maintaining a secure environment within the bounds of the corporate network. Most users hold a preconceived notion that firewalls are only useful for protecting the internal corporate network from the Internet. This idea is furthered by the belief that a single gateway firewall is needed to repel malicious external attacks, but everyone inside the firewall should be trusted (Hwang & Gangadharan, 2001). Many have come to describe this as the *hard exterior with a soft, chewy center.* Many corporate network environments today include thousands of hosts behind the corporate firewall (Meredith, 2003). The ideal that everyone behind the corporate perimeter firewall can be trusted is far outdated.

Evolving Internal Threats

Internal threats on the corporate network have grown in number and monetary liability in recent years. Network administrators understand this and know that the biggest threat is frequently not from the outside, but from both deliberate and unwitting sources on the internal network (Markham & Payne, 2001). Research from a collaboration between the FBI and CSI has shown that insider abuse accounts for 80% of network attacks, and this number continues to grow (Gordon, Loeb, Lucyshyn, & Richardson, 2006; Richardson, 2003). Insiders have access to significantly higher amounts of resources without having to breach an external firewall (Meredith, 2003). Yet, the problem still remains that companies do not focus on internal sabotage, and allow a complete trust relationship between hosts on the internal corporate network (Gahan, 1992; Quigley, 2002).

Several examples of internal security blunders in recent years can be considered; the UBS PaineWebber fiasco of 2004 is one instance. During this internal security breach, the primary cause was the activity of Roger Duronio, a disgruntled administrator for the corporate network. Duronio planted and distribed a logic bomb which brought down 2000 servers on the company's network. While the overall security of the corporate network was sound, there were still areas of concern (Gaudin, 2006). The fact remains that many

corporations hold the idealized notion that all attackers are outside the corporate network and the inside is safe. The UBS Paine Webber case demonstrates the amount of damage an internal user can perpetrate on the corporate network.

The typical context for a firewall is that of a network perimeter security device. More recent research and developments have utilized firewall technologies to protect the internal network from internal threats. The following are two such technologies which can be leveraged to help protect internal resources from resident threats on the corporate network.

Host-Based Firewalls

Host-based firewalls offer protection for an individual host on the network from all other hosts on that same network. The host-based firewall is typically installed as a piece of software on a single system to protect that system from everything else. Many individuals and home offices incorporate host-based firewall solutions due to the small number of hosts connected to the external Internet and, therefore, the lack of need and funds for a larger firewall system (Strassberg et al., 2002). In the corporate environment, host-based firewalls have traditionally only been implemented to protect critical systems. For instance, a file server with important trade secret data may have a host-based firewall installed to add a greater degree of protection for this information. Network administrators are therefore capable of much more fine-grained security for this host (Hwang & Gangadharan, 2001).

The primary disadvantage with host-based firewall technology is the lack of scalability for the entire organization. In a corporate environment, which may contain thousands of networked machines, host-based firewalls have not historically offered centralized manageability (Pan, Yang, & Lee, 2004; Strassberg et al., 2002). Therefore, each time an individual needs to change their personal firewall, an administrator must personally make this modification or give the individual administrative rights on his or her machine, and thereby open the network to an even greater risk of insider abuse or error.

An ideal structure would involve host-based firewalls that were easy for administrators to manage. Implementing a host-based firewall on every machine on the corporate network, including client machines, could help with malicious attacks and code disseminated on the internal network. The primary obstacle is providing for feasible management of these complex distributed systems. By providing a centralized management mechanism for every host-based firewall on the network, firewall security is distributed to every host on the internal network from this centralized management console. Host-based firewalls then become a viable option for providing individual protection for each host on the internal network.

Distributed Firewalls

Distributed firewalls build on host-based firewalls and improve on their disadvantages by offering a coordinated, host-based firewall environment for the entire corporate network. Bellovin first proposed a distributed firewall implementation for protecting every host on the corporate network (Bellovin, 1999). His design requirements for the system includes three components (Bellovin, 1999; Ioannidis, Keromytis, Bellovin, & Smith, 2000; Keromytis, Ioannidis, Greenwald, & Smith, 2003):

1. **Policy language:** The policy language should be able to specify application-specific rules for each and every host in the corporation.
2. **Management system:** The distributed firewall policy specifications must be maintained, updated in, and distributed from a central repository for all hosts on the network.
3. **Network-level encryption:** The distributed firewall management system must provide for safely distributing security policies to all hosts.

Using the design specifications above, the progression of events for each host would be as follows: (1) the system starts up; (2) before allowing user access, the system retrieves its specific firewall configuration information using the specified policy language from the management policy server employing an encrypted transmission; (3) once the firewall is configured, the user is allowed to log in. A highly simplified network diagram for a distributed firewall setup is shown in Figure 2.

A distributed firewall implementation on the internal corporate network provides many advantages for security as well as manageability. First, distributed firewalls offer a mechanism for internal security for each host from every other host on the internal network (Bellovin, 1999). Insider abuse is severely suppressed as every host is now protected from a would-be internal attacker. Second, the corporate perimeter firewall can be alleviated of some of the stress placed on it. With

the growing number of protocols and security vulnerabilities, the perimeter firewall has become somewhat of a chokepoint for the entire corporate network. By providing firewalls on each host, many excess rules and restrictions can be removed from the perimeter firewall thereby offering greater overall throughput (Ioannidis et al., 2000). Third, management of host firewalls is greatly eased due to the centralized nature of a distributed firewall implementation. All host-based firewall modifications can be made in a singe location and these changes are disseminated to the proper host machine.

COST-BENEFIT ANALYSIS

The implementation of any IT project is always governed by an overall cost-benefit analysis of the proposed system or solution. All expenditures within an organization must be analyzed both for their potential benefit to the corporation as well as their estimated cost throughout the lifetime of the product or service. Many different strategies are incorporated to help with this analysis. In the area of computer and network security, the typical strategy used is risk assessment.

Risk assessment describes the process used to delineate assets in the organization and threats to those assets. An asset is any item of value to the corporation and is dependent on the type of organization. These assets can typically be broken down into three areas: people, process, and technology. Once assets have been identified, the security risks to those assets must then be thoroughly delineated. These risks typically coincide with the CIA model of protecting Confidentiality, Integrity, and Availability. After assets and their associated threats have been identified, risk assessment can then take place. This can be performed in various ways. A common technique involves identifying all possible interfaces which can be used to access a particular asset and then identifying the threats which can affect the asset through this interface (Scambray & McClure, 2003).

Risk assessment is used as a primary input to the cost-benefit analysis of a project. After the risk assessment process has been completed, these risks can be categorized by their level of importance, likelihood of occurrence, and so on. This information can then be used to decide which assets are the most crucial to the organization and what threats affect those assets. Steps can then be taken to implement security measures to protect these assets from their associated threats.

Figure 2. Distributed firewall network diagram

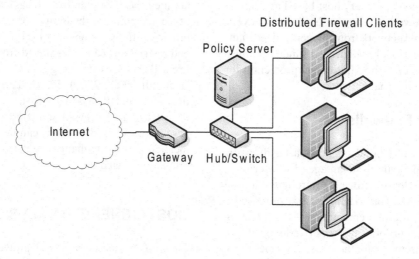

Table 2. Cost-benefit analysis example

Question	Solution	Costs/Benefits
Do you need to monitor closely the payloads of packets entering and leaving your network?	SPI/Application Gateway	(+) able to analyze any part of a packet (-) must configure complex filtering rules (-) slows response time
Do you host services locally for external customers (Web) or employees (e-mail, VPN, etc.)?	DMZ	(+) extra layer of protection from the outside (-) must implement 2 firewalls (-) must manage configurations for 2 firewalls
Do you have a large number of users who need to access the Internet?	NAT	(+) do not have to pay for a large amount of public IP's (-) must account for some protocols
Do you need to provide extra protection for certain key machines?	Host-based firewall	(+) provides protection from internal abuse (-) must configure and manage each firewall separately
Do you have user delineations within your corporation where groups of users should only have access to certain information?	Distributed Firewall	(+) provides centralized management (+) provides added protection for each user on the internal network from other internal users (-) must configure and manage these firewalls

Many factors must be considered when conducting a risk assessment of your organizational firewall implementation and appropriating necessary funds. Table 2 provides a few examples of possible questions to consider when constructing your corporate firewall infrastructure as well as possible solutions to these scenarios. Also, costs incurred as well as benefits gained from the specified implementation are listed. Table 2 is an example starting point for a cost-benefit analysis for firewall implementation. Firewall implementation will depend on many factors which are dependent on the specific network.

SUMMARY

The corporate perimeter firewall is one of the oldest and most implemented network security measures used in contemporary organizations. It offers a first line of defense against all types of external attackers, malware, viruses, and many other types of security threats which aim to compromise the organization's information systems. To effectively manage firewalls, administrators must understand what is available to them and how they interact with other components on the network. Also, a greater understanding of common terminology will allow for greater understanding when buying, upgrading, or modifying your current system. Finally, a greater understanding of related technology as well as future trends will greatly aid in overall network security and health.

Firewalls are essentially dividing devices which separate networks of differing security levels. There are various types of firewalls as well as delineation mechanisms for the different types. The packet filtering firewall is one of the oldest and most well-known firewall technologies. It performs firewall functions by analyzing the contents of packets for specific known security threats. The two main types include static and stateful packet inspection (SPI), as well as a hybrid of the two technologies. Circuit gateways are a type of firewall which acts as a relay agent between clients on the internal corporate network and the external services they desire. Application gateways take circuit gateway technology a step further by adding functionality to analyze packets at the application level.

There are many concepts which are related either directly or indirectly to firewall technologies. The demilitarized zone (DMZ) offers a buffer between the internal corporate network and the external Internet where certain services are typically housed. Network address translation (NAT) was originally designed to alleviate public address depletion problems but serves to hide internal hosts from external threats. Logging is a key component of firewall implementation which provides information for various audits which are (or should) be conducted by the organization. The information from these logs is also useful for reconnaissance information about successful security breaches as well as many real-time intrusion detection systems.

Internal security is an immense problem which has only gained notoriety within the past few years. While traditionally used for perimeter security, newer firewall technologies can offer solutions for many internal security risks. Host-based firewalls offer greater protection for certain key hosts which may be of greater value on the corporate network. Distributed firewall technology builds on host-based firewalls by offering protection for every host on the network while alleviating the management burden by incorporating a centralized management and policy system.

Implementing any IT software and/or hardware solution has both advantages and disadvantages. Those in charge of the decision must conduct a cost-benefit analysis to decide if what they wish to implement is truly possible. Implementation of security measures requires a risk assessment of the company's assets and the threats which could compromise those assets

according to the CIA model. In the end, it all comes down to to the final assessment of risk and benefit to the company.

REFERENCES

Bellovin, S.M. (1999). Distributed firewalls. *Login*, 37-39.

Bragg, R., Phodes-Ousley, M., & Strassberg, K. (2004). *Network security: The complete reference*. Emeryville, CA: McGraw-Hill/Osborne.

Cheswick, W.R., & Bellovin, S.M. (1994). *Firewalls and internet security: Repelling the wily hacker*. Reading, MA: Addison-Wesley.

Gahan, C. (1992, July 1-9). Protecting your organisation's most valuable asset [LAN security]. *IEEE colloquium on designing secure systems (IEEE)*.

Gaudin, S. (2006). UBS trial aftermath: Even great security can't protect you from the Insider. *Finance Tech*. Retrieved May 2, 2008, from http://www.financetech.com/showArticle.jhtml?articleID=191601061

Goncalves, M. (2000). *Firewalls: A complete guide*. New York: McGraw-Hill Companies, Inc.

Gordon, L.A., Loeb, M.P., Lucyshyn, W., & Richardson, R. (2006). *2006 CSI/FBI computer crime and security survey*. Computer Security Institute.

Hwang, K., & Gangadharan, M. (2001). Micro-firewalls for dynamic network security with distributed intrusion detection. *IEEE international symposium on network computing and applications, NCA 2001* (pp. 68-79).

Ioannidis, S., Keromytis, A.D., Bellovin, S.M., & Smith, J.M. (2000). Implementing a distributed firewall. *ACM*, 190-199.

Keromytis, A.D., Ioannidis, S., Greenwald, M.B., & Smith, J.M. (2003). The STRONGMAN architecture. In *Proceedings of DARPA information survivability conference and exposition, (IEEE)* (Vol. 1, pp. 178-188).

Markham, T., & Payne, C. (2001). Security at the network edge: A distributed firewall architecture. In *Proceedings of the DARPA Information Survivability Conference & Exposition II, DISCEX '01(IEEE)* (Vol. 1, pp. 279-286).

Meredith, L.M. (2003). A summary of the autonomic distributed firewalls (ADF) project. In *Proceedings of the DARPA Information Survivability Conference and Exposition, (IEEE)* (pp. 260-265).

Pan, C.-C., Yang, K.-H., & Lee, T.-L. (2004). Secure online examination architecture based on distributed firewall. In *Proceedings of the 2004 IEEE International Conference on e-Technology, e-Commerce and e-Service* (pp. 533-536).

Pohlmann, N., & Crothers, T. (2002). *Firewall architecture for the enterprise.* New York, NY: Wiley Publishing, Inc.

Quigley, A. (2002). Inside job. *netWorker, 6*(1), 20-24.

Rekhter, Y., Moskowitz, R.G., Karrenberg, D., Groot, G.J.D., & Lear, E. (1996). *Request for comments: 1918.* Retrieved May 2, 2008, from http://www.faqs.org/rfcs/rfc1918.html

Richardson, R. (2003). CSI/FBI computer crime and security survey. *Computer security institute,* (pp. 21).

Scambray, J., McClure, S. (2003). *Hacking exposed: Windows server 2003.* Emeryville, CA: McGraw-Hill/Osborne.

Strassberg, K., Gondek, R., & Rollie, G. (2002). *Firewalls: The complete reference.* Berkeley, CA: McGraw-Hill/Osborne.

Whitman, M.E., & Mattord, H.J. (2005). *Principles of information security* (2nd ed.). Boston: Thompson Course Technology.

Zalenski, R. (2002). Firewall technologies. *IEEE Potentials, 21*(1), 24-29.

Zwicky, E.D., Cooper, S., & Chapman, D.B. (2000). *Building internet firewalls* (2nd ed.). Sebastopop, CA: O'Reilly & Associate, Inc.

KEY TERMS

The following terms were derived from Strassberg et al. (2002).

Application Gateway (Proxy Server): A circuit gateway which adds the functionality for analyzing packets at the application level.

Circuit Gateway: A relay agent which acts as an intermediary between internal and external hosts.

Demilitarized Zone (DMZ): A buffer between two networks of differing security levels which usually contains certain services/hosts to which both networks require access.

Distributed Firewall: A coordinated, centrally managed, host-based firewall environment for all hosts on the corporate network (Bellovin, 1999).

Firewall: A device and/or software designed to protect networks of differing security levels.

Network Address Translation (NAT): The process of converting internal private addresses to one or more external addresses.

Packet Filtering: Examining the header and/or data of each a packet against known security vulnerabilities to decide whether or not to pass the packet along the network to the next hop or rejecting the packet.

Stateful Packet Inspection (SPI): A packet filter which keeps track of existing communications and only allows communications between the hosts involved in the current transmission.

Chapter X
An Immune–Inspired Approach to Anomaly Detection

Jamie Twycross
University of Nottingham, UK

Uwe Aickelin
University of Nottingham, UK

ABSTRACT

The immune system provides a rich metaphor for computer security: anomaly detection that works in nature should work for machines. However, early artificial immune system approaches for computer security had only limited success. Arguably, this was due to these artificial systems being based on too simplistic a view of the immune system. We present here a second generation artificial immune system for process anomaly detection. It improves on earlier systems by having different artificial cell types that process information. Following detailed information about how to build such second generation systems, we find that communication between cells types is key to performance. Through realistic testing and validation, we show that second generation artificial immune systems are capable of anomaly detection beyond generic system policies. The chapter concludes with a discussion and outline of the next steps in this exciting area of computer security.

INTRODUCTION

The work discussed here is motivated by a broad interest in biologically-inspired approaches to computer security, particularly in immune-inspired approaches to intrusion detection. The first part of this chapter gives a brief overview of biologically-inspired computing and computer security, and introduces the field of artificial immune systems. We have developed an immune-inspired process anomaly detection system. Process anomaly detection is an important technique in computer security for detecting a range of attacks, and the second part of this chapter introduces and reviews current approaches to process anomaly detection, relat-

ing our work to other work in this area. The third section of this chapter introduces our own efforts to develop a prototype immune-inspired realtime process anomaly detection system. However, our interests are also wider, and address issues concerning how artificial immune systems are modelled and implemented in general. We have implemented a system, `libtissue`, in which immune-inspired algorithms can be developed and tested on real-world problems. The design and implementation of this system is briefly reviewed. The final part of this chapter presents and discusses the results of validation tests using `libtissue`. A number of datasets containing system call and signal information were generated and a simple algorithm was implemented to test the `libtissue` system. The behaviour of the algorithm is analysed and it is shown how the `libtissue` system can be used to build immune-inspired algorithms that detect anomalies in process behaviour.

BIOLOGICALLY-INSPIRED APPROACHES

Biological approaches to computer security are appealing for a number of reasons. Williamson (2002) discusses some of these reasons and their impact on the design of computer security systems. Biological organisms have developed many novel, parsimonious, and effective protection mechanisms. As computer systems and networks become more complex traditional approaches are often ineffective and suffer from problems such as scalability, and biologically systems are important sources of inspiration when designing new approaches. The short position paper of Morel (2002) discusses the general design of cyber-security systems that provides a large distributed computer network with a high degree of survivability. He proposes that a cyber-security system emulates the architecture of the biological immune system. As in this chapter, the innate immune system is considered as central to the immune response, processing information and controlling the adaptive immune system. An effective cyber-security system should emulate key features, most importantly distributed control, of the biological system, it should provide multiple information gathering mechanisms, and it should coevolve with the threat.

In another interesting position paper, Williams (1996) explores the similarities between people's health and the security of complex computer systems. Humans are composed of distinct but tightly integrated multilayer systems, have external interfaces which can receive a wide range of input, and which carefully balance security and functionality, and have internal interfaces with protection mechanisms. They are not born with many of their defenses, but learn to protect themselves against recurring threats such as viruses, and are able to identify and develop defenses for new threats. The body is able to detect conditions that are likely to lead to injury. It is surrounded by a skin which, if damaged, leads to further response. Williams suggests that computer systems also need to have virtual skins with a similar functionality. He highlights the importance of the balance between functionality, security, and flexibility. Humans, as

with computer systems, live a complex environment where conditions change over time. Both computer and biological systems are very sensitive to the input they receive. Biological systems check and filter input at many levels, and he suggests security systems need to do the same. He also emphasises the impossibility of accurate measurement of health in humans, which is reflected in the difficultly of measuring the security of computer systems. His general view is that the computer security industry is becoming as specialised as the healthcare industry, with security engineers akin to doctors.

Our interest is in immune-inspired approaches to intrusion detection. The field of artificial immune systems began in the early 1990s with a number of independent groups conducting research which used the biological immune system as inspiration for solutions to problems in other domains. There are several general reviews of artificial immune system research (Dasgupta, 2006; Hart & Timmis, 2005), and a number of books including Dasgupta (1999) and de Castro and Timmis (2002) covering the field. Large bibliographies have been collated by Dasgupta and Azeem (2006) (over 600 journal and conference papers), and an annual international conference has been held since 2002 (Proceedings of the International Conference on Artificial Immune Systems, http://www.artificial-immune-systems.org/). Specifically of relevance to this chapter is the review of artificial immune system approaches to intrusion detection by Aickelin, Greensmith, and Twycross (2004).

Intrusion detection systems are software systems designed to identify and prevent the misuse of computer networks and systems. Still a relatively young field, first discussed by James Anderson in his seminal 1980 paper (Anderson, 1980), and with the first working system described in Dorothy Denning's 1987 paper (Denning, 1987), intrusion detection still faces many unresolved research issues. Many intrusion detection systems have been developed, representative samples of which are reviewed in Kemmerer and Vigna (2002) and Venter and Eloff (2003). Several excellent review papers (Axelsson, 2000; Bace & Mell, 2001) and books (Northcutt & Novak, 2003) on intrusion detection approaches have also been published. There are a number of different ways to classify intrusion detection systems (Axelsson, 2000). In their paper, Jansen and Karygiannis (1999) discuss the shortcomings of current intrusion detection system technology and the advantages of and approaches to applying mobile agents to intrusion detection and response. They highlight the issue of false positives as the primary problem facing the intrusion detection system community, and this is one of the key issues which this chapter seeks to address, particularly in terms of the detection of novel attacks.

PROCESS ANOMALY DETECTION

In the classic paper *"An Evening with Berferd in which a Cracker is Lured, Endured, and Studied"* (Cheswick, 1992), Cheswick describes the activities of a cracker who is allowed to gain access to a monitored machine. Other more recent publications (Mitnick & Simon, 2005) which have deconstructed real-world attacks have painted a similar picture. Often, the initial goal of an attack is to gain administrator privileges or *"get root"* on a machine, and so give the attacker free reign on the system. If the attacker does not have an account on the system, then they may try to exploit a vulnerability in a network service running on the target remote machine to gain access. This is termed a remote-to-local attack. Buffer overflow exploits are often used to subvert remote services to execute code the attacker supplies and, for example, open a remote command shell on the target machine. Sometimes, the attacked service will already be running with administrator privileges, in which case the initial attack is complete. Otherwise, the attacker will have access to the machine at the same privilege level that the attacked service is running at. In this case, or if the attacker already has a local user account on the target machine, they will need to perform a privilege escalation attack, called a user-to-root attack. Often, this will involve attacking a privileged program, such as a program running with administrator privileges, and, once again, subverting its execution to create a command shell with administrator privileges. After the initial goal of unrestricted access is achieved, the attacker may install rootkits to hide their presence and facilitate later access. Data can be copied to and from the machine, remote services such as filesharing daemons can be started, and, in the case of worms, this may all be done automatically without human intervention.

Process anomaly detection systems are designed to detect and prevent the subversion of processes necessary in such remote-to-local and user-to-root attacks. A number of host-based intrusion detection systems have been built around monitoring running processes to detect intrusions, and are discussed in detail in the next section. In general, these intrusion detection systems collect information about a running process from a variety of sources, including from log files created by the process, or from other information gathered by the operating system. The general idea is that by observing what the process is currently doing (e.g., by looking at its log files), we can tell whether the process is behaving normally, or has been subverted by an attack. While log files are an obvious starting point for such systems, and are still an important component in a holistic security approach, it is fairly easy to execute attacks which do not cause any logging to take place, and so evade detection. Because of this, there has been a substantial amount of research into other data sources, usually collected by the operating system. Of these, system calls have been the most favoured approach. This section begins with a brief background on system calls and then reviews current system call-based approaches to process anomaly detection.

Processes and System Calls

A process is a running instance of a program. On modern multitasking operating systems many processes are effectively running simultaneously. For example, a server may be running a web server, email servers and a number of other services. A single program executable, when run, may create several child processes by forking (Fork, 2007) or threading (Pthreads, 2007). For example, web servers typically start child processes to handle individual connections once they have been received. The process which created the child process is called the parent process. Child processes themselves may create children, sometimes generating a complex process tree derived from a single parent process node created when the executable is first run. The operating system is responsible for managing the execution of running processes, and associates a number, called a process identifier, with each process. This number uniquely identifies a process. Essentially, the operating system initialises a counter and assigns its value to a new process, and then increments the counter. When a process is started, the operating system associates other metadata with it too, such as the process identifier of the parent process that created it, and the user who started the process. The process is also allocated resources by the operating system. These resources include memory, which stores the executable code and data, and file descriptors, which identify files or network sockets which belong to the process.

System calls (syscalls) are a low-level mechanism by which processes request system resources such as peripheral I/O or memory allocation from an operating system. As a process runs, it cannot usually directly access memory or hardware devices. Instead, the operating system manages these resources and provides a set of functions, called syscalls, which processes can call to access these resources. On modern Linux systems, there are around 300 syscalls, accessed via wrapper functions in the libc library. Some of the more common syscalls are summarised in Table 1. At an assembly code level, when a process wants to make a syscall, it will load the syscall number into the EAX register, and syscall arguments into registers such as EBX, ECX or EDX. The process will then raise the 0x80 interrupt. This causes the process to halt execution, and the operating system to execute the requested syscall. Once the syscall has been executed, the operating system places a return value in EAX and returns execution to the process. Operating systems other than Linux differ slightly in these details; for example, BSD puts the syscall number in EAX and pushes the arguments onto the stack (Bovet & Cesati, 2002; Syscalls, 2007). Higher-level languages provide library calls, which wrap the syscall in easier-to-use functions such as printf.

Syscalls are a much more powerful data source for detecting attacks than log file entries. All of a monitored application's interactions with the network, filesystem, memory, and other hardware devices can be monitored. Most attacks which subvert the execution of the monitored application will probably have to access some of these resources, and so will have to make a number of syscalls. In other words, it is much harder to evade a syscall-based intrusion detection system. However, monitoring syscalls is more complex and costly than reading data from a log file, and usually involves placing hooks or stubs in the operating system, or wrapping the monitored process in a sandbox-like system. This increases the runtime of the monitored process, since for each syscall the monitor will spend at least a few clock ticks pushing the data it has collected to a storage buffer. Syscall interposition systems, which, in addition to passively gathering syscall information, also decide whether to permit or deny the syscall, can add additional runtime overheads. Also, processes can generate hundreds of syscalls a second, making the data load significantly higher. Other factors also need to be taken into account when implementing a syscall monitoring or interposition system. Incorrect replication of operating system state or other race conditions may allow syscall monitoring to be circumvented. These factors are addressed in detail by Garfinkel (2003).

Current Approaches

The `systrace` system of Provos (2003) is a syscall-based confinement and intrusion detection system for Linux, BSD, and OSX systems. A kernel patch inserts various hooks into the kernel to intercept syscalls from the monitored process. The user specifies a syscall policy which is a whitelist of permitted syscalls and arguments. The monitored process is wrapped by a user-space program, which compares any syscalls a process tries to make (captured by the kernel hooks)

Table 1. Common system calls (syscalls)

Number	Name	Description
1	exit	terminate process execution
2	fork	fork a child process
3	read	read data from a file or socket
4	write	write data to a file or socket
5	open	open a file or socket
6	close	close a file or socket
37	kill	send a kill signal
90	old_mmap	map memory
91	munmap	unmap memory
301	socket	create a socket
303	connect	connect a socket

with this policy, and only allows the process to execute syscalls which are present on the whitelist. Execution of the monitored process is halted while this decision is made, which, along with other factors such as the switch from kernel- to user-space, adds an overhead to the monitored process. However, due in part to the simplicity of the decision-making algorithm (a list search on the policy file), as well as a good balance of kernel- vs. user-space, this performance impact on average is minimal, and `systrace` has been used to monitor processes in production environments. As an intrusion detection system, `systrace` can be run to either automatically deny and log all syscall attempts not permitted by the policy, or to graphically prompt a user as to whether to permit or deny the syscall. The latter mode can be used to add syscalls to the policy, adjusting it before using it in automatic mode. Initial policies for a process are obtained by using templates or by running `systrace` in automatic policy generation mode. In this mode, the monitored process is run under normal usage conditions and permit entries are created in the policy file for all the syscalls made by the process. The policy specification allows some matching of syscall arguments as well as syscall numbers.

Gao, Reiter, & Song (2004) introduce a new model of syscall behaviour called an execution graph. An execution graph is a model that accepts approximately the same syscall sequences as would a model built on a control flow graph. However, the execution graph is constructed from syscalls gathered during normal execution, as opposed to a control flow graph which is derived from static analysis. In addition to the syscall number, stack return addresses are also gathered and used in construction of the execution graph. The authors also introduce a course-grain classification of syscall-based intrusion detection systems into white-box, black-box and gray-box approaches. Black-box systems build their models from a sample of normal execution using only syscall number and argument information. Gray-box approaches, as with black boxes, build their models from a sample of normal execution but, as well as using syscall information, also use additional runtime information. White-box approaches do not use samples of normal execution, but instead use static analysis techniques to derive their models. A prototype gray-box anomaly detection system using execution graphs is introduced by the authors, and they compare this approach to other systems and discuss possible evasion strategies in Gao et al. (2004).

Sekar, Bendre, Dhurjati, and Bollineni (2001) implement a realtime intrusion detection system which uses finite state automata to capture short and long term temporal relationships between syscalls. One advantage of using finite state automata is that there is no limit to the length of the syscall sequence. Yeung and Ding (2003) describe an intrusion detection system which uses a discrete hidden Markov model trained using the Baum-Welch re-estimation algorithm to detect anomalous sequences of syscalls. Lee (2000) explores a similar Markov chain model. Krugel, Mutz, Valeur, and Vigna (2003) describe a realtime intrusion detection system implemented using Snare under Linux. Using syscall audit logs gathered by Snare, their system automatically detects anomalies in syscall arguments. They explore a number of statistical models which are learnt from observed normal usage. Endler (1998) presents an offline intrusion detection system which examines BSM audit data. They combine a multilayer perceptron neural network which detects anomalies in syscall sequences with a histogram classifier which calculates the statistical likelihood of a syscall. Lee and Xiang (2001) evaluate the performance of syscall-based anomaly detection models built on information-theoretic measures such as entropy and information cost, and also use these models to automatically calculate parameter settings for other models.

Forrest, Hofmeyr, Somayaji and other researchers at the University of New Mexico have developed several immune-inspired learning-based approaches. In Forrest, Hofmeyr, and Somayaji (1997) and Hofmeyr and Forrest (2000) a realtime system is evaluated which detects anomalous processes by analysing sequences of syscalls. Syscalls generated by an application are grouped together into sequences, in this case sequences of six consecutive syscalls. This choice of sequence length is discussed in Tan and Maxion (2003). A database of normal sequences is constructed and stored as a tree during training. Sequences of syscalls are then compared to this database using a Hamming distance metric, and a sufficient number of mismatches generates an alert. No user-definable parameters are necessary, and the mismatch threshold is automatically derived from the training data. Similar approaches have also been applied by this group to network intrusion detection (Balthrop, Esponda, Forrest, & Glickman, 2002; Hofmeyr & Forrest, 2000). Somayaji (2002) develops the immune-inspired pH intrusion prevention system which detects and actively responds to changes in program behaviour in realtime. As with the method

Figure 1. The architecture of `libtissue`; *hosts are monitored by* `libtissue` *antigen and signal clients, which in turn provide input data to the artificial immune system algorithm, run on a* `libtissue` *server; algorithms are able to change the state of the monitored hosts through response clients*

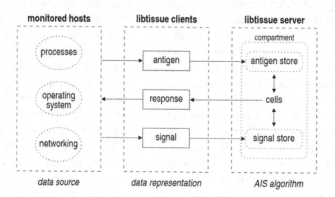

just described, sequences of syscalls are gathered for all processes running on a host and compared to a normal database using a similar immune-inspired model. However, if an anomaly is detected, execution of the process that produced the syscalls will be delayed for a period of time. This method of response, as opposed to more malign responses such as killing a process, is more benign in that if the system makes a mistake and delays a process which is behaving normally, this may not have a perceptible impact from the perspective of the user. The idea of process homeostasis, with pH maintaining a host machine within certain operational limits, is introduced. This approach was effective at automatically preventing a number of attacks.

THE `libtissue` SYSTEM

The broader aim of the research presented here is to build a software system which allows researchers to implement and analyse novel artificial immune system algorithms and apply them to real-world problems. We have implemented a prototype of such a system, called `libtissue`, which is being used by ourselves and other researchers (Greensmith, Aickelin, & Twycross, 2006a; Greensmith, Twycross, & Aickelin, 2006b; Twycross & Aickelin, 2006) to build and evaluate novel immune-inspired algorithms for process anomaly detection. This section briefly reviews the design and implementation of the `libtis`-`sue` system, more detail of which can be found in Twycross and Aickelin (2006).

`libtissue` has a client/server architecture pictured in Figure 1. An artificial immune system algorithm is implemented as part of a `libtis`-`sue` server, and `libtissue` clients provide input data to the algorithm and response mechanisms which change the state of the monitored system. This client/server architecture separates data collection by the `libtissue` clients from data processing by the `libtissue` servers and allows for relatively easy extensibility and testing of algorithms on new data sources. `libtissue` was coded in C as a Linux shared library with client and server APIs, allowing new antigen and signal sources to be easily added to `libtissue` servers from a programmatic perspective. Because `libtissue` is implemented as a library, algorithms can be compiled and run on other researchers' machines with no modification. Client/server communication is socket-based, allowing clients and servers to potentially run on separate machines; for example, a signal or antigen client may in fact be a remote network monitor.

Artificial immune system algorithms are implemented within a `libtissue` server as multiagent systems of cells. Cells exist within an environment, called a tissue compartment, along with other cells, antigen, and signals. The problem to which the algorithm is being applied is represented by `libtissue` as antigen and signals. Cells express various repertories of receptors and producers which allow them to interact with antigen and control other cells through signalling networks. `libtissue` allows data on implemented algorithms to be collected and logged, allowing for experimental analysis of the system. A libtissue server is in fact several threaded processes running asynchronously. An initialisation routine is first called which creates a tissue compartment based on user-supplied parameters. During initialisation a thread is also started to handle connections between the server and libtissue clients, and this thread itself starts a separate thread for each connected client. After initialisation, cells, the characteristics of which are specified by the user, are created and initialised, and the tissue compartment populated with these cells. Cells in the tissue compartment then cycle and input data is provided by connected libtissue clients.

libtissue clients are of three types: antigen, signal, and response. Antigen clients collect and transform data into antigen which are forwarded to a libtissue server. Currently, a systrace antigen client has been implemented which collects process syscalls using systrace (Systrace Homepage, http://www.systrace.org/). Signal clients monitor system behaviour and provide an artificial immune system running on the tissue server with input signals. A process monitor signal client, which monitors a process and its children and records statistics such as CPU and memory usage, and a network signal client, which monitors network interface statistics such as bytes per second, have been implemented. Two response clients have been implemented, one which simply logs an alert, and another which allows an active response through the modification of a systrace syscall policy. All of these clients are designed to be used in realtime experiments and for data collection for offline experiments with tcreplay.

The implementation is designed to allow varied artificial immune system algorithms to be evaluated on real-world, realtime systems and problems. When testing intrusion detection systems it is common to use preexisting datasets such as the Lincoln Labs dataset (Lincoln Labs, 2007). However, the project libtissue has been built for is focused on combining measurements from a number of different concurrent data sources. Preexisting datasets which contain all the necessary sources are not available. Therefore, to facilitate experimentation, a libtissue replay client, called tcreplay, was also implemented. This client reads in log files gathered from previous realtime runs of antigen and signal clients. It also has the facility to read logfiles generated by strace (Strace Homepage, http://sourceforge.net/projects/strace/) as an optional source of antigen in place of the systrace client. It then sends the information in these logs to a libtissue server. Variable replay rates are available, allowing data collected from a realtime session to be used to perform many experiments quickly. Having such a replay facility is important in terms of reproducibility of experiments. In reality, the majority of experimental runs are scripts which take data and parameter files as input and run a tissue server and tcreplay client.

VALIDATION OF APPROACH

We wanted to verify that useful algorithms could be implemented and applied to a real-world problem. This section reviews the details of this validation. It discusses how data on a process anomaly detection problem was generated. It then presents a simple anomaly detection algorithm which we have implemented to test the libtissue system. Results from an analysis of the behaviour and performance of the libtissue system and the algorithm are then presented. Lastly, an example of how this algorithm and the libtissue system can be used to detect anomalies in process behaviour is given.

Dataset Generation

In order to gather data for the process anomaly detection problem, a small experimental network with three hosts was set up. One host, the target, runs software—in this case, a Redhat 6.2 server, with a number of vulnerabilities. The other two hosts act as clients which interact with the target machine, either attempting to exploit its vulnerabilities or simulating normal usage. Because the experimental network contains vulnerable hosts, access between it and the public campus network is tightly controlled. While minimal, this setup permits realistic network-based attack and normal usage scenarios to be played out. Physically, the network exists on a single Debian Linux host running two VMware guest operating systems. The host and guests are connected via a virtual VMware host-only network. This setup was chosen as it allows for relatively fast configuration and restoration of the experimental network when compared with one in which each host is a physically separate machine connected via the standard network infrastructure of switches and so on. Redhat 6.2 was chosen because the default installation installs a number of programs with vulnerabilities (Redhat Linux 6.2 Security Advisories, https://rhn.redhat.com/errata/rh62-errata-security.html), and because many well-documented exploits are available for these vulnerabilities. Tests were carried out with the `rpc.statd` daemon (rpc.statd, 2007), which provides a status monitoring service to other NFS clients and servers. The default version of `rpc.statd` shipped with Redhat 6.2 has a format string vulnerability which allows a remote user to execute arbitrary code with root privileges on the server (Multiple Linux Vendor rpc.statd Remote Format String Vulnerability, http://www.securityfocus.com/bid/1480). An exploit, `statdx2` (Bugtraq: statdx2 - Linux rpc.statd revisited, 2002), has been released which levers this vulnerability and, by default, injects shellcode which causes a remote root shell to be opened on the attacker's machine, allowing unrestricted access to the server. This vulnerability has also been used in automated attacks such as the Ramen worm.

In order to collect the data, that is process syscall information and appropriate context signals, the target system was instrumented. The Redhat nfslock init script was modified to start `rpc.statd` wrapped by `strace` (Strace Homepage), which logged all the syscalls made by `rpc.statd` and its children. At the same time, a specially written application called `process_monitor` was started which monitors a process and all of its child processes. At regular intervals, one tenth of a second in this case, it takes a snapshot of the process table which it then traverses, recording the process identifiers of all the processes which are children of the monitored process. The monitor then logs the current name of the monitored process, the total number of children including itself owned by the process, the total CPU usage of the process and its children, and the total memory usage of the process and its children. Pairs of `strace` and `process_monitor` logs were collected on the instrumented target machine while `rpc.statd` was utilised in a number of

different scenarios. These logs were then parsed to form a single `tcreplay` logfile for each of the scenarios. An antigen entry in the `tcreplay` log was created for every syscall recorded in the `strace` log. A signal entry was created for each recording of CPU usage in the `process_monitor` log. While the `strace` log actually contains much more information, the use of just the syscall number is more than sufficient for testing the example algorithm described in the next section. It would be expected that a more complex algorithm would require additional complexity in both the antigen and range of signals it is provided with, such as the addition of information about syscall arguments, sequences of syscalls, or instruction pointer addresses.

The monitored scenarios are divided into three groups based on whether the type of interaction with the `rpc.statd` server is a successful attack, a failed attack, or normal usage. Statistics for the datasets are given in Table 2. All the datasets followed a similar pattern. The data was generally very bursty in terms of syscalls per second, with relatively long periods of no syscalls punctuated by bursts of up to 1102 syscalls per second (`success1`). All datasets contain an initial one second burst of 405 syscalls executed by `rpc.statd` during normal startup. Syscalls generated by `rpc.statd` at shutdown, a burst of between 17 and 29 syscalls caused by typing halt on the server, are also present in the normal and failure datasets. They are not present in the success datasets as the `rpc.statd` process is replaced by a shell process during the exploit and so not able to go through normal shutdown. In both successful attacks there are three bursts of between 98 and 1102 syscalls. The user interaction on the resulting remote shell (typing `exit`) creates 5 syscalls. The unsuccessful attacks produced a single burst of 96 and 62 syscalls (`failure1` and `failure2` respectively). The actions of the NFS client in `normal2` result in a single burst of 16 syscalls.

Table 2. Statistics for the six datasets gathered

dataset	total time	total antigen	max antigen rate
success1	55	1739	1102
success2	36	1743	790
failure1	54	518	405
failure2	68	495	405
normal1	38	434	405
normal2	104	450	405

Figure 2. The two different cell types implemented in `twocell`

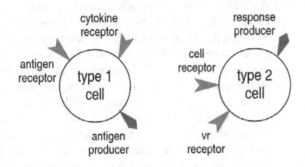

The `twocell` Algorithm

The cells in `twocell`, shown in Figure 2, are of two types, labelled Type 1 and Type 2, and each type has different receptor and producer repertories, as well as different cell cycle callbacks. Type 1 cells are designed to emulate two key characteristics of biological APCs: antigen and signal processing. In order to process antigen, each Type 1 cell is equipped with a number of antigen receptors and producers. A cytokine receptor allows Type 1 cells to respond to the value of a signal in the tissue compartment. Type 2 cells emulate three of the characteristics of biological T cells: cellular binding, antigen matching, and antigen response. Each Type 2 cell has a number of cell receptors specific for Type 1 cells, VR (variable-region) receptors to match antigen, and a response producer which is triggered when antigen is matched. Type 2 cells also maintain one internal cytokine, an integer which is incremented every time a match between an antigen producer and VR receptor occurs. If the value of this cytokine is still zero, that is no match has occured, after a certain number of cycles, set by the `cell_lifespan` parameter, then the values of all of the VR receptor locks on the cell are randomised.

A tissue compartment is created and populated with a number of Type 1 and 2 cells. Antigen and signals in the compartment are set by `libtissue` clients based on the syscalls a process is making and its CPU usage. Type 1 and 2 cells have different cell cycle callbacks. Type 1 cells ingest antigen through their antigen receptors and present it on their antigen producers. The period for which the antigen is presented is determined by a signal read by a cytokine receptor on these cells, and so can be made dependant upon

CPU usage. Type 2 cells attempt to bind with Type 1 cells via their cell receptors. If bound, VR receptors on these cells interact with antigen producers on the bound Type 1 cell. If an exact match between a VR receptor lock and antigen producer key occurs, the response producer on Type 2 cells produces a response, in this case a log entry containing the value of the matched receptor.

System Dynamics

In experiments it is important to have a baseline with which to compare algorithmic performance. In terms of syscall policies such a baseline can be generated, and is here termed a naive policy. A naive syscall policy is generated for a process, such as `rpc.statd`, by recording the syscalls it makes under normal usage, as in the `normal1` and `normal2` datasets. A permit policy statement is then created for all syscalls seen in the datasets. This baseline is not too unrealistic when compared to how current systems such as `systrace` automatically generate a policy. Similarly to a naive policy, one way in which `twocell` can be used to generate a syscall policy is by running it with normal usage data during a training phase. During the run, responses made by Type 2 cells are recorded. At the end of each run, a syscall policy is created by allowing only those syscalls responded to, and denying all others. Since interactions in `libtissue` are stochastic, looking at the average results over a number of runs helps to understand the behaviour of implemented algorithms. A script was written to start the `twocell` server and then after 10 seconds start the `tcreplay` client and replay a dataset in realtime. `twocell` was allowed to continue running for a further minute after replay had finished. This process was repeated 20 times for both the `normal1` and `normal2` datasets, yielding 40 individual syscall policies. A single average `twocell` policy was then generated by allowing all syscalls which were permitted in any of the 40 individual policies. It was found that all of the 38 syscalls that were permitted in the naive policy were also permitted in the average policy.

In order to examine more closely how `twocell` responds, a single run of the `twocell` algorithm was observed. Following the same general procedure as the previous experiment, `twocell` was run once with the `normal2` dataset. The resulting policy is shown in Table 3, along with the frequencies with which the permitted syscalls were responded to. Dur-

Table 3. The syscall policy generated by `twocell` *for the* `normal2` *dataset and the frequency of response for each syscall*

syscall	frequency
gettimeofday(78)	1
listen(304)	1
send(309)	1
select(142)	2
poll(168)	3
recvfrom(312)	8
fcntl(55)	9
fstat(108)	9
open(5)	22
close(6)	34

ing the run, the time at which a Type 2 cell produced a response to a particular syscall was also recorded, and the rate at which these responses occured was calculated. This clearly showed a correlation between the rate of incoming syscalls and the rate of responses produced by Type 2 cells. Cells initially do not produce any response until syscalls occur, and then produce a burst of responses for a relatively short period before settling down to an unresponsive state once again. This is to be expected, as antigen (syscalls) enter and are passed through `twocell` until their eventual destruction after being presented on Type 1 cell antigen producers.

Classification Accuracy

An example is now given of how the classification accuracy and error of a `libtissue` algorithm can be evaluated. In terms of syscall policies, a particular policy can be considered successful in relation to the number of normal syscalls it permits vs. the number of attack syscalls it denies. The naive policy and average `twocell` policy generated from datasets `normal1` and `normal2` in the experiment above were evaluated in such a way. The number of syscalls both policies permitted and denied when applied to the four datasets in the attack and failed attack groups was recorded. Syscalls within these groups were labelled as either generated by an attack or by normal usage. For each dataset, Table 4 shows the percentages of attack and normal syscalls in the dataset, together with the percentage of syscalls permitted by the naive and `twocell` policies. From the results, the tendency of the naive policy was to permit the vast majority of syscalls, whether attack related or not. The `twocell`-generated policy behaved much more selectively, denying a slightly larger proportion of syscalls in the `success1` and `success2` datasets than it permitted. For the `failure1` and `failure2` dataset the converse was true.

Discussion

The dataset, algorithm and experiments presented in this section show how a novel algorithm has been developed and applied using the `libtissue` system. Runs used on average around 1%, and never more than 3%, of the available CPU resources, showing that it is computationally viable to process realtime data using our approach. The collection and analysis of the `rpc.statd` data has brought to light the potential

Table 4. Comparison of the performance of a naive policy and a `twocell` *policy generated from the* `normal2` *dataset*

dataset	success1	success2	failure1	failure2
normal syscalls	23%	23%	81%	87%
attack syscalls	76%	76%	18%	12%
naive permit	90%	90%	99%	99%
naive deny	9%	9%	0%	0%
twocell permit	47%	47%	69%	68%
twocell deny	52%	52%	30%	31%

usefulness of a number of novel data sources which can be use in conjuction with syscall information. The experiments we conducted compared an algorithm, `twocell`, implemented with `libtissue`, to a baseline standard approach, and showed how the agents in `twocell` responded in different ways to normal and attack sessions. By measuring the response of the agents, we use our algorithm to classify sessions as normal or attack. This experiment showed that the performance `twocell` is at least comparable to current approaches.

More widely, the validation experiments with the `twocell` algorithm and the `rpc.statd` dataset show the feasibility of using `libtissue` to implement artificial immune systems as multiagent systems and apply them to real-world problems. The `twocell` algorithm has also provided a necessary stepping-stone on the route to developing more complex algorithms. We are preparing to publish results of experiments with an algorithm which is able to detect a number of novel attacks with a low false-positive rate. To evaluate this and other algorithms we have created a second dataset which contains a wider range of normal and attack usage that the `rpc.statd` dataset. The new dataset, which was created by monitoring a `wuftpd` FTP server, contains syscalls and 13 different signals including CPU usage, memory usage, and socket and file usage statistics.

In order to generate realistic normal usage of the `wuftpd` server, we recreated normal sessions seen on a production network on an instrumented experimental network much like the setup for the `rpc.statd` dataset. Data on real FTP client-server interaction can be readily obtained from network packet traces collected by network-based monitors. Such packet traces are technically fairly easy to gather but, more importantly, traces are also already available publically, removing the need to gather this data altogether. Use of public datasets also contributes to the reproducibility of experiments. By reassembling network packets transmitted between client and server a sufficiently complete record of an FTP session can be reproduced. The dataset used (LBNL-FTP-PKT dataset, 2003) contains all incoming anonymous FTP connections to public FTP servers at the Lawrence Berkeley National Laboratory over a ten-day period and is available from the Internet Traffic Archive (http://ita.ee.lbl.gov/). The traces contain connections between 320 distinct FTP servers and 5832 distinct clients and provide a rich source of normal usage sessions, and we initially used the traces for one FTP server over two days.

CONCLUSION

In this chapter, we have given an overview of biologically-inspired approaches to computer security, in particular immune-inspired approaches. We then discussed in detail an intrusion detection problem, process anomaly detection, and reviewed current research in this area. A system, `libtissue`, which we have built for implementing immune-inspired algorithms was then detailed, and the results of validation experiments using an artificial immune system implemented with `libtissue` and applied to process anomaly detection were presented and discussed.

REFERENCES

Aickelin, U., Greensmith, J., & Twycross, J. (2004). Immune system approaches to intrusion detection—a review. In *Proceedings of the 3rd International Conference on Artificial Immune Systems* (LNCS 3239, pp. 316-329). Catania, Italy.

Anderson, J.P. (1980). *Computer security threat monitoring and surveillance*. Fort Washington, PA: James P. Anderson Co.

Axelsson, S. (2000). Intrusion detection systems: A survey and taxonomy. *Technical Report 99-15*. Department of Computer Engineering, Chalmers University.

Bace, R., & Mell, P. (2001). Intrusion detection systems. *Technical Report NIST Computer Science Special Reports SP-800-31*. National Institute of Standards and Technology.

Balthrop, J., Esponda, F., Forrest, S., & Glickman, M. (2002). Coverage and generaliszation in an artificial immune system. In *Proceedings of the 4th Annual Genetic and Evolutionary Computation Conference* (pp. 3-10).

Bovet, D.P., & Cesati, M. (2002). *Understanding the Linux kernel*. O'Reilly and Associates.

Bugtraq. (2000). *statdx2—Linux rpc.statd revisited*. Retrieved May 2, 2008, from http://seclists.org/lists/bugtraq/2000/Oct/0170.html

Cheswick, B. (1992). An evening with berferd in which a cracker is lured, endured, and studied. In

Proceedings of the 1st Winter USENIX Conference (pp. 163–174). San Francisco, CA.

Dasgupta, D. (1999). *Artificial immune systems and their applications*. Springer Verlag.

Dasgupta, D. (2006). Advances in artificial immune systems. *IEEE Computational Intelligence Magazine, 1*(4), 40-49.

Dasgupta, D., & Azeem, R. (2007). *Artificial immune system: A bibliography*. Retrieved May 2, 2008, from http://ais.cs.memphis.edu/papers/ais_bibliography.pdf

de Castro, L.N., & Timmis, J. (2002). *Artificial immune systems: A new computational intelligence approach*. Springer.

Denning, D.E. (1987). An intrusion detection model. *IEEE Transactions on Software Engineering, 13*(2), 222–232.

Endler, D. (1998). Intrusion detection applying machine learning to solaris audit data. In *Proceedings of the IEEE Annual Computer Security Applications Conference* (pp. 268–279). Scottsdale, AZ.

Fork. (2007). *Linux man page (2)*.

Forrest, S., Hofmeyr, S., & Somayaji, A. (1997). Computer immunology. *Communications of the ACM, 40*(10), 88-96.

Gao, D., Reiter, M.K., & Song, D. (2004). On gray-box program tracking for anomaly detection. In *Proceedings of the 13th USENIX Security Symposium* (pp. 103-118). San Diego, CA.

Garfinkel, T. (2003). Traps and pitfalls: Practical problems in system call interposition based security tools. In *Proceedings of the Network and Distributed Systems Security Symposium* (pp. 162-177).

Greensmith, J., Aickelin, U., & Twycross, J. (2006a). Articulation and clarification of the dendritic cell algorithm. In *Proceedings of the 5th International Conference on Artificial Immune Systems* (LNCS 4163, pp. 404-417). Oeiras, Portugal.

Greensmith, J., Twycross, J., & Aickelin, U. (2006b). Dendritic cells for anomaly detection. In *Proceedings of the IEEE World Congress on Computational Intelligence* (pp. 664-671). Vancouver, Canada.

Hart, E., & Timmis, J. (2005). Application areas of AIS: The past, the present and the future. In *Proceedings of the 4th International Conference on Artificial Immune Systems* (LNCS 3627, pp. 483-497). Banff, Canada.

Hofmeyr, S., & Forrest, S. (2000). Architecture for an artificial immune system. *Evolutionary Computation Journal, 8*(4), 443-473.

Jansen, W., & Karygiannis, T. (1999). Mobile agent security. *Technical report, NIST Special Publication* (pp. 800-819).

Kemmerer, R., & Vigna, G. (2002). Intrusion detection: A brief history and overview. *Security and Privacy, Supplement to IEEE Computer Magazine* (pp. 27-30).

Kruegel, C., Mutz, D., Valeur, F., & Vigna, G. (2003). On the detection of anomalous system call arguments. In *Proceedings of the 8th European Symposium on Research in Computer Security* (pp. 326-343). Gjovik, Norway.

LBNL-FTP-PKT Dataset. (2003). Retrieved May 2, 2008, from http://www-nrg.ee.lbl.gov/LBNL-FTP-PKT.html

Lee, W., & Xiang, D. (2001). Information-theoretic measures for anomaly detection. In *Proceedings of the IEEE Symposium on Security and Privacy* (pp. 130-143).

Lincoln Labs. (2007). *DARPA intrusion detection evaluation datasets*. Retrieved May 2, 2008, from http://www.ll.mit.edu/IST/ideval/

Mitnick, K.D., & Simon, W.L. (2005). *The art of intrusion: The real stories behind the exploits of hackers, intruders and deceivers*. Wiley.

Morel, B. (2002). Immunology and the survivability of mission critical cyber-based systems. In *Proceedings of the 4th Information Survivability Workshop* (pp. 21-24).

Northcutt, S., & Novak, J. (2003). *Network intrusion detection, third edition*. New Riders.

Provos, N. (2003). Improving host security with system call policies. In *Proceedings of the 12th USENIX Security Symposium* (pp. 257-272). Washington, D.C.

Pthreads. (2007). *Linux man page (7)*.

rpc.statd (2007). *Linux man page (8)*.

Sekar, R., Bendre, M., Dhurjati, D., & Bollineni, P. (2001). A fast automaton-based method for detecting anomalous program behaviors. In *Proceedings of the IEEE Symposium on Security and Privacy* (pp. 144-155).

Somayaji, A. (2002). *Operating system stability and security through process homeostasis*. PhD thesis, University of New Mexico.

Syscalls. (2007). *Linux man page* (2).

Tan, K., & Maxion, R. (2003). Determining the operational limits of an anomaly-based intrusion detector. *IEEE Journal on Selected Areas in Communications, 21*(1), 96-110.

Twycross, J., & U. Aickelin, U. (2006). Libtissue—implementing innate immunity. In *Proceedings of the IEEE World Congress on Computational Intelligence* (pp. 499-506). Vancouver, Canada.

Venter, H., & Eloff, J. (2003). A taxonomy for information security technologies. *Computers and Security, 22*(4), 299-307.

Williams, J. (1996). Just sick about security. In *Proceedings of the New Security Paradigms Workshop* (pp. 139-146). ACM Press.

Williamson, M.M. (2002). Biologically inspired approaches to computer security. *Technical Report HPL-2002-131*. HP Laboratories, Bristol.

Ye, N. (2000). A Markov chain model of temporal behavior for anomaly detection. In *Proceedings of of the 2000 IEEE Workshop on Information Assurance and Security* (pp. 171-174).

Yeung, D.Y., & Ding, Y. (2003). Host-based intrusion detection using dynamic and static behavioral models. *Pattern Recognition, 36*(1), 229-243.

KEY TERMS

Artificial Immune System: A relatively new class of metaheuristics that mimics aspects of the human immune system to solve computational problems. This method has shown particular promise for anomaly detection. Previous artificial immune systems have shown some similarities with evolutionary computa-

tion. This is because they focus on the adaptive immune system. More recent approaches have combined this with aspects of the innate immune system to create a second generation of artificial immune systems.

Adaptive Immune System: Central components of the adaptive immune system are T cells and B cells. The overall functionality of the adaptive immune system is to try and eliminate threats through antibodies, which have to be produced such that they match antigen. This is achieved in an evolutionary-like manner, with better and better matches being produced over a short period of time. The adaptive system remembers past threats and hence has the capability of responding faster to future similar events.

Dendritic Cells: These belong to the class of antigen presenting cells. During their life, dendritic cells ingest antigen and redisplay it on their surface. In addition, dendritic cells mature differently depending on the context signals they are exposed to. Using these two mechanisms, these cells differentiate between dangerous and non-dangerous material and then activate T cells.

Innate Immune System: Central components of the innate immune system are antigen presenting cells and in particular dendritic cells. Until recently, the innate system was viewed as less important than the adaptive system and its main function was seen as an information pre-processing unit. However, the latest immunological research shows that it is the innate system that actually controls the adaptive system. Above all, dendritic cells seem to be the key decision makers.

Process Anomaly Detection: A method of detecting intrusions on computer systems. The aim is to detect misbehaving processes, as this could be a sign of an intrusions. The detection is based on syscalls (i.e., activities by the processes), and context signals (e.g., CPU load, memory usage, or network activity).

T Cells: Created in the thymus (hence the "T"), these cells come in different subtypes. Cytotoxic T cells directly destroy infected cells. T helper cells are essential to activate other cells (e.g., B cells). T reg cells suppress inappropriate responses.

Chapter XI
Cryptography for Information Security[1]

Wasim A. Al-Hamdani
Kentucky State University, USA

ABSTRACT

This chapter introduces cryptography from information security phase rather than from deep mathematical and theoretical aspects, along with cryptography application in information security. The chapters introduce classical cryptography, block, stream cipher, and public key family, and with the most advance systems as elliptic curve, digital signature, cryptography key managements, and the last part of the chapter are the cryptography application in protocols, communications, e-mails, and the most advance research topics.

INTRODUCTION

The word *cryptography* means "secret writing." Some define "cryptography" as "*study of mathematical techniques*". *Cryptography* is a function which transfer "*plain text*" p_t in to "*ciphertext*" c_t, and decryption is the inverse function which transfer "*ciphertext*" into "*plain text.*"

Cryptographic Goals

The cryptography goals are: *Privacy* or *confidentiality*, *data integrity*, *authentication* and *nonrepudiation*.

Cryptography Classification

CRYPTO system could be classified generally as "unkeyed" (key is not required for encryption and decryption) base algorithms and "keyed" (key is required for encryption and decryption) based. Unkeyed

base classified farther to "hash functions" (a method of turning data into a (relatively) small number that may serve as a digital "fingerprint" of the data), "pseudorandom generator" (an algorithm generates a sequence of numbers that approximate the properties of random numbers). Keyed base is classified into "symmetric" key ("secret key") (uses identical key for encryption and decryption) and "asymmetric" ("public key") (the key for encryption and decryption are not identical). Symmetric algorithms are classified into: "block cipher" (encryption and decryption accomplish on fixed size of plain text/ciphertext called block of bits), "stream ciphers" (encryption and decryptions are accomplished on sequence of bits one bit at a time), "digital signatures" (an electronic signature that can be used to authenticate the identity of the sender of a message or the signer of a document), hash functions, pseudorandom generator, "identification" (identifying something, map a known entity to unknown entity to make it known), and "authentications" (who or what it claim to be). Asymmetric are classified into: digital signatures, identification, and authentications.

The Symmetric could be classified as "conventional" or "classical" and "modern "algorithms." The classical are classified into: "transposition "and "substitution;" another type of cryptography is called the "hybrid" which combines Symmetric and asymmetric to form hybrid ciphers.

ATTACKS on crypto system are "passive attacks" (called "traffic analysis" in which the intruder eavesdrops, but does not modify the message stream) and "active attack" (intruder modify (delete, replay) the massage) (Stallings, 2005). There are many different attacks such as: "ciphertext-only attack" (the attacker has one or more ciphertext messages), "known-plain text attack" (the attacker has one or more plain text messages and the associated ciphertext messages), "chosen-plain text attack" (the attacker can choose a plain text message and find out the associated ciphertext message), "adaptive chosen-plain text attack" (similar to chosen-plain text attack but the ciphertext messages gathered by the attacker can be used to determine the choice of the next plain text message to work with dynamically), "chosen-ciphertext attack" (the attacker can choose a ciphertext message and find out the associated plain text message), "adaptive chosen-ciphertext attack" (similar to chosen-ciphertext attack, but the plain text messages gathered by the attacker can be used to determine the choice of the next ciphertext message to work with dynamically), "frequency analysis" (attempts to break an encryption algorithm by studying the frequency of words and patterns in the ciphertext messages to figure out the encryption key; simple substitution and transposition ciphers are vulnerable to frequency analysis), "algebraic attack" (attempts to break an encryption algorithm by studying the mathematical structure of the algorithm), "analytic attack" (attempts to break an encryption algorithm by using algebraic manipulation to reduce the complexity), "statistical attack" (attempts to break an encryption algorithm by exploiting the statistical weaknesses in the design of the algorithm), "differential cryptanalysis" (is a chosen-plain text attack; it attempts to break an encryption algorithm by using pairs of plain text messages with specific differences between the two messages of each message pair, and analyzing the effect of these differences on the associated ciphertext messages), "linear cryptanalysis" (is a known-plain text attack. It attempts to break an encryption algorithm by using linear approximations to describe the behaviors of the algorithm), "meet-in-the-middle attack" (is a known-plain text attack in which the attacker half-encrypts a plain text message with all possible first-half keys and half-decrypts the associated ciphertext message with all possible second-half keys and hopes to get the same value.), "man-in-the-middle attack" (an attacker is able to read, insert and modify a messages between two parties without either party knowing that the link between them has been compromised), "exhaustive key search" or "brute force attack" (decrypt a ciphertext message by trying every possible key value until the resulting plain text message is meaningful) and "birth day attack" (probability that two or more people in a group of 23 share the same birthday is greater than 1/2; such a result is called a birthday paradox).

MATHEMATICS BACKGROUND

Probability Theory

A *probability distribution* P on a sample space S is a sequence of numbers $P_1, P_2, \ldots, P_n$ that are all nonnegative and sum 1. A probability distribution P on S is a function $P : S \rightarrow [0,1]$ such that $P(x_1) + P(x_2) + \ldots + P(x_n) = 1$. The number P_i is the *probability* of S_i being the outcome of the experiment. An *event* E is a subset of the sample space S. The *probability* that event E occurs, denoted P(E).

Why do we need Probabilities with cryptography? The studies of probability are required for birthday attack, statistical analysis and classical attack.

Birthday Problems

Given a group of people, what is the probability of two people in the group having the same birthday? For a group of 400 people, guaranteed (a probability of one) since there are only 365 possible birthdays to go around. If there were only two people in the group, the chance that those two people share the same birthday is quite small (near to 0.) Generally, the birthday problem solved using the equation

$$1 - \frac{(366)(366-1)(366-2)\ldots(366-n)}{366^n}$$

Why do we need to know birthday bay problem? It been used in several attacks.

Number Theory

A branch of pure mathematics concerned with the properties of integers.

Divisibility

The set of integers is denoted by the symbol □. When a, b integers; then a *divides* b if there exists an integer c such that b = ac. If a divides b, then this is denoted by a | b. Example -3|18, since 18 = (-3)(-6).

An integer c is a *common divisor* of a and b if c|a and c|b. A nonnegative integer d is the *greatest common divisor* (gcd) of integers a and b, denoted d=gcd (a, b). Example: The common divisors of 12 and 18 are1, 2, 3, 6 and gcd (12, 18) = 6. *Euclidean algorithm* is used for computing the gcd of two integers, if a and b are positive integers with a > b, then gcd(a, b) = gcd(b, a mod b).

Why do we need divisibility and GCD with cryptography? They are used in classical and public key encryption.

Prime Numbers

Two integers a and b are said to be *relatively prime* if gcd (a, b) = 1. An integer p $\geq$ 2 is said to be *prime* if its only positive divisors are 1 and p. Otherwise, p is called *composite*. If n is composite integer, then n has a prime divisor less than or equal to $\sqrt{n}$. Example: 101 is prime, since $\sqrt{101} \approx 10$, and 1|101, 2$\not|$101, 3$\not|$101, 5$\not|$101, 7$\not|$101.A prime p is said to be a *strong prime* if the following three conditions are satisfied= p – 1, p + 1 and r-1 has a large prime factor.

Why do we need prime number with cryptography? Used in public key, it has been proven the prime number must be strong and required by the standard ANSI X9.31 (Digital Signatures, 1998).

Euler Phi (φ) Function

For n $\geq$ 1, $\phi(n)$ the number of integers in the interval [1, n] which are relatively prime to n. The function φ is called the *Euler phi function;* Example φ(31) =30.

Why do we need φ? It used in RSA and other public key cryptography system.

Congruence Arithmetic's

n positive integer, if a and b are integers, then a is said to be *congruent* to b *modulo* n, written a $\equiv$ b (mod n), if n divides (a,b). The integer n is called the *modulus* of the congruence. Example: 24 $\equiv$ 9 (mod 5) since 24 - 9 = 3 *5 · The *multiplicative inverse* of a modulo n is an integer x: ax = 1 (mod n).

Why do we need multiplicative inverse? RSA needs to use it for key generation process.

Chinese Remainder

If the integers $n_1, n_2, \ldots, n_k$ are pair wise relatively prime, then the system of x $\equiv a_1$ (mod n_1), x $\equiv a_2$ (mod n_2), $\cdots$, x $\equiv a_k$ (mod n_k) has a unique solution modulo $n_1, n_2, \ldots, n_k$.

Where does Chinese remainder theorem used? SSL Accelerator Card uses Chinese Remainder Theorem (CRT) (HP AXL600L SSL Accelerator Card, 2005), and it has been used in secret sharing (Iftene, 2005).

Polynomials

A *polynomial is* any expression of the form $f(x) = a_0 x^0 + a_1 x^1 + a_2 x^2 + \ldots + a_{n-1} x^{n-1} + a_n x^n = \sum a_n x^n$ Example: $f(x) + g(x) = x^3 + x^2 + 2x + 1$

Why do we need to know polynomial? Polynomials is the basic idea for stream cipher and advance encryption standard.

Note: What is true for integer number is true for polynomial.

MATHEMATICAL PROBLEMS

There are some mathematical problems concurring cryptography; these are:

- **The Integer Factorization Problem:** Given a positive integer n, find its prime factorization.
- **Primality Testing and Factoring:** To deciding whether an integer is composite or prime.
- **Discrete Logarithm Problem:** Given a prime p , a generator g mod p and a value y $\in \mathbb{Z}_p^*$ find x such that y = g^x (mod p)
- **The RSA Problem:** Given a positive integer n that is a product of two distinct odd primes p and q, a positive integer e such that

gcd(e, (p-1)(q-1)) = 1 , and an integer c, find an integer m such that m^e =c (mod n).

CLASSICAL CRYPTOSYSTEM

Transposition Algorithms

It is "rearranging the plain text in different way to construct the ciphertext." "To be or not to be" will generate ciphertext "EBOTTONROEBOT."

Substitution

The plain text alphabet is substituted by another set of alphabets (symbols).

Simple Substitution

Example: Morse coding, P_t = "come at once", then C_t is " -.-.x ---x -- x . xx .- x - xx ---x -.x-.-.x . xx."

Direct Standard

A C_{ti} = (P_{ti} +k) mod 26 , Where $1 \leq i \leq 26$; example: P_t ="To be or not to be is a matter of life" and k=3 then C_t C_t ="WREH RUQRWWREHMVDPDW-WHURIOMIH."

Multiplicative

A C_{ti} = (P_{ti} *k) mod 26 with condition of gcd(26,k)=1 ; P_t ="this is the way" and k=7, gcd (26,7)=1 then the ciphertext is "MXEWEWDXCYAM."

Polyalphabetic Substitution

In this type of algorithm, more than one character is mapped into one character. The bases for this type of algorithms is to make the character distribution in the ciphertext as flat as possible. A letter "A" could be encrypted with the same key as "B" and second time as "F."

Vigenere

The Vigenere system uses the equation of $C_{ti} = P_{ti} + k_i$ mod 26 where $1 \leq i \leq n$, n is the size of the message, Plain text is" it is the time to go back and

collect the information", key is" computer science is the best" the C_t =" KHUHN AIKAO MXBIS JSVRE OHUHN ZQRNM LVAPN SEOEBAHU." There are many versions of this system.

Hill

The algorithm uses a linear transformation on the block of plain text P_t to generate a block of C_t. The algorithm uses a simple equation which is C_t = (M* P_t) mod 26 and generally

$$C_t = \begin{pmatrix} C_{t1} \\ C_{t2} \\ .... \\ C_{tm} \end{pmatrix} = \begin{pmatrix} k_{11} & \cdots & km \\ \vdots & \ddots & \vdots \\ k_{m1} & \cdots & k_{mm} \end{pmatrix} \begin{pmatrix} P_{t1} \\ P_{t2} \\ .... \\ P_{tm} \end{pmatrix} \mod 26 .$$

The key matrix must be "GOOD" matrix. A GOOD matrix is: If the key matrix is defined as $\begin{pmatrix} a & b \\ c & d \end{pmatrix}$ Then gcd((ad – bc), 26) = 1.

CLASSICAL SYSTEM ATTACKS

Statistical Attack

The attack is the major theme for this section especially the attack on classical algorithms and systems; basically, there are: ciphertext, minimal knowledge on the type of algorithm and no key, no other information. The minimal knowledge about the algorithm is "*this is a classical type algorithm.*"

To attack a ciphertext encrypted using classical algorithms, there are several techniques. Before explained these techniques now we will review some concepts:
1.   The Ciphertext language properties.
2.   The Ciphertext statistics.

Using the following GROUP category:

1.   E
2.   T,A,O,I,N,S,H,R
3.   D,L
4.   C,U,M,W,F,G,Y,P,B
5.   V,K,J,X,Q,Z

Box 1.

$$I_c(x) = \sum_{i=0}^{25} \frac{f_i(f_i - 1)}{n(n-1)}$$

0

Key length	1	2	3	4	10	lager
I_c	0.066	0.052	0.047	0.045	0.041	0.38

Index of Coincidence (Friedman, 1987)

The technique is used to find the key size and defined in Box 1.

BLOCK CIPHER FAMILY

Encrypts a message into block then maps n-bit plain text to n-bit ciphertext, where n is the block size, defined as in equation $C_t = E(k, P_t)$, $P_t = D(k, C_t)$. A block ciphers system evaluated according to: key size, block size, security level, complexity, data expansion, error propagation.

Block Cipher Modes of Operation (DES Mod of Operations, 1980)

The block cipher works with a message of block size n bits (for example DES n=64), a message M which exceed the size of n bits must be partition into m block, then linking these blocks in certain mechanism. The method of combining all encrypted blocks is called *Mode of Operations*. There are four basic modes of operations, which are: ECB Electronic Code Book, CBC Cipher Block Chaining, CFB K-bit Cipher Feedback, and OFB K-bit Output Feedback.

ECD Electronic Code Book

Each block encrypted separately, disadvantage is that identical plain text blocks are encrypted into identical ciphertext blocks, Encryption $C_{ti} = E(k, P_{ti})$, and Decryption $P_{ti} = E(k, C_{ti})$, i is the number of blocks. one or more bit errors in a single ciphertext block affect decryption of that block only.

CBC the Cipher Block Chaining

The plain text is XORed with the previous encrypted block before it is encrypted. Encryption is $C_{ti} = E(k, P_{ti} \oplus C_{ti-1})$, $C_{t0} = IV$, and decryption is $P_{ti} = D(k, C_{ti}) \oplus C_{ti-1}$, $C_{t0} = IV$. One-bit change in a plain text affects all following ciphertext blocks, and a bit change to the ciphertext causes complete corruption of the corresponding block of plain text, and inverts the corresponding bit in the following block of plain text.

Initial Vector used with CBC is: Fixed, Counter IV, Random IV, and Nonce-Generated IV

CFB Cipher Feedback

CFB decryption is almost identical to CBC decryption performed in reverse: $C_{ti} = E(k, C_{ti-1}) \oplus P_{ti}$, $P_{ti} = D(k, C_{ti-1}) \oplus C_{ti-1}$, $C_{t0} = IV$, the IV need not be secret. Ciphertext block C_{ti} depends on both C_{t-1} and preceding plain text P_t. One or more bit errors in any single bit ciphertext block affects the decryption of that and the next ciphertext blocks. This is useful for applications that require low latency between the arrival of plain text and the output of the corresponding ciphertext, such as certain applications of streaming media.

Output Feedback (OFB)

K-bit Output Feedback (OFB) mode is similar to the CFB-mode, $C_{ti} = P_{ti} \oplus Out_i$, $P_{ti} = C_{ti} \oplus Out_i$, $Out_i = E(k, Out_{i-1})$, $Out_0 = IV$. One or more bit errors in any ciphertext affects the decryption of only that block.

Counter Mode

The initial vector a number that is the same size as the block of the block cipher; the number is incremented, and the incremented number is used in encryption.

Modes as Stream Ciphers

CBC mode may also be considered a stream cipher with n-bit blocks playing the role of very large characters. These modes of operation allow one to define stream ciphers from block ciphers.

Data Encryption Standard (DES) (Simovits, 1995)

DES is used for the protection of unclassified computer data and it is not approved for protection of national security classified information (Data Encryption Standard (DES), 1988). DES applies a 56-bit key to each 64-bit block of data. The process involves 16 rounds with major two processes: key and plain text.

The Plain Text Process

Initial permutation and denoted IP.

The permuted block is split into two equally sized blocks (L_0, R_0) which become the input for the first round.

The round manipulates these two blocks and the output becomes input for new two blocks (L_1, R_1)
$L_1 = R_0$, $R_1 = L_0 \oplus f(R_0, K_1)$

The DES rounds: $L_n = R_{n-1}$, $R_n = L_{n-1} \oplus f(R_{n-1}, K_n)$ and last round, $L_{16} = L_{15} \oplus f(R_{15}, k_{16})$, $R_{16} = R_{15}$

The two blocks are finally subject to a final permutation which is the inverse of the initial permutation.

The Function f

This function has two inputs: a 48-bit key and 32-bit block. The 32 bits are input to the expansion permutation function E. The E is the expansion permutation which takes the 32-bit block as an input and yields a 48-bit output.

The Key Scheduler Algorithm

The key is 64 bits, but the effective use of these key limits to 56 bits (by removing the parity bit). The key is first subject to an initial permutation, then divided into two 28-bit blocks, and is then $(C[0], D[0])$ subject to a left shift according to a shift-table.

Analysis of the Data Encryption Standard

Complement property: $E(\bar{k}, \bar{P_t}) = \overline{E(k, P_t)}$

Weak Keys: 01010101 01010101 or FEFE FEFE FEFEFEFE
Semi-Weak Keys: 01FE 01FE 01FE01FE or E0FEE0FE F1FEF1FE
Possibly Weak Keys: 1F1F0101 0E0E0101

DES Attack

The main attacks are: related keys, differential, linear, and (Al-Hamdani, 1999) state the bio attack.

DES Key Search Machine

A machine built by cryptography research advanced wireless technologies, and demonstrated fast key search for the data encryption standard (DES).

Multiple Encryptions

Triple-DES

(3DES) is a 64-bit block cipher with 168-bit key and 48 rounds, 2^{56} times stronger than DES, and uses three times the resources to perform the encryption/decryption process compared to DES.

DES-EEE3 – 3 different keys
DES-EDE3 – 3 different keys
DES-EEE2 – 2 different keys
DES-EDE2 – 2 different keys

x DES

Also called Fenced DES, this has some change in the outer layers of dealing with DES.

DES-X

DESX is a strengthened variant of DES supported by RSA Security's toolkits. The difference between

Box 2.

System	Round	Block size	Key size
FEAL-4	4	64 bits	64 bits
FEAL-K	K		
	18 Feistel Network + 16 Mixing	64 bits	0...128
RC5	0...225	32,64 and 128	0...2040
RC6	20	128 bits	0...2040 (128, 192, and 256 bits

DES and DESX is that, in DESX, the input plain text is bitwise XORed with 64 bits of additional key material before encryption with DES, and the output is also bitwise XORed with another 64 bits of key material (RSA Laboratories, http://www.rsasecurity.com).

Advanced Encryption Standard (AES)

"Rijndael" designed to use simple byte operations, the key size and the block size may be chosen from of 128, 192, or 256 with a variable number of rounds. The numbers of rounds are:

*   Nine if both the block and the key are 128 bits long.
*   11 if either the block or the key is 192 bits long, and neither of them is longer than that.
*   13 if either the block or the key is 256 bits long.

The total number of rounds key bits is equal to block length multiplied by the number or rounds plus one.

The General Process of SAE

The first (r-l) rounds are similar, and they consist of four transformations called:

*   **ByteSub:** Substitution bytes
*   **ShiftRow:** Shift rows
*   **MixColumn:** Multiply columns
*   **AddRoundKey:** XORed by the key

The last round only perform the transformations:

*   **ByteSub**
*   **ShiftRow**

*   **AddRoundKey**

International Data Encryption Algorithm IDEA

IDEA operates on 64-bit blocks using a 128-bit key, and eight rounds and an output transformation (the half-round). It has been used with PGP.

Other Block Cipher Algorithms

See Box 2.

STREAM CIPHER

Stream Cipher Foundation

One time pad system (Vernam Cipher) is defined as $C_{ti}=P_{ti} \oplus K_i$ for i=1,2,3,4...n where $P_{t1},P_{t2},P_{t3},...P_{tn}$ plain text bits, $k_1,k_2,k_3....k_n$ key bits, $C_{t1},C_{t2},C_{t3},...C_{tn}$ ciphertext bits, and $\oplus$ is the XOR function. The decryption is defined by $P_{ti}=C_{ti} \oplus K_i$ for i=1,2,3,4. See Exhibit 1.

Synchronous and Self-Synchronizing Stream Ciphers

Synchronous Stream Cipher is one in which the key stream is generated independently of the plain text/ciphertext. *Self-Synchronizing* or *asynchronous* stream cipher is one in which the key stream is generated as a function of the *key* and a *fixed number of previous ciphertext* bits. When ciphertext bits are deleted or inserted, it will cause a fixed number of plain text characters to be unrecoverable.

Exhibit 1. General model of a stream cipher encryption/decryption

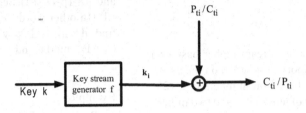

Exhibit 2. Key generator function

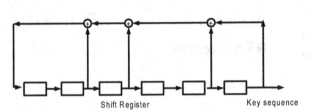

Exhibit 3.

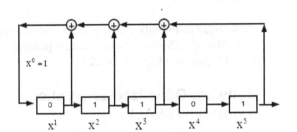

Key Generator

A key generator normally consists of shift register(s), XOR function, and a feedback function. See Exhibit 2.

The key generator is mapped from a polynomial function; for example, a polynomial function of $f(x)= x^5+x^3+x^2+x+1$ has a hardware of feed back shift register as shown in Exhibit 3.

If the polynomial is primitive (similar to prime number), then the maximum sequence generated is $2^5-1 =31$. Bit sequences will be generated 10110100 0011001001111101100010; after that, the sequence repeated itself.

Statistical Properties of Key Generator Sequences

The generated sequence (m) should have a good statistical sequence, and must satisfy the *randomness* tests, such as Golomb's randomness postulates and the five tests (*frequency* (mono-bit), *serial, poker, runs,* and *autocorrelation* test).

140-1 Statistical Tests for Randomness (Security Requirements, 1994)

Specifies four statistical tests for randomness; the string bits must be of length 20,000 bits. The tests are: monobit, (frequency), poker, runs, and long run test.

Stream Cipher Generators

There are three type of generators: *Linear* (as seen before); *Non linear* as AND, JK, Jeff, Plesse's, and Multiplexer; and the third one is *software generator* as de Bruijn FSR.

Well-Known Generators

CRC-12: $1+x+x^3+x^{11}+x^{12}$,
CRC-16: $1+x^2+x^{15}+x^{16}$
CCITT: $1+x^5+x^{12}+x^{16}$
A5 is European cellular telephone algorithm: $1+x+x^2+x^5+x^{19}$, $1+x+x^5+x^9+x^{22}$, $1+x+x^3+x^4+x^{23}$, GPS satellites: $1+x^3+x^{10}$, $1+x^2+x^3+x^6+x^8+x^9+x^{10}$

Other Stream Cipher

RC4

RC4 is a software type of stream cipher based on tables and internal memory. It is based on the use of a random permutation based on numbers 0. . . 255 represented as an array of length 256 and two indices in this array.

The Use of RC4

RC4 is most commonly used to protect Internet traffic using the SSL (Secure Sockets Layer) protocol and Wired Equivalent Privacy (WEP).

Software-Optimized Encryption Algorithm (SEAL)

Software-optimized encryption is designed for software implementation and, in particular, for 32-bit processors. Key generation has three procedures: preprocessing, pseudorandom function, and target platform.

The Combination of DES and Stream Cipher

DES algorithm is a linear function; it has been used as a key generator for Stream Cipher. DES generate 64 bit to be used as a key for the Stream Cipher. The LFSR input to DES is 64 bit size $C_{ti} = DES(k, L_{64}) \oplus Pti$ where L is LFBR.

PUBLIC KEY

The idea of public key is a one-way function. One-way function: it is easy to compute f(x) from x computation of x from f(x), and should be hard for the crypto attacker. The legal receiver should have a *trapdoor* available.

RSA

Publicly described in 1977 (Rivest, Shamir, & Adleman, 1978). RSA is widely used in electronic commerce protocols. It uses three parts: key generation, encryption, and decryption.

Key generation: Primes p and q such that n=pq and $\varphi = (p-1)(q-1)$. Select e with $1 < e < \varphi$ and gcd (e, φ) =1. (In other words, e is relatively prime to φ), then find d with $1 < d < \varphi$ with ed = 1(mod φ), *Encryption*: $C_t = P_t^e$ mod n and *Decryption*: $P_t = C_t^d$ mod n.

Example:
    p = 61, q = 53, n = p*q = 3233, $\varphi = (p-1)(q-1)$ = 3120, e = 17, d = 2753, public key is (e,n), private key is d. Encrypt = (P_t^e) mod n = (P_t^{17}) mod 3233

Decrypt $(C_t) = (C_t^d)$ mod n = (C_t^{2753}) mod 3233.

RSA Security

Key Size

1024-bit RSA keys are equivalent in strength to 80-bit symmetric keys, 2048-bit RSA keys to 112-bit symmetric keys and 3072-bit RSA keys to 128-bit symmetric keys. RSA claims that 1024-bit keys are likely to become crackable some time between 2006 and 2010, and that 2048-bit keys are sufficient until 2030. An RSA key length of 3072 bits should be used if security is required beyond 2030. NIST key management guidelines further suggest that 15360-bit RSA keys are equivalent in strength to 256-bit symmetric keys.

RSA Attacks

Factorization, small exponent e, small exponent d, search, homomorphic, Modulus, Message concealing, cycling, Fixed Point.

RSA in Practice

Digital Signatures

Digital signatures and hand-written signatures both rely on the fact that it is very hard to find two people with the same signature (see Digital Signature on page 16).

Digital Envelope

The digital envelope consists of a message encrypted using secret-key and an encrypted secret key. Digital envelopes usually use public key cryptography to encrypt the secret key.

PGP: Pretty Good Privacy. PGP combines some of the best features of both conventional and public key RSA cryptography. PGP is a hybrid cryptosystem (see Cryptography Applications).

Secure Sockets Client

One of the most common uses of public key technology is in the Secure Sockets Layer (SSL) protocol, and use Web browsers for secure communications over the internet. (see Cryptography Applications).

RABIN

Based on two (distinct) p and q primes, n= p q, encryption: $C_t = P_t^2$ mod n decryption: Square roots m1, m2 m3, and m4 of C_t mod n^2.

ElGamal

Based on: Prime number p and generate α a random integer a , $1 \le a \le p-2$, Encryption: $C_t = (\gamma, \delta)$ where k, $1 \le k \le p-2$ (gcd((p-1),k)=1 and $\gamma = \alpha^k$ mod p , $\delta + Pt$ $((h)^k$ mod p) mod p , Decryption:

$P_t = \gamma^{-a} \ \delta \ \mathrm{mod} \, p$.

Security of ElGamal

The problem of breaking the ElGamal Encryption scheme is equivalent to solving the Diffie-Hellman problem (The *Diffie-Hellman problem* is the following: "given a prime p, a generator α of Z_P^*, and elements α^a mod p and a^b mod p , find α^{ab} mod p").

Elliptic Curve

Elliptic curves are mathematical constructions from number theory and algebraic geometry, which in recent years have found numerous applications in cryptography. An elliptic curve can be defined over any field (e.g., real, rational, complex). Elliptic curves can provide versions of public key methods that, in some cases, are faster and use smaller keys, while providing an equivalent level of security. Their advantage comes from using a different kind of mathematical group for public key arithmetic.

Elliptic Curves Over Real Numbers

They are named because they are described by cubic equations. In general, cubic equations for elliptic curves take the form $y^2 + axy + by = x^3 + cx^2 + dx + e$ where a,b,c,d and e are real numbers and x and y take on values in the real numbers. It is sufficient to be limited to equations of the form $y^2 = x^3 + ax + b$ (Cubic). Also included in the definition is a single element denoted **O** and called the *point at infinity* or the *zero point*, which we. To plot such a curve, we need to compute $y = \sqrt{x^3 + ax + b}$ for given values of a and b, the plot consists of positive and negative values of y for each value of x.

Elliptic Curve Security

The best attack on the elliptic curve is general brute-force methods. The current lack of more specific attacks means that shorter key sizes for elliptic cryptosystems appear to give similar security as much larger keys that might be used in cryptosystems based on the discrete logarithm problem and integer factorization. For certain choices of elliptic curves, there are efficient attacks.

DIGITAL SIGNATURE (ALSO CALLED ELECTRONIC SIGNATURE)

The process has three parts: Key Generation, Signature, and Verification. There are other terms comes in association with Digital Signature such as *Digital Certificates (DC)*. This certificate includes: *Certificate Authority* (CA), the date of validity of the certificate, Certificate Signer/Provider, Sites/Hosts, Code Signer/Provider, Cross-Certification, Personal, File, Key Recovery, PKCS #12.

How Does It Work?

Hash function (Signature Information) = Hash value Asymmetric funtion (Key, Difgital Signature) = Decrypted signature
Digital Signature = (key, Asymmetric funtion (Hash Value = Hash funtion (M)))
The second part with each Digital signature is the verification

$$\text{Equal} \begin{cases} \text{Hash Function(Signature Information)} = \text{HashValue} \\ \text{Asymetric Function(Key, Difgital Signature)} \\ = \text{Decrypted Signature} \end{cases}$$

Steps of Digital Signature

Signature:

Sender: $E_{\text{Sender private key}}$ (h(Message) =Hashed) + Message

Verification:

Receiver: h(M) =$D_{\text{Sender publick key}}$ (Hashed

The *Digital Signature Standard* (DSS) is based on the *Digital Signature Algorithm* (DSA). DSS is the format for digital signatures that has been endorsed by the U.S. government. The DSA algorithm consists of a private key that only the originator of the document (signer) knows, and a public key. DSS is specified in Federal Information Processing Standard (FIPS) 186 (Digital Signature Standard (DSS), 2000).

Classification of Digital Signature Algorithms

Two general classes of digital signature algorithms: *digital signature algorithms with appendix* and *digital signature algorithms with plain text recovery*.

RSA Signature

Each Sender and Receiver (A and B) creates an RSA public key and a corresponding private key. Each entity Sender and Receiver should do the following: generate two large distinct random primes p and q, each roughly the same size, compute n = pq and φ = (p - 1)(q - 1), select a random integer e, $1 < e < \varphi$, such that gcd(e,φ) = 1, use the Euclidean theory to compute the unique integer d, $1 < d < \varphi$, such that ed = 1 (mod n)a's public key is (n,e); a's private key is d. Sender A signs a message m $\in$ M, A Receiver B can verify A's signature and recover the message m from the signature.

RSA Signatures in Practice

To use RSA in practice some consideration must be taken in account such as: reblocking problem, redundancy functions, system-wide parameters, short vs. long plain texts, and performance.

ISO/IEC 9796 Formatting (Information Technology, 1991)

ISO/IEC 9796 is the first international standard for digital signatures with the following features: it is based on public key cryptography; the particular signature algorithm is not specified but it must map k bits to k bits; it provides plain text recovery; and it specifies the plain text padding.

Public Key Standards (RSA Cryptography Standard, http://www.rsasecurity.com/)

PKCS #1 defines mechanisms for encrypting and signing data using the RSA public key cryptosystem.
PKCS #3 defines a Diffie-Hellman key agreement protocol.
PKCS #6 is being phased out in favor of version 3 of X.509.

ElGamal Signature

Randomized signature mechanism, generates digital signatures with appendix on binary plain texts of arbitrary length, and requires a hash function h : {0,1}* $\to \mathbb{Z}_p$ where p is a large prime number. The DSS is a variant of the ElGamal signature mechanism.

Other Digital Signature Algorithms

Digital Signature Algorithm (DSA), Fiat-Shamir, Nyberg One-Time Signatures, ESIGN.

HASH FUNCTIONS

A *Hash Function* takes a message of any length as input and produces a fixed length string as output and referee to as a *message digest* or a *digital fingerprint*. A cryptographic hash function is a hash function with certain additional security properties to make it suitable for use in various information security applications, such as authentication and message integrity. Encryptions may be either by using a public key or private key algorithm. Encryption of digest prevents active attacker from modifying the message and re-calculating its checksum accordingly. Hash functions have the following two properties: *compression* and *ease of computation*.

Types

There are major two types of hash functions: *modification detection codes* (MDCS) (also known as *manipulation detection codes* or *message integrity codes* (MICS)), and *message authentication codes* (MACs). The purpose of an MDC is *hash* with *additional* properties. MDCs are a subclass of unkeyed hash functions, and they are two types: *One-Way Hash Functions* (OWHFs) and *Collision Resistant Hash Functions* (CRHFs)—finding any two inputs having the same hash-value is difficult. The purpose of a MAC is has *without additional* mechanisms. The differences between the *key Hash Function* and *unkeyed Hash Function* based on further properties are: preimage resistance, 2nd-preimage resistance, and collision resistance (Menezes, van Oorscho, & Vanstone, 1996)

Cryptography Hash Function

Characteristics:
Models: Iterated, serial, and parallel.
Flow If either h_1 or h_2 is a collision resistant, then $h(x) = h_1(x) \| h_2(x)$.
Data representation: different data representations (e.g., ASCII vs. EBCDIC) must be converted to a common format before computing hash-values.
Padding and length-blocks: Extra bits appended before hashing.

Security

Attacks on: bit size of an MDC, MAC key space, or bit size of a MAC, precomputations, parallel targets for OWHFs, and long-message for 2nd-preimage.

Unkeyed Cryptography Hash Functions (MDCs)

There are three categories: customized, based on block ciphers, and based on modular arithmetic. The customized are those which are specifically designed "from scratch" for the explicit purpose of hashing, with optimized performance in mind (Menezes et al., 1996).

Cryptography Hash Functions Based on Modular Arithmetic

The basic idea is mod m arithmetic as the basis of the function. A major factors with this type is to meet the required security level, and a significant disadvantage is speed.

MASH

MASH-1 (Modular Arithmetic Secure Hash, Algorithm 1) has been proposed for draft ISO/IEC standard. MASH-1 involves use of an RSA-like modulus m, whose bit length affects the security; m should be difficult to factor, and for m of unknown factorization.

Other Cryptography Hash Functions

There are other types of cryptography Hash Functions based on different ideas such as: cellular automaton, knapsack, and algebraic matrices. The most well-known unkeyed hash functions are the MD Family (MD2, MD4 and MD5), SHA Family (1, 256, 384, and 512), as well as the RIPEMD-160.

MD Family (MD2, MD4 and MD5)

MD is a message digest developed by Rivest (RSA Laboratories) and customized, the most use is MD4, the number 4 in a series number, and MD4 was designed specifically for software implementation on 32-bit machines.

SHA Family (1 , 256,384 and 512)

Published in 1993 from National Institute of Standards as the Standard, FIPS PUB 180 and now referred to as "SHA-0" in 1995 in FIPS PUB 180-1, and commonly referred to as "SHA-1." SHA-1 appears to provide greater resistance to attacks; SHA-0 and SHA-1 produce a 160-bit (Secure Hash Standard, 1995). The family consists of 160, 256, 384, and 512. All algorithms are iterative. See Box 3.

CRYPTOGRAPHY KEY MANAGEMENT

Key management deals with generation, distribution, and storage of keys. Once a key is generated, it must

Box 3.

Algorithm	Message Size (bit)	Block size (bit)	Word size (bit)	Message Digest Size (bit)	Security (bit) (Birthday attack)
SHA-160	$< 2^{64}$	512	32	160	80
SHA-256	$< 2^{64}$	512	32	256	128
SHA-244	$< 2^{64}$	512	32	244	112
SHA-385	$< 2^{128}$	1024	64	384	192
SHA-512	$< 2^{128}$	1024	64	512	256

remain secret to avoid accident. In practice, most attacks on public key systems are probably aimed at the key management level, rather than at the system itself (RSA Laboratories). With "key management," there are two basic techniques (Bellovin & Housley, 2005): *automated key management* and *manual key management*. They provide very different features and characteristics.

Automated Key Management

Used in the following conditions: a party will have to manage n^2 static keys, where n may become large. Any stream cipher (such as RC4) is used. An IV might be reused, especially an implicit IV. Large amounts of data might need to be encrypted in a short time, causing frequent change of the short-term session key. Long-term session keys are used by more than two parties. Multicast is a necessary exception. Examples: IPsec IKE and Kerberos. S/MIME and TLS also include automated key management functions.

Manual Key Management

Maybe use in the following situations: The environment has very limited available bandwidth or very high round-trip times. Public key systems tend to require long messages and lots of computation; symmetric key alternatives, such as Kerberos, often require several round trips and interaction with third parties. The total volume of traffic over the entire lifetime of the long-term session key will be very low.

Key Size and Random Values

When manual key management is used, long-term shared secret values should be at least 128 bits and

"random" values, ensuring that an adversary will have no greater expectation than 50% of finding the value after searching half the key search space.

Diffie-Hellman (D-H) Key Exchange

This is a protocol that allows two parties that have no prior knowledge of each other to jointly establish a shared secret key over an insecure communications channel. This key can be used to encrypt subsequent communications using a symmetric key cipher. The Diffie-Hellman key exchange includes: agreement, establishment, negotiation, and exponential key exchange.

Although the Diffie-Hellman key agreement itself is an anonymous (nonauthenticated) key agreement protocol, it provides the basis for a variety of authenticated protocols.

CRYPTOGRAPHY APPLICATION (HANSCHE, BERTI, & HARE, 2003; JAVVIN TECHNOLOGIES, 2006; STALLINGS, 2006; WAN, 2003)

Internet Protocol

IPSec

It is a framework that extends the IP for secure data transmission between computers or networks. It is used as an add-on to IPV4, and built into IPV6 and works at the network layer. The security services provided by IPSec are confidentiality, integrity, authentication, and protection against replay attack. IPSec supports different encryption (e.g., DES, 3DES) and hashing (e.g., SHA-1, MD5) algorithms. The keys used in IP-

Sec can be installed manually, or through automated means.

Protocols

It has two protocols: *Authentication Header (AH)* provides integrity and authentication by using a keyed-hashed function to calculate the hash value (MAC) for each data packet. *Encapsulating Security Protocol (ESP)* provides: encryption, integrity, and authentication by using symmetric and hashing. Before encrypting a packet, padding is used to ensure that the packet ends on a 32-bit boundary.

Operating Modes

Transport mode: protects the payload of a packet and *Tunnel mode* protects the header and the payload of a packet.

Security Association

Agreements on some parameters is the first step in communicate using IPSec using the handshaking process. A *Security Association (SA)* is used to store the negotiated parameters, including the agreed authentication and encryption algorithms, keys, keys lifetime, and the source IP addresses. *A Security Parameter Index (SPI)* is a 32-bit identifier that is put into the packet header of a protected packet.

Simple Key Management for Internet Protocol (SKIP)

This is a session-key management protocol for use with IPSec. It does not require prior communication to exchange keys and establish sessions. Therefore, there is no connection setup overhead.

Internet Key Exchange (IKE)

It is for exchanging session keys and parameters in the negotiation or handshaking process between two communicating parties in the IPSec framework. It contains two main protocols: *Internet Security Association* and *Key Management Protocol (ISAKMP)*. It provides the framework for the negotiation process.

Web

SSL/TLS: Secure Socket Layer (SSL) and Transport Layer Security (TLS) Protocols

Secure Socket Layer (SSL) and Transport Layer Security (TLS) Protocols provide privacy and integrity between two applications. The protocol is composed of two layers: the TLS Record Protocol and the TLS Handshake Protocol. It supports different symmetric systems: (DES, 3DES, and so on), hashing (MD5, SHA-1), digital signature (RSA or DSS), and key exchange (RSA or Diffie-Hellman) algorithms.

Hypertext Transport Protocol (HTTP)

For sensitive information, a server should encrypt the information (Cookies) before storing them as cookies on a client machine.

Secure HTTP (S-HTTP)

S-HTTP is designed to integrate with HTTP applications. It provides a variety of security mechanisms, providing the security service options appropriate to the wide range of potential end uses. S-HTTP provides symmetric capabilities to both client and server. Several cryptographic message format standards may be incorporated into S-HTTP clients and servers.

HTTPS (HTTP over SSL)

It is standard for HTTP security, and is more popular than S-HTTP. The whole communication channel or session between a client and a server is encrypted, rather than messages being encrypted individually as in S-HTTP.

Secure Electronic Transaction (SET)

Secure Electronic Transaction (SET) designed to protect credit card transactions on the Internet. It is not a payment system; rather, it's a set of security protocols and formats enabling users to employ the existing credit card payment infrastructure on an open network in a secure fashion. The purchase request consists of four messages: Initiate Request, Initiate Response, purchase request, and purchase response

Data Communication

For there are two approaches of encryption implementation:

Link Encryption (Online Encryption)

Encryption and decryption are carried out at every intermediate node of a communication path at the data link layer. All traffic (including the header, trailer and payload of every packet) over a communication link is encrypted. Every packet needs to be decrypted at every node in order for the router to read the address information in the header for routing. The packet is then re-encrypted and forwarded.

End-to-End Encryption

Encryption and decryption are carried out at the two end-systems at the network (or upper) layer. Only the payload of a packet is encrypted.

E-Mail

Multipurpose Internet Mail Extension (MIME)

Extends to the Internet-based text format used by *Simple Mail Transfer Protocol* SMTP (is the standard for e-mail transmissions across the Internet) to allow the exchange of nonASCII data in an e-mail (e.g., video, audio, and image). Many client software support MIME. Based on the MIME headers of an e-mail, e-mail client software can recognize the data type and handle the data accordingly.

Secure MIME (S/MIME)

It extends to the MIME standard. Provide confidentiality, integrity, authenticity, and nonrepudiation for e-mail and attachments using public key. The crypto systems used in S/MIME are: DES, 3DES or RC4, Hashing—MD5 or SHA-1, Digital signature—DSA or RSA, Key exchange Diffie-Hellman or RSA, Public key certificate—X.509v3.

Privacy-Enhanced Mail (PEM)

It uses a hierarchical trust model similar to a PKI, though not as flexible. It allows only a single path from the root to an end entity (i.e., no cross-certification). It uses MD2 or MD5 for hashing, DES in CBC mode for encryption, RSA for key management and digital signature, and X.509 for certificate format.

Message Security Protocol (MSP)

It is a military standard of secure e-mail application. It is a X.400 compatible application level protocol. It provides the flexibility of using different encryption, hash values, and digitally sign. It also provides return receipts.

Pretty Good Privacy (PGP)

It provides the flexibility of using different algorithms to encrypt messages (3DES, IDEA or CAST), calculate hash values (MD5 or SHA-1), digitally signature (RSA or DSA), and exchange keys (RSA or Diffie-Hellman). A user's key pair (private and public key) is generated when the application asks the user to randomly type on the keyboard. The random keystroke timing and the keys struck are used to generate the key pair. Each user distributes his or her public key certificate(s) to others. Users sign the public key certificates of those they trust to form a community of users who trust each other, a "Web of trust." Two *"key ring"* files are used to store the keys on a PGP node *Private-key ring* and *Public key ring*.

OTHER SERVICES

Secure Shell (SSH)

It uses public key cryptography to establish a secure tunnel for terminal-like access between two computers. It provides confidentiality, integrity, and authenticity. It supports different encryption (e.g., 3DES, Blowfish), hashing (e.g., SHA-1, MD5), and authentication (e.g., password, RSA, DSA) algorithms. It is a secure replacement for programs like telnet, ftp.

Secure Remote Procedure Call RPC (S-RPC)

Secure RPC uses a simple version of the Diffie-Hellman exponential based method for determining a common DES key.

Secure DNS

Digitally signs DNS data before sending the data to a client, so it can be assured that the data comes from the correct DNS server and has not been modified in an unauthorized manner.

FUTURE TRENDS(CAO & CAO, 2006; DWORK, 2006; SHOUP, 2005; TARTARY & WANG, 2006)

The major research areas in cryptography are:

- High-performance Encryption Methods
- Public Key Cryptography and Infrastructures
- Key agreements
- Electronic Cash and related Electronic Commerce Infrastructure
- Internet Security Protocols
- Computational Number Theory
- Intellectual Property and Content Protection Mechanisms
- Watermarking
- Fighting Pirates
- Finger Mark
- The Secure PC
- Key Exchange
- Authentication/Signatures
- Proxy-Signatures
- Boolean Functions and Stream Ciphers
- Cryptographic protocols
- Quantum Cryptography

REFERENCES

Advanced Encryption Standard (FIPS 197). (2001). Federal Information Processing Standards.

Al-Hamdani, W. (1999). Computing the IP & IP-1 table for Des algorithm (attack based on genetic programming). *National Computer Center Journal, 35.*

Bellovin, S., & Housley, R. (2005). Guidelines for cryptographic key management. In *Request for Comments* (4107). Retrieved May 2, 2008, from http://www.faqs.org/rfc/rfc4107.txt

Cao, F., & Cao, Z. (2006, December 8–10). Security model of proxy-multi signature schemes. In *Proceedings of Cryptology and Network Security5th International Conference, CANS 2006 Suzhou, China* (Vol. 4301). Springer, Lecture Notes in Computer Science.

Data Encryption Standard (DES) (FIPS PUB 46-2). (1988). Federal Information Processing Standards Publication.

DES Mod of Operations (FIPS PUB 81). (1980). Federal Information Processing Standards Publication.

Digital Signature Standard (DSS) (FIPS 186-2). (2000). Federal Information Processing Standards.

Digital Signatures Using Reversible Public Key Cryptography for the Financial Services Industry (rDSA) (Document# ANSI X9.31-1998). (1998). American National Standards Institute.

Dwork, C. (Ed.). (2006, August 20–24). Advances in cryptology. In *Proceedings of CRYPTO 200626th Annual International Cryptology Conference, Santa Barbara, California, USA* (Vol. 4117). Springer, Lecture Notes in Computer Science.

Electronic Frontier Foundation. (1998). *Cracking DES.* Electronic Frontier Foundation.

Friedman, W. (1987). *The index of coincide and its application in cryptograph.* Agent Park Press.

Hansche, S., Berti, S., & Hare, C. (2003). *Official (ISC)2 guide to the CISSP exam.* Auerbach.

HP AXL600L SSL accelerator card for proliant servers. *The white paper* (DA-11419 U.S., Version 9). (2005, May 16). HP Products.

Iftene, S. (2005). *Compartmented secret sharing based on the Chinese remainder theorem.* International Association for Cryptography Research, Cryptology ePrint Archive.

Information Technology - Security Techniques - Digital Signature Scheme Giving Message Recovery (INCITS/ISO/IEC 9796-1991). (1991). America National Standard Institute Standards.

Information Technology - Security Techniques - Digital Signature Schemes Giving Message Recovery - Part 3: Discrete Logarithm Based Mechanisms (INCITS/ISO/IEC 9796-3-2000). (2000). America National Standard Institute Standards.

Information technology - Security techniques - Digital signature schemes giving message recovery Part 2: Integer factorization based mechanisms (INCITS/ ISO/IEC 9796-2-2002). (2002). America National Standard Institute Standards.

Javvin Technologies. (2006). *Network protocols handbook* (3rd). Javvin Technologies, Inc.

Menezes, A.J., van Oorscho, P.C., & Vanstone, S.A. (1996). *Handbook of applied cryptography.* CRC.

Rivest, R., Shamir, A., & Adleman, L. (1978). A method for obtaining digital signatures and public-key cryptosystems. *Communications of the ACM, 21*(2).

Simovits, M. (1995). *The DES: An extensive document and evaluation.* Agent Park Press.

Shoup, V. (Ed.). (2005, August 14–18). Advances in cryptology. In *Proceedings CRYPTO 2005 25th Annual International Cryptology Conference, Santa Barbara, California, USA* (Vol. 3621). Springer, Lecture Notes in Computer Science.

Stallings, W. (2005). *Cryptography and network security: Principles and practices, fourth edition,* (pp. 13). Prentice Hall.

Stallings, W. (2006). *Network security essentials: Applications and standards, third edition.* Prentice Hall.

Tartary, C., & Wang, H. (2006, December 8–10). Achieving multicast stream authentication using MDS codes. In *Proceedings of Cryptology and Network Security 5th International Conference, CANS 2006 Suzhou, China* (Vol. 430). Springer, Lecture Notes in Computer Science.

Wan, K. (2003). *CISSP exam notes.* KP Lab Limited.

KEY TERMS

Asymmetric Key Cryptography: Uses different cryptography key encryption and decryption.

Block Cipher: A symmetric key cipher which operates on fixed-length groups of bit.

Cryptography: The "Study of mathematical techniques" and its goals are: Confidentiality, Data Integrity, Authentication and Nonrepudiation.

Digital Signature: Also called electronic signature, it is used to indicate that the plain text or file that it is attached to an electronic mail is originated by the sender. The process has three parts: Key Generation, Signature, and Verification. There are other terms comes in association with Digital Signature, such as Digital Certificates (DC).

Elliptic Curve Cryptography (ECC): An approach to public-key cryptography based on the algebraic structure of elliptic curves over finite fields.

Public Key Cryptography (PKC): Also known as asymmetric cryptography, it uses two keys—a "public key" and a "private key" —to implement an encryption.

Stream Cipher: Also called one time pad system (Vernam Cipher), it is a symmetric type, where plain text bits are combined with a key stream bits using exclusive, or XOR, operation.

Symmetric Key Cryptography: Uses identical cryptography key for encryption and decryption.

ENDNOTE

[1] Most of the material are adopted from COS533 lecture notes "Introduction to Cryptography" at Kentucky State University

Chapter XII
Memory Corruption Attacks, Defenses, and Evasions

Carlo Belletini
Università degli Studi di Milano, Italy

Julian L. Rrushi
Università degli Studi di Milano, Italy

ABSTRACT

The chapter introduces and describes representative defense mechanisms to protect from both basic and advanced exploitation of low-level coding vulnerabilities. Exploitation of low-level coding vulnerabilities has evolved from a basic stack-based buffer overflow with code injection to highly sophisticated attack techniques. In addition, pure-data attacks were demonstrated to be as efficient as control-data attacks and quite realistic. On the other hand research on assessment of the robustness of proposed mitigation techniques revealed various weaknesses in them leading to design and implementation of evasion techniques. Most of the defensive techniques protect only from a limited set of attack techniques, thus a defense employment requires multiple complementary mitigation techniques. Furthermore, there are few mitigation techniques designed to counter pure-data attacks. In response to these limitations, current research proposes better defensive mechanisms such as pointer taintedness detection and attack data burning capable of countering any kind of control-data or pure-data attack.

INTRODUCTION

Low-level coding vulnerabilities have been widespread in modern operating systems. These vulnerabilities account for the majority of CERT advisories released in recent years. Attack techniques which exploit low-level coding vulnerabilities evolved from a basic stack-based buffer overflow to actual highly sophisticated forms. These attack techniques have demonstrated to be quite devastating and fully applicable to real world target programs, and are considered to be among the main attack techniques employable to get intruded into target operating systems or take destructive actions against them. Besides being used directly by attackers

or being embedded in automatic attack tools, attack code which exploits low-level coding vulnerabilities performs as well when incorporated in autonomous attack agents. It was the case of the historical Morris worm, Code Red, Code Red II, or Blaster for instance. The efficiency of such attack techniques is derived directly from a high control on sensitive data in the memory of a running program acquirable from the nature of vulnerabilities they exploit.

The overall objective of this chapter is to provide thorough defense intelligence to protect computer systems from exploitation of low-level coding vulnerabilities. This chapter covers fundamental defensive approaches result of significant defensive research on the field. For each one of these defensive approaches this chapter describes the defense coverage, limitations, particular requirements, computational cost and applicability to real-world computer systems. In addition, this chapter gives an overview of both basic and advanced attack techniques derived from significant research on offensive attack capabilities carried out mainly by hackers underground, and provided in the form of nontraditional publications in highly technical hacker journals and hacker mailing lists. This chapter also provides information about evasion techniques built upon research on assessments of the robustness of operational defensive approaches.

WHAT ARE LOW-LEVEL CODING VULNERABILITIES AND HOW ARE THEY EXPLOITED?

These vulnerabilities may be defined as programming errors which open the way to an attacker to corrupt the memory of a program. Exploitation of such vulnerabilities generally takes the form of control-data or pure-data attacks. Control-data attacks corrupt memory management data for the purpose of transferring control to binary code inserted into the address space of a target process, or to existing arbitrary instructions which usually are forced to take attacker supplied data as arguments. Pure-data attacks (Chen, Xu, Sezer, Gauriar, & Iyer, 2005a; Pincus, & Baker, 2004) are built upon corruption of noncontrol data (i.e., computational data usually held by global or local variables in a program, such as, for example, user identification data, configuration data, decision making data, file descriptors, RPC procedure numbers, and so on).

Array Overflows

An array overflow is a programming error which occurs when no range checks are performed on a value which is used to index an array. The danger rises when such a value may be directly or indirectly affected by an attacker, and the array is filled with user-supplied data.

Buffer Overflows

A buffer overflow vulnerability is a programming error which allows data to be stored beyond the boundaries of a destination buffer, therefore overwriting adjacent memory locations and possibly further away. Buffer overflows may be caused by instructions which do not perform any bounds checking on a destination buffer when storing data into it. Some functions such as *strncpy()* allow a programmer to explicitly specify the number of bytes to copy to a destination buffer, but do not null-terminate the destination buffer. These apparently safe functions may lead to the creation of adjacent not null-terminated buffers. Such a situation in conjunction with a vulnerable function may cause an excessive amount of data to be copied to a destination buffer, thus overflowing it. In fact, the intention to copy one of these buffers to a destination buffer may copy the intended buffer along with one or more adjacent buffers causing an overflow of the destination buffer. A stack-based buffer overflow attack in one of its very first forms consists in injecting binary code and overwriting the saved instruction pointer stored on stack with the address of the injected code (Aleph1, 1996).

If executable memory areas where an attacker could inject binary code is not available or the available buffers are too small to hold the entire injected binary code, the attacker may overwrite the saved instruction pointer on stack with the address of existing instructions. The attacker may specify possible arguments by injecting them on stack along with the corrupting address. A common approach is to overwrite the saved instruction pointer with the address of the *system()* function of the libc dynamic library along with injecting on stack the address of the string that represents a command the attacker aims at executing on a target system. This attack technique is referred to as return-into-library (Nergal, 2001; Solar Designer, 1997). As a result of errors in handling the index of arrays in looping and iteration, a destination buffer may be overflowed by just a few bytes, more commonly by one byte or by five bytes.

Although such a buffer overflow is limited, it may be sufficient for an attacker to reach and corrupt the least significant byte of the saved frame pointer in a Little Endian architecture, and consequently dictate the address where the operating system pops a saved instruction pointer (Klog, 1999). Heap overflow attacks (Anonymous, 2001; Conover, 1999; Kaempf, 2001) are built upon the fact that most of the memory allocator algorithms such as System V in Solaris, Doug Lea's Malloc used by the GNU C Library, RtlHeap in Windows, and so on, store heap management data in band on the heap itself. By overflowing a buffer on heap, an attacker may corrupt such data and consequently force the execution of macros such as *unlink* or *frontlink* and make them use corrupted values in both sides of various assignments. This enables an attacker to write arbitrary values to memory locations of his choice.

In an indirect pointer overwrite (Bulba & Kil3r, 2000), an attacker overflows a buffer to overwrite a data pointer in which attacker supplied data is to be written. The attacker makes such a pointer point to a memory address where control data or sensitive pure data are stored. When the corrupted data pointer is dereferenced attacker supplied data overwrite the aforementioned control data or sensitive pure data. Similarly, through a buffer overflow an attacker may overwrite function pointers with the address of injected binary code.

Format String Vulnerabilities

A format string vulnerability is a programming error which consists in allowing an attacker to specify the format string to a format function. An attacker may have the possibility to specify a format string directly, such as, for example, when a programmer writes *printf(buff)* instead of *printf("%s," buff)* where *buff* is user supplied data, or indirectly when before being used by a vulnerable format function user supplied data is stored in other variables, possibly in a formatted form by other format functions. Format functions parse a format string one byte at a time. If a read byte is not equal to *%,* the format function copies this byte directly to output, otherwise, it means that a format directive is encountered and the corresponding value is retrieved from a memory address stored on stack. By providing format directives in a format string an attacker has the possibility to force a format function to operate on values, part of which are user supplied, stored on stack. For instance, by providing *%x* or *%s* an attacker could view memory content and by providing *%n* an attacker may write the number of bytes printed that far into the memory location pointed by an address retrieved from stack. An attacker could specify this address where to write at or read from by including it in the format string and popping values from the stack till reaching it. At that point, the inserted format directive will be processed by the vulnerable format function which will use it in these read/write operations. In the case of the *%n* format directive, the attacker in the format string may also define each byte of the value to be written

in the memory address specified in the format string as well (Scut & Team Teso, 2001; NOP Ninjas, 2001; Gera & Riq, 2002).

Integer Overflows

Integer errors are of two kinds, namely integer overflows and integer sign errors. An integer overflow occurs when an integer variable is assigned a value which is larger than the maximum value it can hold. When an integer variable is overflowed no buffers are smashed, thus an integer overflow vulnerability is not directly exploitable. Nevertheless, according to (JTC 1/SC 22/WG 14. ISO/IEC 9899, 1999), an overflown, unsigned integer variable is subject to a modulo of MAXINT +1, and the result of this operation becomes the new value of such a variable. The actual value of an overflown integer variable may become too small; therefore, it may be quite problematic when used as a size value in memory allocation operations in programs that are not prepared for such a failure. As a consequence of an integer overflow, too little memory may be allocated possibly leading to an overflow of a buffer on heap if such memory holds the destination buffer of an unprepared memory copy operation. An integer sign error occurs when a function which expects an unsigned integer variable as an argument is passed a signed integer variable instead. Such a function then implicitly casts the signed integer into an unsigned one. The danger stands in the fact that a large negative value may pass several maximum size tests in a program, but when implicitly cast into an unsigned integer and used in memory copy operations it may cause a buffer overflow.

Dangling Pointers

A dangling pointer vulnerability occurs when a pointer referenced by a program refers to already deallocated memory. Such a vulnerability may cause a program assume abnormal behavior, and in the case of a double free vulnerability, it may lead to a complete program exploitation (Dobrovitski, 2003). A double free occurs when deallocated memory is deallocated a second time. After a chunk on heap is freed twice, its forward and backward pointers will point to that chunk itself. If the program requests the allocation of a chunk of the same size as the double freed chunk, and the later chunk is first unlinked from the list of free chunks, after the unlink the forward and backward pointers of the doubled free chunk will still point to that chunk itself. Thus, the doubled free chunk will not really be unlinked from the list of free chunks. The memory allocator algorithm though assumes that this chunk is effectively unlinked, and the vulnerable program will use the user data part of the double freed chunk. The attack at this point proceeds as in a heap overflow exploitation.

RESEARCH ON DEFENSE AND EVASION

As different manifestations and new kinds of low-level coding vulnerabilities were discovered, and their exploitation got more and more sophisticated, the research directions on defense from such vulnerabilities also evolved in order to respond to functional limitations in current defensive techniques and protect from as many attack techniques as possible. In fact, a well-known problem in defensive research is the so-called problem of incomparability of mitigation techniques (Pincus & Baker, 2004). This problem is formulated as follows: for any two categories of mitigation techniques A and B, there are exploits prevented by A which are not prevented by B, and vice versa. Furthermore, the majority of significant defensive approaches is oriented towards control-data attacks (i.e., attacks which corrupt memory management data to alter control flow in a target program). This is due to the fact that pure-data attacks (i.e., attacks which corrupt noncontrol data) were believed to be quite rare against real-world programs.

Nevertheless, the research described in Chen et al. (2005a) demonstrates that pure-data attacks are realistic and such attacks could result in a security compromise equivalent to a security compromise caused by a control-data attack exploiting the same low-level coding vulnerability.

Representative Defense Mechanisms

The chapter provides a description of representative vulnerability mitigation techniques employed in protection from both basic and advanced exploitation of low-level coding vulnerabilities. A summary of these vulnerability mitigation techniques is given in Table 1. In Table 1, and throughout the remaining of this chapter, these techniques are treated according to an order defined by the time they were first presented, although some of them evolved to reflect several evasion techniques and limitations in their first releases. Randomizing the instruction set for each process performs well against code injection, but in its very design, such technique does not counter return-into-library attacks. Randomization of the address space layout provides good protection, but in a 32-bit architecture, the randomization granularity is not sufficient to resist brute force derandomization attacks. Thus, this technique is much more robust when employed in 64-bit architectures. The canary mechanism protects control-data on stack or heap if an attacker performs a sequential memory write from the injection point till reaching control data, but such mechanism is not designed to protect from straight memory corruption which leaves canaries intact. A dual stack mechanism preserves the integrity of saved instruction pointers, but leaves unprotected all other control data.

Denying a specific vulnerability conditions prevents the exploitation of that vulnerability. Nevertheless, its defense coverage is quite limited. Implementing nonexecutable memory pages provides good protection against execution of injected binary code, and it is quite useful when complementing address space layout randomization. Pointer encryption protects control data, but it is vulnerable to a combination of brute forcing with a partial pointer overwrite attack. Most of the mitigation techniques provided by research on defense suffer from the problem of incomparability of mitigation techniques and are oriented towards protection from control-data attacks. As pure-data attacks have been demonstrated to be realistic, such a problem has been addressed in later research. The pointer taintedness detection and the FireBuff defensive approach all alone can protect from any kind of low-level coding vulnerability exploitation including pure-data attacks. Taking into account that these techniques neutralize the usability of input data as an attack instrument, they are expected to protect from novel control-data or pure-data attacks.

Nonexecutable Memory Pages

The Openwall kernel patch (Solar Designer, 2006) makes the stack, heap and static data areas nonexecutable in order to counter execution of injected binary code. Nevertheless, a successful return-into-library attack would result in evasion of such a security mechanism (Alexander, 2005). Furthermore, a nonexecutable stack may break code with legitimate executable stack needs. PaX Team, along with ASLR against return-into-library attacks propose the NOEXEC functional-

Table 1. A summary of mitigation techniques and their defense coverage

Defense mechanism	Attack vectors it aims at defending against	Attack techniques or attack support vectors not defended against	Evasion techniques
Nonexecutable memory	Code injection	Return-into-library Pure-data attacks	-
Canaries	All memory corruption attacks targeting control data saved on stack Heap overflow attacks	Format string attacks or indirect pointer overwrite corrupting control data other than those saved on stack Pure-data attacks besides those carried out through a heap overflow	-
Dual stack	All memory corruption attacks targeting the saved instruction pointer	Frame pointer overwrite Format string or heap overflow attacks targeting control data other than the saved instruction pointer Pure-data attacks	-
Denial of specific vulnerability conditions	Format string attacks Stack-based overflows	Heap overflows Pure-data attacks	-
Instruction set randomization	Code injection	Return-into-library Pure-data attacks	Incremental key-guessing (return & jump techniques)
Address space randomization	Return-into-library Pure-data attacks	Code injection	Brute-force derandomization
Data stream cipher encryption	All memory corruption vulnerabilities	-	Partial pointer overwrite (in the case of PointGuard only)
Pointer taintedness	All memory corruption vulnerabilities	-	-

ity which disallows the creation of writable/executable memory mappings. PaX marks each page that it intends to make nonexecutable as requiring root privileges. Such a marking is performed through page privilege flags. When one of these pages is accessed, a page fault is generated. Consequently, PaX checks to determine whether the access to the protected page was a data access or the CPU tried to execute an instruction. In the later case, PaX deems a code injection attacks is in place and aborts program execution.

Canaries

A method for protecting from exploitation of buffer overflows carried out as a control-data attack is to place between pure data and control data a boundary word referred to as a canary. The integrity of the canary is checked right before using control data. If the canary

has been modified, it means that a buffer overflow has occurred, and action may be taken. There are three kinds of canaries, namely:

- Terminator canaries whose value is composed of string terminators such as *0x0d* (carriage return), *0x0a* (line feed), *0x00* (Null), and *0xff* (end of file). If not overwritten, these bytes terminate string copy operations.
- Random canaries whose value is generated randomly.
- Random XOR canaries whose value is the result of an XOR between a randomly generated word and specific control data.

StackGuard's (Cowan, Pu, Maier, Hinton, Bakke, Beattie, Grier, Wagle, & Zhang, 1998) aims at detecting corruption of a saved instruction pointer before a function returns. During a function prologue StackGuard stores a random canary next to the saved instruction pointer on stack. When such a function enters its epilogue StackGuard checks that the canary is intact before allowing this function to return. If the original value of the canary has been corrupted, it means that a stack overflow has occurred; consequently, StackGuard reports the incident in a log file and aborts program execution. Thus, in practice, StackGuard focuses exclusively on the prevention of stack-based buffer overflow attacks which corrupt the saved instruction pointer. Nevertheless, overflowing a buffer on stack and performing a sequential write of bytes till overwriting a saved instruction pointer is just one way to corrupt such a saved instruction pointer. As shown by Bulba and Kil3r (2000), an attacker may bypass StackGuard protection by performing essentially an indirect pointer overwrite or overflowing long jump buffers, both not necessarily located on stack. Furthermore, obviously, a format string attack or a heap overflow attack may corrupt a saved instruction pointer without corrupting the canary.

In response to such a limitation, authors of StackGuard proposed to employ a random XOR canary instead of a random canary (i.e., XOR the random canary with the saved instruction pointer). During a function epilogue, StackGuard XORs the canary with the actual saved instruction pointer. If an attacker has corrupted the saved instruction pointer anyhow, the recomputed canary and the original value of the canary will mismatch. This scheme does not protect other control data saved on stack such as a saved frame pointer or saved register values. A frame pointer overwrite attack could still corrupt a saved frame pointer and exploit a stack-based buffer overflow without being caught by the canary mechanism. StackGuard dealt with this limitation by storing the canary between control data and noncontrol data in each stack frame (Wagle & Cowan, 2003). StackGuard has been implemented as a patch to GCC, and it has employed all the three kinds of canaries. The performance overhead induced by StackGuard is reported to be modest.

Other canary-based approaches have been built upon StackGuard. ProPolice (Etoh & Yoda, 2000), for instance, is based on StackGuard and protects the saved instruction pointer and the saved frame pointer from stack-based buffer overflows by storing on stack a randomly generated guard variable (i.e., a random canary) between these saved pointers and noncontrol data. Like in StackGuard the integrity of the canary is checked during a function epilogue before using

any of the protected pointers. Microsoft Visual C++ .NET compiler provides the /GS flag for the activation of a canary-based security mechanism (Bray, 2002). /GS causes the generation of a random cookie value with the same size as a pointer. The randomness of such a canary comes from processor counters. During a function prologue, the canary is XORed with the saved instruction pointer and is saved between control data and noncontrol data on stack. During a function epilogue, the canary is XORed with the actual value of the saved instruction pointer, and if the resulting value of the canary is not the same as its original value, a dialog box is displayed saying "Buffer overrun detected" and subsequently the program is terminated. The performance overhead, in most cases, does not exceed 2%.

ContraPolice (Krennmair, 2003) provides a canary-based mechanism for protecting from heap overflow attacks. When memory is allocated on heap, ContraPolice places a random canary before and after the allocated memory. Integrity checks on the canaries are performed before exiting from any function which has copied data into the canary confined memory. If canaries do not match, ContraPolice aborts execution of the protected program. ContraPolice is implemented as an extension to the *libc* library, but its performance cost is generally noticeable.

Dual Stack

StackShield (StackShield, http://www.angelfire. com/sk/stackshield) creates a separate stack to store a copy of a function's saved instruction pointer. During the prologue of each function, StackShield copies the corresponding saved instruction pointer to such separate stack, and during a function epilogue StackShield copies the copy of the saved instruction pointer from the separate stack back to the saved instruction pointer location on stack. Thus, StackShield forces a function to correctly return to its original caller. The protection provided by StackShield is quite limited as it exclusively focuses on protection from attacks which corrupt the saved instruction pointer. All other control data remain unprotected. As demonstrated in Bulba and Kil3r (2000), a frame pointer overwrite attack could exploit a program without being blocked by StackShield. Libverify (Baratloo, Singh, & Tsai, 2000) is a library which creates a separate canary stack located on heap. Libverify alters functions in such a way that a function during its prologue saves a copy of the saved instruction pointer on the canary stack. During function epilogue, the actual value of the stored instruction pointer on stack is compared with the value saved on canary stack. If these two values are not equal, Libverify rises a security alert and aborts execution of the program. RAD (Chiueh & Hsu, 2001) (i.e., return address defender) is quite similar to StackShield. When a new stack frame is created, RAD stores a copy of the saved instruction pointer. Before a function returns, the saved instruction pointer about to be referenced is compared with the saved value, and if they are not equal, the program is halted. These defensive approaches are quite limited, as they protect saved instruction pointers only, leaving all other control data unprotected.

Denial of Specific Vulnerability Conditions

FormatGuard (Cowan, Barringer, Beattie, Kroah-Hartman, Frantzen, & Lokier, 2001) is a mitigation technique against format string attacks. FormatGuard compares the number of actual parameters that a programmer has passed to a format function against the number of parameters the format string in the format function calls for. If the number of actual parameters is found to be less than the number of parameters the format string calls for, then FormatGuard considers such a fact as an indication of an ongoing attack. Consequently, FormatGuard reports the possible incident in a log file and aborts program execution. FormatGuard is reported to impose a 1.3 % run time overhead in the worst case, and in most cases, such an overhead is quite lower than that. Libformat (Robbins, 2001) is a library which checks if a program calls a format function with a format string that is writable and contains a *%n* format directive, in which case Libformat aborts program execution. As a writable format, string and a *%n* format directive are both legal Libformat may raise false positives.

Libsafe (Baratloo, Singh, & Tsai, 2006) is a library which intercepts each call to a library function vulnerable to buffer overflows. Libsafe directs such a call to a function which implements the same functionality as the original function but in a way that any buffer overflows are contained within the current stack frame. Libsafe automatically estimates the maximum safe size of a buffer by realizing that such a buffer cannot extend beyond the boundary of the current stack frame. The substitute version of the original vulnerable function limits any buffer write within the estimated buffer size. In its 2.0 version, Libsafe protects from format string attacks by rejecting dangerous format directives such as %n which write to the location where the saved instruction pointer is saved. Libsafe, however, cannot protect from exploitation of heap overflows or from corruption of data pointers or function pointers.

Instruction Set Randomization

Seeking inspiration from biological systems, Forrest, Somayaji, and Ackley (1997) propose randomization as a potential instrument to acquire software diversity. Their research is based on the fact that diversity is a source of robustness in biological systems; therefore, randomization could potentially increase the robustness of software systems. Instruction set randomization (Barrantes, Ackley, Forrest, Palmer, Stefanovic, & Zovi, 2003; Kc, Keromytis, & Prevelakis, 2003) is a technique devised along this line to disrupt the attack usability of binary code injected into the address space of a protected process. The main idea behind instruction set randomization is to create a randomized instruction set for each process. These process-specific instruction sets are to be kept secret from attackers. If an attacker carries out a code injection attack against a protected process, and does not know how to produce machine code according to the instruction set of the protected process, then the attacker will end up with injecting invalid binary code.

A common method of generating a process-specific instruction set is to encrypt the instructions of a program with a random key. Program instructions are then loaded into main memory as cipher text, and each instruction is decrypted right before being processed by the CPU. The decryption of each instruction is to be performed in such a way that no instruction is ever present in main memory in a decrypted form. A cryptographic key is generated randomly and it is associated with a specific process. A common cryptographic scheme is to encrypt program instructions by XORing them with the associated key, and decrypt encrypted program instructions by XORing them again with the associated key.

(Barrantes et al., 2003) propose an instruction set randomization technique implemented as a proof of concept tool at machine emulator level called RISE (randomized instruction set emulator). RISE aims at preventing both local and remote code injection attacks. Their approach generates at load time a pseudo-random cryptographic key to be employed in the creation of a private instruction set for a process. The cryptographic key is stored in the process address space and its length is equal to the number of bits of the overall program instructions. Program instructions are encrypted all at one time by being XOR'ed with the key when they are loaded into the emulator. At run time, each instruction gets decrypted separately when it is fetched for execution by the emulator. RISE has notable difficulties in supporting dynamic libraries whose code is shared among different processes as each process has its own private key and must use the same instruction set as the libraries it requires. When RISE encrypts dynamic library code with a process key, the operating system performs a copy-on-write and stores a private copy of these encrypted instructions in the virtual memory of the protected process. This method allows coexistence of instruction set randomization and shared libraries, but wastes a considerable amount of main memory, therefore it is in conflict with the usefulness of shared libraries themselves. RISE is based on the Valgrind x86 emulator (Seward & Nethercote, 2003) and adds an execution latency of 5% to a program running under Valgrind. Kc et al. (2003) also propose instruction set randomization to prevent any kind of code injection attack. They demonstrate their instruction set randomization scheme in protection of both binary programs and programs written in an interpreted language such as Perl. With regard to the protection of binaries (Kc et al., 2003) generate a 32-bit key for each binary and perform ELF binary rewriting through an extended *objcopy* utility to encrypt existing instructions with the cryptographic key. As an encryption scheme, they propose the XOR scheme or a secret 32-bit transposition. The decryption key is then embedded in the executable's header. At load time, the operating system extracts the decryption key from the program header and stores it in the process control block. At run time, a special instruction called *GAVL* is used to copy the decryption key from the process control block to a special CPU register which holds the key during program execution. Each program instruction is decrypted with the key in the special CPU register when it is fetched from main memory and before it gets executed by the CPU. The approach proposed by Kc et al. (2003) is oriented towards attacks targeting remote services and does not address locally mounted attacks. In addition, this approach does not handle dynamic libraries, thus it requires a program to be statically linked, and its performance cost is quite high. Kc et al. (2003) implemented their approach in bochs-x86 Pentium emulator (Lawton, 2006) to demonstrate the feasibility of their approach. While countering code injection represents a conquest, the overall defense

against exploitation of low-level coding vulnerabilities provided by instruction set randomization is limited. Even at design level, instruction set randomization cannot prevent attacks carried out in a return-into-library form. In this exploitation technique, no injected binary code is ever needed, as existing instructions are used to subvert a target program. Obviously, instruction set randomization cannot do anything to protect from pure-data exploits.

Research carried out by Sovarel, Evans, and Paul (2005) shows that a determined attacker may be able to circumvent instruction set randomization by determining the randomization key. Their work describes two incremental key-guessing attacks, namely the return attack and the jump attack, applied against a program running on an x86 processor and protected by instruction set randomization. These two attacks are demonstrated assuming the target program is vulnerable to a stack-based buffer overflow. The return attack consists in injecting into an executable memory location within the address space of the target process a near return control instruction encrypted with a guessed key. Such an instruction $0xc3$ is one byte long, thus the correct key may be found with at most 256 key guesses. During the buffer overflow, the saved instruction pointer is overwritten with the address where the injected return instruction encrypted with a guessed key is stored, the saved frame pointer is preserved, and the original saved instruction pointer is stored just above the overwritten instruction pointer, assuming the stack grows downwards. If the guess is correct, when the vulnerable function returns the injected return instruction will be decrypted correctly and will be executed.

After its execution, the original saved instruction pointer is used as a return address and the program resumes its execution as if no control hijacking took place. Nevertheless, an attacker usually does not know in advance the saved instruction pointer or the saved frame pointer stored in the stack frame of a vulnerable function. The jump attack consists in injecting a near jump instruction ($0xeb$) with an offset of -2 ($0xfe$), thus two bytes altogether, encrypted with a guessed key. During the buffer overflow the saved instruction pointer is overwritten with the address where the injected near jump instruction encrypted with a guessed key is stored. If the guess is correct, then when the vulnerable function returns the injected instruction is decrypted correctly and is executed by the CPU. When executed, the injected near jump jumps back to itself causing an infinite loop. The jump attack is feasible when carried out against programs which when executing normally keep a socket open to the client. If after the jump attack the socket remains open, it means that the program has fallen into an infinite loop, thus the guess is correct.

If the socket gets closed, it means that the program crashed due to the incorrect decryption of the injected jump instruction, thus the guess is wrong. After successfully carrying out a return attack or a jump one, an attacker has guessed correctly one or two bytes, respectively. In order to guess the remaining key bytes, an attacker changes the position of the guessed byte and goes ahead like in the first step. In the case of the return attack, for instance, if in a first successful attack the attacker has guessed the first byte of the key he injects the near return instruction encrypted with a guessed byte in the next position, and overwrites the saved instruction pointer with the address of the next position, and so on. The return and the jump attack are feasible in programs which allow an attacker to distinguish between correct and incorrect guesses. As failed key guesses will make the target process crash, incremental key guessing attacks are feasible when carried out either against programs whose instructions are encrypted with the same key each time they are executed, or against programs whose forked children are encrypted with the same key and the attack is directed towards a child.

Address Space Randomization

PaX ASLR (Address Space Layout Randomization) (PaX Team, 2006) is a kernel patch which randomizes at load time the addresses used by a process created from an ELF executable making use of ELF dynamic libraries and running on a 32-bit x86 architecture. It does so for the purpose of building a barrier against attacks which exploit low-level coding vulnerabilities in these processes, since such attacks generally are built upon prior knowledge of certain memory addresses. PaX ASLR initializes with random values three variables, namely *delta_exec*, *delta_mmap*, and *delta_stack*, which it adds to the base address of the memory area containing executable code, initialized data and uninitialized data, to the base address of the memory area containing the heap, dynamic libraries, thread stacks and shared memory, and to the base address of the area containing the main stack, respectively. The *delta_exec* and *delta_mmap* variables are limited to 16 bits of randomness, while the *delta_stack* variable is limited to 24 bits of randomness.

Bhatkar, DuVarney, and Sekar (2003) randomize at compile and link time the base address of the program code, stack, and heap memory areas. Furthermore, this approach randomizes the distances between functions and adds a random space between adjacent functions. Nevertheless, this approach produces a static address space randomization which makes it less difficult for an attacker to evade it compared to dynamic address space randomization. Xu, Kalbarczyk, and Iyer (2003) modify the dynamic loader to perform a load-time address space randomization similar to PaX ASLR. In addition their approach randomizes the location of GOT (global offset table), patches PLT (procedure linkage table) and does not require any kernel modifications. Nevertheless, the address randomness introduced by this approach is limited to 13 bits, three bits less than PaX ASLR.

Shacham, Page, and Pfaff (2004) evade PaX ASLR in a few minutes by employing a brute-force derandomization attack on the *delta_mmap* variable. As this variable's randomness is limited to 16 bits, a brute force attack is quite feasible to determine its value. Once the value of *delta_mmap* is determined the authors use it to mount a return-into-library attack. The work described in Shacham et al. (2004) evades also the approach described in Xu et al. (2003), as the later uses only 13 bits of randomness, and the aforementioned attacks do not need information on GOT or PLT.

Xu and Chapin (2006) devise an address space randomization technique to protect from return-into-library attacks, assuming that other complementary mechanisms are deployed to protect from execution of injected binary code. Such a technique consists in partitioning a program into small blocks referred to as islands, and randomly mapping them at load time into the address space of a protected program. The partition is such that from one island attackers can deduce little information about other islands. Every island is compiled into a separate shared library and the ABI (application binary interface) is used to access code and data on different islands. This allows PLT (procedure linkage table) and GOT (global offset table) to be distributed into islands and to be mapped randomly into the address space along with islands in order to reduce possible memory information leakage. Xu and Chapin (2006) devised a new relocation algorithm in the dynamic loader in order to reduce loading and randomization time to quite acceptable values.

Data Stream Cipher Encryption

PointGuard (Cowan, Beattie, Johansen, & Wagle, 2003) is a compiler technique which encrypts pointers with a random key the length of a memory word through the XOR operation when they are stored in main memory. PointGuard decrypts encrypted pointers by XOR'ing them again with the same encryption key when they are loaded into CPU registers. As attackers do not know the encryption key, they cannot corrupt any pointer in main memory with a value that is such, that when decrypted would result in a value useful to the attack. After being loaded into registers, pointers are consequently decrypted, but in that stage, attackers cannot corrupt them as registers are not addressable. PointGuard provides protection from any kind of control-data attack and from a part of pure-data attacks, namely from those pure-data attacks which corrupt function pointers or data pointers.

PointGuard may be evaded by a partial pointer overwrite (Alexander, 2005), which generally consists in corrupting just one byte of a pointer. On a Little Endian architecture, for instance, an attacker may overflow a buffer on stack and corrupt the least significant byte of a pointer as such byte is stored at a lower address and will be the first byte of the pointer to be corrupted. The remaining uncorrupted bytes of the pointer will be decrypted correctly by PointGuard; therefore, the overall value of the partially corrupted pointer may point to a memory location whose three most significant bytes are the same as a memory location which is of interest to an attacker. The attacker then may employ brute forcing to partially corrupt a pointer possibly falling into injected code or existing program instructions other than the intended ones. The same attack goal may be achieved on any architecture through a format string attack or a heap overflow attack to corrupt any byte of an encrypted pointer.

FireBuff (Bellettini & Rrushi, 2006) is a defensive approach which is intended to protect from any kind of control-data or pure-data attack. Although FireBuff has been implemented under Linux as a proof of concept, its conceptual design is acceptably OS independent. FireBuff encrypts in a stream cipher way with a random key all data that are input to a protected program. These data are preserved as cipher text in main memory. When program instructions need to process user supplied data, such data are first copied to a memory region referred to as temporary storage area. The temporary storage area is mapped memory made readable and writable but not executable through the *mprotect()* system call. The encrypted data are decrypted in the temporary storage area as many bytes at a time as the number of bytes processed by the instruction at a time. For instance, if an instruction such as *printf()* processes data one byte at a time, the data in the temporary storage area to be processed by such instruction will be decrypted one byte at a time. Decrypted data in the temporary storage area are destroyed immediately after being processed by program instructions. FireBuff definitely thwarts any kind of attack technique exploiting control data or pure data as such data will be corrupted with the result of the encryption with a random key of the original values specified by attackers. In addition, FireBuff protects from code injection. Binary code injected into the address space of a FireBuff protected process will be encrypted while residing in main memory, therefore the CPU will not recognize such encrypted data as valid machine code.

Pointer Taintedness

Pointer taintedness detection (Chen, Xu, Nakka, Kalbarczyk, & Iyer, 2005b) is an architectural technique which protects from both control-data attacks and pure-data attacks. It has been implemented on the Simple Scalar processor simulator. Such a defensive approach extends the existing memory system by adding an additional taintedness bit which is associated with each byte. CPU registers are also extended to include a taintedness bit for each byte. A taintedness bit is set if the respective byte is part of input data. Thus, input data are marked tainted and taintedness bits are properly propagated through the memory when tainted data are used as source in CPU operations. If a tainted word is used as an address to access data or code, the CPU raises an exception. Upon receiving such an exception, the operating system aborts the execution of a protected program in order to block an ongoing attack.

CONCLUSION

Protection from memory corruption attacks is of paramount importance to the security of computer systems. In fact, the low-level coding vulnerabilities which those attacks exploit are subject to most of the security advisories made public by CERT. Further, memory corruption attack techniques have evolved from very basic stack smashing techniques to highly advanced offensive capabilities evading several intrusion prevention and/or detection systems. This chapter has focused on the main vulnerability mitigation techniques which have been devised and implemented for the purpose of countering memory corruption attacks exploiting low-level coding vulnerabilities. The chapter has provided a description of the main research ideas behind those run-time defensive techniques, their defense coverage area, their feasibility and limitations, and the evasion techniques which were subsequently devised to bypass their protective capabilities. In conclusion, the chapter highlights approaches such as Chen's pointer taintedness detection technique and the FireBuff host-based intrusion prevention technique which are proposed as stand-alone defensive techniques against both control-data and pure-data attacks, thus moving towards an alleviation of the problem of incomparability of mitigation techniques.

REFERENCES

Aleph1. (1996). Smashing the stack for fun and profit. *Phrack Magazine, 7*(49).

Alexander, S. (2005). *Defeating compiler-level buffer overflow protection.* j-LOGIN, 30(3), 59-71.

Anonymous. 2001. Once upon a free(). *Phrack Magazine, 9*(57).

Baratloo, A., Singh, N., & Tsai T. (2000). Transparent run time defense against stack smashing attacks. In *Proceedings of the USENIX 2000 Annual Technical Conference* (pp. 251-262). San Diego, CA.

Baratloo, A., Singh, N, & Tsai T. (2006). *Libsafe: Protecting critical elements of stacks.* Retrieved May 2, 2008, from http://www.bell-labs.com/org/11356/libsafe.html

Barrantes, E.G., Ackley, D.H., Forrest, S., Palmer, T.S., Stefanovic, D., & Zovi D. (2003). Randomized instruction set emulation to disrupt binary code injection attacks. In *Proceedings of the 10th ACM Conference on Computer and Communications Security (CCS2003)* (pp. 281-289). Washington, U.S.A.

Bellettini, C., & Rrushi, J. L. (2008). Enforcing logical boundaries on potentially hostile data to defend against memory corrupted attacks. In *Proceedings of the 2nd Annual IFIP Working Group 11.10 International Conference on Critical Infrastructure Protection,* George Mason University, Arlington, VA.

Bellettini, C., & Rrushi, J.L. (2006). *FireBuff: A defensive approach against control-data and pure-data attacks.* Technical Report of Università Degli Studi di Milano.

Bhatkar, S., DuVarney, D., & Sekar, R. (2003). Address obfuscation: An efficient approach to combat a broad range of memory error exploits. In *Proceedings of the 12th USENIX Security Symposium* (pp. 105-120). Washington D.C., U.S.A.

Bray, B. (2002). *Compiler security checks in depth.* Retrieved May 2, 2008, from http://msdn.microsoft.com/library/default.asp?url=/library/enus/dv_vstechart/html/vctchcompilersecuritychecksindepth.asp

Bulba, & Kil3r. (2000). Bypassing stackguard and stackshield. *Phrack Magazine, 10*(56).

Chen, S., Xu, J., Sezer, E.C., Gauriar, P., & Iyer, R.K. (2005). Noncontrol-data attacks are realistic threats. In *Proceedings of the 14th USENIX Security Symposium* (pp. 177-192). Baltimore, U.S.A.

Chen, S., Xu, J., Nakka, N., Kalbarczyk, Z., & Iyer, R.K. (2005). Defeating memory corruption attacks via pointer taintedness detection. In *Proceedings of the IEEE International Conference on Dependable Systems and Neworks* (pp. 378-387). Yokohama, Japan.

Chiueh, T., & Hsu, F. (2001). RAD: A compile-time solution to buffer overflow attacks. In *Proceedings of the 21th International Conference on Distributed Computing Systems (ICDCS).* Phoenix, AZ.

Conover, M. (1999). w00w00 security team. *w00w00 on Heap Overflows.* Retrieved May 2, 2008, from http://www.w00w00.org/files/articles/heaptut.txt

Cowan, C., Barringer, M., Beattie, S, Kroah-Hartman, G., Frantzen, M, & Lokier, J. (2001). FormatGuard: Automatic protection from printf format string vulnerabilities. In *Proceedings of the 10th USENIX Security Symposium* (pp. 191-200). Washington, District of Columbia, U.S.A.

Cowan, C., Beattie, S., Johansen, J., & Wagle P. (2003). PointGuard: Protecting pointers from buffer overflow vulnerabilities. In *Proceedings of the 12th USENIX Security Symposium* (pp. 91-104). Washington, District of Columbia, U.S.A.

Cowan, C., Pu, C., Maier, D., Hinton, H., Bakke, P., Beattie, S., Grier, A., Wagle, P., & Zhang, Q. (1998). StackGuard: Automatic adaptive detection and prevention of buffer-overflow attacks. In *Proceedings of the 7th USENIX Security Conference* (pp. 63-77). San Antonio, TX.

Dobrovitski, I. (2003). Exploit for CVS double free() for linux pserver. *Bugtraq mailinglist*. Retrieved May 2, 2008, from http://seclists.org/lists/bugtraq/2003/Feb/0042.html

Etoh, H., & Yoda, K. (2000). *Protecting from stack-smashing attacks*. Retrieved May 2, 2008, from http://www.research.ibm.com/trl/projects/security/ssp/main.html

Forrest, S., Somayaji, A., & Ackley, D. (1997). Building diverse computer systems. In *Proceedings of the 6th Workshop on Hot Topics in Operating Systems* (pp. 67-72). Cape Cod, MA.

Gera, & Riq. (2002). Advances in format string exploitation. *Phrack Magazine, 11*(59).

JTC 1/SC 22/WG 14. ISO/IEC 9899. (1999). *Programming languages—C*. Technical report, International Organization for Standards.

Kaempf, M. (2001). Vudo—an object superstitiously believed to embody magical powers. *Phrack Magazine, 8*(57).

Kc, G.S., Keromytis, A.D., & Prevelakis V. (2003). Countering code-injection attacks with instruction-set randomization. In *Proceedings of the 10th ACM Conference on Computer and Communications Security* (pp. 272-280). Washington, U.S.A.

Klog. (1999). The frame pointer overwrite. *Phrack Magazine, 9*(55).

Krennmair, A. (2003), *ContraPolice: A libc extension for protecting applications from heap-smashing attacks*. Retrieved May 2, 2008, http://www.synflood.at/papers/cp.pdf

Lawton, K. (2006). *Bochs emulator*. Retrieved May 2, 2008, from http://bochs.sourceforge.net

Nergal. (2001). The advanced return-into-lib(c) exploits: PaX case study. *Phrack Magazine, 11*(58).

NOP Ninjas. (2001). *Format string technique*. Retrieved May 2, 2008, from http://doc.bughunter.net/format-string/technique.html

PaX Team. (2006). *Documentation for the PaX project*. Retrieved May 2, 2008, from http://pax.grsecurity.net/docs

Pincus, J., & Baker, B. (2004). *Mitigations for low-level coding vulnerabilities: Incomparability and limitations*. Retrieved May 2, 2008, from http://research.microsoft.com/users/jpincus/mitigations.pdf

Rivas, J.M.B. (2001). *Overwriting the .dtors section*. Retrieved May 2, 2008, from http://synnergy.net/downloads/papers/dtors.txt

Robbins, T.J. (2001). *Libformat*. Retrieved May 2, 2008, from http://the.wiretapped.net/security/host-security/libformat

Scut, & Team Teso. (2001). *Exploiting format string vulnerabilities version 1.1*. Retrieved May 2, 2008, from http://julianor.tripod.com/teso-fs1-1.pdf

Seward, J., & Nethercote, N. (2003). Valgrind: A program supervision framework. *Electronic Notes in Theoretical Computer Science, 89*(2).

Shacham, H., Page, K., & Pfaff, B. (2004). On the effectiveness of address-space randomization. In *Proceedings of the 11th ACM conference on Computer and Communications Security (CCS)* (pp. 298-307). Washington, District of Columbia, U.S.A.

Solar Designer. (2006). *Openwall: Nonexecutable stack patch*. Retrieved May 2, 2008, from http://www.openwall.com/linux

Solar Designer. (1997). *Getting around nonexecutable stack (and fix)*. Bugtraq Mailing List.

Sovarel, A.N., Evans, D., & Paul N. (2005). Where's the FEEB? The effectiveness of instruction set randomization. In *Proceedings of the 14th USENIX Security Symposium* (pp. 145-160). Baltimore, MD, U.S.A.

Xu, J., Kalbarczyk, Z., & Iyer, R. (2003). Transparent runtime randomization for security. In *Proceedings of the 22nd Symposium on Reliable Distributed Systems* (pp. 260-269). IEEE Computer Society, Florence, Italy.

Xu, H., & Chapin, S.J. (2006). Improving address space randomization with a dynamic offset randomization technique. In *Proceedings of the ACM Symposium on Applied Computing* (pp. 384-391). Dijon, France.

Wagle, P., & Cowan, C. (2003). StackGuard: Simple stack smash protection for GCC. In *Proceedings of the GCC Developers Summit* (pp. 243-256). Ottawa, Ontario, Canada.

KEY TERMS

Canary: A word placed on the boundary of a buffer in order to detect sequential overwrites of that buffer. Detection is performed by checking the integrity of a canary.

Control-Data Attack: Exploitation of a vulnerability built upon corruption of data which are used by a target process for memory management purposes.

Injection: Insertion of attack data into the address space of a target process. Generally, the attack data are machine executable code or parameters to be passed to program functions.

Low-Level Coding Vulnerability: A programming language weakness which, when combined with a programming error, could enable an attacker to cor-

rupt the memory of a given process and consequently violate the security of a computer system.

Memory Overflow: The phenomenon of writing beyond the boundaries of a destination buffer in memory.

Pointer: A data type whose value is the address of the memory location where another value is stored.

Pure-Data Attack: Exploitation of a vulnerability built upon corruption of computational data of a target process.

Run-Time Vulnerability Mitigation: A defensive technique which intervenes in the execution of a process to be protected while the latter is running.

Stream Cipher: Symmetric cryptography whose encryption and decryption operations typically consist in XOR'ing a secret key with plain text bits and cipher text bits, respectively.

Tainted Pointer: A pointer whose value originates from input data.

Chapter XIII
Design and Implementation of a Distributed Firewall

Dalila Boughaci
LRIA-USTHB, Algeria

Brahim Oubeka
LRIA-USTHB, Algeria

Abdelkader Aissioui
LRIA-USTHB, Algeria

Habiba Drias
LRIA-USTHB, Algeria

Belaïd Benhamou
Technopôle de Château-Gombert, France

ABSTRACT

This chapter presents the design and the implementation of a decentralized firewall. The latter uses autonomous agents to coordinately control the traffic on the network. The proposed framework includes a set of controllers' agents that ensure the packets filtering services, a proxy agent that plays a role of a proxy server and an identifier agent which is responsible for user authentication. The decentralization of the different agents' activities is managed by an administrator agent which is a core point for launching the most important operations of the access control. A prototype has been designed and implemented. Furthermore, the authors hope that the underlying framework will inform researchers of a possible way to implement a decentralized firewall to improve the current solution, and will help readers understand the need for techniques and tools such as firewalls that are useful to protect their network traffic.

INTRODUCTION

A firewall is a software program or a hardware device operating as packet filters or an application level gateway. It permits to analyze the network traffic and allow or disallow the transfer of data on base of certain rules.

In a central firewall solution, all traffic from internal corporate network to the Internet and vice versa has to pass through the firewall. However, an increasing bandwidth causes problems to that solution.

Also, bottlenecks and potential vulnerabilities for the whole network communication may be caused by the central solution.

To improve the classical solution, some approaches have been proposed. Among them, we cite: the smart data servers to manage distributed personnel firewalls with a central tool proposed in Haffner, Roth, Heuer, Engel, and Meinel (2001). In Bellovin (1999) and Ioannidis, Keromytis, Bellovin, and Smith (2000), the authors propose a distributed firewall where IPsec is used to distribute credentials that express parts of the overall network policy. A prototype using KeyNote (Blaze, Feigenbaum, and Keromytis, 1999) trust management system is implemented in (Ioannidis et al., 2000). Al-Shaer and Hamed (2004) and Al-Shaer, Hamed, Boutaba, and Hasan (2005) propose a set of techniques to automatically discover policy anomalies in centralized and distributed firewalls, and recently, Wang, Behera, Wong, Helmer, Honavar, Miller, and Lutz (2006), Boughaci, Drias, Bendib, Bouznit, and Benhamou, (2006a), and Boughaci, Oubeka, Aissioui, and Benhamou (2006b) use agents to implement some security tools.

In the following, we will provide a possible way to implement a decentralized firewall by the use of autonomous agents.

The implementation of firewalls with agent technology is one of the new paradigms for the access control for computer systems. In this chapter, an agent-based firewall is proposed. It uses autonomous agents to coordinately control the traffic on the network. The proposed system allows controllers and proxy agents to collaborate to provide a complete system permitting the distribution of the access control and the automation of the complex administration tasks. A prototype has been designed and implemented.

The utilization of agents in the domain of computer network security for the access control is justified by the fact that the cooperative work offered by agents can help firewalls to decrease the congestion by distributing the access control on different intelligent entities (agents) and automating the complex administration tasks.

The chapter is organized as follows. The following section gives some background on both firewalls and software agents. The third section describes our proposed firewall. Some implementation details are given in the fourth section. Finally, the fifth section concludes and gives some future works.

BACKGROUND

This section is intended to give the reader a basic understanding of traditional firewalls and software agents.

Firewall

A firewall is a security tool used to protect a computer network from unauthorized access. It may be a hardware device, a software program, or a combination of both (Brown, Davies, & Price, 1995; Mogul, Rashid, & Accetto, 1987).

The firewall is used mainly for controlling the traversal of packets across the boundaries of the computer network based on a specific security policy defined by the network administrator. However, the configuration of the firewall requires a considerable understanding of network protocols and of computer security. A small mistake can make the security of the network in a danger.

Types of Firewalls

There are two main categories of firewalls: network layer firewalls and application firewalls.

- **Network layer firewall** called also *packet filter* that operates as IP-packet filter. It allows or disallows the transfer of data on base of certain rules defined by the firewall administrator. It can filter the network traffic based on many packet attributes like: the source IP address, the source port, the destination IP address, the destination port, the protocol type (TCP/UDP), and also the destination service, like www or FTP.
- **Application firewall or proxy** that can be viewed as a relay that sits between a client application and a real server. It is used to filter all requests entering and leaving the network. It can also hide the true network addresses of protected hosts.

Firewall Implementations

Firewall can be implemented in both hardware and software, or a combination of the two. In the following, we cite some existing firewall implementations taken from the free encyclopedia Wikipedia at the Web site http://en.wikipedia.org/wiki/Firewall_(networking).

Software Implementation:

- Dotdefender (Firewall)
- eBox Platform (GPL)
- Gibraltar Firewall
- ipchains
- IPCop (GPL)
- IPFilter
- ipfirewall
- Microsoft Internet Security and Acceleration Server
- Netfilter/iptables
- Symantec
- pfSense (BSD-style license)
- WinGate (computing)

Hardware Implementation:

- Cisco PIX
- DataPower
- Juniper Networks NetScreen
- Secure Computing Sidewinder Appliance
- NetASQ
- Fortinet
- Lightning MultiCom VPN Firewall
- Lucent VPN Firewall
- Nortel Stand-alone and Switched Firewall
- Sarvega
- Watchguard

Software Agents

An agent (Franklin & Graesser, 1996; Wooldridge & Jennings, 1995) is an autonomous entity, reactive and able to communicate with knowledge-based systems. A multiagents system is a system that understands a set of agents. If agents are in coordination, we said that the system is cooperative. If agents are in competition, then we said that the agents system is competitive.

The agents have been used with great success in different domains in particular in eCommerce (Boughaci & Drias, 2005; Guttman & Maes, 1999; Noriega & Sierra,1999; Suwu & Das, 2001), in telecommunications (Gaiti & Martikainen, 2002; Dillenseger, et al., 2002) and in computer security (Boughaci et al., 2006a; Boughaci et al., 2006b; Wang et al., 2006).

Franklin and Graesser (1996) define *an autonomous agent as a system situated within and a part of an environment that senses that environment and acts on*

it, over time, in pursuit of its own agenda and so as to effect what it senses in the future.

Agent Classification

Based on Franklin and Graesser (1996), we list in the following the main agent's properties:

- **Reactive:** Able to act and respond at time to changes in its environment.
- **Autonomous:** Proactive, and can take decision and exercises control over its own actions.
- **Temporally continuous:** Persistence of identity and is a continuously running process.
- **Communicative:** Able to communicate with other agents.
- **Cooperative:** Able to collaborate with other agents to achieve a common goal.
- **Adaptive:** Able to learn and changes its behavior with experience.
- **Mobile:** Able to migrate from one machine to another.

FIRE-AGENT: A FIREWALL USING AGENTS

This section summarizes the design of the proposed distributed firewall using autonomous agents. The agent-based unified modeling language (AUML) is used for the modeling of the proposed agent-based system.

The Design of the Distributed Firewall

The agent-based system that we propose here is based on a set of agents. It includes a set of controllers' agents that ensure the packets filtering services, a proxy agent that plays a role of a proxy server, and an identifier agent which is responsible for user authentication. In addition, the decentralization of the different agents' activities is managed by an administrator agent, which is a core point for launching the most important operations of the access control. Especially, firewall rules sets have to be distributed to the set of controllers' agents scattered on some network nodes.

As you can see on Figure 1, our architecture includes four different types of agents: the administrator agent,

Figure 1. The general diagram of the distributed firewall

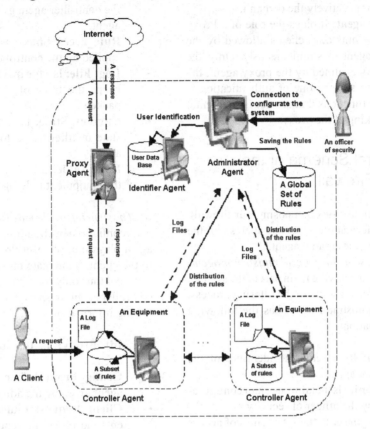

the controller agent, the proxy agent, and the identifier agent. The communications between the agents are by exchanging messages structured according to the KQML, and navigate on the Internet in a transparent way. It can also support several clients the Knowledge Query Manipulation Language, which is a language and protocol for communication among software agents and knowledge-based systems; see KQML[1] Web Site for further details about this language.

On the other hand, we have used the Agent Unified Modeling Language, AUML[2] (Bauer, Van Dyke Parunak, & Odell, 2001) for modeling the agents' activities and interactions. Some useful diagrams are given in the subsection below.

The main components of our firewall are detailed as follows:

- **The administrator agent:** It initiates all relative actions to the filtering process. It ensures the good working of the system. Firstly, the

administrator agent distributes the set of rules already defined by the officer of a security and stocked in the global rules base. These rules will be shared between the different controllers' agents. To guarantee some suppleness and avoid agent's congestion, the administrator agent doesn't intervene in the rules sharing process.

- **The controller agent:** Is mainly a packet filter. It analyzes the source and target address of each data packet, checks its port and accepts the packet if one of them is allowed to pass or reject it if one of them is disallowed to pass. The trace of filtered packets is registered in a log file and sent to the administrator agent.

- **The identifier agent:** Is responsible for checking authorization. It contains the basic functionality for session handling. The authentication is initiated by the administrator agent that sends to the identifier agent the name and the password of a user. The identifier agent looks in its data base for a corresponding registration and acquit positively or negatively the demand.

- **The proxy agent:** It plays the role of a Proxy server. It permits only clients allowed by the controller agent to simultaneously. Only the role of proxy is aimed by the proxy agent, the role of hides and the one of authentication is appendices functions that are not fundamental for the working of the proxy.

The Structural Schema of the Distributed Firewall

Here, we detail the entities composing our firewall. We give some information about our agents and the objects handled by these same agents.

The structural schema of the administrator agent: the administrator agent is the main part of the system. It initiates all actions relating to the filtering process. In short, the administrator agent has the following important information:

- **Idf_Admin:** Represents the identifier of the administrator agent.
- **Config_Admin:** Is the administrator configuration given by the officer of security.
- **Rule_acces_base:** Is the set of rules of access control edited by the officer of security.
- **All_agent_list:** Is the list of the agents of access control to be connected to the system and their identifier.
- **Actif_agent_list:** Is the list of the active agents.
- **Config_agent_list:** Is the list of configuration of all the agents made by the officer of security.
- **Idf_proxy_list:** Is the list of the proxy agents and their identifier.

The structural schema of the controller agent: the controller agent is the entity responsible for the traffic filtering. It captures packets, extracts information necessary to filtering, and compares this information with those of the recorded rules in its data base in order to make a decision whether to accept or reject the packets. The controller agent keeps a trace of filtered packets in a log file to be sent to the administrator agent. In short, the controller agent has the following information:

- **Idf_Cagent:** Is the identifier of the controller agent in our system.

- **Config_Cagent:** Represents the configuration of the controller agent given by the administrator agent.
- **Rule_acces_Sbase:** Is a subset of rules to be applied by the controller agent.
- **Log_File:** Is a file in which the controller agent keeps the trace of the entering and leaving packets.
- **Current_State:** Is a plug keeping the current state of filtering performed by the controller agent.
- **Rout_Table:** Is the routing table associated with the equipment lodging the controller agent.

The structural schema of the proxy agent: after has been configured by the administrator agent, the proxy agent plays the role of a Proxy. It makes it possible to the client to navigate on Internet in a transparent way, and thus only for connections authorized by the controller agent. In short, the proxy agent has the following information:

- **Idf_Proxy:** Is the identifier of the proxy agent.
- **Config_Proxy:** Is the configuration of the proxy agent given by the administrator agent.
- **Client_Request_table:** Is the table of the clients those making requests through the proxy agent.
- **Server_Answer_table:** Is the table of the servers from where expects answers.

The structural schema of the identifier agent: the identifier agent is the entity responsible for users' management and in particular the authentication. This authentication is initiated by the administrator agent that sends to the identifier agent the name of the user and his password. The identifier agent seeks in its data base a corresponding data and reply positively or negatively to the request. The results will be directly communicated to the administrator agent that decides the opening or not of the session.

In addition to the four agents, there are other entities in our architecture that play an important part for the system like: the packet and the administrator classes.

The packet class: is the principal entity of the system. The packets convey the data between the various stations of the network. They offer a good means to control the traffic. Each packet has the following information: the source IP address, the destination

Figure 2. The sequence diagram of the activity of the opening of a session

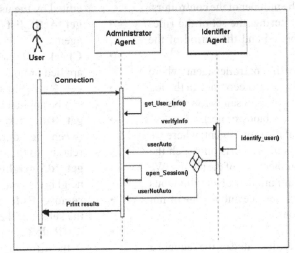

IP address, the source port, the destination port, the protocol type, and so on. In short, the packet class contains the following attributes:

- **Adresse_Sourc:** Is the source IP address of the packet.
- **Adresse_Dest:** Is the destination IP address of the packet.
- **Port_Sourc:** Is the the number of the source port of the packet.
- **Port_Dest:** Is the number of the destination port of the packet.
- **Protocol:** Is the protocol type concerned with the packet.
- **Ack_Flag:** Is the flag Ack for the TCP protocol.

The administrator class: in order to manage the different users of our system, we have added an administrator class that represents the officer of security of the system. Its description is as follows:

- **Password:** Is a single number identifying the network administrator,
- **User_Name:** Is the name given to the network administrator.

The Functional Schema of the Distributed Firewall

Here, we describe the main activities of our firewall illustrated as sequence diagrams.

Activity1. The opening of a session: when a user presents himself, the system requires of him to be identified. The user enters his password and his login. This information is collected by the administrator agent and is transmitted towards the identifier agent. The latter checks this information and returns the result of the authentication. The operation is illustrated as a sequence diagram in Figure 2 where:

- **get_User_Info ():** the administrator agent gets the name and the password of the user.
- **open_Session ():** opening a session by a user.
- **identify_user ():** The identifier agent verifies the authenticity of the user.
- **verifyInfo:** Send the name and password for verification.
- **userAuto:** The user is identified.
- **userNotAuto:** The user is not identified.

Activity2. The Initialization of the system: before launching the filtering process, the configuration of the agents is necessary. To be done, the administrator follows the three steps given as follows:

a. The configuration of the administrator agent: where we specify the number of the controllers' agents implied in filtering, the set of the rules of control to be applied and the period of the control message.

b. The configuration of the controller agent: where we specify the protocols to keep trace in the log file, we describe the policy of safety towards the unknown protocols (to block or not).

c. The configuration of the proxy agent: where we specify the numbers of the ports on which the proxy agent waits connections of the clients. We specify the maximum number of simultaneous connections for each service and to loge or not the client connections.

The overall operation is illustrated on the sequence diagram in Figure 3.

Activity 3. The launching of filtering: The administrator agent diffuses the rules to the controllers' agents. Each one of them recovers a copy and enters in interaction with the other agents to share these rules, in order to configure the mechanisms of access control in the most powerful possible way (by applying a protocol of rules sharing which will be described in the next subsection).

The activity is illustrated on the sequence diagram in Figure 4 where:

- **load_Rule_base ():** Load the base of the rules edited by the user.
- **get_Actif_list ():** Get the list of the active agents.
- **Check_All_rule ():** To check if all the rules are applied or not.
- **get_Rule_Sbase ():** Get a subset of rules which can be applied by the controller agent.
- **get_Rule_dest ():** Calculate the distance between the addresses of source or destination relating to the rule and the controller agent.
- **get_Idf_neighbor ():** Get the identity of the neighbor agents.
- **remove_Rule_Sbase ():** Remove a rule from the subset of the controller agent rules.
- **diffRuleBase:** Diffusion of the rules of filtering to the different controllers agents.
- **startFiltr:** To launch filtering.
- **sendRegSbase:** Sending of the subset of the rules.
- **askReg:** Applied rule ask.
- **Accpask:** Accepted ask.
- **notAccpask:** Refused ask.

Activity4. Get the log file: When the administrator wishes to get the log file, the administrator agent sends a request to the controller agent. The latter recovers a copy of the log file and sends it to the administrator agent.

To implement the agent-based firewall, two components are necessary:

Figure 3. The sequence diagram of the activity of the initialization of the system

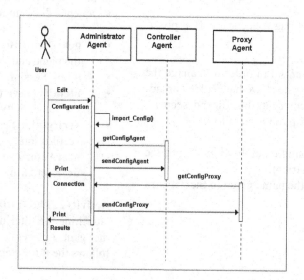

Figure 4. The sequence diagram of the activity of the launching of filtering

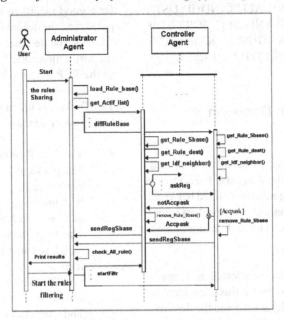

a. A language for expressing policies and resolving requests.
b. A mechanism for safety distributing security policies between agents.

The two components are detailed in the following.

The Expression of the Access Control Policy

We have defined a Language of Description of Politics of the Access Control (LDPAC) to permit the expression of the access control policy to be distributed to controllers' agents. In LDPAC language, an access control policy is defined by a set of rules. Each rule is a set of conditions and an action is executed when all the conditions are fulfilled. The general form of a rule is given as:

Rule: IF <Conditions> THEN <Action>

All conditions have the same generic structure expressed as:

Condition: <ACCESS CONTROL PARAMETER> <RELATIONAL OPERATOR> <VALUE>

- **ACCESS CONTROL PARAMETER:** The most parameters which we consider are those usually used to achieve the packets filtering (for example: the address information, the source and destination ports, the flags in the case of the TCP, connections, and so on).
- **RELATIONAL OPERATOR:** Are the different logical operators as: =, >, < plus the keyword "INCLUDE IN" to specify beaches of addresses.
- **VALUE:** It is the value associated to the parameter of a control. It can be the IP address, the number of the port, the name of protocol[3] and True or False for the Ack flag. In the case of any address, we use the keyword "ALL."

The Action indicates if the connection described by conditions must either be allowed or forbidden. It can take three possible values: "ACCEPT," "REJECT," and "INGNOR." The first value describes an authorized connection, the second for a forbidden connection and the third indicates that the agent is not concerned by the connection.

An example of the access control rules is given as:

R1: IF (IP_SRC_ADDRESS = 192.165.203.5) AND (IP_DST_ADDRESS = "ALL") AND (SRC_PORT > 1023) AND (DST_PORT = 80) AND (PROTOCOL =

TCP) THEN ACCEPT;
R2: IF (IP_SRC_ADDRESS = "ALL") AND (IP_DST_ADDRESS = 192.165.203.5) AND (SRC_PORT = 80) AND (DST_PORT > 1023) AND (PROTOCOL = TCP) AND (TCP_FLAG = FALSE) THEN ACCPET

The Control and the Decision Between Agents

The firewall rules sets have to be distributed and shared between the controllers' agents. Therefore, a protocol of the rules sharing must be defined between the different agents participating in the packets filtering services. Three assertions are defined and given in the following.

a.   **Assertion 1:** A rule can be allotted to an agent contained in equipment only if this one is located on the way between the source and the destination described by the rule.

b.   **Assertion 2:** If a rule can be allotted to agents located on several equipments in cascade, the rule should be allotted only to the agent located on the nearest equipment to the ends.

C.   **Assertion 3:** If the address source or the address destination includes the party of network supervised by a controller agent. The latter break up this rule and takes only the addresses that belong to him.

IMPLEMENTATION DETAILS

This section gives some implementation details about our distributed firewall. The Java programming language is used in the implementation.

Our Fire-agent has been implemented using JAVA[4] of Sun micro systems on Windows 2000 professional. To capture packets, we have used WinPcap tool that constitutes an interfacing between the physical layer and the network layer of the TCP/IP protocol. For testing the prototype, we have used a local area network consisted of at least two stand-alone machines.

The architecture of our agents is based on the utilization of interacted modules which are implemented as a thread or a set of threads. Packets are the main entities of the firewall system. They transport data between the different stations of the network and offer a good means to control the traffic. Each packet possesses the following information: the source IP address, the destination IP address, the source port, the destination port, the protocol and other information as the TCP flags (Ack, Urg, and so on).

The Tools. To implement our prototype, we need some tools and standard given as follows:

*   The Java Programming language.
*   The package Jpcap[5] which is a network packet capture library for applications written in Java. It is useful for developing packet capture applications in Java.
*   The Java Database Connectivity (JDBC) API which is a standard SQL database access interface.
*   MySQL[6] which is the world's most popular open source database.
*   The threads to program the different agents. The Java Virtual Machine allows an application to have multiple threads of execution running concurrently.

Two type of communication are used:

*   The Java Remote Method Invocation (Java RMI) that provides a simple and direct model for distributed computation with Java objects.
*   The socket that establishes bidirectional communication between a server program and one or more client programs.

The overall of our prototype is depicted in Figure 5 below.

The Internal Architecture of Our Agents

The architecture of our agents is based on the utilization of interacted modules which are implemented as a thread or a set of threads.

The Internal Architecture of the Controller Agent

The controller agent is composed of a set of modules described as follows:

Figure 5. The overall schema of the distributed firewall

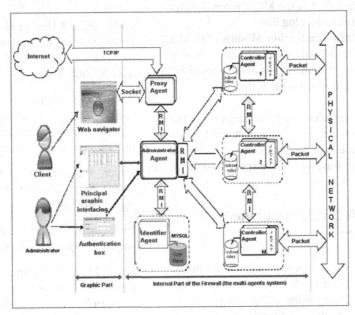

- **The Capture Packet Module (CPM):** It is the module that waits in the interfacing network the arrived packets As soon as a packet arrived, it is captured (using Jpcap library) and transmitted to the Traffic Filtering Module (TFM).
- **The Traffic Filtering Module (TFM):** It represents the mechanisms of the control access implemented by the controller agent. It receives rules from the Control Central Module (CCM). Then it loads these rules in a memory. The results corresponding to the application of these rules will be recorded in a log file.
- **The Control Central Module (CCM):** It is the central module of the controller agent. It is warned of the arrival of each new rule of the access control by the Exchange Message Module (EMM) module. The CCM verifies if a rule it can be applied to the equipment by the means of the Routing Information Module (RIM).
- **The Exchange Message Module (EMM):** It creates a Remote Method Invocation (RMI) register joined to the agent since its creation.
- **The Rules Sharing Module (RSM):** It provides to the CCM the information concerning a good positioned equipment that already applies a rule "r". To provide this information, the RSM interacts with the RSM of the neighboring agents

using the protocol of rules sharing already given in the preview section.
- **The Routing Information Module (RIM):** It is used by the CCM to know if the relative connection to a rule "r" is passed by the equipment on which is installed the agent. When the network topology is changed, the RIM informs the RSM to take in account the new topology.
- **The Graphic Interfacing Module (GIM):** Is a window containing two zones of text, one for the IP address of the administrator agent and the second for the number of the controller agent.

The Internal Architecture of the Proxy Agent

The proxy agent is composed of a set of modules given as follows:

- **The Port Listening Module (PLM):** Its role consists in monitoring on the specific ports for every service. It creates a process of the Server Socket class that waits for Clients' connections. As soon as a connection is accepted, it passed to the AEM module that treats the request.
- **The Address Extraction Module (AEM):** This module extracted the relative information to the

received request of the PLM. This information will be transmitted to the MCM module, after their registration in a log file.

- **The Maintain Connection Module (MCM):** This module permits the multiple customer management. It implements the "Runnable" interfacing and spreads the Socket class.

For the other modules, the CCM stays up to the good working, of the agent. The Exchange Message Module (EMM) and the Graphic Interfacing Module (GIM) have similar functions viewed previously with the controller agent.

The Internal Architecture of the Identifier Agent

The identifier agent is composed of a set of modules. The User Authentication Module (UAM) is the module responsible for user authentication. It manages a user data base enriched by the CCM module.

CONCLUSION AND FUTURE WORK

In this chapter, a distributed firewall is proposed. It uses autonomous agents to coordinately control the traffic on the network. Our contribution consists of using the agents to implement a distributed firewall to improve the performance of classical ones. The originality of our model reside in the fact that it allows agents to collaborate with other tools to provide a complete system permitting the access control in the network and the mandating of clients of the internal network during their accesses to the external network.

Several perspectives proved out to be promising and can bring a more to our distributed firewall. These perspectives are the following: for the identifier agent, a global strategy of authentication of clients of the network protected by our system will be added. Finally, the use of mobile agent seems to be a solution to automated management, so the administrator is not obliged to displace between the different equipments of the network to place controllers' agents.

REFERENCES

Al-Shaer, E., & Hamed, H. (2004, April). Modeling and management of firewall policies. *IEEE eTransactions on Network and Service Management, 1*(1). Retrieved May 3, 2008, from http://www.etnsm.org/

Al-Shaer, E., Hamed, H., Boutaba, R., & Hasan, M. (2005). Conflict classification and analysis of distributed firewall policies. *IEEE Journal on Selected Areas in Communications (JSAC), 23*(10).

Bauer, B., Van Dyke Parunak, H., & Odell, J. (2001). *Extending UML for agents*. http://www.erim.org/~vparunak/

Bellovin, S.M. (1999). Distributed firewalls. *login: magazine, special issue on security, November.*

Blaze, M., Feigenbaum, J., & Keromytis, A. (1999), KeyNote: trust management for public key infrastructures. In *Proceedings of the 1998 Cambridge Security Protocols International Workshop* (Vol. 1550, pp. 59-63) Springer.

Brown, R., Davies, N.D.W., & Price, W.L. (1995). *Sécurité dans les réseaux informatiques*. AFNOR, document in French.

Boughaci, D., & Drias, H. (2005). Taboo search as an intelligent agent for bid evaluation. *International Journal of Internet and Enterprise Management, Inderscience Publisher, 3*(2), 170-186.

Boughaci, D., Drias, H., Bendib, A., Bouznit, Y., Benhamou, B. (2006a, May 25–27). A Distributed Intrusion Detection Framework based on Autonomous and Mobile Agents. In *Proceedings of IEEE Computer Society International Conference on Dependability of Computer Systems (DEPCOS-RELCOMEX'06)* (pp. 248-255).

Boughaci, D., Drias, H., Oubeka, B., Aissioui, A., & Benhamou, B. (2006b). A distributed firewall using autonomous agents. In *Proceedings of depcos-relcomex, International Conference on Dependability of Computer Systems (DEPCOS-RELCOMEX'06)* (pp. 256-263).

Dillenseger, B., Tagant, A.-M., & Hazard, L. (2002). Programming and executing telecommunication service logic with moorea reactive mobile agents. *MATA 2002, LNCS, 2521/2002*, 48-57.

Franklin, S., & Graesser, A. (1996). Is it an agent, or just a program? A taxonomy for autonomous agents. In *Proceedings of the Third International Workshop on Agent Theories, Architectures, and Languages.* Springer-Verlag.

Gaiti, D., & Martikainen, O. (2002). Intelligent agents for telecommunication environments. *Innovative Technology Series, Information Systems and Networks.* Lavoisier Library.

Haffner, E.G., Roth, U., Heuer, A., Engel, T., & Meinel, C. (2001). Managing distributed personal firewalls with smart data servers. In *Proceedings of the World Conference on WWW and Internet, AACE WebNet 2001* (pp. 466-471). Orlando, FL.

Guttman, R., & Maes, P. (1999, March). Agents that buy and sell. *Comm. ACM*, 81-91.

Ioannidis, S., Keromytis, A.D., Bellovin, S.M., & Smith, J.M. (2000). Implementing a distributed firewall. In *Proceedings of the ACM Conference on Computer and Communication Security* (pp. 190-199).

Mogul, J., Rashid, R., & Accetto, M. (1987, November). The packet filter: An efficient mechanism for user-level network code. In *Proceedings of the Eleventh ACM Symposium on Operating Systems Principles* (pp. 39-51).

Noriega, P., & Sierra, C. (Eds.). (1999). *Agent-mediated electronic commerce, LNAI 1571.* Springer.

Wang, Y., Behera, S., Wong, J., Helmer, G., Honavar, V., Miller, L., & Lutz, R. (2006). Towards automatic generation of mobiles agents for distributed intrusion detection systems. *Journal of Systems and Software, 79*, 1-14.

Wooldridge, M., & Jennings, N.R. (1995). Intelligent agents: Theory and practice. *Knowledge engineering Review*, 115-152.

Suwu, W., & Das, A. (2001). An agent system architecture for e-commerce. In *Proceedings of the 12th International Workshop on Database and Expert Systems Applications, dexa* (pp. 0715).

KEY TERMS

Computer Security: Techniques and measures used to protect data stored in a computer or circulated on the network from unauthorized accesses. Among the security tools, we find firewalls, intrusion detection system, antivirus, data encryption, and passwords systems.

Hacker: An intruder who gains unauthorized access to computer system.

IP Spoofing: A technique to gain unauthorized access to network. The hacker can do it by modifying the packet header then sending messages to a computer with an IP address indicating that the message is coming from a trusted host.

Network Firewall: A device used to control access between a trusted network and an untrusted network based on certain configured rules.

Packet: Called also datagrams, it is a piece of a message (data and destination address) transmitted over a packet-switching network.

Packets Filtering: A technique for controlling access to a network by analyzing the traversal packets and allowing or disallowing them passing based on the IP addresses of the source and destination.

Ping: A utility to determine whether a specific IP address is accessible.

Proxy: A relay which sits between a client application and the real server permitting to intercept all requests on the network. The proxy server effectively hides the true network addresses.

Router: A device that forwards data packets along networks.

ENDNOTES

[1] KQML Web site, http://www.cs.umbc.edu/kqml

[2] AUML Web site, http://www.auml.org

[3] IP: short for Internet Protocol that deals with packets.
TCP: short for Transmission Control Protocol that enables two hosts to establish a connection and exchange streams of data .
FTP: short for File Transfer Protocol which is the protocol for exchanging files over the Internet.

ICMP: short for Internet Control Message Protocol which is an extension to the Internet Protocol (IP) supporting packets containing error, control, and informational messages.
UDP: short for User Datagram Protocol.

[4]   The Java home page, http://java.sun.com
[5]   http://jpcap.sourceforge.net/
[6]   http://www.mysql.com

Chapter XIV
A Formal Verification Centred Development Process for Security Protocols

Tom Coffey
University of Limerick, Ireland

Reiner Dojen
University of Limerick, Ireland

ABSTRACT

This chapter concerns the correct and reliable design of modern security protocols. It discusses the importance of formal verification of security protocols prior to their release by publication or implementation. A discussion on logic-based verification of security protocols and its automation provides the reader with an overview of the current state-of-the-art of formal verification of security protocols. The authors propose a formal verification centred development process for security protocols. This process provides strong confidence in the correctness and reliability of the designed protocols. Thus, the usage of weak security protocols in communication systems is prevented. A case-study on the development of a security protocol demonstrates the advantages of the proposed approach. The case-study concludes with remarks on the performance of automated logic-based verification and presents an overview of formal verification results of a range of modern security protocols.

INTRODUCTION

The security of electronic networks and information systems is a critical issue for the use of new technologies in all fields of life. Mobile and fixed networks are trusted with highly sensitive information. Thus, security protocols (also called cryptographic protocols) are required to ensure the security of both the infrastructure itself and the information that runs through it. These security protocols can be thought of as the keystones of a secure architecture. Basic cryptographic protocols allow agents to authenticate each other, to establish fresh session keys for confidential communication and to ensure the authenticity of data and services. Building on such basic cryptographic protocols, more advanced services like nonrepudiation, fairness, electronic payment, and electronic contract signing are achieved.

The massive growth in communications technologies—in particular in the wireless sector—causes an ever-changing environment for today's communication services. The pervasive nature of emerging Information and Communications Technologies has added new areas of concern to information security. For example, the increased virtual and physical mobility of users enhances their possibilities for interaction, but leads to an increasing demand for reliable trust relationships. To address new security risks and threats arising from such changes in the communication environment, a constant supply of novel security protocols is required.

However, security protocols are vulnerable to a host of subtle attacks, and designing protocols to be impervious to such attacks has been proven to be extremely challenging and error-prone. This is evident from the surprisingly large number of published protocols, which have later been found to contain various flaws, in many cases, several years after the original publication (Brackin, 2000; Coffey, Dojen, & Flangan, 2003a, 2003b, 2003c, 2003d; Huima, 1999; Gürgens & Rudolph, 2002; Newe & Coffey, 2002; Ventuneac, Coffey, & Newe, 2004; Ventuneac, Dojen, & Coffey, 2006; Zhang & Fang, 2005; Zhang & Varadharajan, 2001).

Motivation

The importance of formal verification of cryptographic protocols during the development process cannot be overstated (Coffey et al., 2003a), as the absence of formal verification of these protocols can lead to flaws and security errors remaining undetected. However, an ad-hoc survey carried out at the Data Communication Security Laboratory, UL in 2005 on over 200 recent papers on cryptographic protocols revealed that only 15% of these publications contained formal verifications.

The BCY protocol (Beller, Chang, & Yacobi, 1993) provides a very interesting case study to highlight the problems with the correct design of security protocols. Published in 1993, the BCY protocol demonstrated the feasibility of public-key cryptography in mobile communications. Subsequently, Carlsen (1994) discovered weaknesses in the protocol and published an amended protocol. Weaknesses in Carlsen's amended protocol were discovered by Mu and Varadharajan (1996), and another modified protocol was published. Horn, Martin, and Mitchell (2002) identified a weakness in the Mu and Varadharajan version of the BCY protocol, but did not publish a corrected version. Coffey et al. (2003a) published formal verifications of the BCY protocol and its derivates. In addition to all previously identified weaknesses, a hitherto unknown flaw in the BCY protocol and its derivatives was detected. A corrected protocol was proposed and also formally verified. This case study highlights that the design of security protocols is a highly complex and error-prone

process. It also shows that formal verification is an imperative step in the design of security protocols.

This chapter advocates the use of formal verification during the development of modern security protocols. It discusses the importance of formal verification of security protocols prior to their release by publication or implementation. A discussion on logic-based verification of security protocols and its automation provides the reader with an insight into the current state-of-the-art of formal verification of security protocols. The authors propose a formal verification centred development process for security protocols. This approach results in a strong confidence in the correctness and reliability of the designed protocols and prevents the usage of weak security protocols in communication systems. Further, a case-study demonstrates the advantages of the proposed approach to the design of security protocols. This case study provides a discussion on the difficulties involved in designing correct and reliable security protocols. As an example, the authentication and key-agreement protocol by Beller, Chang, and Yacobi (1993) is taken. The BCY protocol contains a number of well-known weaknesses and, thus, the ability of the proposed process to detect these weaknesses is demonstrated. The case-study concludes with remarks on the performance of automated logic-based verification and presents an overview of formal verification results of a range of modern security protocols.

FORMAL VERIFICATION OF SECURITY PROTOCOLS

Needham and Schroeder (1978) are generally credited with the introduction of formal methods as a possible tool for cryptographic protocol analysis. However, the first experimental work in this area was done by Dolev, Even, and Karp (1982) and by Dolev and Yao (1983), who developed a set of polynomial-time algorithms for deciding the security of a restricted class of protocols. It was soon found that relaxing the restrictions on the protocols made the security problem undecidable (Even & Goldreich, 1983). However, Dolev and Yao's work was significant in that it was the first to develop a formal model that provided:

1. The possibility of multiple executions of the protocol running concurrently.
2. Cryptographic algorithms behaving like black boxes, obeying a set of algebraic properties.

3. A model of an intruder who can read, alter and destroy traffic, and who can also control some legitimate members of the system.

Based on the Dolev-Yao model, new verification techniques for the analysis of security protocols have been developed. These can be divided by their underlying principles into:

1. State-Space-based techniques like The Interrogator (Millen, Clark, & Freedman, 1987), Murφ (Dill, 1996), FDR (Lowe, 1996), NRL Protocol Analyser (Meadows, 1996), Huima's model checker (Huima, 1999), Brutus (Clarke, Jha, & Marrero, 2000) and Athena (Song, Berezin, & Perrig 2001).
2. Logic-based techniques using logics of belief and/or knowledge like the BAN logic (Burrows, Abadi, & Needham, 1990), the GNY logic (Gong, Needham, & Yaholom, 1990), AUTLOG (Kessler & Wendel, 1994), SVO (Syverson & van Oorschot, 1994), CS logic (Coffey & Saidha, 1997), KM logic (Kudo & Mathuria, 1999), ZV logic (Zhang & Varadharajan, 2001), SW Logic (Stubblebine & Wright, 2002) and CPL (Kramer, 2004).
3. Theorem Proving Techniques based on generic theorem provers like Isabelle (Paulson, 1998), or on special purpose theorem proving techniques developed for formal verification of cryptographic protocols like CSP (Schneider, 1998) and TAPS (Cohen, 2000).

Logic-Based Techniques

Logic-based formal verification of cryptographic security protocols proves the correctness of the protocol against its goals. The technique of logic-based formal verification is accredited largely to Burrow et al. (1990), developers of the BAN logic. This work initiated intense research in the area of logic-based formal verification and several logics, such as the logics of Gong et al. (1990), Syverson and van Oorschot (1994), Coffey and Saidha (1997), and Kudo and Mathuria (1999) have been developed on the basis of BAN.

Logic-based verification of cryptographic protocols involves a process of deductive reasoning, where the desired protocol goals are deduced from the initial assumptions and message exchanges of the protocols as illustrated in Figure 1.

The first steps in logic-based verification involve specifying the protocol steps, the initial assumptions, and the protocol goals in the language of the logic. The final verification step concerns the application of logical postulates to establish the beliefs and possessions of protocol principals. The objective of the logical analysis is to verify whether the desired goals of the protocol can be derived from the initial assumptions and protocol steps. If such a derivation exists, the protocol is successfully verified; otherwise, the verification fails. A successfully verified protocol can be considered secure within the scope of the logic. On the other hand, even the results of a failed verification are useful, as these may point to missing assumptions or weaknesses in the protocol. If a weakness is discovered, the protocol should be redesigned and reverified.

Logic-based techniques have an advantage in that they are usually decidable and often efficiently computable, and thus can be completely automated (Brackin, 2000; Dojen & Coffey, 2005; Kessler & Wedel, 1994). Numerous protocol flaws in security protocols have been detected by researchers employing modal logics (Brackin, 2000; Burrows et al., 1990; Coffey & Dojen, 2003; Coffey et al., 2003a, 2003b, 2003c; Coffey & Saidha, 1997; Coffey, Saidha, & Burrows, 2003; Gong et al., 1990; Kessler & Wedel, 1994; Newe & Coffey, 2002; Newe & Coffey, 2003a, 2003b, 2003c; Syverson & van Oorschot, 1994; Ventuneac, Coffey, & Newe, 2004; Zhang & Varadharajan, 2001).

Automation of Logic-Based Verification

The manual application of formal techniques remains difficult and error-prone. As a result, the use of formal verification techniques for cryptographic protocols has not found widespread use outside the research community. It is important to get the advancements in formal verification techniques out to the people who can make best use of them, namely the designers and evaluators of the cryptographic systems that are being deployed in today's communication networks. Probably the highest obstacle currently prohibiting widespread use of formal techniques at the early development stages of cryptographic protocols is the complexity of their application. While some techniques have been already automated, often the use of these automated tools remains similarly complex to manual application.

Logic-based techniques are often developed with manual application in mind. Most current attempts to automate verification logics use generic theorem

Figure 1. Process of logic-based verification

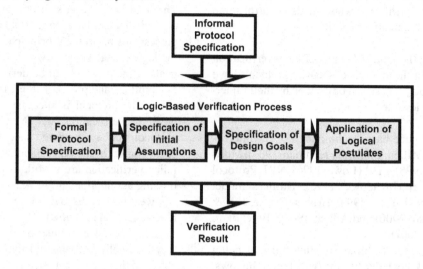

Figure 2. Traditional development process of security protocols

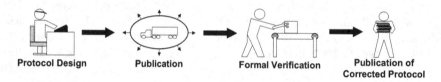

provers, such as HOL, Coq, Isabelle, or PVS. However, logics often need to be modified to be automated by such generic theorems provers. Further, theorem provers usually only return results of the performed proofs, but will not provide any details of how these are achieved. However, in the case of security protocol verification, such details are very useful for the protocol designer. This is particularly true in the case of a failed verification, as the details of the proof are helpful in identifying the exact cause of the verification failure. Specialised automation techniques can be used to overcome such limitations. For example, Dojen and Coffey (2005) developed a novel automation technique for logic-based verification of security protocols. The main advantages of the novel technique include low resource requirement, traceability of verification results and the ability to accurately model manual verification logics.

A FORMAL VERIFICATION-CENTERED DEVELOPMENT PROCESS FOR SECURITY PROTOCOLS

The design of reliable and correct security protocols is an intricate and error-prone process. This is evident from the large number weaknesses found in protocols, in many cases years after their publication. While it can be shown that complete protocol security is undecidable (Cervesato, Durgin, Lincoln, Mitchell, & Scedrov, 1999), formal verification provides a level of confidence in the security of protocols unrivalled by informal or intuitive techniques.

Traditionally, such informal techniques are used to verify security protocols during the development process. However, the absence of formal verification of these protocols prior to their publication can lead to flaws and security errors remaining undetected. Frequently, such flaws are discovered by subsequent formal verification of published protocols and amendments are proposed (Coffey et al., 2003a; Gürgens &

Rudolph, 2002; Huima, 1999; Newe & Coffey, 2003a; Ventuneac et al., 2004; Zhang & Fang, 2005). Figure 2 illustrates this approach to security protocol design.

The large number of published protocols, which have later been found to contain various flaws, shows that this traditional development process is inadequate and can result in weak protocols being employed in communication systems. The main difficulty in the development of effective security protocols is to address the vast possibilities of adversaries to gain information (Dojen & Coffey, 2005). In contrast to communication protocols, where the main issues are reachability of all legal states and avoidance of infinite loops, security protocol verification deals with the gain of information by adversaries. The adversaries can be either passive or active. Further, adversaries might use simultaneous protocol runs to gain information. One has to keep in mind that adversaries will not play fair by any rules. Therefore, formal verification should be considered an imperative step in the design of security protocols (Coffey et al., 2003a). As a consequence, the authors propose a formal verification centred development process as illustrated in Figure 3.

In this development process, a draft of the protocol is subject to formal verification prior to its publication. If any weaknesses of the protocol are discovered during the formal verification, the draft is passed back to the design stage and corrected. This corrected version of the protocol will be again subject of the formal verification process. Design and Verification of a security protocol are considered two inseparable steps: protocol design and formal verification are iterated until formal verification does not reveal any weaknesses of the protocol. Only then is the protocol published or implemented. The incorporation of formal verification as an integrated part of the development process significantly increases the confidence in the correctness of the security protocol and, thus, risk of using faulty protocols in electronic networks or information systems is drastically minimized.

CASE-STUDY: DESIGNING A PROVABLY SECURE CRYPTOGRAPHIC PROTOCOL

This case-study demonstrates the advantages of the proposed development process by applying it to the BCY protocol (Beller, Chang & Yacobi, 1993). The BCY protocol is chosen, as it contains a number of well-known problems. The original protocol is treated as an initial draft of a newly designed protocol, and subject to formal verification. Subsequently, the protocol is redesigned to address the detected weaknesses. Thus, the ability of the proposed development process to prevent the usage of weak protocols is demonstrated.

Formal verification during this case study is performed by an automated verification system that is based on Layered Proving Trees (Dojen & Coffey, 2005) and the GNY Logic (Gong et al., 1990). Figure 4 outlines the structure of the verification system. It features a library incorporating definitions of the verification logics, including the logical postulates and the grammar for the logic. The user inputs the formal protocol specification which consists of the initial assumptions, the protocol steps and the protocol goals and selects the logic to be used from the library. The system will automatically apply the logical postulates and provides the verification results.

A successfully verified protocol can be considered secure within the scope of the logic. The results of a failed verification help to identify any weaknesses in

Figure 3. Proposed development process for security protocols

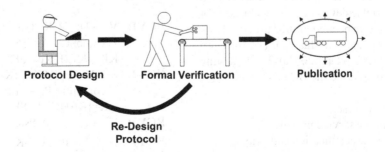

169

Figure 4. Verification system overview

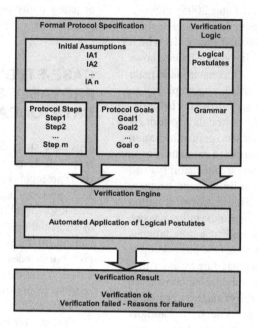

the protocol or any missing initial assumptions. Thus, the reasons for protocol failure are detected and can be corrected. The corrected version of the protocol should be again subject to formal verification.

The BCY Protocol

The protocol by Beller et al. (1993), referred to as the BCY protocol is aimed at providing authentication and key agreement in low-power portable devices such as mobile phones. It demonstrates the computational feasibility of using public-key cryptography in mobile communications. The protocol combines a Diffie-Hellman key exchange (Diffie & Hellman, 1976) with the modular square root (MSR) encryption technique (Rabin, 1979) to reduce the computational burden on the low-power portable device. Some weaknesses of the BCY protocol have been identified previously by Carlsen (1994), Mu and Varadharajan (1996), Horn et al. (2002), and Coffey et al. (2003a). The following notation is used to describe the BCY protocol.

U: An identifier of the user.
V: An identifier of the service provider.
S: An identifier of the certification authority.

Nx: A random nonce generated by X.
TSx: An expiration time for the certificate for X.
Kx+: public key of X.
Kx-: private key of X.
KK: a key-encrypting key.
SK: a session key.
dataX: identification data for X

As the service provider uses two public keys, one for Diffie-Hellman key agreement and one for MSR encryption, these will be termed Kvd+ and Kvm+ respectively. Certificates, denoted by (X1,...,Xn)Ks-, contain the components X1 to Xn signed by a certification authority. The steps of the protocol are as follows:

BCY1: V → U: {V, Kvd+,Kvm+}Ks-
        U computes Y = {Nu}Kvm+,
        KK={Kvd+}Ku-, SK = {Nu}KK
BCY2: U → V: Y, {{U,Ku+}Ks-}Nu
        V computes R$_U$ ={Y}Kvm-,
        KK={Ku+}Kvd-, SK = {Nu}KK
BCY3: V → U: {dataV}SK
BCY4: U → V: {dataU}SK

Formal Logic-Based Verification of the BCY Protocol

The initial protocol is created and is subject to formal verification. In order to verify a security protocol, it must be translated into the language of the used verification technique. The following input script represents the formal protocol specification, and has been used to verify the BCY protocol with the automated verification system:

```
// BCY Formal Protocol Specification
// Assumptions
A1 : U possess KuPriv;
A2 : U possess {U,KuPub}KsPriv;
A3 : U possess dataU;
A4 : U possess Nu;
A5 : U possess KsPub;
A6 : U believe fresh(Nu);
A7 : U believe recognised(dataV);
A8 : U believe recognised(V);
A9 : U believe hasKey(S,KsPub);
A10: U believe S hasJurisdiction S believe
allStatement;
A11: U believe S hasJurisdiction hasKey(V,
KvmPub),hasKey(V,KvdPub);
A12: V possess KvdPriv;
A13: V possess KvmPriv;
A14: V possess {V,KvdPub,KvmPub}KsPriv;
A15: V possess dataV;
A16: V possess KsPub;
A17: V believe recognised(dataU);
A18: V believe recognised(U);
A19: V believe hasKey(S,KsPub);
A20: V believe S hasJurisdiction S believe
allStatement;
A21: V believe S hasJurisdiction
hasKey(U,KuPub);

// Steps
S1 : U told notHere({(V,KvdPub,KvmPub),[S
believe hasKey(V,KvmPub),
    hasKey(V,KvdPub)]}KsPriv);
S2 : V told notHere({notHere(Nu)}KvmPub),no
tHere({notHere({(U,KuPub),
    [S believe hasKey(U,KuPub)]}KsPriv)}Nu);
S3 : U told notHere({dataV}{Nu}{KvdPub}KuP
riv);
    S4 : V told notHere({dataU}{Nu}{KuPub}K
vdPriv);

// Goals
G1 : U believe hasKey(V,KvmPub),hasKey(V,K
vdPub);
G2 : U possess {Nu}{KvdPub}KuPriv;
G3 : U believe fresh({Nu}{KvdPub}KuPriv);
G4 : U believe shareKey(U,{Nu}{KvdPub}KuP
riv,V);
```

```
G5 : U believe V conveyed {dataV}{Nu}{KvdP
ub}KuPriv;
G6 : U believe fresh({dataV}{Nu}{KvdPub}Ku
Priv);
G7 : V believe hasKey(U,KuPub);
G8 : V possess {Nu}{KuPub}KvdPriv;
G9 : V believe fresh({Nu}{KuPub}KvdPriv);
G10: V believe shareKey(V,{Nu}{KuPub}KvdPr
iv,U);
G11: V believe U conveyed {dataU}{Nu}{KuPu
b}KvdPriv;
G12: V believe fresh({dataU}{Nu}{KuPub}Kvd
Priv);
```

The assumptions section of the script identifies the possessions and believes of protocol participants at the beginning of a protocol run. Here, the assumptions A1 to A5 model U's possession of its own private key, certificate, identification data, random nonce and the certification authority's public key, respectively. The next assumptions model U's believe in the freshness of its nonce (A6), its own ability to recognise both V's identification data (A7) and name (A8). Further, U believes that KsPub truly is the certification authority's proper public key (A9) and that the certification authority is honest (A10) and can be trusted to provide public keys for V (A11). The assumptions A12 through to A21 model the matching possessions and believes for V (note that V has two public/private keys and V has no information about Nu).

The steps section models the message exchange between principals. Note that GNY's message extensions are indicated with square brackets. These message extensions are used to convey some principal's beliefs to other principals.

The goals section states the expected believes and possessions required for a successful verification of the protocol. Here, the goal G1 asserts that U believes the received public keys truly belong to V. Goals G2, G3, and G4 model key agreement for U, i.e. that U possesses the session key believes it to be fresh and that it is a suitable key for use with V. Authentication of V by U is modelled through goals G5 and G6 by stating that U believes that message BCY3 has been sent by V, and that it has been sent during the current protocol run. The goals G7 through to G12 assert the matching conditions for V.

After completion of the verification process, the following results are obtained for the BCY protocol:

```
(1) : U believe hasKey(V,KvmPub),h
asKey(V,KvdPub)is False
(2) : U possess {Nu}{KvdPub}KuPriv is
```

Figure 5. Browsable result view sample for Goal 5

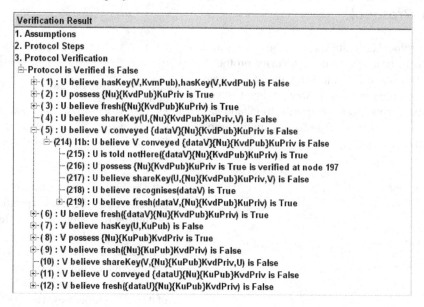

```
True
    (3) : U believe fresh({Nu}{KvdPub}KuPriv)
is True
    (4) : U believe shareKey(U,{Nu}{KvdPub}K
uPriv,V) is False
    (5) : U believe V conveyed {dataV}{Nu}{K
vdPub}KuPriv False
    (6) : U believe fresh({dataV}{Nu}{KvdPub
}KuPriv) is True
    (7) : V believe hasKey(U,KuPub) is
False
    (8) : V possess {Nu}{KuPub}KvdPriv is
True
    (9) : V believe fresh({Nu}{KuPub}KvdPriv)
is False
    (10): V believe shareKey(V,{Nu}{KuPub}Kv
dPriv,U) is False
    (11): V believe U conveyed {dataU}{Nu}{K
uPub}KvdPriv is False
    (12): V believe fresh({dataU}{Nu}{KuPub}K
vdPriv) is False
```

These results identify the following failed goals:

1. U cannot establish validity of V's public keys/certificate (Goal 1)
2. U cannot establish key agreement with V (Goal 4)
3. U cannot authenticate V through message BCY 3 (Goal 5)

4. V cannot establish validity of U's public key/certificate (Goal 7)
5. V cannot establish key agreement (Goals 9, 10)
6. V cannot authenticate U through message BCY 4 (Goals 11,12)

These failures stem essentially from two weaknesses of the protocol:

- The principals cannot validate the certificates.
- V cannot establish that the session key is fresh.

Due to these weaknesses, the original BCY protocol provides neither authentication nor key agreement.

The used automated verification tool presents the verification results in a browsable tree, which provides detailed information about the performed reasoning. This allows the use to investigate the reasons for any identified protocol failures. As an example, Figure 5 outlines the reasoning used to establish Goal 5. Here, the result shows that Goal 5 fails, since U does not believe that SK is a suitable shared key with V (node 217).

Redesign of the BCY Protocol

In light of the weaknesses discovered in formal verification and analysis, the redesign of the BCY protocol can be implemented with focus on two aspects:

- Validate freshness of the certificates exchanged in the key agreement stage.
- Enhance the session key so that V can establish its freshness.

The following amendments are proposed:

- First, an expiration time TS is included in U's and V's certificate. Thus, the certificates are changed to {U,KuPub,TSu}KsPriv and {V,Kv1Pub,Kv2Pub,TSv}KsPriv respectively. These amendments to the certificates avoid attacks where an intruder replays a compromised certificate.
- Second, a nonce Nv, created by V, is added and included in the construction of the session key (i.e., SK becomes {Nu,Nv}{Kv1Pub}KuPriv and {Nu,Nv}{KuPub}Kv1Priv for U and V respectively). As both parties now contribute towards the session key, each can confirm its freshness. In particular, V is now able to confirm freshness of SK and, consequently, is able to derive that SK is a suitable secret shared with user U. This results in the following amended protocol:

BCY'1: V → U: {V, Kvd+,Kvm+, TSv}Ks-
U computes Y = {Ru}Kvm+,
KK={Kvd+}Ku-, SK = {Ru,Rv}KK

BCY'2: U → V: Y, {{U,Ku+, TSu}Ks-}Ru
V computes Ru = {Y}Kvm-,
KK={Ku+}Kvd-, SK = {Ru,Rv}KK

BCY'3: V → U: {dataV}SK

BCY'4: U → V: {dataU}SK

The following input script to the verification system details the redesigned BCY protocol.

```
// Amended BCY Formal Protocol Speci-
fication
// Assumptions
A1 : U possess KuPriv;
A2 : U possess {U,KuPub}KsPriv;
A3 : U possess dataU;
A4 : U possess KsPub;
A5 : U possess Nu;
A6 : U believe fresh(Nu);
A7 : U believe recognised(dataV);
A8 : U believe recognised(V);
A9 : U believe hasKey(S,KsPub);
A10: U believe S hasJurisdiction S be-
lieve allStatement;
A11: U believe S hasJurisdiction hasKey
(V,KvmPub),hasKey(V,KvdPub);
```

```
A12: U believe fresh(TSv);
A13: U believe shareKey(U,{Nu,Nv}{KvdPu
b}KuPriv,V);
A14: V possess KvdPriv;
A15: V possess KvmPriv;
A16: V possess {V,KvdPub,KvmPub}KsPriv;
A17: V possess dataV;
A18: V possess KsPub;
A19: V possess Nv;
A20: V believe fresh(Nv);
A21: V believe recognised(dataU);
A22: V believe recognised(U);
A23: V believe hasKey(S,KsPub);
A24: V believe S hasJurisdiction S be-
lieve allStatement;
A25: V believe S hasJurisdiction
hasKey(U,KuPub);
A26: V believe fresh(TSu);
A27: V believe shareKey(V,{Nu,Nv}{KuPub}
KvdPriv,U);

// Steps
S1 : U told notHere(Nv, notHere({(V,KvdP
ub,KvmPub,TSv),[S believe
    hasKey(V,KvmPub),hasKey(V,KvdPub)]}KsPri
v));
S2 : V told notHere(notHere({Nu}KvmPub),
{Nv,{(U,KuPub,TSu),[S believe
    hasKey(U,KuPub)]}KsPriv}Nu);
S3 : U told notHere({dataV}{Nu,Nv}{KvdP
ub}KuPriv);
S4 : V told notHere({dataU}{Nu,Nv}{KuPu
b}KvdPriv);

// Goals
G1 : U believe hasKey(V,KvmPub),hasKey(
V,KvdPub);
G2 : U possess {Nu,Nv}{KvdPub}KuPriv;
G3 : U believe fresh({Nu,Nv}{KvdPub}KuP
riv);
G4 : U believe shareKey(U,{Nu,Nv}{KvdPu
b}KuPriv,V);
G5 : U believe V conveyed {dataV}{Nu,Nv
}{KvdPub}KuPriv;
G6 : U believe fresh({dataV}{Nu,Nv}{Kvd
Pub}KuPriv);
G7 : V believe hasKey(U,KuPub);
G8 : V possess {Nu,Nv}{KuPub}KvdPriv;
G9 : V believe fresh({Nu,Nv}{KuPub}KvdP
riv);
G10: V believe shareKey(V,{Nu,Nv}{KuPub
}KvdPriv,U);
G11: V believe U conveyed {dataU}{Nu,Nv}
{KuPub}KvdPriv;
G12: V believe fresh({dataU}{Nu,Nv}{KuPu
b}KvdPriv);
```

The following highlights the differences between the input script for the original BCY and the amended

BCY protocols: U has the added initial believes in the freshness of TSv (A12) and that a Diffie-Hellman key exchange results in a suitable shared key (A13). For V the additional assumptions A19 and A20 state the possession and freshness of V's nonce, and assumptions A26 and A27 add V's initial believes in the freshness of TSu and that a Diffie-Hellman key exchange results in a suitable shared key. The Steps section incorporates the amendments as discussed above. The goals are the same for the amended BCY protocol than for the original BCY protocol. After completion of the verification process the following results are obtained for the BCY protocol:

```
(1) : U believe hasKey(V,KvmPub),hasKey(
V,KvdPub)is True
(2) : U possess {Nu}{KvdPub}KuPriv is
True
(3) : U believe fresh({Nu}{KvdPub}KuPriv)
is True
(4) : U believe shareKey(U,{Nu}{KvdPub}K
uPriv,V) is True
(5) : U believe V conveyed {dataV}{Nu}{K
vdPub}KuPriv True
(6) : U believe fresh({dataV}{Nu}{KvdPub
}KuPriv) is True
(7) : V believe hasKey(U,KuPub) is True
(8) : V possess {Nu}{KuPub}KvdPriv is
True
(9) : V believe fresh({Nu}{KuPub}KvdPriv)
is True
(10): V believe shareKey(V,{Nu}{KuPub}Kv
dPriv,U) is True
(11): V believe U conveyed {dataU}{Nu}{K
uPub}KvdPriv is True
(12): V believe fresh({dataU}{Nu}{KuPub}K
vdPriv) is True
```

This successful verification of the redesigned protocol provides strong evidence in the correctness of the protocol. Thus, the ability of the proposed development process to prevent the use of weak protocols by detecting protocol flaws is demonstrated.

Performance of Automated Logic-Based Verification

The automated verification system has been applied to a range of modern protocols, using different logics. A Pentium® 4 CPU 3GHz with 1GB of RAM running Microsoft Windows XP has been used for the empirical tests. The following gives a summary of some results:

- ASK Protocol (Aydos, Sunar, & Koc, 1998): Verification using GNY logic reveals known weaknesses. Memory 34MB, time 0.8s
- CDFASK Protocol (Coffey et al., 2003c): Verification using GNY logic succeeds. Memory 20MB, time 0.3s
- ASPeCT Protocol (Horn & Preneel, 2000): Verification using GNY logic reveals known weakness. Memory 26MB, time 1.4s
- Boyd-Park Protocol (Boyd & Park, 1998): Verification using CS logic reveals known weakness. Memory 77MB, time 1.3s
- Amended Boyd-Park (Newe & Coffey, 2003a): Verification using CS logic succeeds. Memory 41MB, time 0.8s
- HYS Protocol (Hwang, Yang, & Shiu, 2003): Verification using CS logic reveals known weakness. Memory 33MB, time 0.3s
- 3GPP AKA Protocol (Zhang & Fang, 2005): Verification using CS logic reveals known weakness. Memory 20MB, time 0.2s
- AP AKA Protocol (Zhang & Fang, 2005): Verification using CS logic succeeds. Memory 46MB, time 0.6s.

These results show that verification logics can be efficiently automated. Further, the process of applying the logical postulates is performed in a manner of seconds. This demonstrates the verification system's ability to efficiently verify security protocols.

FUTURE TRENDS

Historically, the formal verification of security protocols has been approached in two fundamentally different ways: one based on the work of Dolev and Yao (1983), and another based on Turing machines.

The approach based on Dolev and Yao assumes perfect cryptography. This assumption states that the content of encrypted messages can only be extracted with the same key (symmetric encryption) or with the inverse key (public key encryption). However, perfect cryptography cannot always be guaranteed: weaknesses are often found in employed cryptographic systems and the continuous increase in computational power enables brute-force attacks that were infeasible only a few years before. Recent work tries to weaken or remove this assumption by adding equational theories (Abadi & Cortier, 2004; Comon-Lundh & Shmatikov, 2003) and modifying the Dolev-Yao model (Baudet,

2005; Lowe, 2004). In general, techniques based on the Dolev-Yao model are often efficiently automated.

In the Turing machine-based approach, no idealization of cryptographic systems is required: cryptographic functions only operate on strings and attackers are modelled as Turing machines. In this framework, correctness is defined in terms of a high complexity and negligible probability of success (Bellare, Kilian & Rogaway, 1994; Goldwasser & Micali, 1984). While this approach appears to be more realistic than the formal approach based on the Dolev-Yao model, its complexity makes it difficult to develop automated or semi-automated verification tools.

In recent years, research has been undertaken to integrate these two approaches. The optimal goal is to prove the security of a protocol in the formal model and then to establish properties of the used cryptographic systems. Both results can then be combined to deduce the security of the protocol in a realistic framework without the perfect cryptography assumption. So far, very restrictive assumptions are required to keep the complexity of the realistic framework computational feasible An example of this approach is (Micciancio & Warinschi, 2004), where the authors prove that under certain conditions security in the formal model also implies security in a well defined more realistic model.

CONCLUSION

The protection of electronic networks and information systems against attack is a critical issue for the use of new technologies in all fields of life. Security protocols are designed to provide such protection. However, the design of correct and reliable security protocols is highly complex and error prone. Therefore, the importance of formal verification of cryptographic protocols during the development process cannot be overstated.

This chapter proposes a formal verification centred development process for security protocols, where design and verification of a security protocol are considered two inseparable steps: protocol design and formal verification are iterated until formal verification does not reveal any weaknesses of the protocol. Only then is the protocol published or implemented. This development process will significantly minimize the risk of using faulty protocols in electronic networks or information systems.

A case study demonstrated this formal verification centred development process using the BCY security protocol. The original BCY protocol was formally verified revealing a number of weaknesses. Subsequently, the protocol was redesigned to address these weaknesses and the amended protocol again subjected to formal verification. As the verification of the modified protocol succeeded, the amended protocol can be considered secure within the limits of its stated goals.

In conclusion, the discovery of various flaws in a surprisingly large number of published protocols, in many cases several years after the original publication, highlight the importance of formal verification and the strength of the proposed development process.

REFERENCES

Abadi, M., & Cortier, V. (2004). Deciding knowledge in security protocols under equational theories. In *Proceedings of 31th International Colloquium on Automata, Languages and Programming ICALP'04* (pp. 46-58) Turku, Finnland.

Aydos, M., Sunar, B., & Koc, C.K. (1998). An elliptic curve cryptography based authentication and key agreement protocol for wireless communication. In *Proceedings of 2nd International Workshop on Discrete Algorithms and Methods for Mobility DIAL M 98* (pp. 1-12). Dallas, USA.

Baudet, M. (2005). Deciding security of protocols against off-line guessing attacks. In *Proceedings of the 12th ACM Conference on Computer and Communications Security CCS05* (pp. 16-25). Alexandria, VA, USA.

Bellare, M., Kilian, J., & Rogaway, P. (1994). The security of cipher block chaining. In Y.G. Desmedt (Ed). *Proceedings of CRYPTO 94* (pp. 341-358). Santa Barbara, CA, USA.

Boyd, C., & Park, D.G. (1998). Public key protocols for wireless communications. In *Proceedings of International Conference on Information Security and Cryptology ICISC '98* (pp. 47-57). Seoul, Korea.

Brackin, S. (2000). Automatically detecting most vulnerabilities in cryptographic protocols. In *Proceedings of DARPA Information Survivability Conference & Exposition* (Vol. 1, pp. 222-236). IEEE CS Press.

Burrows, M., Abadi, M., & Needham, R. (1990). A logic of authentication. *ACM Transactions on Computer Systems, 8*(1), 18-36.

Carlsen, U. (1994). Optimal privacy and authentication on a portable communications system. *ACM Operating Systems Review, 28*(3), 16-23.

Cervesato, I., Durgin, N., Lincoln, P., Mitchell, J., & Scedrov, A. (1999). A meta-notation for protocol analysis. In *Proceedings of IEEE Computer Security Foundations Workshop* (pp. 55-69). Mordano, Italy.

Chang, Y.F., & Chang, C.C. (2005). An efficient authentication protocol for mobile satellite communication systems. *ACM SIGOPS Operating Systems Review, 39*(1), 70-84.

Clarke, E.M., Jha, S., & Marrero, W. (2000). Verifying security protocols with Brutus. *ACM Transactions on Software Engineering and Methodology (TOSEM), 9*(4), 443-487.

Coffey, T., & Dojen, R. (2003). Analysis of a mobile communication security protocol. In *Proceedings of International Symposium on Information and Communication Technologies ISICT03* (pp. 329-335). Dublin, Ireland.

Coffey, T., Dojen, R., & Flanagan, T. (2003a). Formal verification: An imperative step in the design of security protocols. *Computer Networks Journal, Elsevier Science, 43* (5), 601-618.

Coffey, T., Dojen, R., & Flanagan, T. (2003b). On the automated implementation of modal logics used to verify security protocols. In *Proceedings of the International Symposium on Information and Communication Technologies* (pp. 324-347) Dublin, Ireland.

Coffey, T., Dojen, R., & Flanagan, T. (2003c). On different approaches to establish the security of cryptographic protocols. In *Proceedings of Conference on Security and Management SAM'03* (Vol. 2, pp. 637-643). Las Vegas, USA.

Coffey, T., & Saidha, P. (1997). A logic for verifying public key cryptographic protocols. *IEEE Journal Proceedings on Computers and Digital Techniques, 144*(1), 28-32.

Coffey, T., Saidha, P., & Burrows, P. (2003). Analysing the security of a nonrepudiation communication protocol with mandatory proof of receipt. In *Proceedings of International Symposium on Information and Communication Technologies ISICT03* (pp. 351-356). Dublin, Ireland.

Cohen, E. (2000). TAPS: A first-order verifier for cryptographic protocols. In *Proceedings of IEEE Computer Security Foundations Workshop* (pp. 144-158). Cambridge, UK.

Comon-Lundh, H., & Shmatikov, V. (2003). Intruder deductions, constraint solving and insecurity decision in presence of exclusive or. In *Proceedings of the 18th Annual IEEE Computer Society Symposium on Logic in Computer Science LICS'03* (pp. 271-280). Ottawa, Canada.

Diffie, W., & Hellman, M.E. (1976). New directions in cryptography. *IEEE Transactions on Information Theory, 22*(6), 644-654.

Dill, D.L. (1996). The Murφ verification system. In *Proceedings of International Conference of Computer Aided Verification* (pp. 390-393). New Brunswick, NJ, USA.

Dojen, R., & Coffey, T. (2005). The concept of layered proving trees and its application to the automation of security protocol verification. *ACM Transactions on Information and System Security (TISSEC), 8*(3), 287-331.

Dolev, D., Even, S., & Karp, R. (1982). On the security of ping-pong protocols. *Information and Control, 55*(1), 57-68.

Dolev, D., & Yao, A. (1983). On the security of public key protocols. *IEEE Transactions on Information Theory, 29*(2), 198-208.

Even, S., & Goldreich, O. (1983). On the security of multi-party ping-pong protocols. In *Proceedings of IEEE Symposium on the Foundations of Computer Science* (pp. 34-39). Tucson, AZ, USA

Goldwasser, S., & Micali, S. (1984). Probabilistic encryption. *Journal of Computer and System Sciences, 28*(2), 270-299.

Gong, L., Needham, R., & Yahalom, R. (1990). Reasoning about belief in cryptographic protocols. In *Proceedings of IEEE Computer Society Synopsis on Research in Security and Privacy* (pp. 234-248). Oakland, USA.

Gürgens, S., & Rudolph, C. (2002). Security analysis of (un-) fair nonrepudiation protocols. In A.E. Abdallah, P. Ryan, & S. Schneider (Eds.). *Formal Aspects of Security, First International Conference, FASec* (pp. 07-114). London, UK.

Horn, G., Martin, K., & Mitchell, C. (2002). Authentication protocols for mobile network environment value-added services. *IEEE Transactions on Vehicular Technology, 51*(2), 383-392.

Horn, G., & Preneel, H. (2000). Authentication and payment in future mobile systems. *Journal of Computer Security, 8*(2/3), 183-207.

Huima, A. (1999). Efficient infinite-state analysis of security protocols. In *Proceedings of Workshop on Formal Methods and Security Protocols FLOC'99.* Trento, Italy.

Hwang, M.S., Yang, C.C., & Shiu, C.Y. (2003). An authentication scheme for mobile satellite communication systems. *ACM SIGOPS Operating Systems Review, 37*(4), 42-47.

Kessler, V., & Wendel, G. (1994). AUTLOG—An advanced logic of authentication. In *Proceedings of IEEE Computer Security Foundations* (pp. 90-99). Menlo Park, California, USA.

Kramer, S. (2004). CPL: An evidence-based 5-dimensional logic for the compositional specification and verification of cryptographic protocols—part I: Language, process model, satisfaction. In *Proceedings of the LICS/ICALPA Affiliated Workshop on Foundations of Computer Security* FCS04 (pp. 77-96). Turku, Finland.

Kudo, M., & Mathuria, A. (1999). An extended logic for analyzing timed-release public-key protocols. In V. Varadharajan, & Y. Mu (Eds.). *Lecture Notes in Computer Science, Proceedings of the Second International Conference on Information and Communication Security* (Vol. 1726, pp. 183-198). Springer Verlag.

Lowe, G. (1995). An attack on the Needham-Schroeder public-key authentication protocol. *Information Processing Letters, 56*(3), 131-133.

Lowe, G. (2004). Analysing protocol subject to guessing attacks. *Journal of Computer Security, 12*(1), 83-98.

Meadows, C. (1996). The NRL protocol analyser: An overview. *Journal of Logic Programming, 26*(8), 113-131.

Micciancio, D., & Warinschi, B. (2004). Soundness of formal encryption in the presence of active adversaries. In *Proceedings of the Theory of Cryptography Conference* (pp. 133-151). Cambridge, MA, USA.

Millen, J.K., Clark, S.C., & Freedman, S.B. (1987). The interrogator: Protocol security analysis. *IEEE Transactions on Software Engineering, 13*(22), 274-288.

Mu, Y., & Varadharajan, V. (1996). On the design of security protocols for mobile communications. In *Proceedings of Australasian Conference on Information Security and Privacy* (pp. 134-145). Wollongong, Australia.

Needham, R.M., & Schroeder, M.D. (1978). Using encryption for authentication in large networks of computers. *Communications of the ACM, 21*(12), 993-999.

Newe, T., & Coffey, T. (2002). Hybrid mobile security protocol: Formal verification using a new modal logic. In *Proceedings of International Conference on Automation and information ICAI-2002.* Puerto De La Cruz, Tenerife, Spain.

Newe T., & Coffey, T. (2003a). Formal verification logic for hybrid security protocols. *International Journal of Computer Systems Science & Engineering, 18*(1), 17-25.

Newe, T., & Coffey, T. (2003b). Minimum-knowledge schemes for low-power, low-memory devices. *WSEAS Transactions on Circuits and Systems, 2*(2), 460-465.

Newe, T., & Coffey, T. (2003c). On the logical verification of key exchange protocols for mobile communications. In: N.E. Mastorakis, G.E. Antoniou, C. Manikopoulos, Z. Bojkovic, I.F. Gonos (Eds.). *Recent Advances in Communications and Computer Science* (pp. 76-81). WSEAS Press.

Paulson, L.C. (1998). The inductive approach to verifying cryptographic protocols. *Journal of Computer Security, 6*(1-2), 85-128.

Rabin, M.O. (1979). Digitalized signatures and public-key functions as intractable as factorisation. *Technical Report MIT/LCS/TR-212.* Massachusetts Institute of Technology MIT, Cambridge, MA, USA.

Schneider, S.A. (1998). Verifying authentication protocols in CSP. *IEEE Transactions on Software Engineering (TSE), 24*(9), 741-758.

Song, D., Berezin, S., & Perrig, A. (2001). Athena: A novel approach to efficient automatic security protocol analysis. *Journal of Computer Security, 9*(1), 47-74.

Stubblebine, S., & Wright, R. (2002). An authentication logic with formal semantics supporting synchronization, revocation, and recency. *IEEE Transactions on Software Engineering, 28*(3), 256-285.

Syverson, P.F., & van Oorschot, P.C. (1994). On unifying some cryptographic protocols logics. In *Proceedings of IEEE Symposium on Security and Privacy* (pp. 14-28). Oakland, CA, USA.

Ventuneac, M., Coffey, T., & Newe, T. (2004). Reasoning on properties of nonrepudiation security protocols. *WSEAS Transactions on Information Science and Applications, 1*(5), 1262-1267.

Ventuneac, M., Dojen, R., & Coffey, T. (2006). Automated verification of wireless security protocols using layered proving trees. *WSEAS Transactions on Communications, 5*(2), 252-258.

Zhang, M., & Fang, Y. (2005). Security analysis and enhancements of 3GPP authentication and key agreement protocol. *IEEE Transactions on Wireless Communications, 4*(2), 734-742.

Zhang, Y., & Varadharajan, V. (2001). A logic for modelling the dynamics of beliefs in cryptographic protocols. In *Proceedings of Australasian Computer Science Conference* (pp. 215-222). Gold Coast, Queensland, Australia.

KEY TERMS

Authentication: The verification of the identity of the source of information.

Confidentiality: The protection of information, so that someone not authorized to access the information cannot read the information, even though the unauthorized person might see the information's container.

Cryptography: The study of mathematical techniques related to aspects of information security such as confidentiality, data integrity, entity authentication, and data origin authentication.

Data Integrity: The provision of the property that data and data sequences have not been altered or destroyed in an unauthorized manner.

Formal Verification: Application of formal methods to establish the correctness of a system.

Formalisation of a Security Protocol: Specifying the protocol in the language of the logic by expressing each protocol message as a logical formula is known as protocol formalisation (or idealisation). A formal description of the protocol, obtained by formalisation, does not simply list the components of each message, but attempts to show the purpose of these components so as to avoid ambiguity.

Nonce: A large random number that is intended to be employed only once and is used for binding messages to a specific protocol run.

Nonrepudiation: Nonrepudiation is the concept of ensuring that a contract, especially one agreed to via the Internet, cannot later be denied by one of the parties involved. With regards to digital security, nonrepudiation means that it can be verified that the sender and the recipient were, in fact, the parties who claimed to send or receive the message, respectively.

Postulate: A proposition that is accepted as true in order to provide a basis for logical reasoning.

Security Protocol: Also called cryptographic protocol, it constitutes transferring specially constructed encrypted messages between legitimate protocol participants to fulfil objectives such as mutual authentication or key-exchange in a predefined procedure.

Chapter XV
Edge–to–Edge Network Monitoring to Detect Service Violations and DoS Attacks

Ahsan Habib
Siemens TTB Center, Berkeley, USA

ABSTRACT

This chapter develops a distributed monitoring scheme that uses edge-to-edge measurements to identify congested links and capture the misbehaving flows that violate service-level-agreements and inject excessive traffic that leads into denial of service (DoS) attacks. The challenge of this problem is to develop low overhead schemes that do not involve core routers in any measurement to achieve scalability. The main contribution of this work is overlay-based network monitoring schemes for efficient and scalable network monitoring. This monitoring scheme uses edge-to-edge measurements of delay, loss, and throughput to infer the internal characteristics of a network domain. The analytical and experimental results show that a network domain can be monitored with O(n) probes, where n is the number of edge routers. Upon detection of an attack, the routers regulate misbehaving flows to stop it. We introduce a new way to measure communication and computation overhead among monitoring schemes. This comparative study shows that core-assisted network monitoring has higher communication and computation overhead comparing to edge-to-edge network monitoring scheme.

INTRODUCTION

The aim of a Denial of Service (DoS) attack is to consume the resources of a victim or the resources on the way to communicate with a victim. By wasting the victim's resources, an attacker disallows it from serving legitimate customers. A victim can be a host, server, router, or any computing entity connected to the network. In addition to DoS attacks, the quality of service (QoS) enabled networks are vulnerable to service level agreement (SLA) violations—namely, the QoS attacks. An attacker in this environment is a user who tries to get more resources (i.e., a better service

class) than what s/he has signed (paid) for. Legitimate customers' traffic may experience degraded QoS as a result of the illegally injected traffic. Taken to an extreme, that excess traffic may result in a denial of service attack. This creates a need for developing an effective defense mechanism that automates the detection and reaction to SLA violations.

Monitoring of a network domain can ensure the proper operation of a network by detecting possible service violations and attacks. Monitoring network activity is required to maintain confidence in the security and QoS of networks, from both the user (ensuring the service level paid for is indeed obtained) and provider (ensuring no unusual activity or attacks take place) perspectives. Continuous monitoring of a network domain poses several challenges. First, routers of a network domain need to be polled periodically to collect statistics about monitoring parameters such as delay, loss, and throughput.

Second, this huge amount of data has to be mined to obtain useful monitoring information. Polling increases the overhead for high speed core routers, and restricts the monitoring process from scaling to a large number of flows. To achieve scalability, polling and measurements that involve core routers should be avoided.

To detect attacks and service violations, we propose a low overhead monitoring scheme that does not involve core routers for any kind of measurements. Our assumption is that if a network domain is properly provisioned and no user is misbehaving, the flows traversing through the domain should not experience high delay or high loss. An excessive traffic due to attacks changes the internal characteristics of a network domain. This change of internal characteristics is a key point to monitor a network domain. We employ agents on the edge routers of a network domain to efficiently measure SLA parameters such as packet delays, loss, and throughput. The delay is an edge-to-edge latency measurement; packet loss is the ratio of total number of packets dropped from a flow to the total packets of the same flow entered into the domain; and throughput is the total bandwidth consumed by a flow inside a domain. A flow can be a micro flow with five tuples (two addresses, two ports, and protocol) or an aggregate one that is combined with several micro flows. Delay and loss are important parameters to monitor a network domain because these parameters mostly reflect the QoS of user applications. High delay and loss can be used as an indication of service violations. Although, jitter (delay variation) is another important SLA parameter, it is flow-specific, and therefore is not suitable to use in network monitoring.

We develop an overlay-based monitoring scheme that forms an overlay network using all edge routers on top of the physical network. The probing identifies the congested links due to high losses are identified using edge-to-edge loss measurements. To identify the congested links, all edge routers probe their neighbors in clockwise and counter-clockwise direction. This method requires only $O(n)$ probing, where n is the number of edge routers. Through extensive analysis, both analytical and experimental, we show that this identifies the congested links to a close approxima-

tion. If necessary, we refine the solution by searching the topology tree intelligently for probes that can be used to identify the status of the undecided links from earlier probing results. When the network is less than 20% congested the refinement process also requires $O(n)$ probes. If the congestion is high, it requires more probes, however, it does not exceed $O(n^2)$. The congested links are used as a basis to identify edge routers through which traffic are entering into and exiting from the domain. From exiting edge routers, we identify the flows that are violating any SLA agreement. If the SLA is violated for delay and loss, the network is probed to detect whether any user is stealing bandwidth. The service violations can indicate a possible attack on the same domain, or on a downstream domain.

We conclude that the distributed monitoring scheme shows a promise for an efficient and scalable monitoring of a domain. This scheme can detect service violations, bandwidth theft attacks, and tell when many flows are aggregating towards a downstream domain for a possible DoS attack. The scheme requires low monitoring overhead, and detects service violations in both directions of any link in a network domain.

BACKGROUND

DoS attacks are a serious threat for the Internet. The San Diego Supercomputer Center reported 12,805 DoS attacks over a three-week period (Moore, Voelker, & Savage, 2001). The approaches for dealing with DoS attacks can be divided into two main categories: detection and prevention approaches. The prevention approaches (Ferguson & Senie, 2000; Jin, Wang, & Shin, 2003; Park & Lee, 2001) try to thwart attacks before they harm the system. Filtering is the main strategy used in the prevention approaches that identify and drop attack packets before entering a network. Filtering can drastically reduce the DoS attack if a substantial number of domains use it, which hard to deploy. If there are some unchecked points, it is possible to launch DoS attacks from those points. The detection approaches, on the other hand, capitalize on the fact that appropriately punishing wrong doers (attackers) will deter them from re-attacking again, and will scare others to do similar acts. The detection process has two phases: detecting the attack and identifying the attacker. To identify an attacker, several traceback methods (Savage, Wetherall, Karlin, & Anderson, 2001; Snoeren, Partridge, Sanchez, Strayer, Jones, &

Tchakountio, 2001; Yaar, Perrig, Song, 2005) can be used. The obvious way to detect an attack is just waiting till the system performance decreases sharply or even the whole system collapses. We design a more effective method for detecting attacks before they severely harm the system. We propose to use monitoring for early detection of DoS attacks.

Network Monitoring

One obvious way of monitoring is to log packets at various points throughout the network and then extract information to discover the path of any packet (Sager, 1998). This scheme is useful to trace an attack long after the attack has been accomplished. The effectiveness of logging is limited by the huge storage requirements especially for high speed networks. Stone (2000) suggested creating a virtual overlay network connecting all edge routers of a provider to reroute *interesting* flows through tunnels to central tracking routers. After examination, suspicious packets are dropped. This approach also requires a great amount of logging capacity.

Many proposals for network monitoring (Breitbart, Chan, Garofalakis, Rastogi, & Silberschatz, 2001; Dilman & Raz, 2001) provide designs to manage the network and ensure that the system is operating within desirable parameters. In efficient reactive monitoring (Dilman & Raz, 2001), the authors discuss ways to monitor communication overhead in IP networks. Their idea is to combine global polling with local event driven reporting. Breitbart et al. identify effective techniques to monitor bandwidth and latency in IP networks (Breitbart et al., 2001). The authors present probing-based techniques, where path latencies are measured by transmitting probes from a single point of control. The paper describes algorithms to compute an optimal set of probes to measure latency of paths in a network, whereas we focus on measuring parameters without the involvements of the core routers.

For monitoring involving core routers, a large variety of network monitoring tools can be found in IEPM (2002). Many tools use SNMP (Case, Fedor, Schoffstall, & Davin, 1990), RMON (Waldbusser, 2000), or NetFlow (Cisco, 2000), which are built-in functionality for most routers. Using these mechanisms, a centralized or decentralized model can be built to monitor a network. The centralized approach to monitor network latency, jitter, loss, throughput, or other QoS parameters suffers from scalability. One way to achieve scalability is to use a hierarchical

architecture (Al-Shaer, Abdel-Wahab, & Maly, 1999; Subramanyan, Miguel-Alonso, & Fortes, 2000). Subramanyan et al. (2000) design a SNMP-based distributed network monitoring system that organizes monitoring agents and managers in a hierarchical fashion. Both centralized and decentralized models obtain monitoring data by polling each router of a network domain, which limits the ability of a system to scale for a large number of flows. The alternative way of polling is to use an event reporting mechanism that sends useful information typically in a summarized format only when the status of a monitored element changes. A more flexible way of network monitoring is by using mobile agents (Liotta, Pavlou, & Knight, 2002) or programmable architecture (Anagnostakis, Ioannidis, Miltchev, Ioannidis, Greenwald, & Smith, 2002). However, periodic polling or deploying agents in high speed core routers put nontrivial overhead on them. Our goal is to design a low overhead and scalable monitoring scheme.

SLA Verification

In Chan, Lin, and Wang (2000), a histogram-based aggregation algorithm is used to detect SLA violations. The algorithm measures network characteristics on a hop-by-hop basis and uses them to compute end-to-end measurements and validate end-to-end SLA requirements. In a large network, efficient collection of management data is a challenge. While exhaustive data collection yields a complete picture, there is an added overhead. The authors propose an *aggregation* and *refinement* based monitoring approach. The approach assumes that the routes used by SLA flows are known, citing VPN and MPLS (Callon, Doolan, Feldman, Fredette, Swallow, & Viswanathan, 1997) provisioning. Though routes are known for double ended SLAs that specify both ingress (entering router of a domain) and egress (exiting router of a domain) points in the network, they are unknown in cases where the scope of the service is not limited to a fixed egress point. As with RONs (Anderson, Balakrishnan, Kaashoek, & Morris, 2001), we verify SLA violations using average values in a recent time frame. This reduces constraints on the network setup and need for knowledge of the flows traversing through each router.

OVERLAY-BASED MONITORING: ARCHITECTURE AND MEASUREMENTS

Like any inference-based measurement (Duffield, Presti, Paxson, & Towsley, 2001), we convert a network topology into tree structure to apply our edge-to-edge probing to identify congested links using loss inference. The conversion of an arbitrary network topology to a tree topology is discussed in (Bu, Duffield, Presti, & Towsley, 2002). The tree contains core routers as internal nodes and edge routers as leaf nodes. The probing agents sit only at the edge routers or at the measurement boxes connect to the edge router, and know their neighbors. The neighbors are determined by visiting the tree using depth first search algorithm starting from any edge router, and putting all edge routers in an ordered sequence. All probing agents form a virtual network on top of the physical network. We equivalently refer the tree topology or the virtual network to an overlay network. A typical spanning tree of the topology, the corresponding overlay network, and direction of all internal links for each probe are shown in Figure 1.

We use a SLA Monitor (SLAM) to collect statistics and take necessary decision. The SLAM gets feedback about delay, loss, and other parameters from the edge routers. A service provider can also use a dedicated host as a SLAM or any edge router can take the responsibility. The SLAM maintains a table storing delay and loss information of misbehaving flows only. The table is updated on receipt of new values from the egress routers. In addition, the SLAM maintains the SLA parameters for each customer for a certain domain. By comparing the delay and loss measurements against the specific customer SLA, the violations are identified.

Now, we discuss the monitoring algorithm. Then, we elaborate each of the steps involved in monitoring algorithm. The algorithm proceeds as follows:

1. Each ingress router copies the header of user packets with probability p_{probe} to probe the network for delay measurement.
2. The edge routers compute the average edge-to-edge delay updates the average delay to the SLAM.
3. When the delay measurements exceed the predefined threshold, the SLAM signals the appropriate edge routers (based on delay probes) to conduct probing for loss. This time each edge router probes its neighbor in clockwise and counterclockwise direction.
4. The SLAM analyzes the outcome of the two rounds of probing. If necessary, it traverses the tree to look for probes for the advanced probing. In this case, the edge routers are informed who will be the receiver of this probing.
5. The edge routers feedback the outcome of the advanced probing to the SLAM. The SLAM continues the process until it gets a feasible solution.
6. The SLAM probes the network for throughput approximation when the loss is higher than the preconfigured threshold.
7. For users with higher delay, loss, and bandwidth consumption, the monitor decides about possible SLA violation. The monitor knows the existing traffic classes and the acceptable SLA parameters per class. For each violation, it takes proper action, such as throttling the particular user traffic using flow control mechanism.

The challenge of edge-to-edge monitoring is to measure each of the network metrics such as delay, loss, and throughput involving only the edge routers. We now present our measurement methodology that involves only the edge routers.

Delay Measurements

Delay-bound guarantees made by a provider network to customer traffic flows are for the delays experienced by the flows between the ingress and egress edges of the provider's domain. Delay measurements can be done using either real customer traffic or artificially injected traffic. The first is an intrusive approach that encodes timestamps into real traffic and rewrites the original content at the egress after appropriate measurements. The second approach is nonintrusive. Probe packets are injected with desired control information to perform measurements and delete the probes from the traffic stream. We adopt the second approach. With a certain preconfigured probability p_{probe}, the ingress copies the packet IP header into a new probe packet. A timestamp $t_{ingress}$ is encoded into the payload, and an identifier field is marked with a new value in the probe packet. The egress router removes probes from the traffic stream, and computes delay for a packet of flow i as:

Figure 1. Architecture to detect SLA violations; (a) tree topology transformed from a network domain; (b) all probing agents located at the edge routers form a virtual network with both neighbors in an ordered sequence; the direction of internal links of each probing is shown; each edge router reports the outcome of probing to the SLA monitor (SLAM)

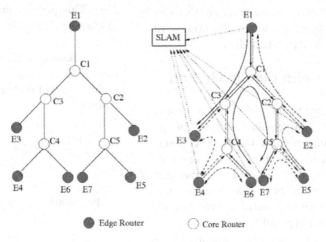

$$delay^i = t^i_{egress} - t^i_{ingress} \qquad (1)$$

The encoded timestamp must follow a well-known format such as the Coordinated Universal Time (UTC), or a standard protocol such as Network Time Protocol (NTP), to obtain the timestamp value at the edge routers. The clock synchronization problem can also be overcome by rerouting the same probe packet from egress to ingress router in the opposite direction. The ingress router then computes the approximate latency from the elapsed time between sending and receiving the probe. At time t, the egress routers classify the packet as belonging to flow i of customer j, and update the average packet delay of the customer traffic as an exponential weighted moving average (EWMA):

$$avgdelay_j(t) = avgdelay_j(t-1) + (1-\alpha)delay_j(t), \qquad (2)$$

where α is a small fraction to emphasize the delay history more than the current sample. If this average packet delay exceeds the delay guarantee in the SLA, we conclude that an SLA violation has occurred. If the network is properly provisioned, and all flows do not misbehave, delay for customer j should not exceed its delay guarantee. The report is sent to SLAM.

Determining the probability with which we should inject probe packets is not an easy task. If there are M edge routers in a network domain, N^i flows (on the

average) passing through an edge router i, and p^{ij}_{probe} is the probability that an edge router i and flow j will be selected to probe for latency, then $MN^i p^{ij}_{probe}$ is the average number of control/probe packets injected into the network domain. To keep the volume of these control messages low, we must select a low probability. However, if the probability is too low, the chance of undetected SLA violations is higher. Therefore, we choose a variable p_{probe} that changes dynamically over time at each edge router.

Loss Measurements: Identifying Congested Links

The following definitions and observations are used to describe the properties of the overlay network, and to identify congested links using edge-to-edge measurement-based loss inference.

Definition 1. Congested link. A link is congested if all loss measurement samples in a given time frame exceed a specified loss threshold.

Definition 2. Probe path. A probe path P is a sequence of routers (either core or edge) $< E_1, C_1, C_2, ..., C_n, E_n >$ where a router exists in the sequence only once. A probe packet originates at the edge router E_1, passes through the core routers C_1, C_2, C_{n-1} and C_n, in the given order, and terminates at the edge router En. We also represent the probe path P by the set of links, $< E_1 \rightarrow C_1, C_1 \rightarrow C_2, ..., C_n \rightarrow E_n >$.

Definition 3. Link direction. A link $u \rightarrow v$ we say link from node u to v, is in inward direction (IN) with respect to node v. Similarly, the same link is in outward (OUT) direction with respect to node u.

Loss Inference with Simple Method

Our solution contains two methods: Simple method and Advanced method. We conduct total two rounds of probing in the Simple method. One in the counter-clockwise direction, and one in the clock-wise direction starting from any edge router. The former one is referred to as *first round* of probing, and the latter one is referred to as *second round* of probing. In each round, probing is done in parallel.

We describe the loss monitoring scheme with a simple network topology. In this example, Figure 2, edge router 1 probes the path 1→3, router 3 probes the path 3→4, and 4 probes the path 4→1. Let P_{ij} be a boolean variable that represents the outcome of a probe between edge routers i to j. P_{ij} takes on value 1 if the measured loss exceeds the threshold in any link within the probe path, and 0 otherwise. Notice that $P_{ij} = 0, \forall_{i,j}, i = j$. We express the outcome of a probe in terms of combination of all link status. Let X_{ij} be a boolean variable to represent the congestion status of an internal link $i \rightarrow j$. We refer X to a *congestion variable*. From Figure 2c, we can write equations as follows:

$$X_{1,2} + X_{2,3} = P_{1,3} \quad X_{3,2} + X_{2,4} = P_{3,4} \quad X_{4,2} + X_{2,1} = P_{4,1}$$

(3)

where (+) represents a boolean *OR* operation. We express status of internal links of any probe path of a network topology in terms of probe outcomes. Note that loss in path 1→3 might not be same as loss in path 3→1. This path asymmetry phenomenon is shown in (Savage, 1999). In general, X_{ij} is independent of $X_{i,j}, \forall_{ij, i \neq j}$.

The second round of probing, Figure 2(a), is done from 1→4, 4→3, and 3→1. We express the outcome of this round of probing in terms of internal links as follows:

$$X_{1,2} + X_{2,4} = P_{1,4} \quad X_{4,2} + X_{2,3} = P_{4,3} \quad X_{3,2} + X_{2,1} = P_{3,1}$$

(4)

For an arbitrary topology,

$$X_{i,k} + \sum_{n=k}^{n=l-1} X_{n,n+1} + X_{l,j} = P_{i,j}$$

(5)

The sets of equations (3 and 4) are used to detect congested link in the network. For example, if the outcome of the probing shows $P_{1,3} = 1$, $P_{1,4} = 1$, and the rest are 0, we get $X_{1,2} + X_{2,3} = 1$ $X_{1,2} + X_{2,4} = 1$. All other probes do not see congestion on its path (i.e., $X_{3,2} = X_{2,4} = X_{4,2} = X_{2,1} = X_{2,3} = 0$). Thus, we get $X_{1,2} = 1$. Similarly, if any of the single links is congested, we can isolate the congested link. Suppose two of the links, $X_{1,2}$ and $X_{2,3}$ are congested. The outcome of probing will be $P_{1,3} = 1$, $P_{1,4} = 1$, and $P_{4,3} = 1$, which makes $X_{3,2} = X_{2,4} = X_{4,2} = X_{2,1} = 0$. This leaves the solution to $X_{1,2} + X_{2,3} = 1$, $X_{1,2} = 1$, $X_{2,3} = 1$. Thus, the overlay-based scheme can isolate links with high loss in this topology.

Figure 2. (a) Spanning tree of a simple network topology; (b) each edge router probes its neighbor edge router in counter-clockwise direction; (c) direction of internal links for each probing

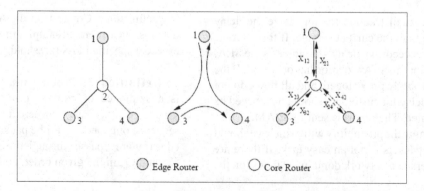

Analysis of Simple Method. The strength of simple method comes from the fact that congestion variables in one equation of any round of probing is distributed over several equations in the other round of probing. If n variables appear in one equation in the first round of probing, no two n variables appear in the same equation in the second round of probing. This property helps to solve the equation sets efficiently. In Theorem 1, we show that the simple method determines the status of a link with very high probability when the congestion is low. Moreover, if any single probe path is congested with arbitrary number of links, the simple method can identify all the congested links.

Lemma 1. *For any arbitrary overlay network, the average length of the probe paths in the Simple Method is ≤ 4.*

Proof. In an overlay network, the number of links are $2(e+c-1)$ considering both directions of a link. The edge routers are the leaves of the topology tree, whereas the core routers are the internal nodes of the tree. The number of leaf nodes is greater than the number of internal nodes. Thus, the number of links is $\leq 2(e + e-1) = 4e$. Number of the probe paths in the first (or second) round of probing is e, and every link appears exactly once in each round. Hence, the average length of a path $\leq \dfrac{4e}{e} = 4$.

Theorem 1. *Let p be the probability of a link being congested in any arbitrary overlay network. The simple method determines the status of any link of the topology with probability* $2(1-p)^4 - (1-p)^7 + 2p(1-p)^{12} - p(1-p)^{24}.$

Proof. Let a particular link l appears in probe paths P_1 and P_2 in the first and second round of probing. The status of a link can be either noncongested or congested. We consider both cases separately and then combine the results.

When l is noncongested. The status of l can be determined if the rest of the links in either P_1 or P_2 are noncongested. Let the length of probe paths P_1 and P_2 are i and k respectively. The probabilities that the other links in P_1 and P_2 are noncongested are $(1 - p)^{i-1}$ and $(1-p)^{k-1}$ respectively. Since only common link

between paths P_1 and P_2 is l, the following two events are independent: $\text{Event}_1 =$ all other links in P_1 are noncongested and $\text{Event}_2 =$ all other links in P_2 are noncongested. Thus, for a noncongested link,

Pr[status of l be determined]
$= (1-p)^{i-1} + (1-p)^{k-1} - (1-p)^{i-1}(1-p)^{k-1}$
$= (1-p)^{i-1} + (1-p)^{k-1} - (1-p)^{i+k-2}$

Using the average length for the probe paths (Lemma 1) (i.e., i=k=4). Pr[Status of l be determined]= $2(1-p)^3 + (1-p)^6$.

When l is congested. If l is a congested link, its status can be determined when all other links that appear on the probe path of l are noncongested and their statuses are determined. Let link l appears on a path in the first round of probing with l_1, l_2, and l_3 (considering the average path length is 4). The probability that l_1 (l_2 or l_3) is noncongested and determined is $(1-p)^4$. The probability to determine the status of these three links is $(1-p)^{12}$. This is true for the equations set in the second round, where l appears with variables other than l_1, l_2, and l_3. Thus, Pr [Status of l be determined] $= 2(1-p)^{12} - (1-p)^{24}$.

For any link l (congested or noncongested), Pr[Status of l be determined]= $(1-p)[2(1-p)^3 - (1-p)^6] + p[2(1-p)^{12} - (1-p)^{24}]$ = $2(1-p)^4 - (1-p)^7 + 2p(1-p)^{12} - p(1-p)^{24}$.

Collorary 1. *If only one probe path P is shown to be congested in the first round of probing, the simple method identifies each congestion link in P.*

Figure 3 shows the probability to determine the status of a link when a certain fraction of the links is actually congested. This figure shows that the simple method determines status of a link with probability close to 0.90 when 10% links of a network are congested. For 20% and 30% congestion, the probabilities are 0.64 and 0.40 respectively. This result is validated with the simulation result for two different topologies (Habib, 2003). The simple method does not help much when 50% or more links are congested. In that case, we use the advanced method to find probes that can decide the status of undecided links in the simple method.

Having congestion on links that affect multiple probe paths might eventually lead to some boolean equations that do not have unique solutions. Thus, the solution of the simple method usually has some links undecided. We identify the status of these undecided links using advanced method, which is discussed next.

Loss Inference with Advanced Method

The algorithm of the advanced method is run as follows: First, we conduct the simple method. Let the set of equations with undecided variables be $\mathbb{E}$. For each variable in equation set $\mathbb{E}$, we need to find two nodes that can be used to probe the network. Each probe requires one start node and one end node. The algorithm uses the same function to find start and end node of a probe. Link direction (Definition 3) plays an important role to find these probes. For example, in Figure 1, if link $C_1 \rightarrow C_3$ is congested, the start probe node can be E_2, E_5, or E_7. On the other hand, if link $C_3 \rightarrow C_1$ is congested, the start probing node can be E_3, E_4, or E_5.

For an undecided link $v_i \rightarrow v_j$, the method looks for leaves descended from node v_i and v_j. First, the algorithm searches for a node in IN direction on a subtree descended from v_i and then in OUT direction on a subtree descended from v_j. For any node v, the advanced method explores all siblings of v to choose a path in a specified direction. The function avoids

previously visited path and known congested path. It marks already-visited paths so that the same path will not be repeated in exploration of an alternate path. If the network is congested in a way that no solution is possible, the advanced method cannot add anything to the simple method. If there is a solution, the advanced method can obtain probes because this is an exhaustive search on the topology tree to find edge-to-edge paths that are not already congested.

Analysis of Advanced Method. The number of probes required in the advanced method depends on the number of congested links existing in a network. The advanced method starts with the undecided links. When the network is sparely congested or densely congested, the algorithm exit with fewer run and the number of trial for each congestion variable is low. To obtain how many trials we need to identify the status of each link, we need the average length of a probe path d and on how many paths b a link lies on. For an arbitrary overlay network, we calculate the approximated value of d and b in (Habib, 2003). Using these two values we show that, Theorem 2, the advanced method identifies the status of a link in O(n) probing with a very high probability when the network is 20% congested or less.

Theorem 2. Let p be the probability of a link being congested. The advanced method detects the status of a link with probability $1 - (1 - (1 - p)^d)^b$,

Figure 3. Probability that the simple method determines the status of a link of any arbitrary topology; x-axis is the fraction of total links that are actually congested; the simple method performs extremely well when less than 20% links of a network are congested; if a network is more than 50% congested, the simple method cannot contribute much

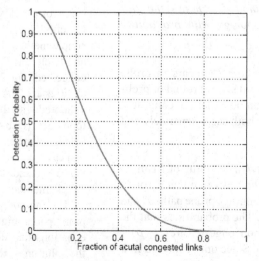

where $d = \dfrac{3e}{2\ln e}$ is the average path length and $b = \dfrac{e(3e-2)}{8\ln e}$ is the average number of paths a link lies on.

Proof. The probability that a path of length d is noncongested $(1-p)^d$. The probability of having all b paths congested is $(1-(1-p)^d)^b$. Thus, the probability that at least one noncongested path exists is $1-(1-(1-p)^d)^b$.

The detection probability in the advanced method (Theorem 2) is plot in Figure 4. This figure shows the probability that a good (noncongested) path exists for any link. The congestion status of the network is varied on the X-axis. Two graphs are shown: one shows the probability that a good path exists. It provides the upper bound because the solution cannot be better than this limit. If no path exists, the advanced method cannot do anything. The other graph shows the probability that a good as well as decided path exists. This provides the lower bound because it uses the decided links from the simple method and the solution cannot be worst than this. The advanced method needs only *one probe* on the average to identify the status of the link when the

network is less than 20% congested. In this case, the total required probes is O(n). Some links might need more than one, which is not high, because a good and decided path exists. If the network is 20-50% congested, the advanced method might need multiple probes to decide the status of one unknown variable in $\mathbb{E}$. If the network is more than 50% congested, the advanced method cannot find a good path easily because the path does not exist, and the advanced method terminates quickly. When the network is highly congested, we need to check almost all the flows any way. Thus, we can go to the detection phase instead of wasting time to rule out very few good links.

The performance of the advanced method is not significant when the network is heavily congested. Then, we can apply only the simple method, and go to the second phase of monitoring directly after that. Thus, we should go to the advanced method if the congestion is below a certain level. The congestion level is determined using the graph of the simple method shown Figure 3. For example, Figure 3 shows that the detection probability is 12% when the network is 50% congested. If congestion level is less than a specified threshold (50%), only then we go to the advanced method. We proceed to the second phase of monitoring with this outcome.

Figure 4. Probability that the advanced method determines the status of a link of topoloogy; the x-axis is the probability that a link to be congested; the y-axis is the probability that a good path (noncongested) exists for any link; the dotted graph shows the probability that a good path exists; the solid graph shows the probability that a good and decided path (from the first round) exists; these two curves provide lower and upper bound of the performance respectively

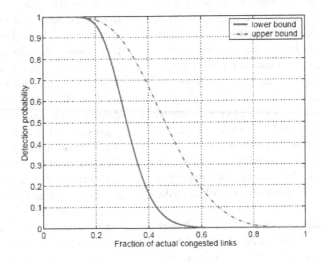

Throughput Measurements

The objective of throughput measurement is to ensure no user is consuming extra bandwidth (beyond its profile) after aggregation within a domain. This cannot be detected by an ingress router if the user sends at a lower rate than its profile through multiple ingress routers. The service provider allows the user to consume extra bandwidth if no other flow suffers degraded performance as a result, so throughput measurement is only performed if a violation has been reported.

The SLAM measures throughput by probing egress routers following a loss or delay violation report. The egress measures the rate at which user traffic is leaving a network domain. This is an average value over time duration and it represents the per-domain throughput for a flow. When the SLAM measures throughput of flows at egress routers, it computes the aggregate throughput for user j as:

$$B^j = \sum_{i=1}^{N_e} B_{ij}. \text{ If } B^j > SLA^j_{bw}$$

then an SLA violation is reported.

DETECTING AND CONTROLLING SLA VIOLATIONS AND ATTACKS

Violation detection is the second phase of our monitoring process. When delay, loss, and bandwidth consumption exceed the pre-defined thresholds, the monitor decides whether the network experiences a possible SLA violation. The monitor SLAM knows the existing traffic classes and the acceptable SLA parameters per class. For each service class, we obtain bounds on each SLA parameter that will be used as a threshold. A high delay is an indication of abnormal behavior inside a network domain. If there is any loss for the guaranteed traffic class, and if the loss ratios for other traffic classes exceed certain levels, an SLA violation is flagged. This loss can be caused by some flows consuming bandwidths above their SLA_{bw}. Bandwidth theft is checked by comparing the total bandwidth obtained by a user against the user's SLA_{bw}. The misbehaving flows are controlled at the ingress routers.

To detect DoS attacks, a set of links L with high loss are identified. For each congested link, $l(v_i, v_j) \in L$, the tree is divided into two subtrees: one formed by leaves descendant from v_i and the other from the leaves descendant from v_j. The former subtree has egress routers as leaves through which high aggregate bandwidth flows are leaving. If many exiting flows have the same destination IP prefix, either this is a DoS attack or they are going to a popular site (Mahajan, Bellovin, Floyd, Ioannidis, Paxson, & Shenker, 2002). Decision is taken by consulting the destination entity. Jung et al. analyze the characteristics of flash crowd and DoS attacks in (Jung, Krishnamurthy, & Rabinovich, 2002), which reveals several distinguishable features between these two. For example, the client distribution of a flash crowd event follows popular distribution among ISPs and networks, however, this is not true for a DoS attack. The other distinguishable features are per client request rate, overlap of clusters a site sees before and after the event, and popularity distribution of the file accessed by the clients. Using these characteristics, the monitor can decide whether it is a DoS attack or a flash crowd. In case of an attack, we control it by triggering filters at the ingress routers, which are leaves of the subtree descendant from v_i and feeding flows to the congested link. For each violation, the monitor takes action, such as throttling a particular user's traffic using a flow control mechanism.

A scenario of detecting and controlling DoS attack is now illustrated using Figure 1(a). Suppose the victim's domain $\mathbb{D}$ is connected to the edge router E_6. The monitor observes that links $C_3 \rightarrow C_4$ and link $C_4 \rightarrow C_6$ are congested for a specified time duration Δt sec. From both congested links, we obtain the egress router E_6 through which most of these flows are leaving. The destination IP prefix matching at E_6 reveals that an excess amount of traffic is heading towards the domain $\mathbb{D}$. To control the attack, the monitor needs to identify the ingress routers through which the suspected flows are entering into the domain. The procedure to identify these ingress routers is discussed next.

An important question is how to identify ingress routers through which the flows are entering into the domain. To identify the flow aggregation, we use delay probes, and assign an ID to each router. An ingress router puts its ID on the delay probe packet. The egress router knows from which ingress routers the packets are coming. For example, in Figure 1(a), say egress router E_6 is receiving flows from E_1, E_2, E_3, and E_5. These flows aggregate during their trip to E_6, and make the link $C_4 \rightarrow C_6$ congested. We traverse the path backwards from the egress router to the ingress routers through the congested link to obtain the entry points of the flows that are causing attacks. In this example, all edge routers can feed the congested links and they all will be candidates for activating filters. Knowing the ingress routers and congested links, we figure out the ingress routers for the flows that are causing the attacks.

COMPARATIVE EVALUATION

We conduct a quantitative analysis of the overhead imposed by core-assisted and overlay-based monitoring schemes. We do not emphasize on numeric overhead value of any specific scheme, rather, we draw a relative comparison among them. For each scheme, we calculate two different overheads: processing and communication. The processing overhead is due to extra processing required at all routers of a domain per unit time. Each router inside a domain requires processing such as address lookup, TTL field decrement, checksum computation, etc. for each monitoring packet. The communication overhead is computed as the number of extra bytes (not packets) injected per unit time. We consider a domain D with M edge routers and N core routers. We assume there are F flows traversing through each edge router and each flow has P packets on average. We define μ as the percentage of misbehaving flows that may cause DoS attacks. For simplicity, we charge α processing units for each packet processed.

Core-Assisted Monitoring. The monitoring schemes inject probe traffic into the network and add processing overheads as well. The total number of injected probes and the size of each probe packet are used to calculate the communication overheads in terms of bytes. The core-assisted scheme depends on the number of packets that core routers send to the monitor to report drop history. The drop history at each core router depends on the flows traversing the network domain and the percentage of these flows that are violating their SLAs at a particular time. For the domain D, if d bytes are required to record the drop information of each flow, then each core needs to send

$$C = \max(\frac{F\mu d}{packet\_size})$$

control packets to the monitor. The *packet_size* is the size of a control packet, which depends on the MTU of the network. To obtain loss ratio, the monitor queries all edges for packet count information of the misbehav-

ing flows. Every edge replies to this query. The total number of packets exchanged among all edge routers and the monitor is $(2M + N)C$ packets. Therefore, the communication overhead is given by:

$$C_{Core} = (2M + N)\max(1, \frac{F\mu d}{packet\_size})packet\_size \tag{6}$$

On average, each probe packet traverses h hops and thus the processing overhead can be calculated as:

$$P_{Core} = (2M + N)\max(1, \frac{F\mu d}{packet\_size})h\alpha \tag{7}$$

Overlay-based monitoring. For our edge-to-edge measurement-based monitoring, each edge router probes its left and right neighbors. If it requires f_d probes per unit time, the communication overhead is:

$$C_{Overlay} = 2Mf_d packet\_size \tag{8}$$

The processing overhead can be calculated as:

$$P_{Overlay} = 2Mf_d h\alpha \tag{9}$$

To visualize the differences among all schemes, we plot the processing and communication overhead for a domain with hundreds of routers. On average, F=100,000 flows pass each edge router per unit time. The number of hop count inside a domain is h=4. On average, f_d= 20 probes are sent per unit time in overlay monitoring.

In Figure 5, we vary the domain size changing the number of routers. The percentage of misbehaving traffic μ is fixed and equals 1%. The figure shows that Core can result in similar computation overhead to overlay-based schemes. Even though the overhead of Core scheme depends on core and edge routers, this scheme reduces processing overhead by aggregating flows when it reports to the monitor. When number of edge routers increases, overhead for both Core and Overlay schemes increase. The core-assisted monitoring has very high communication overhead because the overhead depends on the number of flows, whereas in the overlay-based scheme, the overhead depends on the number of routers and scales well to a large domain with a large number of flows.

Figure 5. The processing and communication overhead for the monitoring schemes when the number of edge routers in a domain is increased; the core scheme has similar processing overhead to overlay-based scheme; however, overlay always impose less communication overhead than the core scheme

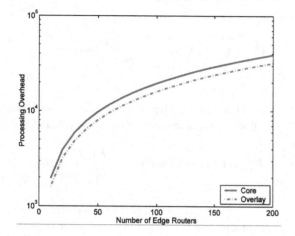
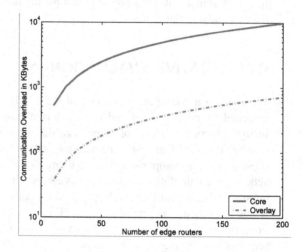

CONCLUSION

The core-assisted monitoring has high overhead for a large network domain. We develop an overlay-based distributed network monitoring scheme to keep a domain safe from service violations and bandwidth theft attacks. We do not measure actual loss of all internal links, instead, we identify all congested links with high losses using overlay networks. Our analytic analysis (verified by simulation in Habib (2003)) shows that even if 20% links of a network are congested, the status of each link can be identified with probability ≥ 0.98. If the network is 40% congested, this probability is still high (0.65). However, if the network is more than 60% congested, this method cannot achieve anything significant since almost every edge-to-edge path has one or more congested links. This new scheme requires only O(n) probes when less than 20% links are congested, where n is the number of edge routers and does not go beyond O(n^2) probes. For an OC3 link, the probe traffic to identify the congested links is 0.002% of link capacity. This monitoring conducts probing in parallel enabling the system to perform real time monitoring. Finally, we have shown that the new scheme scales well for a large network comparing with the core-assisted monitoring.

REFERENCES

Anagnostakis, K., Ioannidis, S., Miltchev, S., Ioannidis, J., Greenwald, M., & Smith, J. (2002, April). Efficient packet monitoring for network management. In *Proceedings of IEEE Network Operations and Management Symposium (NOMS)*. Florence, Italy.

Anderson, D., Balakrishnan, H., Kaashoek, F., & Morris, R. (2001, October). Resilient overlay network. In *Proceedings of ACM Symp on Operating Systems Principles (SOSP)*. Banff, Canada.

Al-Shaer, E., Abdel-Wahab, H., & Maly, K. (1999, May). HiFi: A new monitoring architecture for distributed systems management. In *Proceedings of IEEE 19th International Conference on Distributed Computing Systems (ICDCS '99)* (pp. 171-178). Austin, TX.

Breitbart, Y., Chan, C., Garofalakis, M., Rastogi, R., & Silberschatz, A. (2001, April). Efficiently monitoring bandwidth and latency in IP networks. In *Proceedings of IEEE INFOCOM*. Anchorage, AK.

Bu, T., Duffield, N., Presti, F., & Towsley, D. (2002, June). Network tomography on general topologies. In *Proceedings of ACM SIGMETRICS*. Marina del Rey, CA.

Callon, R., Doolan, P., Feldman, N., Fredette, A., Swallow, G., & Viswanathan, A. (1997, November). *A framework for multiprotocol label switching.* Internet draft.

Case, J., Fedor, M., Schoffstall, M., & Davin, J. (1990, May). *A simple network management Protocol (SNMP).* IETF RFC 1157.

Chan, M., Lin, Y.-J., & Wang, X. (2000, November). A scalable monitoring approach for service level agreements validation. In *Proceedings of International Conference on Network Protocols (ICNP)* (pp. 37-48). Osaka, Japan.

Cisco. (2000, May). *Netflow services and applications.* Retrieved May 3, 2008, from http://www.cisco.com/

Dilman, M., & Raz, D. (2001, April). Efficient reactive monitoring. In *Proceedings of IEEE INFOCOM.* Anchorage, AK.

Duffield, N., Presti, F., Paxson, V., & Towsley, D. (2001, April). Inferring link loss using striped unicast probes. In *Proceedings of IEEE INFOCOM.* Anchorage, AK.

Ferguson, P., & Senie, D. (2000, May). *Network ingress filtering: Defeating denial of service attacks which employ IP source address spoofing agreements performance monitoring.* IETF RFC 2827.

Habib, A. (2003, August). *Monitoring and controlling QoS network domains: An edge-to-edge approach.* Doctoral dissertation. Purdue University.

IEPM. (2002). *Internet end-to-end performance monitoring.* http://wwwiepm.slac.stanford.edu/

Jin, C., Wang, H., & Shin, K. (2003, October). Hop-count filtering: An effective defense against spoofed traffic. In *Proceedings of the 10th ACM conference on Computer and communications security* (pp. 30-41). Washington, D.C.

Jung, J., Krishnamurthy, B., & Rabinovich, D. (2002, May). Flash crowds and denial of service attacks: Characterization and implications for cdns and Web sites. In *Proceedings of World Wide Web (WWW).* Honolulu, HI.

Liotta, A., Pavlou, G., & Knight, G. (2002, May/June). Exploiting agent mobility for large-scale network monitoring. *IEEE Network.*

Mahajan, M., Bellovin, S., Floyd, S., Ioannidis, J., Paxson, V., & Shenker, S. (2002, July). Controlling high bandwidth aggregates in the network. *ACM Computer Communication Review, 32*(3), 62-73.

Moore, D., Voelker, G., & Savage, S. (2001, August). Inferring Internet denial-of-service activity. In *Proceedings of USENIX Security Symposium.* Washington D.C.

Park, K., & Lee, H. (2001, August). A proactive approach to distributed DoS attack prevention using route-based packet filtering. In *Proceedings of ACM SIGCOMM.* San Diego, CA.

Sager, G. (1998, November). *Security fun with OCxmon and cflowd.* Intenet2 working group meeting.

Savage, S., Wetherall, D., Karlin, A., & Anderson, T. (2001, June). Network support for IP traceback. *IEEE/ACM Transaction on Networking, 9*(3), 226-237.

Savage, S. (1999, October). Sting: A TCP-based network measurement tool. In *Proceedings of USENIX Symposium on Internet Technologies and Systems (USITS '99).* Boulder, CO.

Snoeren, A., Partridge, C., Sanchez, L., Strayer, W., Jones, C., & Tchakountio, F. (2001, August). Hashed-based IP traceback. In *Proceedings of ACM SIGCOMM.* San Diego, CA.

Stallings, W. (1998). SNMPv3: A security enhancement for SNMP. *IEEE Communications Surveys, 1*(1).

Stone, R. (2000, August). Centertrack: An IP overlay network for tracking DoS floods. In *Proceedings of USENIX Security Symposium.* Denver, CO.

Subramanyan, R., Miguel-Alonso, J., & Fortes, J. (2000). A scalable SNMP-based distributed monitoring system for heterogeneous network computing. In *Proceedings of High Performance Networking and Computing Conference (SC 2000).* Dallas, TX.

Yaar, A., Perrig, A., & Song, D. (2005, March). FIT: Fast Internet traceback. In *Proceedings of INFOCOM 2005* (Vol. 2, pp. 1395-1406).

Waldbusser, S. (2000, May). *Remote network monitoring management information base.* IETF RFC 2819.

KEY TERMS

Denial of Service: A denial-of-service (DoS) attack is an attempt to make resources unavailable to the legitimate users.

Edge-to-Edge Measurements: An edge-to-edge measurement is a methodology where measuring tools reside only at the edge routers and there is no direct access to the core routers.

Network Monitoring: Network monitoring describes the process of constantly monitoring a computer network to detect failures or attacks and notifies the network administrator when a certain condition is met.

Service Level Agreements: A service level agreement (SLA) is a service contract where the services, priorities, guarantee, etc. collectively, the level of service, is defined. It is a contract that exists between customers and their service provider, or between service providers.

Service Violations: Service violations occur a user or a flow consumes extra resources beyond its service level agreements.

SLA Monitor: SLA Monitor is an entity that collects statistics about network parameters such as latency, loss, throughput from the routers and take necessary decision.

Chapter XVI
A "One–Pass" Methodology for Sensitive Data Disk Wipes

Doug White
Roger Williams University, USA

Alan Rea
Western Michigan University, USA

ABSTRACT

Hard disk wipes are a crucial component of computing security. However, more often than not, hard drives are not adequately processed before either disposing or reusing them within an environment. When an organization does not follow a standard disk wipe procedure, the opportunity to expose sensitive data occurs. More often than not, most organizations do not wipe drives because of the intense time and resource commitment of a highly-secure seven-pass DOD wipe. However, we posit that our one-pass methodology, verified with a zero checksum, is more than adequate for organizations wishing to protect against the loss of sensitive hard drive data.

INTRODUCTION

With the advent of legislation such as the Sarbanes-Oxley Act of 2002 (SOX) (Sarbanes & Oxley, 2002) and the Health Insurance Portability and Accountability Act of 1996 (HIPAA, 1996), there are requirements that commercial organizations take action to ensure that the privacy of both employee and customer data is protected from unplanned disclosure to third parties. Increasing pressure from auditors to adhere to strict principles for sanitization of magnetic media may lead to the expensive and time consuming process for disposal and/or redistribution of hard disk media, unless a more efficient and cost effective approach is implemented.

This research focuses on issues surrounding the practice of sanitizing hard drive diskettes for reuse or disposal with a focus on efficiency in terms of reduction of time and effort devoted to sanitization practices. The primary approach focuses not on information of national security or business critical data, but rather on disks retrieved from end user workstations and laptops containing routine or potentially sensitive (but not classified as sensitive) data. The assumption of this research is that while this information should be considered sensitive (per SOX and HIPAA), it would not be considered "secret" or critical to the business.

However, our assumption does not imply that we do not advocate due care and due diligence in the disposal of media, but rather that in the most common cases, it may be sufficient to perform single wipes rather than the repetitive wipes advocated for critical and secret material. The easier it is to sufficiently wipe disks containing routine data, the more often this process will be implemented in a business environment.

Our research tests a "one-pass" methodology and makes a recommendation for business practitioners to sanitize media. Our findings provide a reference study for the use of one-pass wipes—coupled with chksum as a validation method—for the basic, yet effective, sanitization of magnetic media in a business environment.

OVERVIEW

There have always been concerns that data existent on magnetic media could interfere with new data or create problems. Early ANS standards advocate wiping the entire width of the tape to ensure no residual data remained (Kerpelman, 1970). Moreover, there is a long-standing myth that in order to protect sensitive data from recovery, it is necessary to overwrite the data many times (Joukov, Papaxenopoulos, & Zadok, 2006). A common hacker term is the "DOD 99 wipe" that advocates up to 99 overwrites for media to ensure it is unrecoverable.

Many other papers have been written examining this type of practice for effectiveness (Garfinkel & Shelat, 2003; Joukov et al., 2006). In particular, Gutmann (1996) demonstrated that the use of special equipment, such as Magnetic Force Microscopy (Rugar, Mamin, Guenther, Lambert, Stern, McFadyen, & Yogi, 1990) and other Microscopic techniques (Gomez, Adly, Mayergoyz, Burke, 1992; Gomez, Burke, Adly, Mayergoyz, Gorczyca, 1993; Rice & Moreland, 1991), enabled the recovery from wiped media (wiped in the traditional sense), even with multiple passes.

Gutmann (1996) went on to demonstrate techniques to fully ensure the destruction of data using repeated writing along the lines of the DOD 99 wipe. Related works advocate physical techniques such as degaussing (NSA, 1985) or even physical destruction of the media. The seminal work for this type of approach is the NIST Special publication 800-88 which provides guidelines for media sanitization. This work advocates multiple passes—the DOD seven-pass wipe— only for the most critical data (Kissel, Scholl, Skolochenko, & Li, 2006).

Our research does not criticize these advanced techniques, as they are long established as effective and necessary, but rather we offer proof that in low security situations—such as with a general purpose desktop or laptop—they may not be necessary. Our study describes the need for data to be purged, but it is not expected that complex techniques—which would involve removal of the platters and subsequent microscopic examination as Gutmann and others —would need to be used.

It is common for organizations that dispose or reissue large numbers of general use machines to completely neglect the wiping of drives simply due to time constraints imposed by more complex wiping techniques. DOD 99 wipes that require 99 passes of 0s, 1s, and random 0s and 1s, can take days to perform even on a small drive. Gutmann's improved approach, which is very effective for sensitive material, requires 35 passes of specialized patterns to complete. In fact, some techniques require special equipment and may not prove economically feasible even for more sensitive equipment. Degaussing may require special housings and facilities and may still prove uneconomical (Preston, 1995).

In our research, we propose a control mechanism for practice which advocates that rather than testing overwrites of the data as the criteria, the remaining content of the drive be used as a mechanism to test for content and recoverability. This is accomplished by using the chksum approach to ensure that all bits have a value of zero prior to release of the drive for reuse or disposal. In this manner, organizations can quickly employ and safely reuse disks that have been cleared of potentially sensitive data without expensive equipment and a large time commitment.

Objective

It is commonly the case that business practitioners are faced with external audit review that advocates media be sanitized (e.g., SOX). Our research will demonstrate that while full seven-pass DOD wipes of drives are sometimes mandated, it may be sufficient for organizations to use a "one-pass" wipe coupled with a chksum validation to establish due care and due diligence in regards to meeting sanitized media criteria. It is again worth noting that we are not advocating this technique be used on any equipment which has been classified as sensitive or greater.

Methodology

In order to test the "one-pass" method of disk wipes, we implemented a software tool called "Wiper" (Riggs, 2008). Wiper allows us to write a single pass of all zeros to eliminate the data on a hard drive. The "one-pass" method is compared to the more time-intensive DOD seven-pass wipe. By comparing the before and after images of each disk drive, we were able to determine how effective our "one-pass" method was for removing access to sensitive data that was previously on the drive.

The following sections discuss our test environment, the approach used, and how we measured success. Accompanying this discussion are detailed explanations of the criteria and approaches we used in this experiment so that our approach can be easily duplicated. Our hope is that others will adopt our process and implement it in the business realm.

Safe Boot Environment

Work on drives, and any other sanitization approaches, should be conducted on a safe workstation. This should not be connected to the network and would ideally be booted from sterile, write-protected media (CD-R boots). Typically, a CD-R boot environment with the proper tools is created and this should be used for the entire process on a workstand or clean machine.

Caution About Using chksum as a Validation Tool

Chksum is a simple techniques that starts with bit one and continues to bit n adding the bits together. This is not a valid method to replace a hash, but can be used in the case of a chksum of 0 to prove that all bits are indeed set to zero. With any value > 0, there is no chksum validity as it is possible for any collection of bits to add up to a the same sum depending on their set. For example, consider the sequential bits: 00010000. The chksum of this sequence is 1. The value is 10 hex. If we change this value to 10000000 the chksum is still 1, but the hex value of the information is not 80 rather than 10. This is a critical distinction and illustrates the danger of overuse of chksum for validation purposes.

Media Selection

A group of fifteen random disks was chosen from a storage area where old disks are retained for use in a computer lab at a university. The disks were arbitrarily assigned to one of two experimental groups with five disks being retained in a control group for examination. Each of the disks had not been previously wiped and contained eclectic information that is not documented for privacy sake. Two disks were found to be not in working order and were replaced with working models from the same storage area.

The disk media contained multiple Linux and Windows partitions as they were used in classes where such activity was common. The disks also contained a wide variety of material as they were used in an open lab environment where many users daily used the diskettes in both active (e.g., file saving) and passive (e.g., Web caching) manners.

Write Protection

The Windows OS immediately modifies any media which is detected and writes some minor changes to the media. In order to prevent this, Firefly (Digital Intelligence, 2008), an IDE write blocker, was used to prevent any modification of the drives when they are being examined. Drives being wiped, obviously do not have write blockers in place.

Discussion of Wipe Approaches and Application

Diskettes may be wiped using many different techniques. As is found in Joukov et al. (2006), we see that there are a wide variety of approaches believed to be effective. In our case, we chose to use two extremes which logically should result in the same outcome.

Hypothesis: *A hard drive whose physical chksum equates to zero contains no easily recoverable data.*

The procedure's purpose is to reduce the amount of time used in wiping disks by corporate workers who are now required to protect privacy in machines. The time involved in waiting for wipes to be completed during the DOD wipe process is very lengthy even for smaller (< 20Gb) drives and may take 24 hours or more for larger drives. The "one-pass" methodology process is much faster and typically takes less than an hour to complete even on larger drives.

DOD Wipe Group

Five of the disks were selected for full seven-pass DOD wipes. This represents the extreme in terms of data sanitization (without destruction) as recommended by numerous software vendors' products. In the DOD wipe process, each disk has every bit on the surface map written with a 0, then with a 1, then with a pseudo-random 0 or 1, and each pass is repeated some number of times. This process results in disks that have chksums not equal to 0, but rather some arbitrary sum of bits which has been established to be effective. In this experiment, the product Paragon Disk Wiper (Paragon Software Group, 2008) was used to conduct the DOD seven-pass drive wipe.

One Pass Wipe Group

In the "one-pass" wipe of the disks, each disk was wiped bitwise for all surface bits and each bit was set to 0. This is a much faster process than the DOD wipe with seven passes. It is not possible to use all 1s (which is often an option on software), as this will result in a chksum > 0 which cannot be distinguished from a diskette which has private content still on its surface.

Time Comparison

Given the number of passes using the same drive and machine specifications, it is the logical conclusion that the "one-pass" wipe would be faster. However, the issue to be tested here is the idea that a "one-pass" wipe should be sufficient for most privacy issues concerning data that is not classified as business critical or national security related. Most often, the issue of time is the most compelling reason organizations typically fail to conduct wipes or use the excuse in their argument for not completing this type of task. If we can remove the time component and support the validity of a "one-pass" methodology for secure disk reuse, the argument becomes moot.

Control Group Selection

The control group was not wiped and the disks were merely tested to determine the validity of the imaging process being used.

Examination of Remaining Disk Space Using chksum

On each disk in the "one-pass" group, a chksum was performed and the results found to be zero. This represents the sum of all bits on the surface map being summed. If any bit was not equal to zero, the value would be greater than zero. The DOD-wiped disks have an arbitrary value and reporting chksums in this case is useless because the bits are left in the random state on completion of the wipe. Therefore, the value

of any given chksum on the DOD disks is always greater than zero.

Image Comparison

Prior to wiping any of the disks, each was write-protected and then imaged using the FTK Imager (AccessData, 2008) to create a bitwise forensic image of the media that could then be examined. In each case, a qualified forensics examiner who has been trained in the use of FTK and forensics examination reviewed the material found on the image to determine if any materials existed that would represent a compromise of privacy. The assumption made is that any material that was recognizable would constitute a security breach. In each case, the imaging was done of the physical drive contents, as opposed to the logical drive, so we could examine every bit on the physical media.

Data Carving

Data carving is a common term in forensics investigation used to describe the examination of two key areas of media that are often neglected by individuals seeking to remove information, the slack space and the free space of the drive.

In each case, data carving tools were also used to attempt to determine if any fragments of media might exist on the drive that could be recovered from collections of clusters, unallocated space, or any other area of the media.

Slack Space

Slack space is defined essentially as an artifact of the management of disk clusters as defined by the type of formatting of the hard disk (e.g., NTFS). Because DOS and Windows file systems reserve fixed clusters for data even when it does not need the entire space, there is always some space left over. This leftover space is called slack space. However, when a cluster is reused the new data may not completely fill the space and old data may remain in the remainder of the cluster. Herein lies a potential security breach.

For example, in the NTFS format on a 4Gb drive the cluster size is typically 8Kb. If a cluster called alpha has a collection of social security numbers on it, each social security number is nine bytes stored as XXXXXXXXX. Moreover, with 888 social security numbers in the cluster, it would be almost completely filled. In traditional file deletes—as opposed to wipes—the file is marked for deletion but not actually wiped from the disk. Later, if someone creates a Word document that is written to the SSN cluster marked for deletion, the system begins to overwrite the cluster. However, what if the Word document is only 4Kb long? In cluster alpha, the first 6Kb of the cluster will contain the Word document, but the remaining 2Kb of alpha still contains the social security number database file. Using a slack space recovery tool with a hex editor—such as Cygnus (Softcircuits, 2008)—to review the clusters, it may be possible to recover the SSN data. This is definitely a security breach.

Free Space

Free space is defined as the unused portion of the disk media that is partitioned. This space is "empty" per the file allocation table but may contain data. This may be older data from a past user, the remains of files which have been "deleted," or very commonly, this space contains cached material. Internet browsers and other applications commonly use free space as a holding area for data caches. It is quite common in examinations of media to find entire Web sites cached in the free space. E-mails and all sorts of valuable material may also be found by reviewing this portion of the drive. Again, data carving is used to attempt to discern valuable material in this portion of the drive. This may be done with data carving tools such as Simple Carver (Filesig, 2008), FTK, or by using a hex editor to directly review the drive area.

Unpartitioned Space

Portions of the drive that have not been formatted or partitioned formally (or have had their partitions removed) are called unpartitioned space. This space may not currently be readable, but it may contain old material that remains after the removal of the partition that is a logical change rather than a physical one. Examination of unpartitioned space is conducted through data carving and hex editing tools to review the cluster's contents for valuable material.

EXPERIMENT RESULTS

In each case, the ten hard drives were wiped and examined using Forensics Tool Kit (FTK) and a hex editor to determine if any content remained on the disk that would be readable. If any sensitive content was found, this would constitute a security breach and invalidate the process.

Table 1 demonstrates the findings of the group that was processed using the seven-pass DOD wipe.

In the seven-pass DOD wipe, each of the five drives was fully wiped and while some artifacts were found in free space, these were determined to be typical and consistent for various drives and of no recognizable value. This appears to be an artifact of the process and does not reflect any "real" items found on the disk. Examination with a hex editor determined there was no content in these locations and later testing of zeroed drives revealed the same pattern on the same drive types with respect to their brand. There was no content found in any of the drives either in the normal spaces, slack/free space, unpartitioned space or elsewhere on the disk. In this case, the hex editor view showed only *A*s. This is a typical value for a blank piece of media.

Table 2 demonstrates the findings of the "one-pass" group.

Unlike the *A*s found on the seven-pass DOD drives, these drives are full of zeroes. This result is expected because we wrote all zeros to every physical bit. Again, the disk artifacts were found and are consistent with

Table 1. PARAGON DOD drive wipe

Paragon Drive Wiper (DOD)					
Manufacturer	Model	Serial #	FTK Items Found	FTK Item Type	HEX View
Western Digital	Cavier 36400	WM420 136 2340	246	DriveFreeSpace	All "a"
Western Digital	Cavier 36400	WM420 136 7693	246	DriveFreeSpace	All "a"
Western Digital	Cavier 36400	WM420 136 2590	246	DriveFreeSpace	All "a"
Western Digital	Cavier 36400	WM420 136 2625	246	DriveFreeSpace	All "a"
Seagate	Fireball Plus	88202150650	390	DriveFreeSpace	All "a"

Table 2. Wiper one-pass all zeros

Wiper					
Manufacturer	**Model**	**Serial #**	**FTK Items Found**	**FTK Item Type**	**HEX View**
Western Digital	Cavier 36400	WM420 134 8090	246	DriveFreeSpace	All 0's
Western Digital	Cavier 36400	WM420 136 2351	246	DriveFreeSpace	All 0's
Seagate	Fireball Plus	882021561467	390	DriveFreeSpace	All 0's
Western Digital	Cavier 36400	WM420 136 9964	246	DriveFreeSpace	All 0's
Western Digital	Cavier 36400	WM420 133 4218	246	DriveFreeSpace	All 0's

Figure 1. Chksum 0000 0000 0000 0000

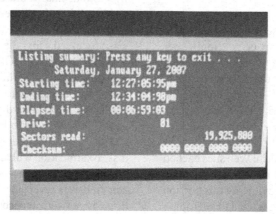

the findings in the seven-pass DOD wipe for the type of drive. Still, the artifacts were reviewed, but found to be inconsequential. In all cases of the "one-pass" wipes, the chksum was 0000 0000 0000 0000 on the drive for its physical contents. This indicates the sum total of all bits on the drive was 0, and that all bits were indeed set to 0. Figure 1 illustrates the chksum results from the zeroed drives. Note the elapsed time was about seven minutes as compared to hours or days required for a DOD-type wipe.

The control disks were imaged and examined, and the contents were found to be intact. There is no value to reporting the contents of these disks, but validation of the disk contents was proven using FTK. Many free space items were found on the unwiped drives. In all cases, FTK produced a wide variety of files, slack space, and free space items from the unwiped drives, including many deleted files and directories. Much information could be gleaned from these drives as opposed to the wiped drives.

DISCUSSION OF FINDINGS

In both the seven-pass DOD and "one-pass" wipes, the drives no longer contained private material and were effectively wiped. There is no reason to indicate that the "one-pass" wipe and writing zeroes was any less effective than wiping all the bits with multiple passes (e.g., seven-pass DOD). While it is the case that esoteric means exist which may enable the recovery of bit settings using electronic recovery, a diskette which has been sterilized and all bits set to zero should be sufficient to remove privacy data that is not deemed of business critical or of national security interest.

Recommendations

It will always be the case when extremely sensitive, national security, or business critical material has been stored on media, that the simplest and most effective solution is the physical destruction of that media after a DOD wipe (Kissel et al., 2006), or Gutmann's (2006) technique if a more complex solution is sought. Yet, for the vast majority of corporate hard drives—from workstations to laptops—a "one-pass" wipe of all zeros should suffice with the chksum validation in place. This process will allow the safe and secure reissue of the hard drive diskette from employee workstations and laptops to other employee systems, or, for that matter, its disposal with some assurance of safety.

Recommended Procedure

In light of these findings, we recommend that a business take the following steps for any machine's drive that is not deemed to hold critical, extremely sensitive, or otherwise secure data whether the drive will be reused or destroyed:

1. Use a disk wiping tool (e.g., Wiper) which writes all zeros to the diskette in a single pass. The write tool must operate on the physical drive (usually device 80 or 81 from most wintel type bios). It is strongly recommended that a workstand or forensics workstation which has no other purpose be used for this process. Any tool which can write bitwise to the physical media should suffice.
2. Upon completion of the wipe, write protect the drive. This will ensure the system will not try and load the drive or write to the drive in any way.
3. Using the forensics boot disk or other safe environment run the chksum program on the physical diskette and validate that the return chksum is 0000 0000 0000 0000.
4. Disconnect the hard drive. Write "chksum 0" on a static-free label and place the label over the drive cable connect port. This will allow for the IT worker to validate the drive wipe and sanitized state before reinstalling any new software or reusing the drive. Drives being disposed or machines with drives being disposed should be in this state with no cables connected. This should be validated before they are released and documented.
5. Include this approach as a policy recommendation to be followed for all drives.
6. Incorporate this as a key control in the process of reissue or disposal and document accordingly for later audit.

Remember that in the event of any doubt about the critical content of the material on the disk media, an organization should physically destroy the disk if it is not to be reused internally or the time for a seven-pass wipe is not viable option. However, techniques such as the DOD seven-pass wipe, or Gutmann's 35-pass wiping approach should be considered and implemented as policy for any media suspected of containing material classified as extremely sensitive or higher, no matter what the disk's intended future use.

CONCLUSION

As with any risk, it is always advisable to validate any methodology before advocating the solution to an organization. This chapter supports the argument that it is not necessary to perform elaborate drive wipes to ensure sanitization when risk is low if the drive wipe is performed correctly and validated by some simple and efficient method, such as a chksum = 0. We provide a set of six steps based on the successful testing of drives to prove the method's approach which may be used as a key control for safe data destruction. It is advisable to categorize or classify media as to its sensitivity and allow only the basic material to be sanitized. Critical media should be subjected to a seven-pass DOD wipe or the 35-pass wipe advocated by Gutmann and then physically destroyed to ensure it is not recoverable.

REFERENCES

AccessData. (2008). *Forensic Toolkit* (computer software). Retrieved May 3, 2008, from http://www.accessdata.com/products/ftk/

Digital Intelligence. (2008). *Firefly IDE blocker* (computer software). Retrieved May 3, 2008, from http://www.digitalintelligence.com/products/firefly/

Filesig. (2008). *Simple carver* (computer software). Retrieved May 3, 2008, from http://www.filesig.co.uk/simplecarver.html

Garfinkel, S.L., & Shelat, A. (2003). Remembrance of data passed: A study of disk sanitization practices. *Security and Privacy Magazine, IEEE 1*(1), 17-27.

Gomez, R., Adly, A., Mayergoyz, I., & Burke, E. (1992). Magnetic force scanning tunnelling microscope imaging of overwritten data. *IEEE Transactions on Magnetics, 28*(5), 3141.

Gomez, R., Burke, E., Adly, A., Mayergoyz, I., & Gorczyca, J. (1993). Microscopic investigations of overwritten data. *Journal of Applied Physics, 73*(10), 6001.

Gutmann, P. (1996, July 22–25). Secure deletion of data from magnetic and solid-state memory. In *Proceedings of the Sixth USENIX Security Symposium* (pp. 77-90). San Jose, CA.

Health Insurance Portability and Accountability Act of 1996 (HIPAA). (1996). *U.S. public law 104-191.* Retrieved on May 3, 2008, from http://aspe.hhs.gov/admnsimp/pl104191.htm

Joukov, N., Papaxenopoulos, H., & Zadok, E. (2006). Secure deletion myths, issues, and solutions. In *Proceedings of the Second ACM workshop on Storage Security and Survivability StorageSS 06* (pp. 61-66). Alexandria, VA.

Kerpelman, C. (1970). Recorded magnetic tape for information interchange (1600 cpi, phase encoded). *Communications of the ACM, 13*(11), 679-685.

Kissel, R., Scholl, M. Skolochenko, S., & Li, X. (2006). Guidelines for media sanitization. *NIST Special Publication,* 80-888.

NSA. (1985). Magnetic tape degausser. *NSA/CSS Specification,* L14-4A.

Paragon Software Group. (2008). *Paragon disk wiper 7.0* (computer software). Retrieved May 3, 2008, from http://www.disk-wiper.com/

Preston, C. (1995). The data dilemma. *Security Management Journal.*

Rice, P., & Moreland, J. (1991). Tunneling-stabilized magnetic force microscopy of bit tracks on a hard disk. *IEEE Trans.on Magnetics, 27*(3), 3452.

Riggs, D. (2008). *Wiper* (computer software). Retrieved May 3, 2008, from http://keycomputer.net/soft-hard.htm?#wiper

Rugar, D.H. Mamin, Guenther, P., Lambert, S., Stern, J., McFadyen, I., and Yogi, T. (1990). Magnetic force microscopy: General principles and application to longitudinal recording media. *Journal of Applied Physics, 68*(3), 1169.

Sarbanes, P., & Oxley, M.G. (2002). *Sarbanes-Oxley act of 2002.* Washington, DC: U.S: Government Printing Office.

Softcircuits Programming. (2008). *Cygnus hex editor* (computer software). Retrieved May 3, 2008, from http://www.softcircuits.com/cygnus/

KEY TERMS

Bitwise Forensic Image: An exact copy of every bit of data found on a disk image. This image is used in forensic investigations to track changes—no matter how minute—in the disk image.

Chksum: This command performs a checksum of the data on a piece of media. The checksum returns a numerical equivalent based on the number of bits present.

Computer Forensics: A discipline that uses analytical and investigative techniques to identify, collect, examine, and preserve evidence or information found on computers or other devices.

Data Carving: An examination of the slack space and free space on a drive. A forensic investigator used tools to "carve" out these sections on a drive and look for data.

Disk Artifacts: In forensic investigations, this refers to leftover information that remains on media even after a wipe has been performed.

Disk Cache: A portion of RAM used to speed up access times. The cache stores the most recently accessed data. When more data is requested, the cache is first checked before accessing the disk again.

Disk Clusters: A group of sectors on a disk. The operating system assigns designations to each cluster and uses them to store and access data.

Disk Wiping Tool: Any software used to remove and/or overwrite data on a disk for security purposes. Wipes can simply write zeroes to a disk (e.g., Wiper) or perform complex writes for increased security (e.g., DOD wipes).

DOD Wipe: The seven-pass Department of Defense disk wipe is the standard used for highly sensitive data. In the first pass, all zeroes are written to the disk.

In the second pass, all ones are written. In subsequent passes a pseudo-random zero or one is written.

Forensics Workstation: A computer specifically designed for forensic investigations. The forensic workstation includes tools to create pristine disk images, as well as a variety of analysis tools. Most workstations allow for multiple types of media to be connected so that information can be analyzed off of a variety of media, such as floppy drives, SCSI, or IDE drives, and so on.

Free Space: The unused portions of a disk that are already partitioned and ready for use.

Gutmann Wipe: A 35-pass wipe consisting of particular patterns of data which remove risk from examination by magnetic microscopy techniques which can be used to reveal previous bit patterns on magnetic media.

Hard Drive Sanitization: The process of securely wiping all data from a hard disk. With a properly sanitized drive it is impossible to recover any data.

Hash: An algorithm or function that translates data into a number. By "hashing" data, one can create a digital fingerprint of the data that can then be compared to see if the data matches. This digital fingerprint is often called a hash value.

Health Insurance Portability and Accountability Act of 1996: HIPAA provide several guidelines and regulations designed to protect individuals and their medical information. Not only does it cover privacy issues, but also a person's right access to all of his or her medical information. Most important to this discussion is the need for organizations to meet the Privacy Rule stipulations in regards to protecting data.

Hex Editor: Computer software that allows a forensics investigator to see the exact contents of a file instead of the data being interpreted by software (e.g., an operating system).

IDE Write Blocker: Most operating systems automatically write some information to a disk when it is connected and the computer is turned on. This hardware device sits between an IDE drive and the computer and does not allow this information to be written to the drive. In forensic investigations, it is crucial to maintain disk image integrity including preventing any data being written from the operating system onto the disk.

One-Pass Methodology: A process by which all zeroes are written to a hard drive or other media in order to sufficiently sanitize the media for reuse within an organization. The one-pass methodology allows for an efficient and effective use of resources (time, personnel, and equipment) so that organizations can safely reuse media that once contained sensitive information.

Sarbanes Oxley Act of 2002: A United States federal law designed to make organizations accountable for their actions. It includes stipulations regarding external audits, governance, and financial disclosures. Most important to this discussion is the need for organizations to meet stipulations in regards to protecting employee, partner, and customer data.

Slack Space: The unused space in a particular file system cluster.

Unpartitioned Space: The unused portions of a disk that are not yet formatted for use.

Chapter XVII
Securing E–Mail Communication with XML Technology

Lijun Liao
Horst-Görtz Institute for IT Security, Germany

Mark Manulis
Horst-Görtz Institute for IT Security, Germany

Jörg Schwenk
Horst-Görtz Institute for IT Security, Germany

ABSTRACT

This chapter deals with the issues concerning e-mail communication security. We analyze the most popular security mechanisms and standards related to the e-mail communication and identify potential threats and vulnerabilities. The most significant drawback of all current approaches is the impossibility of keeping headers information authentic. This leads to possible impersonation attacks and profiling of the e-mail communication, and encourages spam and phishing activities. Furthermore, none of the currently available security mechanisms supports partial signature generation of the e-mail content by distinct signers, which might be useful in commercial scenarios. To handle these problems, we suggest a new approach, called XMaiL, which can be considered as an advanced e-mail security mechanism based on the popular XML technologies. The proposed XMaiL supersedes all currently available e-mail security standards in the sense of the higher flexibility and security.

INTRODUCTION

Sending an *e-mail* is considered today as one oaf the most convenient ways to communicate any kind of digital information, and is of major importance for individuals and commercial organizations. Communication via e-mail provides many advantages compared to classical paper mails. Negligible transport times and costs are surely the most attractive properties of the e-mail-based communication. Another aspect is the digital form of the transmitted information, which allows its subsequent automated processing and back-

up. In many companies, e-mail has become a critical application service and has already replaced paper mails for the communication between employees, business partners and customers. Often information being transmitted is valuable and sensitive, such that effective protection mechanisms are desirable in order to prevent information from being manipulated or to protect confidential information from being revealed by unauthorized parties. As a result, *e-mail security* is paramount concerns, as are e-mail service availability and optimization technologies, including e-mail archiving, not least because of the increased flooding with spam and phishing mails. A large number of e-mail security mechanisms has been meanwhile developed and standardized, building a solid basis for secure e-mail communication. Almost all of these protection mechanisms use cryptography to satisfy the requirements of confidentiality, authentication, and integrity. Still suggested mechanisms, though solving urgent problems, have various scenario-specific limitations, so that interesting research activities continue to arise in this appealing area of communication services.

In this chapter, we give insight into various popular security mechanisms and standards being developed over the past twenty years. Beside overall description we identify strengths and weaknesses of each approach from the perspective of theoretical research and practical deployment. Starting with the description of a plain e-mail format, resulting from the Internet Message Format in RFC 2822, and possibilities of attaching documents via MIME-extensions, we focus on the most popular security formats like (Open) PGP (Pretty Good Privacy) (RFC 2440), PGP/MIME (RFC 3156) and S/MIME (RFC 3851). We make clear that further improvement of the currently existing formats is needed and describe a novel solution that unifies strengths of the previous approaches and provides additional attractive features for the higher flexibility of the e-mail communication achieving the desirable security properties. Our solution, called XMaiL, is a new XML based e-mail format, which combined with popular standards in the area of XML security such as XML Signature (Bartel, Boyer, Fox, LaMacchia, & Simon, 2003) and XML Encryption (Imamura, Dillaway, & Simon, 2002) provides better interoperability and higher security compared to the previous solutions.

PLAIN E-MAIL FORMATS AND TRANSMISSION PROTOCOLS

The current plain *e-mail* format, without any protection mechanisms, results from the general Internet Message Format in RFC 2822. According to this format, a message transmitted over Internet (and e-mail is treated as such) consists of two main parts: the header part, and the body part. The header part consists of various headers, each containing some specific information (the header name and its content is separated by a colon). Table 1 summarizes the most used headers.

The following example is typical for the plain e-mail message. The header part includes information about the source and destination addresses, the date when the message was sent, and its subject. The actual information is located in the body part, which follows the header part.

```
From: alice@example.org
To: bob@example.net
Date: Sun, 5 Nov 2006 12:17:58 -0800
(PST)
    Subject: E-mail Communication Se-
curity

    This is an example e-mail message
for this chapter. Treat it as spam!
```

RFC 2822 specifies syntax only for text messages. In particular, it does not consider transmission of attachments, such as independent text documents, images, audio, or other sorts of structured data. In

Table 1.

Header	Description
From	Specifies the author(s) of the message
Sender	Specifies the mailbox of the agent responsible for the actual transmission of the message. If more authors are specified in the field From, the field Sender must be shown.
To	Specifies the primary recipients of the message.
Cc	Specifies the addresses of others who are to receive the message, though the content of the message may not be directed to them.
Date	Specifies the timestamp of the e-mail submission to the delivery system by the sender.
Subject	Specifies a string identifying the topic of the message.

order to handle this convenient feature extensions, known as Multipurpose Internet Message Extensions (MIME) have been proposed. The following example extends the one above by additional MIME headers. The most important added header is content type that describes the nature of the data (therefore, also called as media type) contained in the body in a way that the receiving e-mail client can present this data using some appropriate media type specific transformation. The content type name consists of the main type and the subtype separated via "/." The top-level content type `multipart/mixed` declares in this case that the content of the e-mail consists of different data types. The content is separated into a part with the content type `text/plain` consisting of the actual text message from the previous example, and a part with the content type `image/jpeg` specifying the attached image document whose description is given in the Base64 data encoding. The header and the individual parts are separated by the specified boundary.

> From: alice@example.org
> To: bob@example.net
> Date: Sun, 5 Nov 2006 12:17:58 -0800 (PST)
> Subject: E-mail Communication Security
> Content-Type: multipart/mixed; boundary="--NextPart_12345"
>
> This is a multi-part message in MIME format.
> ----NextPart_12345
> Content-Type: text/plain; charset=iso-8859-1
>
> This is an example e-mail message for this chapter. Treat it as spam!
> ----NextPart_12345
> Content-Type: image/jpeg; name=water.jpg
> Content-Transfer-Encoding: base64
> Content-Disposition: inline; filename=water.jpg
>
> /9j/4AAQSkZJRgABAgEAYABgAAD/X8gT38g VH+IIFQAAEgAAE0AAE8AAP8vAA==
> ----NextPart_12345--

From the security point of view, upon composing the e-mail message, the sender is free in choosing data of header fields and body. Simple impersonation attacks are thinkable where some incorrect source address is supposed to leave the actual sender anonymous. For example, current spam and phishing e-mails extensively misuse this technique. Even in a case where the sender does not have intentions to provide fake

data, e-mail security strongly depends on the actual transmission process.

The previously described formats for the plain text e-mail and MIME extensions build the content of the transmitted e-mail message. However, every message transmitted over the Internet requires an additional envelope which is given by the actual transmission protocol. Currently, the most popular transmission protocol for e-mail communication is the standardized Simple Mail Transmission Protocol (SMTP). SMTP has been designed for reliable and efficient transmission of e-mails, and provides different procedures (e.g., for session initiation, mail transaction and forwarding, verification of mailbox names, and so on). SMTP is capable of transmitting e-mails to the specified final destination not only in the same network, but also across different networks through a number of intermediate relay or gateway hosts whereby identifying the appropriate next-hop via address resolution based on DNS queries. In the context of the e-mail security, the actual transmission process provides one of the highest risks to the confidentiality, authentication, and integrity of the original e-mail information. The most essential reason is that e-mails are usually transmitted over publicly accessible networks with distributed administrative control over relays and gateways, where eavesdropping and active modification of the transported information is possible (and easy), and thus, critical. We stress that any e-mail sent in the plain text format with or without MIME extensions is susceptible to a large number of attacks. Header fields and bodies of such e-mails can be easily modified resulting in integrity changes, possible impersonation attacks, and simple eavesdropping of the included information.

Obviously, no excessive motivation is required to agree that for achieving security in e-mail communication additional protection mechanisms are indispensable. In general, cryptographic techniques are widely used to address various security issues in e-mail communication.

SECURE E-MAIL FORMATS

In the context of *e-mail* communication security, mostly all available protection mechanisms utilize *digital signatures* and encryption schemes. The main difference between various mechanisms is not the kind of the signature or encryption scheme being used, but the way how the key management is handled and what extensions to the common (plain text) e-mail formats are done. For some introduction to cryptographic techniques, we refer to Menezes, Oorschot, & Vanstone (1996). In the following, we focus on the three most popular security mechanisms: (Open)PGP, PGP/MIME, and S/MIME.

(Open)PGP and PGP/MIME

Pretty Good Privacy (PGP) is the earliest and still one of the most frequently used security solutions for e-mail communication. The latest version of PGP, called *OpenPGP*, is described in RFC 2440. In (Open)PGP, users can achieve confidentiality, integrity, and (sender) authentication for the exchanged e-mail content using the described techniques of asymmetric cryptography. The following example shows an e-mail composed of a message followed by its signature. Note that PGP specific lines point out that the actual message is signed and show the boundaries of the signature. Still, in the sense of the e-mail format from RFC 2822, signed message and the actual signature are treated as a single part within the e-mail body. The encryption is treated in a similar way, except that the plain text is replaced by the cipher text.

> From: alice@example.org
> To: bob@example.net
> Date: Sun, 5 Nov 2006 12:17:58 -0800 (PST)
> Subject: E-mail Communication Security
>
> -----BEGIN PGP SIGNED MESSAGE-----
> This is an example e-mail message for this chapter. Treat it as spam!
>
> -----BEGIN PGP SIGNATURE-----
> iGoEARECADQFAkT1uG0JEKvFAHxhU
> ... C7tIxxBbGljZSA8YWxpY2VAd2luc2Vy-
> dmVyqXD9
> -----END PGP SIGNATURE-----

The PGP/MIME approach described in RFC 3156 specifies the integration of the above PGP approach into the framework of MIME extensions. The following example shows that in PGP/MIME the signed message and the signature are considered as different parts of the body. The top-level content type `multipart/signed` indicates that a message is signed and the attribute `micalg` indicates that the hash function SHA1 has been used. The actual message is indicated by the content type `text/plain`

whereas the attached signature is indicated by the content type `application/pgp-signature`. The media type application is used to indicate that the content can be processed using the appropriate PGP application program.

> From: alice@example.org
> To: bob@example.net
> Date: Sun, 5 Nov 2006 12:17:58 -0800 (PST)
> Subject: E-mail Communication Security
> Content-Type: multipart/signed; boundary="--NextPart_12345"; micalg=pgp-
> SHA1; protocol="application/pgp-signature"
>
> ----NextPart_12345
> Content-Type: text/plain; charset=iso-8859-1
>
> This is an example e-mail message for this chapter. Treat it as spam!
>
> ----NextPart_12345
> Content-Type: application/pgp-signature; name="signature.asc"
> Content-Description: OpenPGP digital signature
> Content-Disposition: attachment; filename="signature.asc"
>
> -----BEGIN PGP SIGNATURE-----
> iGoEARECADQFAkT1uG0JEKvFAHxhU
> ... IxxBbGljZSA8YWxpY2VAd2luc2Vy-
> dmVyqXD9
> -----END PGP SIGNATURE-----
> ----NextPart_12345--

In case of encryption, the top-level content type is set to `multipart/encrypted`, and the e-mail body contains one part with the content type `application/pgp-encrypted` as control part, and one part with the content type `application/octet-stream` which specifies the cipher text. (Open)PGP and PGP/MIME utilize the hybrid encryption approach where the symmetric key used to encrypt the actual message is in turn encrypted with the public key of the receiver and attached to the message. If confidentiality, message integrity, and (sender) authentication is

Table 2.

Type	Subtype	Protocol	Description
multipart	signed	application/pgp-signature	Signed e-mail consisting of two parts: one for the original plain text message, and another one for the signature.
	encrypted	application/pgp-encrypted	Encrypted e-mail contains of two pars, one for the control part, and another one for the encrypted data.
application	pgp-encrypted	-	The control part of multipart/encrypted e-mail.
	pgp-signature	-	The content type for the signature part of the multipart/signed e-mail.
	pgp-keys	-	A MIME body part of this content-type contains ASCII-armored transferable Public Key Packets.

required simultaneously then the message should be first signed and then encrypted. The top-level media type is then set to `multipart/encrypted`. The content of the body is similar to the example above (with the content type `multipart/signed`), except that it is transmitted as a cipher text. Obviously, upon receiving such encapsulated message, the e-mail client must decrypt it before being able to verify the signature. Additionally, PGP/MIME provides the media type `application/pgp-keys` allowing the transmission of the public keys. The Table 2 summarizes various content types available in the PGP/MIME format.

In (Open)PGP and PGP/MIME, the so-called Web of Trust mechanism is used to establish the authenticity of the binding between a public key and a user. Each user has an identity certificate which includes his identity (composed of a real name and a corresponding e-mail address) and a public key. These identity certificates can be signed by other users who attest the association of the public key and the identity. The more signatures a user can obtain for own identity certificate the more "trusted" he is. The assumption is that users holding private keys are independent, so that even if one of them makes a bad judgment, they will not all do so. In practice, the Web of Trust is used very rarely. However, it provides and interesting rating mechanism allowing each user to specify a "trust value" for the identity certificate of another user, and also demand a certain number of independent signatures on the identity certificate before that binding is considered as valid. The main problem in the Web of Trust is the actual assumption on independence of signatures since it is not possible to prevent the case where one user holds several private keys. Another problem is that newly introduced users are likely to

remain untrustworthy until their identity certificates have a sufficient number of associated signatures.

S/MIME

Secure MIME (S/MIME) is another widely used security mechanism that provides extensions to the MIME framework, allowing to achieve message integrity and (sender) authentication (using *digital signatures*), and data confidentiality (using digital encryption). Several versions of S/MIME are currently available; the latest version is S/MIME 3.1 (RFC 3851). The following example shows a signed e-mail with S/MIME extensions. Similar to PGP/MIME, the actual e-mail body consists of the message and the signature. The message part in the body has the content type `text/plain` whereas the content type of the signature part consists of the actual name `application/pkcs7-signature` indicating that the syntax of the attached signature corresponds to the signature format from the industrial standard PKCS#7 (RFC 3852). Note that multiple message parts are possible if a message consists not only of the text information, but has additional binary attachments. In this case, one signature is generated over the whole content.

From: alice@example.org
To: bob@example.net
Date: Sun, 5 Nov 2006 12:17:58 -0800 (PST)
Subject: E-mail Communication Security
Content-Type: multipart/signed; boundary="--NextPart_12345"; micalg=sha1;
  protocol="application/pkcs7-signature"

----NextPart_12345
Content-Type: text/plain; charset=iso-8859-1

This is an example e-mail message for this chapter. Treat it as spam!

```
----NextPart_12345
Content-Type: application/pkcs7-signature;
name=smime.p7s;
Content-Transfer-Encoding: base64
Content-Disposition: attachment;
filename="smime.p7s"
```

MIAGCSqGSIb3DQEHAqCAMIA-CAQVQQDEwV...VQQDEwVBbGljZTEM-MAoGA1UECxMDTkRTM==

```
----NextPart_12345--
```

S/MIME supports different content type values depending on the syntax and the actual security goal. Table 3 summarizes possible content types.

Note that a signed e-mail can be indicated in two different ways: (1) with one body part and the content type `application/pkcs7-mime` with the S/MIME attribute set to `signed-data`; (2) with two body parts such that the top-level content type is `multipart/signed` and the additional low-level type is `application/pkcs7-signature` (as in our example). The first approach can only be used if both the sender's and the recipient's clients are S/MIME capable; otherwise no presentation of the received message is possible. The second approach can be used if both clients are at least MIME capable, so that they can at least present the received message to the user (even without being able to process the signature). The risk of using the second approach is that upon e-mail transport over relay and gateway hosts, possible changes to the complex MIME structure can make the signature invalid; this happens often in practice. E-mails containing encrypted messages have only one part in the body indicated by the content type `application/pkc7-mime` and the S/MIME parameter `enveloped-data`.

The authenticity of the relationship between the public key and the identity (e-mail address) of a user in S/MIME is established based on X.509 certificates (currently in version 3) described in (RFC 3280). These certificates are issued by a strict hierarchical system called Public Key Infrastructure (PKI). The so-called Certification Authority (CA) is at the root of the hierarchy and can sign a X.509 certificate for the user with the own private key after having verified his identity. The trust in X.509 certificates is established under the assumption that CA itself is trusted. Thus, in order to verify the validity of the certificate it is sufficient to verify its CA's signature using the public key of the CA which is included into certificate of the CA and to check that the latter has not been revoked (we refer to RFC 3280 for the certificate revocation techniques). The CA certificate can be signed by some higher level CA or self-signed (in the latter case it is called "root certificate"). This construction ensures that for each issued certificate there exists a path up to some "root certificate." Hence, one particular user's certificate is valid if all certificates in this path are valid too. This is the fundamental difference between S/MIME and Open(PGP) where certificates can be signed by individuals.

Table 3.

Main Type	Sub Type	S/MIME Parameter	Description
multipart	signed	-	Signed e-mail consisting of two parts: one for the original plain text message, and another one for the signature.
application	pkcs7-mime	signed-data	Signed S/MIME data according to PKCS#7.
	pkcs7-mime	enveloped-data	Encrypted S/MIME data.
	pkcs7-mime	certs-only	The data contains only X.509 certificates.
	pkcs7-signature	-	The content type for the signature part of the `multipart/signed` e-mail.
	pkcs10-mime	-	The request for certificate generation according to PKCS#10 (RFC 2986)

Problems with S/MIME and PGP/ MIME Format

As described above, integrity and authentication of the e-mail content can be achieved by digital signatures according to the *S/MIME* and *PGP/MIME* specifications. However, none of the currently available security mechanisms (except for the ad hoc solution in RFC 3851) can be used for the authentication of the information contained in the header lines as noticed in (Ewers, Kubbilun, Liao, & Schwenk, 2005). The only exception concerns e-mail addresses in the headers From and Sender (the latter in case that many authors exist). In order to communicate their authenticity to the receiver, it is necessary for the e-mail client to check that these addresses are included in the PGP identity certificates, or in the Subject or SubjectAltName fields of the X.509 certificates. However, none of the currently popular e-mail clients, including Microsoft Outlook, performs these checks. Therefore, any adversary with his/her own certificate (e.g., for the e-mail address adversary@example.org) can compose an e-mail message signed with his/her own public key, but with a different e-mail address (e.g., ceo@somebank.com) in the header From. This e-mail will be treated by the current available e-mail clients as authentic since the signature remains valid. However, the different address in the header From may cause confusion by the receiver. Authenticity of all other headers, such as To, Date, Subject, and so on can be biased in a similar way. For example, these attacks can be misused for the spam dissemination. Indeed, an automated script can be used to replace the contents of the headers To, Cc, and Bcc for some message which has been previously signed. Each of these generated e-mail messages would have a valid

signature and would not be recognized as spam. Another threat is given by possible replay attacks where a signed e-mail, for example a notification sent by a trusted bank to one particular customer, can be modified by changing the header To with the e-mail address of a different customer and forwarded to this customer who will be assured of its authenticity. Additionally, if the original notification contains a link on the bank's Web site, where the customer have to enter own online banking password, then combining this replay attack with a DNS spoofing attack on the bank's domain name would be a serious threat.

Figure 1 shows an example with the Microsoft Outlook 2007 e-mail client. The figure on the left shows the original signed e-mail sent from alice@foo.org to bob@foo.org, whereas the figure on the right shows the modified version. The header From is changed to ceo@somebank.com, however, Microsoft Outlook gives no warning about this modification. Note also that the headers To, Date, and Subject are modified too; however, the signature is still valid.

S/MIME and *PGP/MIME* e-mails provide confidentiality of the e-mail body, but not of the information in the header fields. Thus, every encrypted e-mail still reveals the subject, the sender address, the issue date, and further information. This information in turn can be misused for the profiling of the e-mail communication of a particular user.

Although S/MIME and PGP/MIME formats support multiple signatures, there is a limitation that all signers must sign the same content. However, there are many scenarios, where a higher flexibility in the sense that different message parts are signed by different signers is desirable. For example, when a company sends a digital invoice to its customer it would be more practical if the technical department could sign the shipping date, and the sales department could sign the recipient address and the total price.

Figure 1.

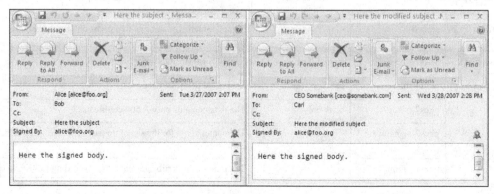

Due to the design drawbacks of the currently available e-mail security mechanisms, the abovementioned problems cannot be solved by extending the existing the specifications. Hence, the specification of an advanced, easily extendable e-mail security format becomes necessary in order to rule out current limitations.

XMAIL

XMaiL (for *XML e-mail*) is a new XML-based e-mail format with the enhanced security properties which utilizes the *XML Security* Standards, including the *XML Signature, XML Encryption, XAdES* (Cruellas, Karlinger, Pinkas, & Ross, 2003), and so on. XMaiL can be transported over *SOAP* (Gudgin, Hadley, Mendelsohn, Moreau, & Nielsen, 2003), *XML-RPC* (Winer, 2008), and via SMTP.

In the rest of this chapter, for brevity, we completely suppress information about XML namespaces and the document <?xml ...> directive.

Building Blocks

In this section, we briefly describe the XML technologies related to our proposal (i.e, XPath (Clark & DeRose, 1999), SOAP, XML Signature, and XML Encryption).

XPath is an expression language for addressing and processing portions of an XML document. The XPath language uses the tree representation of the document, allows the navigation along this tree, and selection of its nodes according to different criteria. The XPath expression /A/B[@type='warning'] selects all B elements that have a @type attribute 'warning' and are children of the A element that forms the outermost element of the XML document.

SOAP is a mechanism for interapplication communication between systems written in arbitrary languages across the Internet. SOAP usually exchanges messages over HTTP: the client POSTs a SOAP request, and receives either an HTTP success code and a SOAP response or an HTTP error code. SOAP messages are XML messages. These messages exchange structured information between SOAP systems. A SOAP message is an ordinary XML document containing a mandatory element <Envelope> that identifies the XML document as a SOAP message. In turn, the element <Envelope> contains an optional child element < Header> and a mandatory element <Body>.

```
<Envelope>
 <Header/>?
 <Body/>
</Envelope>
```

XML Signature defines XML syntax for digital signatures and can be used to sign XML documents. It provides similar functionality as PKCS#7 but is more extensible and tailored towards signing of the XML documents. It is applied in various Web technologies (e.g., SOAP, SAML, and so on).

The <SignedInfo> specifies the signed content and the applied algorithms. The elements <Signature-Method> and <CanonicalizationMethod> are used by the <SignatureValue> and are included in <SignedInfo> to protect them from being tampered. The XML Digital Signature working group suggests two canonicalization algorithms: XML Canonicalization (Boyer, 2001) and Exclusive XML Canonicalization (Boyer, Eastlake, & Reagle, 2002). None of them solves all possible problems that can arise. For the discussion on the appropriate choice of the canonicalization algorithm, we refer to Boyer (2001) and Boyer et al. (2002). A list of <Reference> elements containing @URI references specifies the used resources; this element also specifies the transformations that have to be applied prior to the computation of the hash value with the algorithm from the <DigestMethod>. The <SignatureValue> is the Base64-encoded value of the signature. This value is the signature (produced according to the specification of the <SignatureMethod>) of the <SignedInfo> after its serialization with the algorithm specified by the <CanonicalizationMethod>. The <KeyInfo> is an optional element that enables the recipients to obtain the key needed for the signature verification. Typically, it contains a set of X.509 certificates. If the <KeyInfo> is empty then the recipient is expected to identify the key from the context. The <Object> is optional and contains some additional data (e.g., the signing time).

```
<Signature ID?>
 <SignedInfo>
 <CanonicalizationMethod/>
 <SignatureMethod/>
 (<Reference URI?>
  <Transforms/>?
  <DigestMethod>
  <DigestValue>
 </Reference>)+
 </SignedInfo>
 <SignatureValue>
 <KeyInfo>?
 <Object ID?>*
</Signature>
```

When generating an XML Signature, the following procedure called Core Generation is performed. First, for each resource being signed the transformations described in <Transforms> are applied. Then, the digest value over the resulting data object is calculated and stored in <DigestValue>. Further, the element <SignedInfo> with the child elements <SignatureMethod>, <CanonicalizationMethod> and <Reference>(s), is created and canonicalized. Finally, the <SignatureValue> is calculated over the canonicalization result of <SignedInfo> using the algorithms specified in <SignatureMethod>.

When validating an XML Signature, the following procedure called Core Validation is performed. First, each digest specified in <Reference> is verified by retrieving the corresponding resource information and applying the described transformations and the specified digest algorithm. The resulting value is compared to the content of the <DigestValue>; validation fails if these do not match. Then, the content of the <SignedInfo> is serialized using the canonicalization method specified in <CanonicalizationMethod>, the key data is retrieved using the information in <KeyInfo> (or by other means if the latter is empty), and the signature is verified using the algorithm specified in <SignatureMethod>.

XML Encryption specifies how to encrypt and decrypt XML documents. If the encrypted data contains a cryptographic key, then it is stored in the <EncryptedKey>; otherwise in the <EncryptedData>.

```
<EncryptedData>
 <EncryptionMethod/>?
 <KeyInfo>?
 <CipherData>
 <EncryptionProperties>?
</EncryptedData>
```

When encrypting an XML element (or its content), the <EncryptedData> replaces the plain text element (or its content) in the encrypted version of the XML document. Upon its decryption, the plain text element (or its content) is placed instead of the <EncryptedData>.

The <EncryptionMethod> is an optional element that describes the encryption algorithm applied to the cipher data. If the element is absent, the encryption algorithm must be known by the recipient or the decryption will fail. The <KeyInfo> is an optional element that carries information about the key used

to encrypt the data. The <CipherData> is mandatory and contains the encrypted data specified in <CipherValue> or its reference in <CipherReference>. The element <EncryptionProperties> can contain additional information concerning the generation of the <EncryptedDate> (e.g., a time stamp).

The <EncryptedKey> extends <EncryptedData> with the <ReferenceList> that contains pointers to the data and further keys encrypted using the key from <EncryptedKey>, the <CarriedKeyName> used for to associate the user's name with the key value, and the @ Recipient attribute that specifies the recipient for whom the key from <EncryptedKey> is intended for.

XMaiL Structure Definitions

The structure of *XMaiL* is defined in XML Schema which can be found in the Appendix. To give an overview, we describe in the following the most important components of XMaiL.

XmaiL: The <XMaiL> specifies an XMaiL document which contains either a single XMaiL or an XMaiL embedded into another XMaiL (e.g., an e-mail message embedded into another e-mail message). The <Header> is mandatory and has similar functionality as the usual header fields in the plain text e-mail format. The <Body> is mandatory in case that the XMaiL represents a single e-mail. It defines the content of the XMaiL. The optional <Security> specifies the encrypted session key, the XML Signatures and all related information, such as the signing Certificate.

```
<XMaiL>
 <Security />?
 <Header />
 <Body />?
</XMaiL>
```

Header: The <Header> specifies the information about the XMaiL (e.g., the authors are specified in the child element <From>, the recipients in <To> or <Cc>, the sent date in <Date>, the topic in <Subject>, and so on). For example, the header From: Alice <alice@example.org> in the plain text e-mail is represented in XMaiL by <From>Alice <alice@example.org></From>.

```
<Header>  ...
  <From/> <Sender/>?
  <To/>? <Cc/>?
  <Date/><Subject/>
  ...
</Header>
```

Body: The <Body> specifies the content of the XMaiL. If the XMaiL contains only one type of media (e.g., text, audio, image, video, or application), then the content is stored in the <Media>; otherwise if the message contains only an embedded XMaiL as its content, then this is stored in the <Message>. In all other cases, the <Multipart> is used.

```
<Body>
  <Media/>?
  <Multipart/>?
  <Message/>?
</Body>
```

Media: The <Media> specifies the attached media type. The corresponding information, such as the content type, the encoding, the description, and so on is specified in the <MediaHeader>. The actual content is included in the <Data>; it can be either given within the <Value>, or referenced in the <Reference> element. The significant advantage of the reference method is that one does not need to attach the whole document to an XMaiL which is sent to multiple recipients, but can include a reference to this document instead. The attached media content should be encoded according to the method specified in the <MediaHeader>.

```
<Media>
  <MediaHeader/>
  <Data>
  <Value/>?
  <Reference/>?
  </Data>
</Media>
```

Multipart: The <Multipart> is used if several different types of data are contained in the XMaiL. It corresponds to the media data type multipart in the MIME e-mail format. The attribute @Subtype defines the relationship of the child elements; it can

be mixed, digest, alternative, parallel, or any of the other defined types. How the sub type is used can be found in Section 5.1 of RFC 2046. Unlike the multipart in e-mail, <Multipart> specifies only the content of XMaiL, but not the signatures.

```
<Multipart Subtype>
  <Media/>*
  <Multipart/>*
  <Message/>*
</Multipart>
```

Message: The <Message> is used to embed an XMaiL into another XMaiL. The information about the embedded XMaiL is specified in the <MediaHeader>, and its content is specified in the child element <XMaiL> for which only the <Header> is mandatory.

```
<Message>
  <MediaHeader/>
  <XMaiL/>
</Message>
```

Security: The <Security> specifies the encrypted session key in the child element <EncryptedKeys>, the attached *XML signatures* in <Signature> elements, and other related information, such as the signing certificate. In contrast to the S/MIME and PGP/MIME extensions, signatures in XMaiL are separated from the body. Thus, in XmaiL, it is possible to achieve integrity and authentication for each element and its content separately (e.g., for the information in the <Header> and <Body> elements, and so on).

EncryptedKeys: In XmaiL, it is possible to encrypt signatures and the body using *XML Encryption.* The encrypted data is stored in the <EncryptedData>. Usually, the plain text content is encrypted with a symmetric key, which in turn is encrypted with the recipients' public keys (hybrid approach), and then stored in the <EncryptedKeys>. Each <Encrypted-Key> specifies the encrypted symmetric key for one particular recipient.

```
<EncryptedKeys>
  <EncryptedKey>+
</EncryptedKeys>
```

Plain-Text XmaiL: The following example shows an XMaiL message without any security mechanisms, sent from Alice (`alice@foo.org`) to Bob (`bob@foo.org`). It contains two attached media data, a text and an image, specified in the <Media> elements in lines 10–15 and 16–23, respectively. These different media types are encapsulated into the <Multipart> element in lines 09–24, which is a child element of <Body>.

```
[01]<XMaiL>
[02] <Header>
[03]  <From>alice@example.org, carl@foo.org</From>
[04] <To>bob@example.net</To>
[05] <Date>Sun, 5 Nov 2006 12:17:58 -0800 (PST)</Date>
[06]  <Subject>E-mail Communication Security</Subject>...
[07] </Header>
[08] <Body>
[09] <Multipart Subtype="mixed">
[10] <Media Id='id-text'>
[11]  <MediaHeader>
[12]   <ContentType>text/plain; charset=iso-8859-1</ContentType>
[13]  </MediaHeader>
[14]  <Data><Value>This is an example e-mail message for this chapter.
     Treat it as spam!</Value></Data>
[15] </Media>
[16] <Media Id='id-image'>
[17]  <MediaHeader>
[18]   <ContentType>image/jpeg; name=water.jpg</ContentType>
[19]   <ContentTransferEncoding>base64</ContentTransferEncoding>
[20]   <ContentDisposition>inline;filename=water.jpg</ContentDisposition>
[21]  </MediaHeader>
[22]  <Data><Value>/9j/4AAQSkZJRgABA...AAE0AAE8AAP8vAA==</Value></Data>
[23] </Media>
[24] </Multipart>
[25] </Body>
[26]</XMaiL>
```

(Multiple) Digital Signatures in XmaiL: The following example extends the previous one by the attached XML signatures, specified within the <Signature> elements, which should be inserted between the

lines 01 and 02 in the above listing. For each attached XML signature, there exists its own <Signature> element within the <Security> element.

```
[S01] <Security>
   <!--Signature created by alice-->
[S02] <Signature><SignedInfo>
[S03] <CanonicalizationMethod Algorithm='.../xml-exc-c14n#'/>
[S04]  <SignatureMethod Algorithm= '...#rsa-sha1'/>
[S05]  <Reference>...<XPath>ancestor-or-self::Date[parent::node()=
      /XMaiL/Header</XPath>...</Reference>
[S06]  <Reference>...<XPath>ancestor-or-self::Subject[parent::node()=
      /XMaiL/Header</XPath>...</Reference>
[S07]  <Reference>...<XPath>ancestor-or-self::Body[parent::node()=
      /XMaiL</XPath>...</Reference>
[S08]  </SignedInfo>
[S09]  <SignatureValue/>
[S10]  <KeyInfo/>
[S11] </Signature>
     <!--Signature created by carl-->
[S12] <Signature>...
[S13]  <Reference>...<XPath>ancestor-or-self::Date[parent::node()=
      /XMaiL/Header</XPath>...</Reference>
[S14]  <Reference>...<XPath>ancestor-or-self::Media[self::node()=
      /XMaiL/Body/Multipart/Media[@Id='id-text']</XPath>...</Reference>
[S15] ...</Signature>
[S16] </Security>
```

The signature specified in the <Signature> in lines S02–S10 is created by Alice. The canonization algorithm is Exclusive XML Canonicalization, specified by the attribute @Algorithm of the <CanonicalizationMethod> in line S03. The signature algorithm is RSA-SHA1, specified by the attribute @Algorithm of the <SignatureMethod> in line S14. The signed contents are referenced to by the <Reference>s in lines S05–S07. Position independent references (e.g., via Id) should be avoided as far as possible, due to the wrapping attack described in (McIntosh, & Austel, 2005); therefore, XMaiL uses XPath to reference the signed contents. Alice signs not only the whole <Body>, but also the elements <Date> and <Subject> within the <Header>. The actual signature value is given in the <SignatureValue> in line S09. The <KeyInfo> in line S10 specifies the public key of the signer, its child elements specify the detail information of this key (e.g., the <KeyValue> specifies the key value, and <X509Data> specifies information about the X.509 certificate which contains the public key). The use of child element which specifies directly the key value is not recommended, since this element does not provide any information concerning the association between the signer and the public key. Another possibility to include the key information is to use the <BinarySecurityToken> defined in WS-Security Core Specification 1.1 (WSS Technical Committee, 2006).

The second signature specified in the <Signature> in lines S12–S15 is created by Bob. Unlike Alice, Bob signs only part of the body, namely the first <Media> in lines 10–15 and the <Date> in line 05. Since the <Date> is authenticated by both signatures, any modification of the original date would result in invalid signatures of Alice and Bob. The modification of the subject can only be detected during the verification of the Alice signature, since it is not authenticated by the Bob signature. According to the XML Signature standard the whole <Header> can also be signed. However, some information can be appended to the <Header>. For example, if the same message is submitted to the mail delivery system for the second time, a new <Resent> can be added to the <Header>. The modification of the header information will then invalidate the signature. Therefore, we sign only the individual elements within the <Header>. If the <Date> is not authenticated by the signature, the message transmission is vulnerable to replay attacks. For example, assume that a supplier receives a signed order from its customer but the <Date> is not signed. Replaying this message with a modified (later) date would still result in a valid signature so that the supplier would believe having received a new order from the same customer, but the customer may not have any intention to make this second order.

As already mentioned in the context of PGP/MIME and S/MIME, it is important to provide an authenticated binding between the identity of the signer and the public key used to verify generated signatures. In order to achieve this application of XmaiL, the Public Key Infrastructure (PKI) with X.509 PKI certificates (PKIX) should be applied. Based on the PKI, the recipient's client can verify the validity of the sender's public-key certificate before treating the signature as valid.

In order to use XMaiL in official scenarios concerning the commercial or governmental issues, the *XML Advanced Electronic Signatures (XAdES)* standard can be applied. XAdES extends the XML Signature syntax and processing specification towards additional XML formats that can keep information concerning nonrepudiation valid for some longer period of time. XAdES adds the <QualifyingProperties> element within the elements <Object> in <Signature>, which contains two further child elements: a <SignedProperties> element specifying the properties to be signed, and an <UnsignedProperties> specifying other properties. The XAdES format specifies six different forms for various security levels of a signature: the basic form XAdES, and the extended forms (i.e., XAdES with Time-Stamp (XAdES-T), XAdES with complete validation data (XAdES-C), XAdES with eXtended validation data (XAdES-X), XAdES with eXtended validation data incorporated for the long term (XAdES-X-L), and XAdES with archiving validation data (XAdES-A)). The choice of an appropriate form depends on the stated security requirements.

After receiving an XMaiL with attached signatures, the mail client must first verify all of these signatures. If any signature is invalid, it must make a corresponding error alert. Additionally, the client must be able to show which information in the header and body have been signed by the signer(s). The visualization and verification of distinct signatures in the standard browser has been described in (Gajek, Kubbilun, Psarros, & Schwenk, 2005).

Encrypted Contents in XmaiL: The following example shows an XMaiL with encrypted contents.

```
[01]<XMaiL>
[02] <Security>
[03] <EncryptedKeys>
  <!-- The session key encrypted with the public key
of bob. -->
[04] <EncryptedKey Recipient='bob@example.
net'>
[05]   <EncryptionMethod/><KeyInfo /><Cipher-
Data/>
[06] </EncryptedKey>
  <!-- The session key encrypted with
the public key of alice. -->
[07] <EncryptedKey Recipient='alice@
example.org'/>
[08] <ReferenceList>
[09]   <DataReference URI='#ED-
Body'/>
```

```
[10]  </ReferenceList>
[11]  <Security>
[12]  <Header>
[13]  <From>alice@example.org</From>
[14]  <To>bob@example.net</To>
[15]  <Date>Sun, 5 Nov 2006 12:17:58 -
0800 (PST)</Date>
[16]  <Subject>E-mail Communication
Security</Subject>
[17]  </Header>
[18]  <Body>
[19]  <EncryptedData Id='ED-Body'>
[20]      <EncryptionMethod
Algorithm='...#aes128-cbc'/>
[21]  <CipherData/>
[22]  </EncryptedData>
[23]  </Body>
[24]</XMaiL>
```

The <EncryptedData> in lines 19–22 specifies the encryption of the content of the <Body>. The content is not encrypted with the public keys of recipients directly; otherwise, encrypting it with the public keys of all recipients and authors would require a longer processing time and a higher message size. Hence, the content is encrypted with a symmetric algorithm and the randomly generated symmetric (session) key, which is usually much shorter then the whole message, is encrypted with the public keys of all recipients and authors. The symmetric encryption method in our example is AES128-CBC, specified in the attribute @Algorithm of the <EncryptionMethod> in line 20. The encrypted content is then specified in the <CipherData> in line 21. The encrypted session key is then specified in the <EncryptedKey>s within <EncryptedKeys>.

After receiving an XMaiL with the encrypted information, the mail client finds the <Encrypted-Key> which is encrypted with its public key. If no corresponding element can be found, the client makes an error alert. Otherwise, it decrypts the elements using its own private key and obtains the symmetric session key, which it uses to decrypt the confidential contents. The decrypted plain text content replaces the corresponding <EncryptedData> in the XMaiL document. Finally, the mail client verifies the validity of the XMaiL according to the given schema definition.

Signed and Encrypted Content in XmaiL: In order to sign and encrypt contents in XMaiL simultaneously, the above described "sign-only" and "encrypt-only"

formats can be nested. XMaiL does not make any limitations concerning the order of the signature generation and encryption. The choice on whether the signature on some element is generated prior to its encryption or after it depends on the particular implementation. Note that if the signature is generated prior to the encryption then it is hidden by the cipher text. Otherwise, the signature remains publicly observable. This might be useful in scenarios where signature verification is performed by some other party (e.g., by a mail server which transfers the XMaiL to the receiver's client only if the signature is valid (note that no private key is needed to verify the signature)).

Sending and Receiving XMaiLs

XMaiLs can be transmitted via most of the available XML transport protocols (e.g., SOAP, XML-RPC). If *SOAP* is used, then XMaiL becomes a child element of the <Body> as shown below.

```
<Envelope>
 <Header/>
 <Body>
  <XMaiL xmlns='.../xmail#'>...</XMaiL>
 </Body>
<Envelope>
```

The SOAP header contains the addresses of the recipient mail server and the recipient's e-mail addresses. The sender client sends then this SOAP message to the mail delivery system which transports it to the recipient's mail servers. After receiving the SOAP message, the receiving client checks if the specified recipient address exists and delivers the received XMaiL to this address. In order to receive an XmaiL, the client asks the mail server to send a SOAP message containing either the whole XMaiL or only the information about its header. In the latter case, the server will send the whole XMaiL only after the corresponding request of the client.

While sending XMaiL via SOAP, all sending, transporting, and receiving servers are Web Service points. How does this compare to the existing e-mailing technology SMTP of today? Both systems have their overhead when it comes to processing. SMTP system requires processing of MIME, in order to understand the content of the message. XMaiL via SOAP does not; however, it has the added overhead of SOAP transformation which is a heavy process. Web Service is becoming one of the popular technologies in the last years, the number of Web Service points increases rapidly; and the standard Web services are easy to deploy; hence, distributing XMaiL via SOAP is not a problem. The disadvantage of this method is that the existing e-mail servers, including SMTP, POP3, and IMAP servers, cannot be used.

XMaiLs can be also transmitted using current e-mail formats as follows:

From: <alice@foo.org>
To: <bob@foo.org>
Date: Sun, 5 Nov 2006 12:17:58 -0800 (PST)
Subject: E-mail Communication Security
Content-Type: application/xmail, charset='utf-8'

<XMaiL xmlns='.../xmail#'>
...
</XMaiL>

The Content-Type `application/xmail` indicates that the content is an XMaiL. The headers From, Subject, Date, To, and Cc should be present in the e-mail headers and with the same content as in the embedded XMaiL. In this case, all e-mail servers, including SMTP, POP3, and IMAP servers, can be further be used without any modification.

After receiving XMaiL sent via e-mail, the receiving client removes all e-mail headers, shows and verifies only the contained XMaiL. Hence, the modification of the e-mail headers does not have any influence on the XMaiL.

XMaiL vs. S/MIME and (Open)PGP and PGP/MIME

XML Signature and XML Encryption allow both X.509 and PGP key information to be used for the signature and encryption, respectively. Since XMaiL uses both XML technologies, it supports both X.509 and PGP signature and encryption.

XMaiL provides extended authentication. While in S/MIME, (Open)PGP, and PGP/MIME, only the content can be signed; in XmaiL, one can sign the header information, such as the sent date, subject, addresses of recipients, and senders. This has various advantages against spamming and impersonation attacks. Note that with previous security formats a sender can generate a signed nonXMaiL message, use a script to change the To, Cc, or Bcc fields, and then deliver these automatically generated messages

whereby the signature remains valid despite of the automatic modifications. XMaiL allows avoiding this by defining the following policy for the mail server. First, all fields related to recipients (that is, the <To> and <Cc>, <Bcc> is not allowed in XMaiL) must be signed. Second, only XMaiLs with valid signatures should be forwarded to the recipient.

Another potential threat with the previous security mechanisms is that an adversary can duplicate a non-XMaiL message and resend it later with modified sent date so that recipients would believe having received a new (fresh) message. Additionally, the adversary can modify the To and Cc fields and deliver the message to other recipients who would also believe having received a proper message. Also, if the Sender or From fields are modified then recipients would believe that this message is originated by the sender whose address is specified in these fields. Since in XMaiL the header fields can be authenticated by the signature, any modification to them will be detected.

Another important difference between XMaiL and other formats is the possibility to create different signatures on different contents of one e-mail message. Note that in S/MIME, (Open)PGP, and PGP/MIME, all signatures must authenticate the same content.

Compared to the existing e-mail formats, XMaiL has also some disadvantages. As shown in Mundy and Chadwick (2004), the creation and verification of XML Signatures, and the encryption and decryption in XML format are slower than in ASN.1 format (as in S/MIME). As a result is the creation and verification of XMaiL are less efficient than in S/MIME. Another disadvantage is that there are now much less Web Service servers than e-mail servers; hence, the sending of XMaiL may be some difficult.

Application

Since XMaiL provides all functions of e-mail old formats, it can ultimately replace them. However this needs time. XMaiL should be applied incrementally. As an example, all e-mails exchanged within a company are in XMaiL format. A proxy between the company network and Internet is needed. If an employee wants to send an e-mail to recipients outside of the company, he writes it in XMaiL format. If the receiver server supports XMaiL, the proxy forwards the e-mail; otherwise, the proxy transforms it to the old format and forwards the latter so that the receiver and receiving server understand this e-mail.

Implementation

The prototype implementation of the XMaiL based e-mail communication is still in process. Now (May 2007) we can create plain-text XMaiLs, XMaiLs with only signatures or encryption, XMaiLs with both signatures and encryption. We can verify all signatures in XMaiL and decrypt the encrypted e-mail. In the implementation, we transfer the XMaiLs both via SOAP and via e-mail. As a next task we will test the processing performance of e-mails in XMaiL format compared to those in old formats.

CONCLUSION

The described XML-based e-mail format XMaiL supersedes the currently available security standards for the e-mail communication. It provides a higher level of security, such as authentication and/or confidentiality of the header field information and provides a higher flexibility by allowing multiple signatures over distinct contents of the same XMaiL document. Additionally, XMaiL supports the signature generation and encryption methods specified in the current S/MIME and (Open)PGP formats.

REFERENCES

Bartel, M., Boyer, J., Fox, LaMacchia, B., & Simon, E. (2002, February). XML-signature syntax and processing. *W3C Recommendation*. Retrieved May 3, 2008, from http://www.w3.org/TR/2002/REC-xmldsig-core-20020212/

Boyer, J. (2001, March). Canonical XML version 1.0. *W3C Recommendation*. Retrieved May 3, 2008, from http://www.w3.org/TR/2001/RECxml-c14n-20010315

Boyer, J., Eastlake, D., & Reagle, J. (2002, July). Exclusive XML canonicalization, version 1.0. *W3C Recommendation*. Retrieved May 3, 2008, from http://www.w3.org/TR/2002/REC-xml-excc14n-20020718/

Callas, J., Donnerhacke, L., Finney, H., & Thayer, T. (1998, November). *OpenPGP message format*. RFC 2440.

Clark, J., & DeRose, S. (Ed.). (1999, November). XML path language (XPath), version 1.0. *W3C Recom-mendation*. Retrieved May 3, 2008, from http://www.w3.org/TR/1999/REC-xpath-19991116

Cruellas, J.C., Karlinger, G., Pinkas, D., & Ross, J. (2003, February). *XML advanced electronic signatures (XAdES)*. Retrieved May 3, 2008, from http://www.w3.org/TR/2003/NOTEXAdES-20030220/

Elkins, M., Torto, D.D., Levien, R., & Roessler, T. (2001, August). *MIME security with OpenPGP*. IETF RFC 3156.

Ewers, L., Kubbilun, W., Liao, L., & Schwenk, J. (2005, September). Secure xmail or how to get rid of legacy code in secure e-mail applications. In *CMS '05: Proceedings of the 9th IFIP International Conference on Communications and Multimedia Security* (Vol. LNCS 3677, pp. 291-300). Springer Berlin/Heidelberg.

Gajek, S., Kubbilun, W., Psarros, M., & Schwenk, J. (2005, September). *Trustworthy visualisation and verification of multiple xml-signatures*. LNCS 3677 (pp. 311-320).

Gudgin, M., Hadley, M., Mendelsohn, N., Moreau, J.-J., & Nielsen, H.F. (2003, June). SOAP version 1.2 part 1: Messaging framework. *W3C Recommendation*. Retrieved May 3, 2008, from http://www.w3.org/TR/2003/REC-soap12-part1-20030624/

Housley, R. (2004, July). *Cryptographic message syntax (CMS)*. IETF RFC 3852.

Housley, R., Polk, W., Ford, W., & Solo, D. (2002, April). *Internet X.509 public key infrastructure certificate and certificate revocation list (CRL) profile*. IETF RFC 3280.

Imamura, T., Dillaway, B., & Simon, E. (2002, December). XML encryption syntax and processing. *W3C Candidate Recommendation*. Retrieved May 3, 2008, from http://www.w3.org/TR/2002/REC-xmlenc-core-20021210/

Menezes, A.J., Oorschot P.C., & Vanstone, S.C. (1996, October). *Handbook of applied cryptography*. CRC Press.

Mundy, D., & Chadwick, D.W. (2004, January/February). An XML alternative for performance and security: ASN.1. In *IEE Computer Society, IT Professional*.

McIntosh, M., & Austel, P. (2005). Xml signature element wrapping attacks and countermeasures. In *SWS*

'05: Proceedings of the 2005 Workshop on Secure Web Services (pp. 20-27) New York, NY: ACM Press.

Ramsdell, B. (2004, July). *Secure/multipurpose Internet mail extensions (S/MIME) version 3.1.* IETF RFC 3851.

Resnick, P. (2001, April). *Internet message format.* IETF RFC 2822.

Winer, D. (2008). *XML-RPC specification.* Retrieved May 3, 2008, from http://www.xmlrpc.com/spec

WSS Technical Committee. (2006, February). Web services security: SOAP message security 1.1 (WS-security 2004). *OASIS Standard Specification.* Retrieved May 3, 2008, from, http://www.oasis-open.org/committees/download.php/16790/wss-v1.1-spec-osSOAPMessageSecurity.pdf

KEY TERMS

Canonicalization: A method brings the input data to a normal form.

Secure E-Mail: A signed and encrypted e-mail. The most two popular mechanisms are S/MIME and PGP.

SOAP: A mechanism for interapplication communication between systems written in arbitrary languages. The message is an XML document with the root element <Envelope>.

S/MIME: Secure MIME. S/MIME allows sending signed and encrypted e-mail.

XMaiL: XML e-mail, a new e-mail format based on XML (defined in this chapter).

XML Security: A series of standards that define security properties in XML format, such as XML Signature and XML Encryption.

Chapter XVIII
Aspect–Oriented Analysis of Security in Distributed Virtual Environment

Li Yang
University of Tennessee at Chattanooga, USA

Raimund K. Ege
Northern Illinois University, USA

Lin Luo
Florida International University, USA

ABSTRACT

This chapter describes our approach to handle security in a complex Distributed Virtual Environment (DVE). The modules of such an environment all need to be concerned about security. An object-oriented model of a DVE allows us to capture security in an aspect-oriented fashion as a crosscutting concern among the multiple modules. As DVEs become more complex in content, distribution, and capabilities, the security requirement emerges as a key issue in their design and implementation. In order to control the software complexity, our strategy is to model and analyze the impact of security concerns on the functional model of DVEs via an aspect-oriented technique. This approach is appropriate to be applied at both the system design and modeling stages and provides guidance during the implementation stage. This chapter illustrates an aspect-oriented approach to the impact analysis of security concerns upon the functionalities of DVEs. A design-level security model for DVEs is provided to show how to weave security concerns into the models of DVE designs seamlessly.

ASPECT-ORIENTED ANALYSIS OF SECURITY IN DISTRIBUTED VIRTUAL ENVIRONMENT

Distributed virtual environments (DVEs) are software systems that connect geographically dispersed users into a shared virtual space and support the interaction between the users and the shared world. DVEs have many applications in medicine, robotics, interactive distance learning and online communities. A DVE must satisfy a plethora of requirements so as to maintain realism of the virtual systems for all the users that are presently exploring this cyber environment.

More concisely, the environments should provide a sense of copresence to all participants, offer means for participants to communicate with each other or the world, respond to users' interactions, and support event handling.

As computing power and network bandwidth increase security, issues in DVEs become more critical and draw more attention. More and more DVEs involve sensitive areas (i.e., handle and produce proprietary or classified information, objects, and processes) security becomes a necessity. Given the richness and complexity of DVEs, there are a multitude of security issues requiring consideration during the development process. First of all, tens or hundreds of users may participant in a DVE simultaneously: all of them should be legitimate users as they access the virtual world. Second, a DVE often encompasses numerous multimodal data from multiple resources to provide a comprehensive and convincing 3D virtual space. Such data will contain rich multiple media like 3D graphics, text and streamed audio/video, and so on. Access to the media data may require different levels of confidentiality. Moreover, since participants interact with the system or other participants via advanced multimedia devices checking and enforcing of access privileges poses significant challenges. Any moment during their exploration of the cyberspace, they actively contribute shared information; this directly results in abundant yet frequently-updated data contributed and shared over the network. Such shared data may be a mixture of administrative flow, entity-data update, and streaming video/audio. Both the interaction and the information produced may be sensitive to some degree. In addition, since individual participants join and leave the shared space at will, changes of group membership happen frequently and further aggravate the management of security concerns. Finally, the transmission of the entire data stream, sensitive or not, may take place over untrusted networks where it is exposed to malicious attacks. In summary, adequate security handling is of increasing importance to allow DVE applications to flourish.

However, there is a lack of both analysis methodologies and techniques for DVE security due to the common preference to relax security in favor of performance. Since DVE applications normally entail frequent interaction, rich multimedia content and involve a great deal of distantly separated users, adequate handling of security significantly adds to latency and degrades the overall performance. This strategy was practical and efficient as most of the pioneering and experimental distributed virtual environments were built upon local or private network setting and the chance of a security breach was quite slight. But as distributed virtual systems widely spread from dedicated networking links to unsecured public networks, a higher need for security concern in the design and implementation of DVEs is inescapable.

This chapter provides an approach to analyze the impact of security concerns in DVEs and to weave the requirements into the environments using an aspect-oriented technique. We elucidate how to model design-level security concerns and how to encapsulate them into DVE design models.

The rest of the chapter is organized as follows. First, we outline related efforts regarding security in DVEs. Then we present an object-oriented view of the distributed virtual content and our evolution of a role-based access control security model. The aspect-oriented analysis of the security capability within DVEs is described in the next section, along with the overall woven results. Finally, we summarize and conclude with perspectives for further work.

RELATED WORK

Much research has been conducted on the subject of security and has resulted in copious techniques and approaches to address the issue from different views and to different levels. The key to the development and integration of a secure infrastructure is information assurance (IA), which has five focal pillars: availability, integrity, authentication, confidentiality, and non-repudiation. As a challenging, complicated and sensitive application, a DVE is influenced by all five subjects of IA at varying levels throughout its life cycle.

Despite its importance, security research specific to DVEs has been somewhat limited compared with the fairly well-researched general security of computer systems and networks. In the 30-year evolving history of DVEs, security was usually treated as of lower priority in contrast to performance and reliability issues. In most of the notable early DVE efforts, the security issues rested primarily with dedicated networks with fully trusted users. A good example is SIMNET (Miller & Thorpe, 1995) sponsored by the U.S. Department of Defense. As the first successful implementation of a large-scale real-time DVE, SIMNET utilized dedicated, high-speed networking links to interconnect its participating nodes. As DVEs evolved progressively, techniques to address general network and computer security concerns like password schemas, data encryption, have been brought into the systems to enhance the security capability of DVEs. For instance, digital certificates were introduced and exploited in Bamboo, which is a component framework supporting real-time, networked virtual environments, to authenticate components loaded across the network (Watsen & Zyda, 1998). Researchers in Bullock and Benford (1999) and Pettifer and Marsh (2001) discussed access control in collaborative virtual environment: authentication and integrity is ensured using certificates and password schemas, privacy is achieved through the use of symmetric and asymmetric encryption. The issue of cheating and hacking in online massively-multiplayer gaming, one big branch of DVE applications, such as Age of Empires (Microsoft, http://www.ageofempires3.com/) and Ashron's Call (Turbine Entertainment Software Corporation, http://ac.turbine.com/), has been discussed by Pritchard (2000). In the newest generation of NPSNET, NPSNET-V, the authors argued that security should now be treated with a higher priority than before. Distributed Security Managers (DSM) equipped with multiple security techniques are created to boost the security capability of NPSNET-V, identified layers include data encryption, intrusion/misuse detection (Sallés, Michael, Capps, McGregor, & Kapolka, 2002).

Part of the reason that security lags behind other capabilities of DVEs is this historical tendency to sacrifice security for performance, which has engendered a lack of both the requirement and practical solutions for security issues in DVEs. But the hub is engendered by the complexity and difficulty of the task itself. The emergence of security concerns and requirements drive the evolvement of the DVE design and result in an increase in software complexity. Security concerns arise in more than one dimension of a distributed environment. They tend to span over multiple modules within the system, instead of necessarily aligning with the functional components of the DVE systems (Aldawud, Elrad, & Baden, 2003; Basch & Sanchez, 2003; Clarke & Walker, 2001).

In view of that, we modularize and analyze the security as a crosscutting concern using aspect-oriented technology on top of a base system that utilizes object-oriented methodology to sculpt common behavior of a DVE.

BACKGROUND

In this section, we first discuss our object-oriented model of DVEs and our role-based access control model. Then we investigate how to further enhance security for DVEs.

The Object-Oriented View of DVEs

We start with our analysis of distributed virtual environments (DVEs) in an object-oriented fashion. The analysis considers three modeling planes: (1) the characteristics of the participant in the immersed cyberspace; (2) the characteristics of virtual objects that compose the virtual representation—both individual virtual objects and the hierarchical nature of the virtual worlds; (3) managing components that administrate the running of the virtual space and the sophisticated interaction between participant and the system.

Conforming to the terminology of networked virtual reality environments, a participant refers to a user participating in the distributed virtual environment. Each participant has a corresponding virtual entity called avatar, to represent him/her in the shared virtual world. Through the utilization of the avatar schema, participants can be aware of the presence of each other and interact with each other. The corresponding object-oriented model must also support sophisticated behaviors a participant may have in the rich simulated world. Participant should be able to enter and leave a virtual world at his/her own will. They can walk around, touch/use virtual objects, communicate with each other by gesture or voice, have their favorite places/objects and visit them more frequently than others. In summary, they should be able to explore a new virtual location in a way just like they do in the real world, maybe even more convenient and more powerful.

Virtual objects and the virtual scene are two major entities in the virtual world and are the focus of the DVE modeling. Virtual objects are semantically meaningful building blocks of a virtual presentation. They are compulsory, so that the virtual space can be a realistic reflection of the real world and the participating users can have an immersed experience. Modeling of virtual objects supports identification of individual virtual objects, with their geometry representation such as shape, color, their spatial position and behavior. Virtual Scene is a temporal, spatial, and logical collection of virtual objects.

Figure 1. UML class diagram of DVE classes

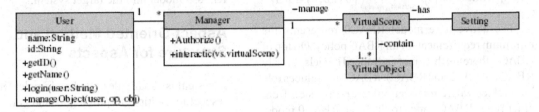

Access Control Models

Access control is to make authorization decision for every request to resources and data of a system and grant or deny the request. Different access control policies can be applied to achieve security objectives. Discretionary (DAC) policies control access based on identity of the requestor and on access control rules stating what requestors are (or are not) allowed to do. It is called *discretionary*, because users can pass their privileges to other users, where granting and revocation of privileges is regulated by an administrative policy. DAC can be bypassed by malicious programs such as Trojan Horses. Mandatory (MAC) policies control access based on mandated regulations determined by a central authority. The most common form of mandatory policy is the multilevel security policy, based on the classifications of subjects and objects in the system. Mandatory policies include secrecy-based mandatory policies and integrity-based policies. A secrecy mandatory policy controls the direct and indirect flows of information to the purpose of preventing leakages to unauthorized subjects via enforcing no-read-up and no-write-down principles. No-read-up principle means a subject is allowed a read access to an object only if the access class of the subject dominates the access class of the object. No-write-down principle means a

The richness and lifelikeness of the virtual representation of the shared world result from the complicated functionalities and services it provides. To offer the services to the participant and govern the system to perform normally, administrating components serve as the bridge between DVE and geographically dispersed users who are sitting in front of their workstations. With respect to the analysis above, we can obtain a group of classes in coarse granularity, which in later demonstration serves as an abstraction of the base system. Figure 1 display the classes using UML Class Diagram notation.

subject is allowed a write access to an object only if the access class of the subject is dominated by the access class of the object. Satisfaction of these two principles prevents information to flow from high level subjects/objects to low level subjects/objects; thereby no process will make sensitive information available to users not cleared from it. Integrity-based mandatory policy, also called Biba model, controls integrity of information by enforcing no-read-down and no-write-up principles. *No-read-down principle* means a subject is allowed a read access to an object only if the access class of the object dominates the access class of the subject. *No-write-up principle* means a subject is allowed a write access to an object only if the access class the subject is dominated by the access class of the object. Satisfaction of these principles safeguards integrity by preventing information stored in low objects or less reliable to flow to higher objects.

We select Role-based Access Control (RBAC) as the underlying security model of DVE systems for the consideration of security aspect modeling. With the RBAC model, access privileges are associated with roles and those roles are assigned to real users based on their responsibilities and qualifications. RBAC has and continues to evolve: the RBAC96 family includes several conceptual models [9]. A formal description of the base RBAC model is as following:

1. U, R, P, and S (users, roles, permissions and sessions respectively), where P is the Cartesian product of operation OP and objects Obj,

2. $PA \subseteq P \times R$, a many-to-many permission to role assignment relation,

3. $UA \subseteq U \times R$, a many-to-many user to role assignment relation,

4. user_sessions: $U \rightarrow 2^S$, a function mapping each user to a set of sessions.

5. session_roles: $S \rightarrow 2^S$, a function mapping each session to a set of roles. $session\_roles \subseteq \{r \mid (user(s), r) \in UA\}$ (which

can change with time) and session s has the permissions $\bigcup_{r \in session\_role(s)} \{p \mid (p,r) \in PA\}$

The above base model RBAC0 represents the minimum requirement for an RBAC policy. On top of RBAC0, there are three more advanced models, namely RBAC1, RBAC2 and RBAC3. RBAC1 introduces role hierarchies where roles can inherit permission from other roles. RBAC2 adds to the basic RBAC0 model static separation of duty (SSD) constraints, which impose restrictions on acceptable configurations of the different components of RBAC: a common example is to define mutually disjoint user assignments with respect to sets of roles. Finally, RBAC3 is a hybrid type combining the merits of both RBAC1 and RBAC2. Figure 2 illustrates the main elements of the RBAC3 model.

ASPECT-ORIENTED APPROACH TO ENHANCING DVE SECURITY

To facilitate the design and analysis of security concerns in distributed virtual environments, aspect-oriented methodology is applied to DVE systems on top of the object-oriented modeling dimension. This section sets off with an introduction of the aspect-oriented paradigm and the issues that arise when incorporating it into the system design of a DVE, followed by an elucidation of role-based access control (RBAC), which serves as the underlying security model of a DVE. To end, the proposed approach is exemplified by

weaving both the core RBAC model and the advanced RBAC3 model into the target system.

Aspect-Oriented Method and Structure for Aspects

A system is usually designed and implemented with respect to multiple requirements and concerns. Object-oriented (OO) methodology provides only one dimension to separate and abstract the concerns. There are some vital requirements to estimate the overall presentation of a distributed virtual environment, such as QoS, fault tolerance and consistency. These requirements tend to crosscut multiple functional modules and therefore violate or interfere with the goal of encapsulation in object-oriented modeling. Figure 3 graphically illustrates the relationship between functional modules and crosscutting concerns, namely aspects. The conventional OO paradigm benefits no longer hold upon such crosscutting features and the aspect-oriented abstraction principle is a more appropriate attempt to tackle this problem. Aspect oriented modeling (AOM) techniques allow system developers to describe solutions that crosscut a design in separate design views called aspects (10). An aspect is a pattern that characterizes a family of concern realizations. An aspect model consists of a set of Unified Modeling Language (UML) diagrams, both structural and behavioral, specifying the internal structure and the behavior of the aspect. An AOM design model consists of one or more aspect models and a primary model, which is specified using a set of UML diagrams. The

Figure 2. Illustration of the advanced RBAC96 family

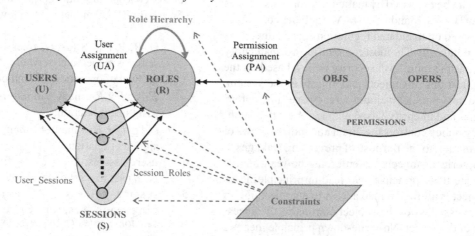

Figure 3. Relationship between aspects and modules

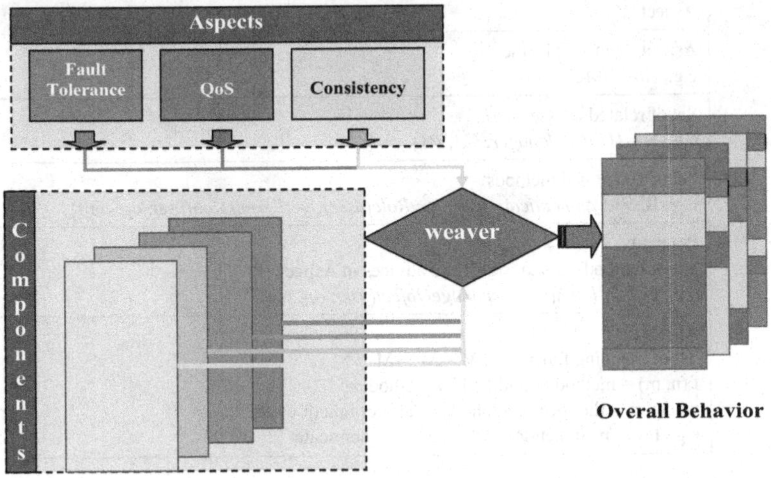

aspect models describe solutions that crosscut the modular structure of the primary model. Using the AOM approach, developers of security-critical systems can separate security treatment strategies from other concerns, by modeling security treatments as aspects. This eases the evolution of security mechanisms, as well as the evaluation of alternative treatment strategies in the trade-off analysis

The basic issues arise during the process of applying aspect-orientation to a target system including how to separate various concerns, and how to weave aspect models into an integrated system.

The first issue, called *separation of concerns,* is to separate the functionality modules from the target aspects, which consists of these steps:

- Identifying and specifying basic functionality components in the system.
- Specifying requirements of the target aspects.
- Defining the crosscutting section (join points) of the functionality components and target aspects.

The second issue, called *aspect weaving,* is to generate an integrated system by weaving aspect models with the functionality components. The steps include:

- Locating the join points where the functionality components and the target aspect interact.
- Defining the behavior of the system in order to

enforce aspect policies on the basic functionality components.
- Integrating aspect models with the functionality components.

The target problem in this presentation is DVE security, which, as a system property of DVEs, fit into the profile of aspects. Thus, we have a motivation to employ aspect orientation of security at the design level to capture the security problem and seamlessly amalgamate the solution into the DVE systems.

Just as the Class in OOP allows us to encapsulate data and methods in one unit, we propose to embody the relation between an aspect and the classes affected by it as illustrated in Table 1. In order to do so, we need the following elements: an identifier, the set of classes that relate to the aspect, the methods modified by it, and finally a function specifying the aspectual behavior that adds to the selected base methods.

Code-driven design limits the ability to understand various kinds of concerns, since it enables expressing the crosscutting nature of software concerns from only one single perspective (a low-level, static, and textual view of the system). This makes it difficult to integrate aspects with other software artifacts and to reason about modules of crosscutting concerns from different perspectives or viewpoints. Indeed, developing aspect-oriented software requires thinking of an aspect as an abstraction that defines a certain interaction context, and offers behavior that can vary depending on certain conditions at runtime (12). Fulfilling such a

Table 1. Structure of aspect

Aspect
Aspect identifier: Name e.g., *coreRBAC*
Set of related Classes e.g., S = {*User, Manager, UA, PA*}
Set of concerned methods e.g., BE = { *authenticate(user), getRole(user), getPermission(user, op, obj)*}
Pointcuts Set of method calls to trigger the advices in Aspect e.g., PC = { *login(user), manageObject(user, op, obj)*}
Advices Set of mapping function f: M × M →M f (n, m) = method *n* modified by method *m* where m is the specification of the aspect functionality e.g., f (*login*, authenticate) = login ≻ authenticate

requirement necessitates the ability to understand and describe the system from multiple viewpoints.

To overcome the shortcomings of current modeling techniques, aspects need to be treated as first-class citizen in advanced modeling languages. We propose to define an aspect as a UML model element that modularizes crosscutting concerns at various levels of abstraction, not only at the code-level.

RBAC0 Enhanced DVE by Aspect-Oriented Design

As a part of the security concern, access control plays an important role for a distributed environment. A DVE provides its users with access to a range of information resources from a wide variety of sources. Explicitly enabling or restricting individual legitimate users' access rights to the protected resources within the DVE means to maintain both the realistic impression and the normal functioning of the system. For example, some virtual entities like a light switch are accessible and operable to all users so that anyone can click on it to turn on/off the light. But access to some resources of associated virtual entities may be restricted to certain groups of members only. Like only users having a role of General can open and view a confidential document in a virtual military simulation space. Access control allows designation of the privileges to arbitrary users upon different available resources, and ensures that

only legitimate users have access to protected entities in the distributed environment.

Identify and Separate the New Aspect Concerns

With the introduction of the role concept from RBAC0, role-based access control becomes a new concern for DVE models. Each user will be assigned certain roles, and permissions to access virtual objects are associated with roles. Coordinator 1 in Figure 4 interfaces with User Class, Manager Class, UA repository Class, and PA repository Class to take care of the role-based authentication and authorization. Authentication checks the user is allowed to use the system or not, the authentication aspect will work with the UA repository class to retrieve the related roles for the current user. And the retrieved roles will be checked against PA repository to decide the permitted operations on the virtual scenes or virtual objects.

Aspects Weaving with Pointcuts

We particularize the weaving processes in ensuing subsections respectively for base RBAC model and the more sophisticated RBAC3 model. The modeling denotation conforms to the standard UML with necessary extension. Separation of concerns is a basic engineering principle that is also the core of object-

Figure 4. Collaboration stereotype with aspects

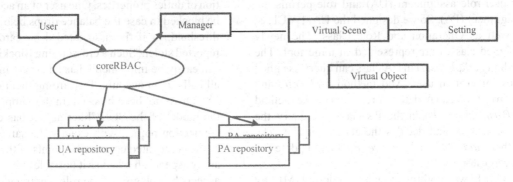

oriented analysis and design methods in the context of the Unified Modeling Language (UML). UML gives the designer a rich, but somehow disorganized, set of views of a model, as well as many features, such as design pattern occurrences, stereotypes or tag values, allowing to add non-functional information to a model (15). Aspect-oriented concepts are applied to manage the multitude of design constraints. We introduce aspect modeling to UML by extending UML with pointcuts that handle the interface between aspects and related classes.

Figure 5 depicts the partial set of classes that are involved in our role-based access control model. Classes unchanged are marked with Time New Roman

font while newly added classes use italic font in class name, attribute name, and method name.

The weaving course is carried out as following: First, we slightly extend the standard UML by <<aspect>>, which is designed for new concerns. For example we design the coreRBAC aspect, which interfaces with the DVE models through two pointcuts. The new designed aspect handles RBAC through authentication and authorization. The former was handled by replacement of login(user) with authenticate(user) where authenticate(user) will check whether that user has been input into the system and has valid roles associated with him/her.

Second, we introduce new classes to handle the coreRBAC related concerns. For instance, we need a

Figure 5. Weave RBAC0 aspect into DVE

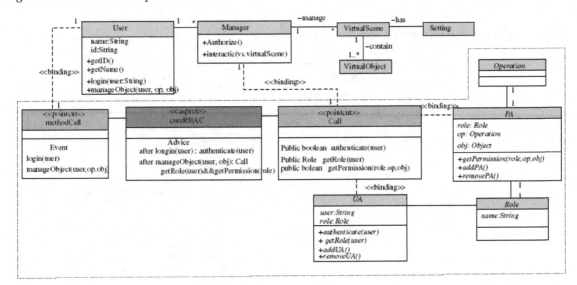

class to store the information and provide operations for user-role assignment (UA) and role-permission assignment (PA). So we designed the UA, PA Class, as well as Operation and Role Class. The newly designed classes are represented in italic font. The method *getRole(user)* in UA class can query assigned roles for certain user. And method *add_UA()* and *remove_UA()* can update UA repository. The method *getPermission(role)* in the PA class can query the PA repository and decides the access request. The method *add_PA()* and *remove_PA()* can update the PA repository.

Third, we slightly extend standard UML by pointcuts, which takes care of the communication between aspects and the classes. For instance, the <<pointcut>> methodCall here specifies the events that will trigger the coreRBAC aspect. When the login(user) method is called, then the advice in coreRBAC is triggered. That means the *authenticate(user)* method will be called, and the <<pointcut>> Call will communicate with the UA class to authenticate the current user. Similarly, when the method *manageObject(user, op, obj)* is called the pointcut will trigger the second advice in the coreRBAC aspect and communicate with UA and PA classes to get roles and permissions for manage the current object's request.

Composition of Aspects

In the configuration model, we can also nicely show aspect composition. To illustrate this idea, we assume that our system must provide further checks for role assignment. For instance, assigned role for one user

must be checked with role hierarchy, and with separation of duties properties. One user of an account must be blocked in case the balance drops below a certain threshold, or if the associated debit card has been reported stolen. Such a crosscutting Blocking feature can easily be implemented as an aspect intercepting all calls to an account, forwarding them only if the account as not been blocked. In this simple example, the model of the SODChker aspect has conjugated connection points, with exactly the same signature as the conjugated connection points of the RoleHierarchy aspect. This makes it possible to compose both aspects by "plugging" the role hierarchy connection point into the separation-of-duty connection point. The RoleHierarchy and SODChker aspects are built on top of the coreRBAC aspect.

It is important for a DVE system to seamlessly adapt to newly emerged and superior techniques so that it can revolutionize and function as best as state-of-the-art technologies can allow it to. In our approach, advanced techniques can be regarded as new aspect and therefore is integrated into the existing based system. Following our RBAC example, we demonstrate by weaving more sophisticated RBAC conceptual model (RoleHierarchy and SODChker) into DVE.

Treating the woven result of the original base system and RBAC0 as the new base system, the process to weave RBAC3 into the DVE is conducted as following:

- First, RBAC1 and RBAC2 are identified as new concerns.

Figure 6. Collaboration stereotype with hierarchical aspects

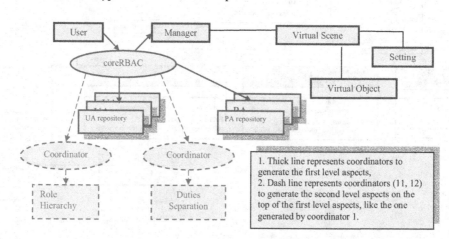

Figure 7. Weave advanced RBAC into DVE

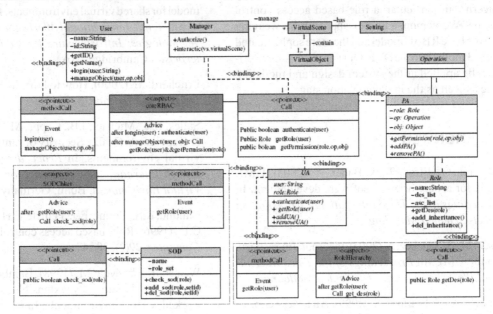

- Second, aspects are designed to handle new concerns. In the aspect handling role hierarchy in RoleHierarchy, we query all descendants of a specific role by the advice call get_Des(role) after getRole(user) method from UA class. The update method includes add_inheritance() and delete_inheritance(): they are now included in order to manage the partial order relationship among roles, which were denoted by bold font. Descendant list and ascendant list are two new attributes introduced to Role class. In aspect handling, separation of duty (SOD) in SODChker, we check SOD constraints by the advice call check_sod(role) after getRole(user) method from UA calss. The update methods include add_sod(role, setid) and del_sod(role, setid). The roles in the set of SOD cannot be assigned to a user in one active session. SOD class maintains a list of SOD sets. Whenever a role will be assigned to a user, the enforce_contraints() method in the SODChker will be called for the reason of separation of duty.
- Third, if there is an existing class with a similar aspect in the base system, merge the methods and attributes of the new class to the base class. Finally, if there is no existing similar class, a new class will be designed and introduced, like UA, PA and Role classes.

- Finally, pointcuts are designed to communicate with the aspects and classes.

FUTURE TRENDS

RBAC models are still evolving. In addition to a standard core RBAC model, extended models (such as RBAC3 used here), and families of models continue to be introduced. Recent RBAC models have studied newer concepts such as delegation and personalization both of which are very important to DVEs. Considering the administration of access models present a meta perspective that is especially important to dynamic DVEs with growing user communities. Thus, aspect-oriented modeling of security remains a fertile area for future research.

CONCLUSION

Security issues in DVEs are getting more and more attention, and security handling is becoming unavoidable with advances in technology of computer graphics and networking. This chapter introduces a novel approach to address access control in DVE systems. Our approach utilizes the aspect-oriented paradigm on top of an object-oriented abstraction of the DVE environments to efficiently abstract and weave security concern—in particular, a role-based access control scheme. We demonstrate our approach by weaving both the base RBAC model and the more sophisticated RBAC3 model into the DVE. Our approach is appropriate to be applied at the system design and modeling stage as well as the implementation stage.

REFERENCES

Aldawud, O., Elrad, T., & Bader, A. (2003). UML profile for aspect-oriented software development. In *Proceedings of the Third International Workshop on Aspect-Oriented Modeling*.

Basch, M., & Sanchez, A. (2003). Incorporating aspects into the UML. In *Proceedings of the Third International Workshop on Aspect-Oriented Modeling*.

Bullock, A., & Benford, S. (1999). An access control framework for multiuser collaborative environments. In *Proceedings of the International SIGGROUP Conference Supporting Group Work*. Phoenix, AZ.

Clarke, S., & Walker, R.J. (2001). Composition patterns: An approach to designing reusable aspects. In *Proceedings of the 23rd International Conference on Software Engineering*. Toronto, Ontario, Canada.

Gelbukh, A., Yáñez, C., & Camacho, O. (2005). A formal foundation for aspect-oriented software development. *Research on Computing Science*, 241-251.

Georg, G., France, R., & Ray, I. (2002). An aspect-based approach to modeling security concerns. In *Proceedings of Workshop on Critical Systems Development with UML*. Dresden, Germany.

Ho, W., Jézéquel, J., Pennaneac'h, F., & Plouzeau, N. (2002). A toolkit for weaving aspect oriented UML designs. In *Proceedings of the First International Conference on Aspect-Oriented Software Development*. Enschede, Netherlands.

Ho, W.M., Pennaneac'h, F., & Plouzeau, N. (2000). UMLAUT: A framework for weaving UML-based aspect-oriented designs. In *Proceedings of the Conference on Technology of object-oriented languages and systems*. Los Alamitos, CA.

Miller, D.C., & Thorpe, J.A. (1995) SIMNET: The advent of simulator networking. In *Proceedings of the IEEE* (Vol. 83, No. 8, pp. 1114-1123).

Pettifer, S., & Marsh, J. (2001). Collaborative access model for shared virtual environments. In *Proceedings of the Tenth International Workshops on Enabling Technologies: Infrastructure for Collaborative Enterprises*. Cambridge, MA.

Pritchard, M. (2000). How to hurt the hackers. *Game Developer Magazine, 6*, 28–30.

Sallés, E. J., Michael, J.B., Capps, M., McGregor, D., & Kapolka, A. (2002). Security of runtime extensible virtual environments. In *Proceedings of the ACM Fourth International Conference on Collaborative Virtual Environment*. Bonn, Germany.

Sandhu, R.S., Coyne, E.J., Feinstein, H.L. & Youman, C.E., (1996). Role-based access control models. *IEEE Computer, 29*(2), 38–47.

Watsen, K., & Zyda, M. (1998). Bamboo: A portable system for dynamically extensible, real-time, networked, virtual environments. In *Proceedings of the IEEE Annual International Symposium on Virtual Reality*. Atlanta, GA.

KEY TERMS

Access Control: Access control is to make authorization decision for every request to resources and data of a system, and grant or deny the request. Different access control policies including Mandatory Access Control (MAC), Discretionary Access Control (DAC), and Role-based Access Control (RBAC) can be applied to achieve security objectives.

Aspect Weaving: Aspect weaving is to generate an integrated system by weaving aspect models with the functionality components. The steps include: (1) locating the join points where the functionality components and the target aspect interact; (2) defining the behavior of the system in order to enforce aspect policies on the basic functionality components; and (3) integrating aspect models with the functionality components.

Aspect-Oriented Modeling: Aspect oriented modeling (AOM) techniques allow system developers to describe solutions that crosscut a design in separate design views called *aspects*.

Aspects: An aspect is a pattern that characterizes a family of concern realizations. An aspect model consists of a set of Unified Modeling Language (UML) diagrams, both structural and behavioral, specifying the internal structure and the behavior of the aspect.

Distributed Virtual Environment (DVE): Distributed virtual environments (DVEs) are software systems that connect geographically dispersed users into a shared virtual space and support the interaction between the users and the shared world. DVEs have many applications in medicine, robotics, interactive distance learning, and online communities.

Role-Based Access Control: With the RBAC model, access privileges are associated with roles, and those roles are assigned to real users based on their responsibilities and qualifications.

Separation of Concerns: To separate the functionality modules from the target aspects, which consists of these steps: (1) identifying and specifying basic functionality components in the system; (2) specifying requirements of the target aspects; and (3) defining the crosscutting section (join points) of the functionality components and target aspects.

Chapter XIX
Information Availability

Deepak Khazanchi
University of Nebraska at Omaha, USA

Andrew P. Martin
University of Nebraska at Omaha, USA

ABSTRACT

This chapter describes the concept of information availability (IAV) which is considered an important element of information security. IAV is defined as the ability to make information and related resources accessible as needed, when they are needed, where they are needed. In the view of the authors, this notion encompasses more than just making sure that the information technology (IT) infrastructure is technically adequate and continuously available, but it also emphasizes other often-ignored attributes of IAV, such as appropriate policies and procedures, an effective security policy, and the establishment of a workable business continuity plan. Thus, the goal of the chapter is to define IAV in the context of information security and elaborate on each of these first and second order determinants of information availability.

INTRODUCTION

As the Internet has matured, enterprises have leveraged information technology (IT) to enhance their operations and improve the services to which consumers have access. The marketplace has embraced these new capabilities, and many consumers now depend upon these services on a daily basis. To meet consumer demands, many businesses now require critical information systems (IS) be online 24 hours per day, seven days per week, and 365 days per year. Due to this increased dependency, the availability of critical IT resources has assumed new importance. While availability is not a new attribute of information, it has dramatically grown in its importance because of the criticality of systems that are now operating in a distributed computing environment. According to recent estimates, the cost of unavailability is astounding and

ranges from $1 to 3 million per hour depending upon the industry sector (Ontrack Data International, 2006). Enterprises require that availability be provided with the same certainty associated with confidentiality and integrity. Therefore, proactive steps need to be taken to mitigate risks that could result in unavailability and procedures need to be in-place to respond to an event that threatens to degrade availability.

Security professionals have developed several protocols, tools, and techniques in an attempt to achieve three generally accepted information attributes (i.e., *confidentiality*, *integrity*, and *availability*), thereby resulting in enhanced Information Security (INFOSEC) (Jonsson, 1998). A system's effectiveness is improved by INFOSEC in that the attributes provided offer defensive capabilities (Maconachy, Schou, Ragsdale, & Welch, 2001). These defensive capabilities are necessary, because information has real value (Denning,

1999) and an organization cannot afford to stand by while its information is made unavailable by natural disaster, hardware or software malfunction, or accidental or intentional loss of resources or data (Hutt, Bosworth, & Hoyt, 1995, pp. 16).

While *Information Availability* (IAV) is well-established as an attribute required for INFOSEC, few security researchers and practitioners have chosen to address IAV with the same enthusiasm as the other security attributes. INFOSEC researchers and practitioners were, and remain, most concerned with maintaining confidentiality and integrity of the information. According to Hosmer (1996), information availability remains mostly misunderstood and unresearched because of the seemingly endless number of potential factors that can impact the availability of information. Hosmer argues that the current availability paradigm is inadequate and emphasizes that *social threats* as well as *technical threats* add to the multifaceted nature of IAV. Furthermore, communications protocols were designed to make information and resource sharing possible; INFOSEC emerged afterwards. IAV was treated as a function of bringing-up an IS and in terms of a user having access to that system. Initially, access was controlled by physical barriers and obstacles. As networking became more popular (and anyone with a computer, a modem, and the knowledge of the operating system (O/S) could remotely access an IS), the need for INFOSEC emerged. IAV was a prerequisite; therefore, INFOSEC researchers and practitioners needed to develop methods and procedures of maintaining confidentiality and integrity. This security paradigm was necessary, but never truly sufficient. For example, if an IS did not have enough modems, then users would receive a busy signal. If the IS was offline, then users could not access the IS. Users accepted the technological constraints of the time, but as technology has improved dramatically over the past decade, and IT resources have become more reliable and pervasive, it seems that the user's tolerance level for downtime has decreased.

The need to address IAV is both past due and necessary, particularly in the context of the information security challenges of today. The paradigm needs to shift (and is to some extent already shifting) from one that assumes IAV to one that provides sustainable IAV—unavailability is not an option in today's context. To achieve this end, a new understanding of IAV and the factors that impact it can help INFOSEC practitioners analyze how each factor can be addressed within the context of their enterprise, and determine

whether or not to initiate changes that will achieve IAV for the organization's critical logical and physical IT resources. Therefore, this chapter has two main objectives: (1) describe the notion of IAV as it relates to information security and identify key first and second order factors that impact Information (IAV) based on an analysis of the *a priori* academic and practitioner literature; and (2) discuss implications for research and practice.

DEFINING INFORMATION AVAILABILITY

Initial research efforts in the area of INFOSEC have focused upon the most needed component: process management. Soon after, access control emerged as a necessary service. "The original motivation for putting protection mechanisms into computer systems was to keep one user's malice or error from harming other users, " (Lampson, 1971). The *reference monitor*, which "controlled sharing of system resources " (Anderson, 1972), was quickly adopted as the basis for assuring that system resources were protected (Brinkley & Schell, 1995). The publications of Bell and LaPadula in 1973 established the first mathematical model for specific access classifications that would satisfy a specific security conditions (LaPadula, 1996). The model concentrates on confidentiality (Schneier, 2000). Further research expanded the reference monitor to the trusted computing base (TCB) which has continued as the premise for modern secure or trusted systems (NRC, 1991).

Confidentiality has been the primary goal of INFOSEC, because there has been and continues to be a desire for systems to be "trusted ", thereby only granting access to users who are authorized to receive the requested information (NCSC, 1992). By controlling access to information and preventing unauthorized disclosure, a system has achieved confidentiality (Brinkley & Schell, 1995). In this chapter, we adopt the definitions of availability, confidentially and integrity shown in Table 1 (Schou, 1996). The objective of *information availability* is to enable access to authorized information or resources to those who need them (CEC, 1991). Thus, for our purpose, IAV is the ability to *make information and related physical and logical resources accessible as needed, when they are needed, and where they are needed*. This notion encompasses more than just making sure that systems and related infrastructure is technically adequate and continuously available, but it also highlights the need to address other often-ignored concerns of IAV such as appropriate policies and procedures, an effective security policy, and the establishment of a workable business continuity plan.

FACTORS IMPACTING INFORMATION AVAILABILITY

It is reasonably well-established in literature and practice that IAV has three first order determinants: Reliability, Accessibility, and Timeliness (Jonsson, 1998). Reliability refers to the degree to which a system performs its purpose for the period of time intended under the operating conditions encountered (Reibman & Veeraraghavan, 1991). For example, a space shuttle's onboard computer and related applications need to work on tasks without interruption and errors in a consistent way. Users do not want to depend upon a system that cannot be trusted to consistently execute their requests. Since a system cannot be reliable if it is not available and secure, the notions of reliability, availability and information security are intricately linked.

Broadly speaking, accessibility refers to the degree to which a system is usable by as many people as possible without modification and is characterized in terms of the ability of users to have physical access to the system, the nature of users' interface with the system, and the ability to physically retrieve potentially relevant information (Culnan, 1985). Authentication is a critical element of accessibility and has been approached from technical, conceptual and organizational levels (Siponen & Oinas-Kukkonen, 2007). At the technical level, there are several access control approaches, such as Mandatory Access Control (MAC) and Discretionary Access Control (DAC), which are supported with access control services such as Role Based Access Control (RBAC) (Sandhu, 1996). At the conceptual level, Siponen and Oinas-Kukkonen (2007) use the example of Access Matrix (Lampson, 1971) which can be utilized to illustrate which users/processes (security subjects) have access to which security objects. At the organizational level, measures to achieve secure access include biometrics, security policy (users' following security guidelines), applying extrinsic deterrence, and ethical responsibility ("employees are responsible for fulfilling the organizational security mission ") (Siponen and Oinas-Kukkonen, 2007).

Timeliness is the responsiveness of a system or resource to a user request. In fact, traditionally IAV has mostly been measured by the amount of time an information resource is either processing or not (uptime and downtime) (Wood, 1995). Users and organizations alike desire instant response to their requests; without good IAV, that desire may not be adequately met.

Second Order Determinants of Information Availability (IAV)

Within the logical and physical domain, *redundancy* (Hutt et al., 1995; Jajodia, McCollum, & Ammann, 1999; Parker, 1992) and thorough *system backups* (Denning, 1999; Hutt et al., 1995; Parker, 1992), *preventative and corrective maintenance* (Hutt et al., 1995), and *disaster recovery* plans (Hutt et al., 1995) increase the availability of IT resources in the event that a threat is realized. The danger in assuming that an information resource (e.g., data file, router or switch, telecommunications pathway, and so on.) will be available is that it is forgotten until that resource is unavailable, at which time, the resource must be immediately restored. Researchers have proposed to quantify availability in terms of latency (Tryfonas, Gritzalis, & Kokolakis, 2000), mean time to fail (MTTF) and mean time to restore (MTTR) (Sun & Han, 2001), maximum waiting time (MWT) (Gligor, 1984), finite waiting time (FWT) (Yu & Gligor, 1990), and probabilistic waiting

Table 1. Definitions of the components of information availability from the ISSO Glossary of INFOSEC and INFOSEC Related Terms Vol. I (Schou, 1996)

Availability	Timely, reliable access to data and information services for authorized users.
Confidentiality	Assurance that information is not disclosed to unauthorized entities or processes.
Integrity	Condition that exists when data is unchanged from its source and has not been accidentally or maliciously modified, altered, or destroyed.

time (PWT) (Millen, 1992). Each metric assesses the amount of time an information resource is unavailable, but from a different perspective. According to Viles & French (1995), most users expect a "100-100 Web: 100 percent availability for all servers and 100 millisecond latency to every server, " which is to say that users desire fast response to a request. This expectation is nearly impossible to sustain given the numerous threats to availability.

In Figure 1, each block on the far left represents an IAV second order factor that impacts the availability of an information resource or the data stored within an information resource. Each factor influences one or more of the first order attributes of information availability, thereby contributing to the overall availability of the information resource and impacting information security. A discussion of each factor and the impacts to the enterprise follows.

Security Policy

An enterprise-wide security policy is the foundation for INFOSEC activities by defining how the enterprise will protect its information resources. The security policy establishes the framework for information processing and use of IT devices within an enterprise. According to Dekker (1997):

A policy is a documented high-level plan for organization-wide computer and information security. It provides a framework for making specific decisions, such as which defense mechanisms to use and how to configure services, and is the basis for developing secure programming guidelines and procedures for users and system administrators to follow.

Without a well-developed security policy, the enterprise is ill-prepared to ensure that information resources will be available and that the data is correct. Due to the increased use of information technology, many organizations have established security policies. Most security policies do not address IAV (Hosmer, 1996; NRC, 1991). In fact, authors of policies generally concentrate predominantly on confidentiality concerns. Distributed Denial of Service (DDoS) attacks specifically challenge availability with immediate and potentially lasting effect and relatively little risk to the attacker. In fact, during such an attack, limiting availability may be the countermeasure to best protect the system. If the security policy does not address availability, the correct actions may not be taken in a timely manner, thereby increasing the potential exposure of the IS and the risk of permanent damage to system.

Figure 1. Factors impacting information availability

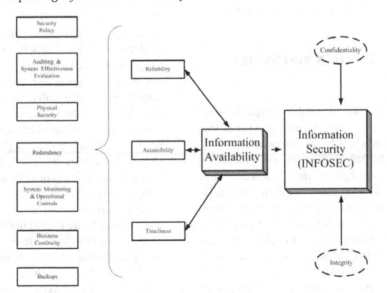

A system security policy should address who is using the system and the enterprise's expectations of users. The enterprise can establish guidelines for appropriate use of the provided information resources by identifying the characteristics of an authorized user. Access control mechanisms can be defined and user privileges can be established. Furthermore, all users should understand their privileges and be aware that system monitoring is used to ensure that online actions are being monitored. In addition, users should be told about the consequences for misuse of the provided information resources and the procedures for reporting suspect or odd behavior. A security policy impacts the reliability of a system by establishing the thresholds within which the system operates. Current and future architecture and design decisions should be based upon the organization's strategic plan and the enterprise security policy. Furthermore, the level of reliability that the organization also desires may impact the amount of preventative maintenance that occurs, the level of system monitoring and auditing, and evaluation of system effectiveness.

Security policy can influence accessibility by setting the access control policies for the system. By doing so, the data contained within the system can be appropriately shared with those users who are authorized, and denied to those who are not. Additionally, physical access to the system is of great concern. Protecting the perimeter (e.g., the campus, the building, the floor on which the computer room resides, or the walls of the computer room) via physical and technological methods is the first line of defense to ensure that authorized users can physically access the system.

Operational Controls and System Monitoring

Creating system security policies that address the availability of resources for the enterprise is a major step toward assuring availability, but the policies require enforcement. If the rules, practices, and procedures set forth in the security policy are not enforced, there is less reason to develop them in the first place. By implementing operational controls within the system, security professionals can set limits that protect the organization's information. Operational controls "are those system rules and guidelines that are necessary to manage the day-to-day activities that occur within an enterprise's information resources" (Weber, 1999). Operational controls are created to implement security

policy, thereby providing a mechanism for enforcing the security policy. There are several areas where operational controls are implemented. According to Weber (1999), tools are most commonly established for computer and network operations, production systems, data storage, technical support, and any outsourced operations. There are several commercial tools that can aid in establishing the required controls that are not inherent within the hardware or software components. Monitoring system performance provides the stakeholders of the enterprise with measurements of how the information resources are operating (Weber, 1999). Moreover, if security personnel have access to real-time monitoring, they can identify potentially unauthorized activity and implement real-time defensive countermeasures to minimize the system's exposure to potential loss. According to Hawkins, Yen, and Chou (2000), the best intrusion protection is constant monitoring for intrusions by utilizing the best protection the organization can afford.

Operational controls and system monitoring can work together to enforce security policy and provide security professionals the capability of defending the system at the desired level. Operational controls affect reliability, accessibility, and timeliness by placing appropriate limits, as deemed necessary within the security policy, on users, applications, hardware, data storage, and support functions.

Auditing and System Effectiveness Evaluation

According to Weber (1999, pp. 10), auditing IT resources is a "process of collecting and evaluating evidence to determine whether a computer system safeguards assets, maintains data integrity, allows organizational goals to be achieved effectively, and uses resources efficiently. " Auditing is used to verify that the operational controls within the system are successfully implemented, and to analyze system behavior to detect misuse or abuse within the system (NRC, 1991). Auditing differs from monitoring in that auditors analyze historical data, whereas monitors trigger alarms based upon real-time activity. Both functions are important and necessary since monitors cannot investigate every anomaly within the system. To that end, thresholds are defined so that the monitoring application will alarm appropriately. Auditors, on the other hand, analyze automatically generated logs and reports of system activity and can identify further trends that may not immediately impact the system, but over time could expand and threaten the availability of the system or even the security of the enterprise.

A system effectiveness evaluation is a specific type of audit that not only analyzes the reports and logs, but takes a macro view of the system, the organization, and its personnel to determine how well the system meets the needs of the organization. This type of evaluation is especially important for availability, in that the availability is a significant dynamic of several factors that a system effectiveness evaluation measures. The results of a system effectiveness evaluation can be used to determine whether or not there is sufficient availability to meet the demands of the enterprise, as well as provide stakeholders with measurements to evaluate how efficiently the system operates within the organization. While the system effectiveness evaluation is based upon user perceptions, the attitudes of the users will significantly determine the success or failure of the system (Weber, 1995).

Auditing and system effectiveness evaluations provide independent assessment of reliability and timeliness factors within the system. The findings of the auditors can be used to determine whether or not the enterprise has sufficient bandwidth within the infrastructure to support the enterprise's information services and users. These evaluations may show trends of inappropriate or unauthorized behavior on the system that is not being caught through real-time monitoring. If that occurs, policymakers and stakeholders have additional information needed to reevaluate the organizational strategy, security policy, monitoring thresholds, and operational controls. Audits are the check and balance to preserve IAV and the enterprise's confidentiality and integrity.

Physical Security

Physical security is a critical prerequisite of IAV. According to the NCES (1998), physical security involves "protecting building sites and equipment from theft, vandalism, natural disaster, manmade catastrophes, and accidental damage ". If an organization does not provide physical security to its systems, then unauthorized personnel would have unchallenged access to the organization's systems. The traditional point of view looks at protecting building sites and equipment from theft, vandalism, natural disaster, manmade catastrophes, and accidental damage (NCES, 1998). Within the context of availability, physical security is extremely important. While information is not directly protected

through physical security, the information resides on hardware that computer security experts are charged to protect, therefore warranting the attention of both information the computer security professionals.

Securing the physical hardware and the communications pathways within the enterprise is an important step in assuring the availability of the system. If the device containing the data a user is requesting is unavailable because the device has been stolen, the power to that device has been cut, or the cable connecting the device is disconnected, the impact to the user or process making the request is the same as if the requestor was not authorized to access that data. That request cannot be fulfilled, thereby negatively affecting the productivity of the requestor and any other requestor attempting to contact the unavailable device. Bois (2002) makes the point that "…it is vital that we acknowledge that people seeking to do harm to our information infrastructure will not stop if they cannot get to us via the Internet. "Without good physical security, the information resources will be attacked, and there will be loss.

Accessibility is impacted if the infrastructure or hardware that facilitates a user's making a request for information and the corresponding response is unavailable. There are several possible reasons why a device may be unavailable, from scheduled maintenance, device or connectivity problems to a malicious attack. Regardless of the reasons behind the unavailability, the end result is the same. Accessibility either is degraded, or completely eliminated for a period of time. Furthermore, the longer the device remains unavailable, the less reliable the system appears to be to the user.

Backups

Backups provide a copy of the data, applications, and O/S settings that are stored within a computer to facilitate recovery if necessary (Schou, 1996). By having backups, an enterprise can minimize the downtime an enterprise experiences following an event that may leave a storage device damaged or erased (Murphy, 1996). Additionally, backups have become necessary because the data stored within the enterprise is valuable (Parrish, 2001). Backups do not protect information; other mechanisms should be in place to protect information. If the situation arises where information is lost, then a set of backups will greatly reduce the amount of downtime and cost of loss felt by the organization.

Backups for both the system and user are required to provide maximum restorable capability to the enterprise. The system is most likely stable, therefore system backups need to be made when the system is initially installed, and subsequent system backups need to be created after changes to the system have been made (Murphy, 1996). User files, on the other hand, are modified quite often, making frequent backups, quite possibly daily, necessary (Murphy, 1996). Physical security of the backup media is crucial, requiring the same level of security for the backup capability as other critical applications (Parrish, 2001). Backups provide a safety net for the enterprise, but the backups must be current, possess integrity, and be available for the system administrator to restore files from the backup media.

Backups address timeliness and accessibility by providing the enterprise the capability to restore lost files in a timely manner. Without backups, the system would need to be recovered by starting with blank storage. This process could be quite time consuming. Furthermore, without proper configuration documentation, there is no guarantee that the system will be recreated in exactly the same way.

Business Continuity

Business continuity is also known as contingency planning or continuity planning or disaster planning and is a key component of any enterprise's plan to maintain operations in the event of a catastrophic event such as a natural disaster or a network attack. It also includes planning for backup operations and post-disaster recovery, to ensure the availability of critical resources (Schou, 1996). Yet, only 20% of existing continuity plans are workable when tested (Brunetto & Harris, 2001). In developing continuity plans, the planners need to understand the organization and analyze the dependencies within the enterprise and with vendors who interact with the organization (Kelly, 2000). Once the dependencies are identified, the areas that could suffer loss and the cost of loss should be estimated (Wilson, 1997). Here, the risk assessment and inventory used to develop the enterprise's security policies can be utilized to develop continuity plans. The security policy and business strategy should identify the requirements for continuity and be included as part of the organization's continuity plan.

Business continuity impacts the timeliness and accessibility of a system by providing a systematic and known process for restoring operations in the least time possible. Without a tested Continuity Plan, the organization has no "insurance " (Facer, 1999) that operations will ever be restored to their pre-event state.

Redundancy

Redundancy relates to the ability of an organization to reconstruct an information element to its last state before disruption and having capabilities to connect to its information resources despite disruptions (Jajodia et al., 1999). The goal of redundancy is to minimize unavailability by utilizing redundant capabilities for restoring the capabilities of an organization's systems (Jajodia et al., 1999). Backing up data provides an extra copy of data, which is restorable in case of failure, sabotage, or natural disaster (Denning, 1999, pp. 384). Furthermore, since failure of any component is possible, the impact of each component being unavailable should be assessed and a redundant equivalent must be available (Hutt et al., 1995). Additionally, having redundant connectivity that has adequate capacity for the traffic load of the organization is an imperative for many organizations today (Hutt et al., 1995).

Based on anecdotal research conducted by the authors, it is clear that redundant systems components are essential to IAV. Our research shows that organizations maintain redundant hardware and software, communications pathways, and data centers (Martin & Khazanchi, 2006). Each company we researched also placed a great deal of confidence in having redundancy to provide IAV in the event of an outage (e.g., natural disaster, manmade catastrophe, accidental or malicious action, or hardware or software failure).

CONCLUDING REMARKS

In this chapter, we have developed a detailed understanding of information availability (IAV) an important attribute of modern information security processes. Based on past literature, we have developed a detailed list of factors that impact information availability and its first order attributes - reliability, accessibility and timeliness.

Implications for Research

The technological advances that have enabled businesses to reliably offer applications and services to internal and external customers through a distributed IT architecture are critical to any business. We believe that given the significance of business requirements upon IAV, there may be justification to separate IAV from information security. Organizations seem to address IAV from a purely operational perspective rather than a broader INFOSEC perspective. Whereas INFOSEC professionals are charged with implementing policies geared toward confidentiality and integrity, business operations personnel have developed infrastructures that support varying levels of IAV. Furthermore, the tools for providing confidentiality and integrity are different from those tools that provide IAV. There also seems to be differing perspectives when discussing confidentiality and integrity and IAV. Therefore, we believe that further empirical research needs to be conducted on the impact of IAV on information security and the antecedents of reliable, accessible, and timely IAV. There is also a need to better understand how IAV models might be adjusted to address the specific needs of smaller businesses.

Implications for Practice

In practice, there is reason to believe that IAV has been an area of great interest. This interest stems from business requirements that are consistent with the business objective of earning profit. Practitioners need to continue to address IAV, but engage researchers in discussions about IAV to better understand its impact on information security. Furthermore, practitioners may consider implementing IAV policies independent of confidentiality and integrity issues in the broader context of information security. By doing so, more focused attention could be devoted to studying how to best provide IAV to meet a business's IAV requirements. Finally, organizations need to develop practical models for addressing IAV that at a minimum address issues of reliability, accessibility and timeliness of information systems and services in the context of all the factors discussed in this chapter—security policy, redundancy, operational controls and systems monitoring, Auditing and system effectiveness, backups, physical security, and business continuity.

REFERENCES

Anderson, J. P. (1972). Computer security technology planning study. *ESD-TR-73-51, Vol. 1*. Retrieved May 4, 2008, from http://csrc.nist.gov/publications/history/#ande72

Bois, J. (2002, April 4). *Protect yourself*. Retrieved May 4, 2008, from http://www.sans.org/reading_room/whitepapers/physcial/271.php?portal=1acb725f82d5 6368553d275ee548be1c

Brinkley, D.L., & Schell, R.R. (1995). Concepts and terminology for computer security. In M.D. Abrams, S. Jajodia, & H.J. Podell (Eds.). *Information Security: An Integrated Collection of Essays* (pp. 11-39). Los Alamitos, CA: IEEE Computer Society Press.

Brunetto, G., & Harris, N.L. (2001). Disaster recovery: How will your company survive? [Electronic version]. *Strategic Finance, 82*(9), 57-61.

Culnan, M. (1985). The dimensions of perceived accessibility to information: Implications for the delivery of information systems and services. *Journal of the American Society for Information Science, 36*(5), 302-308.

Commission of the European Communities (CEC). (1991). *Information technology security evaluation criteria (ITSEC), provisional harmonized criteria: version 1.2* [Electronic version]. Luxembourg: Office for Official Publications of the European Communities.

Dekker, M. (1997). Security of the Internet. *The Froehlich/Kent Encyclopedia of Telecommunications* (Vol. 15, pp. 231–255). Retrieved May 4, 2008, from http://www.cert.org/encyc_article/tocencyc.html

Denning, D.E. (1999). *Information warfare and security*. New York: Addison-Wesley.

Facer, D. (1999). Rethinking: Business continuity [Electronic version]. *Risk Management, 46*(10), 17-18.

Gligor, V.D. (1984). A note on denial-of-service in operating systems. *IEEE Transactions on Software Engineering, SE-10*(3), 320-324.

Hawkins, S., Yen, D.C., & Chou, D.C. (2000). Awareness and challenges of Internet security. *Information Management & Computer Security, 8*(3), 131-143.

Hosmer, H.H. (1996). Availability policies in an adversarial environment. In *Proceedings of the 1996 Workshop on New Security Paradigms, USA,* (pp. 105-117). Retrieved May 4, 2008, from http://doi.acm.org/10.1145/304851.304876

Hutt, A.E., Bosworth, S., & Hoyt, D.B. (Eds.). (1995). *Computer security handbook (3rd edition)*. New York, NY: John Wiley & Sons, Inc.

Jajodia, S., McCollum, C.D. & Ammann, P. (1999). Trusted recovery [Electronic version]. *Communications of the ACM, 42*(7), 71-75.

Jonsson, E. (1998, September 22-26). An integrated framework for security and dependability. In *Proceedings of the 1998 Workshop on New Security Paradigms (Charlottesville, VA), NSPW '98* (pp. 22-29). New York, NY: ACM Press.

Kelley, J. (2000) Business continuity: Battling high-tech exposures [Electronic version]. *Risk Management, 47*(5), 31-33.

Lampson, B.W. (1971). Protection. In *Proceedings of the 5th Annual Princeton Conference on Information Sciences and Systems*. Retrieved May 4, 2008, from http://citeseer.nj.nec.com/287804.html

LaPadula, L.J. (1996). Secure computer systems: Mathematical foundations. In D.E. Bell & L.J. LaPadula. *MITRE Technical Report 2547 (Vol. 1, March 1, 1973)* [Electronic version]. Retrieved May 4, 2008, from http://www.mitre.org/resources/centers/infosec/secure_computers/secure_comp_math.pdf

Maconachy, W.V., Schou, C.D., Ragsdale, D. & Welch, D. (2001). A model for information assurance: An integrated approach. In *Proceedings of the 2001 IEEE Workshop on Information Assurance and Security* (pp. 306-310).

Martin, A. (2003). *Key determinants of information availability: A multiple case study*. Unpublished MS in MIS Thesis, University of Nebraska at Omaha.

Martin, A., & Khazanchi, D. (2006, August 4-6). Information Availability and Security Policy. In *Proceedings of the Americas Conference on Information Systems (AMCIS 2006)*. Acapulco, Mexico. Retrieved May 4, 2008, from http://amcis2006.aisnet.org/

Millen, J.K. (1992). Resource allocation model for denial of service. In *Proceedings of the Symposium on Research in Security and Privacy* (pp. 137-147).

Murphy, M. (1996). *Backup strategy*. Retrieved May 4, 2008, from http://www.linuxjournal.com/article.php?sid=1208

National Center for Education Statistics (NCES). (1998, September 22). Safeguarding your technology: Practical guidelines for electronic education information security [Electronic version]. In T. Szuba. *Technology and Security Task Force of the National Forum on Education Statistics*. Retrieved May 4, 2008, from http://nces.ed.gov/pubsearch/pubsinfo.asp?pubid=98297

National Computer Security Center, (NCSC). (1992). *Guide to understanding security modeling in trusted systems* (Aqua Book) [Electronic version]. Retrieved May 4, 2008, from http://www.radium.ncsc.mil/tpep/library/rainbow/NCSC-TG-010.pdf

National Research Council (NRC). (1991). *Computers at risk: Safe computing in the information age*. Washington, D.C.: National Academy Press.

Ontrack Data International. (2006). *Cost of data loss*. Retrieved May 4, 2008, from http://www.ontrack.com/understandingdataloss/

Parker, D.B. (1992). Restating the foundation of information security. In *Proceedings of the Eighth International Conference on Information Security* (pp. 139-151). Netherlands.

Parrish, S. (2001, August 30). *Security considerations for enterprise level backups*. Retrieved May 4, 2008, from http://rr.sans.org/backup/enterprise_level.php

Reibman, A.L. & Veeraraghavan, M. (1991). Reliability modeling: An overview for system designers [Electronic version]. *Computer, 24*(4), 49-57.

Sandhu, R. (1996). Access control: The neglected frontier [Electronic version]. In *Proceedings of the First Australasian Conference on Information Security and Privacy* (pp. 219-227). Australia.

Schneier, B. (2000). *Secrets and lies: Digital security in a networked world*. New York, NY: John Wiley & Sons, Inc.

Schou, C. (Ed.). (1996). *Information systems security organization (ISSO) glossary of INFOSEC and INFOSEC related terms, Vols. I & II*. Idaho: Idaho State University.

Siponen, M.T., & Oinas-Kukkonen, H. (2007, February). A review of information security issues and respective research contributions. *SIGMIS Database 38, 1*, 60-80.

Sun, H. & Han, J.J. (2001). Instantaneous availability and interval availability for systems with time-varying failure rate: Stair-step approximation. In *Proceedings of the 2001 Pacific Rim International Symposium on Dependable Computing* (pp. 371-374).

Tryfonas, T., Gritzalis, D. & Kokolakis, S. (2000, August). A qualitative approach to information availability. In *Proceedings of Information Security for Global Information Infrastructures (IFIP TC11) Sixteenth Annual Working Conference on Information Security* (pp. 37-47).

Yu, C-F. & Gligor, V.D. (1990). A specification and verification method for preventing denial of service. *IEEE Transactions on Software Engineering, 16*(6), 581-592.

Viles, C.L. & French, J.C. (1995). Availability and latency of world wide Web information servers. *Computing Systems, 8*(1), 61-91.

Weber, R. (1999). *Information systems control and audit.* Upper Saddle Creek, NJ: Prentice-Hall, Inc.

Wilson, K. (1997, September 2). Contingency and recovery planning: Checklist for information systems. Retrieved on May 4, 2008, from http://socrates.berkeley.edu:2001/em/checklist.html

Wood, A. (1995). Predicting client/server availability [Electronic version]. *Computer, 28*(4), 41-48.

KEY TERMS

Accessibility: The degree to which a system is usable by as many people as possible without modification and is characterized in terms of the ability of users to have physical access to the system, the nature of users' interface with the system, and the ability to physically retrieve potentially relevant information.

Auditing: Process of collecting and evaluating evidence to determine whether a computer system safeguards assets, maintains data integrity, allows organizational goals to be achieved effectively, and uses resources efficiently

Backup: Copy of files and programs made to facilitate recovery if necessary.

Business Continuity Planning: A key component of any enterprise's plan to maintain operations in the event of a catastrophic event such as a natural disaster or a network attack. It also includes planning for backup operations and post-disaster recovery, to ensure the availability of critical resources.

Information Availability (IAV): The ability to make information and related physical and logical resources accessible as needed, when they are needed, and where they are needed.

Operational Controls: System rules and guidelines necessary to manage the day-to-day activities that occur within an enterprise's information resources.

Physical Security: Protecting building sites and equipment from theft, vandalism, natural disaster, manmade catastrophes, and accidental damage.

Redundancy: Having an information element stored redundantly or having the ability to reconstruct an information element (Jajodia, *et al.*, 1999).

Redundancy: The ability of an organization to reconstruct an information element to its last state before disruption and having capabilities to connect to its information resources despite disruptions. The goal of redundancy is to minimize unavailability by utilizing redundant capabilities for restoring the capabilities of an organization's systems.

Reliability: The degree to which a system performs its purpose for the period of time intended under the operating conditions encountered. **Security Policy:** A documented high-level plan for organization-wide computer and information security.

Systems Monitoring: Monitoring system performance provides the stakeholders of the enterprise with measurements of how the information resources are operating and allows security professionals to identify potentially unauthorized activity and implement real-time defensive countermeasures to minimize the system's exposure to potential loss.

Timeliness: The responsiveness of a system or resource to a user request. In fact, traditionally information availability has mostly been measured by the amount of time an information resource is either processing or not (uptime and downtime).

Chapter XX
Formal Analysis and Design of Authentication Protocols

Siraj Ahmed Shaikh
United Nations University (UNU), Macau, SAR China

ABSTRACT

The purpose of this chapter is to introduce the reader to the research area of formal analysis of authentication protocols. It briefly introduces the basic notions of cryptography and its use in authentication protocols. The chapter looks at the Needham-Schroeder (1978) protocol as an example of an authentication protocol, and examines the history of the protocol as a stimulus to the formal analysis of such protocols. We then introduce the process algebra CSP (Hoare, 1985) to model authentication protocols and present Schneider's (1998) rank function approach to analysing such protocols. The chapter concludes by describing related ongoing work in this area of research and highlight some of the challenges posed by the problem of analysing and designing protocols.

INTRODUCTION

Modern communications technology allows us to communicate faster than ever before, with much higher capacity for more diverse types of data. Along with its wider reach in society, in the form of both mobility and relatively affordable access, modern communications has transformed the world we live in—serving as bedrock for electronic commerce and, other digital and communication services. The Internet has become an integral part of the personal, professional, and economic spheres of our daily life. Global organisations, whether official, commercial, or social, are relying on the Internet ever more to function, bringing an increasing need for a secure and trusted electronic infrastructure.

The pervasive nature of the Internet, one major factor behind its success, is also proving to be its main threat. Once connected to this global network, no one is more than a few clicks away from Web servers hosting web sites transacting commerce worth millions or critical state-run infrastructures running sensitive operations. Such Internet systems are threatened by both hackers with malicious and fraudulent intent, and software technology designed using indefinite and imprecise methods.

Security protocols, being developed for more than two decades now, aim to protect and secure networked systems from such threats. Using mathematically-sound yet simple cryptographic methods, these protocols are designed to provide a range of communication security services, such as authentication, confidentiality, and nonrepudiation. These protocols allow networked entities to engage with each other and derive guarantees about each other's identity, state of knowledge and participation. An early example of such a protocol is due to Needham and Schroeder (1978), who introduced a two-party protocol to authenticate both participants to each other. The Needham-Schroeder protocol, as it has since come to be known, was a forerunner of the many security protocols that were to follow. While interest in formal design and analysis of security protocols has greatly increased, Needham and Schroeder (1978) made the first suggestion towards such an effort in the seminal presentation of their protocol:

...protocols such as those developed here are prone to extremely subtle errors that are unlikely to be detected in normal operation. The need for techniques to verify the correctness of such protocols is great, and we encourage those interested in such problems to consider this area...

Burrows, Abadi, and Needham (1990) were the first to contribute a formal method to analyse the security goals—particularly the authentication goals—of such protocols as a system of belief logic. Interestingly, the original Needham-Schroeder protocol was formally verified to be correct using the logic.

Significant impetus for such formal analysis and verification, however, was provided much later when "subtle errors" were identified in this very protocol by Needham and Schroeder, as a result of an attack by Lowe (1995). The discovery of such an attack brought to light the difficulty over not only the design of such protocols, but also their formal analysis, stimulating a tremendous research interest. Of the many formalisms introduced to analyse and verify the design of security protocols, Lowe's (1996) model-checking approach using the process algebra *Communicating Sequential Processes* (CSP) (Hoare, 1985), Meadow's (1996) specialist tool—known as the *NRL Protocol Analyzer*—Gordon and Jeffrey's (2001) type-checking approach, and Thayer, Herzog, and Guttman's (1998) *strand spaces* are noteworthy.

A formal approach to analysing such protocols is presented by Schneider (1998). Schneider introduces the notion of *rank functions* and adopts a theorem-proving approach to verifying authentication and confidentiality for protocols. The idea of a rank function helps to partition the protocol message space and provides an insightful analysis of security protocols. Schneider's (1998) approach extends to a complete formal framework providing formal specification of security protocols and their properties in CSP, an analysis of these protocols using the idea of rank function and, finally, the formal verification of these

protocols using a rank function theorem. The approach is aided by specialist tools such as Heather's (2000) *RankAnalyzer* and, Evans and Schneider's (2005) implementation of this approach in the *Prototype Verification System* (PVS).

CRYPTOGRAPHY

Cryptography—derived from the Greek word *kryptos* meaning *hidden*—is to do with *hiding* information. Before we look at cryptographic protocols, it is important to understand cryptography that is commonly employed. The purpose of this section is to discuss some of the methods in cryptography and how they are used.

The purpose of cryptography is to *hide* information so that it is not revealed to everyone. This is made possible by converting the information from its original form, known as *plaintext* (or *cleartext*), to a distorted form, and therefore incomprehensible, known as *ciphertext*. The process of converting plaintext to ciphertext is called *encryption*, and the process of converting ciphertext back to plaintext is called *decryption*. Both operations involve the use of a *cryptographic key* that is essential to converting plaintext to ciphertext and back to the original plaintext.

Both encryption and decryption operations are implemented in the form of algorithms known as *cryptographic algorithms* or *cryptosystems*, where plaintext (or ciphertext) and encryption (or decryption) keys are parameters. We denote the ciphertext produced as a result of encrypting a plaintext m using an encryption key K as $\{m\}_K^E$ and denote the result of decrypting some m using a decryption key K as $\{m\}_K^D$. If both operations are the same, or where it is clear which is intended, then the superscript is omitted and we write $\{m\}_K$. For an encryption key K the corresponding decryption key is denoted as K^{-1}.

A ciphertext $\{m\}_K$ is said to provide *confidentiality* for m such that only those possessing the appropriate decryption key K^{-1} may access m in plaintext form. Not only does the possession of the decryption key, therefore, becomes essential to the retrieval of plaintext from a ciphertext, it also provides us with the means to dictate who can, or cannot, retrieve it (equally, the possession of an encryption key begets the generation of a ciphertext using that key) – a concept exercised in the design of cryptographic protocols. There are two different types of cryptosystems.

Shared-Key Cryptography

This form of cryptography, also known as *symmetric-key* or *secret-key cryptography*, provides a system where the encryption key and the corresponding decryption key are the same. In a *shared-key cryptosystem*, as it is referred to, for some plaintext *m* encrypted with a key *K*

$$m = \{\{m\}_K^E\}_{K^{-1}}^D$$
where
$$K = K^{-1}$$

This form of cryptography is quite conventional and has been in practice for some time, mostly in use where two participants share a key and encrypt their communication under this key, so as to ensure no one else can eavesdrop on their communication. For such a system to work, it is essential that the cryptographic key is only shared between the two (or more) communicating parties and known to no one else. A good example of a shared-key cryptosystem is the *Data Encryption Standard* (NBS, 1977), widely known as *DES*. This algorithm has recently been superseded by the new *Advanced Encryption Standard* (*AES*) algorithm (Daemen & Rijmen, 2002).

Public-Key Cryptography

In contrast to the previous type, the *public-key cryptosystem* first introduced by Diffie and Hellman (1976), makes use of encryption and decryption keys that are different. The mechanisms are often the same but the keys used are such that the possession of one of the key does not allow any knowledge of the other. In such a system

$$m = \{\{m\}_K^E\}_{K^{-1}}^D$$
where
$$K \neq K^{-1}$$

In practice, this allows users of a network to have a pair of keys that are complementary to each other. One of them, called the *public key*, is made public while the other, called the *private key*, is kept private. Any other user could use the public key of a user to encrypt a message with it and send it to the user. Only the user, possessing the corresponding private key, could then decrypt and retrieve the message. For such a system to work, it is essential that the private key for a user remains private to the user and is known to no one else.

Note that for the purpose of protocol analysis in this chapter, we assume all cryptographic methods, discussed in this section so far, to perform as they are described to do so. We assume cryptography to be perfect, that is to say, no plaintext, partly or wholly, can be derived from a ciphertext by an entity unless the appropriate decryption key for the ciphertext is known to that entity.

CRYPTOGRAPHIC PROTOCOLS

A communication protocol is an agreed sequence of actions performed by two or more communicating entities in order to accomplish some mutually desirable goal. The entities may use the protocol to communicate over a wired network or any other medium, such as wireless. In this chapter, we specify protocols informally using the notation

$$(i) \quad X \rightarrow Y : \qquad m$$

to denote the *i*th step of a protocol where entity *X* sends a message *m* destined for entity *Y*. A cryptographic protocol is essentially a communication protocol that makes use of cryptographic techniques, allowing the communicating entities to achieve one or more security goals. A particular protocol, however, may enable the communicating parties to establish one or more of these goals. Some common security goals include (data and entity) *authentication*, *confidentiality* and *integrity*. The term *authentication* has, over the years, come to refer to various notions. One common use of the term refers to *user authentication*, where people are identified and verified for their identity. In the context of protocol design and analysis, authentication refers to either *data authentication* or *entity authentication*. Data authentication ensures that some data (message) has certainly come from the source that it seems to have come from. Entity authentication, which we deal with in detail in this chapter, provides a similar guarantee on the identity of some entity – confirming that a certain entity is indeed currently being communicated with. A protocol providing authentication to (both or one of) the entities involved is known as an *authentication protocol*. The goal of *confidentiality* provides an assurance on the secrecy of some message, using some form of cryptography, whereas the goal of *integrity* ensures that the message is not (intentionally or accidentally) tampered or modified in any way since being sent by its source.

An important part of the design of cryptographic protocols is the use of *nonces*. These are essentially random values (numbers) generated by the participants of a protocol. They are assumed to be distinct in every run and assumed to be unguessable by anyone except the participant who generated it. Typically, a participant (authenticator) would generate a nonce and send it out as a *challenge* to a respondent participant (being authenticated). The respondent responds by producing the challenge nonce in a form different from that in which it was received (according to the format of the protocol). Upon receiving the challenge nonce back, the challenging participant is assured that the corresponding participant has produced the appropriate *response* after it has received the challenge, since the nonce is considered unpredictable by any other participant.

The use of nonces in a *challenge-response* exercise, also referred to as a *nonce handshake*, provides a simple and an easy way of verifying another participant's identity. The use of nonces is also critical in providing recentness, or freshness, of messages. For all protocols described in this chapter, we assume perfect nonce generation. We assume that all participants involved in any run of a protocol, regardless of their honest or malicious intent, are capable of generating random numbers. These random numbers, or nonces, are generated freely and perfectly and, such that they are unguessable by any other participant, particularly an intruder. Implicit here is the assumption that the identity of the participant who originally generated a nonce cannot be derived from the nonce itself. This is important, as it allows an intruder to reuse or replay a nonce from one participant to make it appear as coming from another.

NEEDHAM-SCHROEDER PROTOCOL

One of the first authentication protocols was proposed by Needham and Schroeder (1978) providing authentication for two participants to each other over a computer network. A shortened three-message version of the protocol is shown in Figure 1 (the original seven-message protocol involves A and B communicating with a trusted server to obtain each other's public keys).

The goal of the protocol is to authenticate both A to B and B to A and to allow them to agree on the values of two secret nonces N_A and N_B created by A

Figure 1. Three-message version of the Needham-Schroeder public-key protocol

(1)	$A \rightarrow B$	:	$\{N_A, A\}_{pkB}$
(2)	$B \rightarrow A$	:	$\{N_A, N_B\}_{pkA}$
(3)	$A \rightarrow B$	:	$\{N_B\}_{pkB}$

and B respectively. A initiates the protocol by sending out its own identity concatenated with a nonce N_A and encrypted with B's public key, to B. Once B receives the message, it is aware of A and its nonce N_A. At this stage B decides upon the nonce that it will use for the purpose of this run represented by N_B. B responds to A by sending it the concatenation of the two nonces N_A and N_B. Once A finds B's response satisfactory, it sends back B's nonce N_B encrypted under B's public key. Upon the receipt of the final message of the protocol, B concludes the protocol.

The first attempt at formally verifying cryptographic protocols was introduced more than a decade after the introduction of the Needham-Schroeder protocol. Needham, not surprisingly, along with Burrows and Abadi (Burrows et al., 1990) presented a formal approach to specifying the goals of security protocols by reasoning in terms of *beliefs* held by the protocol participants. BAN logic, as it is known, states beliefs as logical expressions that are constructed according to what could be observed by the participants during a protocol run. A full account of their logic and their analysis of the original Needham-Schroeder (1978) protocol is provided in (Burrows et al., 1990), where Burrows et al. formally verify the correctness of this protocol. Years later, however, Lowe (1995) uncovered a major flaw in this verified protocol. Lowe (1995) presents a man-in the-middle attack on the Needham-Schroeder protocol, such that it allows an intruder to impersonate one participant in a session with another. The attack is shown in Figure 2.

In the attack, A initiates a protocol run with the Intruder I. I, pretending to be A, forwards A's attempt to B by encrypting N_A and A with B's public key. B responds to the request by encrypting the nonce N_A and its own nonce, N_B, and encrypting it under A's public key. I relays this message onto A as a response to A's earlier request. A responds to I by encrypting N_B with I's public key and sending it onto I, who retrieves N_B and sends it onto B encrypted under B's public key, leading B to believe that it has just authenticated A, whereas in actual fact it, has not.

Figure 2. Lowe's attack on the Needham-Schroeder public-key protocol

(1.1)	A → I	:	$\{N_A, A\}_{pkI}$
(2.1)	I(A) → B	:	$\{N_A, A\}_{pkB}$
(2.2)	B → I(A)	:	$\{N_A, N_B\}_{pkA}$
(1.2)	I → A	:	$\{N_A, N_B\}_{pkA}$
(1.3)	A → I	:	$\{N_B\}_{pkI}$
(2.3)	I(A) → B	:	$\{N_B\}_{pkB}$

Note that the protocol still provides authentication, albeit a weaker form of it. In order for B to authenticate A in run 2.x, A has to have decrypted B's response in Step 2.2; where the protocol actually fails is on B being led to believe that it, first, shares the nonce N_B only with A and, secondly, the final message actually comes from A. Also note that A is not misled into any false goals as it intentionally initiates the protocol with I —the goal of an initiator A authenticating a responder B is not violated, but only the converse goal of a responder B authenticating an initiator A is violated.

Lowe's (1995) attack seriously undermined confidence in BAN logic and also uncovered the reality of analysing and verifying authentication protocols—the very subtlety of this problem. It effectively triggered a new era of formal analysis of cryptographic protocols, incorporating various styles of analysis such as model-checking, theorem-proving, and other specialised tools and techniques. Not surprisingly, almost all approaches have used the Needham-Schroeder (1978) protocol and its flaw as one of the benchmarks to demonstrate their effectiveness.

FORMAL ANALYSIS OF AUTHENTICATION PROTOCOLS

Schneider (1998) uses CSP (Hoare, 1985) to model authentication protocols. The protocol participants are modelled as independent processes, interacting with each other by exchanging messages. Different roles are modelled as different processes as necessitated by a protocol, for example, initiator, responder and trusted server; an intruder process is also modelled. The use of CSP to model this type of parallel message-passing distributed system captures the precise specification of a cryptographic protocol. Schneider (1998) attributes CSP to be effective for modelling protocols as "*it is*

close to the level we think of them." For an in-depth study of the language, readers are advised to consult Hoare's (1985) original introduction to CSP, Roscoe's (1997) work, and Schneider's (1999) treatment.

We introduce the basic building blocks in CSP, describing the notation and features of the language relevant to this chapter. We then describe Schneider's use of CSP to model the cryptographic protocol environment and describe his rank functions approach. We use an authentication protocol by Woo and Lam (1992) as a running example to demonstrate Schneider's formal approach.

Introduction to CSP

A CSP system is modelled in terms of processes and events that these processes can perform, which are essentially instances of communication, usually involving a channel and some data value. Events may be atomic in structure or may consist of distinct components.

Processes: The CSP expression $a \rightarrow P$ describes a process that initially performs event a, and then behaves as process P. For example, consider a process *PRINT_ONE* that only accepts one document and prints it off, represented by events *accept* and *print*

$$PRINT\_ONE = accept \rightarrow print \rightarrow STOP$$

The aforementioned expression describes a process that can perform the event accept and then print, after which it simply stops. The process *STOP* is the simplest CSP process that can be described; it has no event transitions and does not engage in any events. The process *PRINT_ONE* would simply make no further progress once it reaches *STOP*. We develop the process further to describe *PRINTER* recursively as

$$PRINTER = accept \rightarrow print \rightarrow PRINTER$$

This allows *PRINTER* to accept documents, print them off, and return to the original state to accept more documents.

For the purpose of communication, a process may be described using compound events such as $c.m$ which describes a message m being communicated on channel c. Channels are also assigned types, so if T is the type of channel c, then $\{c.t \mid t \in T\}$ describes the set of events associated with channel c. The communication of a process can be described as input or output, where

$c!v \rightarrow P$ describes a process that will output value v on channel c and then behaves as P. The expression $c?x \rightarrow P(x)$ describes a process P accepting input x on channel c where the behaviour of P after the input is described as $P(x)$, determined by input x.

External Choice: The *external choice* operator $\square$ provides the option of running either of the two processes P or Q when put together as $P \square Q$, where the choice between these two processes is determined by the environment. This operator can also be used in an indexed form where for an indexing set I, $\square_{i \in I} P_i$ describes the option of running any one of the indexed processes P_i.

Parallel Composition: The *parallel* operator $\|$ is used to force P and Q to run in parallel and synchronise on events in the set of events A. This is written as $P \| Q$. P and Q may perform any events that are not in A independently, without the need for any synchronisation. A process P may be restricted on certain events in A, expressed as $P \| STOP$ which prevents P from being able to perform any event in A.

The *interleaving* operator $\|\|\|$ is used to allow P and Q to run in parallel, but not interact with each other at all. This is written as $P\|\|\|Q$ and is equivalent to parallel composition over the empty set. For a larger number of processes, an indexed form of the interleaving operator can be used. For a finite indexing set I and process P_i defined for each $i \in I$, $\|\|\|_{i \in I} P_i$ describes the interleaving of all processes P_i.

Traces: The trace semantics in CSP allows us to capture the sequence of events performed by a communicating process as a trace, and then use the trace to model the behaviour of the process. A trace of a process is a finite sequence of events that it may perform. A sequence of events tr is a trace of a process P if some execution of P performs exactly that sequence of events. This is denoted as $tr \in traces(P)$, where $traces(P)$ is the set of all possible traces of P. Every process has an empty trace, and therefore, the set of its traces is always nonempty. Also, for every process, the set of its traces is prefix-closed, that is to say, if tr is a possible trace of P, then so is any prefix of tr.

The only trace of the simple process $STOP$ is an empty sequence $\langle \rangle$

$traces(STOP) = \{\langle\rangle\}$

For the process $PRINTER$ previously described, we have

$traces(PRINTER) = \{\langle\rangle, \langle accept\rangle, \langle accept, print\rangle, \langle accept, print, accept\rangle, ...\}$

A concatenation of two traces tr_1 and tr_2 is written as $tr_1 {}^\wedge tr_2$, which is the sequence of events in tr_1 followed by the sequence of events in tr_2. A trace tr of the form $\langle a\rangle^\wedge tr'$ expresses event a followed by the remainder of the trace tr'. A prefix tr' of tr is denoted $tr' \leqslant tr$. The length $\#tr$ of a trace is the number of elements that it contains so that for example $\#\langle a,b,d\rangle = 3$. The set of events appearing in a trace tr is denoted as $\sigma(tr)$; the operator σ also extends to processes where $\sigma(P)$ is the set of events that appear in some trace of P.

For a set of events A, the projection operation $tr \upharpoonright A$ describes the maximal subsequence of tr, all of whose events are drawn from A. Another form of projection is on the set of channel names where $tr \Downarrow C$ describes the sequence of messages passed on a set of channels C.

Trace semantics are used by Schneider (1996) to specify security properties for protocols as *trace specifications*. This is done by defining a predicate on traces and checking whether every trace of a process satisfies the trace specification. For a process P and a predicate S, P satisfies S if $S(tr)$ holds for every trace tr of P, that is, P **sat** $S \Leftrightarrow \forall\ tr \in traces(P) \bullet S(tr)$.

We can use trace specifications to express causal precedence on events. For some events a and b, we describe a predicate 'a precedes b' where

$$P \text{ sat } a \text{ precedes } b \Leftrightarrow \forall\ tr \in traces(P) \bullet (tr' {}^\wedge \langle b\rangle \leqslant tr \Rightarrow \langle a\rangle \text{ in } tr')$$

This means that any occurrence of b in any trace tr of P is preceded by an occurrence of a in tr.

SCHNEIDER'S CSP APPROACH

We describe a set of all atoms that could ever appear in a message of a protocol. Consider the set of all participant identities that may take part in a protocol as $\mathcal{U}$, the set of nonces used by participants in protocol runs as $\mathcal{N}$, the set of timestamps used by participants as $\mathcal{T}$ and a set of encryption keys used as $\mathcal{K}$, which may include different types of keys such as public keys and private keys (denoted pkA and skA for a participant A). The set of all such atoms $\mathcal{A}$ is defined as

$$\mathcal{A} ::= \mathcal{U} \mid \mathcal{N} \mid \mathcal{T} \mid \mathcal{K}$$

We use $\mathcal{A}$ to define a message space $\mathcal{M}$ that contains all the messages that may ever appear during a protocol's execution

$$\mathcal{M} ::= \quad \mathcal{A}$$
$$\quad | \; \{\mathcal{M}\}_k \quad \text{encryption of message } \mathcal{M} \text{ with key}$$
$k \, (\in \mathcal{K})$
$$\quad | \; \mathcal{M}.\mathcal{M} \quad \text{concatenation of messages}$$

Schneider (1998) models the protocol as a network where an arbitrary number of participants engage with each other along communication channels. The participants are modelled as CSP processes acting in parallel and an intruder process is modelled to run alongside, with capabilities as defined by Dolev and Yao (1983). These capabilities include blocking, replaying, spoofing and manipulating any message that appears on any of the communication channels in the network. In order to model such capabilities, Schneider (1998) introduces a generates "⊢" relation to characterise what messages may be generated from a given set of messages. The rules that define this relation are as follows, where S is some set of messages, m is a message and k is some key

- $m \in S$ then $S \vdash m$
- $S \vdash m$ and $S \subseteq S'$ then $S' \vdash m$
- $S \vdash m_i$ for each $m_i \in S'$ and $S' \vdash m$ then $S \vdash m$
- $S \vdash m \wedge S \vdash k \Rightarrow S \vdash \{m\}_k$
- $S \vdash \{m\}_k \wedge S \vdash k \Rightarrow S \vdash m$
- $S \vdash m_1.m_2 \Leftrightarrow S \vdash m_1 \wedge S \vdash m_2$

The relation can be extended to simulate further properties of cryptography or message extraction.

We introduce two channels *send* and *receive*, each of type $\mathcal{U}.\mathcal{U}.\mathcal{M}$, which all processes use to transmit and receive messages on. The event *send.i.j.m* represents the transmission of a message m from a participant i

to a participant j on channel *send* while *receive.j.i.m* represents the reception of a message m by a participant j from a participant i on channel *receive*.

A CSP process $USER_i$ is used to describe the behaviour for each participant $i \in \mathcal{U}$. An *Intruder* process is introduced and is modelled in parallel to synchronise with all participants on all *send* and *receive* events. We describe the complete network NET consisting of all $USER_i$ processes running in parallel with the *Intruder* process as

$$NET = (\|\|_{i \in \mathcal{U}} USER_i) \quad \underset{\{send,receive\}}{\|} \quad Intruder$$

where the *Intruder* process is defined as follows

$$Intruder(S) = (send?i?j?m \rightarrow Intruder \, (S \cup \{m\}))$$
$$\square$$
$$(\underset{i,j \in \mathcal{U}, S \vdash m}{\square} \quad receive!i!j!m \rightarrow Intruder \, (S))$$

The process is parameterised by a set of messages S that constitute the intruder's knowledge and is defined to allow it to either

- Receive any message m, sent by any participant i to any participant j along channel *send*, and then behave as the intruder with that additional message m in its set of knowledge S, or
- Send any message m, generated under ⊢ from set S, to any participant i pretending to come from any participant j along channel *receive*, and remain with the same set of knowledge S.

The *Intruder* process is described to precisely model the behaviour of an intruder who may wish to block, spoof or manipulate some (or all) messages and, also allow it to possess any initial public knowledge about the network (such as participant identities and

Figure 3. Woo-Lam protocol

(1) A → B	: A
(2) B → A	: N_B
(3) A → B	: $\{N_B\}_{KAS}$
(4) B → S	: $\{A, \{N_B\}_{KAS}\}_{KBS}$
(5) S → B	: $\{N_B\}_{KBS}$

their respective public keys). A set of such initial knowledge is denoted *IK* and is modelled to be in the possession of the *Intruder* to start with. The *Intruder* process is specified as *Intruder = Intruder(IK)*.

Woo-Lam Protocol

We describe an authentication protocol introduced by Woo and Lam (1992) and use it as an example to demonstrate Schneider's approach. Woo and Lam (1992) introduce a protocol that provides one-way authentication of protocol initiator *A* to responder *B*. The protocol uses shared-key cryptography and a trusted server *S*, with whom *A* and *B* share long-term symmetric keys.

The protocol is shown in Figure 3, where $\{m\}_k$ represents message *m* encrypted under key *k,* and "," represents the concatenation operator. The keys K_{AS} and K_{BS} represent the long-term keys that *A* and *B* share with server *S*. The goal of the protocol is for *B* to authenticate *A* using nonce N_B.

A starts the protocol by sending its identity to *B*. *B* replies by sending a freshly generated nonce N_B. *A* encrypts N_B with key K_{AS} and sends it back to *B*. *B* concatenates *A*'s reply with the identity of *A*, encrypts it with key K_{BS} and sends it to the server *S*. *S* sends out N_B back to *B* encrypted under K_{BS}. *B* compares the nonce it receives from *S* with the one it sent out to *A*. If they match, then *B* is guaranteed that the initiator of the protocol is in fact the principal claimed in the first step of the protocol. We model the three participant roles *A*, *B* and *S* as processes $User_A$, $User_B$ and *Server*. We parameterise process $User_B$ as $User_B(n_B)$ to represent each unique run of *B* with respect to the nonce it generates.

To help specify authentication properties for protocols, Schneider (1996) introduces *signal* events into these models to indicate the various stages of a protocol run. These events are used in trace specifications to express the authentication property the protocol needs to satisfy and are described more formally by Shaikh, Bush, and Schneider (2005). For process $User_A$, we specify a *Running.A.b.n* signal and introduce it in *A*'s run at a point when *A* is aware of its involvement in a run with *b* using nonce *n*. For process $User_B$, we specify a corresponding $Commit.B.a.n_B$ signal and introduce it once *B* has authenticated *a* using nonce n_B and completed its run.

$$User_A = \square_{b \in \mathcal{U}}$$

$$send.A!b!A \rightarrow$$
$$receive.A.b?n \rightarrow$$
$$Running.A.b.n \rightarrow$$

$$send.A!b!\{n\}_{KAS} \rightarrow STOP$$

$$User_B(n_B) = receive.B?a.a \rightarrow$$
$$send.B!a!n_B \rightarrow$$
$$receive.B.a?y \rightarrow$$
$$send.B.S.\{a,y\}_{KBS} \rightarrow$$
$$receive.B.S.\{n_B\}_{KBS} \rightarrow$$
$$Commit.B.a.n_B \rightarrow STOP$$

$$Server = receive.S?b?\{a,\{n\}_{Kas}\}_{Kbs} \rightarrow$$
$$send.S.b.\{n\}_{Kbs} \rightarrow STOP$$

We express the authentication property for the Woo-Lam protocol as a trace specification. We consider a specific run of the protocol where *B* attempts to authenticate *A* using a nonce N_B shown in Figure 4.

The authentication property for the protocol would require if *B* has completed a protocol run with *A* using N_B, then *A* must have taken part in the run with *B* using N_B. We use particular signal events from Figure 4 to indicate these stages for the two processes $User_A$ and $User_B$ and state the property: if $User_B$ performs a $Commit.B.A.N_B$ signal, then $User_A$ must have performed the corresponding $Running.A.B.N_B$ signal prior to it. We express this as a trace specification as

$$Running.A.B.N_B \text{ precedes } Commit.B.A.N_B$$

To prove the protocol correct, we check whether the network NET satisfies this specification. This entails checking if a $Commit.B.A.N_B$ event occurs in any possible trace of NET, then a $Running.A.B.N_B$ event has occurred prior to it in the trace. We achieve this by restricting NET on the particular $Running.A.B.N_B$ event and checking whether the corresponding $Commit.B.A.N_B$ event can possibly occur in any of its traces. If a $Commit.B.A.N_B$ event does occur without being preceded by the $Running.A.B.N_B$ event, the condition has been violated. Schneider (1998) introduces the notion of rank functions to help verify this condition. The idea is to partition the message space into those messages that are allowed to circulate in the restricted network and those that are not due to the restriction.

RANK FUNCTIONS

A rank function is defined as a function from the message space $\mathcal{M}$ to the set of integers

$\rho: \mathcal{M} \to \mathbb{Z}$

The function is lifted to events, sequences and sets as follows:

- $\rho(c.m) = \rho(m)$, $m \in \mathcal{M}$
  the rank of an event *c.m* is the rank of message *m* communicated on channel *c*
- $\rho(S) = \min\{\rho(s) \mid s \in S\}$, $S \subseteq \mathcal{M}$
  the rank of a set *S* is the smallest rank of elements of *S*
- $\rho(tr) = \min\{\rho(s) \mid s \text{ in } tr\}$
  the rank of a sequence *tr* is the smallest rank of elements in *tr*

The rank function is used to characterise those messages in a message space that an intruder may get hold of and those that the intruder cannot. With respect to the restricted NET described in the previous section, we assign a positive rank to messages that are allowed to circulate the network and a nonpositive rank to those that are restricted.

We say a process *P maintains rank* with respect to a rank function ρ, if it cannot introduce any message of a nonpositive rank after receiving messages of positive rank. In other words, if all that the process has ever received are messages of positive rank, then all it should ever send out are messages of positive rank. We formalise this as follows

P maintains $\rho \Leftrightarrow \forall\, tr \in traces(P) \bullet \rho(tr \Downarrow receive) > 0 \Rightarrow \rho(tr \Downarrow send) > 0$

Schneider (1998) presents a general-purpose rank function theorem that is central to his proof strategy.

Rank Function Theorem. If, for some set of events *R* and *T*, there is a rank function $\rho: \mathcal{M} \to \mathbb{Z}$ satisfying

R1) $\forall\, m \in IK \bullet \rho(m) > 0$
R2) $\forall\, S \subseteq \mathcal{M},\, m \in \mathcal{M} \bullet ((\forall m' \in S \bullet \rho(m') > 0) \wedge S \vdash m) \Rightarrow \rho(m) > 0$
R3) $\forall\, t \in T \bullet \rho(t) \leqslant 0$
R4) $\forall\, i \in \mathcal{U} \bullet User_i \underset{R}{\|} STOP$ maintains ρ

then   **NET sat R precedes T**

The theorem, the proof of which is available in

(Schneider, 1998), states that if we find a rank function ρ that satisfies the four conditions R1 to R4, then the network NET satisfies *R* precedes *T*. The four conditions of the theorem ensure

- The intruder should not be in possession of any messages of nonpositive rank to start with (R1),
- Given a set of messages of positive rank the intruder should only be able to generate messages (under the generates relation "$\vdash$") of positive rank (R2),
- No honest participant, restricted from executing events in *R*, introduces a message of nonpositive rank unless it receives a message of nonpositive rank (R4), and
- Events in set *T* are of nonpositive rank (R3).

The final condition R4 of the rank function requires checking of CSP processes against a particular specification. In order for an individual process to satisfy condition R4, we need to check whether the process *maintains rank* while being restricted on events in *R*.

A number of specialised proof rules that help establish condition R4 are available by Schneider (1998). We do not list these in this chapter for the sake of brevity and refer the reader to consult (Ryan, Schneider, Goldsmith, Lowe, & Roscoe, 2001; Schneider, 1998) for an exhaustive list of these rules.

Analysing the Woo-Lam Protocol

To demonstrate the rank function theorem, we analyse the Woo-Lam protocol as an example and attempt to verify the protocol for the authentication property described earlier. The property requires us to check whether $Running.A.B.N_B$ precedes $Commit.B.A.N_B$ for all traces of NET. Recall that the rank function theorem is defined in terms of general sets *R* and *T*. We assign $Running.A.B.N_B$ and $Commit.B.A.N_B$ to sets *R* and *T* respectively, that is, $R = \{Running.A.B.N_B\}$ and $T = \{Commit.B.A.N_B\}$. We identify ranks on the message space for NET and construct a rank function shown in Figure 5.

The rank function assigns all user identities in the set $\mathcal{U}$ a positive rank. The identity of all users is assumed to be known to the intruder and therefore could be impersonated by the intruder. All the nonces in $\mathcal{N}$, including N_B are assigned a positive rank. *B* sends out N_B in cleartext, and therefore, an intruder can easily get

Figure 4. A specific run of the Woo-Lam protocol involving A and B using nonce N_B

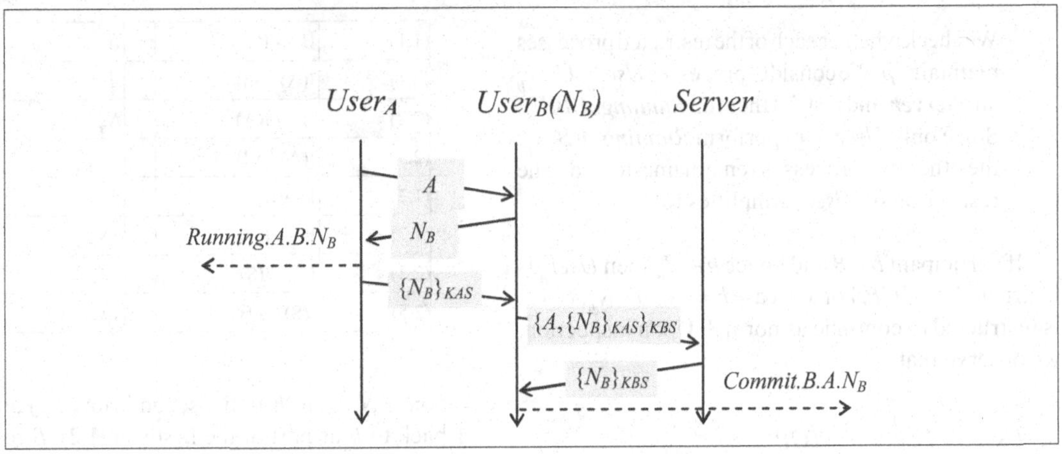

Figure 5. A rank function for the Woo-Lam protocol

$\rho(\mathcal{U}) = 1$ (including A, B and S)

$\rho(\mathcal{N}) = 1$ (including N_B)

$$\rho(\mathcal{K}) = \begin{cases} 0 & \text{if } k = K_{AS} \\ & \text{or } k = K_{BS} \\ 1 & \text{otherwise} \end{cases}$$

$$\rho(\{m\}_k) = \begin{cases} 0 & \text{if } \{m\}_k = \{N_B\}_{KAS} \\ & \text{or } \{m\}_k = \{A,\{N_B\}_{KAS}\}_{KBS} \\ & \text{or } \{m\}_k = \{N_B\}_{KBS} \\ \rho(m) & \text{if } \rho(k) = 1 \\ 1 & \text{otherwise} \end{cases}$$

$\rho(m_1,m_2) = \min\{\rho(m_1),\rho(m_2)\}$

$\rho(Running.A.B.N_B) = 1$

$\rho(Commit.B.A.N_B) = 0$

hold of it. The two shared keys used in the protocol, K_{AS} and K_{BS}, are both assigned a nonpositive rank, as they are supposed to be private to participants A and B. Since we consider NET to be restricted on *Running.A.B.N$_B$*, the three messages (see Figure 4) that follow this event, $\{N_B\}_{KAS}$, $\{A,\{N_B\}_{KAS}\}_{KBS}$ and $\{N_B\}_{KBS}$, are assigned a nonpositive rank. We now consider each of the conditions of the Rank Function Theorem and check whether the rank function in Figure 5 satisfies them.

R1: $\forall\, m \in IK \bullet \rho(m) > 0$

The set IK contains all the agent identities. There is nothing in this set that is of nonpositive rank. The condition is satisfied.

R2: $\forall\, S \subseteq \mathcal{M}, m \in \mathcal{M} \bullet ((\forall m' \in S \bullet \rho(m') > 0) \wedge S \vdash m) \Rightarrow \rho(m) > 0$

This conditions checks whether a message of nonpositive rank can be generated under the "$\vdash$" relation from a set of messages of positive rank. None of the messages identified as of positive rank, shown in Figure 5, let the intruder generate any messages that are of nonpositive rank. The three messages of nonpositive rank, $\{N_B\}_{KAS}$, $\{A,\{N_B\}_{KAS}\}_{KBS}$ and $\{N_B\}_{KBS}$, are encrypted under keys K_{AS} and K_{BS}, both of which are of nonpositive rank. This prevents an intruder from generating these messages as it has no way of acquiring these two keys. The condition is satisfied.

R3: $\forall\, t \in T \bullet \rho(t) \leqslant 0$

This condition requires none of the events in T to be of positive rank. The only event in set T is the signal event *Commit.B.A.N$_B$* of nonpositive rank. This condition is satisfied.

R4: $\forall\, i \in \mathcal{U} \bullet User_i \underset{R}{\|} STOP$ sat maintains ρ

We check whether each of the restricted processes maintains ρ. We consider processes $User_A$, $User_B$ and $Server$, and restrict them on $Running.A.B.N_B$. Since only $User_A$ can perform $Running.A.B.N_B$, the other two processes remain unaffected. The restriction on $User_A$ simplifies to

If participant $b = B$ and nonce $n = N_B$, then $User_A$ is instructed to $STOP$. For any case $b \neq B$ or $n \neq N_B$, $User_A$ is instructed to continue as normal. Upon inspection, we observe that

$$User_A \underset{Running.A.B.N_B}{\|} STOP$$

fails to maintain rank. Consider a run where participant A initiates the protocol with some participant C, and is intercepted by an intruder I, as shown in Figure 6.

In this case, the process $User_A \underset{Running.A.B.N_B}{\|} STOP$ behaves as follows

$$send.A!C!A \rightarrow$$
$$receive.A.C?N_B \rightarrow$$
$$\qquad if\ b = B \wedge n_b = N_B$$
$$then\ STOP$$
$$\qquad else\ Running.A.C.N_B \rightarrow$$
$$\qquad\quad send.A!C!\{N_B\}_{KAS} \rightarrow STOP$$

where it outputs the message $\{N_B\}_{KAS}$ while communicating with C. This shows that $User_A$ fails to maintain rank as $\{N_B\}_{KAS}$ is of nonpositive rank. The condition R4 is therefore not satisfied. We have shown that the rank function from Figure 5 fails to meet all the conditions of the Rank Function Theorem. To demonstrate a flaw in the protocol as a result of this failure, we consider the attack shown in Figure 7.

The attack shows an authentication attempt initiated by B (1.1) with an intruder I, who is also a valid participant of the network. I then pretends to be A and initiates a second run with B (2.1). I obtains the

Figure 6. A possible run of the Woo-Lam protocol

(1)	$A \rightarrow I(C):$	A
(2)	$I(C) \rightarrow A:$	N_B
(3)	$A \rightarrow I(C):$	$\{N_B\}_{KAS}$

Figure 7. An attack on the Woo-Lam protocol

(1.1)	$B \rightarrow I$	:	B
(2.1)	$I(A) \rightarrow B$	:	A
(2.2)	$B \rightarrow I(A)$	:	N_B
(2.3)	$I(A) \rightarrow B$	:	X
(1.2)	$I \rightarrow B$	:	N_B
(1.3)	$B \rightarrow I$	:	$\{N_B\}_{KBS}$
(2.4)	$B \rightarrow I(S)$	:	$\{A,X\}_{KBS}$
(2.5)	$I(S) \rightarrow B$	:	$\{N_B\}_{KBS}$

nonce N_B from B in the second run (2.2) and sends it back to B as part of the first run (1.2). B responds by encrypting it with the key K_{BS} that it shares with the server S (1.3). This first run is similar to the possible run shown in Figure 6, and is only used by I to manipulate B into encrypting the nonce N_B with the key B shares with S. Once I has the nonce encrypted with K_{BS}, it pretends to be S and sends it back to B as part of the second run (2.5), allowing B to believe that it has just authenticated A, whereas A has not even taken part in any of these runs. The attack is complete.

FUTURE TRENDS AND CONCLUSION

The previous section has demonstrated the effective use of rank functions to analyse a flawed version of the Woo-Lam protocol. An amended version of the same protocol is also presented by Woo and Lam (1994); interested readers are encouraged to apply the rank functions approach to the correct version, for the purpose of both exercise and a full proof of correctness. Other protocols analysed using this approach include the Needham-Schroeder (1978) protocol in (Schneider, 1998), the Yahalom protocol (Burrows et al., 1989) in (Ryan et al., 1999), and a biometric authentication protocol for 3G mobile systems (Dimitriadis & Polemi, 2005) in (Shaikh & Dimitriadis, 2006).

In recent years, the standard approach has been developed and extended on many fronts. Schneider (2002) has used rank functions to reason about the algebraic properties of real cryptographic mechanisms, such as the exclusive-or operator. Delicata and Schneider (2005) extend the notion of a rank function to a *temporal rank function* to analyse *forward secrecy* properties of key establishment protocols. Shaikh et al.

(2005) propose a formal structure for signal events to specify authentication properties in CSP, and specify a range of different authentication properties to demonstrate the effectiveness of signals. Their work is important in helping protocol designers to precisely model authentication and specify the subtle variations that exists within the concept.

Schneider's theory of rank functions allows us to reason about the protocol message space in a clear and rigorous manner. The rank function theorem builds on it to provide a powerful technique to verify authentication protocols. The task of identifying ranks to messages manually, however, is arduous and nontrivial. Shaikh et al. (2006) present a heuristic approach to aid the manual construction of candidate rank functions. The heuristic is designed to help in the reasoning and deduction of rank assignment to messages, providing a structured way of conducting this exercise. Heather and Schneider (2005) present an approach that allows verifying a protocol running on an infinitely large network. They achieve this by reducing the problem to that of verifying a network with a limited number of protocol participants and runs, and as a result, a smaller message space. They present a decision procedure, in the form of an algorithm, with which the security of a protocol on a large network may be decided by constructing a rank function for a relatively small and more limited network.

The manual checking of proof conditions for the rank function analysis remain labour-intensive and error-prone. Over the years various tools have been introduced to mechanise the repetitive procedures involved in such analysis in an attempt to reduce the possibility of human-error. This includes Heather's (2000) bespoke tool, known as *RankAnalyzer*, and Evans and Schneider's (2005) use of the general-purpose theorem-proving tool by Owre, Rushby, and Shankar (1992), known as the *Proof Verification System* (PVS). Heather's (2000) *RankAnalyzer* is purpose-built to allow an automated analysis of authentication protocols, requiring little human effort to operate. The protocols are input in a notation very similar to the standard informal specification and require no further human interaction. Evans and Schneider's (2005) use of PVS has developed the rank function analysis further to not only provide tool support, but also to extend it to a practical framework, analysing a wider variety of security properties including nonrepudiation and time-dependent security properties for protocols.

Research into formal analysis of cryptographic protocols has been going on for over two decades now and still continues. With a wide variety of formalisms and strategies used, the research community deserves credit for addressing and successfully solving the original problem of analysing protocols to an extent. Future directions of this research aim at extending the boundaries of this intruder model and incorporating further properties of existing cryptographic primitives and modelling new primitives (Backes & Schunter, 2003), tackling new types of threats such as the Denial of Service (DoS) attacks (Yasinsac, 2001), and finally, analysing large complex protocols such as the Internet Key Exchange (IKE) operating in a real world environment (Meadows, 2003). While there is no doubt that work has already started in the pursuit of such research goals (Meadows, 2003), there is also a need to re-examine the existing formal approaches and improve upon them. The goal is to enhance these approaches so as to make them more efficient and also more accessible to those outside the formal community.

ACKNOWLEDGMENT

I am grateful to Dr. Vicky J. Bush and Prof. Steve A. Schneider for their comments and feedback on various parts of this chapter.

REFERENCES

Backes, M., & Schunter, M. (2003). From absence of certain vulnerabilities towards security proofs: pushing the limits of formal verification. In *Proceedings of the 2003 workshop on New security paradigms* (pp. 67-74). New York: ACM Press.

Burrows, M., Abadi, M., & Needham, R.M. (1990). A logic of authentication. *ACM Transactions on Computer Systems (TOCS), 8*(1), 18-36.

Daemen, J., & Rijmen, V. (2002). *The design of Rijndael: AES—the advanced encryption standard.* Berlin: Springer-Verlag.

Delicata, R., & Schneider, S.A. (2005). Temporal rank functions for forward secrecy. In *Proceedings of the 2005 IEEE Computer Security Foundations Workshop* (pp. 126-139). Washington: IEEE Computer Society Press.

Diffie, W., & Hellman, M.E. (1976). New directions in cryptography. *IEEE Transactions on Information Theory, 22*(6), 644-654.

Dimitriadis, C.K., & Polemi, D. (2005). A protocol for incorporating biometrics in 3G withrespecttoprivacy. In *Proceedings of the 3rd International Workshop on Security in Information Systems (WOSIS'2005), Miami, U.S.* (pp. 123-135). Setúbal: INSTICC Press.

Dolev, D., & Yao, A.C. (1983). On the security of public key protocols. *IEEE Transactions on Information Theory, 29*(2), 198-208.

Evans, N., & Schneider, S.A. (2005). Verifying security protocols with PVS: Widening the rank function approach. *Journal of Logic and Algebraic Programming, 64*(2), 253-284.

Gordon, A.D., & Jeffrey, A. (2001). Typing correspondence assertions for communication protocols. *Electronic Notes in Theoretical Computer Science (ENTCS), 45*, 1-22.

Heather, J. (2000). *"Oh!...Is it really you?"—using rank functions to verify authentication protocols.* Doctoral Thesis, Royal Holloway University of London.

Heather, J., & Schneider, S.A. (2005). A decision procedure for the existence of a rank function. *Journal of Computer Security, 13*(2), 317-344.

Hoare, C.A.R. (1985). *Communicating sequential processes.* Prentice-Hall International

Lowe, G. (1995). An attack on the Needham-Schroeder public key protocol. *Information Processing Letters, 56*(3), 131-133.

Lowe, G. (1996, March 27-29). Breaking and fixing the Needham-Schroeder public-key protocol using FDR. In T. Margaria, & B. Steffen (Eds.). *Tools and Algorithms for Construction and Analysis of Systems, Proceedings of the Second International Workshop, TACAS '96, Passau, Germany* (Vol. 1055 of LNCS, pp. 147-166). Berlin: Springer-Verlag.

Meadows, C. (1996). The NRL protocol analyzer: An overview. *Journal of Logic Programming, 26*(2), 113-131.

Meadows, C. (2003). Formal methods for cryptographic protocol analysis: Emerging issues and trends. *IEEE Journal on Selected Areas in Communication,*

Special Issue on Formal Methods for Security, 21(1), 44-54.

National Bureau of Standards (NBS). (1977, January). *Data encryption standard.* U.S. Department of Commerce, FIPS Publication 46, Washington, D.C.

Needham, R., & Schroeder, M. (1978). Using encryption for authentication in large networks. *Communications of the ACM, 21*(12), 993-999.

Owre, S., Rushby, J.M., & Shankar, N. (1992). PVS: A prototype verification system. In D. Kapur (Ed.). *Proceedings of the 11th International Conference on Automated Deduction: Automated Deduction* (Vol. 607 of LNCS, pp. 748-752). London: Springer-Verlag.

Roscoe, A.W. (1997). *The theory and practice of concurrency.* Prentice-Hall International.

Ryan, P., Schneider, S.A., Goldsmith, M., Lowe, G., & Roscoe, A.W. (2001). *Modelling and analysis of security protocols.* London: Addison-Wesley.

Schneider, S.A. (1996). Security properties and CSP. In *Proceedings of the 1996 IEEE Symposium on Security and Privacy* (pp. 174-189). Washington: IEEE Computer Society Press.

Schneider, S.A. (1998). Verifying authentication protocols in CSP. *IEEE Transactions on Software Engineering, 24*(9), 741-758.

Schneider, S.A. (1999). *Concurrent and real-time systems: the CSP approach.* London: Addison-Wesley.

Schneider, S.A. (2002). Verifying authentication protocol implementations. In *Proceedings of the IFIP TC6/WG6.1 Fifth International Conference on Formal Methods for Open Object-Based Distributed Systems V* (pp. 5-24). Deventer: Kluwer.

Shaikh, S.A., Bush, V.J., & Schneider, S.A. (2005). Specifying authentication using signals events in CSP. In D. Feng, D. Lin, & M. Yung (Eds.). *Conference on Information Security and Cryptology (CISC'2005), Beijing, China* (Vol. 3822 of LNCS, (pp, 63-74). Berlin: Springer-Verlag.

Shaikh, S.A., & Bush, V.J. (2006). Analysing the Woo-Lam protocol using CSP and rank functions. *Journal of Research and Practice in Information Technology (JRPIT), 38*(1), 19-29.

Shaikh, S.A., Bush, V.J., & Schneider, S.A. (2006). A heuristic for constructing rank functions to verify authentication protocols. In *Proceedings of the 3rd International Verification Workshop (VERIFY'06)* (pp. 112-127). Seattle, U.S.

Shaikh, S.A., & Dimitriadis, C.K. (2006, April 18-21). Analysing a biometric authentication protocol for 3G mobile systems. In J.A. Clark, R.F. Paige, F.A.C. Polack, & P. Brooke (Eds.). *Security in Pervasive Computing, Third International Conference, SPC, York, UK* (Vol. 3934 of LNCS, pp. 211-226). Berlin: Springer-Verlag.

Thayer, F.J., Herzog J.C., & Guttman, J.D. (1998). Strand spaces: Why is a security protocol correct? In *Proceedings of the IEEE Symposium on Security and Privacy* (pp. 160-171). Washington: IEEE Computer Society Press.

Woo, T.Y.C., & Lam, S.S. (1992). Authentication for distributed systems. *Computer, 25* (1), 39-52. Washington: IEEE Computer Society Press.

Woo, T.Y.C., & Lam, S.S. (1994). A lesson on authentication protocol design. *ACM SIGOPS Operating Systems Review, 28*(3), 24-37. New York: ACM Press.

Yasinsac, A. (2001). Dynamic analysis of security protocols. In *Proceedings of the 2000 workshop on New security paradigms* (pp. 77-87). New York: ACM Press.

KEY TERMS

Attack: An attack refers to the violation of the security goal of a system or a protocol. The term is commonly used to describe intentional (as opposed to accidental) violations, and involves an intruder actively (or passively) manipulating protocol messages and interactions with other participants.

Authentication: Authentication is a security goal and refers to the verification of a real or digital identity of a person, an electronic node, or device. In the context of protocols, this refers to the verification of a message sender's or protocol participant's identity.

Communicating Sequential Processes (CSP): A formal language for describing patterns of interaction for concurrent systems (in computer science). First described by Sir Professor Tony Hoare at Oxford in 1978, it is a member of the family of mathematical theories of concurrency known as process algebras. It is traditionally written in a fairly mathematical notation with special symbols representing its operators, and is typeset more like mathematics than a typical programming language.

Intruder: The term intruder is used to refer to an entity that interacts with or takes part in a protocol with intent to undermine the goals of the protocol. Also known as an enemy, attacker, spy, eavesdropper, penetrator, opponent, or an insider.

Nonce: Also known as a cryptographic nonce, it refers to a random or pseudorandom number particularly used to ensure the freshness (or recentness) of some message or communication in protocols.

Protocol: A set of guidelines for governing communication between two or more electronic entities. Protocol are usually characterised by communication or security goals they are designed to provide (such as reliability, confidentiality, or authentication), the communication medium they are designed to operate on (such as wired or wireless), or some specific functionality (such as tunnelling).

Rank Function: A rank function is a function from a set of messages (or a message space) to the set of integers. The purpose of this function is to partition the messages, so as to characterise those messages that an intruder may get hold and those that an intruder may not get hold of. In the context of protocol analysis, this is helpful in analysing those messages that are critical to the correctness of the protocol, but are leaked to the intruder during execution.

Chapter XXI
Access Control Frameworks for a Distributed System

Rajeev R. Raje
Indiana University-Purdue University Indianapolis, USA

Alex Crespi
Indiana University-Purdue University Indianapolis, USA

Omkar J. Tilak
Indiana University-Purdue University Indianapolis, USA

Andrew M. Olson
Indiana University-Purdue University Indianapolis, USA

Carol C. Burt
2AB Inc., Helena, AL, USA

ABSTRACT

Component-based software development offers a promising technique for creating distributed systems. It does require a framework for specifying component properties, analyzing the behaviors of a system before composition, and validating them during operation. This chapter focuses on access control properties of a distributed system. It provides a framework that addresses the following issues: (a) specifying access control properties for individual components, (b) identifying components with required access control properties, and (c) formulating compositional models for predicting the access control properties of a composed system from those of its individual components.

INTRODUCTION

Although component-based software development is a valuable approach for creating a complex distributed system, it requires a framework for specifying component properties in order to analyze the system's behavior before its assembly and, then, validate it during operation. Both functional and quality of service (QoS) features of components require specification. One common QoS characteristic is security, whose importance cannot be understated in many sensitive application domains, such as medical or military applications. A framework that supports composing and predicting a distributed system's security characteristics from the properties of its individual components would aid in the creation of more secure systems for such sensitive domains. Access control is an important type of security. Thus, any framework to specify and predict the security properties of a composed system from the properties of individual components should provide a means to model and predict the system's access control properties. This chapter describes one such framework based on the principles of UniFrame (UniFrame Project, 2006)—an on-going research effort that aims to automate the creation of Distributed Computing Systems (DCS) from geographically scattered, heterogeneous software components.

The specific objectives of this chapter are to provide a means of:

- Expressing the access control characteristics of individual software components within the UniFrame paradigm.
- Identifying individual software components on a network that meet system access control requirements.
- Predicting the access control behavior of an integrated system based on the properties of its individual components.

BACKGROUND

There have been many attempts made at modeling access control in computing systems. This section describes a few prominent efforts.

Access Matrix

The basic model for access control is the access control matrix, which consists of a two dimensional matrix relating subjects to objects. Each cell in the matrix contains the access privileges of one subject for accessing one object (Saunders, Hitchens, & Varadharajan, 2001). This matrix can be extremely large for large systems and may be sparsely populated, leading to great inefficiencies in implementation (Sandhu & Samarati, 1994). Therefore, most systems implement access control models that can be mapped back to the concept of the access control matrix while avoiding these inefficiencies.

Access Control Lists (ACL)

ACL are a means of implementing efficiently access control matrices. Each secured object has an ACL that consists of data from a column of the access control matrix. Only entries for subjects allowed to use the object are present in the ACL, thereby eliminating the access control matrix's inefficiencies. Replacing the ACL for an object is easy, but determining all of the privileges for a single subject is difficult in such a system (Sandhu & Samarati, 1994). For instance, if all of the access privileges of a subject must be revoked, then all ACLs must be examined. This may still be more efficient than examining the whole matrix.

Discretionary Access Control (DAC)

In DAC, an owner of an object determines if a given subject may be allowed access to that object or not. Thus, a DAC policy consists of a subject's identity, pertinent object identities, and a series of rules decided by the object's owner. This policy specification determines whether or not a particular subject may perform a specific operation on an object. Closed DAC systems only allow access when the policy specifically allows the access, whereas an open DAC system only disallows access when the policy denies access. One weakness of DAC is that once a user gains access to information, potentially nothing prevents it from sharing the information with an unauthorized user (Sandhu & Samarati, 1994). In addition, with DAC systems, it can be difficult to represent and maintain complex access control policies for a large organization.

Mandatory Access Control (MAC)

MAC assigns each object a security level (e.g., Top Secret, Secret, Confidential, and Unclassified), and each subject a clearance level (i.e., Top Secret, Secret, Confidential, and Unclassified) reflecting the subject's trustworthiness. A subject may access an object only if the subject's clearance level is sufficiently high to permit access to the object's security level. A subject may read objects of equal or lower security level than the subject's clearance level, whereas the subject may write only to objects that are of equal or higher security level than the subject's clearance level. This structure ensures that information from an object with a higher security level does not get written to a document with a lower security level, thus preventing a breach in security (Sandhu & Samarati, 1994).

Role-Based Access Control (RBAC)

Role-based access control is a variation on DAC where there is an additional level of indirection between subjects and their privileges (Ferraiolo & Kuhn, 1992; Saunders et al., 2001). The users are assigned to one or more roles, and roles are linked to access control privileges. In such a system, it is possible to design roles to match an organization's structure and to change a user's roles easily as their position in the organization changes. RBAC can also incorporate hierarchical relationships among roles as well as among permissions and roles, and users and roles. Thus, RBAC possesses a management flexibility that DAC does not.

Model Driven Access Control

One way of modeling access control in a system, independently of specific technologies or policy models, is to develop a more general access control model that can be refined into any of the major existing access control models. Burt, Bryant, Raje, Olson, and Auguston (2003) discuss such a platform independent model (PIM) that can be mapped onto platform specific models (PSM) for creating distributed systems. A PIM of access control that accommodates currently existing access control models, provides an abstract view of access control that is useful to parameterize domain models. This enables transforming PIMs to PSMs by incorporating access control points. Three pieces of information needed during the parameterization of the PIM include identification of: the resources that require protection, the points within the application where the access control checks are made, and the application specific context/attribute information necessary at each access control checkpoint.

Common Criteria

The Common Criteria (CC) approach provides a means to evaluate the effectiveness of access control in the context of additional security properties. The result of an effort to develop an international standard for evaluating the security characteristics of information technology products, the CC represents an alignment of preexisting U.S., Canadian, and European standards (Common Criteria Project Sponsoring Organizations, 2004). The designers of this new standard hope that it will result in the world wide recognition of evaluation results for IT products. Common Criteria require-

ments break down into two categories: functional requirements, which specify security behavior, and assurance requirements, which form the basis for gaining confidence that the desired security properties of a product are effective and implemented correctly. The CC does not address the composition of security properties. According to Katzke (2002), there is no formal/mathematical approach for determining the security properties of a system composed of evaluated products. Therefore, CC does not provide any direct guidance for developing a means of composing access control specifications of components into the specifications of a system.

This section has provided a brief overview of various approaches to modeling access control. In contrast to model-driven access control and the CC, the other approaches here do not specifically tackle access control in the context of component-based distributed systems. As with the CC, model-driven access control does not address the issue of predicting a system's access control features from those of its components. The UniFrame-based access control model described in the following section tackles these issues.

UNIFRAME

UniFrame (Raje, Bryant, Auguston, Olson, & Burt, 2001) provides a process for specifying and discovering individual components for a DCS, predicting its properties and generating it from the components. The foundation of the UniFrame process is a knowledge base (KB) that experts from a particular application domain create. The KB contains details about architectural designs of component-based distributed systems (CBDS) in the domain and the types of components that integrate each. A Unified Meta-component Model (UMM) (Raje, 2000) specification defines each component in the KB using multiple levels. A developer who wishes to create and validate specific components for a CBDS consults the KB to follow the UMM specifications encoded there. The developer also creates a detailed UMM specification for each component created and successfully validated and deploys them on a network. These components register with the UniFrame Resource Discovery System (URDS) (Olson, Raje, Bryant, Burt & Auguston, 2005; Siram, 2002). URDS is a hierarchical and proactive discovery service that uses the principles of multi-level matching (Katuri, 2006). A system developer desiring to create a CBDS for a specific application issues a query consisting of the requirements the CBDS must meet. The query processor consults the KB for the design of an appropriate CBDS. If the KB contains a design meeting these requirements, the processor divides the query into subqueries, each representing the specification of a single component. It passes these subqueries to the URDS, which searches for appropriate matching component specifications among those the component developers supplied. If it finds a set that matches all the subqueries, it returns the corresponding set of components to the system developer, who then selects a sufficient subset, provides any proprietary components and requests the process to assemble the integrated CBDS according to the design. The UniFrame System Generator (Huang, 2003) performs this assembly. This task may require *glue code* to bridge the differences between components. This code may also serve for providing the necessary instrumentation to measure the assembled system's QoS during testing. As the chapter's focus is the access control models of the components and the assembled system, it does not describe further the unrelated aspects of the UniFrame research. It discusses only the aspects related to the specification and discovery of components based on their access control properties and prediction of the access control features of the system composed from the components.

Case Study

This chapter presents its basic ideas in the context of a case study involving a simplified university student information system. This case is appropriate because the university must protect sensitive student information while permitting access to various stakeholders in the university. The student information system provides the basic functionality used to store and retrieve academic and financial information about students enrolled at a university. The goal here is not to model a comprehensive student information system, but instead, to use the system's representative functionality to provide a realistic setting with which to test the access control model presented. Therefore, the system functionality will be limited to the following actions: *Create* a new student record and *Read/Save* student records. The *Read student record* command will attempt to read the information for the indicated student from each of the servers (e.g., *Academic Server* and *Financial Aid Server*) in the system. Access control policies may permit a user to read only portions of the student's record, thus acting as a filter of information

in this situation. The *Save student record* action will attempt to write portions of the student's record to various servers in the system. This action will succeed only if each portion of the record being written is successfully stored. In this case, the access control infrastructure acts like a gate that either allows the entire action or cancels the action altogether.

To implement the basic functionality described above, the student information system instance in this case study consists of five separate components: User Terminal, Record Server, Academic Server, Financial Aid Server, and the Student Employment Server. User Terminal (UT) provides a uniform access point for all users across the system. Record Server (RS) acts as the main contact point for all requests. It holds general information about all students in the system. Academic Server (AS) holds transcripts and degree program information (e.g., requirements) for each student. Financial Aid Server (FAD) holds student loan, grant, and scholarship information about each student in these programs. Student Employment Server (SES) holds student employment information about students working at the university. Users submit requests via the UT, which routes them through the RS before they pass to one or more lower level servers. A server is a logical entity, not necessarily a single physical entity. This architecture creates a variety of situations in which one request requires access control verifications across multiple, distributed components.

UniFrame's Access Control Framework

Model Driven Access Control and the Common Criteria both suggest that the key parts of the access control framework for components include the naming of resources in the system and the identification of resources that are protected by access control guards in components. These two pieces of information, contained resources and protected resources, form the basis of a searching mechanism for locating software components with the desired access control properties. The student information system (SIS) name space contains a resource called student_record (sr), which contains four sections: general_student_information (gsi), academic_record (ar), financial_aid (fa), and student_employment (se). Each of these four can be further broken down into more finely grained parts. For instance, the resource name for a particular student's transcript is shown below. It refers to the transcript for a student with the student ID of a student Smith.

ResourceName = {student_record = fsmith, section = academic_record, part = transcript}

Using this naming structure permits expressing a specific resource name with a single string: *fsmith.academic_record.transcript,* or more succinctly, *fsmith.ar.transcript*. The wildcard symbol, *, represents all pertinent records as a group. For instance, *. ar* represents the set of academic records for all students, indicating in an access control policy (e.g., that an academic advisor may have read access to the academic records of all students). In addition to a name, each resource is also mapped to a set of operations performable on the resource.

UniFrame requires a component's developers to write a UMM specification that describes the resources the component contains. Due to the chapter's space restrictions, it does not show the UMM specification's exact format. Please refer to Crespi (2005) for more details. A *contained resource* means that the component carries out operation(s) on the resource under its control. By having each component specify which resources it contains, it is possible to analyze the scope of a component's effects on resources within the system. It is assumed that a unique component contains a resource, so that another component needing access to that resource must act on it via the containing component. In addition to specifying the resources a component contains, the component developer must specify which resources it protects via access control guards. Clearly, the *protected resources* in a component will be a subset of its *contained resources*.

As indicated in an earlier subsection, the DCS developer issues a query to the URDS to locate the necessary components for generating the DCS. Although, the discovery and matching process considers both the functional and QoS features for identifying and selecting appropriate components from those available on a network, this chapter focuses only on the matching process related to the access control features. The combination of *contained* and *protected resources* for each component forms the basis of the matching algorithm for access control properties. The DCS developer specifies the resources to be protected in the new system, defining, thusly, the search criterion. The matching logic proceeds as follows: For each resource requiring protection, determine whether or not a component under consideration contains the resource. If the component contains that resource, then determine whether or not the component protects the resource from unauthorized operations. If this examination

results in a "yes" for each resource requiring protection, then that component matches the DCS developer's requirements. Otherwise, the component is discarded. This process repeats for all possible components that are available on the network.

The mechanisms for stating the access control policies and associated matching of queries map well with the declarative features of the logic programming model (i.e., "what," not the "how" the imperative programming model implies). Hence, UniFrame's approach employs logic programming in Prolog to implement this access control matching. In such a program, a list of names of resources to be protected expresses the system's requirements. For instance, the following fact says that the general student information and student employment portions of any student record require access control protection. Each * in this expression indicates every student's record.

require_protect(['.gsi','*.se'])*.

In addition to the specification of what needs protection in the system, facts must be present to indicate the contained and protected resources in each component available on the network. The following two facts state that the component *StudentEmploymentServer1* contains the student employment portion of all student records and that it also ensures that a guard protects this resource.

contain('StudentEmploymentServer1','.se')*.
ensure_protect('StudentEmploymentServer1','.se')*.

The following predicate serves to represent components without resources (i.e., neither containing nor protecting any resources).

consider('StudentEmploymentServer1').

In addition to the necessary Prolog facts concerning the containment and protection of resources in the required DCS and the available components, are predicates to support matching these components to the DCS specification. The first of these is a predicate that determines whether or not a component protects the resources it contains and whether those resources are present in the list of system resources requiring protection. A recursive predicate that successively investigates each resource in the list of system resources needing protection represents this. The base case of the recursion assumes that all components protect an empty list of resources. The predicate returns true if, for each resource requiring protection, the component contains and protects the resource or does not contain the resource.

> protects(_, []).
> protects(Component,[Resource|OtherResources])
> :-
>   (contain(Component,Resource),ensure_protect(Component,Resource) ;
>   (not contain(Component,Resource))),
>   protects(Component,OtherResources).

Finally, the following predicate evaluates to true if a component is to be considered and meets the criteria about protecting the required resources.

> match(Component) :- consider(Component), require_protect(Resources),
>   protects(Component,Resources).

Components within a DCS interact with each other through the methods in their interfaces, and these interactions form the basis of the composition of the DCS from individual components. Logic programming can model such a composition by expressing each method as a predicate. When a call to a method of one component involves calls to one or more methods of other components, evaluating the predicate of the originating method requires evaluating the predicates defining the calls on the other components. For instance, the following predicate models the invocation of the *saveStudentRecord* method of the component called *record_server1*. For this predicate to evaluate to true, each resulting call to the financial aid, academic record, and student employment servers must also succeed.

> *saveStudentRecord(P,S,SR):- saveFinancialAid(P,S,SR), saveAcademicRecord(P,S,SR),*
> saveStudentEmployment(P,S,SR).

Here, P indicates the principal, S the student ID, and SR the student record. The *saveStudentRecord* method on the record server results, in part, in saving the general student information section to the record server. If this operation involves an access control authorization, then the preceding predicate would be modified to include a guard for protecting the write access to the general student information section of the student record.

With this Prolog modeling approach, each component's access control model consists of a predicate for each of its methods plus predicates for representing access control guards within the component. If the model follows proper conventions for naming predicates, the predicates for all components in a system can be combined into a single Prolog database representing the entire system. For instance, the *saveStudentRecord* predicate for the *UserTerminal* model would include a reference to the *saveStudentRecord* predicate in the *RecordServer* model, but both component models cannot use identical names for their predicates.

Beyond representing component interfaces, the access control model also includes information about potential users of the system. Each user has credentials identifying security attributes that the access control model uses to determine the user's access privileges. A combination of functors model this information by creating a fact that relates a user ID to information such as roles, groups, and access ID. For example,

> *authenticate(fsmith, credential(accessID(fsmith), role([student]), group([student]))).*

indicates that the user *fsmith* has credentials such that the access ID is *fsmith*, role is *student*, and group is *student*. Two situations in the model access the information in this fact. The first identifies a principal via the predicate *principal(AID,P):-authenticate(AID,P)*. This retrieves the credentials of a principal with an access ID through queries like *principal(fsmith,P)*, which binds *fsmith*'s credentials to the variable *P* during Prolog's resolution process. Second, the model can also determine whether or not a user is a student by examining the user's credentials to see if the student role is present in the list of roles.

The component developer can implement a component's guard(s) any appropriate way. Depending on the component's model, a guard may consult a dynamic attribute server in order to retrieve any dynamic security attributes that it may need to make access control decisions. This particular access control functionality is generally necessary only in advance systems, but the discussion mentions it here to demonstrate how to handle it. The guard would then consult the access control policy to determine whether or not the access request is authorized. To perform such a check, the guard needs three pieces of information:

the principal's credentials, the resource's name, and the operation requested. *P, R*, and *O* represent these, respectively, in the following predicate:

guard(P,R,O):- dynamicAttributes(P,NEWP,R), accessControl (NEWP,R,O).

The variable *NEWP* represents the principal's set of modified attributes the dynamic attribute server returns for the guard to use when evaluating the access request. This modification permits the system to account for dynamic attributes. In order to model the action of a dynamic attribute server, it may be necessary to model some of the data stored in a component. Sometimes access control decisions depend on context information, such as time, ownership, or geographic location and their effects are encoded in the dynamic attribute server. In case the student information system allows students to access their own records, there must be a way to determine whether a user is the owner of a student record or not. Each component that stores information may potentially need to model it in Prolog so that it represents the dynamic security attributes properly. In this case study, the necessary dynamic attribute information is retrievable from the resource name, because a student's ID links the student to the student's record. If the principal's access ID is the same as the record's student ID, then the dynamic attribute predicate will append the role of student owner to the security attributes. Exactly how each component implements these actions depends upon the component developer.

For simplicity of this chapter, the UniFrame access control framework assumes a uniform access control policy for all components in a system. The goal, then, is only to determine how particular policies impact the ability of a DCS's users to perform certain actions. Therefore, in the Prolog-based model, a single predicate called *accessControl(P,R,O)*, with P, R and O representing the principal's security attributes, resource name, and operation, respectively, evaluates the access control policy. The DCS developer designs this predicate to represent the desired policy.

To facilitate composing individual component specifications into a system level specification, the DCS developer follows a series of conventions to avoid conflicts in predicate naming when combining components' predicates. First, each component in the model must have a unique name to prevent distinct components from having the same name. The name of a predicate for each of a component's methods is the con-

catenation of the component's name with the method's name. This eliminates the possibility the definitions of a *Liveness* predicate of two different components colliding. The previous *saveStudentRecord* example, when created by a component named *record_server_1*, would result in the following predicate:

record_server_1_saveStudentRecord(P,S,SR) :- guard(P,[[sr,S],[section,gsi]],write),
    financial_aid_server_1_saveFinancialAid(P,S, SR),
    academic_record_server_1_saveAcademicReco rd(P,S,SR),
    student_employment_server_1_saveStudentEmp loyment(P,S,SR).

Notice that the three component names prefix each of their corresponding predicates, *saveFinancialAid, saveAcademicRecord,* and *saveStudentEmployment.* This avoids name collisions.

This section has presented a method for using logic programming to perform static and dynamic testing of access control properties before a DCS is actually composed. The next section explores the creation of an additional system model based on TLA (Temporal Logic of Actions) that permits determining whether the access control system can induce deadlocks and evaluating in more detail the dynamics of the composed DCS.

VALIDATION OF ACCESS CONTROL BEHAVIOR

The use of Temporal Logic of Actions (TLA) (Lamport, 2002) allows the validation of safety and liveness properties associated with the behavioral model of a distributed system. Whereas the goal of the Prolog-based DCS model in the previous section was to validate that access to system resources properly depends, statically, on access control guards and policies, the TLA-based model, introduced here to extend the control framework, serves to validate dynamic system properties to ensure that access control behaviors and policies do not detrimentally affect the dynamics of component interactions.

A single mathematical statement, in TLA, can represent the behavioral specification of a system, as shown below, where *Init* represents an initial predicate that specifies the set all of possible initial values for variables in the system and the *Next* predicate expresses the relation between the current and next state of the system. With the temporal operator □ (box) asserting that a formula is always true, $\Box[Next]_{vars}$ states that *Next* is true for every step in the system's behavior. The TLA formula for a system specification also contains of the *Liveness* predicate expressing the liveness requirements of the system

$$Spec == Init \wedge \Box[Next]_{vars} \wedge Liveness$$

The five components of the case study described earlier each have variables determining their state and are interconnected via communications channels that are also modeled as variables. The *Init* predicate is a conjunction of the initial predicate for each component as well as predicates defining the set of users in the system and the communications channels between the components.

> *Init* == /\ *UserTerminal_Init*
> /\ RecordServer_Init
> /\ AcademicServer_Init
> /\ FinancialAidServer_Init
> /\ StudentEmploymentServer_Init
> /\ Users_Init
> /\ Channels_Init

To describe how the system's state can change, the definition of the *Next* predicate also involves predicates defined for each system component and requires that there exist (∃) a thread *t* such that at least one of the component predicates is true. In other words, at any point, at least one component in the system can step to the next state in the system's evolution.

> *Next* == ∃ *t* ε *Threads:(UserTerminal(t)* \/
> RecordServer(t) \/
> AR_Server(t) \/
> FA_Server(t) \/
> SE_Server(t))

A TLA function models the synchronous communications channels between pairs of components; a record for each element of the set *Threads* in the function allows multiple concurrent communications channels to be active at any given time. Each record contains fields for the state of its channel, the request data being transmitted and a message from the replying component. The data field is also a record including information concerning the principal (*p*), the student record being accessed (*r*), the command to execute

(*c*), and any data needed to execute the command (*d*). Initially, all of the channels are set to the *ready* state and contain no information. Refer to Lamport (2002) for a discussion of the complete syntax of TLA. A total of eight channel variables are necessary to model communications among the five components in the case study. Because the user terminal can read only student records on the record server, the TLA-based model represents this as one channel where the following TLA expression initializes its value. The variable *ut_rs_save* represents the state of the channel between the *User Terminal* (ut) and the *Record Server* (rs) for executing the save command.

> *ut_rs_save = [t ε Threads |-> [state |->"ready",*
> *data |->[p|->("":>""), r|->"", c|->"", d|->""],*
> *message |->("":>"")]]*

A component responds to the caller by changing the state argument to "replied" and sending a message back to the caller in the following manner. TLA notation uses the ' (prime) to indicate the value of a channel variable after a transition. Therefore, the following statement defines the possible future value of the channel variable *ut_rs_save* in terms of the current state of the system. The new value *ut_rs_save*' is the same as the current value *ut_rs_save* except that its state argument becomes "*replied*", and it carries a response message for the current thread *t*. Through actions like these, TLA can model the communications between components.

> *ut_rs_save'=[ut_rs_save EXCEPT ![t]=[state |-> "replied",*
> *data |-> ut_rs_save[t].data,*
> *message |-> ("response" :> "student information"]]*

As with the previous Prolog modeling, it is necessary to use TLA to model user attributes, resource names, access control policies, and mechanisms for evaluating these policies within the TLA definition of each component. A function defines user attributes by mapping each attribute name to a value.

> *attribute = ("accessid" :> {"jdoe"} @@*
> *"roles" :> {"bursar"}@@*
> *"groups" :> {"employee"})*

The Prolog-based model represented resource names as a list of lists: *[[sr,S],[section,gsi]]*. A TLA-based model employs a function for the resource name. For instance, the following function represents all portions of the general student information of the student record for "hblake," so *resource["section"]* would return *"gsi."*

> *resource=("sr" :> "hblake" @@*
> *"section" :> "gsi" @@*
> *"part" :> "all")*

A single TLA operator models the policy evaluator. Given this basic user and resource information, it returns true or false after considering a series of logical conditions that represent the access control policy.

> *PolicyEvaluator(a,r,o) == ∨(∧r["section"]="gsi"*
> *∧ o="save" ∧ "owner" ε a["roles"])*
> ∨(∧r["section"]="gsi" ∧ o="load" ∧(∨ "student"
> ε a["groups"]
> ∨ "staff" ε a["groups"]))

This particular policy evaluator operator will give only students the ability to save their own general student information, but will allow any student or staff member to read the general student information for any student record. This form of policy is adequate for this case study, though it is possible in TLA to define custom operators with Java references that access some external policy evaluator rather than using a pure TLA model of the policy. With such a custom operator, it would be possible to perform a model check using the actual access control policy that is to be implemented in the final system rather than using a TLA representation of the policy. This would reduce the likelihood of error being introduced into the model.

With user security attributes and resource names defined as functions and operations represented with simple strings, it is now possible to define how to model access control guards. As before, the guard needs three pieces of information: user security attributes, resource name, and the operation to be performed. As with the Prolog-based model, it is possible to add dynamic attributes to the security attributes before evaluating the policy. The following example guard, from a record server, determines whether or not the user making the request is also the owner of the student record.

RS_Guard(a,r,o) == PolicyEvaluator([a EXCEPT
!["roles"]=IF (r["sr"] ε a["accessid"])
THEN a["roles"] U {"owner"}
ELSE a["roles"]], r, o)

If this is true, then it adds the dynamic attribute *owner* to the roles attribute using the set union operation, which TLA denotes with *"U."* It then submits the resulting new attributes, original resource name and operation to the policy evaluator operator. The *RS_Guard* operator will be a guard in the record server protecting access to any particular resource and is available for use in other TLA expressions to determine access authorizations. If it evaluates to true, then the record server returns a message containing a function mapping the general student information to "READ," indicating success in reading the record; otherwise, it sets the message to "BLOCKED," which indicates authorization failure. The follow predicate defines *ut_rs_read'* with respect to *ut_rs_read* when it includes the *RS_Guard* predicate.

```
ut_rs_read'=[ut_rs_read
        EXCEPT ![t]=[ state|->"replied",
                data|->ut_threads_data[t],
                message |->( "gsi" :> (IF RS_
Guard(ut_rs_read[t].data.p,

                        ut_rs_read[t].data.r,
                        ut_rs_read[t].data.
c)

                THEN "READ"
                ELSE "BLOCKED")
@@
                "ar" :> sr_ar_read[t].mes-
sage @@
                "fa" :> sr_fa_read[t].mes-
sage @@
                "se" :> sr_se_read[t].mes-
sage
                )                ]
```

Without defining liveness properties, there is no guarantee the system will ever take an action, even with properly defined *Init* and *Next* predicates. By defining *Liveness* with the weak fairness expression $WF_{vars}(Next)$, the specification at least guarantees that a *Next* step will eventually occur if *Next* is enabled forever.

Liveness == WF_{vars}(Next)

However, TLA allows validation of quite complex liveness properties using model checking. The following *Self_Read* predicate states, for all threads, that if the thread represents a student who is attempting to read her or his own student record, then eventually (~>) the communications channel will return that information. Therefore, such predicates are useful for verifying that the system specification allows all students to read their own student records.

Start_Read_Self(t) == /\ ENABLED(UT_Send_Read(t))

/\ ut_threads_data[t].r \in ut_threads_data[t].p["accessid"]

End_Read_Self(t) == /\ ENABLED(UT_Receive_Read(t))

/\ ut_threads_data[t].r \in ut_threads_data[t].p["accessid"]
/\ ut_rs_read[t].message["gsi"]="READ"
/\ ut_rs_read[t].message["ar"] ="READ"
/\ ut_rs_read[t].message["fa"] ="READ"
/\ ut_rs_read[t].message["se"] ="READ"

Self_Read ==\A t \in Threads: Start_Read_Self(t) ~> End_Read_Self(t)

By carefully designing TLA predicates representing system properties, the TLA model checker can evaluate all possible state transitions to validate that each property always holds. In this manner, is it possible to validate also that students can never change any other student's information and are always able to save their own information.

PROPERTY Self_Read Other_Student_Read Other_Student_Save Self_Save

TLA can model access control constructs in this way. With the help of such specifications, it is possible to validate that the composed TLA specifications are deadlock free and possess defined liveness properties.

A combination of Prolog-based and TLA-based models provides the DCS system developer with information for statically and dynamically validating a system composition before deployment, as well as for testing the impact of access control policies on the functionality of the system.

FUTURE TRENDS

The access control model presented above is a part of the ongoing UniFrame research effort. So, there are several areas where it can extend this model in the future. One is to automate the composition of a DCS's TLA specification from those of its components. Given a system design from the KB, the process of generating this model is systematic and should lend itself to automation. A tool for accomplishing this would speed the model checking process.

The Prolog-based access control modeling could be modified to provide better handling of the access control-based filtering of results. The current Prolog model is of a limited use in such situations because it gives no indication of what information the system releases.

The existing UniFrame System Generator and URDS systems include neither access control modeling nor additional security properties (such as encryption). These may be worthy of investigation and inclusion into the UniFrame Framework to strengthen it.

CONCLUSION

This chapter has presented an access control model for the UniFrame Approach that facilitates the inclusion of access control properties into the semiautomated process of generating distributed computing systems as advocated by the UniFrame research. The work presented here is partially inspired by that of Burt et al. (2003) on model-driven access control. Interpreting the Prolog-based and TLA-based models as platform independent models, Guard operators identify access control points in them and simple constructs identify resources in each model. This separates the access control policy from the component models and their implementations. This hides the policy model from components because each principal provides security attributes for itself at runtime. A principal simply submits these to the access control points that use them during policy evaluation; this happens outside of the components, so the business logic need not concern these attributes or their evaluation.

A component model may also possess a *Dynamic-ContextServer* for providing dynamic attributes to a principal's security attribute list when appropriate. The UniFrame research has successfully implemented, and experimented with, a prototype based on these models. Thus, the access control framework described in this chapter is a promising approach to making access control characteristics of individual software components composable, thereby rendering the properties of systems specifiable and predictable.

ACKNOWLEDGMENT

This material is based on the work supported by the U.S. Office of Naval Research under award number N00014-01-1-0746.

REFERENCES

Burt, C., Bryant, B., Raje, R., Olson, A., & Auguston, M. (2003). Model driven security: Unification of authorization models for fine-grain access control. In *Proceedings of the 7ᵗʰ IEEE International Enterprise Distributed Object Computing Conference* (pp. 159-173) Los Alamitos, CA: IEEE Press. Retrieved May 5, 2008, from http://www.cs.iupui.edu/uniFrame

Common Criteria Project Sponsoring Organizations. (2004). *Common criteria for information technology security evaluation, part 2: Security functional requirements, version 2.3.* Retrieved May 5, 2008, from http://www.commoncriteriaportal.org/public/files/ccpart2v2.3.pdf

Crespi, A. (2005). *An access control model for the uniframe framework.* Unpublished M.S. Thesis, Department of Computer and Information Science, Indiana University Purdue University Indianapolis, Indiana. Retrieved May 5, 2008, from http://www.cs.iupui.edu/uniFrame/

Ferraiolo, D., & Kuhn, R. (1992). Role-based access controls. *15ᵗʰ National Computer Security Conference.* Retrieved May 5, 2008, from http://csrc.nist.gov/rbac/Role_Based_Access_Control-1992.html

Huang, Z. (2003). *The UniFrame system-level generative programming framework.* Unpublished M.S. Thesis, Department of Computer and Information Science, Indiana University Purdue University Indianapolis, Indiana. Retrieved May 5, 2008, from http://www.cs.iupui.edu/uniFrame/

Katuri, P. (2006). *Experimenting with multilevel matching concepts for software components.* Unpublished M.S. Project, Department of Computer and Information Science, Indiana University Purdue

University Indianapolis, Indiana. Retrieved May 5, 2008, from http://www.cs.iupui.edu/uniFrame/pubs-openaccess/katuriProjectFinal.pdf

Katzke, S. (2002). *Future directions of the common criteria (CC) and the common evaluation methodology (CEM).* National Institute of Standards and Technology. Retrieved May 5, 2008, from http://www.ipa.go.jp/security/fy13/evalu/event/20020328/docs/29-2Katzke.pdf

Lamport, L. (2002). Specifying Systems: The TLA+ Language and Tools for Hardware and Software Engineers. Boston, MA:Addison Wesley Publication Company.

Olson, A., Raje, R., Bryant, B., Burt, C., & Auguston, M. (2005). UniFrame: A unified framework for developing service-oriented, component-based, distributed software systems. In Z. Stojanovic, & A. Dahanayake (Eds.). *Service Oriented Software System Engineering: Challenges and Practices*, (Chapter IV, pp. 68-87). Hershey, PA: Idea Group, Inc.

Raje, R. (2000). UMM: Unified meta-object model for open distributed systems. In *Proceedings of 4ᵗʰ IEEE International Conference on Algorithms and Architecture for Parallel Processing* (pp. 454-465). Los Alamitos, CA: IEEE Press. Retrieved May 5, 2008, from http://www.cs.iupui.edu/uniFrame

Raje, R., Auguston, M., Bryant, B., Olson, A., & Burt, C. (2001). A unified approach for the integration of distributed heterogeneous software components. In *Proceedings of the Workshop on Engineering Automation for Software Intensive System Integration*, SEAC technical report (pp. 109-119). Monterey, CA: U.S. Naval Postgraduate School. Retrieved May 5, 2008, from http://www.cs.iupui.edu/uniFrame

Sandhu, R., & Samarati, P. (1994). Access control: Principles and practice. *IEEE Communications Magazine, 32*(9), 40-48.

Saunders, G., Hitchens, M., & Varadharajan, V. (2001). Role-based access control and the access control matrix. *ACM SIGOPS Operating Systems Review, 35*(4), 6-20.

Siram, N. (2002). *An architecture for discovery of heterogeneous software components.* Unpublished M.S. Thesis, Department of Computer and Information Science, Indiana University Purdue University Indianapolis, Indiana. Retrieved May 5, 2008, from http://www.cs.iupui.edu/uniFrame/

UniFrame Research Group. (2006). *UniFrame home site*. Retrieved May 5, 2008, at http://www.cs.iupui.edu/uniFrame

KEY TERMS

Access Control: An access control is a mechanism to enforce access privileges to different entities in a computing system.

Contained Resource: A resource is contained in a component if the component encapsulates the resource and carries out operations on the resource.

Distributed Computing Systems (DCS): A distributed computing system consists of networked processors, each with its own memory, that communicate with each other by sending messages.

Guard: A guard is a logical condition that evaluates to true or false for protecting a resource within a component.

Prolog: Prolog is a logic programming language that acts as a theorem prover.

Protected Resource: A resource is a protected if the component that encapsulates that resource protects it via access control guards.

Student Information System: It contains necessary information about students enrolled in a university. It serves here as a simplified case study for describing the proposed model of access control.

Temporal Logic of Actions (TLA): TLA is a technique for specifying the behavior of concurrent systems.

UniFrame: This is a unifying framework that supports a seamless integration of distributed and heterogeneous components.

UniFrame Resource Discovery System (URDS): URDS provides an infrastructure for proactively discovering components deployed over a network.

Chapter XXII
Implications of FFIEC Guidance on Authentication in Electronic Banking

Manish Gupta
State University of New York, Buffalo, USA

JinKyu Lee
Oklahoma State University, USA

H. R. Rao
State University of New York, Buffalo, USA

ABSTRACT

The Internet has emerged as the dominant medium in enabling banking transactions. Adoption of e-banking has witnessed an unprecedented increase over the last few years. In today's online financial services environment, authentication is the bedrock of information security. Simple password authentication is the prevailing paradigm, but its weaknesses are all too evident in today's context. In order to address the nature of similar vulnerabilities, in October 2005, the Federal Financial Institutions Examination Council (FFIEC)—which comprises the United States' five federal banking regulators—published joint guidance entitled Authentication in an Internet Banking Environment, recommending that financial institutions deploy security measures to reliably authenticate their online banking customers. The analysis of FFIEC guidance presented in the article are with the view to equip the reader with a glimpse of the issues involved in understanding the guidance for specific banking organization that may help towards learned and better decisions regarding compliance and improved security. The chapter will allow Information Technology managers to understand information assurance issues in e-banking in a holistic manner, and help them make recommendations and actions to ensure security of e-banking components.

INTRODUCTION AND BACKGROUND

The Internet is an integral part of our daily lives, and the proportion of people who expect to be able to manage their bank accounts anywhere, anytime is constantly growing and Internet banking has come of age as a crucial component of any financial institution's multichannel strategy (Hiltgen et al., 2006). Information about financial institutions, their customers, and their transactions is, by necessity, extremely sensitive; thus, doing such business via a public network introduces new challenges for security and trustworthiness (Hiltgen, Kramp, &Weigold, 2006). Adoption of e-banking has witnessed an unprecedented increase over the last few years. 20% of Internet users now access online banking services, a total that will reach 33% by 2006, according to the Online Banking Report (Gupta, Rao, & Upadhyaya, 2004). By 2010, over 55 million U.S. households will use online banking and e-payments services, which are tipped as "growth areas." Any Internet banking system must solve the issues of authentication, confidentiality, integrity, and nonrepudiation, which means it must ensure that only qualified people can access an Internet banking account, that the information viewed remains private and cannot be modified by third parties, and that any transactions made are traceable and verifiable (Hiltgen et al., 2006).

INTERNET BANKING AND AUTHENTICATION

The actual and perceived threats to Internet-based banking define the need for a set of interrelated security services to provide protection to all parties that can benefit from Web banking in a secure environment (Gupta et al., 2004). The risks of doing business with unauthorized or incorrectly identified persons in an Internet banking environment can result in financial loss and reputation damage through fraud, disclosure of customer information, corruption of data, or unenforceable agreements.

Security for financial transactions is of vital importance to financial institutions providing or planning to provide service delivery to customers over the public Internet, as well as to suppliers of products, services, and solutions for Internet based e-commerce. With security incidents such as identity theft and account hijacking undermining customer confidence, slowing adoption rates and threatening profits, it is very evident that requirement to go beyond mere passwords for authentication is real and important. The recent FFIEC guidance on authentication in online banking reports "Account fraud and identity theft are frequently the result of single factor (e.g., ID/password) authentication exploitation" (FFIEC, 2005). In today's online financial services environment, authentication is the bedrock of information security. Username/password authentication is the prevailing paradigm, but its weaknesses are all too evident on today's Web. Password reuse, insecure passwords, and poor password

management practices open a world of attacks by themselves (Jones, 2006). It is high time for financial institutions re-evaluate authentication strategy, in light of the fact that cyber attacks are only going to grow in sophistication and in impact.

CHAPTER ORGANIZATION AND CONTRIBUTION

The chapter discusses impact and issues surrounding FFIEC guidelines for stronger authentication requirements for online banking. The chapter analyses the opportunities and costs of initiatives that financial institutions have to undertake to comply by these guidelines. First the chapter discusses implications, requirements, and risks involved with the authentication guideline and how they interact with one another in determination of an execution plan. This encompasses the assessment phase of the guidance evaluation. Then, the chapter discusses various state-of-art authentication technologies, processes, and methods that can be reviewed and investigated further for their appropriateness in a specific organizational and business context. This is the compliance and implementation phase. Here, the chapter demonstrates how components of assessment phase interact with compliance and implementation phase. Figure 1 illustrates the architecture of the guidance evaluation methodology and interactions amongst its components. The chapter concludes with commentary on the analyses and recommendations.

THE FFIEC GUIDANCE

The Federal Financial Institutions Examination Council (FFIEC) is an interagency council set up to develop standards for the federal auditing of financial institutions by bodies such as the Federal Reserve System and the Federal Deposit Insurance Corp. (FDIC). In October 2005, the Federal Financial Institutions Examination Council (FFIEC)—which comprises the United States' five federal banking regulators—published joint guidance entitled *Authentication in an Internet Banking Environment*, recommending that financial institutions deploy security measures to reliably authenticate their online banking customers. The new guidelines are not a law, but are more like best practices that banks will be audited against by the

Figure 1. Framework for evaluation of FFIEC guidance in a specific business

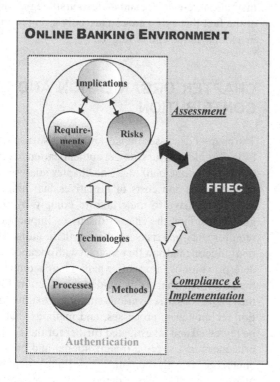

end of 2006, a spokesman from the Federal Reserve said. At that time, federal examiners will begin documenting situations where financial institutions are not yet in compliance (ComputerWorld, http://www.computerworld.com/securitytopics/security/story/0,10801, 105599,00.html). In this guidance, the FFIEC makes it clear that it considers single-factor authentication, *"as the only control mechanism,"* inadequate for online banking (Epaynews, http://www.epaynews. com/statistics/bankstats.html).

ASSESSMENT PHASE

Regarding its guidance, the FFIEC says, banks should assess their own risk and decide which solutions best meet their individual needs. It strongly recommends that all financial institutions undertake a comprehensive assessment of the risks associated with their online banking services—including customer authentication, verification of new customers, and monitoring and reporting—and adopt authentication methods that reduce these risks. These methods are described as mul-

tiple-factor authentication, layered security, or *"other controls"* that supplement single-factor authentication. The five regulators involved have stated that financial institutions will be expected to achieve compliance with the FFIEC's guidance by the end of 2006. This section will outline the nature of the guidance and shows how to make it operational. Here, we will also provide a discourse on business risk and necessity management issues along with authentication strategies. This section can help technology and security managers comprehend what does the guidance mean to their organization insight of specific organizational and business characteristics.

Implications

There are several factors banks should consider while evaluating solutions and approach for their e-authentication efforts including: supporting industry and technology standards—both present and future, utilizing of vendor-supported, commercial off-the-shelf (COTS) software, gaining buy-in from agency stakeholders, conducting operational pilots, and incorporating lessons learned into the program an tracking program milestones and performance measures in a strategic business plan. Banks should adopt a holistic view of solution costs in their evaluation of authentication solutions. Specifically, the following types of costs ought to be considered in order to better understand a solution's total cost of ownership (TCO) (Yeo, 2007):

- **Acquisition costs:** This category refers to upfront infrastructure costs and can include both hardware (e.g., server) and software (e.g., licensing) costs, and future requirements for extended capabilities.
- **Deployment costs:** This category encompasses factors such as internal IT employees and vendor time required to deploy the solution (plan, install, and configure the solution). Additionally, this category should also include the cost of shipping the authentication devices to customers and provisioning them for the first time.
- **On-going costs:** This category includes maintenance and support expenses, as well as hardware replacement, due to failure or built-in obsolescence, are examples of on-going costs.

Surveys have indicated that between 15-30% of tokens, for example, are lost and need to be replaced annually. As such, this usually constitutes the largest cost component (up to 70% in larger scale deployments) and is usually attributable to replacement, distribution and re-provisioning costs (Yeo, 2007). On-going administration costs are also included and this refers to costs to maintain the deployment as well as end-user support and helpdesk costs. Support and help desk costs are typically the hidden costs of deploying a strong authentication solution.

Requirements

The FFIEC guidance provides high level guidelines for financial institutions to approach compliance in following three broad stages:

1. Identification and assessment of risks associated with its Internet-based technologies and services. Risks should be evaluated in light of the type of customer, the customer's transactional capabilities, the sensitivity of customer information, the ease of using the communication method, and the volume of transactions.

2. Assessment of the adequacy of authentication techniques and adjust its information security program in light of any relevant changes in technology, the sensitivity of its customer information, new or changing risks and the evolving sophistication of compromise techniques, and other internal or external threats to information. The compliance and assessment phase of this chapter discusses this in greater details.

3. Implement effective risk mitigation strategies.

Yeo (2007) proposes the following five evaluation criteria for choosing a suitable authentication solution:

- **Ease of Use.** User acceptance is a critical success factor for any security solution. If a particular approach is too cumbersome or confusing, users—especially in the consumer domain—will either turn to expensive alternative channels or disengage completely. Both of these outcomes negate any potential positive impact from improved security.

- **Security.** Naturally, the solution must adequately defend against phishing, spyware, hacking, man-in-the-middle attacks, and other threats driving organizations to adopt strong authentication. The solution must provide protection during "normal" usage, as well as during loss periods pending replacement of a device or card. Authentication solutions must provide mechanisms to determine the authenticity of the Web site being accessed, as well as provide the user's online identity better protection by providing an additional factor for authentication beyond the password.

- **Flexibility.** Increasingly, authentication is being performed in conjunction with an assessment of risk. For example, a user checking their account balance from home has a different risk profile than attempting an interbank transfer from a foreign country. Online organizations must be able to choose from a variety of authentication methods that best align with the risk of a given transaction. This also allows authentication to be only as invasive as required by the risk to improve user acceptance.

- **Scalability and Cost-Effectiveness.** The chosen authentication solution should be able to meet the evolving needs of a growing bank. As such, they should reflect the financial realities of deploying to a large, diverse customer population. Banks may need to look at the total cost for the solution, including: the original license costs, annual maintenance fees, the cost of distribution and loss replacement if there's a physical element of the solution, and the maintenance implications based on the device's resilience (hardiness) and longevity. Without addressing these considerations, any mutual and strong authentication solution risks not being effective at protecting online identities and restoring customer confidence in online services.

- **Accessibility across different interaction channels.** Given the efforts to implement and roll out consumer strong authentication for Internet activity, smart organizations will leverage the solution beyond the standard Web browser environment. They will prefer a solution that works with Web-enabled Personal Digital Assistants, in phone interactions, at ATMs, and at tellers and other points of service.

Financial institutions should also pay attention to legal considerations such as (Hayes, Judy, & Ritter, 2006):

- **Licensing of new technologies.** When new authentication technologies are acquired, the related purchase or licensing agreements provide an opportunity for institutions to consider and allocate some of the new types of risks associated with those technologies. For example, biometric technologies, which require the capture and storage of new identifying data, may justify special terms regarding warranties, security controls, and allocation of liability in the event of service failures.

- **Customer service agreements.** Existing customer service agreements may require amendment in order to obtain the consent of customers to the new authentication methods. In addition, terms addressing limitations of liability should be examined in order to confirm that those terms work effectively with the potential liabilities presented by the new authentication technologies.

- **Privacy policies.** Various authentication technologies can involve the capture of additional personal information—or different uses of personal information—that has already been captured and stored by a financial institution. Existing privacy policies may require revision to accommodate these practices; of course, these revisions may be accomplished in many instances concurrently with related customer service agreement revisions.

Risks

Many institutions adopt a standardized view of electronic transactions, implementing similar procedures and authentication controls for transactions with widely varying economic value and risks. As part of the required risk assessments, financial institutions may conclude that different terms and conditions are appropriate based on the nature of the transactions with which the new authentication methods will be employed.

Designing security levels commensurate with risk levels has a long history and is formally described in a number of sources (Anderson & Rayford, 1991; Baker, 1992). The risk assessment requirement in the guidance implies that banks have an existing risk assessment process and methodology, which should form the basis of evaluating and justifying additional controls beyond usernames and passwords. There are three general risk management strategies that financial institutions could adopt to meet the new regulatory requirements for online authentication (Hayes et al., 2006):

- **Standardized procedures** that require multifactor authentication for all transactions and for all online customers.
- **Layered authentication** based on the transaction type. Under this approach, accessing informational features or account balances requires minimal authentication. However, fund transfers to third parties or bills payments require higher levels of authentication.
- **Per-transaction, real-time risk assessment.** This approach uses sophisticated software to assess the risk index associated with each individual transaction in real time and assign a degree of authentication based on a risk score.

Banks should understand the relative costs and benefits of these different risk management strategies and tailor one which best suits their scope of services and customer risk profile. Standardized procedures could result in an increased burden on customers who use online services only or principally for low-risk transactions such as checking account balances or interest rates (Yeo, 2007). Layered authentication may provide an easier sign-on process for customers seeking only information, but may require costly partitioning and re-programming of online services. Per-transaction risk assessments are likely to produce the most user-friendly customer experience, but require the use of expensive software and may result in banks' dependence on particular software vendors.

IMPLEMENTATION AND COMPLIANCE PHASE

There are a variety of technologies and methodologies financial institutions can use to authenticate customers. These methods include the use of customer passwords, personal identification numbers (PINs), digital certificates (Schneier, 2005) using a public key infrastructure (PKI), physical devices such as smart cards, one-time passwords (OTPs), USB plug-ins or other types of "tokens", transaction profile scripts, biometric identification, and others. The level of risk protection afforded by each of these techniques varies. The selection and use of authentication technologies and methods should depend upon the results of the financial institution's risk assessment process (FFIEC, 2005). The section discusses these authentication technologies and methodologies in depth. For example,

Table 1. Authentication

Strong Authentication Considerations (FinanceTech, http://www.financetech.com/news/showArticle.jhtml?articleID=192202387)
Be easy for customers to use
Allow customers to use it anywhere
Be cost-effective
Provide appropriate levels of security
Be easily manageable
Work across different channels of interaction

for confidentiality and integrity, Secure Sockets Layer/ Transport Layer Security (SSL/ TLS) is the de facto Internet banking standard, whereas for authentication and nonrepudiation, no single scheme has become predominant yet (Hiltgen et al., 2006). This Section of the chapter explains costs and benefits offered by various authentication technologies, methodologies. Basically, this section will aid managers understand various aspects of authentication implementation based on their particular needs as would be evidenced by the previous phase on assessment. The chapter concludes by summarizing the analyses of the two complementary phases of the evaluation process of FFIEC guidance in form of operational recommendations.

Authentication Technologies and Processes

Faced with an impending deadline, many organizations are taking a phased approach to getting compliance today that can easily evolve to include multifactor authentication over time. We discuss some of the most common authentication technologies and processes next that can aid managers in financial services understand the nature and scope of available technologies as they could pertain to achieving compliance with the FFIEC guidelines.

In general, the three factors that might be used in an authentication system are:

- Something a user knows (a password or Personal Identification Number (PIN));
- Something a user has (a device such as a smart card or token);
- Something a user is (biometrics).

Traditionally, passwords and PINs have been used as the most commonly used authentication factor. The benefits and drawbacks of a number of technologies addressing each of the above factors are discussed next:

i. Passwords
ii. Smart Cards and Tokens
iii. USB Authentication Tokens
iv. Number Generation Tokens
v. Biometrics

i. Passwords

Using "something that a user knows" to authenticate an individual usually means requiring them to demonstrate knowledge of a password or a pass phrase. PINs may be viewed as a specific subset of passwords comprising of numeric characters only. The idea of authentication-by password is a simple one. The individual lays claim to a particular identity, often represented by a username, and then supports this claim by demonstrating knowledge of some "secret" information known only to that individual and stored by the authenticating system for validation.

TECHNICAL REVIEW AND USER IMPACT ASSESSMENT

Passwords have been built into systems and used effectively as the sole authentication mechanism for many years. It is a technically mature technology, although passwords suffer from two conflicting requirements: the passwords must be sufficiently "random" to prevent them being guessed by an attacker, yet simultaneously not too difficult for the user to remember. The security of a password-based authentication system relies on achieving the right balance between the two. The concept of a user ID and password is a cost effective and efficient method of maintaining a shared secret between a user and a computer system. Identifying a user is essential for the application of security in the form of permissions to various objects, processes and access to resources. User authentication in computer systems based on passwords has been a cornerstone of computer security for decades. The authentication process is embedded in many systems, in many different variations. In each case, one common aspect is the focus on mapping authentication data to specific authorized users for a specific application (Conklin, Dietrich, & Walz, 2004). This can be represented as presenting something you know and others would not know. An example is a user ID and password combination, one of the simplest forms of user authentication (Anderson & Rayford, 1991; Manber, 1996; Menkus, 1988; Riddle, Miron, & Semo, 1989). Remembrance of passwords is one of the cornerstones of the current password-based authentication system (Adams & Sasse, 1997; Pond et al., 2000; Smith, 1987; Zviran & Haga, 1999). Complex passwords will often be written down, making them vulnerable to discovery, whereas passwords that are easier to remember will be easier to crack through dictionary and social engineering attacks. Widespread usage of password-protected systems accessed by the Internet has caused an explosion in the number of accounts per user and is revealing issues associated with users' difficulty in remembering passwords (Jones, 2002; Microsoft Canada, 2000; Swanson, 2003).

Note on Costs: Password systems are often cheapest to implement than other authentication mechanisms because they tend to require less investment in hardware and generality of the software. However, this lower initial expenditure does not necessarily mean that a password system is a cheaper option, as there are hidden costs involved in managing and maintaining passwords. Mindful of the fallibility of conventional passwords, several researchers have suggested simple, cost-effective techniques that might be useful adjuncts to them (Smith, 1987; Zviran & Haga, 1990; Zviran & Haga, 1994). Users will always forget their passwords (whether or not they are complicated), so there needs to be a mechanism in place to deal with forgotten (or compromised) passwords. For large networks this may require the provision of a dedicated password helpdesk. To make matters even more complicated, it is good security practice to force users to change their passwords on a regular basis.

ii.   Smart Cards and Tokens

Since 1970s, magnetic cards have enabled a quick and reliable identification, based on information stored on the magnetic stripe. In 1990-e5 the smart card was introduced (Cagliostro, 2004; DiGiorgio, 2006). Smart card is a flat plastic card with a chip in it, generally credit card-sized, following the ISO 7816 standard. They can perform multiple functions, for example combining IT network and building access control with storage of information such as medical records, financial information and biometric templates. There are large-scale deployments of smart cards today, such as payment EMV (Europay, Mastercard, and Visa) cards and the US Department of Defense (DOD) Common Access Cards (CACs). Smart card is a commonly accepted name for every such card, but there are two main categories of smart cards: Memory card and Smart card. Memory cards only have a memory chip, with nonprogrammable logic on it with only purpose to store data. Smart cards have a chip, which is essentially a microprocessor with internal memory. Smart cards can further be divided in two additional categories: *contact* smart cards and *contact-less* smart cards. The contact smart card requires insertion into a smart card reader in order to be used. The reader is connected directly to a conductive micro-module on the surface of the card, through which physical commands and data are transmitted to the card. A contact-less smart card requires no physical contact to the reader and is sufficient to bring the card close to the card reader in order to initiate the transmission of data and commands. One advantage of contact-less smart devices is a longer hardware lifetime, as there is no wear through contact with a reader for most applications. Apart from their low-cost to banks, smartcards are seen to be able to support merchant loyalty schemes and to provide convenience to consumers (Visa, 1997).

Technical Review and User Impact Assessment

Though Smart cards are technically mature and widely used., they can be exposed to two types of attacks. Invasive attacks can be carried out by physical re-engineering of the card's integrated circuit to expose the information stored within the card. However, smart cards are tamper evident and an invasive attack will cause some damage to the card's surface, thereby alerting the owner to the attack. Noninvasive attacks rely on observing and manipulating the card's operat-

Figure 2. Smart card

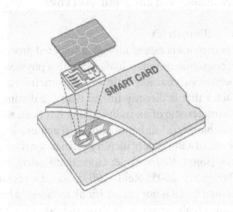

ing environment and/or the signals that it transmits or receives in an attempt to gather useful information. If the authentication secret held on a smart card becomes compromised, it can be easily revoked. A new secret or a new card can be issued to the authorized user. Smart cards are widely used, as they are acceptable to most users. Various smart card products have been certified to EAL4 under the Common Criteria scheme. An example of smart card is in Figure 2.

Note on Costs: Since smart cards require a reader device, the rough cost of a PKI enabled contact smart card and reader will be in the range of $30-$60 each based on a distribution base of 1000, while contactless smart card cost could be range of $100. Also should be noted the deployment and support costs associated with maintaining infrastructure for smart cards.

iii.   USB Authentication Tokens

USB authentication token is small hardware devices that plug directly into the computer's USB port. Typically such tokens consist of a hard plastic outer casing that houses the electronic circuit and a metal USB port connector at one end. Although their appearance is completely different, USB authentication tokens are functionally very similar to the smart cards discussed in the previous section (Pomeroy & Shorter, 2006). A picture of USB authentication is as shown in Figure 3.

Technical Review and User Impact Assessment

One drawback of USB authentication tokens over smart cards is the amount of information or personalization that can be displayed on their surface. Although tech-

nically mature, USB authentication tokens take up a very small share in today's market, and are mainly used for network access purposes. USB tokens are bulkier than smart cards, but may be carried easily on a key ring and can be used in PKI environments (Pomeroy & Shorter, 2006). An example of this token is shown in Figure 3. They are more robust than smart cards as the chip is held within a hard outer casing. They could also be filled with hard epoxy resin, and therefore there is more scope for tamper resistance measures. However, these tokens can be less tamper evident than smart cards (Pomeroy & Shorter, 2006). If an attacker is able to remove and subsequently replace the hard plastic casing, attacks on the chip may go unnoticed. To avoid this, tamper evident seals can be incorporated onto the token surface. Most of the USB authentication tokens use electronic chips that are evaluated at E4 security level (equivalent to EAL5). FIPS 140-1 Level 2 certification (demonstrating tamper-evident seals or coatings) is also achieved by the main vendors of USB tokens.

Note on Costs: As they do not require a separate reader, the cost of USB authentication tokens is lower than that of smart cards. Token cost per user is likely to be in the region of $50. As with smart cards, there will be other costs associated with the implementation of this technology, such as PKI and underlying system costs as well as support costs.

iv.   Number Generation Tokens

Password-generator tokens are calculator-like devices that generate dynamic passwords that the user types in. The token is synchronized with the authentication system, which contains the same code as the token. Thus, this technology is based upon the fact that the system generates the same sequence of numbers at the same time. The user enters the number provided by the token onto the system and is authenticated if this number matches that produced by the system itself. For two-factor authentication, a keypad can be put on the token to allow PIN authentication to the token itself. The value of such a design is that there is no way of deducing the secret value. Even malicious software running in the machine to which the token is connected cannot determine the secret value.

Technical Review and User Impact Assessment

This technology is technically mature. The tokens are commonly used, mainly for remote authentication. The tokens are robust and tamper modification resistant as the chip is encased in a hard shell. This technology does not require any hardware for reader. The token has a numeric keypad with which to enter the number onto the system. However, as the number must be physically entered, the process is more user intensive and prone to human error. The requirement for the user to type in a long string of digits, plus the bulkiness of the devices means that user acceptance of this technology may be lower than that of smart cards and USB authentication tokens (Pomeroy & Shorter, 2006). As these tokens are continually performing calculations, they use a relatively large amount of power. In the absence of a reader, the power source is internal, and thus these tokens have a limited lifespan. This authentication technology relies on the fact that the user will enter the same sequence of numbers as is produced by the system within a brief window of time. The major drawback to such a system is that it relies on synchronization between the token and the authenticating system that requires more maintenance. Number generation tokens are not suitable for use with a PKI as there is no scope for storing private keys on them. There is also no electronic interface to the system, which would be essential for PKI functions (Pomeroy & Shorter, 2006). As there is no electronic interface with the computer system, the risks of electronic attack are reduced. The attacker must obtain the token before performing such attacks. This technology uses symmetric keys in the process of generating the "pseudorandom" number. This is a potential weakness of the authentication process, but as the symmetric key is combined with a timestamp, this makes the task of the attacker much more difficult because they must also correctly deduce the time and combination method used. Number generation tokens can be revoked if they become compromised, and new tokens can be issued easily. Figure 4 shows ActiveCard®, an example of random number generator product.

Note on Costs: The cost of a number generation token is roughly $15, based on user base of 1000. Extra

costs will be required, such as server software for this technology and annual support costs.

v   Biometrics

Biometrics is essentially an automated process of the recognition of individuals through a physiological or behavioral characteristic. Since biometrics is the only factor that is directly linked with the distinguishing characteristic of an individual, it has been advocated that biometric authentication will achieve increasing levels of assurance of identity verification (Ortega-Garcia, Bigun, Reynolds, & Gonzalez-Rodriguez, 2004; Palmgren, 2005; Reid, 2004). Recent research has shown that it is not very difficult to "steal" a biometric trait, create its copy, and use the fake trait to attack biometric systems (Leyden, 2002; Thalheim et al., 2002; Kinstey, 2002). One such biometric fingerprint reader product by Digital Persona, a security product company is shown in Figure 5.

Figure 4. ActivCard random number generator

Figure 5. DigitalPersona fingerprint scanner

Figure 3. USB authentication tool

Technical Review and User Impact Assessment

As with other technologies, biometric authentication systems are vulnerable to attacks, such as transmission, replay, and spoofing. The advantage of biometrics is that, for most cases you don't leave home without them, and they cannot be forgotten. Disadvantages are many, including not being able to change them if needed, or use them for all functions as they are not secret and are not possessed by nonhuman entities needing authentication (Matyas & Riha, 2003). There are many different types of biometric, although the most commonly used are physiological ones: fingerprint and hand geometry, facial recognition, and iris scanning. For the authentication of a user, a capture device (biometric reader) takes a measurement, known as a template, of the particular characteristic (e.g., an electronic representation of the fingerprint) and this measurement is compared with a previously stored template. The authentication decision is then made based on the result of this comparison. Examples of the biometric methods employed today include (Langenderfer & Linnhoff, 2005):

- **Fingerprint verification:** Used by police organizations around the world, fingerprint verification is the most common biometric authentication method in use today. Improvements to scanning techniques and enrollment methods have reduced the instances of false rejection experienced in many early fingerprint verification systems.
- **Retinal and iris scanning:** These biometric processes involve examination of patterns found

in the human eye. Retinal scanning is very accurate but requires a user to place his or her eye very close to a scanner.

- **Voice verification:** This form of biometric requires a user to speak a specified phrase into a microphone. Speech patterns are analyzed and compared to the user's prerecorded voiceprint.

This technology is not as technically mature as the cards and tokens discussed previously. However, the rate of development and adoption has increased recently in response to the threat of terrorism, the U.S. Enhanced Border Security Act and identity theft crackdown. The major uses of biometrics today are in prisons, at airports, passport/visa integration, and for immigration purposes. Unlike passwords, cards and tokens, the use of biometrics as the authentication mechanism is an inexact science. For any one individual, it is highly unlikely that two measurements taken of the same characteristic will be exactly the same. Unfortunately, there is a low user acceptance of biometrics. There are several reasons for this, including health and safety issues, association with criminal databases and users' fears that a third party may be able to deduce sensitive personal information such as certain medical conditions from the stored information (Pomeroy & Shorter, 2006). Some users may be unable to use the system at all. As the biometric characteristic is part of the user, it cannot be forgotten, lost or stolen. Therefore this technology is more convenient than devices that a user must carry around and certain types of attack relevant to cards or tokens are eliminated. It is also unlikely that this form of authentication technology would be "shared"

Table 2. Examples of common two-factor authentication with PC, ActivCard, and GSM mobile phones (Jorgensen, 2007)

TECHNOLOGY	TWO FACTOR AUTHENTICATION	
	A secret the user has	*A secret the user knows*
PC with signature file.	A secret key stored in the signature file.	A password. The password is required for each use of the private key.
ActivCard: Processor capable of cryptographic operations.	A secret key stored on the ActivCard.	A PIN code. The PIN code is required each time the card is used to generate a password.
GSM mobile phone: Processor on SIM-card is capable of cryptographic operations.	A secret key stored on the SIM-card.	A PIN code. The PIN code is required when the phone is switched on.

with a colleague for convenience (Pomeroy & Shorter, 2006). Storing users' biometric templates means that the Data Protection Act will apply with the use of this technology.

Note on Costs: *The cost of a biometric reader will be in the region of $30 each based on a user-base of 1000. There are also associated annual support costs to be taken into consideration.*

DISCUSSIONS AND CONCLUSION

Financial organizations have traditionally been at the forefront of security, and they should maintain this posture in the Internet era (Slewe & Hoogenboom, 2004). Countering the threat of fraud is a continuing process requiring constant vigilance and keeping one step ahead of the fraudsters. Ultimately, the choice of authentication solutions will also be different for each bank, depending on its assets, the risks the organization considers acceptable, and the costs of the (considered) security measures.

We have analyzed several relevant authentication technologies that can aid managers in financial services to make informed decisions in complying with the FFIEC guidelines. However, there are further issues that must be addressed and questions that must be answered when considering which technologies to deploy in a specific environment. One helpful consideration is to determine to what extent the technology should be compatible with existing infrastructure and ever more changing regulatory and technological landscapes. Finally, current policy should be analyzed and a gap analysis undertaken and resolved, where appropriate, with respect to using the technology in the planned environment. No single security technology offers a "silver bullet." The choice of an authentication system requires trade-offs against customer convenience and acceptability (Wheatley, 2005). The discussions and presentations in this chapter provide insights into details of compliance with the FFIEC guidelines in form of a comprehensive dissertation on implications, requirements, risks and technologies.

REFERENCES

Adams, A., & Sasse, M.A. (1997). Users are not the enemy. *Communications of the ACM, 42*, 41-46.

Anderson, J., & Rayford, Vaughn. (1991, September). Guide to understanding identification and authentication in trusted systems (light blue book). *National Computer Security Center NCSC-TG-017.*

Baker, D.B. (1992, May). Assessing controlled access protection (violet book). *National Computer Security Center NCSC-TG-028.*

Cagliostro, Charles. (2004). *Smart cards primer.* Retrieved May 6, 2008, from http://www.smartcardalliance.ordindustriyn fo/smart cards orimer.cfni

Conklin, A., Dietrich, G., & Walz, D. (2004, January 5-8). Password-based authentication: A system perspective. In *System Sciences Proceedings of the 37th Annual Hawaii International Conference* (pp. 10).

DiGiorgio, R. (2006). *Smart cards: A primer.* Retrieved May 6, 2008, from http://www.iavaworld.com/iavaworld/1i2w--1997/iw-12-iavadev nhtml

Federal Financial Institutions Examination Council (FFIEC). (2005). *Authentication in an Internet banking environment.* Retrieved May 6, 2008, from http://www.ffiec.gov/pdf/authentication_guidance.pdf

Gupta, M., Rao, R. & Upadhyaya, S. (2004, July-September). Electronic banking and information assurance issues: Survey and synthesis. *Journal of Organizational and End User Computing, 16*(3), 1-21.

Hayes, B.S., Judy, H.L., & Ritter, J.B. (2006). FFIEC issues new guidance on authentication in online transactions. *Banking & Financial Services Policy Report, 25*(2), 1-3.

Hiltgen, A., Kramp, T., &Weigold, T. (2006, March/April). Secure Internet banking authentication. *IEEE Security and Privacy.*

Jones, M.B. (2006, March). The identity metasystem: A user-centric. *Inclusive Web authentication solution position paper for the W3C workshop on transparency and usability of Web authentication.* New York City. Retrieved May 6, 2008, from http://research.microsoft.com/~mbj/papers/InfoCard_W3C_Web_Authentication.pdf

Jones, T. (2002). Too many secrets? Password proliferation leads to user fatigue. *Columbia News Service—Columbia University Graduate School of Journalism.* New York.

Jorgensen, Neils. (2007). New Technologies in e-banking: Convenient and trustworthy. In H.R. Rao, M. Gupta, & S. Upadyaya (Eds.). *Stronger Authentication: Responding to the crisis of confidence, Managing Information Assurance in Financial Services.* Hershey, PA: Idea Group Publishing, ISBN: 978-1-59904-171-1.

Kingstey, D. (2002, June). Fingerprint security easy to fool. *News in Science, 20.* Retrieved May 6, 2008, from http://lwww.abc.net.au/science/news/stories/s585792.htm

Langenderfer, J., & Linnhoff, S. (2005). The emergence of biometrics and its effect on consumers. *The Journal of Consumer Affairs, 39*(2), 314-336.

Leyden, J. (2002). Gummi bears defeat fingerprint sensors. *The Register.* Retrieved May 6, 2008, from

   http://www. theregister.com/2002/05/16/gummi~bears~defeat-fingerprint-sensors

Manber, U. (1996). A simple scheme to make passwords based on one-way functions much harder to crack. *Computers & Security, 15,* 171-176.

Matyas, J., Vaclav, & Riha, Z. (2003). Toward reliable user authentication through biometrics. *IEEE Security & Privacy, 1,* 45-49.

Menkus, B. (1988). Understanding the use of passwords. *Computers & Security, 7,* 132-136.

Microsoft Canada. (2000). Information overload: Canadians have too many passwords. *Microsoft Canada, 2003.*

Ortega-Garcia, J., Bigun, J., Reynolds, D., & Gonzalez-Rodriguez, J. (2004, March). Authentication gets personal with biometrics. *IEEE Signal Processing Magazine, 21*(2), 50-62.

Palmgren, K. (2005). Biometric authentication, an introduction. *SecurityDocs.* Retrieved May 6, 2008, from http://www.securitydocs.c0milibrary/3003

Pomeroy, B., & Shorter, K. (2006). *Authentication technologies, trusted information management, QinetiQ.* Retrieved May 6, 2008, from http://www.qinetiq.com/home/security/securing_your_business.QuickNavPar.0006.File.pdf

Pond, R., Podd, J., Bunnell, J., & Henderson, R. (2000). Word association computer passwords: The effect of formulation techniques on recall and guessing rates. *Computers & Security, 19,* 645-656.

Reid, P. (2004). *Biometrics for network securiy.* Upper Saddle River, NJ: Prentice Hall PTR.

Riddle, B.L., Miron, M.S., & Semo, J.A. (1989). Passwords in use in a university timesharing environment. *Computers & Security, 8,* 569-579.

RSA. (2006). http://www.rsasecurity.com/node.asp?id=2970

Schneier, B. (2005, April). Two-factor authentication: Too little, too late. *Communications of ACM, 48*(4), 136.

Slewe, T., & Hoogenboom, M. (2004). Who will rob you on the digital highway? *Communications of the ACM, 47*(5), 56-60.

Smith, S.L. (1987). Authenticating users by word association. *Computers and Security, 6,* 464-470.

Swanson, S. (2003). Way too many passwords, not enough protection. *Chicago Tribune,* online edition, pp. 1.

Thalheim, L., Krissler J., & Ziegler, P. (2002). Body check: Biometric access protection devices and their programs put to the test. *C'TMagarine, 11,* 114. Retrieved May 6, 2008, from http://www.heise.de/ct/englisWO2/1/1I 14/

Visa. (1997). *Visa sets global strategy to evolve core businesses using innovative new chip technologies.* Retrieved May 6, 2008, from http://www.visa.com/cgibin/vee/vw news/keylist.html?2+0

Wheatley, M. (2005). *Frontiers in finance.* KPMG Financial Services Practice.

Yeo, A. (2007). Stronger authentication: Responding to the crisis of confidence. In H.R. Rao, M. Gupta, & S. Upadyaya (Eds.). *Managing Information Assurance in Financial Services.* Idea Group Publishing, ISBN: 978-1-59904-171-1

Zviran, M., & Haga, W.J. (1990). Cognitive passwords: The key to easy access control. *Computers and Security, 9,* 723-736.

Zviran, M., & Haga, W.J. (1993). A comparison of password techniques for multilevel authentication mechanisms. *Journal of Computing, 36,* 221-237.

Zviran, M., & Haga, W. (1999). Password security: An empirical study. *Journal of Management Information Systems, 15*, 161-185.

KEY TERMS

Authentication Factor: A piece of information or process that is used to authenticate or verify an individual's identity.

Biometric Authentication: The method for uniquely identifying individuals based on one or more intrinsic physiological or behavioral traits.

Electronic Banking: Also called Internet banking, this is a term used for performing banking transactions, payments, and other services over the Internet through a financial institutions' secure Web site.

The Federal Financial Institutions Examination Councile (FFIEC) Guidance for Authentication: The FFIEC—which comprises the United States' five federal banking regulators—published joint guidance entitled *Authentication in an Internet Banking Environment*, recommending that financial institutions deploy security measures to reliably authenticate their online banking customers.

Smart Cards and Tokens: A credit card-sized device that contains an integrated chip that holds and protects information regarding the bearer that can be used for authentication. This is most common form of authentication factor for "something you have."

Technology Evaluation: Also called *assessment*, this is study and evaluation of new technologies to understand their relative benefits and costs in context of their proposed implementation. During evaluation, user interaction issues such as use of ease, use of deployment, security, invasiveness, and so on are also considered.

Two-Factor Authentication: A system where two different authentication factors are used to authenticate. These two have to be from commonly accepted three factors: (1) "something you know" (such as a password or PIN), (2) "something you have" (such as a smart card or USB security token), and (3) "something you are" (such as a fingerprint, a retinal scan, or other biometric authentication).

Chapter XXIII
Disruptive Technology Impacts on Security

Sue Conger
University of Dallas, USA

Brett J. L. Landry
University of Dallas, USA

ABSTRACT

Historically, companies have automated a security model that analogizes the concept of a "guardian" who monitors incoming and outgoing activities and data, and this has worked with emerging technologies to this point. This chapter introduces imminent technologies (RFID chips, GPS, and smart motes) and discusses their disruptive effects on network security. Options for mitigating the risks are developed. These technologies are sufficiently disruptive to require a paradigm shift in securing and safeguarding data.

BACKGROUND

In the real world, security operates on a model of a physical guard who protects business premises from unwanted intruders. In the real world, as threats increase, the human guards are supplemented with x-ray or other inspection technology to ensure that admitted persons do not bring unwanted items into the premises. In the automated realm, computer security analogizes from the real world model to develop guardian-like software that inspects and accepts or rejects digital objects (e.g., e-mail, documents, transactions, etc. as well as viruses, worms and malware, etc.) before it enters or leaves the computing silo.

Emerging technologies that provide portable, hidden, and readily-available appropriation of corporate information are changing the focus of security issues to a need for capabilities that can find hidden devices throughout the organization, its employees, and the domiciles of employee tele-commuters. First,

three technologies that challenge the current security paradigm are defined and discussed, threats from such technologies are developed, and legal and practical remedies are described. Based on this discussion, we develop the security issues with which companies must now deal—those beyond network based security. Research directions for those issues and practical guidance to organizational security specialists are provided.

NEW TECHNOLOGIES CHALLENGE SECURITY PARADIGMS

Three technologies—Radio Frequency Identification (RFID), Global Positioning Systems (GPS), and smart motes—will force organizations to change the way they perceive security needs in the coming years. Rogers (1995) defined an S-curve of innovation that projects market growth over time (see Figure 1). Each of these technologies is in a different stage of maturation (see Figure 1), but each promises to change privacy issues and extend challenges to individuals in protecting their personal information. GPS, introduced in 1978, and imbedded in all U.S. cell phones, is a maturing industry for hand-held GPS with a U.S. market expected to reach $22 billion in 2008 and a global market about triple at $60 billion (David, 2003; ETRI, 2005). Therefore, GPS is toward the top of the diffusion growth curve and represents a relatively mature technology. RFID, developed in the 1940s, is still finding its market. While it has had significant press, primarily because of privacy concerns, the technology is still in a growth phase, represented in the figure as mid-way up the S-curve. Smart motes enjoy limited commercialization and are still under development (Warneke & Pister, 2004). As such, they are the least mature technology and are about at the beginning growth inflection point on the S-curve.

These technologies are representative of technology directions in that they are pervasive, portable and embedded. As nano-technologies develop more fully in the coming decade, they will offer more novel disruption to corporate security paradigms. The three technologies here provide a "warm-up" for companies to become agile and clever in security management.

RFID

Developed in the 1940s, RFID is a technology that uses wireless computer chips to track items at a distance (Anonymous, 2002). RFID systems require two basic elements: a transponder and an interrogator. The RFID tag (see Figure 1) is the transponder composed of an integrated circuit fused to a small antenna, and, if passive, requires no internal electrical power (Alien Technology, 2007).

RFID chips ranges from passive to active[1]. *Passive* RFID does not transmit until a reader "requests" data from a chip, has no energy source imbedded in the chip, and is limited to reading from about 10 feet (3 meters) (Anonymous, 2007b). An RFID chip consists of an antenna and a transponder. The antenna in Figure 2 is the concentric ring of metallic coil. They can be printed using magnetic ink with special printers, bringing the cost of the cheapest chip to about US $.02. The transponder is the information source and is contained in the small square at the center of the chip in Figure 2. The interrogator is in a separate device that sends a powerful radio frequency signal to passive RFID in the form of radio waves. This signal gives power to the transponder that emits its signal, thus completing a "read."

In contrast, *active* RFID transceivers contain a battery, memory, and ability to continuously monitor and record sensor inputs. Active RFID transmit continuously and are readable by any reader within 30 meters, about 90 feet. They are re-programmable and vulnerable to worms and software attacks (Miller, 2006; Ricker, 2006). Transceivers for active RFIDs can be as small as 2x3 inches and are installed in thousands of door portals and can read data from thousands of tags a minute, from over 300 feet (100 meters), moving at 100 mph (Anonymous, 2002). Active RFID are

Figure 1. S Curve of innovation and emerging technologies

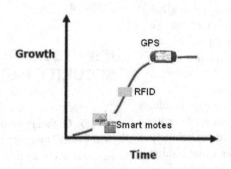

Figure 2. RFID Chip (Gadgetell.com, 2007)

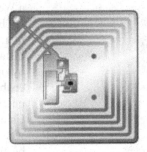

amenable to hostile environments such as ship cargo holds, deserts, or warehouses. One issue with active RFID is their continuous sending which can confound readers and confuse location identification if not set up properly.

RFID are used in every conceivable product including metals, liquids, textiles, plastics, pharmaceuticals, and others. For instance, they are imbedded in children's pajamas, robots to guard playgrounds, and even shaving gear (Alien Technology, 2007; Gilbert, 2005; IDTechEx, 2007; Olsen, 2007; Sullivan, 2005).

The global market for RFID is huge and growing, including governments and businesses in every industry. Sales are predicted to hit $1 trillion by 2012 (IDTechEx, 2007). The price of RFID chips falls between 5 percent and 10 percent a year (Cannell, 2006). Many experts predict a world with RFID chips "incorporated into ... everyday objects ... wherein virtually everything is networked through the Web" (Cannell, 2006). The new generation of RFID chips coming on the market contains electronic product codes (EPC), which are a 96-bit code capable of uniquely identifying *everything on the planet* (EPC Global, 2005). And, there are some people who think that recording everything about a person may have some use (Bell, 2004).

RFID is not all bad. RFID can accelerate, simplify, and improve repetitive counting tasks, such as taking a physical inventory that morphs from onerous, backbreaking, days-long work to a walk down each aisle (Schuman, 2006). Shrinkage, the euphemism for stolen, lost, or otherwise missing goods, transforms from a rising percentage of retail costs to almost a thing of the past, simply by placing RFID sensors at all ingress/egress points. In addition, shoplifters who might "hide" goods on their person while they checkout other goods will be discovered and charged

for the items. Traffic jams are reduced by toll tags, and transit tickets, identification of luggage at airports or containers in shipping yards all are easily identified and experience speedier processing with embedded RFID. Similarly, transactions are quicker with the use of Speed Pass® and other smart cards with embedded RFID, as is identification and return of stray animals that have been "chipped." These are clearly desirable outcomes of RFID use for corporations and society.

Global Positioning Systems

The next technology that threatens current corporate security methods, Global Positioning System technology (GPS), is available as stand-alone devices or imbedded in devices such as cell phones and cars (see Figure 3). While a researcher at Raytheon Corporation, Ivan Getting envisioned GPS in the 1950s (Anonymous, 2007a; Anonymous, 2007c). Getting left Raytheon and started his own company where he realized his dream for GPS in the 1960s (Anonymous, 2007a; Anonymous, 2007c). GPS is enabled by a constellation of 27 earth-orbiting satellites, 24 of which are in active operation at any one time. Each satellite circles the globe twice a day with orbits arranged so that at any time, anywhere on earth, there are at least four satellites "visible" in the sky. A GPS receiver is a device that locates at least three satellites to determine its distance to each and use this information to deduce its own location (Anonymous, 2007a; Brain, 2007).

Location identification is based on a mathematical principle called trilateration. Trilateration is the location of a single point in space relative to its distance from three other known points. The GPS receiver calculates location and distance from each of the satellites by timing how long it takes a signal to come from each. Plus, devices at known locations such as

Figure 3. Garmin GPS (From Hart, 2006)

Figure 4. Trilateration example (Brain, 2007)

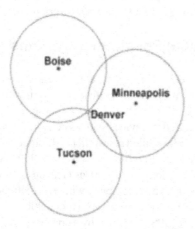

Boise, Tucson, and Minneapolis are also plotted. By computing the difference in time from each satellite to each known point, an exact fourth point (Denver in Figure 4) is identified, and it is accurate to within 10 feet (Anonymous, 2007a; Brain, 2007). GPS can tell you how far you have traveled, how long you have been traveling, your current and average speeds, and the estimated time of arrival at current speed. Further, a "bread crumb" trail showing where you have traveled is available to track your trip. GPS tracking data can be stored inside the unit, or sent to a remote computer

by radio or cellular modem. Some systems allow the location to be viewed in real-time on the Internet with a Web browser (Brain, 2007).

Enhanced 911 (E-911) telephone services required that, as of October, 2001, in the U.S., GPS locators be installed in every cellular telephone and able to be read by operators when cell calls to 911 are made. E-911 enables location-based commerce (L-comm) to help phone companies recoup the cost of E-911 service. Using L-comm, one might program his phone to call when he's within two blocks of a Starbucks. Stores will be able to push advertisements to people in the area for special sales. Or, retailers might track how many cars pass their location and how many stop, without letting the car passengers know they are being watched (Said & Kirby, 2001). Location tracking requires that an RFID tag be placed on the object to be track. Then, the GPS receiver locates the object. Together, RFID and GPS provide location identification of anything on earth. The RFID identifies the individual; the GPS tracks them.

On the positive side, E-911 allows the finding of cars under water, children stranded with only a phone, and so on. E-911 also makes stolen goods a thing of the past because everything can be tracked. Yet, as the PC, PDA, RFID, GPS, telephone, and fast Internet access converge and miniaturize into a single pocket-sized device, security as a corporate silo must also change.

Smart Motes

Now we turn to the technology that has the most serious implications for industrial espionage and loss of control over everything for everyone everywhere: *Smart motes.* Smart motes, also known as smart dust, will eventually be sand speck-sized sensors, or "motes" each of which is a "'complete, wireless subsystem,' running tiny operating systems, and outfitted with an antenna connector, serial interface, analog inputs, and digital inputs and outputs" (Dustnetworks.com, 2007). Currently they are highly miniaturized micro-electromechanical devices (MEMs) with imbedded intelligence that pack wireless communication in the digital circuitry (see Figure 5). The "Spec" mote in Figure 5 was five square centimeters, but every year since the Berkeley mote project began (Warneke & Pister, 2004) has seen an order of magnitude more miniaturization along with more sophisticated software, based on the Tiny OS, and high-cognitive functioning. Since motes are self-powered, they are

Figure 5. Berkeley "Spec" Mote, 2003

active only about 10 percent of the time. This allows them to have an active life of about three years.

Each mote digitizes the data collected by an attached sensor and uses an onboard radio to send it in packet form to neighboring motes. Motes are compact, ultra low-power, wireless network devices that provide modular connections to a wide range of sensors and actuators. The unique low-power capabilities of smart mesh enable network topologies where all motes are routers and all motes can be battery-powered (Dustnetworks.com, 2007).

Smart motes are already used in energy and military applications but they have similar capabilities to RFID with the added benefit that they can be engineered to adhere to desired surfaces, imbedded invisibly in paint, in joint compound, aerosoled into a situation ingested by humans and animals, reprogrammed dynamically from "home," and report "in" to "home" by piggybacking through any available wireless network. Thus, motes have infinite capacity to invade and erode security.

The "spec" mote in Figure 5 evidences the recent state of the art. This "Berkeley mote" is battery powered with bi-directional wireless communication and sensing. From university lab to commercialization took about four years but the demand for these small devices is going to be boundless when they become a few millimeters smaller and a few megahertz more more powerful. Intel began commercial manufactur-

ing their mote based on the Berkeley research starting around 2004.

Smart motes are a form of nanotechnology that now costs less than $1 each to create in volume. These mechanisms form self-organizing, intelligent, networks programmed to perform some task, usually surveillance of some type. In addition to obvious problems with organizational security, they can remove any vestige of personal privacy as well. If inhaled, motes might even report on the inner health of individuals (Warneke & Pister, 2004). Now imagine that all of collected data were reported back to a competitor company with digital, photographic, audio, or even video recordings and information and the magnitude of the security compromises becomes inescapable.

THREATS

Confidentiality, Integrity, and Availability (CIA) are the three elements required for secure computing. Confidentiality is threatened by invisibility and hacking, integrity by theft and corruption, and availability by denial of service. Much of the discussion focuses on RFID, because it has garnered the most attention to date. Each security concern and its CIA issues are discussed next.

Invisibility

Invisibility is an enabling characteristic. The remaining security concerns all are heightened as a result of this invisibility. No one currently can detect imbedded RFID which can be as small as the dot on the letter "i." RFID are capable of being "printed" with virtually imperceptible antennae. Because transceivers (RFID readers) can be imbedded in buildings, roads, street corners, traffic lights, containers, trucks, ships, aircraft, or other infrastructures, RFID are being read everywhere. Door portals contain RFID readers that can identify the movement of individual by reading smart cards, tracking movements with floor sensors while hidden cameras, microphones, and heat sensors monitor activities. Thus, RFID and the other surveillances have led to eavesdropping concerns (Albrecht, 2002). RFID chips are being imbedded in some clothing items with the intention of being active for many years.

GPS as embedded in phones is invisible but tracking devices also are invisible, about the size of a cell phone. "A new device, the 'GemTek' personal tracking device ... allows consumers to remotely track the position of a loved one, ... asset, or another important item" (Gemini Technology, 2007). This device easily can be hidden on one's person so while not invisible, it is small enough to be unseen.

Motes are nearing the nanometer size. Ingested, painted, embedded (e.g., in carpeting), or implanted ones are invisible and may be unknown recorders of corporate actions, troop strengths, or medical states capable of surveillance for several years (Chromatius, 2006; Kitchener, 2006; Singer, 2003; Williams, 2006).

Tracking and Profiling

The same capabilities that solve some business problems, such as preventing shrinkage and taking inventory, allow any person or company with an RFID reader to "spy" on individuals' behaviors. Further, RFID can be invisible to the naked eye, robust in hostile contexts, and continue sending their information for years (Albrecht, 2002; Albrecht & McIntyre, 2004; OECD, 2006). Illicit tracking is difficult to identify or track since readers are everywhere and determining which reader was used for the illicit activity is difficult to track unless a crime is committed and the perpetrator apprehended with an RFID reader on his person (OECD, 2006).

In addition, the ACLU alleges that U.S. citizens and corporations, post-2001, have "unknowingly becoming targets of government surveillance" (Anonymous, 2007b). Post-2001 "erosion in protections against government spying and the increasing amount of tracking being carried out by the private sector (which appears to have an unappeasably voracious appetite for consumer information) and the growing intersection between the two" (Albrecht, 2002) have led to the increase in surveillance of all types by all types of organizations and their business partners with whom they share data. Governments are active and prolific data collectors and aggregators for purposes of tracking and monitoring everyone in their databases.

Organizations in the U.K. decry the surveillance society that they have become with national identify cards that contain both identifying and health information. New Zealand's Privacy Commissioner has warned about RFID as a data threat (Jackson, 2007)

GPS similarly are able to track individuals, but as the technology blends into daily use users forget they are being tracked. Google's "My Location" widget software has caused significant warnings of privacy

transgressions. Lane (2007) sites Google's ability to track "device and hardware IDs, device type, request type, carrier, your carrier user ID, and the content of your request" at a minimum. Lane's article sites concerns from privacy advocates such as Marc Rotenberg of the Electronic Privacy Information Center (EPIC) and Jeff Chester of the Center for Digital Democracy. Chester says Google's "data collection-dependent business model is increasingly a ... threat to consumer welfare" (Lane, 2007).

Google is not the only GPS threat. Anyone with a reader, such as GemTek, can track specific devices. Anyone with a bit of technical savvy can track any devices, opening up new avenues for stalking and other forms of tracking. About half of the cell phone users in one Japanese survey believe mobile GPS is a privacy threat (Y-N, 2007) while the Communication, Electric, and Plumbing Union (CEPU) in Australia has declared GPS an "unacceptable" technology for their trucks (Corner, 2007).

Motes provide new means of clandestinely seeding a person or device to provide traceability. As motes get even smaller, the ability to aerosol them into a situation will be largely untraceable. Therefore, the threats from RFID and GPS also are present in motes.

Data Theft, Replay, and Cloning

New types of theft involve several types of transgressions: Theft, replay and cloning. Both replay and cloning give rise to integrity issues. First is data theft that comes from clandestine RFID readers being built into door portals, highway systems, street corners, and other public places to read the RFID chips that pass by (Faber, 2007). Anyone with a smart card, building radio card, toll tag, and so on is being scanned and read, that is being eavesdropped on, daily (OECD, 2006). This hidden eavesdropping is a form of theft enabled by the invisibility of the devices.

Replay attacks can occur when an attacker captures network traffic and then replays it again. These replay attacks can be used to manipulate inventory levels or to generate traffic to crack encryption schemes. In the case of RFID, replay attacks could be used to fool physical access controls and payment systems (Rieback, Crispo, & Tanenbaum, 2006a). For GPS, alternative locations could be falsely used to hide the location of an item. Smart motes could be used to determine if luggage contained explosive by spraying them near luggage. The motes would determine if it was safe and report back. However, a replay attack could give an all-clear signal from luggage containing explosives by canceling out, blocking and then replaying a previous good transmission. Rieback, Simpson, Crispo, & Tanenbaum (2006b) discuss that is possible to reduce the attack surface by requiring authentication procedures between the devices and the backend systems.

The other type of theft is "cloning" in which the cloner palms a coil that is the antenna for a wallet-sized cloning device, which is "currently shoved up his sleeve. The cloner can elicit, record, and mimic signals from smart card RFID chips. [The cloner] takes out the device and, using a USB cable, connects it to his laptop and downloads the data from the 'card for processing'" (Newitz, 2006). The OECD identifies this as one of the most serious problems with unprotected RFID since it is virtually undetectable and difficult to trace (OECD, 2006). One California college student used an RFID reader about the size of a deck of cards to scan items and download them to his computer from which he then changed prices, walked back through a store, and changed the prices of desired items (Newitz, 2006). Other similar tales of foiling building security based on RFID, hotel room keys spoofing smart cards with RFID tags, overriding RFID tag information to obtain, for instance, free gas, and to clone implanted RFIDs all have occurred (Newitz, 2006).

While GPS, per se, is not generally programmable, software such as Google's My Location will be subject to hacker and cracker threats. Should hacks be made generally available, GPS will be subject to similar data theft of any information about the device and its history of use.

Motes use the "Tiny OS" operating system. No known problems exist with it, but no known external verification of its hackability exists to date. As motes are more often deployed, the ability to exploit mote operating systems will come to be an issue.

Data Corruption

Integrity's threat is the corruption of information. This happens when an unauthorized alteration of information whether stored on a system, or some media or in transit across the network occurs. The same methods used in the theft section can be used for more malevolent uses to corrupt data and therefore, create havoc in computer infrastructures around the globe. Session hijacking can occur in either in a wireless communication with RFID, GPS or motes and the interrogators

or in a wired network between the interrogators and the backend databases and systems.

Active RFID chips suffer a buffer overflow bug, similar to that Microsoft's operating systems that can be used to inject a worm or obtain the contents of the chip. Researchers have demonstrated how to inject malware into RFID chips, thereby disrupting not just chip operation but the readers as well (Naraine, 2006). Active RFID, GPS, and smart motes' operating systems are amenable to viruses, worms, and hacks. The RFID used in Netherlands passports was hacked by a high school student in four hours; this is the same chip used in U.S. e-Passports (Ricker, 2006). Worms, injected into the operating system in an active RFID or smart mote network have the potential to cause havoc in the injected environment (Rieback et al., 2006b). For instance, if a suitcase contains an active RFID chip that is infected it could infect every other RFID chip in the airport. The chip is read as the traveler enters the airport and promptly infects the airport systems. The infection will spread to all luggage similarly equipped with active RFIDs, and so on, as the worms spreads around the globe (OECD, 2006). Not only are all of the chips in the luggage now unusable but every computer that has read the infected chips are also ruined. The re-programming job involved with such mobility of devices will be endless as infected luggage continues to proliferate and spread the problem. RFID, GPS, and smart motes change the perimeter of the network and, thus, require different security measures (Chromatius, 2006; Rieback et al., 2006a).

Availability

Because RFID, GPS, and smart motes all eventually interact with other possibly infected and compromised computers, they are also at risk. Availability's threat is denial of service. Any intentional degradation or blocking of traffic to a particular computer or network resource can be considered reduction or loss of availability. Loss of availability also can be caused by unintentional actions such as power outages, hardware or software failures, or disasters. Distributed Denial of Service (DDOS) attacks in which the radio frequency channel is jammed with "noise" to prevent communication are added problems in addition to the spoofing, cloning, and worms discussed above. It is possible that a DDOS could be generated from infected PCs within a company's intranet. To protect interrogators and access points, these devices need to incorporate firewall and screening protection. In today's computing environment with Wireless networks, VPN connections, and 3G cellular networks, a porous perimeter exists that can no guaranty the security of the intranet. With this in mind, all of these devices must be cataloged as possible threat agents.

In addition to buffer overflow problems discussed in the previous section, spurious data attacks that take advantage of poorly coded database access queries, for instance, are an additional source of vulnerability. These vulnerabilities reside not only in the RFID chip-reader interface, but also in the RFID reader—RFID middleware interface, any interfaces with EPC software, and any EPC connectivity (Konidala, Kim, & Kim, 2006). There are technical responses to each of these threats, none of which are present in current RFID designs.

Currently the RFID environment is "open" so that all readers are considered authentic and allowed to read a chip. This both gives out the maximum information to the maximum number of readers, but also opens the chip to being read, spoofed, cloned, and so on by unauthorized sources. Malicious RFID reading might become a new form of corporate espionage that is carried out by employees who simply carry an RFID jammer, spoofer, or so on in a pocket at work. While the effects of most jamming exercises would be inconvenient, in the case of medical identification, the results could be fatal in the devices were rendered useless (Rieback et al., 2006a). In examining each of these items, all must be present for the information to have meaning and be reliable. With the exception of military scenarios, end users and corporations do not have a means to police shared use radio spectrums for blockers and jammers.

As nanotechnology techniques become more sophisticated, smart motes will get both smaller and smarter. Eventually, they will be reprogrammable "bot" armies that are global, self-reproducing and capable of currently unimaginable intelligence (Anonymous, 2006; Singer, 2003; Warneke & Pister, 2004). In addition, most intelligence won't be used against just individuals, it will be turned against corporations and governments as well (Singer, 2003).

SOLUTIONS

The solutions are corporate self-regulation, legislation, and technical controls. Each is discussed in this section followed by an assessment of their effectiveness to date.

Corporate Self-Regulation

No industry likes legislated regulation so companies always profess to be able to self-regulate. Several groups have developed guidelines for self-regulation, making it easier on companies not to have to develop their own. Two groups, The Center for Democracy and Technology and Electronic Product Code Global (EPC Global) have issued standards and guidelines for corporate self-regulation, including:

- Notices on packages of RFID tagging
- Education of consumers to recognize EPC tags
- Choice information about discarding, removing, or deactivating RFID chips in products.
- Record use, retention, and security guidelines propose that the RFID chips not "contain, collect, or store any personally identifiable information" (OECD, 2006, p. 21).

These guidelines all relate to personal information privacy of consumers, not to a company protecting itself from the same technologies. Notices on packages, retention and deactivation policies, and even acceptable use statements will not keep the technology from being used against the organization. Organizations need to be aware that these technologies can and might be sued against them from competitors or disgruntled employees.

Legislation

Legislative means of regulating RFID exist in Europe via Directives 94/46/EC and 2002/58/EC and the U.S. via Section 5 of the FTC Act (OECD, 2006). Plus, the OECD's 1980 *Guidelines on the Protection of Privacy and Transborder Flows of Personal Data* contains eight principles that also apply to RFID privacy that were the basis for the EPC suggestions above. One of the eight recommendations related to corporate security: "Security safeguards should protect against loss and unauthorized access, modification or disclosure" (OECD, 2006).

The OECD guidelines are strictly followed because of EU legislation for transborder data flows, but not for RFID or other methods of data collection. In addition, Australia, most Asian countries, some South American countries, and Europe have privacy laws that cover most situations in which data collection, data aggregation of the collected data, and use of collected data all apply.

Technical Controls

The first solution, corporate self-regulation, is not being practiced. Evidence amasses of corporate transgressions of the innocence and trust of consumers. Companies assume their security silos are impenetrable (Albrecht & McIntyre, 2004; OECD, 2006). Technical controls will be most effective alternative to mitigating emerging technology threats. But, technical control implementation is at the whim of executives who need to balance their cost of security against the risk of losing control. At the moment, the economics of security cost do not support the expenditures however, economics does not prevent the wholesale loss of security control that can occur when these technologies emerge.

Konidala, et al. (2006) developed a detailed report on all of the vulnerabilities of RFID at each stage of the technology and their interactions—six stages in all. They further detailed technical mitigations of each risk for each level of technology. If there were any question on what actions were needed, one need only reference their report. Thus far, these technologies have proven too costly or beyond the technical capability of current RFID technology without sacrificing size or weight in the process.

Research at Carnegie-Mellon University also seeks to allow location-based devices, such as RFID, GPS, and motes to be used in ways that preserve user privacy. This research is in its infancy, but the authors assert that technical preservation of user privacy is the most promising line of research to solving this knotty problem (Tang, Keyani, Fogarty, & Hone, 2006).

The threats to security from mobile technology has also received the attention of the Network Working Group of the Internet Engineering Task Force (IETF) (Haddad, Nordmark, Dupont, Bagnulo, Park, Patil, et al., 2006). This report describes how mobile device IDs become knowable any time there is a send/receive action. Any malicious eavesdropper in the same geographic area can identify a user's MAC address, IPv6 address and the data sequence number (Haddad et al., 2006). Once this information is known, it may be feasible to discern some personal information through monitoring of the actual messages being sent/received.

Security Issues

Thus far, we have defined and described the capabilities of three technologies that will disrupt security

in organizations. Also, the methods currently being applied to control use of the technologies, mostly aimed at protecting consumer privacy, are shown to be largely ineffective. In this section, the security issues that companies need to grasp are explained with security decisions identified. The paradigm shift for organizations to adopt is the acceptance of an invisible threat. Today, security guards at corporate offices check for weapons via metal detectors, look for large IT hardware (they will stop someone with a server on a hand truck), and verify access with card access either via magnetic strips or RFID. Most organizations do not search laptops, because everyone has them and they are supposed to have them. The same is true for cellular telephones and portable memory devices. The invisible threat may be in the vending machine that dispenses coins that include smart motes. It could be in combined GPS and RFID attack discussed earlier.

The only legal means to effectively block GPS signals are submerging the organization deep in the earth or providing a shielded computer room that blocks the signal. With that in mind, it would not be difficult to track the movement of every employee in the organization. How? Take the employee phone list that contains cell phone numbers and now the hacker has a list of people, department, and a means to track them. Now that the hacker knows who the employees are and where they are at all times, the employees can be stalked and opportune time to attack found. There are two clear options at this point, 1) steal assets such as laptops and other data devices or 2) clone their identity with RFID hacking tools. The first option is more of a temporary issue, because so many devices today are not encrypted. As encryption becomes more standard with BitLocker in Windows Vista and other third party tools for laptops and memory devices, this threat will reduce.

For non-repudiation (i.e., one cannot prove "It was not me") for access to critical locations to be supported, we must have at least two of the four methods of authentication: What you know, what you have, what you are, and more recently, what you do. A solution with RFID is to move beyond RFID tags alone. RFID ID cards only cover one of these authentication methods—what you have. Therefore critical location access needs to be supplemented with passwords (what you know) or biometrics (what you are). In any case, RFID cards are not secure and can be used by anyone with a card. Also, with GPS, an employee might gain illegal access to otherwise inaccessible information if it is transmitted via a GPS solution. Two-factor authentication to a GPS device mitigates this problem, but mitigating sniffer attacks that capture traffic signals require GPS-encryption.

The question is what about the smart motes? By comparison, jump drives are huge compared to smart motes, however organizations do not check for jump drives today, so how are they going to check for these? How will organizations scan their entire infrastructure for these high tech bugs that are in the fibers of the carpet transmitting data out? Will firms decide to actively block wireless signals not used for business purposes? If so what will be the legal and healthcare issues for the employees involved? How do you sterilize an environment without damaging the legitimate computing devices? These are all questions that must be addressed in the next 10 years, because this is new reality that will make jump drives and open 802.11 wireless seem secure and insignificant.

CONCLUSION

Most of the transgressions relating to new technologies extend existing situations to which the original security paradigms were applied. Emerging technologies make those discussions moot since they can easily circumvent the security silos of the past. Of possible solutions to security issues, corporate self-regulation and legislative regulations are unlikely to be effective.

Technology controls, while articulated and appearing complete, have, to date not been implemented. As companies realize the security implications of RFID, GPS, and smart motes, they need to start thinking beyond the firewall and toward the identification of nanotechnologies as the challenges most urgently needing solutions.

REFERENCES

Albrecht, K. & McIntyre, L. (2004). RFID: The Big Brother bar code. *ALEC Policy Forum, 6*, 49-54.

Albrecht, K. (2002). Supermarket cards: The tip of the surveillance iceberg. *Denver University law Review, 79*, 535-554.

Alien Technology (2007). RFID. Alien Technology [Online].

Anonymous (2002). Part I: Active and passive RFID: Two distinct, by complementary, technologies for real-time supply chain visibility. http://www.autoid.org/2002_Documents/sc31_wg4/docs_501-520/520_18000-7_WhitePaper.pdf

Anonymous (2006). Data takes on a life of its own. http://www.mobius.com/mobius/collateral/articles/BST_Data_Lifecycle_May06.pdf

Anonymous (2007a). AIB error led 15,000 customers to get details of other accounts. *Irish Times*, November 30.

Anonymous (2007b). Famous Inventors. http://www.famous.inventors.com/invention-of-gps.html

Anonymous (2007c). Private information stolen from civil servant's home. *CBC News*, November 16.

Bell, G. (2004). A personal digital store. *Communications of the ACM, 44*, 86-94.

Brain, M. (2007). *Introduction to how GPS works*. http://howstuffworks.com/mote.htm

Cannell, P. (2006). Writing for academic journals - Murray, Rowena. *British Journal of Educational Technology, 37*, 495.

Chromatius (2006). Dust: A ubiquitous surveillance technology. http://blogcritics.org/archives/2006/02/19/111529.php

Corner, S. (2007). Telstra Union says GPS in trucks "unacceptable threat to privacy". *iTWire, November 3*.

Dustnetworks.com (2007). Smart dust. http://www.dustnetworks.com

EPC Global (2005). Guidelines on EPC for consumer products. http://www.epcglobaline.org/public/ppsc_guide

Faber, P. (2007). RFID strategy -- RFID privacy and security issues. *Industry Week Online*

Gemini Technology (2007). GemTek GPS tracker. http://www.gem-tek-tracker.com/index2.html

Gilbert, A. (2005). Will RFID-guided robots rule the world? http://news.com.com/2101-7337_3-5778286.html

Haddad, W., Nordmark, E., Dupont, F., Bagnulo, M., Park, S. S. D., Patil, B. et al. (2006). Anonymous identifiers (ALIEN): Privacy threat model for mobile and multi-homed nodes. Network Working Group. http://tools.ietf.org/html/draft-haddad-momipriv-threat-model-02

IDTechEx (2007). The RFID knowledgebase. http://rfid.idtechex.com/knowledgebase/en/nologon.asp

Jackson, R. (2007). "Promiscuous" RFID a data threat, warns Privacy Watchdog. *Computerworld.*

Kitchener, G. (2006). Pentagon plans cyber-insect army. http://www.bbc.co.uk,/2/hi/americas/480342.stm

Konidala, D., Kim, W. S., & Kim, K. (2006). *Security Assessment of EPCGlobal Architecture Framework.* Korea: Auto-ID Labs White Paper, #WP-SMNET-017.

Lane, F. (2007). Google's "My Location" a threat to privacy. *Sci-Tech Today.*

Miller, P. (2006). German hackers clone RFID e-passports. http://www.engadget.com/2006/08/03/german-hackers-clone-rfid-e-passports/

Naraine, R. (2006). Dutch researchers create RFID malware. *eWeek Online*

Newitz, A. (2006). The RFID hacking underground. *Wired,* http://www.wired.com/wired/archive/14.05/rfid_pr.html

OECD (2006). Report on cross-border enforcement of privacy laws. *Organization for Economic Co-operation and Development (OECD).*

Olsen, S. (2007). RFID coming soon to scooters, diapers. *ZDNet,* http://www.zdnet.com.au/news/hardware/soa/RFID_coming_to_scooters_diapers/0,130061702,339272981,00.htm?ref=search

Ricker, T. (2006). Dutch RFID e-passport cracked – US next? http://www.engadget.com

Rieback, M., Crispo, B., & Tanenbaum, A. (2006a). RFID malware: Truth vs. myth. *IEEE Security and privacy, 4,* 70.

Rieback, M. R., Simpson, P. N. D., Crispo, B., & Tanenbaum, A. S. (2006b). RFID malware: Design principles and examples. *Pervasive and Mobile Computing, 2,* 405-426.

Rogers, E. (1995). *Diffusion of Innovations.* (4th ed.) New York: The Free Press.

Said, C. & Kirby, C. (2001). GPS cell phones may cost privacy. *San Francisco Chronicle.*

Schuman, E. (2006). The RFID hype effect. *eWeek,* February 27.

Singer, M. (2003). Smart dust collecting in the enterprise. http://www.siliconvalley.internet.com/news/

Sullivan, L. (2005). Apparel maker tags RFID for kid's pajamas. *Information Week Online*

Tang, K., Keyani, P., Fogarty, J., & Hone, J. I. (2006). Putting people in their places: An anonymous and privacy-sensitive approach to collecting sensed data in location-based applications. In.

Warneke, B. A. & Pister, K. S. J. (2004). An ultra-low energy microcontroller for smart dust wireless sensor networks. In Williams, M. (2006). The knowledge: Biotechnology's advance could give malefactors the ability to manipulate life processes -- and even affect human behavior. *MIT Technology Review.*

Y-N, Ken (2007). Nearly half consider mobile GPS a privacy threat. *What Japan Thinks,* March 30.

KEY TERMS

Availability: The ability of a computer component or service to perform its required function at a stated time or over a stated period of time.

Confidentiality: Managing and maintaining information such that it is known no more widely than necessary.

Corporate Self-Regulation: A method of management for privacy that is free of government regulation and relies on the beneficent actions of corporations acting as 'good citizens.'

GPS: Global Positioning System is a device that uses a government-controlled satellite system to provide location identification to within 9 feet (2 meters) of its earth-bound position.

Integrity: The assurance that information is untainted. This strictly means that the information put into the computer is the same as the information that comes back later. Integrity is often also used to mean data is accurate.

Nanotechnologies: The field of applied science that seeks manufacturing and control of devices and materials at a scale 100 nanometers or smaller.

RFID: Radio Frequency Identification hardware and software built into some type of tag (e.g., cloth, paper, plastic) that acts as a transponder to emit a signal that can uniquely identify the device to which it is attached.

Security: The management of risk such that the probability of intrusions, breaches, and leaks is minimized, and that, should a problem occur, that it is identified, managed, and prevented from future occurrence.

Smart Motes: Very small (soon to be nano-sized) self-managing networks of wireless microelectrome-chanical sensors (MEMS) capable of wireless communication for up to several years. At present their functioning is limited to environmental sensing such as light and temperature. The ultimate goal is for smart motes to become artificially intelligent robots capable of complete interpretation of their environment via aerosol, paint, ingestion, or other novel methods of delivery.

Vulnerability: Any weakness in a system (typically a computer system) that poses a risk of attack to the owner.

ENDNOTE

1   There are actually five classes of RFID, dumb passive, passive with some functionality and/or encryption, semi-passive which use broad-band communication, active which communicate via broadband and peer-to-peer and with both tags and readers, and active which can give power to the three passive classes and communicate wirelessly. (Sensitech, http://www.sensitech.com/pdfs/Beyond_Passive_RFID.pdf , 2003)

Section III
Security Policies and Procedures

Chapter XXIV
Internal Auditing for
Information Assurance

Sushma Mishra
Virginia Commonwealth University, USA

Amita Goyal Chin
Virginia Commonwealth University, USA

ABSTRACT

Internal auditing has become increasingly important in current business environments. In this era of the Sarbanes-Oxley Act and other similar legislations, regulatory compliance requires elaborate organizational planning. Auditing helps organizations in internal control assessment, change management, and better governance preparedness, thus enhancing information assurance. Various facets of internal auditing are discussed in this chapter and the role of internal auditing in information assurance is analyzed. Future issues and trends with internal auditing are also presented.

INTRODUCTION

Regulations including the Sarbanes-Oxley Act (SOX), the Health Insurance Portability and Accountability Act (HIPAA), the USA Patriot Act, and a plethora of others have created an urgency among business organizations for rapid compliance with governmental standards. Internal auditors play an increasingly important role in today's business scenario, and therefore, have become in great demand. This is clearly evident from the recent surge in the job satisfaction and salary of internal auditors (Oxner & Oxner, 2006). Businesses often use internal auditors as in-house consultants, relying on them for adding value to a wide range of initiatives including management controls, financial reporting, information systems design, and fraud detection. Auditing plays an important role in securing information systems within organizations by including

functions such as internal control assessment, controls over financial reporting, designing and implementation of information systems, vulnerability management, risk analysis, segregation of duties, adequacy of business controls, and the physical security of assets.

Recent developments in the regulatory environment have brought significant changes to the organizational outlook regarding internal auditing. Internal auditors are aware of these increased responsibilities and concentrate on discovering new ways of assuring the public about the integrity of organizational reports (Verschoor, 1991). Today's business environment requires an audit process that supports the continuous assessment of the goals and objectives of information assurance. Organizational strategic goals must be tactically executed with performance measuring capability. For information assurance purposes, there should be close coordination between the audit team, the security team, and the information technology operations (Bunker, 2003).

Information assurance (IA) can be viewed as an objective that involves all of the people, activities, and technologies employed to ensure that the fundamental properties of security—confidentiality, integrity, availability—are met throughout the lifecycle of a system (McEvilley, 2002). IA can be viewed as a process centric phenomenon that is comprehensive enough to include definition, implementation, and verification level operations. IA also includes day-to-day operations and the maintenance of the integrity of systems in such operational transactions. Assurance is subjective in nature and needs to be clearly explained to all involved in the security process.

Increasingly complex auditing functions require auditors to possess a deep knowledge about the organization and its business processes. Auditors should show an adequate understanding of the organizational culture, of the key players in the organization, and of the competitive environment in which the organization exists. Some audit practices that are becoming of heightened importance in today's context include risk management and risk assessment. Recent research from the Institute of Internal Auditor's Global Auditing Information Network (GAIN) indicates that given the various tools and techniques currently available to auditing teams, managing risks as well as consulting with management on aligning organizational goals within departments are considered extremely important. Audit functionality plays an important role in securing information systems in organizations by performing functions such as internal control assessment, risk analysis, segregation of duties, adequacy of business controls, and physical security of assets. Process and plan should have a clear statement of roles and responsibilities. An audit is also a means by which to ensure accountability from the management level of organizations. Accountability in management structures ensures better security management since governance objectives of securing informational assets can be reached in a systematic fashion. An accountability map provides security management programs with this critical component (Bunker, 2003).

This chapter explores the role of information technology (IT) auditing in the overall organizational information assurance functionality. Internal as well as independent audit functionalities are becoming a common practice for security purposes and there are various ways in which auditing can add value to an organization. The main objectives of this chapter are: to provide a background about audit functionality and discuss its expected functions; to provide an assessment of the importance of the role of auditing for information assurance purposes; to present the current audit practices for IT in general, and specifically, for information assurance purposes; and to discuss some future trends regarding the role of auditing in assurance.

BACKGROUND

The Institute of Internal Auditors (2006) defines the role of audit as:

Internal auditing is an independent, objective assurance and consulting activity designed to add value and improve an organization's operations. It helps an organization accomplish its objectives by bringing a systematic, disciplined approach to evaluate and improve the effectiveness of risk management, control, and governance processes (p. 11)

Internal auditing has a broad focus, including individual transactions, control systems, and program operations. There are certain basic assumptions regarding the professionals in this field, necessitating that auditors retain the defining characteristics of credibility. To add value to an organization, auditors should be:

- Unbiased in their assessment. They are not just employees of a corporation but have a bigger societal responsibility.
- Systematic in their approach to collect and analyze information.
- Organized in using various criteria for formulating conclusions. Some of these criteria could include industry standards, goals/targets, benchmarks, and laws.
- Able to use widely accepted professional audit standards.

An organization has various stakeholders and public firms have an accountability towards their shareholders. Regulatory bindings require that the management of such public firms must periodically account to their investors for their use and stewardship of resources and to the extent to which the public's objectives have been accomplished (The Institute of Internal Auditors, 2006). An effective audit activity reduces the risks inherent in an organization's operational environment and strengthens the relationship between the shareholders and the management. The market relies upon the auditor to provide an independent, objective evaluation of the accuracy of an organization's accounting. Additionally, the auditor should present other risk mitigating plans in order to provide assurance in the information provided by the organization. The need for a third party to attest to the believability and credibility of the financial reporting, performance results, compliance, and other measures arises from several factors inherent in the relationship between the investors and an organization (The Institute of Internal Auditors, 2006):

- **Moral hazards:** Conflicts of interest: Management may use their resources and authority to benefit their own interests, rather than the public's interests.
- **Remoteness:** Operations may be physically removed from the management's direct oversight.
- **Complexity:** The management may not possess the technical expertise needed to oversee the activity.
- **Consequence of error:** Errors may be costly when management uses large amounts of resources acquired from the public and are responsible for programs affecting citizens' lives and health.

Organizations should develop an enterprise-wide, completely integrated audit and control model that can be used for improving audit results, corporate governance, and regulatory compliance (Robitaille, 2004). Such practices lead to a high level of assurance, increased profitability, control documentation, and control training. Maintaining an audit issue database to house all outstanding audit issues is a good step towards ensuring better assurance (Robitaille, 2004). Each issue identified during the audit process should be registered and corrective action should be taken against it. This database can help in consolidating a world-class audit, control, and corporate governance practices for enterprise wide risk management.

Even though many organizations dread auditing opportunities, in reality, the assessments provided by auditors offer valuable benefits (Perkins, 2006). For example, auditor inputs provide IT staff and senior managers with a rare opportunity to step back from day-to-day concerns and re-evaluate direction, change

strategy, and enter new markets (Perkins, 2006). In addition, assessments often help to improve perceptions of the IT organization. An effective audit team may provide good assessments that offer an impartial and comprehensive picture of IT concerns across the enterprise. They must clearly describe the business demand for IT services as well as the cost of those services. They must also provide an analysis of the IT staff's capability to deliver the services. These reports may be crucial in the efforts for compliance with governmental regulations. In addition, auditors are responsible for providing recommendations for strategic changes and clear definitions of the projected benefits to be derived from the recommended changes.

MAIN FOCUS OF THE CHAPTER

IT audit plays a crucial role in assuring investors as to an organization's business process integrity and the credibility of the organization's financial reports. Auditors are an integral part of the information assurance practices of an organization.

COMPLIANCE

Information systems security and assurance have become inevitable issues. The Common Criteria for Information Technology Security Evaluation (CCI-TSE), usually referred to as the Common Criteria (CC), establishes a level of trustworthiness and confidence that should be placed in the security functions of products or systems and the assurance measures applied to them (Yavagal, Lee, Ahn, & Gandhi, 2005). Such a level of assurance can be achieved by evaluating the product or system conformance with a common set of requirements set forth by the Common Criteria Board.

Auditing plays an important role in ensuring that organizations are compliant with various mandatory legislations. The compliance process may involve multiple arduous steps by which organizations can implement and instill new changes in the business process. The audit process helps organizations in adapting various change initiatives and also in sustaining these changes at an optimal level.

Auditors help in leveraging compliance activities to long-term costs and review organizational code of conduct to ensure all policies are communicated to the employees (Whitley, 2005). Repeat compliance planning and the whistle-blowing role have to be performed diligently in order to keep corporate objectives transparent.

INTERNAL CONTROL ASSESSMENT

The Sarbanes-Oxley Act requires the timely disclosure of internal control effectiveness and verification of such disclosure through external auditors. This law requires that an adequate system of internal accounting control exist and has forced organizations to revisit their internal as well as external audit capabilities. This could imply that computer administrators may be responsible for the analysis and documentation of computer-based controls in order to facilitate effective interaction with the auditors who are performing control evaluations.

The evidence gathered by the auditor to support an opinion on the financial statements includes data produced by the computer system; thus, a review of the controls on the computer system and of the reliability of the data produced by the system has become an integral part of most audits (Litecky & Rittenberg, 1981).

The role of the internal auditor is dictated by the management's efforts to evaluate the control structure of the information systems (Litecky & Rittenberg, 1981). Thus, internal auditors are expected to look at the adequacy of internal controls and management controls for regulating business functionalities. Internal auditors may also become involved with systems development audits, data security audits, application audits, as well as, on occasion, the evaluation of the various efficiencies of an operation (Litecky & Rittenberg, 1981).

The Sarbanes-Oxley Act mandates the performance of assessments from neutral, external auditors. These auditors have a responsibility to the general public regarding the authenticity of the audit reports. External auditors check for errors or irregularities that might occur in systems, and in controls which might prevent or detect such errors or irregularities. The effectiveness of such controls is extremely important because simply having the right controls in the various places may not suffice. The controls should be able to provide reasonable assurance that the systems are adequately secure (Litecky & Rittenberg, 1981).

SYSTEMS DEVELOPMENT

Internal auditors play an important role in systems development and EDP auditing. An auditor typically invests more time performing compliance audit tasks and less time evaluating systems development activities. The involvement of auditors in systems development needs to increase (Greenberg & Murphy, 1989) for a multitude of reasons. For example, an auditor should ensure that systems that are developed are auditable and the internal control environment is adequate (Greenberg & Murphy, 1989). In the post Sarbanes-Oxley Act era, it is necessary that the compliance requirements of system development practices be planned a priori and check points be developed throughout the development process (Mishra & Weistroffer, 2006). Compliance with the Sarbanes-Oxley Act may prove costly if such measures are added only as an afterthought, following system deployment. Adhering to an established framework or developing an in-house compliance plan, which is embedded in the development methodology, is required. An effective internal auditing functionality can help in meeting such objectives.

Auditing is also required post-implementation of newly developed information systems. Assessment of the control environment and a periodic review of the system is required by law.

GOVERNANCE

Auditors play a crucial role in the change management initiatives within an organization. Managing all business processes at an optimum level and allowing room for change requires infrastructural and strategic support. Auditors can provide both (maintenance and transition towards change) in an organization. Auditing is integral to the governance structure within an organization, and can add significant value to such initiatives. A simplified checklist detailing all of the activities that an auditor can perform in order to add value does not exist because value-adding techniques are unique for each organization (Bookal, 2002).

Proving better information assurance requires good governance practices. Audit initiatives should be viewed as a value-adding process not only to the governance process but also to the overall strategic direction of the organization. Auditors need to be a part of the solution, not just a part of the problems plaguing the organization. With reference to Section 404 of the Sarbanes-Oxley Act, auditors have never played a more decisive position in governance than now. They are expected to play the role of "independent insiders." For transparent governance practices, the board should seek independent advice from internal auditors. This will encourage the culture of accountability and enhance the perception of the organization in the eyes of the investors. In addition, this may improve the performance of the business.

Management counts on internal auditing to improve the governance process. In response to increased governmental regulations, auditing can play a strategic role in the organizational efforts towards information assurance. Auditors need to assist the board of directors in governance, self-assessment, and best practices ideas for internal control and risk management (Whitley, 2005).

CURRENT PRACTICES IN INTERNAL AUDIT

IT auditing is a very challenging job. Internal auditors have to focus on the risks and controls that are vital to sound corporate governance practices. The need for sound internal auditing within corporate governance structures has never been more clearly demonstrated than by recent events (Bookal, 2002). Auditors have to be professional and competent to do the expected job properly. The demanding job profile of auditors forces them to play a strong and visible role in governance, risk management, and internal control processes (Bookal, 2002). Some of the basic requirements to be an effective auditor and add value to the organization are:

- **Knowledge about organization and technology:** A deep understanding of technology and its impact on business process is required. This includes all of the technical capabilities, formal structures, and informal working relationships in the organization (Roth, 2003).
- **Leadership initiatives:** Internal auditors should have a strong working relationship with management, external auditors, and the board. There should be a free flow of information between all of these groups. This calls for strong leadership initiatives from the auditing team and the organization in order to provide enough resources as well as a degree of independence.
- **Unconventional:** To add value to a business and possibly see unforeseen problems requires unconventional and innovative methods. Audi-

tors are supposed to think "outside the box" and provide new directions to businesses. There is a huge societal responsibility placed on auditors, who are responsible for disclosing accurate information. Fulfilling such a promise requires constant work and innovative methods for keeping the business safe. Talented and motivated staff is required and this staff has to be involved in the decision making process in order to output good solutions.

- Participative and real time risk assessment: Auditors need to be continuously involved in the risk assessment process. Risk models developed by the audit team need to be real time based. Cyclical audits are becoming less prevalent (Roth, 2003) as it is believed that audit teams can add value throughout the business process. Multidisciplinary audit teams, including members from engineering, law, accounting, finance, and management, are required to continuously add value to the organization and to align organizational strategic IT with organizational objectives.

While a list of best practices for auditing may be used as a blue print, a comprehensive audit program which is specific to the needs of the organization and based on the organizational culture, organizational environment, and client needs should be created for internal audit purposes (Roth, 2003).

Risk Based Approach

Internal control assessment is an important aspect of an auditor's job. There are two primary ways of approaching the evaluation of internal controls (Litecky & Rittenberg, 1981).

- **Positive approach (often termed as the objectives approach):** In this approach, auditors assess whether sufficient controls exist in an organization to meet information assurance objectives. Interviews, observations, and analysis of flowcharts are used by auditors in their assessment.
- **Negative approach:** This approach concentrates on the effectiveness of the controls. A risk assessment approach is used to determine various irregularities in the system, and controls are identified as preventive or detective in nature.

It is also determined whether such controls can provide reasonable assurance. Questionnaires are used to identify the types of controls that should exist and interviews are conducted in the next stage.

Both of these approaches can be used in conjunction to yield a better assessment. A recent survey of auditors regarding the importance of various internal controls for assurance purposes suggests that program (computer software) change controls, online controls, and segregation of duties controls are the most important. An emphasis on these controls is becoming inevitable, given that an ever-increasing number of organizations are depending on computers and technology for the maintenance and flow of information.

Organizational risk management is better served by a risk based auditing approach. Therefore, the auditing approach should be risk based, emphasizing the purpose of the controls rather than the efficiency of the control implementation (McNamee & Selim, 1999). Excessive layers of control slow down the business process. Many organizations have began using control self assessment (CSA) to address management's concern in terms of risk and control (McNamee & Selim, 1999). Irrelevant controls are identified and discarded during the use of the CSA tool. Avoiding risk becomes the focus and may involve the redesign of business processes in order to mitigate inherent risk.

Elevated organizational ranks for risk managers, such as chief risk officer, are an indicator that audit functionality is gaining top governance priority (McNamee & Selim, 1999). Effective audit plans that incorporate the dynamic assessment of risks throughout business processes are crucial in ensuring effective assurance practice.

Process Based Approach

Information assurance practices can be divided into various stages with each stage having a different role in overall security management. In each stage, auditors are expected to contribute in different ways in order to ensure success of the assurance program. Some of these stages are (McEvilley, 2002):

- **Analysis:** Security problems can be identified in a rational assessment stage of organizational business process and information flow. Risk assessment is performed, control points at various stages are identified, and security solutions

are suggested. Each and every activity in the business process supports or provides a necessary and sufficient part of the solution. The assessment portion involves data collection to define the problem. This includes vulnerability, risk and threat identification and assessment, site surveys, penetration testing and analysis, and auditing (McEvilley, 2002). The auditors involved in this stage of assurance should help in identifying control points and methods to secure such points.

- **Planning:** The planning activities should include the establishment of an organization-wide infrastructure for the formal management of security endeavors. Such activities include the development of policy, standards, and procedures to govern all phases of the system lifecycle. This stage also prepares for the future maintenance of the systems by educating and training users. An assessment of the technical requirements of the organizations as well as the strengths and weaknesses is also provided. The auditors identify weaknesses in information flow, and provide a risk assessment of the vulnerabilities that can arise. Risk based audit, where auditors are an integral part of the business process and suggest remedies throughout the year, is currently the most popular audit approach.

- **Technical support:** In this stage the security plan is technically implemented. This may involve the development of the technical architecture and infrastructure, access control, installation of firewalls, and so on. Components are selected or designed, developed, and integrated into the architecture and infrastructure in order to construct the technology portion of the solution. Auditors help in ensuring that the organization has all of the requisite technical skills and solutions for assurance. Therefore, auditors are also required to have sufficient knowledge of technologies.

- **Maintenance and feedback:** This phase ensures that the security plan works and that business continuity is maintained. The security plan should be able to solve the business problem and add value to the organization by ensuring business continuity. An incident response plan, disaster recovery techniques, and continuous assessment of the policies are required. Auditors help in providing a unique outsider perspective regarding the effectiveness of various security solutions. A feedback cycle helps in improving the assurance plan and in continuously improving any identified shortcomings.

Internal auditors need continuous support from management in order to convey their change initiatives to business process owners within an organization. Conflict resolution between various stakeholders is a job requirement for auditors and must be properly managed for overall assurance purpose (Allen, 1996). An auditor's primary responsibility is to provide assurance to clients (Marks, 2001) and other stakeholders. Critical thinking about technology is often a key to success. An auditor must think beyond the obvious, assess unforeseen risks using the latest technologies, and suggest innovative and adaptive methods for combating issues.

FUTURE TRENDS

Today's changing business scenario arguably requires a plan to engineer effective and measurable security into organizational systems that provide critical functions and services. There are various ways through which internal auditors can add value to the business processes and enhance assurance. Auditors can help in improving cycle times, productivity, quality, employee turnover, customer satisfaction, and financial results (Berk, 2006).

Internal auditors have a unique role to play in this ever changing and confusing business landscape—that of risk managers and consultants for assurance initiatives (Marks, 2001). The job of auditing presents a plethora of challenges and more real time solutions are required. The skill set and expertise of auditors working with technology have to be sufficient in order to understand the intricacies of the business world. Auditing as a profession is rapidly changing and providing new ways of information assurance.

Several aspects of auditing require more vigilant attention and emphasis in the future. For example, embedding a control culture within an organization is an important area of future research. Some essential actions stated in Section 404 of the Sarbanes-Oxley Act are: setting the tone at the top, providing adequate control documentation, improving operational effectiveness, strengthening other non-computer related internal controls, and improved information systems security (Rittenberg & Miller, 2005). Internal controls provide a solid conceptual foundation for effective

information assurance process. The establishment of a strong auditing culture in an organization should be followed by embedding "control-centric" thinking into process flow and breeding a philosophy of continuous improvement.

In order to further elevate the importance of internal audit in information assurance practices of organizations, there is a demand for providing the profession of internal auditors the same status as that of doctors or lawyers. The communication with management and its auditors should be considered privileged and protected by law (Ferenzczy, 2004). Auditors have access to the most confidential information in the organization and their assessment of business processes is provided as a report which acts as a bridge of trust between investors and the management of organizations. Communication of any sorts between internal departments of organizations and auditors, in the process of assessment, should be protected from outsiders (Ferenzczy, 2004). Even though internal audit reports and the analysis in such files may be protected, the information contained in such files is not currently protected by law.

CONCLUSION

Information assurance should be viewed as an enabler for businesses providing infrastructural support for various processes. Information assurance objectives can only be realized through an effective systems audit team. Only an effective security program, developed through rigorous audit functionality, can incorporate assurance principles in the fabric of organizational activities. Security solutions engineered and entwined with audit and assurance processes can provide stability to businesses. Internal auditing plays an important role in the assurance program of an organization.

REFERENCES

Allen, R. (1996). Managing internal audit conflicts. *The Internal Auditor, 53*(4), 58-61.

Berk, J. (2006). Change champions. *The Internal Auditor, 63*(2), 64-69.

Bookal, L. (2002). Internal auditors: Integral to good corporate governance. *The Internal Auditor, 59*(4), 44-49.

Bunker, E. (2003). Optimizing an organization's security effectiveness by using vulnerability management to support the audit function. *Information Systems Control Journal, 4*, 28-30.

Dhillon, G. (2006). *Principles of information systems security: Text and cases.* John Wiley &Sons.

Ferenzczy, J. (2004). The privilege of internal auditing. *The Internal Auditor, 61*(2), 74-81.

Greenberg, R. & Murphy, D. (1989). Systems development and the internal auditor: Where are we. *The Internal Auditor, 46*(4), 52-57.

Information Systems Audit and Control Association (2004). *CISA Review Manual, 2004 Edition.* Rolling Meadows, IL: ISACA.

Litecky, C. & Rittenberg, L. (1981). The external auditor's review of computer controls. *Communications of the ACM, 24*(5), 288-295.

Marks, N. (2001). The new age of internal auditing. *The Internal Auditor, 58*(6), 44-49.

McEvilley, M. (2002). The essence of information assurance and its implications for the Ada community. *Proceedings of SIGAda'02,* December 8-12, Houston, TX, USA.

McNamee, D. & Selim, G. (1999). The next step in risk management. *The Internal Auditor, 56*(3), 35-38.

McQuay, P. (2005). Systems development audits. *The Internal Auditor, 62*(6), 58-63.

Mishra, S. & Weistroffer, R. (2006). A framework for integrating Sarbanes-Oxley compliance into the software development process. *Proceedings of the 9th Southern Association of Information Systems Conference,* Jacksonville, March 10-12.

Oxner, T. & Oxner, K. (2006). Boom time for internal audit professionals. *The Internal Auditor, 63*(3), 50-58.

Perkins, B. (2006). Assessments are opportunities. *Computerworld.* Retrieved on December 20, 2006 from http://www.computerworld.com/action/article.do?command=viewArticleBasic&articleId=274359

Rittenberg, L. & Miller, P. (2005). The good news about compliance. *The Internal Auditor, 62*(3), 55-61.

Robitaille, D. (2004). World-class audit and control practices. *The Internal Auditor, 61*(2), 74-81.

Roth, J. (2003). How do internal auditors add value? *The Internal Auditor, 60*(1), 33-37.

The Institute of Internal Auditors (IIA) (2006). The role of auditing in public sector governance. Retrieved on December 19, 2006 from http://www.theiia.org/index.cfm?bhcp=1

Verschoor, C. (1991). The impact of legislation and regulations on internal auditing. *The Internal Auditor, 48*(3), 96-100.

Whitley, J. (2005). Internal auditing's role in corporate governance. *The Internal Auditor, 62*(5), 21-22.

Yavagal, D., Lee, S., Ahn, G., & Gandhi, R. (2005). Common criteria requirements modeling and its uses for quality of information assurance (QoIA). *Proceedings of 43rd ACM Southeast Conference,* March 18-20, Kennesaw, GA.

KEY TERMS

Information Assurance (IA): A process centric phenomenon that is comprehensive enough to include definition, implementation, and verification level operations.

Information Systems Security: Information systems security is the process of protecting all information assets from misuse, harm or any other unintended result. This includes securing information in computers, maintaining integrity of business processes, retaining skilled knowledge workers with their implicit knowledge and also encouraging employees to claim ownership of their share of information assets (Dhillon, 2006).

IT Governance: IT governance can be defined as the structure of relationships and processes to direct and control the enterprise. IT governance helps the organization achieve its goal by adding value while balancing risk and return over IT and its processes (ISACA, 2004).

Internal Control: Internal controls are a means to provide reasonable assurance that an organization will achieve its business objectives while avoiding undesired risks (ISACA, 2004). Internal controls are policies, procedures, practices, and organizational structures put in place to reduce business risks in organizations.

Role of Audit: Internal auditing is an independent, objective assurance and consulting activity designed to add value and improve an organization's operations. It helps an organization accomplish its objectives by bringing a systematic, disciplined approach to evaluate and improve the effectiveness of risk management, control, and governance processes (Institute of Internal Auditors, 2006).

Chapter XXV
IT Continuity in the
Face of Mishaps

William H. Friedman
University of Central Arkansas, USA

ABSTRACT

This chapter is management oriented. It first proposes a general theoretical context for IT disasters within the wider class of all types of disasters to which a business is subject—whether caused by natural or human action. After this theoretical discussion, numerous practical and proactive prevention methods then are suggested that can be applied both before and after an IT disaster. Implementation of these measures should contribute greatly to reducing both the occurrence of disasters and the damage that might be wrought by most adverse events not under our control.

INTRODUCTION

Adversity planning has come to the forefront of the public's concerns because of both the scope and frequency of news making natural disasters. "Ordinary" computer and networking failures, no matter how far reaching the consequences and importance of the entities affected, are reported with such regularity as hardly to cause a stir in the public arena—except among those affected, for example, the investment community (Campbell, Gordon, Loeb, & Zhou, 2003; Cavusoglu, Mishra, & Raghunathan, 2004). Both these realizations point to the need for reassessing the nature of past and probable future problems as well as instituting effective preventive and recovery measures. A theoretic context is provided for the subsequent discussion of disasters.

This chapter considers topics related to disasters in a natural progression:

- What we think about disasters in general and why we need to revise the conventional "wisdom" about disasters
- Why disaster matters so much—its consequences
- Legal requirements and methods for disaster planning
- How to be successful in minimizing loss from a disaster and instituting controls
- Ensuring physical security
- Post-disaster IT` continuity and recovery

REVISING COMMON ASSUMPTIONS ABOUT DISASTER

First we need to revise our assumptions about disasters:

1. **Catastrophes occur independently of one another.** Comment: Any given disaster may be due to a cause that does not disappear after the first strike. Malware creators propagate their exploits in waves.
2. **Disasters tend to repeat themselves with only minor differences.**
3. In the short term, the chances of experiencing a calamity are low.
4. It is unlikely that a calamity like the last one will occur any time soon.
5. The number of calamitous events in any narrow timeframe or given place will be constant over time

With knowledge gained through bitter and repeated experience, organizations would do well to call into question the guiding assumptions mentioned above and consider the following points (which counter the above assumptions):

1. Weather, seismic, and especially socially caused traumatic events seem to feed off one another.
2. Greater communication and transportation resources are now available to ill-intentioned people. Comment: Even without any apparent communication, a relatively recently noted phenomenon is the simultaneous discovery and creation of new behaviors—both good and ill—in geographically separated locales. Ideas, which crop up in one place, may arise in another at approximately the same time. This situation is evidently part of nature. For instance, Japanese primatologists observed a single macaque monkey who learned how to wash sweet potatoes before eating them and that this learned procedure spread to the entire troupe (Narby, 2005). Other instances of primate learning have spread to other locations without any apparent communication.
3. Increased extremism and climatic changes (brought about by greater industrial activity, perhaps) trigger more human-made disasters.
4. Ideologically motivated damage and employee sabotage are increasingly the norm.
5. One calamitous event can be seen to stimulate a recurrence rather quickly. An instability here and now augments instability later and nearby.
6. The pace of adverse happenings is quickening.
7. New kinds of items causing disaster are emerging, for example, denial of service attacks, rootkits.

CONSEQUENCES OF DISASTER

Three factors in any discussion of the topic of this article must be explicated:

1. Hoepman and Jacobs (2007) define *exposure* of a system as the "likelihood of successful attack" (one can add for purposes of this more general article, "likelihood of *disaster*") irrespective of any damage that might result. However, other sources explain it as the "condition of being exposed to danger or loss" (*Webster's*, 1981) or the **"amount of possible financial loss"** (*Encarta Dictionary*, 1992). These latter two definitions are better able to preserve the distinction from *risk*, because risk is often explained in terms of likelihood or probability.
2. Hoepman and Jacobs explain *risk* to a system as its "exposure in view of the extent of the *expected* harm," which agrees with *Webster's*, namely, **"the possibility of loss"** (*Webster's*, 1981). Clearly, both definitions imply that it is a matter of probability.
3. Finally, Hoepman and Jacobs define the *security* of a system as "an objective measure of the number of its vulnerabilities and their severity" (2007). This latter notion can be augmented by saying security also involves the ability to detect, anticipate, and avoid attack or calamity.

To preserve IT *continuity*, one must find a way to reduce exposure and risk and increase security. Insufficient proactive behavior to provide security to critical IT systems and, of course, its crucial data underscores the exposure and risk that jeopardize the organization. A representative sample of common detrimental consequences of poor security for crucial IT systems given below; several are mentioned in PriceWaterhouseCoopers (2007):

1. Loss of productivity
2. Delay of project development
3. Lawsuits and governmental action over insufficient protection of data important to others
4. Loss of organizational knowledge
5. Loss of revenues from valuable technology and intellectual property
6. Brand damage due to loss of confidence by stakeholders (internal and external)
7. Reduced short-term cash flow and increased financial obligations.
8. Falling short of market expectations.
9. Credit rating is in jeopardy of being downgraded.
10. Financial scandal and accounting irregularities
11. Shareholder defections
12. Litigation
13. Large judgments
14. Dimished reputation.
15. Inability to continue to function and/or even continue to exist as an organization

While the above effects of IT mishaps can bring down a company—especially the last, one should bear in mind that trumpeting a proven track record on IT security can provide a company with considerable competitive advantage (Kroenke, 2007). Customers and investors will be much more comfortable with a company that has safe, reliable information systems.

GENERAL PREPAREDNESS

Legal Requirements to Provide Safeguards

If the consequences of IT failure cited above are not sufficient incentive towards IT vigilance, the government of the United States recently has mandated compliance in the areas of security, privacy, and financial accuracy in the form of various bills:

1. The Gramm-Leach-Blilely Act (GLBA), which requires organizations to protect "their customers' financial records" and "take all reasonable measures to detect, prevent, and respond to attacks, intrusions, or other systems failures" (Carr & Snyder, 2007).

2. The Health Insurance Portability and Accountability Act (HIPAA), which is designed to protect the health records of individuals. Organizations must control "access, policies, procedures, and technology to restrict who has access to the information and (especially importantly for IT) requires establishment of security mechanisms to protect data that are electronically transmitted" (Carr & Snyder, 2007).

3. The Sarbanes-Oxley of 2002 (Pub. L. No. 107-204, 116 Stat. 745, also known as the **Public Company Accounting Reform and Investor Protection Act of 2002**) (Wikipedia, 2007). A corollary of the act's requirement is that C-level officers attest to their companies' having proper 'internal controls.' It's hard to sign off on the validity of data if the systems maintaining them aren't secure" (Carr & Snyder, 2007).

In order to provide the mandated disaster planning, a company must strive to be legally blameless by setting up and prove (if the need arises) that it has an adequate disaster plan. There should be a planning team an extensive risk assessment, test runs, training and general orientation for employees, and finally revisiting the plan to see what can be improved (*Business*, 2002)

Systematizing the Development of a Security Plan

In order to develop a satisfactory security system, it would be a good idea to institute a security system development cycle, much like a general systems development life cycle. This cycle might consist of these steps:

1. Preparedness for an organization requires a detailed knowledge of what its critical systems and data stores are. These are systems, which if suddenly rendered inoperable might cause the demise of the organization. Such systems and data stores make possible the flow of information and materials within an organization and govern the relationships with external entities like customers and governmental agencies.

2. It is not practical to protect all such items, so one must select the ones that can be feasibly safeguarded.

3. Once these systems/data stores are identified, one needs to examine the likely threats.

4. Determine what protections are in place now and how well they have served.

5. Next comes the installation of new or augmented mitigation measures and controls. Comment: these include firewall rules, router ACLs (access control lists), IDS (intrusion detection systems), and IPS (intrusion prevention-management systems).

6. The last step (before repeating the cycle) is to monitor the security of the systems as well as any *residual* vulnerabilities that either resulted in damage (despite the defenses), were overlooked, or that one might expect to be exploited in the future. Comment: A useful tool, generically known as a "compliance dashboard" continually examines the "key performance indicators" of systems—especially those linked to compliance issues and makes the results known immediately and, frequently, in graphic form.

One more security measure ought to be mentioned in the context of development. Counterintuitively, Hoepman and Jacobs argue surprisingly coercively that open source (!) security systems are more secure than closed source. (2007) Keeping a security system closed is useless, they contend, since "tools like debuggers and disassemblers allow attackers to find vulnerabilities in applications without access to the source relatively quickly." Moreover, because of openness, many legitimate persons are able to find and patch vulnerabilities.

SUCCESS FACTORS IN MINIMIZING RISK AND LOSS

There are certain common principles to be observed in the introduction of any system (adapted from Hayes, 2007). Management should

1. Provide "visible, consistent support and an active role in communication and reward."

2. Assure linkage of IT security to corporate strategies. Comment: Alignment is typically measured through psychometric surveys of employees who report their answers on a Likert scale, which is then summarized demographically.

3. Clearly prioritize development and implementation of security measures (relative to other initiatives, programs, and priorities).

4. Require the use of facts and data to support actions at all levels of decision-making.

5. Create accountabilities, expectations, roles, and responsibilities for the organization.

6. Conduct and attend regular reviews to assure and verify progress.

7. Establish a documented 1-year security project inventory (and refresh regularly).

8. Assign a Champion and Black Belt to each project and hold them accountable (also see Burbridge & Friedman, 1988).

9. Purchase business insurance (McNamara, 2007):
   ○ Liability
   ○ Life (for critical personnel)
   ○ Workman's compensation
   ○ Property damage
   ○ Business interruption

Controls

Special controls not unique to IT security include items from this checklist (Turban, Mclean, & Wetherbee, 2001)

- Detect problems as early as possible
- Deter intentional acts
- Enhance recovery systems
- Correct [existing] problems

PHYSICAL SECURITY

In first considering security issues, it is understandable that one would immediately think of mishaps affecting IT operations due to human neglect (e.g., carelessness, about passwords, omitted backups, etc.) or intentional tampering (planting malware that will sabotage a system)—in other words, incidents involving software and data. However, equal attention should be directed at preventable threats emanating from purely physical causes and deploying appropriate defense mechanisms.

- A large department store chain has built a windowless, concrete bunker to house its main computing equipment and data next to its corporate headquarters. This facility has its own generators and a reserve supply of fuel in case of power outage.

- A site should have fireproofing and special protection for extinguishing fires without damaging equipment (e.g., Halon gas).
- The site should have (electrical) surge protection and uninterruptible power supplies (e.g., backup batteries).
- Climate (e.g., temperature and humidity) controls are essential.
- There should be shielding against electromagnetic fields—these can emanate from either natural sources or from saboteurs.
- Physical intrusion alarms (e.g., motion detectors) ought to be installed in computer centers.
- Restrictions on physical access should be instituted (e.g., man traps, pass cards, biometric IDs, etc.)
- IT can be distributed to several locations to avoid having all an organization's eggs are in one basket.
- All IT activity can be continuously replicated at one or more (distant) sites, ready to take over in case of emergency or normal downtime, say, for upgrading a system.
- An organization can combine the above two strategies of distributing and replicating IT services. For instance, if New York provides the primary service for just the East Coast of the U.S., Chicago for the Midwest, and San Francisco for the Pacific Coast—a distributed IT department; then mirror sites with replicated transactions could be safely located in Philadelphia, St. Louis, and Los Angeles respectively.
- In the above example, an organization might be well advised to choose locations (outside of California), that is, places known historically to be free from earthquakes, forest fires, floods, El Nino (and other severe storms).

PROVIDING FOR IT SYSTEMS CONTINUITY AFTER A DISASTER

Numerous sources have warned organizations and individuals about backing up their important data as a wise protective measure in the event of a disaster. However, two other aspects of this very important topic are not often given sufficient attention, namely, data recovery and continuing operations—seamlessly, if possible. Organizations and private individuals need to have an *operational* fallback to maintain their normal activities. It is not just data that need to be preserved, but also the ability to function continuously, even when a catastrophe interrupts operations.

Typically, in order to function properly off-site, an organization should look for

1. Adequate infrastructure (space, air conditioning, etc.)
2. Guaranteed use of similar hardware and software in case of need
3. A platform-independent network
4. Adequate storage
5. End-user recovery capability
6. Voice recovery capability
7. Mobile recovery capability
8. Ample security at recovery sites too (!)
9. Backup procedures to the emergency sites

IT Continuity Measures

Given the scope of recent disasters, for example, storms and terrorist attacks, it is clear that one needs to plan organizational continuity outside their normal locus: the home, the office, the city, or even the wider region, if similarly susceptible.

There are several precautionary technologies and strategies presently available, all designed to ensure continuity of operations for a company.

1. **Failover** (ability of a system automatically and transparently to switch to a working database, server, or network in case the primary system fails). Accessibility is, of course, vital for mission-critical applications. Still, physical damage, system failures, data center outages, and network downtime regularly cause important applications to fail. Certain tools can mirror application data in real-time and transmit to an organization's local or remote backup system via a typical network connection. By automating complex failover and failback processes, such tools allow companies to resume normal operations quickly without human intervention or the long delays associated with recovery from tape.

2. **Hot site.** An organization arranges with a special provider or department to establish a disaster recovery facility that copies computer transactions as they occur, for example, the organization's production databases are replicated in real-time. Ideally this facility should be located in a zone previously unaffected by the type of disasters one might expect in the present location. The

305

idea is that when the main center is disabled, the hot site can kick in immediately or as shortly as possible.

3. **"Warm site."** This is a less elaborate arrangement, calling for duplicating records at intervals rather than in real-time. The tradeoff is in lower cost and fewer complexities.

4. **"Cold site."** If an organization arranges with a service provider or reciprocal partner to provide space or equipment when needed, they both have more security and chances of continuing their normal functions.

5. **Mobile van.** There are providers who maintain a type of moving recovery site (hot, warm, or cold), that can show up on the doorstop of an organization experiencing a problem with a ready-to-use mobile recovery unit. The mobile provider supplies both technology and replicated data to ensure continuous operations outside the original center. Obviously, however, if the area affected makes this impossible, it would be necessary to meet the van at some distance. The main advantage of the mobile van then is tremendous flexibility.

CONCLUSION

It is never too early to initiate implementation of these suggestions. An organization should plan in advance how to protect its people, assets, and information resources. Each organization should also conduct the requisite feasibility studies in anticipation of the most common and the most deleterious disasters. The expenditures on protection naturally ought to be commensurate with the values being protected. Needless to say, all controls and safeguards decided upon should be tested for reliability under extreme conditions before a company can be confident it has done all it can to mitigate disaster..

REFERENCES

Burbridge, J., & Friedman, W. (1988). The roles of user and sponsor in MIS projects. *Project Management Journal, 19*(2), 71-76.

Business, the ultimate resource (2002). Cambridge, MA: Perseus Publishing, pp. 492-493.

Carr, H., & Snyder, C. (2007). *Data communications and network security*. Boston: McGraw-Hill Irwin.

Cavusoglu, H., Mishra, B., & Raghunathan, S. (2004). The effect of Internet security breach announcements on shareholder wealth: Capital market reactions for breached firms and internet security developers. *International Journal of Electronic Commerce, 9*(1), 69-104.

Coffee, P. (2007). Security: Next steps. *eWeek, 24*(37).

Campbell, K., Gordon, L., Loeb, M. & Zhou, L. (2003). The economic cost of publicly announced information security breaches: Empirical evidence from the stock market. *Journal of Computer Security, 11*(3), 431-448.

Encarta Dictionary: English (North America) in Microsoft Office Word 2003 based on The American heritage Dictionary of the American Language (1992). (3rd ed.). Boston: Houghton Mifflin Co.

Friedman. W. (2005). Organizational continuity is vital in face of catastrophe. *Log Cabin Democrat, Business/Farm*. Sunday, September 18, 4B

Hayes, B. (n.d.). Six sigma critical success factors. Retrieved May 20, 2007 from http://www.isixsigma.com/library/content/c020415a.asp

Hoepman, J-H & Jacobs, B. (2007). Increased security through open source. *Communications of the ACM, 50*(1), 79-83.

Kroenke, D. (2007). *Using MIS*. Upper Saddle River, NJ: Pearson, Prentice Hall

Labovitz, G. & Rosansky V. (1997). *the power of alignment: how great companies stay centered and accomplish extraordinary things*. New York: John Wiley & Sons.

McNamara, C. (n.d.). Business insurance. Retrieved May 20, 2007 from http://www.managementhelp.org/insurnce/insurnce.htm

Narby, J. (2005). *Intelligence in nature*. New York: The Penguin Group.

OneSwitchTM Overview: Automated enterprise replication & failover/failback for Windows applications at the push of a button. Retrieved May 20, 2007 from http://www.messageone.com

Poulsen, K. (2003). Windows root kits a stealthy threat. Retrieved May 21, 2007 from http://www.theregister. co.uk/2003/03/07/windows_root_kits_a_stealthy/

PriceWaterhouseCoopers. (n.d.). What if: How to prepare and respond to a corporate crisis. Retrieved May 20, 2007 from http://www.pwc.com/images/us/ eng/main/view3/bigwhatif.pdf

Sarbanes-Oxley Act. *Wikipedia,* (n.d.). Retrieved May 20, 2007 from   http://en.wikipedia.org/wiki/ Sarbanes-Oxley_Act

Turban, E., Mclean, E., & Wetherbee, J. (2001). *Information technology for management.* New York: John Wiley & Sons.

Webster's third new international dictionary of the English language unabridged (1981). Springfield: G. & C. Merriam Co.

KEY TERMS

Champion: A person of prestige in an organization who can ensure that a project will progress as expected.

Close Source: A program with a restrictive license designed to maintain a degree of secrecy about the code; only the execution modules are distributed.

Cold Site: A relatively inexpensive alternative to other backup sites, since there is no hardware or transmitted data already in place to resume operations.

Exposure: Amount of possible financial loss in a disaster.

Failback: Resumption of operations at restored site of disaster.

Failover: Ability of a disrupted system to switch to a working system with seamless continuity.

Halon Gas: An agent for extinguishing fires without causing damage to equipment that water might bring about.

Hot Site: Backup site usually operated by a service company enabling a company to resume its IT processing. Data are transmitted to the site in real time, so the site has immediately current data. The hardware is already in place to continue processing.

IT: Abbreviation of information technology; the functional unit in an organization that processes data to yield information.

Open Source: The actual coding statements in a program are made publically available, without charge; responsible programmers are free to suggest, or in some cases, modify or add to the program.

Risk: Probability of a loss; sometimes, the probability of a loss multiplied by the exposure.

Rootkit: Software that introduces and hides running programs, either legitimate or illegitimate from the operating system and may take control of a computer. A rootkit is notoriously difficult to detect and remove (Poulsen, 2003).

Security of a System: "An objective measure of the number of its vulnerabilities and their severity;" also the ability to detect, anticipate, and avoid attack or calamity.

Warm Site: Backup location where data are transmitted only periodically instead of continuously. The hardware is already in place to continue processing from the last transmission of data.

Chapter XXVI
Business Continuity and Disaster Recovery Plans

Yvette Ghormley
Saint Leo University, USA

ABSTRACT

This chapter describes the tools that businesses can use to create a Business Continuity and Disaster Recovery Plan. Utilizing business modeling, business impact analysis, risk analysis, and mitigation strategies, businesses can analyze their operations to learn the business critical functions that must be recovered as quickly as possible during any type of disaster. These processes are illustrated using the case study of a hypothetical small manufacturing business located in California. Specific information technology solutions are also discussed and the necessity of integrating them into the overall plan. Businesses that are prepared to face any kind of disaster with an implemented and tested Business Continuity and Disaster Recovery Plan are much more likely to survive than businesses that do not have such a plan. It is hoped that the contents of this chapter will spur business owners that have not yet adopted such a plan to do so.

INTRODUCTION

Disasters have affected businesses in all shapes and forms for hundreds of years. However, with the advent of high-speed communication, computers, digitized data, and vastly increased reliance on databases and electronic storage of information, businesses have a lot more to lose than hardware if a disaster strikes. Many business also operate in a "24/7" environment and are global in their scope of operations. A high percentage of small businesses are also Internet-based, or have a significant portion of income derived from the Internet, a marketing and selling resource system that 15 years ago was little more than a curiosity.

Consider the following facts: (a) 80 percent of businesses affected by a major "incident" close within

18 months, (b) 90 percent of businesses that lose data as a result of a disaster close within two years, and (c) 58 percent of UK businesses were disrupted by a manmade disaster over 3,000 miles away in another country (the World Trade Center terrorist attacks of September 11, 2001 in New York) (Taylor, 2006). It is clear that all businesses, from large multinational corporations down to the "mom and pop" business selling services on Internet, must develop a disaster recovery (DR) plan and prepare for business continuity (BC) following an incident that affects business operations.

It used to be that BC and DR plans were the domain of IT departments, and while some of the mission-critical items are certainly IT-related, the functions of IT must be integrated into the overall plan (Taylor

2006; Vijayan, 2005). D'Amico (2006) recommends a three-pronged approach to preparing BC and DR plans. First, the Resolve Phase, which involves assessing the risks, whom should be involved, what units of the business are most critical, and what steps can be taken to minimize risk. Second, the Respond Phase, which includes formation of the disaster response team, how information will be disseminated to employees, how customers and suppliers will be notified, and where personnel will operate and with what equipment. Third, the Rebuild Phase, which includes the decision of which personnel will be directly involved in damage assessment and rebuilding, adjustments to business operations while rebuilding is in progress, and the maintenance of operations so that business can proceed. This is the approach adopted for the chapter.

The chapter comprises four main sections: (a) background, which includes categories of disasters that can impact businesses, consequences, and an outline of business continuity and disaster recovery methodologies; (b) the three-phase approach to BC and DR, which includes (1) constituting a BC & DR team, (2) assessing the risks of likely disasters, (3) forming a priority list of business-critical functions, (4) mitigating the risks, (5) creating operations plans in the event of a disaster, (6) writing the BC & DR plan in simple manual form, (7) implementing and testing the plan, and (8) specific IT and engineering functions that must be integrated into the overall plan, which include backup and distribution of company data and records, provision of hardware and software backup, specific supplier and intercompany agreements, satellite and voice-over IP (VOIP) telephone switching, utility backup, temporary employee and business relocation, and restoration of critical systems on a priority basis; (c) future trends; and (d) conclusions.

The chapter will be most geared toward small and medium-sized businesses and entities.

BACKGROUND

Types of Disasters

Several descriptors exist that can help define a disaster from the point of view of a business. The first is the scale or geographic footprint. An onsite disaster is one that only affects a business' operations at a given location. A denial-of-service attack aimed at a company's servers, or the broken water pipe that showered a Pennsylvania hospital's data center (Buckley, 2002) are both examples of this category. The next higher level is the local disaster, which typically affects a community. For example, a fire that damaged a main communications cable in Manchester, England on March 29, 2004 left 130,000 homes and businesses without phone or Internet services (Taylor, 2006). Higher still is the regional-level disaster, typified by Hurricane Katrina, whose damaging winds and resultant storm surge caused 1,570 deaths in Louisiana and $40-50 billion in economic losses (Kates, Colten, Laska & Leatherman, 2006). At the highest level of the scale are national and international disasters. If the H5N1 influenza strain ever develops into a pandemic, this will be one unwelcome example (Maldin, Inglesby, Nuzzo, Lien, Gronvall, Toner, et al., 2005).

The second is the type of disaster: manmade or natural. Earthquakes, floods, hurricanes, and tornadoes, are examples of the latter, while the attacks of September 11, 2001 or the Phillips Petroleum chemical explosion in Pasadena, Texas, exemplify the former. However, there can also be a gray area insofar as the impact of a natural disaster can be far larger when inappropriate risks or actions are taken. Thus one might argue that the flooding of New Orleans after the passage of Hurricane Katrina was a result of poor levee maintenance, rather than an exceptionally severe hurricane.

The third parameter is the duration of the initial event that constitutes the disaster. Usually this is measured in minutes or hours, but certain incidents, such as flooding or snowstorms, can have durations of several days or even weeks.

The final descriptor is whether any warning occurs, and the length of the warning preceding the disaster. Most disasters have little or no warning, although there might be useful imminent signs, particularly with natural disasters, that are probability-related.

Occasionally, disasters can occur that have more of a diffuse geographic nature, but which nevertheless still impact business. Coombs (2004) lists several examples that do not fit the classic disaster profile, such as product tampering (e.g., the Tylenol tampering cases involving cyanide), a technical error accident, which can be exemplified by the crash of an airliner, or a technical error recall, such as a product failure in the marketplace.

Consequences of Disasters for Businesses

On first analysis, the parameters of the disaster will seem to dictate the impact it will have on a given business, and this is true to a certain extent. However, more important, is the degree to which critical functions of a business are affected. For example, in a study of the unavailability of health management information systems (HMIS) on healthcare maintenance organizations (HMOs), Bandyopadhyay (2001) found that loss of HMIS lasting < 24 hours would be critical for 26.7 percent of HMOs. This clearly points the way to having alternate data sites, and recovery methods that bring such centers quickly online. However, for many businesses, loss of communications and power are also critical aspects of disasters.

The experience of Hurricanes Katrina and Rita during the summer of 2005 showed many Gulf-Coast companies just how vulnerable their communication networks were, both within the company, and those affecting supply chains, and customers. Many chemical companies were forced to use satellite-based Internet and phone connections because more than three million telephone lines were out of operation, as well as more than 1,000 cellular transmitting sites that were inoperative (Seewald & D'Amico, 2005). Therefore, any DR plan must address alternate ways of setting up vital communications.

While power outages are not uncommon, due mostly to storm-related damage and natural disasters, as well as the occasional accidental severance of neighborhood cables, few business owners think about the state of the nation's electricity grid system. A stark reminder came on August 14, 2003, when a cascade failure of power management in a small Midwest utility company swiftly led to the collapse of the national grid in the northeast and central parts of the country, with outages lasting up to five days, and business losses of $6 billion (Taylor, 2006).

Power is basic. Onsite emergency generators can help keep critical systems operational for several days or weeks, but for power-intensive businesses, such as manufacturing, unless the facility has a power cogeneration plant, there are likely to be sustained financial losses from an inability to produce goods. As a result, analysis during DR planning should tackle mechanisms that might mitigate such losses, such as business interruption insurance (Gebhardt, 2000; Wong, Monaco, & Louise, 1994), or the cost-effectiveness of alternate power sources.

DR planning should also investigate how the disaster is managed, both from an external point of view, such as a customer, and internally, such as perceived by affected employees. In some cases, this is referred to as crisis management. Poorly managed disasters carry a message into the future that can negatively affect the management and perception of how subsequent disasters are handled. A case in point is the explosion that happened at the Phillips Petroleum plant in Pasadena, Texas, on March 27, 2000, when people were reminded of the far deadlier blast that occurred in 1989 that killed 23 workers (Coombs, 2004). In such instances, Coombs (2004) found that the impact of prior disasters can be negative even if the current disaster is not the fault of the business organization, if the disaster history of the company is made public at the time. This finding is part of Situational Crisis Communication Theory.

Another facet that should not be overlooked is how the DR team and the employees of a business are affected by a disaster. In disasters of extensive magnitude, first responders are routinely debriefed in a process termed Critical Incident Stress Management (CISM) (Hammond & Brooks, 2001). CISM is usually conducted in group sessions 48-72 hours after the incident and is designed to assist participants in emotionally and cognitively processing the events that have happened to mitigate the stressful reactions that are generated by disasters, and to lessen the risk of PTSD (posttraumatic stress disorder) from occurring (Dyregrov, 1989; Mitchell, 1983). CISM sessions are usually conducted by a mental health professional and a member of the DR team that was not involved in the actual incident, and consist of individuals relating what happened to them, and what actions they performed. The emphasis is on understanding the stressful and emotional reactions that accompanied the disaster.

In addition, the psychological reaction of employees and their families to a disaster, particularly one that involves injuries or death, and/or extensive damage, should be addressed. Failure to do so can result in psychological disturbances and trauma that can be long lasting in the post-impact phase (Somasundaram, Norris, Asukai, & Murthy, 2003; Thomas, 2006). Intervention should be initiated at the early stages for those most at risk of developing PTSD, severe anxiety, or depression (Somasundaram et al, 2003).

Business Continuity and Disaster Recovery Methodologies

Several methodologies are used in conjunction to develop a BC and DR plan. These include business modeling, business impact analysis (BIA), risk analysis, and mitigation strategy development

Business Modeling

The purpose of business modeling is to elicit the relationships between people, processes, hardware, and software applications. For small businesses of perhaps less than 20 employees, this exercise can be conducted on paper, perhaps with the aid of simple mapping software, such as Microsoft Visio (Erlanger, 2006). However, the larger and more sophisticated the business is, the more will be the need for software the guide the BC & DR team. For example, Paragon, a Sungard product, is a software package that guides users along the business continuity pathway, and includes diagramming capabilities; Strohl Systems LDPRS can also model a dependency map, allowing users to assess what would happen to other systems if a single process is disrupted.

Erlanger (2006) also stresses that finding a framework for business modeling can be helpful. For governance, bridging the gap between control requirements, technical issues, and business risks, COBIT (controlit. org) is a possibility. For IT contingency planning, both COSO (coso.org) and ITIL (itil-toolkit.com) contain useful documents.

The output of business modeling can directly feed into BIA, since it highlights how critical systems are connected.

Business Impact Analysis

Deciding what is most critical to a business is the function of BIA. There has been little research conducted about the best way to conduct a BIA—for example, whether directors, executives, or other personnel should be consulted (Erlanger, 2006)—but at the end of the day the process is about discovering the different layers that exist and their interrelationships within and between the different systems that might support multiple business operations. Although many executives might indicate that the functions under their domain are critical, when considerable money has to be spent ensuring that they can be quickly brought up after a disaster, it is often determined that cheaper alternatives can be found. At a minimum, the following items should be assessed, according to Keahey (2006): (a) financial impact due to disruption of operations, (b) loss of assets (human, equipment, infrastructure), (c) violation of laws and regulations, and (d) effect on public perception. Conducting a BIA can also uncover hidden interdependencies that might be the result of gradual process improvements. The reason the BIA is key, is that it identifies the processes or functions that are mission-critical, and which will constitute the driving input for the disaster recovery plan (DRP) (Bandyopadhyay, 2001).

Bandyopadhyay (2001) suggests that the BIA process first examine how long the organization can function without key computer and database support, which functions are most essential to continuing business operations (Coleman, 1993), and which are most vulnerable to a disaster (Wong et al, 1994). Following this analysis, priority items can be ranked and financial losses estimated for each critical function should it cease operations during a disaster. In essence, BIA is a cost-benefit exercise. After ranking mission-critical elements, the team asks what measures can be instituted to ensure that critical elements are preserved during a disaster, what each measure costs, and what the likely losses would be if the element failed during a disaster. For example, if the unavailability of an inventory database paralyzes the shipping of goods from several geographic locations, and the financial losses are estimated at $40,000 per day, and it would cost $50,000 to set up a mirror site at a different geographical location, updated daily, with recurring annual costs of $5,000, then it would make sense to think about investing in such a system. For a smaller business with estimated daily losses of $2,000 this might not be a cost-effective solution; a better answer might be the provision of a back-up inventory on paper, updated nightly.

Risk Analysis

Risk analysis has always been part of the information security life cycle: risk analysis → cost-benefit implementation → vulnerability assessment (Peltier, 2004). At its heart, the object of a formal risk analysis is to list all the possible threats to a business' operations, quantify as far as possible the probability of such a threat materializing, and assess the impact of the threat. Threats are grouped into three categories: natural, human, and environmental. For each specific threat, an estimate of its occurrence (probability) over a one-year timeframe (usually next year) is obtained, and the impact of such a threat materializing is assessed.

Probabilities of threats can be obtained from a variety of sources. For example, the USGS (United States Geological Survey) can provide the likelihood of a damaging earthquake for a specific locale, and insurance companies/local law enforcement can provide statistics for the kinds of human threats that are envisaged. There are also a number of risk assessment tools, such as the Disaster Risk Index, Disaster Financing Deficit Index, and Risk Management Index, that can help companies with international operations quantitatively assess the risks of different types of disaster in various countries or regions of the world, estimate economic loss risks, and determine which countries are better able to manage disaster risks, and absorb economic losses/recovery costs of major disasters (Dilley, 2006). For some specific threats it might be impossible to estimate exact probabilities, in which case the threat should be categorized as low, medium, or high. A high probability can be envisaged as an event with a 10 percent or more chance of occurring on annual basis, whereas, a low probability might be around 0.01 percent.

Impact is the consequence of the threat materializing and should be categorized into high, medium, and low. A high impact might mean the very survival of the company is at stake. A medium impact will cause considerable financial hardship or disruption to the activities of the business, but will be limited, and a low impact has minimal effect.

For a small business, a dedicated team comprised of individuals from different departments should suffice to brainstorm a list of possible threats. However, the larger the company or the more diverse the operations that the business carries out, the more experts (internal and external) will need to be brought into the picture. For example, as part of its risk mapping analysis for disaster recovery, a team led by the Global Risk Manager of Cemex, a multinational cement-products producer and trader in 23 countries, conducted an in-depth assessment of worker occupational risks to employees and benchmarked locations in terms of risk using the ESIS "AAA" Safety & Health Risk Assessment Process, global safety standards and the company's safety benchmarks (Wayne, 2000).

Mitigation Strategy Development

When both BIA and risk analysis has been completed, the next step is to develop strategies or specific proposals to mitigate the risk of each threat. Four outcomes are possible: (a) a cost-effective solution that will eliminate or reduce the risk to an acceptable level, (b) solutions that can reduce the risk, though the cost might be unacceptable, (c) accepting the risk as defined (no action), and (d) cases in which no strategy can be found to mitigate the risk of a threat. Strategies might also be found that mitigate more than one risk.

Defining risks that are acceptable is a judgment call upon the part of senior management, but the decision can be aided by developing a probability/impact matrix (Peltier, 2004). This is a method of classifying probabilities of events into high, medium, and low and assigning a high, medium, or low impact to each event. For example, if the probability of utility water loss for 1-2 days occurring at the locations of a business' geographic area is low, of the order of < 0.01 percent, and the impact is low, then this clearly is an acceptable risk. On the other hand, an event that has a medium impact, but which has a medium probability—for example, a major fire onsite—is an event that needs development of a mitigation strategy.

Once mitigation strategies are developed for specific threats, it is advisable to re-perform the BIA and risk analysis for the threat with the proposed solution in place to ensure it is going to be effective. In addition, a cost-effectiveness analysis should be performed for each strategy, to determine "bang for the buck." Marginal cost-effective strategies might be useful against those threats for which there are few options, and for which high impact exists, but for low impact threats, they might be shelved. For natural hazards, such as earthquakes, floods, and wind, several tools, such as the Geographic Information System- (GIS) based loss estimation methodology, have been developed to model the hazards in terms of damage, and proposed changes can be factored into these tools to determine their cost-effectiveness (Iwan, Cluff, Kimpel, Kunreuther, Masaki-Schatz, Nigg, et al., 1999).

In cases in which no specific strategy can be developed to minimize the risk of the threat, one alternative is to use risk management so that in the event that the threat materializes, the inoperability of the affected system can be distributed to other systems, thus minimizing the impact. Jiang and Haimes (2004) detail one such study.

THE THREE-PHASE APPROACH TO BUSINESS CONTINUITY AND DISASTER RECOVERY

Throughout this section, a hypothetical small plastics company, Sunward Plastics, with 60 employees and two locations in southern California, will be used as a case study to illustrate the BC and DR process.

The Business Continuity and Disaster Recovery Team

Two main criteria should be followed when considering the makeup of a BC & DR team for the Resolve Phase. The first is that representatives from every major department should be on board. The second is that the team leader and his or her deputy should come from different locations, if the company has more than one location. The reason for this idea is that if a disaster strikes, the team leader might be indisposed, injured, or killed, in the worst-case scenario. It is also a good practice to create a succession list, so that the decision-making mantle passes to those personnel on the team who are available to direct operations when others are indisposed.

In the case of Sunward Plastics, the team consists of the CEO (team leader), Safety Officer (deputy), and six other members drawn from Manufacturing, Sales & Marketing, Accounting, Purchasing, and IT. Other experts both within and outside of the company are added to specific meetings as needed. The IT department also has a small subteam, since its operations heavily impact the company, and many of the BC and DR plan elements will fall into its domain.

In the Respond Phase, the team leader or the deputy will normally declare whether a disaster has occurred and assume control, forming the Disaster Response Team. At one end of the disaster scale, this means exercising intelligent judgment as to whether an event merits implementing the BC & DR plan. For example, at Sunward Plastics, a logistical problem with the railroad that stops railcars from being moved for three days might constitute a disaster. (For other manufacturing companies it might take only a day.) At the other end of the scale, a major earthquake in the area of one geographic location (Sunward's two locations are 75 miles apart) might mean that the first team member to assume control onsite is the person who starts implementing the BC & DR Plan.

During the Respond Phase, the most critical items following implementation of the plan are to assess the consequences of the disaster, and communicate the nature and scope of the disaster to all employees, customers, and suppliers as necessary. Communications need to be redundant, which means making use of an Intranet (if one exists), the Internet, and telephone (landline, cellular, VOIP [Voice Over Internet Protocol], and satellite) as necessary. The nature of the disaster will dictate how this is accomplished. For example, a local power outage might be obvious to personnel at the location affected, but a software problem that crashes database servers might not be readily apparent to everyone. In the latter case, Sunward might choose to disseminate the following bulletin:

At 10:05 PST, on Jul 7, 2007, a software error caused all the company's database servers to crash, and we have declared a disaster. Finished Inventory, Raw Materials, EDI, Accounting, Payroll, and HR database functions are offline indefinitely. Please notify customers, suppliers, and other entities as appropriate.

As the situation moves from the Response to the Rebuild Phase, the response team will take measures to ensure that the company keeps its critical functions operating while it determines how best to repair the damage.

If Sunward had experienced a major earthquake at one of its locations, in the absence of information from the affected site, it is likely that the response team would have been initially drawn from the unaffected site, and that the deputy would have called the disaster. For companies with multiple locations, it is vital that the team take control from whichever location can best handle the disaster and this might initially involve some duplicative effort in the case of a major disaster until communication links are firmly established with the disaster site.

Business Critical Functions and Risk Assessment

During the Resolve Phase, determining which functions of the business are the most critical, and developing a threat risk/impact table for each function, are the most important items for the BC & DR Team to tackle. Tools, such as BIA and business modeling, will enable the team to rank order functions that can quickly halt important operations or cause the most financial impact. Because Sunward had no particular expertise in this area, it hired a risk analysis consultant to guide them through the process, and made use of an accounting expert to develop financial loss projections. Table 1 shows a list of initial critical functions that the team developed in this phase, and from this first pass, detailed financial loss projections were developed, enabling the team to rank the order of these functions.

The team then carried out a threat risk/impact analysis to determine what kinds of threat existed to its operations, the probability that each might occur over a one-year timeframe, and the impact of each to its operations (Table 2). Both these types of information were then utilized in the development of risk mitigation strategies. Bearing in mind the cost-effectiveness of solutions, the team then created a list of risk mitigation strategies for each of its business critical functions, some of which overlapped, and presented them to the business owners.

Threat Mitigation Strategies

An earthquake of magnitude > 6.0 was judged to be the most dire threat to the facility manufacturing injection molded products, which also served as the company's headquarters. At the other location producing pipe products, a raw materials shortage was deemed the most dire threat, since the company had streamlined raw materials delivery two years ago. On the IT side, however, the company was vulnerable if its electronic databases and EDI (electronic data interface) became incapacitated for more than one day, since this progressively impacted the company's ability to service customers, and make and receive payments. A denial-of-service attack on the company's Web server was also deemed important, as many customers would be unable to place orders.

Although the solutions to the IT domains were relatively straightforward, there were no easy or inexpensive solutions to mitigate damage from a large-magnitude earthquake. Nevertheless, Sunward produced a multi-year plan to address these concerns (Table 3). Ironically, the improvement in efficiency that had been obtained by just-in-time (JIT) raw materials and product shipment now worked against Sunward as far as earthquake and raw material shortage threat mitigation was concerned. However, the analysis also produced a bonus in that it clearly identified a vulnerability: the injection molding operations were far more vulnerable than the pipe extrusion operations in terms of raw material shortages, and the effects of a large earthquake. While the structural modifications at L1 (the headquarters, and location for injection molding

[IM] operations) were ultimately vetoed by the business owners on cost grounds, the owners did see the logic in the other proposed strategies, primarily because they reduced the vulnerability of IM, lowered the risk of running out of raw materials, dovetailed with the expansion plans at L2 where the PE operations were located, and increased the possibility for more flexibility by relocating some of the more critical IM operations to L2.

The analysis also pointed out the vulnerability of the electronic databases and the Web server, and the possibility of prolonged communications breakdown at either location. The mitigation strategy was to ultimately create a hot site at L2, which would become the back-up site for all critical IT operations, improve the power backup facilities at L1, so that computer, telecommunications, and EDI operations could be maintained, albeit at the expense of manufacturing operations, develop a better system for protecting the Web server from outside threat, and spend more time ensuring that software applications ran smoothly. Finally, the addition of satellite phone capability would help to ensure that in the worst-case scenario, communications between the two locations could be established.

The BC & DR Plan, however, is incomplete; still to be discussed is how to keep operations ongoing after a disaster strikes.

Operations Plans

Although we have addressed how to mitigate the risks and consequences of threats, if disaster does strike, what can be done to keep business ongoing? This part of the Resolve Phase studies some possibilities for each type of threat, given the information and mitigation strategies that will be implemented, to maintain the critical business functions.

In the case of Sunward, it is important to maintain manufacturing operations and shipping of products as much as possible, and ensure that database, EDI, and Web server functions are operational. For example, if there is a power outage at L1, electrical generation capacity will ensure that the latter are online, but manufacturing will come to a halt. If the power outage is likely to be prolonged (several days or weeks), decisions will need to be made regarding production at L2 and whether to activate the reciprocal BC plan. For example, some production might be shifted to L2, and contingency planning for manufacturing at the reciprocal company activated. By working through

Table 1. List of critical business functions and consequences of loss developed at Sunward Plastics

Function	Consequences of Loss
Injection molding manufacturing operations	Financial impact (late ship dates after 2 days; product shortfalls after 5 days)
Pipe extrusion manufacturing operations	Financial impact (late ship dates after 4 days; product shortfalls after 10 days)
Product shipping	Financial impact (consequences per manufacturing operations)
Reception of plastic raw materials	Progressive shutdown of manufacturing operations, starting at 4 days for certain products. At 10 days critical for 50% of products
EDI (Electronic Data Interface)	Unable to receive or make payments
Web server	Customers unable to place orders
Finished inventory (electronic database)	Immediate loss of potential sales; problems with tracking larger-volume products
Accounting (database)	Unable to keep track of or process some receivables

Table 2. Threat risk/impact chart developed for Sunward Plastics. P = probability, over a one-year timeframe (annual rate of occurrence). Note: this chart was developed for one of Sunward's two physical locations

Threat Category	Specific Threat	P	Impact
Natural	$\geq$ Magnitude 6 earthquake	0.04	High
	Flood	1×10^{-3}	Medium
	Landslide	1×10^{-4}	High
	Storm/wind-related damage	1×10^{-3}	Low
Human	Server attack	0.5	Medium
	Computer virus	0.25	Medium
	Application software bug	0.05	High
	Defective product recall	$< 1 \times 10^{-6}$	High
	Theft (external threat)	0.02	Low
	Theft (employees)	0.1	Low
	Raw material shortage > 2 days	0.01	Medium
	Area terrorist attack	$< 1 \times 10^{6}$	Medium
Environmental	Fire	1×10^{-4}	High
	Power outage > 1 day	1×10^{-3}	Medium
	Loss of water > 1 day	1×10^{-4}	Medium
	Gasoline shortage	0.1	Low
	Telecommunications outage > 1 day	1×10^{-3}	Medium

various scenarios in this fashion, the team will be better armed to deal with the real McCoy if disaster strikes.

Writing, Implementing, and Testing the Plan

The object of writing the plan is to create a manual that is easy for all employees to use, can be simply updated, and provide critical information and one or two pages of to-do checklists in the event of a specific type of emergency. While no plan can be perfect, it is a starting place. For example, if there is an abrupt loss of landline telecommunication service at one business location, a series of actions designed to switch or activate alternate forms of communication can be swiftly performed by the relevant personnel to ensure business continuity.

Testing the BC & DR Plan is critical. Bandopadhyay (2001) found that almost half the HMOs he surveyed had never tested or updated their plans. An untested plan is a liability rather than an asset. By testing plans, one exposes weaknesses, pitfalls, or poor assumptions that need to be corrected (Terry, 1995), and has the

Table 3. Risk mitigation strategies for Sunward Plastics. Note: L = location; IM = injection molding; PE = pipe extrusion

Strategy	Threat Addressed	Business Function Helped	Cost & Timing
Structural modifications to buildings, outside facilities, rail spur at L1	Earthquake (L1); landslide (L1)	IM operations; product shipping	Expensive; 5-year implementation
Relocation and expansion of certain injection molding operations to L2	Earthquake; power outage > 1 day (L1); fire (L1)	IM operations; product shipping	Moderately expensive, but can be tied in with planned expansion; 2-year implementation starting immediately
Expansion of rail spur at L2	Earthquake (L1); raw material shortage > 1 day	IM operations; PE operations; product shipping	Expensive; start in 18 months time
Truck leasing agreement (L2)	Raw material shortage > 1 day	Reception of plastic raw materials; product shipping; IM operations; PE operations;	Cheap; start immediately
Contingency arrangements for emergency production at other companies (reciprocal BC plan)	Earthquake; power outage > 1 day; raw material shortage > 1 day	IM operations; PE operations	Cheap; start immediately
Second raw material source qualification for certain product lines	Earthquake (L1); raw material shortage > 1 day	Reception of plastic raw materials; IM operations; PE operations;	Inexpensive; start immediately
Expansion of power generation capability at L1	Earthquake (L1; power outage > 1 day (L1)	EDI; finished inventory DB; accounting DB	Moderately expensive; start immediately
Satellite phone acquisitions	Earthquake (L1 & L2); tele-communications outage (L1 & L2)	All functions	Inexpensive; start immediately
Hot site provision at L2 for IT functions (primarily data back-up)	Earthquake; power outage > 1 day (L1); computer virus; fire (L1); application software bug	Finished inventory; accounting DB	Moderately expensive; start in 6 months with cold site provision first; hot site capability by 18 months
More sophisticated firewall and automated intrusion monitor software	Web server attack	Web server availability	Relatively inexpensive; start immediately
Better scrutiny of application software	Computer virus; application software bug	EDI, finished inventory DB; accounting DB	Inexpensive; start immediately

opportunity to improve. The initial test should be a realistic as possible, though in some cases simulation might have to suffice. For example, one might simulate a major fire, but create a situation in which personnel have to carry out authentic reactions and document what they have done using checklists within the plan manual. Testing should not be carried out until all employees have received adequate training in the plan section for which they might be responsible, should a disaster strike. If testing proves the plan to be inadequate, subsequent brainstorming by the team must devise better solutions. Once the plan has proved

satisfactory, it is recommended that subsequent testing be carried out at least annually, and after major amendments to the plan.

Specific IT and Engineering Functions

In the context of the BC and DR Plan, IT is most concerned with the integrity of data, the software and hardware that enables applications to run, and the communications that permit access to the data.

Several options exist regarding back up and recovery of critical data. Magnetic tape storage is still common, and elegant robotic tape libraries can automatically store, code, and file terabytes of data using gigabit Ethernet-based networks that are segmented PNs (private networks), or SANs (storage area networks), which are often fiber-optic based (Hinegardner, 2003). Centralized disk storage systems that are NAS-based (Network Area Storage), which employs a TP/IP network (Transfer Packet Protocol/Internet Protocol), or SAN-based have also come onstream. NAS-based systems are better suited to storage of Web pages and e-mail, while SANs are typically used to back up relational databases, such as those existing on Oracle or Microsoft SQL servers (Hinegardner, 2003). Smaller businesses that do not need such elaborate systems can also store data on individual CDs or DVDs.

Most important is when and where the data are stored. For some businesses, weekly or overnight back up after the end of the business day is sufficient, while for others, several snapshots taken during a 24-hour period might be more appropriate. Where should the storage media be located? The answer depends on the risk of the storage data being damaged beyond repair at the location at which it is stored. That risk can be quantified during the risk/threat analysis and the result used to drive the decision-making. If the probability is anything but extremely low, thought should be given to duplicating the data and systems offsite, either by using a vendor that specializes in such operations, such as SunGard or IBM, or creating a specific offsite location that is geographically separated from the primary storage site (Tabar, 2002). Such locations can be "cold," which means the data is simply stored; "hot," which means that equipment at the alternate site is in place and can be quickly configured to recover the data and duplicate critical business functions; or warm, implying a site that needs some upgrading of resources or work to recover data and provide critical business functions from that site (Bandyopadhyay, 2001).

Another solution is to find a company that is willing to enter into an agreement to provide offsite data storage, and perhaps the provision to restore critical business functions if a disaster occurs. If such a reciprocal agreement is contemplated, it is important that the two companies be separated by considerable geographic distance, and that the vulnerabilities of one company do not mirror those of the other.

The other important point to address is communications. Natural disasters, such as hurricanes and earthquakes that have a large geographic footprint or manmade disasters that involve the accidental severance of major data cables, are relatively common and can significantly affect communications for a long period of time. Options to work around communications blackouts include satellite phones, portable wireless networks for businesses that need internal communications (Arnold, Levine, Manmatha, Lee, Shenoy, Tsai et al., 2004), and VOIP, which can be configured at alternate business locations in conjunction with employees to answer phone calls destined for specific numbers or extensions.

Finally, provision might need to be made for the use of temporary employees at other business locations or the temporary transfer of employees from one location to another while the Rebuild Phase is in progress. Figuring out how this could be done for specific types of disaster in advance is far better than scrambling to do it after a disaster has occurred.

FUTURE TRENDS

Threats to business operations are increasing—both in probability and the emergence of new types of threats. The impact of global warming and subsequent climate change continues to tax different parts of the world, particularly as businesses impinge upon what are seen as vulnerable areas. The aging electrical grid in the USA, the possibility of pandemics, the rise of terrorism, including the increased attacks against servers and computer systems are all threats that must be addressed in a timely fashion.

The capabilities of IT technology in mitigating the consequences of disasters are also improving, but so is the complexity of businesses and the need to keep critical functions operational on a 24/7 basis. The challenge for businesses will be to integrate IT solutions into their own BC and DR plans, and stay abreast of developments. Businesses that do not might be "lucky" for a while, but risk going out of business if a major disaster strikes.

CONCLUSION

Many tools exist for a business to create a successful BC and DR plan. Using BIA, business modeling, and risk analysis, corporations can analyze their vulnerabilities to perceived threats and develop specific strategies to mitigate the consequences of a disaster. It is also important to create a plan that is tested frequently, and updated as appropriate, especially when new systems are brought online. Being prepared for the worst does not mean that a business will not be financially damaged as a result of disaster, but it will help ensure business continuity and minimize the human, financial, and material costs associated with disasters.

REFERENCES

Arnold, J. L., Levine, B. N., Manmatha, R., Lee, F., Shenoy, P., Tsai, M. C., et al. (2004). Information-sharing in out-of-hospital disaster response: The future role of information technology. *Prehospital and Disaster Medicine, 19*(2), 201-207.

Bandyopadhyay, K. (2001). The role of business impact analysis and testing in disaster recovery planning by health maintenance organizations. *Hospital Topics, 79*(1), 16-22.

Buckley, M. C. (2002). Calm during the crisis: Pennsylvania hospital averts IT catastrophe by following its comprehensive disaster recovery plan—assisted by a little on-the-spot ingenuity. *Health Management Technology, 23*(11), 42-44.

Coleman, R. (1993). Six steps to disaster recovery. *Security Management, 37*(2), 61-64.

Coombs, W. T. (2004). Impact of past crises on current crisis communication. *Journal of Business Communication, 41*(3), 265-289.

D'Amico, V. (2006). Streamlining the phases of disaster recovery. *Accounting Today, 29*(9), 26, 29.

Dilley, M. (2006). Setting priorities: Global patterns of disaster risk. *Philosophical Transactions A: Mathematics, Physics, and Engineering Sciences, 364*(1845), 2217-2229.

Dyregrov, A. (1989). Caring for helpers in disaster situations: Psychological debriefing. *Disaster Management, 2,* 25-30.

Gerbhardt, K. (2000). Easing coverage conflicts. *Best's Review, 101*(7), 102.

Hammond, J., & Brooks, J. (2001). The World Trade center attack. Helping the helpers: The role of critical incident stress management. *Critical Care, 5,* 315-317.

Hinegardner, S. (2003). Data storage for managing the health enterprise and achieving business continuity. *Journal of Healthcare Information Management, 17*(2), 32-36.

Iwan, W. D., Cluff, L. S., Kimpel, J. K., Kunreuther, H., Masaki-Schatz, S. H., & Nigg, J. M. et al. (1999). Mitigation emerges as major strategy for reducing losses caused by natural disasters. *Science, 284*(5422), 1943-1947.

Jiang, P., & Haimes, Y. Y. (2004). Risk management for Leontief-based interdependent systems. *Risk Analysis, 24*(5), 1215-1229.

Kates, R. W., Colten, C. E., Laska, S., & Leatherman, S. P. (2006). *Proceedings of the National Academy of Science, 103*(40), 14653-14660.

Keahey, K. (2006). Diversify your network as part of a disaster-recovery plan. *The Central New York Business Journal*, September 15, 38-39.

Maldin, B., Inglesby, T. V., Nuzzo, J. B., Lien, O., Gronvall, G. K., Toner, E., et al. (2005). Bulls, bears, and birds: Preparing the financial industry for an avian influenza pandemic. *Biosecurity and Bioterrorism: Biodefense Strategy, Practice, and Science, 3*(4), 363-367.

Mitchell, J. T. (1983). When disaster strikes ... the critical incident stress debriefing team. *Journal of Emergency Medical Services, 8,* 36-39.

Seewald, N., & D'Amico, E. (2005). Can you hear me now? *Chemical Week*, October 26, 38.

Somasundaram, D., Norris, F. H., Asukai, N., & Murthy, R. S. (2003). Natural and technological disasters. In B. L. Green et al. (Eds.), *Trauma interventions in war and peace* (pp. 291-318). New York: Springer.

Tabar, P. (2002). Data security and recovery. Planning ahead for business as usual. *Healthcare Information, 19*(2), 36-38.

Taylor, D. (2006). Continuity errors. *Financial Management*, March, 25-28.

Terry, R. J. (1995). Organizing a contingency plan for success. *Disaster Recovery Journal, 8*(2), 43-46.

Thomas, C. R. (2006). Psychiatric sequelae of disasters.

Journal of Burn Care Research, *27*(5), 600-605.

Vijayan, J. Data security risks missing from disaster recovery plans. *Computerworld*, *39*(41), 1, 16.

Wayne, C. R. (2000). Business continuity planning. *Occupational Hazards*, *69*(10), 178-180.

Wong, B. K., Monaco, J. A., & Louise, S. C. (1994). Disaster recovery planning: Suggestions to top management. *Journal of Systems Management*, *45*(5), 28-34.

KEY TERMS

Business Impact Analysis: The process of delineating the functions most critical to the survival of a business.

Business Continuity: The continuance of business operations regardless of disasters that befall it.

Business Modeling: A process of mapping all the functions of a business from a relationship point of view.

Cold Site: A location remote to the normal geographic locations of a business, which stores business-critical data.

Disaster Recovery: The process of bringing business-critical functions back online as soon as possible.

Disaster Footprint: The size of a disaster in terms of geographic area affected and the level of destruction.

Hot Site: A location remote to the normal geographic locations of a business, which stores business-critical data and has the systems in place to restore and bring online business-critical functions.

Mitigation Strategies: Strategies developed to minimize the threats to a business and their impact during a disaster.

Risk Analysis: The process of analyzing possible threats to a business, and estimating their probability and impact.

Chapter XXVII
Security Policies and Procedures

Yvette Ghormley
Saint Leo University, USA

ABSTRACT

The number and severity of attacks on computer and information systems in the last two decades has steadily risen and mandates the use of security policies by organizations to protect digital as well as physical assets. Although the adoption and implementation of such policies still falls far short, progress is being made. Issues of management commitment, flexibility, structural informality, training, and compliance are among the obstacles that currently hinder greater and more comprehensive coverage for businesses. As security awareness and security-conscious cultures continue to grow, it is likely that research into better methodologies will increase with concomitant efficiency of security policy creation and implementation. However, attacks are becoming increasingly more sophisticated. While the human element is often the weakest link in security, much can be done to mitigate this problem provided security policies are kept focused and properly disseminated, and training and enforcement are applied.

INTRODUCTION

In the days of mainframes, users were given a username and password, and perhaps an electronic badge to admit them to a computer facility. Those days have long evaporated. With the advent of private broadcast networks, intranets, portable media devices, laptops, and the commercial development of the Internet, security for any kind of business has become a lot more complicated. Moreover, it is costing more. The average loss from unauthorized access to data increased by 488 percent from $51,545 in 2004 to $303,234 in 2005, according to the most recent Computer Security Institute/FBI Computer Crime and Security Survey (McFadden, 2006). For larger companies, recent se-

curity breaches were estimated by Ernst and Young to range from $17 to $28 million per incident (Garg, Curtis, & Halper, 2003), and Austin & Darby (2003) reported that the cost of security breaches to businesses in the USA was $17 billion. Further, correcting the long-term damage, which includes loss of customer confidence, damage to the company's image, and financial consequences, such as stock devaluation for public companies, can be extremely costly, although difficult to estimate. Therefore, developing an effective security policy, implementing it, and ensuring that it is understood and practiced by all employees is essential.

The Approach to Security Policies and Procedures

Companywide policies should be initiated and enforced from the top, and that includes IT security policies. That does not mean to say that technical policies, such as those developed by IT departments, cannot have a specific focus, but the level of technical complexity itself should not be regarded as a barrier that top management can ignore. Tuesday (2002) cites a case study in which an old approved policy was updated at a lower level but ignored by a CEO's assistant, who was essentially acting as the gatekeeper. The eventual result was that the CEO applied for an exception dispensation; however, the antics of the assistant probably caused sufficient disruption that enforcing the updated policy was difficult.

Policies must focus on the most important aspects of security rather than comprise a long list of laundry items in a 200-page manual. For example, one of the most productive ways to review security from scratch is for each business unit to determine what devices and associated data (digital assets) are the most important (Austin & Darby, 2003). From this data, common policies can be formulated, with the establishment of exception procedures for those groups that are not impacted, or who require a different solution.

The creation of simple, nonspecific technology-dependent policies allows for the possibility of change, and flexible approaches. Tomorrow's security problems are not necessarily going to be solved by today's solutions. Both threats and technology change, and policies should be broad enough to accommodate these facts.

Enforcement of policies is also important. Policies can be written and implemented, but if breaches occur, they must be addressed. Not reacting to breaches in policy causes employees to think that a policy can be safely ignored, and increases the risk that real damage will be done the next time an incident occurs.

Last, the roles of individuals in shaping, implementing, and enforcing security policies must be delineated. If responsibilities are not created, there is a tendency for some individuals to assume roles and proceed unilaterally, and others to ignore situations that must be addressed.

This chapter comprises six main sections: (a) methods to determine the constitution of security policies (frameworks, scope, and creation), (b) adoption and implementation of policies into specific procedures, (c) exception procedures, (d) training in security

policies, (e) enforcement of security policies, and (f) leadership roles in security policies. Rather than focusing on specific technologies, the intent of the chapter is to create a framework from which security policies and procedures can be derived for any type of business entity. These elements, with emphasis on the constitution of security policies, are discussed in terms of (a) the research that has been conducted, and (b) practical advice that can be utilized.

BACKGROUND

Constitution of Security Policies

Developing Frameworks

Many IS (information security) researchers express skepticism about the use and effectiveness of security policies (Höne & Eloff, 2002), citing perception of security controls as barriers to efficiency and progress, which leads to circumvention (Wood, 2000). To be effective, IS security policies depend must on the specific organization and its environment (Karyda, Kiountouzis, & Kokolakis, 2005). These twin issues must always be borne in mind when creating security policies.

Several approaches have been taken regarding frameworks for security policies. Baskerville (1993) notes that the development of information security systems (ISS) in general has proceeded by generation, starting with the first generation, which relied upon checklists or security management standards; the second, which were mechanistic in nature, focusing on functional, technical, and natural science factors in ISS design, and neglecting the social nature of organizations; and the third, comprising logical modeling methods that abstract ISS problems. Siponen (2005) advances these concepts, describing five paradigms in modern ISS approaches, which include the viable and survivable, security-modified, responsibility modeling, business process, and information modeling. The reader might ask what relation this fundamental research has to do with security policies, and the answer is that the future fifth generation, which Siponen (2005) advocates, incorporates the use of social techniques, such as user participation to ensure the social acceptance of security techniques and procedures. In addition, although the use of sanctions and deterrents needs justification, such practices should be accepted by all the employees of an organization. In other words, future ISS designs will be synonymous with security acceptability. Details of these ISS approaches can be found in the papers by Baskerville and Siponen (2002), and Siponen (2005).

Karyda et al. (2005) base the framework of their approach to security policies on the theory of contextualism (Pettigrew, 1987). In essence, contextualism seeks to analyze the relationship and interaction between the content of strategic change, the context of that change, and the process involved in managing that change (Pettigrew & Whipp, 1993). The interrelationships transform dynamically over time, as a result of both outer contexts, such as the economic, social, competitive factors found in an organization's external environment, and inner contexts, such as the structural, political, and cultural factors present within an organization. By investigating security policy content, formulation processes, implementation, and adoption in this manner at three levels—organization, work system, and information technology—Karyda, et al. (2005) made four crucial findings in two case studies. First, employees with increased responsibilities and varied activities have higher security awareness. The corollary to this is that organizations with rigid, hierarchical structures will likely develop problems in the application of security policies. Second, organizations with coherent cultures, especially codes of ethics, have an easier time of adopting and implementing IS security policies. Third, the more management participates and visibly supports security policies, the better the outcome. Finally, security awareness and security policy evaluation programs assist in promoting successful adoption and implementation.

Alignment is another concept that has implications for the development of security policies. In her case study of eight companies Chan (2002) discovered that aligning IS and business strategies improved IS performance, but another key finding was that informal organization mattered more than formal structure. These results bear on another alignment, that between information security policy (ISP) and the strategic information systems plan (SISP), of which the latter is aligned with corporate strategy (Doherty & Fulford, 2006; Doherty, Marples, & Suhami, 1999). According to Doherty and Fulford (2006), the traditional method of SISP is to assemble a team, conduct a situation analysis, formulate, and then implement a strategy, and modify it as necessary after review. These researchers suggest that during the formulation phase, the SISP should be created or modified, and when the review is

phase is conducted, the ISP should then be reviewed and modified in parallel. This linkage ought to provide several benefits: (a) imbue the ISP with a stronger business orientation; (b) provide advance warning of security risks or the need for new controls when new SISP directives are initiated; (c) move the security culture from one of reactive to proactive; (d) incorporate security management issues into user manuals, training, and procedures prior to the introduction of new systems; and (e) raise awareness of security breaches in management. The findings of Chan (2002) suggest that this process is best carried out using maximum flexibility and informal structure, rather than a rigid, completely defined structural organization.

Maynard and Ruighaver (2001) adapted software quality factors to create a framework for the quality of information security policies, utilizing measures of functionality, reliability, usability, efficiency, maintainability, and compliance. Functionality focuses on the appropriateness of security policies, whether the policies operate as intended in "real life," avoidance of contradiction (corollary harmony), and a careful balance between unintended disclosure of sensitive information versus the need by employees to comprehend all policies. Reliability highlights the developing maturity of security policies as they are reviewed and modified, and the ability of the policies to tolerate faults and not "fail hard." Usability is the ability to easily comprehend the policies, obtain them in a variety of formats, and execute them without going against psychological norms. Being able to easily update and implement policies without inordinate consumption of time or resources constitutes efficiency. Measures of maintainability focus on the ease with which deficiencies can be analyzed, rectified or changed, while compliance tests the ability of the policies to adhere to the standards of the organization, as well as legislative or regulatory requirements.

Scope of Security Policies

Baskerville and Siponen (2002) have proposed three levels of security policies: high-level reference, lower-level reference, and meta-policies. High-level reference security policies emanate from and are written by top management. Lower-level reference policy documents address specific departments, areas, or processes and are more concrete in nature, describing specific procedures to control authorization, protect assets, or minimize vulnerabilities. Security meta-policies are concerned with policy-making—for example, which entities or individuals are responsible for making policies, or when activities should trigger policy-making.

In practice, the scope of security policies is linked to the perceived strategic importance of information and security management practice. Some research shows that this is influenced by the risk perceptions of senior management and board of a company, and by internal or external events that are deemed significant by a company's decision-makers (Ezingeard, Bowen-Schire, & Birchall, 2004). In support of their findings, Ezingeard et al. (2004) also cite the novel security issue, which reduces to difficulty in judging the impact of a security problem if it has never been experienced (Frank, Shamir, & Briggs, 1991). There is also the sequential attention to goals issue, which manifests itself in change as a result of a major incident, and reversion to old practice for other reasons some time later (Cyert & March, 1992). This occurrence has been used to explain paradoxical decision in IS strategy (Hirscheim & Sabherwal, 2001). In addition, Doherty and Fulford (2005), who surveyed IT managers of large UK organizations, found no statistical association between the adoption of information security policies and the incidence or severity of security breaches. Distilled, this research intimates that both the scope and development of security policy content as currently practiced have a long way to go to reach maturity.

Security policy content has often developed from the BS 7799 standard that became the ISO 17799 standard in 2000. Doherty and Fulford (2006) have elaborated individual components of this standard as follows: personal usage of information systems (rights and responsibilities), disclosure of information (restrictions), physical security of infrastructure and information resources, violations and breaches of security, prevention of viruses and worms, user access management (who has access to what), mobile computing (security controls), Internet access, software development and maintenance, encryption (when and how), and contingency and continuity planning. Based on a validated survey of large UK companies, Fulford and Doherty (2003) determined that ≥ 89 percent of these components were covered in security policies, with the exception of software development, encryption, and contingency planning, with figures of 27 percent, 55 percent, and 18 percent, respectively. The factors affecting the success of information security policies identified as most important by respondents, which are listed in ISO 17799, were visible commit-

ment from management, a good understanding of security risks, distribution of guidance on IT security policy to all employees, and a good understanding of security requirements. However, adoption of these success factors appears to be substantially lacking and worrisome (Fulford & Doherty, 2003).

Dhillon and Torkzadeh (2006) proposed a value-focused assessment of information system security as the baseline for developing an instrument for measuring IS security concerns. According to Keeney (1992; 1999), by identifying values, individuals can decide what they want and how to obtain it. The methodology involves three steps: (a) interviews with appropriate individuals to elicit values in the decision context, which typically produces long lists of wishes; (b) conversion to a common format (object and preference); and (c) classification of objectives into fundamental with respect to context, or a means to support/inform fundamental objectives (means objectives) (Dhillon & Torkzadeh, 2006). Based upon this approach, these authors interviewed 103 user managers from a broad range of industries and obtained 86 objectives, which were grouped into 25 clusters. Fundamental objectives included maximize awareness, maximize data integrity, maximize organizational integrity, whereas means objectives included improve authority structures, understand work situation, maximize access control, and maximize fulfillment of personal needs. What is most interesting is that this approach could be used to define the scope of security policies that moves beyond the ISO standards.

Security Policy Creation

Baskerville and Siponen (2002) advocate three imperatives for the creation of security meta-policies: flexibility (responsiveness), political simplicity, and criterion-orientation. Political simplicity in this context refers to due consideration of compliance by policy makers so that exceptions to policies can be explicit and reasoned, and criterion-orientation to the focus on the organization's priorities without exact specification on how the criteria should be met. In addition, the objective of such policies is to identify and classify security subjects and objects, which are the employees, business partners, and third parties associated with the organization, and the organization's assets, respectively (Baskerville & Siponen, 2002). Further, meta-policies are concerned with what type of access security subjects have to security objects.

In general, formulation of a security policy according to Karyda et al. (2005) is accomplished at three levels: organizational level, works system level, and the information technology level. The organizational level embodies structure, management style, norms and culture, defines the role and support of management, and describes both internal and external relationships. The work system level encompasses IS users, business processes, customers or users, and the technology and information utilized. Finally, the information technology level elaborates the specifications and configurations of technical components, as well as the software and hardware for implementation. The process of security policy creation follows the input → activities → output schema, in which input is typified by risk evaluation assessment, legal requirements, structural and cultural characteristics of the organization, existing security practices, knowledge of IT technology and security controls, and management standards and best practices. Activities constitute the identification of security requirements and controls, compilation of the policy document, the writing of individual procedures, and assemblage of the specifications for technical security controls. Finally, the output is in the form of a security policy for information systems and specifications for countermeasures. Separating IT security policies that are focused toward IT employees from those targeting all employees (Vijayan, 2006) can be easily accomplished using this methodology.

Adoption and Implementation of Security Policies

While creation of a security policy is the first step, is must be adopted and implemented or it is useless. Recent research in the UK shows that 60 percent of all companies surveyed have still not implemented a security policy (DTI, 2006), and even among larger companies, adoption is still an issue (DTI, 2006; Fulford & Doherty, 2003). May (2003) suggests that this is a result of security policies not being placed high enough on the agenda of company boards.

Karyda et al. (2005) suggest that the activities involved in adoption of a security policy include establishing norms that support security management, promoting the issue of security to IT users, and resolving conflicts and difficulties found in the application of security controls. They also suggest keeping users and management informed regarding IS security agenda. Through their contextual analysis, these investigators also studied two organizations, following security

policy creation, adoption, and implementation. In one of these case studies, the Social Security Institute in the UK, management supported the creation of the security policy but failed to provide a linkage between security and the overall strategy of the organization. After creation of the policies, adoption and implementation stalled. Lack of flexibility in organizational structure and employing qualified personnel, competitive relationships, unbalanced workload in the IT department, and lack of understanding by users on security issues, as well as the security policy were among the reasons cited for the lengthy delays.

Behavioral research can provide insight into adoption and implementation. For example, by creating responsibility and accountability in structures, management can ensure that employees have a sense of ownership regarding security measures (Mishra & Dhillon, 2006). However, if these "top-down" directives are absent or half-hearted, one can see why members of an organization might not take security policies seriously. Other behavioral facets impinging on security concerns include alignment (if the goals of individuals are not aligned with those of the organization, security threats from the "inside" are likely) (Loch & Conger, 1996; Stanton, Stam, Mastrangelo, & Jolton 2005); ownership (employees should be treated as owners of information assets) (Adams & Sasse, 1999); and environment (a proactive environment promoting the importance of security behavior is important) (Dhillon & Torkzadeh, 2006; Vroom & Solms, 2004). All these factors are likely to enhance the goal of adopting and implementing a security policy once it has been formulated.

Physical implementation of IT security policies occurs at the works system or information technology levels. Although a technical discussion is beyond the scope of this chapter, the modeling approach exemplified by the work of Nagaratnam, Nadalin, Hondo, McIntosh, and Austel (2005) will be used as an illustration. Initially, a security policy officer and business analyst translate the security policy and using a business model, analyze and design the security requirements for the application, with the assistance of security and application architects. Implementation begins by writing the application policy, followed by building and testing the secure application. Deployment of the policy follows under the auspices of the application or security administrator by configuring the infrastructure for the application security, customizing the policies, and developing a list of subscribers who will utilize the policy. Finally the specific policy is managed and monitored under IT administration, with changes as necessary. Ultimately, many IT security policies depend on the utilization of service-oriented architecture templates for process mapping, efficiency, and elimination of redundancy in conjunction with mark-up using the appropriate machine language, for example, BPEL (Business Process Execution language). Once a specific policy is in place, it should be periodically audited. Bishop and Peisert (2006) caution that because of the complexity of modern systems, it is not always apparent that the low-level policy actually reflects the high-level policy. This could be the result of a "lost-in-translation" problem because "not only must a higher-level policy language be transformable into an implementation of a policy (or set of policies) on systems, but also deriveable from the existing configuration of systems. This means that mechanisms to handle contradictions must be defined, as must syntax and semantics to handle procedures external to the computer" (Bishop & Peisert, 2006, p. 1).

Exception Procedures, Training, Enforcement, and Leadership Roles

Exception Procedures

A good security meta-policy attempts to maximize compliance without outlawing noncompliance (Baskerville & Siponen, 2002). Following this, while adherence to security policies is important, cultural, legislative, and technological factors might make full compliance difficult to achieve (Maynard & Ruighaver, 2006). These are instances in which exceptions or deviations from policy can be created. In each case, a formal request for exemption should be made with documented reasons. An example of this would be the adoption of handheld BlackBerry 7200s by Unilever for their top executives, in which an exception from the policy of using the BlackBerries for both voice and data was granted in the form of permitting executives to use cell phones or smart phones for telephone conversations (McFadden, 2006).

Another historical example of the development of exceptions was reported by Couger (1986), which was a case study that involved approaches to configuration control of desktop computers. Three approaches were categorized: laissez faire (basically a free hand), hard controls (no exception to standardized configuration, under penalties), and soft controls (encouragement of desktop technology acquisition through a centralized

agency by the addition of supplementary budgets). The first two approaches resulted in incompatible desktop technology, but the third did not, because of incentives and market-driven standards, and the fact that internal economics forced exceptions to be well justified (Baskerville & Siponen, 2002). However, if the number of exceptions reached critical mass, the central standard was changed.

Training

McCarthy (2006) reported that in a survey conducted by the Computing Technology Association in 2006, just 29 percent of respondents indicated that information security training was required at their companies. Yet of those 29 percent, 84 percent indicated that such training had reduced the number of major security breaches since implementation. Further, those respondents that did not mandate security training said that it was not a departmental or business priority or top management support for it was lacking.

Training has been referred to as a key ingredient to ensuring that a security policy is successful by a number of researchers. Maynard and Ruighaver (2006) link training to the learnability element. Besides the learning of the security policy itself, the complexity or simplicity of the policy will dictate the amount of training required. Overly complex policies can fail because users do not understand them no matter how much training they receive. Training is also one of the five emergent themes found in behavioral analysis of information systems security governance research and helps the implementation and communication of policies, as well as raising awareness of security issues, and improving efficiency (Mishra & Dhillon, 2006). Additionally, it results in improved internal control management. In their case study of the Social Security Institute, lack of training was also cited by Karyda et al. (2005) as a prime cause for failure to implement a security policy.

Enforcement

The foundation for any kind of enforcement policy as it pertains to security policies, whether it contains deterrent action, sanctions, or punishment are the various behavioral theories borrowed from psychology and the social sciences (Mishra & Dhillon, 2006). Foremost are the deterrence theories (Straub & Welke, 1998; Theoharidou & Kokolakis, 2005) that discuss individual and group behavior, and relate to the intention to commit crime. In our context, this would be breaking the rules embedded in the security policy. Theories of reasoned action (Loch & Conger, 1996; Park, 2000) and planned behavior try to understand how individuals react to security issues in a behavioral context and how superimposed control is perceived. Research from social bond theory (Lee, Lee, & Yoo, 2004; Theoharidou & Kokolakis, 2005) suggests that strong normative pressure forces individuals to behave correctly, while results from social learning theory (Hollinger, 1993; Theoharidou & Kokolakis, 2005) provide insight into why peer pressure can force individuals to do certain things that they would not otherwise do. In connection with this concept, the research conducted by Milgram (1963), suggests that certain actions can be brought about when the agent for instruction is perceived as an authoritative figure. Mathias (2004) describes such a real-life incident involving the installation of unauthorized application processors that occurred due to lack of policy awareness and because a supervisor told an employee "it was okay to do it." Finally, social engineering, based on a knowledge of the beliefs, values, and attitudes of individuals seeks to impose a set of values or beliefs to given situations and is commonly used in the security industry (Loch & Conger, 1996).

In an ideal world, security policy enforcement would not be necessary. However, enforcement is necessary in order to reinforce a normative culture that "security policies matter." What form enforcement takes is a matter for discussion within an organization, and should be predicated on an assumption that (a) security policies are widely available via a number of media types within an organization; (b) that all employees have received training in security policies (initial and recurrent as necessary); so that (c) there is not only an awareness, but a comprehension of such policies as they apply to individuals within organizations. Enforcement can take forms of reminders or reprimands for "first offenses," or mandatory retraining or dismissal for severe breaches of security policy and repeated offenses.

Leadership Roles

Throughout this section, the recurrent theme of leadership has been emphasized with regard to the formulation and implementation of security policies. Many case studies have amply demonstrated that if senior management and the board of a company are not actively involved in security policies, the result will either be no security policy or one that takes an inordinate amount of time and resources to become operational. However, leadership roles do not cease with senior management. Lower and middle management must also be on board. This helps develop a security-conscious culture and prevents conflicts from emerging or behavior that runs contra to the security policy.

PRACTICAL GUIDANCE FOR SECURITY POLICIES

Creation, Adoption, and Implementation

Earlier it was indicated that IT-related policies should be separated from non-IT-related security policies targeting all employees. However, that should not imply that there would be two entirely separate "teams" dealing with such policies. Top management, and/or the board of an organization should kick off the security policy initiative in a variety of ways via companywide memos, meetings with employees, and use any available intranet. The point is to instill into the organization a firm top-down commitment to the project, begin the process of building a security-conscious culture, and delineate the general procedures by which the security policies will be created, adopted, and implemented. This should not be a one-time event for top management, especially for those companies that are not heavily invested in IT operations. Indeed, the involvement of senior management in all phases of the project is encouraged.

How should the security policy teams be constituted? This will depend on the size of the organization, its complexity, as well as its level of IT operations. One answer is to create the position of a security officer (if such a position does not already exist), a tsar-like figure who will guide the whole process and be answerable to the board or top management (Karyda et al., 2005). Another solution might be to appoint co-team leaders, one of whom is familiar with the strategic goals of the organization, the other an individual from the IT department who has a detailed working knowledge of its operations. One or more teams might necessary in large organizations, but if this route is chosen, it will be crucial to have a coordinator (who could also be the security officer) to ensure that all policies are harmonized and interoperable.

Although it is important to outline the structure of teams and identify the roles of members, it should be remembered that flexibility and informality are the keys to success. Rigidity and inflexible hierarchies can at best impede progress, or worse cause the project to languish. The composition of teams should reflect all interests of departments, divisions, or groups within an organization so that end users of the security policies—also the equivalent to all stakeholders—are not ignored. In some cases, the creation of meta-policies, with active direction from senior management might precede the creation of individual security policies in order to provide guidance on what is permissible.

In consideration of the content of security policies, while the overall accent is on the protection of assets, it is crucial not to be overly swayed by security incidents that have happened within the company. Such a view can produce bias. On the other hand, team members should be aware of incidents that have happened industrywide and have kept abreast of industry developments in order to achieve a balance. Case studies have shown that attitudes of "It can't happen here," or "We don't have the budget for that kind of security," or not uncommon. If consensus cannot be achieved within the company on what should be protected and to what degree, it might be useful to hire an outside expert to obtain a second opinion.

Drafts of security policies must be modeled or tested to ensure that they will work "as advertised." Assuming that a given procedure will work as written is likely to create a false sense of security, which is why the emphasis in this chapter has been on iterative processes in which review, feedback, and modification are important elements. Once the procedures have been tested, policies can be written and organized into manuals for dissemination.

The methods by which security policies are disseminated have been criticized as being insufficient and based too often on only one method (Fulford & Doherty, 2003). Consider not only using paper manuals but web-based applications, which have the option of being interactive to facilitate learning. For larger organizations pilot schemes can also be utilized in which security policies are implemented for small units to determine factors or modes of success or failure.

Other Factors

One of the essential factors to the success of security policies is training. Too many case studies have shown that failure was the result of lack of employee awareness. In addition, training can assist in building a security-conscious culture in which security of assets and data is considered a norm. Training should be thorough, companywide (which also includes all levels of management), and conducted during the implementation phase. Recurrent or refresher training is also smart as it keeps the skills of individuals better honed. Training after major configuration changes or the adoption of new infrastructure developments is also vital. The take-home message is that training should not be a one-time event. Most organizations are dynamic in structure, responding to new developments, and both security policies and the training associated with them should reflect this state.

Security policies must be enforced and individuals who willfully break security policies should be reprimanded. Without internal controls, it is unlikely that individuals will take security policies seriously, and will likely think that small transgressions are permissible. The majority of security breaches are caused by human error—that it to say from the failings of individuals rather than equipment or faulty procedures. If that error can be minimized, the security policies in place will succeed.

Even with internal controls present, errant human behavior will occur. Some individuals will perceive the security policy as too onerous, or "not applying to him or her." This kind of behavior is risky for the organization in that it can be contagious—"If she's doing it, so can I"—and can also facilitate attacks from outside the organization. However, the most dangerous individuals are those who have an axe to grind, and have the access authority to wreak havoc on security controls from within the company. Investing in monitoring equipment is a good idea, although if it is done with a heavy hand it might lead to resentment by individuals. The bottom line of an organization, however, is that the breaching of security policies should not be tolerated under any circumstances.

Finally, the issue of exception merits comment. Onerous processes—and security policies are no exception—often provoke an attitude of "that doesn't apply to me," particularly if the individual is at a high level within the organization, or commonly operates outside of the physical structures of the organization, such as a salesperson. Problems with security policy compliance should be reported to the individuals responsible for security and promptly, whether they are bona fide problems or gripes. It might be that a given procedure is poorly written, does not reflect original intention, or is simply too arduous, and is affecting a large group of individuals, in which case the procedure needs to be rethought. Individual or group exceptions to a stated policy should be decided upon by the security officer or other authority in a fair, rational manner without granting special status because of rank, power, or situation.

CONCLUSION

Security policies are a must for all organizations conducting business regardless of size or type. By protecting assets—human, physical, electronic, and digital—in a systematic way, organizations can focus most on what they do best: their business. Research shows that the creation, adoption, and implementation of security policies, however, is still lacking in many aspects. Issues of lack of management commitment, training, flexibility, and poor alignment with business strategic goals, as well as "knee-jerk" reflex action toward major security breaches are identified as the "usual suspects." Nevertheless, progress is being made in both the scope and execution of security policies in business today.

REFERENCES

Adams, A., & Sasse, M. A. (1999). Users are not the enemy. *Communications of the ACM, 42*(12), 40-46.

Austin, R. D., & Darby, C. A. R. (2003). The myth of secure computing. *Harvard Business Review, 81*(6), 121-126.

Baskerville, R. (1993). Information systems security design methods; implications for information systems development. *ACM Computing Surveys, 25*(4), 375-414.

Baskerville, R., & Siponen, M. (2002). An information security meta-policy for emergent organizations. *Logistics Information Management, 15*(5-6), 337-346.

Bishop, M., & Peisert, S. (2006). Your security policy is *What*?? Retrieved December 26, 2006 from http://www.cs.ucdavis.edu/research/tech-reports/2006/CSE-2006-20.pdf

Chan, Y. E. (2002). Why haven't we mastered alignment? The importance of the informal structure. *MIS Quarterly Executive, 1*(2), 97-112.

Couger, J. (1986). Pluribus computum. *Harvard Business Review, 86*(5), 87-91.

Cyert, R. M., & March, J. G. (1992). *A behavioral theory of the firm*, pp. 62, 166. Englewood Cliffs, NJ: Prentice-Hall.

Dhillon, G., & Torkzadeh, G. (2006). Value-focused assessment of information system security in organizations. *Information Systems Journal, 16*(3), 293-314.

Doherty, N. F., & Fulford, H. (2005). Do information security policies reduce the incidence of security breaches: An exploratory analysis. *Information Resources Management Journal, 18*(4), 21-39.

Doherty, N. F., & Fulford, H. (2006). Aligning the information security policy with the strategic information systems plan. *Computers and Security, 25*, 55-63.

Doherty, N. F., Marples, C. G., & Suhaimi, A. (1999). The relative success of alternative approaches to strategic information systems planning: An empirical analysis. *Journal of Strategic Information Systems, 8*(3), 263-283.

DTI. (2006). Information security breaches survey, 2006. Department of Trade and Industry. Retrieved January 10, 2007 from http://www.pwc.com/extweb/pwcpublications.nsf/docid/7FA80D2B30A116D7802570B9005C3D16

Ezingeard, J. N., Bowen-Schrire, M., & Birchall, D. (2004). *Triggers of change in information security management*. Paper presented at the ISOneWorld Conference, Las Vegas, Nevada, April. Retrieved December 27, 2006 from

http://www.information-institute.org/security/3rdConf/Proceedings/53.pdf

Frank, J., Shamir, B. & Briggs, W. (1991). Security-related behavior of PC users in organizations. *Information and Management, 21*, 127-135.

Fulford, H., & Doherty, N. F. (2003). The application of information security policies in large UK-based organizations: An exploratory study. *Information Management and Computer Security, 11*(3), 106-114.

Garg, A., Curtis, J., & Halper, H. (2003) Quantifying the financial impact of information security breaches. *Information Management and Computer Security, 11*(2), 74-83.

Hirscheim, R., & Sabherwal, R. (2001). Detours in the path toward strategic information systems alignment. *California Management Review, 44*(1), 87.

Hollinger, R. (1993). Crime by computer: Correlates of software piracy and unauthorized account access. *Security Journal, 4*(1), 2-12.

Höne, K., & Eloff, J. (2002). What makes an effective security policy? *Network Security, 6*(1), 14-16.

Karyda, M., Kiountouzis, E., & Kokolakis, S. (2005). Information systems security policies: A contextual perspective. *Computers and Security, 24*, 246-260.

Keeney, R. L. (1992). *Value-focused thinking*, p. 5. Cambridge, MA: Harvard University Press.

Keeney, R. L. (1999). The value of Internet commerce to the customer. *Management Science, 45*(4), 533-542.

Lee, S. M., Lee, S., & Yoo, S. (2004). An integrative model of computer abuse based on social control and general deterrence theories. *Information and Management, 41*(6), 707-718.

Loch, K. & Conger, S. (1996). Evaluating ethical decision making and computer use. *Communications of the ACM, 39*(7), 74-83.

Mathias, T. (2004) Security policy: A paper tiger. *Computerworld, 38*(19), 28.

May, C. (2003). Dynamic corporate culture lies at the heart of effective security strategy. *Computer Fraud and Security, 2003*(5), 10-13.

Maynard, S., & Ruighaver, A. B. (2006). *What makes a good information security policy: A preliminary framework for evaluating security policy quality.* Paper presented at the 5th Annual Security Conference, Las Vegas, Nevada, April. Retrieved December 28, 2006 from http://www.dis.unimelb.edu.au/staff/sean/research/Maynard-PolicyQaulity.pdf

McFadden, B. (2006). Security from scratch. *Baseline*, May 15, 60-61.

McCarthy, B. (2006). Close the security disconnect between awareness and practice. *Electronic Design*, September 1, 20.

Milgram, S. (1963). Behavioral study of obedience. *Journal of Abnormal and Social Psychology 67, 371-378.*

Mishra, S., & Dhillon, G. (2006, June). Paper presented at the Ninth Annual NYS Cyber Security Conference Symposium on Information Assurance, Albany, NY. Retrieved January 5, 2007, from http://www.albany.edu/iasymposium/mishra.pdf

Nagaratnam, N., Nadalin, A., Hondo, M., McIntosh, M., & Austel, P. (2005). Business-driven application security: From modeling to managing secure applications. *IBM Systems Journal, 44*(4), 847-867.

Park, H. S. (2000) Relationships among attitudes and subjective norms: Testing the theory of. reasoned action across cultures. *Communication Studies, 51*(2), 162-175.

Pettigrew, A. (1987). Context and action in the transformation of the firm. *Journal of Management Studies, 24*(6), 649-670.

Pettigrew, A., & Whipp, R. (1993). *Managing change for competitive success,* pp. 11-34. Oxford, England: Blackwell.

Siponen, M. T. (2005). Analysis of modern IS security development approaches: Towards the next generation of social and adaptable ISS methods. *Information and Organization, 15*(4), 339-375.

Stanton, J. M., Stam, K. R., Mastrangelo, P., & Jolton, J. (2005) An analysis of end user security behaviors. *Computers and Security, 24*(2), 124-133.

Straub, D., & Welke, R. (1998). Coping with systems risk: Security planning models for management decision making. *MIS Quarterly, 22*(8), 441-465.

Theoharidou, M., & Kokolakis, R. (2005). The insider threat to information systems and the effectiveness of ISO 17799. *Computers and Security, 24*, 472-484.

Tuesday, V. (2002). No good policy should go unbroken. *Computerworld, 36*(36), 36.

Vijanayan, J. (2006). Data security policies need focus, execs say. *Computerworld*, April 10, 12.

Vroom, C., & Solms, R. V. (2004). Towards information security behavioral compliance. *Computers and Security, 23*(3), 191-198.

Wood, C. (2000). An unappreciated reason why security policies fail. *Computer Fraud and Security, 10*, 13-14.

KEY TERMS

Alignment: The degree to which strategic or corporate goals are in harmony with security policies.

Information Security (IS): The securing of information identified as confidential by computer-based and human-based procedures.

Information Security System (ISS): A framework that encompasses the methodology by which information will be identified as confidential and kept secure.

Information Security Policy (ISP): A written document specifying how the digital and electronic equipment assets of an organization will be protected through the use of individual procedures.

Information Technology (IT): The technology that supports access, processing, and dissemination of data (information).

Security Awareness: The perception by individuals within an organization that security is important to the conduct of business.

Security Meta-Policy: A policy that describes what is permissible in broad terms of security issues without specifying exact technological solutions.

Security Policy: A written document specifying how all assets of an organization will be protected through the use of individual procedures.

Strategic Information Systems Plan (SISP): A plan that describes how information will be collected, processed, and disseminated within and outside of an organization.

Chapter XXVIII
Enterprise Access Control Policy Engineering Framework

Arjmand Samuel
Purdue University, USA

Ammar Masood
Purdue University, USA

Arif Ghafoor
Purdue University, USA

Aditya Mathur
Purdue University, USA

ABSTRACT

This chapter outlines the overall access control policy engineering framework in general and discusses the subject of validation of access control mechanisms in particular. Requirements of an access control policy language are introduced and their underlying organizational philosophy is discussed. Next, a number of access control models are discussed and a brief outline of various policy verification approaches is presented. A methodology for validation of access control implementations is presented along with two approaches for test suite generation, that is, complete FSM based and heuristics based. This chapter is aimed at providing an overview of the access control policy engineering activity and in-depth view of one approach to device test cases for an access control implementation mechanism.

INTRODUCTION

With the increase in information and data accessibility, the concern for security and privacy of data is also increasing, accentuating the need to protect system resources from vulnerabilities introduced as a result of security system design. Engineering access control mechanisms for an enterprise entail a number of closely related activities which include selection of an appropriate security model, creation of access control policy, verification of policy for inconsistencies, and validation of access control implementations.

The wide scale application of access control policies in an enterprise make it imperative that the underlying access control software (system) is correct in that it faithfully implements a policy it is intended to; hence testing of access control system becomes critical. The challenge is in devising such testing techniques that are scalable and effective in detecting those faults that can occur in an access control system.

In this chapter we introduce the overall policy engineering activities with stress on issue of test generation for access control systems using automata theoretic approaches to provide cost effective solutions for conformance and functional testing of an access control mechanism.

BACKGROUND

Security requirements of information systems include protection against unauthorized access to or modification of information, and against denial of service to authorized users. Access control is the key security service providing the foundation for information and system security. An access control implementation is responsible for granting or denying authorizations after the identity of a requesting user has been validated through an appropriate authentication mechanism. Operating systems, database systems, and other applications employ policies to constrain access to application functionality, file systems, and data. Often these policies are implemented in software that serve as front end guard to protected resources, or is interwoven within the application. Examples of application of such controls in securing system resources abound in commercial and research domains (Bhatti, 2005; Notargiacomo, 1996; Tripathi, 2003; XACML, 2005).

A number of reported common vulnerabilities and exposures are related to design and/or coding flaws in access control modules of an application. Testing remains indispensable despite advances in the formal verification of secure systems (Ahmed, 2003; Alpern, 1989; Clarke, 2000; Hansen, 2005; Landwehr, 1986; Lupu, 1999), and in static or dynamic program-analysis based techniques (Cowan, 2003; Livshits, 2005; Martin, 2005) because verification only guarantees correctness of the design under certain assumptions. Any faults in the implementation due to, for example, coding errors, incorrect configuration, and hidden or "backdoor" functionality could jeopardize the effectiveness of corresponding (access control) specification (Thompson, 2003).

Validation of access control implementations is essential because security and privacy issues are now a significant cause for concern amongst the developers of embedded systems such as those found in healthcare, nuclear, automotive, and other industries (Gupta, 2005;

Ravi, 2004). The authentication and access control mechanisms in such environments pose a significant challenge to the designer and tester. The testing of authentication and access control mechanisms, carried out to ensure correctness of the underlying implementation, is necessary for enforcing accountability. Authentication establishes the identity of a user and is a prerequisite for access control.

REQUIREMENTS OF ENTERPRISE ACCESS CONTROL POLICY LANGUAGE

Figure 1 depicts the relationship between security requirements of an enterprise and corresponding access management policy language. While the stated enterprise requirements address the issues of interoperability and scalability, they also drive the important language design parameters of context sensitivity and ease of administration. The enterprise requirement of attribute-based control sets the stage for highly granular and flexible control of users and resources. The autonomy requirement of domains and sub-domains in the enterprise opens opportunities for collaboration with other enterprises. Next we discuss the requirements of a policy-based access management language in detail.

Declarative Rules

Declarative rules in an access management policy language allow each enterprise to compose rules which are both flexible and scalable. The rules can be modified without any effect on the application code and can be composed individually by participating sub-domains by using a common vocabulary and composition rules. Once created, they can be applied across domains with similar efficacy.

Use of declarative rules enables autonomy of control within a domain as well as de-centralized administration in a cluster of domains interoperating with each other. The issues of autonomy and de-centralized administration are fundamental to the design of an access control policy language for an enterprise which seeks to be part of a collaboration or federation with other enterprises. The principle of local autonomy suggests that each sub-domain of an enterprise and indeed each collaborating enterprise in inter-enterprise coloration, retain control over its

Figure 1. Requirements of enterprise access management policy language

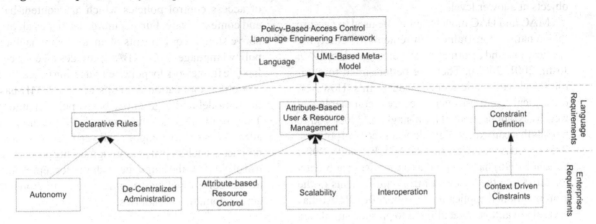

resources. De-centralized administration enables all participating sub-domains to retain local autonomy for creating and implementing access control policies in a de-centralized fashion.

Attribute-Based User and Resource Management

While access management in a single domain with a few users, permissions, and resources effectively can be achieved by User IDs and resource names, it is not possible to do the same in an enterprise with thousands of users collaborating with other enterprises of similar scale. Using credential attributes of users and resources effectively circumvents this scalability challenge. Credentials also can be shared across enterprise boundaries resulting in an interoperable collaboration with no restrictions on the number of users and resources being shared. Consequently, attribute-based user and resource management addresses the challenges of interoperability and scalability in enterprise access management.

Constraint Definition

Specification of semantic and contextual constraints is an important aspect of design of access management policies for enterprises and inter-enterprise collaboration. In order to maintain integrity of access control, semantic constraints such as Separation of Duty (SoD), and cardinality (Joshi, 2005) have to be defined for users and resources. Contextual constraints such as

time, activity, location, and so on, associated with a request, play an important role in the access control decision. Definition of constraints also can change with change in contractual obligations of enterprises and hence need to updated.

ACCESS CONTROL MODELS

The many access control models, proposed in the literature to address diverse security requirements of information systems, can broadly be classified into two categories: Discretionary Access Control (DAC) (Graham, 1972; Harrison, 1976; Jajodia, 1997; Lampson, 1974; Sandhu, 1994) and Mandatory Access Control (MAC) (Bell, 1976; Biba, 1977; Lampson, 1973; McLean, 1990). In DAC, the basic premise is that subjects have ownership over objects of the system and subjects can grant or revoke access rights on the objects they own to other subjects at the original subjects' discretion. Subjects can be users, groups or processes that act on behalf of other subjects. However, lack of any system control in DAC can allow users to access unauthorized objects. MAC limits the high degree of flexibility permitted to subjects in DAC by strict enforcement of system wide constraints in controlling subjects' access of objects. The subjects and objects are classified based on some predefined security levels, which leads to various clearance levels for access control. The unauthorized flow of sensitive information is controlled by two principles of "no read-up" and "no write-down," that is users with low clearance level are not permitted to read high level objects and users at a higher level cannot write to objects at a lower level.

MAC and DAC models cannot be used to capture the dynamic constraint requirements of emerging applications and information systems (Bertino, 1999; Joshi, 2001, 2001a). They are better suited to environments with static security constraints. However, the critical requirements for secure e-commerce and web-based applications (Thuraisingham, 2001) require models that can express flexible access control policies. Role Based Access Control (RBAC) (Ferraiolo, 2001; Sandhu, 1996) has emerged as a promising approach for satisfying the access control requirements of the aforementioned applications (Ahn, 2000). RBAC has several advantages that allow it to provide simplified security management (Bertino, 1999). These include the abstraction of roles and use of role hierarchy, principle of least privilege, separation of duty (SoD), and policy neutrality (Joshi, 2001). These advantages distinguish RBAC from other models as a powerful model for specifying policies and rules for a variety of organization-specific security models. Furthermore, RBAC is capable of modeling a wide range of access control policies including those modeled using DAC and MAC (Osborn, 2000).

In order to control the time-sensitive activities present in various applications like work flow management systems and real time databases, access control systems are required to be augmented with temporal constraints. As an example workflow applications used in healthcare setups are also required to enforce temporal access constraints in order to ensure security of patient records (Malamateniou, 1998). One such constraint is to allow a doctor access to the patient record for only a specified duration. Temporal RBAC (TRBAC) (Bertino, 2001) and Generalized Temporal RBAC (GT-RBAC) (Joshi, 2005) extended RBAC with temporal constraints to enforce time based access control requirements. While authorization for use of resources based on time allows organizations to exercise fine grained temporal control, the importance of spatial context is also being realized lately. This realization has been amplified with the advent of mobile computing devices utilizing wireless networks and allowing users to access computing resources while on the move. The Generalized Spatio-Temporal RBAC (GST-RBAC) model (Samuel, 2007) allows specification of rich spatial constraints based on topological relationship between locations.

XML GT-RBAC (X-GTRBAC), the recently defined GT-RBAC policy model using XML (Bhatti,

2006), provides a compact and generic representation of access control policies which are content-based and context-aware. Further more, it satisfies all of the above stated requirements of an access management policy language. X-GTRBAC provides a generic and flexible framework for policy engineering in healthcare and other application domains using a UML-based meta-model and a grammar based policy language. The use of UML in this approach allows the policy administrators to compose and verify access control policies at each step of policy engineering process. The use of XML as the language of choice for representing access control policies permits it to be interoperable across domains boundaries.

VERIFICATION OF ACCESS CONTROL POLICIES

Access control policy analysis and verification recently has been an active area of research. Ahmed and Tripathi (Ahmed, 2003), have proposed static verification of security requirements for CSCW systems using finite-state techniques. Model checking helps in automating analysis of complex systems and properties (Clarke, 1997). A technique for the extraction of abstract finite-state machines directly from finite-state programs and satisfaction of a formula by the abstract machine is given in (Clarke, 1994). This methodology is the basis of subsequent model checking approaches. Schaad (2006) has proposed a model-checking approach for automated analysis of delegation and revocation functionalities in the context of a work flow requiring static and dynamic separation of duty constraints. Zhang (2005) has proposed a model-checking algorithm which can be used to evaluate access control policies. As has been noted here, verification of access control policies is in itself a daunting task and its details are not being addressed here. Interested readers are referred to the above mentioned references.

VALIDATION OF ACCESS CONTROL SYSTEMS

We now present a test generation technique for generating tests for implementations of access control policies. Our test generation strategy is based on three procedures which constructs Finite State Machine

(FSM) based models of a set of role based access control (RBAC) policies and utilizes W method (Chow, 1978) for test generation from these models. The first procedure constructs and uses a complete FSM for each policy for test generation and as a result is able to achieve excellent fault detection capability.

Two approaches are presented to reduce the size of the generated test suite. One approach is based on a set of heuristics that reduce the size of the original model and hence that of the generated test suite. The second approach directly generates a significantly smaller test suite from the finite state model using random selection of paths, alleviates the need for an in-memory representation of the model, and exhibits high fault detection effectiveness. The proposed approaches for test generation were evaluated empirically using a new fault model specifically targeted at implementations of access control policies.

Testing Context

Figure 2 shows the context of applicability of the proposed test generation approach. As shown, the access enforcement module is the system under test (ACUT). Prior to testing, the ACUT is initialized with a policy P. It is assumed that a Policy processor performs this initialization task. The Policy processor constructs an internal representation of P for subsequent access by the ACUT. Often the internal representation is a table containing various relations. This division of tasks between two sub-modules allows for flexibility in the specification of policies. For example, P could be represented using XML (Bhatti, 2006) or it could be specified using a GUI (Koch, 2003) attached to the Policy processor.

A request received by the ACUT is authenticated against the policy and, if *granted* passed to the Application. The Test harness contains the test cases generated using the finite state model of the given RBAC policy P. Test cases are to test the policy enforcement mechanism, not the application. Each test case t could assume one of two forms: (r, q) or (r, rp), where $r=r_1, r_2, \ldots, r_{k-1}, r_k$ is a sequence of $k>0$ requests that belong to the input alphabet I, $q=q_1, q_2, \ldots, q_{k-1}, q_k$ is the expected state transition sequence, and $rp=rp_1, rp_2, \ldots, rp_k$ is the expected response sequence.

Testing is performed by applying all the test cases in succession to the ACUT. A test t is executed against the ACUT by sending each request in t to the ACUT and observing the state changes for correctness. An ACUT which passes all the tests is considered conforming to P with respect to the given test set.

Fault Model

The fault detection effectiveness of proposed test generation strategy is evaluated using a fault model shown in Figure 3. The proposed RBAC fault model consists of three types of faults: user-role assignment, user-role activation, and permission-role assignment. As in Figure 3, each fault is further categorized into two subcategories. Fault type UR1 restricts an authorized user from being assigned to a role or leads to an unauthorized de-assignment. Fault type UR2 may lead to unauthorized role assignments. PR1 faults restrict a permission being assigned to an authorized role or cause an unauthorized de-assignment. PR2 faults assign permission to an unauthorized role. UA1 and UA2 faults are similar to UR1 and UR2 and impact role activation.

Figure 2. Interaction between an application, access control enforcement module (ACUT), and the protected resources

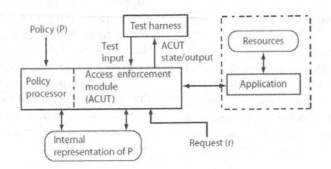

Figure 3. A fault model for evaluating the effectiveness of tests for RBAC implementations

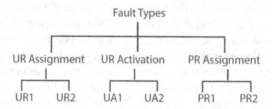

The proposed fault model is complete in that any violation of an RBAC policy corresponds to at least one of the six fault types. For example, suppose that role r_1 can be activated by at most one user at any instant. Now, suppose that while u_1 has activated r_1, a request for activation of r_1 by u_2 is allowed. This is an instance of the UA2 fault. Examples of other fault types can be constructed similarly.

FSM Based Test Generation

We propose a test generation procedure (Procedure A) which constructs a FSM model M of the given RBAC policy and then generate tests from the model using a well known automata theoretic method, (Chow, 1978). A state in M is a sequence of pairs of bits, one pair for each user-role combination as in the table below. For example, given two users, u_1 and u_2, and one role, r_1, a state is represented as a pattern of two consecutive pairs of bits. In this case, 1011 indicates that u_1 is assigned to role r_1 but has not activated r_1 and u_2 is assigned to r_1 and has activated it.

Pattern	Role	
	Assigned	Activated
00	No	No
10	Yes	No
11	Yes	Yes
01	Not Used	Not Used

Although several methods are available for generating a test suite from an FSM, we used the W method (Chow, 1978) for its good fault detection ability. The W method works by first generating a test tree from the FSM model and then concatenating the test sequences (generated from the test tree) with the determined state characterization set (W). The W set consists of input

sequences that can distinguish between behaviors of every pair of states in the minimal FSM.

The FSM modeling of an RBAC policy makes the specified behavior explicit, thus allowing one to investigate the conformance of an ACUT with respect to the specified behavior. As a result of the complete modeling of the ACUT behavior this test generation strategy turns out to be highly effective in detecting access-related faults defined above; however this strategy can become impractical due the astronomical size of the complete FSM. As an example, the number of states in a complete FSM model of the expected behavior of ACUT can easily reach 3^{50} in an application with ten users and five distinct roles.

Reducing the Number of Tests

We consider two approaches to reduce the number of tests: Procedure B which utilizes a set of six heuristics to reduce the size of the model and hence of the generated test suite, and Procedure C which directly generates a significantly smaller test suite from the complete FSM (as used in Procedure A) using Constrained Random Selection of Paths (CRPS) and alleviates the need for an in-memory representation of the model.

Procedure B: The heuristics are derived from knowledge of the structure of access control policies. While the heuristics did lead to a drastic reduction in the size of the model, they also can result in reduced fault detection effectiveness if each heuristic is applied in isolation with the other heuristics. The "isolationist" nature of each heuristic is by virtue of the reason that the FSMs generated using a heuristic contains only "local" information about a policy. Therefore we recommend combining the test suites generated using individual heuristics so as to exploit the locality information across the FSMs that can likely lead to an adequate test suite.

Procedure C: The CRPS strategy is precisely aimed at achieving the goal of a reduction in the size of the test suite without incurring the loss of reduced system view as is the case for heuristics used in Procedure B. The strategy here is that given the complete FSM M corresponding to P, tests are derived by randomly selecting paths of fixed length from M. One could use some statistical criterion, such as the rate of ACUT failure, or an economic criterion such as the maximum number of test sequences, as a criterion to determine the total number of tests in the CRPS test suite. The lengths of tests are selected to be close to the length of longest test generated by using Procedure A.

The fault detection effectiveness of CRPS is likely to be better than the tests generated using Procedure B because the tests are generated from the complete FSM and hence maintain the global view of the system. While the complete FSM is astronomically large, CRPS strategy can be easily coded without the need to actually represent the model in internal memory. The effectiveness would likely increase as the length and number of tests in CRPS test suite increases.

Empirical Evaluation

We have conducted an empirical study to assess the cost, fault detection effectiveness, and cost-benefit ratio (CBR) of the three procedures earlier. The cost of each procedure is measured in the total length of all tests in its test suite. Program mutation (DeMillo, 1978) and manual injection of malicious faults were used to measure the fault detection effectiveness.

The cost-benefit ratio is the ratio of the cost of the tests generated using a procedure to their fault detection effectiveness. The study was based on an implementation of a generic access control mechanism named (Bhatti, 2006).

X-GTRBAC is a generic policy enforcement system that provides both authentication and access control. It can serve as a front-end to any application that needs to enforce access control based on an RBAC policy. In the case study, our focus is on the access control functionality of X-GTRBAC. It is a Java-based system in which the RBAC policy is specified using XML policy files. The access control is implemented using two sets of modules: a policy initializer and a policy enforcer. Only the policy enforcement subsystem of X-GTRBAC was the target of the case study.

Two types of faults were injected into the policy enforcement module (ACUT): first order mutants (referred as simple faults) and malicious faults. Mutation operators as defined in the muJava system (Ma, 2005) are used to generate 349 mutants of the ACUT. Malicious faults were manually injected to create 8 malicious versions of the ACUT. Procedure A, as expected, was able to provide complete fault coverage for both the simple and malicious faults, but at the expense of very high CBR.

Procedure B also achieved complete coverage for simple faults but failed to detect one malicious fault. Despite the low CBR of Procedure B, its use would not be recommended for purely black box ACUT's in which white box coverage measures cannot be used to determine coverage of a test suite. Procedure C detected all the simple and malicious faults while having a good CBR measure which is slightly above the CBR measure of Procedure B.

CONCLUSION

In this chapter we have outlined the components involved in enterprise access control policy engineering. We spell out the enterprise access control policy language requirements and introduce the various access control models being used today. We discuss the issues involved in the process of validation of access control policy implementation software and provide an in-depth treatment of the subject. We have treated in details two approaches for the creation of test suites which have been shown to be effective in testing of such software. The heuristic based approach can be effectively used to reduce the size of the test set but at the same time maintain a high level of effectiveness.

REFERENCES

Ahmed, T. & Tripathi, A. R. (2003). Static verification of security requirements in role-based CSCW systems. *SACMAT 03,* 196-203

Ahn, G.-J. & Sandhu, R. (2000). Role-based authorization constraints specification. *ACM Transactions on Information Systems Security, 3*(4), 207-226.

Alpern, B. & Schneider, F. B. (1989). Verifying temporal properties without temporal logic. *ACM Trans-*

actions on Programming Languages and Systems, *11*(1), 147-167.

Bell, D. E., & LaPadula, L. J. (1976). Secure computer system: Unified exposition and multics interpretation. *MTR-2997,* MITRE Corp

Bertino, E., Bonatti, P. A., & Ferrari, E. (2001). TRBAC: A temporal role-based access control model. *ACM Transaction on Information and System Security,* *4*(3), 191-233.

Bertino, E., Ferrari, E., & Atluri, V. (1999). The specification and enforcement of authorization constraints in workflow management systems. *ACM Transaction on Information and System Security,* *2*(1), 65-104.

Bhatti, R., Ghafoor, A., & Bertino, E. (2006). X-Federate: A policy engineering framework for federated access management. *IEEE Transactions on Software Engineering,* *32*(5), 330-347.

Bhatti, R., Ghafoor, A., Bertino, E., & Joshi, J. B. D. (2005). X-GTRBAC: An XML-based policy specification framework and architecture for enterprise-wide access control. *ACM Transaction on Information and System Security,* *8*(2), 187-227.

Biba, K. (1977). Integrity considerations for secure computer systems. *MTR-3153,* MITRE Corp.

Chow, T. S. (1978). Testing software design modeled by finite state machines. *IEEE Transactions on Software Engineering,* *SE-4*(3), 178-187.

Clarke, E. M. (1997). Model checking. *Lecture notes in Computer Science,* *1346,* 54-56, Springer Verlag KG.

Clarke, E. M., Grumberg, O. & Long, D. E. (1994). Model checking and abstraction. *ACM Trans. Program. Lang. Syst,* *16*(5), 1512-1542.

Clarke, E. M., Grumberg, O., & Peled, D. A. (2000). *Model checking.* MA: The MIT Press.

Cowan, C., Beattie, S., Johansen, J., & Wagle, P. (2003). PointGuard: Protecting pointers from buffer overflow vulnerabilities. *USENIX Security Symposium,* CVE (2006), Common Vulnerabilities and Exposures, http://www.cve.mitre.org/

DeMillo, R. A., Lipton, R. J., & Sayward, F. G. (1978). Hints on test data selection. *IEEE Computer,* *11*(4), 34-41.

Ferraiolo, D. F., Sandhu, R., Gavrila, S., Kuhn, D. R., & Chandramouli, R. (2001). Proposed NIST standard for role-based access control. *ACM Transaction on Information and System Security,* *4*(3), 224-274.

Graham, G., & Denning, P. (1972). Protection - - Principles and practice. *Spring Joint Computer Conference.*

Gupta, P., Ravi, S., Raghunathan, A., & Jha, N. K. (2005). Efficient finger print-based user authentication for embedded systems. *42nd Design Automation Conference, DAC'05,* 244–247.

Hansen, F. & Oleshchuk, V. (2005). Lecture notes in computer science. Chapter: Conformance Checking of RBAC Policy and its Implementation. *Proceedings of Information Security Practice and Experience: First International Conference, ISPEC 2005.*

Harrison, M. A., Ruzzo, W. L. & Ullman, J. D. (1976). Protection in operating systems. *Communications of the ACM,* *19*(8), 461-471.

Jajodia, S., Samarati, P., Subrahmanian, V. S., & Bertino, E. (1997). A unified framework for enforcing multiple access control policies. *Proceedings of the 1997 ACM SIGMOD International Conference on Management of Data, SIGMOD '97,* 474-485.

Joshi, J. B. D., Aref, W. G., Ghafoor, A., & Spafford, E. H. (2001). Security models for Web-based applications. *Communications of the ACM,* *44*(2), 38-44.

Joshi, J., Ghafoor, A., Aref, W. G., & Spafford, E. H. (2001a). Digital government security infrastructure design challenges. *Computer,* *34*(2), 66-72.

Joshi, J. B. D., Bertino, E., Latif, U., & Ghafoor, A. (2005). A generalized temporal role-based access control model. *IEEE Transactions on Knowledge and Data Engineering,* *17*(1), 4-23.

Koch, M. & Parisi-Presicce, F. (2003). Visual specifications of policies and their verification. *Lecture Notes in Computer Science,* *2621,* 278-293, Springer-Verlag.

Lampson, B.W. (1973). A note on the confinement problem. *Communications of the ACM,* *16*(10), 613-615.

Landwehr, C. E., Gerhart, S. L., McLean, J., Good, D. I., & Leveson, N. (1986). NRL invitational workshop on testing and proving: Two approaches to assurance. *SIGSOFT Software Engineering Notes,* *11*(5), 63-85.

Livshits, V. B. & Lam, M. S. (2005). Finding security errors in Java programs with static analysis. *Proceedings of the 14th Usenix Security Symposium.*

Lupu, E. C. & Sloman, M. (1999). Conflicts in policy-based distributed systems management. *IEEE Transactions on Software Engineering, 25*(6), 852-869.

Ma, Y. S., Offutt, J. & Kwon, Y. R. (2005). MuJava: An automated class mutation system: Research articles. *Softw. Test. Verif. Reliab., 15*(2), 97-133.

Malamateniou, F., Vassilacopoulos, G., & Tsanakas, P. (1998). A workflow-based approach to virtual patient record security. *IEEE Transactions on Information Technology in Biomedicine, 2*(3), 139-145.

Martin, M., Livshits, B., & Lam, M. S. (2005). Finding application errors and security flaws using PQL: A program query language. *OOPSLA '05: Proceedings of the 20th annual ACM SIGPLAN Conference on Object Oriented Programming, Systems, Languages, and Applications,* 365-383.

McLean, J. (1990). Security models and information flow. *IEEE Symposium on Security and Privacy,* 180-189.

Notargiacomo, L. (1996). Role-based access control in ORACLE7 and Trusted ORACLE7. *Proceedings of the first ACM Workshop on Role-based Access Control, RBAC '95,* 65-69.

Osborn, S. L., Sandhu, R., & Munawer, Q. (2000). Configuring role-based access control to enforce mandatory and discretionary access control policies *ACM Transactions on Information and System Security, 3*(2), 85-106.

Ravi, S, Raghunathan, A., & Chakradhar, S. (2004). Tamper resistance mechanisms for secure, embedded systems. *17th International Conference on VLSI Design,* 605–611.

Samuel, A. & Ghafoor, A. (2007). Framework for specification and verification of generalized spatio-temporal role based access control model. *CERIAS Technical Report,* TR 2007-08.

Sandhu, R. & Samarati, P. (1994). Access control: Principles and practice. *IEEE Communications, 32*(9), 40-48.

Sandhu, R. S., Coyne, E. J., Feinstein, H. L., & Youman, C. E. (1996). Role-based access control models. *IEEE Computer, 29*(2), 38-47.

Schaad, A., Lotz, V. & Sohr, K. (2006). A model-checking approach to analyzing organizational controls in a loan origination process. *SACMAT 06,* 139-149.

Thompson, H. H. (2003). Why security testing is hard. *IEEE Security and Privacy, 1*(4), 83-86.

Thuraisingham, B., Clifton, C., Gupta, A., Bertino, E., & Ferrari, E. (2001). Directions for Web and e-commerce applications security. *10th IEEE International Workshops on Enabling Technologies, WETICE '01,* 200-204.

Tripathi, A. R., Ahmed, T., & Kumar, R. (2003). Specification of secure distributed collaboration systems. *The Sixth International Symposium on Autonomous Decentralized Systems (ISADS'03),* 149-15.

XACML (2005). eXtensible Access Control Markup Language (XACML), *OASIS,* http://www.oasis-open.org/committees/tc_home.php?wg_abbrev=xacml

Zhang, N., Ryan, M., & Guelev, D. P. (2005). Evaluating access control policies through model checking. *ISC 05,* 446-460.

KEY TERMS

Definition 1: RBAC Fault Model: The RBAC fault model consists of three types of faults: user-role assignment, user-role activation, and permission-role assignment.

UR Assignment Faults: These faults are subsequently classified into two types: UR1—faults because of which an *authorized* user is restricted from assignment to a role or gets improperly de-assigned from the assigned role, UR2—faults by virtue of which an *unauthorized* user is assigned to a role. As already mentioned before, *authorized* user imply such a user who can be assigned to or can activate a role under *R(P)*. UR1 fault in an ACUT' constrain a user from accessing the authorized permissions, whereas UR2 fault allows access to unauthorized permissions.

UR Activation Faults: These faults can also be classified into two types: UA1—faults because of which an *authorized* user is restricted from activating a role or the activated role is improperly deactivated, UA2—faults by virtue of which an *unauthorized* user can activate a role. As noted previously, an authorized user can activate a role either by virtue of direct user assignment to that role or by being assigned to a role senior to the target role in A-hierarchy semantics. UA2 fault in an ACUT' can result into serious compromise of confidentiality and integrity of the system resources because, in RBAC users are only able to access system resources through the mechanism of user-role activations.

PR Assignment Faults: Like two previous kind of faults these faults can also be categorized into two types, PR1 and PR2 faults, where former are the faults in which a permission-role assignment allowed by P actually does not exist in the ACUT' and later are the one in which the situation is otherwise, that is, such a permission-role assignment exists in the ACUT' which is not permitted by the policy. In case of PR1 faults the authorized permission-role assignment, required

to be valid in the ACUT', can be either by virtue of direct permission assignment to the role or assignment through inheritance semantics.

Definition 2: Complete FSM based test suite generation technique. In this procedure tests are generated from the complete FSM, derived from the policy P, as per the steps outlined in (Chow, 1978). The complexity of this procedure not only depends on the size of M but also on the observability of states in the ACUT.

Definition 3: Heuristics based test suite generation technique. In this procedure heuristics are used to reduce the size of the model and of the test set. These heuristics are similar to the concept of state abstractions as used in various verification techniques.

Chapter XXIX
Information Security Policies:
Precepts and Practices

Sushil K. Sharma
Ball State University, USA

Jatinder N.D. Gupta
The University of Alabama at Huntsville, USA

ABSTRACT

The purpose of the information security policy is to establish an organization-wide approach to prescribe mechanisms that help identify and prevent the compromise of information security and the misuse of organization's data, applications, networks, and computer systems to define mechanisms that protect the organization from its legal and ethical responsibilities with regard to its networks' and computer systems' connectivity to worldwide networks. Most of the organizations worldwide already have formulated their information security policies. Having a security policy document in itself is not enough, the document must be complete. This paper examines security policies of 20 different academic organizations with standard security policy framework and attempts to answer questions such as: are these security policy documents complete? Are they fully up to date? Does the precept match the practice? These are kind of questions that are addressed in this study.

INTRODUCTION

Over the years, the number of personal computers and information technology (IT) devices and networks has explosively increased in organizations and this has created unprecedented challenge of protecting not only these devices but also information assets in organizations. Thus, organizations have an imperative to formulate an information security policy that states the different measures an enterprise plans to take to protect computers, networks, IT devices, and information assets from deliberate or inadvertent unauthorized acquisition, damage, disclosure, manipulation, modification, loss, or use (Baskerville & Siponen, 2002). Usually, it is the responsibility of information technology departments to maintain the confidentiality, integrity, and availability of an organization's information. The basis of how this is done is described in an organization's security policy. A security policy is a statement that spells out exactly what defenses will be configured to block unauthorized access, what constitutes acceptable use of network resources, how the organization will respond to attacks, and how employees should safely handle the organization's resources in order to discourage loss of data or damage to files (Doughty, 2003; Holden, 2003). The information security policy also includes an organization's plan to educate, aware, and train its employees to protect the company's information assets. Policy reflects the philosophy and strategy of management with regard to information security (Höne & Eloff, 2002).

A good organizational information security policy should include such elements as: the need for security, access control, accountability, and employee and user responsibilities to ensure the confidentiality, integrity, and availability of information. The CIA Triangle stands for Confidentiality, Integrity, and Availability. Confidentiality ensures that information is accessible only to those authorized to have access. This refers not only to the prevention of unauthorized disclosure of the contents of data, but also the unauthorized disclosure of the existence of the data. Integrity refers to the completeness, correctness, and trustworthiness of the information. Availability means that information is available to those approved at any given time. Non-repudiation proves that a transaction really took place. All these help an organization protect, control, and keep safe its information, assuring that they are free from danger (Doughty, 2003). Information security is critical to supporting and maintaining the ongoing functions of the organization, protecting the organization's assets, safeguarding the privacy of the organization's employees and customers, and preventing the use of the organization's systems for malicious attacks.

BACKGROUND

Organizations have been spending tremendous amounts of money on deploying firewalls, Intrusion Detection Systems (IDS) software, and encryption equipment and human resources for information security (Doherty & Fulford, 2005). But if an organization just haphazardly puts together these security tools and devices without formulating an organizational information security, nothing good will come of it. A security policy for a system is like a foreign policy for a government because it defines the aims and goals. Any company should have interest in protecting its assets against undesired events. A security policy should address the information assets of the organization, the threats to those assets, and the measures that management has decided are reasonable and proper to protect

those assets (Fulford & Doherty, 2003). Organizations are also supposed to comply with governmental legislations such as the Health Information Privacy and Protection Act (HIPPA), Sarbanes-Oxley Act, Gramm-Leach-Bliley Act (GLBA), Child Online Privacy and Protection Act (COPPA), and the Patriot Act (Tulu & Chatterjee, 2003; Ma & Pearson, 2005).

Many academic organizations or universities have been claiming that they have formulated effective information security policies to protect their information assets. The study was undertaken to examine security policies of 20 different academic organizations to asses whether security policy of these organizations match the standard security policy framework. The standard information security policy framework chosen is the National Institute of Standards and Technology (NIST) based Federal Information Security Management Act (FISMA) Policy framework which is recommended for information security (Warkentin & Vaughn, 2006).

Methodology

We examined security policies of 20 different academic organizations. The policies of these 20 organizations were obtained through online resources. These security policies are examined with standard security policy framework recommended by the National Institute of Standards and Technology (NIST). Each of the 20 organizational information security policy is assessed whether standard security policy components such as: scope of security explaining definition and domains of security, standard guidelines outlining what standards need to be met, roles and responsibilities of individuals, compliance and penalties in case of any violations, mention of incident response, back up and recovery plans, information security education, awareness and training, employee accountability, management responsibilities including handling incidents, mention of relevant laws and acts, allowable and prohibitive use, rights to monitor and intercept, contact information and roles are mentioned in the policy document.

Information Security Policy Framework

The information security policy framework provides the overall model for developing a comprehensive security program. The framework helps organizations to classify systems as defined in FIPS Publication 199 by continuously monitoring the configuration, inventory, and networking activity of machines on the network. This enables security administrators to target and automatically provision their policies based on the classification and behavior of systems. The framework suggests that organization should dynamically classify groups of systems and enforce integrated host-level access controls that are aligned with business processes and the roles of users, systems, and applications (Maynard & Ruighaver, 2006; Tishkov, Kotenko, & Sidelnikova, 2005).

The framework suggests that organizations should perform a comprehensive risk analysis of various vulnerabilities and the potential financial losses. Risk consists of a combination of information resources that have value and vulnerabilities that are exploitable. The magnitude of the risk is the product of the value of the information and the degree to which the vulnerability can be exploited. Thus, a comprehensive risk assessment exercise must be the first phase of the policy development process. Such risk analysis exercise will help organizations' management to understand the amount of financial investment in security and consequences in case of any security breach (Doherty & Fulford, 2006).

The information security policy framework can also be formulated based on the principles and guidelines described in the Foobar Information Security Framework document. The Foobar Information Security Framework describes that all Foobar network equipment (routers, servers, workstations, etc.) shall be classified according to the standard Foobar classification scheme and placed in a network segment appropriate to its level of classification. All users hosts and data must be classified and all physical network segments, IP subnets and other IP traffic carriers must be classified in the same way (Medlin, Cazier, & Dave, 2006).

The information security policy framework also suggests that organizations should evolve a security culture and it should be discussed in security policy document (Von Solms & Von Solms, 2004). The people or employees are known to be the weakest link in the security chain (Schultz, 2005). Many organizations understand security only in terms of investing in firewalls, intrusion detection systems and routers. Considering this weak link, organizations need to create a security culture that is conducive to the implementation of security policies. For creating security culture, organizations not only need to communicate with their employees on a regular basis but have to train, make aware and educate them about security

(Thomson & von Solms, 1998). There should be a reward system in place for good security practice. Similarly, organizations should specify disciplinary action against staff for non-compliant or negligent behavior. Organizations should give employees clear guidelines of acceptable behavior, and clearly spell out the consequences of breaching those guidelines. All staff should be made to sign a document stating their acceptance of the principles of the security policy. This forces staff to read and understand the policy and gives organization legal recourse in the case of security breaches (Kim, Kim, & Na, 2005).

Information security policy document should also mention about physical security to protect physical access to resources, commensurate with the identified level of acceptable risk. These may range in scope and complexity from extensive security installations to protect a room or facility where server machines are located, to simple measures taken to protect a user's display screen. Once an organization has a system of security policies in place, it will be necessary to determine the efficacy of the policies within the context of the organization. The proper way to do this is, of course, via another risk assessment exercise, thus completing the security cycle.

Data Analysis and Finding

After evaluating the information security policies of 20 academic organizations based on the criteria mentioned in methodology, it was found that only two of the 20 organizations had security policies that met 80 percent of all the requirements for a standard information security policy framework. The policy of two organizations is divided into sections and subsections which make for an easy read. Expectations and rules are clearly laid out for the reader to cipher through and understand. General rules are listed at the beginning, which give the reader an exact idea of what is expected of them right away. As the reader progresses through the policy they are informed of specific policies and procedures that they will be expected to follow and adhere to which solidify the points given at the beginning of the policy.

Majority of the organizations in their security policy had mentioned scope of security explaining definition and domains of security and roles and responsibilities of individuals. Only 40 percent of organizations had mentioned standard guidelines outlining what standards need to be met. Only 20 percent organizations had mentioned compliance and penalties in case of any violations in the security policy. It now is generally recognized that business continuity planning and disaster recovery planning are vital activities of a security plan. A sound disaster recovery/business continuity plan is essential to protect the well being of an organization. This cannot be over emphasized yet many enterprises still side step the issue or hold plans which are clearly out of date or inadequate. It was interesting to note that only 10 percent of organizations had discussed disaster recovery/business continuity plan in their security policy document.

In a majority of organizations, the policy is undefined and cumbersome and seems to be of not much use. Many terms are defined and reasons for investigating security concerns are listed, but there is no mention of what kind of system security implementations are used or what are the procedures recommended to use the resources. Backup data seems to be important, but it never is clarified how the data will be backed up. Vital data must be maintained in secure offsite storage but where and how often backups are made are never mentioned. Electronic mail or network traffic monitoring usage and blockage on the network is needed information that the security policy should state for users. More informative information and suggestions for personnel and network users could assist in their willingness to implement and enforced the policy themselves which would make the network more secure.

Majority of organizations' security policy was very generic and did not discuss incident response, business continuity and disaster recovery in the policy document. Only 5 percent of organizations had mention of relevant laws and acts in their policy. It was interesting to know that only 1 percent of organizations had mention about rights to monitor and intercept in their security policy. Only 45 of percent organizations had a statement of allowable and prohibited use as part of security policy. The majority of these 45 percent had a generic statement

Users must not interfere with, or attempt to interfere with, the normal use of IT resources by other users. Interference includes: denial of service attacks, misusing mailing lists, propagating chain letters or hoaxes, and intentional or unintentional sending of unwanted e-mail to users without specific authorization or a way to opt-out ("spamming"). Other behaviors that cause a network traffic load or computing load that interferes with the normal and intended use of the IT resources is also prohibited.

One thing that was common in all the organizations was that all had mentioned contact information and roles in their security policy. A discussion of the need for security and the impact on account of the occurrence of potential threats were left out by the majority of the organizations. The most significant finding, however, was that 11 of the organizations failed mention about risk analysis in their security policy. The risk analysis is said to be the most critical and integral part of an organization's security policy. Although some defined risk, they failed to give examples for any possible threats they may face. Some of the policies included a list of the assets belonging to the organization, but were still missing the threats, probabilities, vulnerabilities, consequences, and safeguards for the company.

FUTURE TRENDS

Malicious code and other attacks are increasing in intensity and the damage that they cause. With little time to react, organizations have to become more proactive in their security stance. Reactive security will no longer work (Wood, 2000). Therefore organizations need to better understand what the future trends, risks and threats are so that they can be better prepared to make their organizations as secure as possible (Maynard & Ruighaver, 2006). The information security policy of organizations must take account of personnel security, user access control, network security and regulatory aspects all embedded into one document. It should integrate technology, people and processes (Thomson & von Solms, 1998).

CONCLUSION

Information security policy is an important part of security plan. Information security policy should specify all the safeguards both technology and human that are taken to protect information and networking assets (Schultz, 2005). It may be necessary to make some far-reaching changes to organizational structure and culture before policies can effectively achieve the organization's security objectives. Foremost among these changes are the designation of responsibility and the commitment of funds. Policy document must be simple, easy to access, use, and understand. It is one thing to have a security policy in place but it is far more important to have a proper security policy document that meets all the requirements of standard security policy framework. The study found that although all the 20 academic organizations had security policies in place, many of their security policies did not meet the standard security policy framework.

REFERENCES

Baskerville, R., & Siponen, M. (2002). An information security meta-policy for emergent organizations. *Logistics Information Management, 15*(5-6), 337-346.

Doughty, K. (2003). Implementing enterprise security: A case study. *Computer & Security, 22*(2), 99-114. Elsevier Ltd.

Doherty, N. F., & Fulford, H. (2005). Do information security policies reduce the incidence of security breaches: An exploratory analysis. *Information Resources Management Journal, 18*(4), 21-39.

Doherty, N. F., & Fulford, H. (2006). Aligning the information security policy with the strategic information systems plan. *Computers and Security, 25*, 55-63.

Fulford, H., & Doherty, N. F. (2003). The application of information security policies in large UK-based organizations: An exploratory study. *Information Management and Computer Security, 11*(3), 106-114.

Holden, G. (2003). Guide to network defense and countermeasures. Course Technology.

Höne, K., & Eloff, J. (2002). What makes an effective security policy? *Network Security, 6*(1), 14-16.

Kim, G., Kim, J., & Na, J. (2005). Design and implementation of policy decision point in policy-based network. *ACIS International Conference on Computer and Information Science (534-538)*. IEEE Press.

Ma, Q., & Pearson, J.M. (2005). ISO 17799: Best practices in information security management? *Communications of the AIS, 15*, 577-591.

Maynard, S., & Ruighaver, A. B. (2006). *What makes a good information security policy: A preliminary framework for evaluating security policy quality*. Paper presented at the 5th Annual Security Conference, Las Vegas, Nevada. Retrieved December 28, 2006 from http://www.dis.unimelb.edu.au/staff/sean/research/Maynard-PolicyQaulity.pdf

Medlin, B. D., Cazier, J. A., Dave, D. S. (2006). Password security issues on an e-commerce site. In M. Khosrow-Pour (Ed.), *Encyclopedia of e-commerce, e-government, and mobile commerce*. Hershey, PA: Idea Group Reference.

Schultz, E. (2005). The human factor in security. *Computer & Security, 24*, 425-426. Elsevier Ltd.

Tishkov, A., Kotenko, I., & Sidelnikova, E. (2005). Security checker architecture for policy-based security management. *Lecture Notes in Computer Science, 3685*, 460-465. Springer Press.

Thomson, M. E., & von Solms, R. (1998). Information security awareness: Educating your users effectively. *Information Management & Computer Security, 6*(4), 167-173.

Tulu, B., & Chatterjee, S. (2003). *A new security framework for HIPAA-compliant health information systems*. Ninth Americas Conference on Information Systems, Tampa, FL.

Von Solms, R., & Von Solms, B. (2004). From policies to culture. *Computers & Security, 23*(4), 275-279.

Warkentin, M. & Vaughn, R. (2006). *Enterprise information systems assurance and system security: Managerial and technical issues*. London: Idea Group Publishing.

Wood, C. (2000). An unappreciated reason why security policies fail. *Computer Fraud and Security, 10*, 13-14.

KEY TERMS

Allowable use is legal use for other purpose that does not impinge on Acceptable use. The amount of Allowable use will vary over time based on the capacity reserve of information technology resources available beyond Acceptable use.

Information Security: The protection of confidentiality, integrity, and availability of information assets.

Information System: A system consisting of hardware, software, network, and recording media, that is installed in an organization for business processing.

Policy: Policy is a set of rules. They're the dos and the don'ts of information security, again, within the framework of the philosophy.

Practices: Practices simply define the how of the organization's policy. They are a practical guide regarding what to do and how to do it.

Prohibited use is illegal use and all other use that is neither Acceptable nor Allowable.

Risk is the possibility of harm or loss to any software, information, hardware, administrative, physical, communications, or personnel resource.

Threat is an event or activity, deliberate or unintentional, with the potential for causing harm to an IT system or activity.

Vulnerability is a flaw or weakness that may allow harm to occur to an IT system or activity.

Chapter XXX
A Guide to Non-Disclosure Agreements for Researchers

Paul D. Witman
California Lutheran University, USA

Kapp L. Johnson
California Lutheran University, USA

ABSTRACT

This chapter provides a set of guidelines to assist information assurance and security researchers in creating, negotiating, and reviewing non-disclosure agreements, in consultation with appropriate legal counsel. It also reviews the use of non-disclosure agreements in academic research environments from multiple points of view. Active academic researchers, industry practitioners, and corporate legal counsel all provided input into the compiled guidelines. An annotated bibliography and links are provided for further review.

INTRODUCTION AND OBJECTIVES

Non-Disclosure Agreements (NDAs) are an important and necessary tool for researchers, particularly in information security and assurance. Research subjects may require agreement to a NDA before allowing researchers access to data, to protect the research subject's proprietary data, procedures, and identity. Likewise, researchers may require agreement to a NDA to protect the creation of intellectual property as a result of the research. Failure to execute a proper NDA could result in legal disputes, fees, and liability, as well as an inability to use the data collected for research purposes.

The objective of this chapter is to provide the reader with a set of guidelines and observations about NDAs

that are specific to the needs of the academic. Most NDAs are executed between commercial enterprises, and as a result it is difficult to find reference material that provides guidance appropriate to information security researchers on this critical topic.

BACKGROUND

These guidelines were developed as the result of a research project to seek out information about academic NDAs. The research was conducted as an e-mail-based survey, using open-ended questions. A request for suggested guidelines went to the ISWorld distribution list, an e-mail distribution delivered to a global community of Information Science (IS) researchers, students, and faculty members. The request was not country-specific, nor specific to any particular segment of IS.

Eleven contributors, including 10 in academia, self-selected and responded to the initial request. Of those 10, at least two had some industry experience as well. One contributor is a corporate legal counsel who provided significant reviews and provided guidance both from the corporate perspective and what academics should consider.

Of the 11 contributors, nine were based in the United States, one in the United Kingdom, and one in Canada. Of the 10 in academia, eight were faculty members, and two were students.

The research is exploratory in nature, and is not intended as an exhaustive guide to the topic. The research focuses primarily on United States legal definitions and practices, but we anticipate that many of the guidelines may apply in other jurisdictions.

LEGAL OVERVIEW

A Non-Disclosure Agreement is an "agreement restricting the use of information by prohibiting a contracting party from divulging data" (Beyer, 2001). NDAs arise out of a relationship whereby one or both parties to the agreement seek to contractually articulate the respective rights and responsibilities of the parties with regard to some kind of intellectual property. Generally speaking, Intellectual Property is any property that can be protected by law including copyrights, ideas, inventions, and other forms of the intellect that has independent commercial value and is not generally known.

For the researcher, it is very important to determine what rights apply to the work to be produced that is, the researcher's results, papers, and products. The researcher should ask the question as to whether the property is primarily functional or aesthetic. Functional elements are protected by utility patents and trade secrets. Nonfunctional or aesthetic elements are protected by trademarks, copyrights and patents. The researcher may ask the question: "Does this creation accomplish a task or goal or is it done primarily to appeal to the senses or provide information or entertainment?" (Milgrim, 2006a, Chapter 9.04).

Thus courts apply property rules when it comes to intellectual product. Because intellectual product is considered property, the issue for the researcher is to identify who is the "owner" of the property. This is critical because the owner of intellectual property has

the right to use it and disclose it to others or restrict its use and disclosure as the case may be (Milgrim, 2006b, Chapter 2.01).

Consequently, the identification of the type of intellectual property law applicable to the researcher's activity is very important. Intellectual property law involves several distinct legal disciplines which at times overlap (Milgrim, 2006a, Chapter 9.02). There are four types of Intellectual Property laws which are generally applicable to the activities of researchers: patent law; copyright law; trademark law; and trade secret law.

Briefly, patents are of two types of interest to security researchers: utility and design. The most common patent is utility patents and is granted to the inventor of a new, non-obvious invention. A design patent is granted for a new but nonfunctional design (USPTO, 2006b).

Copyrights are granted to authors of "original works of authorship" that include dramatic, musical, artistic, computer programs, and certain other intellectual works, both published and unpublished. Copyrights protect the form of expression rather than the subject matter of the writing, that is, copyrights do not protect ideas and facts, only the manner in which the ideas and facts are expressed (USPTO, 2006a).

Trademark or Servicemark law protects a word, name, symbol, or device that is used in trade with goods to indicate the source of the goods as distinguished from the goods of others (USPTO, 2006c).

Lastly, which will be of most interest to researchers, trade secret law protects any confidential information that gives the creator or holder of the secret a competitive advantage, that is, the information has independent economic value derived from the fact that it is secret. By definition, trade secrets are confidential information, and the owner of the trade secret can prevent others from using the information (NCCUSL, 1985, Section 1[4]).

As is often the case, intellectual property overlaps and the researcher should be aware that patent, copyright, trademark/servicemark, and trade secrets can overlap with regard to a particular product, service, or information. For instance, it is very difficult, if not impossible, to pursue a patent application, while at the same time keeping the invention as a trade secret. In addition, it is not unheard of for a product to be protected under both trademark and copyright law. Finally, patent law can intersect with copyright and trademark/servicemark law in the manner or appearance of an item as well as its design and non-obvious functionality (Milgrim, 2006b, Chapter 9.04).

Researchers must also be aware that it is the nature of confidentiality that creates the need for a nondisclosure agreement. While confidentiality may be implied from the relationship of the parties or the nature of the communication between the parties, express nondisclosure agreements are the safest means for a researcher to protect him/herself from violating a confidential duty as well as protecting their intellectual interests which arise out of the relationship. Therefore, NDAs can differ on the nature and scope of the disclosure, but NDAs must include a clear description of the information held to be confidential, how the confidential information may or may not be used, the duty of confidentiality, choice of law and venue, remedies for breach including injunctive relief, duration of the agreement, scope of activities, who owns the confidential information, protection of marginal matter, as well as post employment activities.

Finally, it must be noted that nondisclosure agreements are contractual. In other words, the law of contracts controls the analysis and the rules a court (whether state or federal) will apply in the case of a breach. Because commercial agreements are in the domain of state law, state law will apply, even if one party is allowed to bring the cause of action in federal court, the federal court will apply the applicable state law (Milgrim, 2006b, Chapter 4.01).

Thus as a matter of law, NDAs are very important in protecting the rights of the owner of the confidential information as to its disclosure and use in a public way.

LITERATURE REVIEW

The literature review provides a framework for other researchers to consider as they review their own needs for confidentiality agreements. While little in the way of concrete guidelines exists in the literature, much is published on the topics of industry-university research collaboration, intellectual property, and the impact of confidentiality agreements on various parts of the research community.

At least since the mid-1980s, universities struggled with how to balance the needs of openness and proprietary control (GUIRR, 1997). This dilemma came about because of the 1980 change in US federal law that made copyright the primary protection for computer software (Peterson, 1985), with its somewhat less rigorous protection for ideas rather than embodiment (Oppedahl & Larson LLP, 1995). The issues that arise

generally center on the classic tension between the academy's desire for open, free sharing of information, and the commercial world's desire to maintain trade secrecy of certain information for commercial purposes.

The reality, however, is rarely so clear cut. Academics also need to keep certain information secret (e.g., confidentiality of the identity of research subjects, delays to allow patent filing). Commercial researchers are sometimes motivated to publish and make a name for themselves or for their employer, both in academic and in trade journals (Newberg & Dunn, 2002). An institution that wishes to commercialize the results of its research may impose publication restrictions both to allow time for patent filings and to allow establishing spin-off business units to bring an idea or invention to market.

Newberg & Dunn (2002) documented several organizational models for Industry-University Research Collaboration, each of which may impact the need for and use of non-disclosure agreements. These include:

1. University to Industry Technology Licensing, where the university clearly owns and is selling or licensing a technology to industry for commercialization
2. Industry-Sponsored University Research, where it is important to establish intellectual property ownership, given that industry is sponsoring and paying for the research
3. Spin-off Companies, often with lead researchers and students taking academic research into the commercial domain, that require appropriate confidentiality and intellectual property ownership agreements; and
4. Idea Labs, such as MIT's Media Lab (Newberg & Dunn, 2002, p. 205), where ongoing cutting-edge research is conducted in an established organizational setting.

Each of these organizational models carries with it potentially different implications about the ownership of intellectual property, and the level of protection that must be accorded to its information. As such, the organizational context of the research must be considered as an aspect of the design of any non-disclosure agreement.

In the case of a formal research consortium inside the university, it may be appropriate to require separate NDAs between the consortium and its researchers, employees, and visitors (Newberg & Dunn, 2002). This approach simplifies relationships with organizations (their NDA could be with the consortium), and may serve to enable free exchange of information among the researchers within the consortium.

The process of establishing ownership of intellectual property is one that can be dealt with in an ad hoc fashion, or can be a very structured part of the campus research environment. Carnegie Mellon University (CMU) is often cited for its highly structured approach. CMU (2001) uses a detailed model identifying the various ways in which intellectual property can be created, and who contributes to that process. From this model, the policy then dictates the ownership of the property. It further prescribes how any economic benefits from that property are to be shared between the researchers, the university, and the sponsors.

Confidentiality agreements may impair the researcher's ability to publish—either by constraining what can be published, by delaying the publication, or by preventing it entirely. NDAs may also impact the researcher's legal right to do the ethically correct thing (e.g., publish results of a study showing impact of chemicals on public health) (GUIRR, 1997).

It is also important for the researcher to understand that even data that is provided under a NDA may lose its confidential status in a number of ways. For example, information that is generally known in the industry of the provider of the information, or information that is generally available to the public, may not be need to be treated as confidential by the researcher (Volonino, 2005). These conditions may vary based on the applicable laws. Therefore, it is important to seek appropriate legal counsel.

At least one study out of the dot-com era also identified potential negative impacts to students. Based on confidentiality agreements signed with one professor, students were in some cases unable to complete assignments given by another professor due to the overlap in the assignment vis-a-vis the confidential information (Marcus, 1999). There remains some dispute about the cause of this issue; it has been represented that the assignment was given as a deliberate form of industrial espionage against another professor. Whatever the facts may be in this case, the potential remains for this problem to occur.

Figure 1 shows a sample of the various entities and constraints that may need to be considered as a non-disclosure agreement is negotiated (modeled after Newberg & Dunn, 2002, p. 225).

Legal and Regulatory factors impact both the researcher and the organization, and may drive some aspects of the non-disclosure agreement, particularly related to the level of protection required. Institutional requirements impact the researcher as well (e.g., intellectual property creation and ownership policies).

Vendors may provide technology and services for a project, and the researcher needs to consider, before launching the project, how and whether any confidential data may be shared with them. Lastly, other people may be exposed to confidential data through participation in the project in a variety of roles, and it may be appropriate to establish constraints around what may or may not be shared with them. Students involved in the research project should also sign a NDA. Stim and Fishman (2001) provide a sample NDA to be used with students to protect confidential information held by a professor.

GUIDELINES

The following guidelines represent the collective wisdom of the respondents to the original query to ISWorld, along with an informal review by a corporate attorney (Anonymous, 2005; Clay, 2005; Edgington, 2005; Kaiser, 2005; Kitchens, 2005; McLaren, 2005; Newman, 2005; Overby, 2005; Straub, 2005; Westerman, 2005).

Starting Points

1. Note that the NDA is not the same as a contract for employment. The NDA defines what each party can and can't disclose to others. An employment contract may or may not cover the same ground, but will also cover such issues as compensation, deliverable expectations, and ownership of intellectual property.
2. Treat the relationship with the organization as a relationship, not as a transaction (Grossman, 2004, pp. 35-38). Take the time to build relationships with your sponsor and with other key participants, so that the NDA is more of a natural part of the process, rather than being the very first step in a relationship.

In other words, don't view the NDA as a contract for a single transaction by which you get some data, publish something, and then move on. Develop a relationship in which you provide interesting analysis and insight to the organization, help them understand some questions, etc. If you develop a group of organizations that enjoy working with you and will share data over time, what a great asset to have as a researcher! (Overby, 2005)

3. Expect to work from the organization's standard NDA. In general, that will make the process simpler than asking them to sign yours. However, if the organization is small and doesn't have a standard NDA, having one of your own as a template is to your advantage.

4. It is also helpful to create standard wording elements that you would like to see in the NDA so that you can suggest specific clauses for their legal counsel to respond to.

5. Be clear about why you need changes; for example,

I want to make these changes because our situation is different from the typical situation covered by this NDA. Of course, I need to protect your confidentiality. But, as an academic, I also need to be free to use my research outputs in teaching and publishing. So, let's see if these changes can protect your interests while also giving me the freedom I need for my career. (Westerman, 2005)

6. Consider making the agreement only between yourself and the organization, and exclude your

university. This separation also simplifies the process. That said, it is important to understand your university's policies and ensure that they are not liable by implication for your work, and that its policies don't require any specific clauses or process.

7. Consider whether the relationship might become one of mutual disclosure, and whether your own, or your university's confidential information needs to be protected as well, possibly for commercialization. Particularly in this latter case, the Bayh-Dole Act of 1980, which affects ownership of intellectual property developed under federal funding, should be factored into the language of the NDA (Foley, 2004).

8. Avoid vague language in the agreement, and gain an understanding of such common legal terms as "prorated" and "reasonable."

Time Limits

9. If possible, obtain permission to publish freely after three years (this is the standard timeframe, though it can be negotiated). Some organizations will have difficulty with such a clause. Even though technology does move quickly, legacy systems often don't, and you could still be in possession of information of value to the

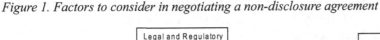

Figure 1. Factors to consider in negotiating a non-disclosure agreement

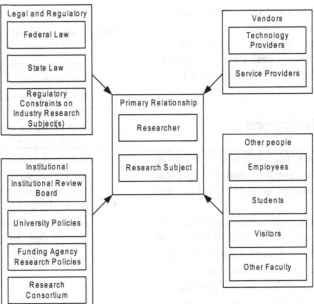

organization which could be detrimental if freely disseminated.

10. The organization may view a time limit as unacceptable, but it is still worth asking.

Approval Requirements

11. If you can, avoid a requirement for explicit approval by the organization. It will certainly simplify the publication process. Many respondents were more vociferous than that. Approval requirements were, in their minds, something to be avoided at all costs. Alternatively, you might seek agreement that the organization has a right to review how they are identified (or disguised), and will have the opportunity to comment (for correctness, within a reasonable timeframe) on any other part of the work. That would be a reasonable compromise.

12. A planned review of the findings by the organization can both strengthen your validity as well as improve the possibility of approval by your local Institutional Review Board.

13. Consider an annotation in the NDA that you retain the right to publish your research, with the exception of the organization's right to retain anonymity and prevent publication of proprietary information, and that both parties will work in good faith to make that possible.

14. Consider offering to co-author with an organization employee if you will be publishing in a trade journal as one of your outlets. This option could help build their stature in the market, and motivate them to participate.

15. Be careful that any approvals language does not require a new approval each time you speak or write about the research you conducted with this data.

Courts and Jurisdictions

16. Note that laws vary from state to state and from country to country. You will need to be sure that your agreement is appropriate for the laws that govern it.

17. Some respondents indicated that courts will often rule against the party that drafted the agreement. However, the corporate counsel who participated in this study indicated that this assumption is generally a myth, and that courts in general will rule against the party that wrote the agreement

only in the case of an ambiguity in the terms that is material to the dispute. It is also worth noting that the party with the burden of proof is more likely to lose the case.

18. The agreement should specify both what laws apply (generally, in the U.S., which state's laws), and in which court system (generally, in the U.S., which county's courts).

Original Documents

19. It is commonplace to be asked to return originals. It is also reasonable for the organization to request return, especially if the relationship sours for any reason. Don't offer this option in the NDA if it is not requested.

20. Be careful to define clearly what needs to be returned, as your derivative works need to be retained to document your work.

21. Don't allow either an implication or an explicit statement that everything coming from the organization is proprietary. Consider asking for proprietary documents and works to be explicitly labeled as such.

22. If your research data includes personal information, try to get that data "anonymized" before you take possession. Anonymization helps protect the organization and you from liability.

23. Ensure that you understand and adhere to any regulatory requirements that apply to the industry under research (e.g., health care and banking privacy regulation).

Disguising the Organization

24. To help smooth the process of obtaining publication approval, consider disguising the name of the organization(s). Even if the financials and other demographics might make it identifiable, you might be able to reduce those numbers by some factor. If there are multiple organizations involved, reducing all numbers by the same factor for all subject organizations might achieve the same result.

25. It is likely the organization would view this request as reasonable. However you need to ensure that the disguising you provide is real and permanent.

Derivative Works

26. Make sure you own your work product and all derivative works[1], unless you're being paid for the work, in which case ownership should be defined by the contract for the work.
27. You need to establish your right to create research papers, and derivative works based on those papers, from the information obtained from the organization.
28. The organization will likely take the position that they own your work product and derivative works from those, so you'll need to establish that ownership explicitly.

A model non-disclosure agreement, for reference purposes only, may be found in the Appendix to this chapter. The model is designed to provide an example of clauses in an agreement that a researcher might expect to see from a research subject, along with specific clauses that the researcher would like added or modified to be more amenable to their needs.

FUTURE TRENDS

While the foundations of intellectual property law are long-standing, it is reasonable to anticipate changes in such laws as they are interpreted both across national boundaries, and as the impact of new technologies continues to be felt. For example, Grossman (2004) notes issues such as the potential invisible violation of trademark via meta-tags on HTML pages. Such issues may seem to have an obvious answer, but will likely take years to work through the courts and legislatures and be embodied in updated legislation.

Globalization is affecting intellectual property rights. Globalization is creating cross-border research and development. To date, there is no international patent, which means that a patent is enforceable only in the jurisdiction where it is granted. To exacerbate the problem, United States patent law does not include extraterritorial effect and generally does not restrict potential infringement outside the borders of the United States. However, this issue is before the U.S. Court of Appeals (*Voda v. Cordis Corp.*). Here the court is being asked to consider whether patent matters arising under foreign law maybe heard under U.S. jurisdiction. Until this matter is heard, practitioners may have to be careful in the important freedom-to-operate and infringement clauses of their agreements.

Where these clauses reference foreign activities, they may want to assess the impact of an adjudication by a forum other than that originally contemplated.[2]

CONCLUSION

This set of guidelines has been used in multiple negotiations, and its parameters provided useful guidance to help structure the discussion with counsel. For example, the need to provide the right to publish anonymized data was not one that was initially acceptable to the research subject, but with appropriate attention to the relationship (Guidelines 2 and 5) with the subject, and by communicating the reason for the need (Guideline 13), an acceptable clause was created and agreed upon.

While finalizing a non-disclosure agreement clearly is an event that warrants the attention of qualified legal counsel, the element required in NDAs that meet the needs of the academic community is not apparently well known in the legal community. As such, we believe it is helpful for researchers to be armed with guidance that can help inform their discussions with counsel, resulting in agreements that appropriately protect all the parties involved.

LIMITATIONS AND DIRECTIONS FOR FUTURE RESEARCH

Contributors to this set of guidelines were not country-specific in their suggestions. This research could be extended to look more closely at laws and regulations outside the United States, and to the effects of cross-border research teams (Shippey, 2002). The Wiki containing the living version of this chapter is shown in Appendix I, and other researchers may contribute to the knowledge base residing there. Formal review by representative legal counsel from the university and corporate settings would be valuable to strengthen the validity and reliability of the data.

A database of best practice clauses, accessible based on the characteristics that the researcher is seeking, might be built to provide a robust collection of material from which to craft future agreements. A survey of the users of these guidelines might also be conducted to evaluate their value to the community, and to further enhance and build on the collected expertise.

DISCLAIMER

This chapter is not represented to be, nor should it be construed as, legal advice. You will need to consult with appropriate legal counsel to obtain a proper assessment of any legal document with which you are presented or which you intend to prepare.

NOTE

A portion of this material is drawn from Witman's (2005) article, which first appeared in the Communications of the Association for Information Systems.

ACKNOWLEDGMENT

The authors greatly appreciate the contributions of Paul Clay, Theresa Edgington, Kate Kaiser, Fred L. Kitchens, Tim McLaren, Julian Newman, Eric Overby, Terry Ryan, Detmar Straub, and George Westerman, as well as the helpful comments from Nathan Garrett and Rich Burkhard.

REFERENCES

Anonymous (2005). *Review of NDA guidelines*. Simi Valley, CA, May 17.

Beyer, G. W. (2001). *Modern dictionary for the Legal Profession* (Third ed.). Buffalo, NY: William S. Hein & Co., Inc. .

Clay, P. (2005). *Response to NDA query*. Simi Valley, CA, May 9.

CMU. (2001). IP Policy mark-up, including changes proposed by the University Research Council, November. Retrieved July 1, 2005, from http://www.andrew.cmu.edu/org/fac-senate/docsDec01/markedIPPol.pdf

Edgington, T. (2005). *Response to NDA query*. Simi Valley, CA, May 9.

Foley, J. (2004). Bayh-Dole act bad for computing research? *Computing Research News, 16*(1), 4, 7.

Garner, B. A. (2004). *Black's Law Dictionary* (Vol. 1). St Paul, MN: Thomson/West.

Grossman, M., Esq. (2004). *Technology law: What every business (and business-minded person) needs to know*. Lanham, MD: The Scarecrow Press, Inc.

GUIRR. (1997). Openness and secrecy in research: Preserving openness in a competitive world. October. Retrieved June 12, 2005, from http://www7.nationalacademies.org/guirr/Openness_and_Secrecy.html

Kaiser, K. (2005). *Response to NDA query*. Simi Valley, CA, May 11.

Kitchens, F. L. (2005). *Response to NDA query*. Simi Valley, CA, May 10.

Marcus, A. D. (1999). Class struggle: MIT students, lured to new tech firms, get caught in a bind --- They work for professors who may also oversee their academic careers --- Homework as "Nondisclosure." *Wall Street Journal (Eastern Edition)*, A.1.

McLaren, T. (2005). *Response to NDA query*. Simi Valley, CA, May 11.

Milgrim, M. R. (2006a). *Milgrim on trade secrets* (Vol. 2). New York: Matthew Bender & Company.

Milgrim, M. R. (2006b). *Milgrim on trade secrets* (Vol. 1). New York: Matthew Bender & Company.

NCCUSL. (1985). Uniform Trade Secrets Act WITH 1985 amendments. August 9. Retrieved November 27, 2006, from http://www.law.upenn.edu/bll/ulc/fnact99/1980s/utsa85.htm

Newberg, J. A., & Dunn, R. L. (2002). Keeping secrets in the campus lab: Law, values and rules of engagement for industry-university R&D partnerships. *American Business Law Journal, 39*(2), 187-240.

Newman, J. (2005). *Response to NDA query*. Simi Valley, CA, May 9.

Oppedahl & Larson LLP. (1995). Comparing patents and copyrights, June 29. Retrieved July 3, 2005, from http://www.patents.com/patents.htm#compare-copyright

Overby, E. (2005). *Response to NDA query*. Simi Valley, CA, May 12.

Peterson, I. (1985). Bits of wownership: Growing computer software sales are forcing universities to rethink their copyright and patent policies. *Science News, 128*(12), 189-190.

Shippey, K. C. (2002). *A short course in international intellectual property rights: Protecting your brands, marks, copyrights, patents, designs, and related rights worldwide.* Novato, CA: World Trade Press.

Stim, R., & Fishman, S. (2001). *Nondisclosure agreements: Protect your trade secrets and more* (1st ed.). Berkeley, CA: Nolo Press.

Straub, D. (2005). *Response to NDA query.* Simi Valley, CA, May 9.

USPTO. (2006a). General information concerning patents - "What is a Copyright?" November 6, Retrieved November 28, 2006, from http://www.uspto.gov/web/offices/pac/doc/general/index.html#copyright

USPTO. (2006b). General information concerning patents - "What is a Patent?" November 6, Retrieved November 28, 2006, from http://www.uspto.gov/web/offices/pac/doc/general/index.html#patent

USPTO. (2006c). General information concerning patents - "What is a Trademark or Servicemark?" November 6, Retrieved November 28, 2006, from http://www.uspto.gov/web/offices/pac/doc/general/index.html#mark

Volonino, L. (2005). *Editing feedback on manuscript.* Simi Valley, CA, July 8.

Westerman, G. (2005). *Response to NDA query.* Simi Valley, CA, May 9.

Witman, P. (2005). The art and science of non-disclosure agreements. *Communications of the AIS, 16*(11), 260-269.

ADDITIONAL SOURCES

Sample Non-Disclosures from Institutions

- From the University of Wisconsin – Milwaukee's Center for Industrial Mathematics. Commentary on non-disclosures and a sample NDA: http://www.uwm.edu/Dept/CIM/indmath8.html
- From the University of Connecticut's Office of Sponsored Research. Provides three forms of NDA, including one-way disclosure in each direction, and mutual exchange: http://www.osp.uconn.edu/non-disclosure.html

Sample Non-Disclosures from the View of Researcher as Discloser

- NDA from Columbia University's Science and Technology Ventures. Assumes that the University is disclosing *its* confidential information to a third party: http://www.stv.columbia.edu/guide/agreements/nondisclosure
- NDA from Southern Methodist University, Focusing on the researcher's work as an "Inventor": http://www.smu.edu/research/Limited%20Use%20and% 20Non-Disclosure%20Agreement.doc

SAMPLE NDA FOR CLINICAL TRIALS

- University of Minnesota's Research Services Organization guidelines. Focuses to some extent on clinical trials, but basic guidelines are provided that could be applicable to other fields: http://www.ahc.umn.edu/research/rso/information/sponsors/instructions/home.html

WIKI FOR DISCUSSION

The basic guidelines presented in this paper are captured on a Wiki, located at http://academicnda.schtuff.com where they can be edited and extended by anyone in the community:

KEY TERMS

Confidentiality: Restrictions on the dissemination of information (Garner, 2004, p. 318).

Copyright: "A property right in an original work of authorship ... giving the holder exclusive right to reproduce, adapt, distribute, perform, and display the work" (Garner, 2004, p. 361).

Intellectual Property: "A category of intangible rights protecting commercially valuable products of the human intellect," including but not limited to trademark, copyright, patent, and trade secret rights (Garner, 2004, p. 824).

Non-Disclosure Agreement: A contract promising "not to disclose any information shared by or discovered from a trade secret holder" (Garner, 2004, p. 1079).

Patent: "The right to exclude others from making, using, marketing, selling ... or importing an invention for a specified period" (Garner, 2004, p. 1156).

Trade Secret: "A formula, process, device, or other business information that is kept confidential to maintain an advantage over competitors" (Garner, 2004, p. 1533).

Trademark: "A word, phrase, logo, or other graphic symbol used ... to distinguish a product ... from those of others" (Garner, 2004, p. 1530).

ENDNOTES

[1] A derivative work, for copyright purposes, is a new work that is created substantially from an original work [Radcliffe & Brinson, 1999]. Examples might be a translation of a book into another language, or in research terms, reusing a large portion of an existing paper to create a new paper with theoretical extensions.

[2] *Voda v. Cordis Corp.*, Appeal No. 05-1238, 2005 WL 2174497 at *11 (Fed. Cir. June 6, 2005).

APPENDIX

Nondisclosure Agreement

AGREEMENT made this [*specify day*] day of [*specify month and year*] between [*name of first party*], and [*name of second party*].

1. Addresses. [*name of first party*] is a [*specify whether individual or business entity*] located at [*identify address*]. [*name of second party*] is a [*specify whether individual or business entity*] located at [*identify address*].

2. Purpose. [*name of first party*] wishes to engage the services of [*name of second party*] (the "Engagement") and in connection with such services, [*name of first party*] may disclose to [*name of second party*] certain confidential technical and business information which [*name of first party*] desires [*name of second party*] to treat as confidential.

3. Definition. "Confidential Information" as used in this Agreement means information or material that is not generally available to or used by others, or the utility or value of which is not generally known or recognized as standard practice whether or not the underlying details are in the public domain, including without limitation: (a) Information or material that relates to [*first party's*] inventions, technological developments, "know how", purchasing, accounting, merchandising or licensing; (b) Trade secrets; (c) Software in various stages of development (source code, object code, documentation, diagrams, flow charts), drawings, specifications, models, date and customer information; and (d) Any information of the type described above that [*first party*] treats as proprietary or designates as confidential, whether or not owned or developed by [*first party*].

4. Nonuse and Non-Disclosure of Confidential Information. During the term of this Agreement, [*second party*] will have access to and become acquainted with various propriety information of Employer, including discoveries, developments, designs, formulas, patterns, devices, secret inventions, processes, software programs, technical data, customer and supplier lists, and compilations of information, records, and specifications , and other matters consisting of trade secrets, all of which are owned by [*first party*] and regularly used in the operation of [*first party's*] business. [*Second party*] may also have access to the confidential information of third parties that has been provided to [*first party*] subject to a Confidential Disclosure Agreement.

All proprietary information and all files, records, documents, drawings, specifications, equipment, computer files, computer records, computer programs, and similar items relating to the business of [*first party*], whether they are prepared by [*second party*] or come into [*second party's*] possession in any other way and whether or not they contain or constitute trade secrets owned by [*first party]*, are and shall remain the excusive property of [*first party*] and shall not be removed from the premises of [*first party*], or reproduced or distributed in any manner, under any circumstances whatsoever without the prior written consent of [*first party*].

[*second party*] promises and agrees that [*she or he*] shall not misuse, misappropriate, or disclose any proprietary information or trade secrets described herein, directly or indirectly, or use them in any way, either during the term of this agreement or at any time thereafter, except as required in the course of the Agreement.

5. Obligations of Confidentiality not Applicable. Obligations of Confidentiality imposed by this Agreement will not apply to confidential information that (a) Is or has been generally available to the public by any means, through no fault of [*second party*], and without breach of this Agreement; (b) Is or has been lawfully disclosed to [*second party*] by a third party without an obligation of confidentiality being imposed on [*second party*]; (c) Has been disclosed without restriction by [*first party]* or by a third party owner of confidential information.

6. Academic Use of Confidential Information. Notwithstanding anything above, [*second party*] may use the above identified Confidential Information for not for profit educational or research activities ultimately leading to publication in academic or trade journals (the "Academic Activities"). If the Confidential Information is used for the Academic Activities, [*second party*] shall protect the anonymity of the Confidential Information as well as the source of the Confidential Information. [*Second party*] shall not publish or otherwise disseminate in writing or otherwise the result of the Academic Activities without the prior consent of [*first party*], such consent to be withheld only as necessary to ensure the anonymity of the Confidential Information. The parties agree that the [*second party*] has the right to produce derivative publications subject to this Agreement.

7. Ownership of Work Product. The parties agree that any and all intellectual properties, including, but not limited to, all ideas, concepts, themes, inventions, designs, improvements, and discoveries conceived, developed, or written by [*second party*], either individually or jointly in collaboration with others, pursuant to this Agreement, shall belong to and be the sole and exclusive property of [*first party*].

Notwithstanding the above, the parties agree that the ownership of derivative work product shall belong to and be the sole and exclusive property of [*second party*]. A "derivative work" is herein defined as a new work based upon an original work to which enough original creative work has been added so that the new work represents an original work of authorship.

8. Term. The obligations of [*second party*] under this Agreement shall survive until such time as all Confidential Information disclosed under this Agreement becomes publicly known and made generally available through no action or inaction of the [*second party*].

9. Return of Materials. [*second party*] agrees to deliver to [*first party*], promptly on request, or thirty days from the date of termination of this Agreement, all confidential material herein identified, in the possession of [*second party*] pertaining to the business of [*first* party] and originating with [*first party*] that came into the possession of [*second party*].

10. Remedies. The parties to this Agreement acknowledge and agree that it is impossible to measure in money the damages which will accrue to the [*first party*] if [*second party*] shall breach or be in default of any of [*second party's*] representations or agreements set forth in this Agreement. Accordingly, if [*second party*] breaches or is in default of any of the representations and agreements set forth above, will cause irreparable injury to [*first party*] and that, in addition to any other remedies that may be available, in law, equity or otherwise, [*first party*] shall be entitled to obtain injunctive relief against the threatened breach of this Agreement or the continuation of any such breach, without the necessity of proving actual damages.

11. Non-interference. For the period of one (1) years after the termination of this Agreement, with or without cause, [*second party*] shall not interfere with the relationship of [*first party*] and any of its customers, employees, agents, representatives or supplier.

12. Non-solicitation. For the period of one (1) years after the termination of this Agreement, with or without cause, [*second party*] shall not solicit, operate, be employed by or otherwise participate in the business or operations of any of the [*first party's*] clients.

13. Miscellaneous. This Agreement shall bind and inure to the benefit of the parties and their successors and assigns. This Agreement supersedes any and all other agreements, either oral or in writing, between the parties with respect to the services provided under this Agreement, and contains all of the covenants and agreements between the parties with respect to the services provided herein. Each party to this agreement acknowledges that no representations, inducement, promises, or agreements, orally or otherwise, other than those set forth herein, have been made by any party, or anyone acting on behalf of any party, and that no other agreement, statement, or promise not contained in this agreement shall be valid or binding. Any modification of this agreement shall

be effective only if it is in writing signed by the party to be charged. This agreement shall be governed by and construed in accordance with the laws of the state of [*state*]. If any provision in this agreement is held by a court of competent jurisdiction to be invalid, void, or unenforceable, the remaining provisions shall nevertheless continue in full force without being impaired or invalidated in any way.

FIRST PARTY

[*signature*]

SECOND PARTY

[*signature*]

Chapter XXXI
Assurance for Temporal Compatibility Using Contracts

Omkar J. Tilak
Indiana University-Purdue University Indianapolis, USA

Rajeev R. Raje
Indiana University-Purdue University Indianapolis, USA

Andrew M. Olson
Indiana University-Purdue University Indianapolis, USA

ABSTRACT

Software realization of a large-scale Distributed Computing System (DCS) is achieved through the Component-based Software Development (CBSD) approach. A DCS consists of many autonomous components that interact with each other to coordinate each system activity. The need for such coordination, along with requirements such as heterogeneity, scalability, security, and availability, considerably increases the complexity of code in a distributed system. This chapter depicts a formal method to specify component interactions involving temporal constraints. Using the component interactions, various types of temporal interaction compatibility classes are defined. A simple case study is presented that indicates the benefits of the component interaction specifications discussed in this chapter.

INTRODUCTION

A major component of quality in software is assurance: a system's ability to perform its job according to the specification and to handle abnormal situations (McGraw, 1999). Assurance is particularly important in the CBSD method because of the special role given by the method to reusability. It is important to obtain reusable software components whose assurance can be trusted in order to create a reliable system from such components.

Reliable software systems can be built using several methods (Musa, 1999). Static typing, for example, is

a major help for catching inconsistencies before they have had time to become defects. Reusability also helps, using component libraries produced and (presumably) validated, rather than developing new software for the same purpose. But this is not enough. To be sure that DCS will perform properly, a systematic approach to specifying and implementing object-oriented software elements and their relations in a software system is needed. One such approach is known as design by contract, in Beugnard & Jezequel, et al., 1999. Under the Design by Contract theory, a software system is viewed as a set of communicating components whose interaction is based on precisely defined specifications of the mutual obligations known as contracts. The design by contracts, in a way, is a mechanism to achieve the correctness, and thereby a higher assurance, by a construction paradigm advocated by Dijkstra (1975).

Some benefits of Design by Contract include the following:

- A better understanding of the DCS.
- A systematic approach to building defect-free DCS.
- An effective framework for debugging, testing and, more generally assuring quality.
- A method for documenting software components.

Typically, contracts for software components have been specified at the syntactical level, which provides a description of type information for a particular method of a component. In a DCS, many other aspects of a component need to be considered and hence, Kumari (2004) and Zaremski et al. (1997) have proposed a multi-level contract for components. It augments the basis syntactic level of contract with behavior, synchronization, and quality of service. Thus, the use of such a multi-level contract, during the design and development of a component, increases the assurance about a component provides a better assurance about a DCS made of such components.

The four levels of contract mentioned above are certainly important for developing a component that is to be used in a DCS; however, many DCS are time-sensitive. Hence, it is equally important to consider the timing constraints as a part of a multi-level contract for a component. Another level for component contracts called the temporal level, is proposed in Tilak (2006). In addition to providing the formal mechanism for describing the temporal level contract, Tilak (2006) also discusses the issues of compatibility and replaceability. This chapter presents the details related to the issue of compatibility and how it plays a role in providing timing-related assurance about DCS made from time-sensitive individual components.

This chapter is organized as follows. Section 2 presents a brief overview of the related work and section 3 gives the design details of the Temporal Interaction Contract specifications. Section 4 describes the algorithms to check compatibility between Temporal Interaction Contracts. Section 5 describes an example for an experimental analysis of these concepts. Section 6 provides the conclusion of this research work with the possible future enhancements.

RELATED WORK

Components with Contracts

Beugnard and Jezequel, et al. (1999) define a general model for software contracts for components. These contracts provide parameters against which the components can be verified and validated. Four classes of contracts are defined in the context of software components: syntax, behavioral, synchronization and quantitative. This classification is based on the increasingly negotiable properties of the various levels of contract. We use the idea of multi-level contracts and extend it, by creating a Temporal Interaction Contract, to describe the component interactions and provide a compatibility analysis. This research briefly mentions a technique to represent component interactions using high-level Petri nets. However, it does not deal with matching component specifications for the purpose of analyzing compatibility. Also, it does not take into consideration the time constraints associated with component interactions. The goal of the present chapter's work is to provide operators to perform the component compatibility analysis based on temporal component interaction specifications of components.

Synchronization and Quality of Service Specification and Matching of Software Components

Kumari (2004) extends the research described in Zaremski and Wing (1997) by providing a mechanism for the formal specification and matching of a component's properties at the synchronization and the Quality of Service levels. Two types of matches are defined: replaceability or compatibility. Replaceability is the ability of two components to replace each other within a system and compatibility is the ability of two components to interoperate, communicate, and cooperate with each other when brought together to form a system. Although these two efforts provide matching techniques for syntax, semantics, synchronization, and QoS level in the component contract, they do not take into consideration the timing constraints associated with the component interaction. The chapter extends the concepts of specification matching, described in Kumari (2004) and Zaremski and Wing (1997), by providing compatibility criteria in the context of temporal interaction constraints.

Behavior Protocols for Software Components

Plasil and Balek (1998) propose a notation to enhance an architecture description language with a description of the component behavior. This notation depicts the interaction on the component's interfaces and reflects step-by-step refinement of the component's specification during its design. It also allows for formal reasoning about the correctness of the specification refinement. The research proposes to employ behavior protocols that are based on a notation similar to regular expressions. As a proof of the concept, the behavior protocols are used in the SOFA (SOFtware Appliances) (Plasil & Balek, 1998), architecture description language at three levels: interface, frame, and architecture. By using SOFA tools, the designer can verify the adherence of a component's implementation to its specification at run time, while the correctness of refining the specification can be verified at design time. A SOFA specification captures component interactions by using agents and an events framework. However, it does not provide any formal mechanism to match component specifications based on the time constraints associated with component interactions.

Extending CORBA Interfaces with Protocols

Canal and Pimentel (2001) describe an extension of the CORBA IDL for describing object service interactions, It concentrates on the interoperability of reusable components at the interaction level which deals with the relative order among their incoming and outgoing messages, and their blocking conditions. An extension to CORBA IDL is proposed that supports the description of the interactions of CORBA objects, in addition to the static description of the object services (i.e., method signatures) provided by the standard CORBA IDL facilities. This approach enriches IDLs with information about the way objects expect their methods to be called, how they use other objects' methods, and even interaction semantic aspects of interest to users, deployers, and implementers of objects. Interactions are described separately from the IDLs using a sugared subset of the polyadic π - calculus (Milner, 1993). However, this approach does not present a formalism to match component specifications and the use of polyadic π - calculus to specify component interactions requires a high degree of mathematical rigor which may or may not offer significant practi-

cal advantages. In contrast, this chapter presents a pragmatic approach to temporal interactions using an easy-to-understand formalism.

Formal Specification of CORBA Systems

Bastide and Sy (1999) extend the CORBA interface definition of distributed objects by a behavioral specification based on high-level Petri nets (Peterson, 1981). This technique allows specifying in an abstract, concise and precise way the behavior of CORBA servers, including internal concurrency and synchronization. It also enables early prototyping and testing of a distributed object system as soon as the behaviors of individual objects have been defined. Again, however, this research does not deal with matching component specifications for compatibility analysis using the temporal constraints.

DIL (Distributed Interaction Language)

DIL (Sturman, 1996) provides an abstraction that presents an interface representing the interaction policy while hiding the details of the coordination mechanisms used to implement the policy. In DIL, each protocol describes a customized response to events within the system. Based on the interaction policy, DIL protocols may dynamically modify the system behavior. Events also may be programmer-defined. A combination of system and programmer-defined events together defines an interaction policy; the protocol provides an implementation for these events and, therefore, an implementation for the policy. DIL allows modular specification of interaction policies in distributed systems. However, DIL focuses mainly on describing properties of interaction such as atomicity and reliability. So, it describes component interactions at a fairly low level of abstraction, whereas this chapter focuses at a higher level of abstraction to describe the temporal constraints.

Midas

Midas (Pryce, 2000) is used to define interactions between components. Midas definitions are compiled into runtime support code that makes use of the underlying transport framework. This componentization of the transport protocol allows the designer to select the most appropriate protocol for each binding and insert additional functionality, such as compression or encryption, above existing protocols. The component interaction specification is supported by including specifications of the component interactions that can be checked mechanically for the deadlock or violation of user-defined constraints. Midas implements strict separation of concerns: programmers can select combinations of mechanisms within a binding to achieve the behavior required for their particular context. Moreover, the Midas language links the design and construction phases by generating objects that can be inserted into bindings to check that components interacting over those bindings conform to the interaction protocol specified by the Midas definition. However, Midas does not provide any formalism to specify time constraints on interactions and thus, does not offer the possibility of specifying compatibility of components.

TEMPORAL INTERACTION CONTRACTS

None of the approaches mentioned in the previous section provides a mechanism for specifying time constraints associated with the method invocations of components nor provides mechanisms to determine whether or not one component can replace another from the perspective of the temporal constraints associated with them. This section introduces the notion of temporal interaction contracts for components in order to accomplish this.

Definitions

The interaction behavior of each component in the DCS is represented by a Temporal Interaction Contract (TIC). Every component in the system is assumed to have the following properties: (i) It responds to external events, (ii) Its lifecycle can be modeled as a progression of states, transitions and events, and (iii) Its current behavior depends on its past behavior and may have associated timing constraints.

Formally, we define TIC $\equiv$ (States, StartState, EndStates, Messages, Transitions) where:

1. States is a set of component states. It has cardinality n.
2. Start $\subset$ States is the initial state.
3. End $\subset$ States is a set of final states.

4. MNT is a finite set of non-temporally constrained messages in a TIC. Non-temporally constrained messages do not have any fixed time value (within which they need to be invoked) associated with them.
5. MT is a finite set of temporally constrained messages in a TIC. Temporally constrained messages have a fixed time value associated with them, within which they need to be invoked.
6. Messages is a finite set of messages. We define Messages $\equiv$ MNT $\cup$ MT. It has cardinality m.
7. Transitions $\equiv$ {Ti} where Ti = (Si, Sj, Mk) is a finite set of transitions where Si, Sj $\subset$ States and Mk $\subset$ Messages. Each transition (Si, Sj, Mk) consists of a source state Si, a target state Sj and a message Mk.
8. InitialTimeSlice is a 2-D an array of size n $\times$ m. InitialTimeSlice stores initial values of time availability (i.e., the time duration in which the message can be invoked) for different messages. These values are used for the calculation of TimeSlice.
9. TimeSlice is a 2-D array of size n $\times$ m. TimeSlice is used to store the information about all the methods that can be invoked at a given state and associated time constraints.
10. InteractionTrace is a 3-D array of size n $\times$ n $\times$ m. InteractionTrace is used to store the information of common messages between two TICs. This information is used in determining compatibility between any two component TICs.

In addition to these data structures, the compatibility analysis employs the following functions:

1. float getDuration(String S1, String M1) returns the temporal activation constraints on M1, which is an output message in the state S1.
2. boolean Transition(String S1, String S2, String M1) denotes that tuple (S1, S2, M1) $\subset$ Transitions. Here, S1 is the source state, S2 is target state and M1 is the associated message that causes the state transition from S1 to S2.
3. String Direction(String S1, String M1) returns value 'IN' if M1 is an input message for state S1, 'OUT' if M1 is an output message for state S1 or NULL otherwise.
4. String Spawn(String S1) returns all non-temporally constrained output messages from a state S1.
5. TimeSlice Add(TimeSlice T[s,m], float x) adds value 'x' to each member element of TimeSlice

[s,m]. So, it is formally defined as Add(T[s,m], x) = ([Ti + x, Tj + x], S); $\forall$ ([Ti, Tj]; S) $\subset$ T[s,m].

6. boolean Overlap (([T1,T2],S1), ([T3,T4],S2)) returns true if the two time durations [T1,T2] and [T3, T4] overlap, i.e., Overlap (([T1,T2],S1), ([T3,T4],S2)) = true iff T1 $\leq$ T3 $\leq$ T2.

7. TimeSlice Normalize(TimeSlice T) returns the normalized form of the input TimeSlice. To normalize a TimeSlice, overlapping TimeSlice tuples that are associated with the same state are combined, i.e., $\forall$ (([Ti, Tj], Si) and ([Tl, Tk], Sj)) $\subset$ T where Si = Sj and either Tl $\leq$ Ti $\leq$ Tk or Tl $\leq$ Tj $\leq$ Tk are replaced with ([Min(Ti, Tl), Max(Tj, Tk)], Si) after normalization.

COMPATIBILITY ANALYSIS

Software component reuse entails the ability to locate the appropriate component from a given repository. So, the algorithms that automate the task of component specification matching are of a great benefit in the reuse process. This chapter looks into matching components in the context of compatibility based on temporal interactions. As stated earlier, compatibility refers to checking whether or not a component "A" can interact with another component "B" from the perspective of time constrained and non-time constrained interactions. Two classes of compatibility, partial and complete, are discussed below. As TIC is another level in the multi-level contracts for components, its compatibility analysis is to be performed after the compatibility analysis is carried out at the other four levels (i.e., syntax, semantics, synchronization, and QoS) of contracts, indicated in Dijkstra (1975) and Sturman (1996).

Control Flow for the Compatibility Analysis

A TIC, T1, is said to be partially compatible to another TIC, T2, iff, some input message of T1 is contained by output messages of T2 or some output message of T1 is contained by input messages of T2. A TIC, T1, is said to be completely compatible to another TIC, T2, iff, starting from the initial state, every input message of T1 can be contained by an output message of T2 or every output message of T1 can be contained by an input message of T2.

Suppose that we want to determine if two TICs, T1 and T2, are partially compatible. First, we calculate InitialTimeSlice values for both TICs (InitialTimeSlice1 and InitialTimeSlice2). Then these values are used to calculate TimeSlice values of both TICs (TimeSlice1 and TimeSlice2) and TimeSlice1 and TimeSlice2 are used to calculate InteractionTrace of T1 and T2. We then determine if T1 and T2 are partially compatible by checking these interaction traces.

We determine if two partially compatible TICs are completely compatible or not by using the equivalence relation between them. All these algorithms are described below.

Initialize Algorithm

Figure 1 shows the Initialize algorithm, which is used to deduce the values of InitialTimeSlice array for a TIC. Each InitialTimeSlice array element is of type ([t1, t2], S1). InitialTimeSlice [S1, m1] = ([t1, t2], S2) means that, if a component is in state S1 and receives a message m1 within time interval t 1 to t2, then it changes its state to S2. In other words, in the state S1, the message m1 can be invoked between time duration t1 to t2 and it causes the component to change its state after the invocation of m1. Thus, InitialTimeSlice array holds the invocation validity information for all the states of a component.

CalculateTimeSlice Algorithm

Figure 2 shows the CalculateTimeSlice algorithm. This algorithm computes the TimeSlice array from the InitialTimeSlice array. The elements of the TimeSlice array are similar to the elements of the InitialTimeSlice array and they have the same semantics. The TimeSlice value is calculated from the values in InitialTimeSlice array by considering the transitive closure of all temporal transitions from each state.

CalculateInteractionTrace Algorithm

The CalculateInteractionTrace algorithm that calculates an interaction trace between two TICs is shown in Figure 3. This interaction trace contains all possible messages that can interact between these two TICs. The interaction trace information is stored in an array named InteractionTrace. So, if InteractionTrace[S1, S2, m1] = ([t1, t2], (S3, S4)) then it means that the message m1 is common between states S1 and S2 of

Figure 1. Initialize algorithm

```
input  : A Temporal Interaction Contract
         T = (States, Start, End, Messages, Transitions)
output: InitialTimeSlice

1.1  Begin ;
1.2  Duration = +∞ ;
1.3  foreach s ∈ States do
1.4      foreach m ∈ Messages do
1.5          InitialTimeSlice [s,m] = φ
1.6      end
1.7  end
1.8  foreach s ∈ States do
1.9      if ((∃s₁ ∈ States) ∧ (Transition(s, s₁, m_time)) ∧ (m_time ∈ M_T)) then
1.10         Duration = getDuration(s, m_time) ;
1.11         foreach m_spawn ∈ Spawn(s) do
1.12             if ((∃s_spawn ∈ States) ∧ (Transition(s, s_spawn, m_spawn))) then
1.13                 InitialTimeSlice [s,m_spawn] = ([0, Duration ], s_spawn) ;
1.14             end
1.15         end
1.16     end
1.17     else
1.18         foreach m_spawn ∈ Spawn(s) do
1.19             foreach (Transition(s, s_spawn, m_spawn)) do
1.20                 InitialTimeSlice [s,m_spawn] = ([0, Duration ], s_spawn) ;
1.21             end
1.22         end
1.23     end
1.24     Duration = +∞ ;
1.25 end
1.26 Return InitialTimeSlice;
```

Figure 2. CalculateTimeSlice algorithm

```
input  : A Temporal Interaction Contract
         T = (States, Start, End, Messages, Transitions)
output: TimeSlice

2.1  Begin ;
2.2  InitialTimeSlice = Initialize(T) ;
2.3  while (∃s_input ∈ States) do
2.4      LastState = s_input, TimeElapsed = 0, Temp = {φ}.
2.5      StateSetArray [s_input] = {s_input} ;
2.6      foreach message ∈ M_NT do
2.7          TimeSlice [s_input, message ] = {φ} ;
2.8      end
2.9      while (Temp ≠ StateSetArray [s_input]) do
2.10         Temp = StateSetArray [s_input] ;
2.11         if ((∃s' ∈ States) ∧ (Transition(LastState, s', m)) ∧ (m ∈ M_T))then
2.12             StateSetArray [s_input] = StateSetArray [s_input] ∪ {s'} ;
2.13             TimeElapsed = TimeElapsed + getDuration(LastState, m) ;
2.14             foreach m' ∈ Spawn(s') do
2.15                 TimeSlice [s_input, m'] = Normalize(TimeSlice [s_input, m']
                         ∪ Add(InitialTimeSlice [s', m'], TimeElapsed));
2.16             end
2.17             LastState = s' ;
2.18         end
2.19         else
2.20             foreach m' ∈ Spawn(LastState) do
2.21                 TimeSlice [s_input, m'] = Normalize(TimeSlice [s_input, m']
                         ∪ Add(InitialTimeSlice [LastState, m'], TimeElapsed));
2.22             end
2.23         end
2.24     end
2.25     States = States − s_input ;
2.26 end
2.27 Return TimeSlice;
```

Figure 3. CalculateInteractionTrace algorithm

```
      input  : Two Temporal Interaction Contracts
               T₁ = (States₁, Start₁, End₁, Messages₁, Transitions₁) and
               T₂ = (States₂, Start₂, End₂, Messages₂, Transitions₂)
      output: InteractionTrace
3.1  Begin ;
3.2  Combined = {(Start₁, Start₂)}, StartSet = {φ} ;
3.3  TimeSlice1 = CalculateTimeSlice(T₁) ;
3.4  TimeSlice2 = CalculateTimeSlice(T₂) ;
3.5  while ∃(temp₁, temp₂) ∈ Combined do
3.6      StartSet = StartSet ∪ {(temp₁, temp₂)} ;
3.7      Combined = Combined- StartSet;
3.8      foreach (m ∈ Spawn(temp₁) ∧ m ∈ Spawn(temp₂)) do
3.9          if Direction (temp₁,m) ≠ Direction(temp₂,m) then
3.10             foreach (([t₁,t₂],s₁) ∈ TimeSlice1 [temp₁,m]) ∧ (([t₃,t₄],s₂)
                    ∈ TimeSlice2 [temp₂,m]) do
3.11                if Max(t₁,t₃) ≤ Min(t₂,t₄) then
3.12                   minimum = Min(t₂,t₄), maximum = Max(t₁,t₃) ;
3.13                   InteractionTrace [temp₁,temp₂, m] = InteractionTrace
                         [temp₁,temp₂, m] ∪ {([minimum, maximum ], (s₁,s₂))} ;
3.14                   Combined = Combined ∪ {(s₁,s₂)}
3.15                end
3.16             end
3.17          end
3.18      end
3.19  end
3.20  Return InteractionTrace;
```

TIC1 and TIC2 respectively. This message has different direction (one "IN" and other one "OUT" or one "OUT" and other one "IN") in both TIC1 and TIC2. Thus, this message represents a possible interaction between these two components. Also, this interaction is valid only for time period t1 to t2. If this message is invoked in the given time period, TIC1 will transit to state S3 and TIC2 will transit to state S4.

Contains Algorithm

This algorithm checks whether or not the time duration [t1, t2] is contained in a TimeSlice T[s, m]. The algorithm searches a set of n elements (([ti1, tj1], sk1), ([ti2, tj2], sk2) , .. , ([tin, tjn], skn)) ∈ T[s, m] such that the time interval [t1, t2] is contained by the union of these n elements. This algorithm is used to check complete compatibility between two given TICs.

EquivalentUnderCompatibility Constraint Algorithm

As shown in Figure 4, this algorithm checks the equivalence of one TIC T1, with another TIC, T2, under compatibility constraint. A TIC, T1, is said to be equivalent under compatibility constraint to another TIC, T2, iff, starting from the initial state, every input message of T1 can be contained by an output message of T2 or every output message of T1 can be contained by an input message of T2. This equivalence is used to determine complete compatibility between two TICs. The algorithm uses TimeSlice values of both the TICs as shown in the Figure 4.

Partial and Complete Compatibility

The above algorithms are used to determine whether or not a TIC is partially or completely compatible with

Figure 4. EquivalentUnderCompatibilityConstraint algorithm

```
input : Two Temporal Interaction Contracts
         T₁ = (States₁, Start₁, End₁, Messages₁, Transitions₁) and
         T₂ = (States₂, Start₂, End₂, Messages₂, Transitions₂)
output: 'True' if T₁ is equivalent to T₂ under compatibility constraint else
         'False'

6.1   Begin ;
6.2   Combined = {(Start₁, Start₂)}, StartSet = {φ}, Equivalent = False ;
6.3   TimeSlice1 = CalculateTimeSlice(T₁) ;
6.4   TimeSlice2 = CalculateTimeSlice(T₂) ;
6.5   while ∃(temp₁, temp₂) ∈ Combined do
6.6       StartSet = StartSet ∪ {(temp₁, temp₂)} ;
6.7       Combined = Combined- StartSet;
6.8       foreach (m ∈ Spawn(temp₁) ∧ m ∈ Spawn(temp₂)) do
6.9           if Direction (temp₁, m) ≠ Direction(temp₂, m) then
6.10              foreach (([t₁, t₂], s₁) ∈ TimeSlice1 [temp₁, m]) do
6.11                  if Contains(([t₁, t₂], s₁), TimeSlice2 [temp₂, m]) then
6.12                      Equivalent = True ;
6.13                  end
6.14              else
6.15                  Return FALSE ;
6.16              end
6.17              if (∃([t₃, t₄], s₂) ∈ [temp₂, m]) ∧ (Max(t₁, t₃) ≤ Min(t₂, t₄))
                  then
6.18                  Combined = Combined ∪ {(s₁, s₂)}
6.19              end
6.20          end
6.21      end
6.22  end
6.23  end
6.24  Return Equivalent;
```

Figure 5. TimeSlice for the C1 Component

```
TimeSlice[Start1, m1] = [0.0,Infinity]$1
TimeSlice[1, m2] = [0.0,10]$2
TimeSlice[2, m3] = [0.0,Infinity]$End2
All other elements are NULL.
```

another TIC. The definitions of partial and complete compatibility, mentioned earlier, are restated in the context of these algorithms as:

A TIC, T1, is said to be partially compatible with another TIC, T2, iff its InteractionTrace with T2 is not null. If the InteractionTrace between two TICs is not null then, there is at least one possible interaction common between two TICs.

A TIC, T1, is said to be completely compatible with another TIC, T2, iff T1 is equivalent to T2 under the compatibility constraint (see Figure 4). If T1 and T2 are completely compatible then all the messages in T1 have a one-to-one match with messages in T2 and vice versa.

A SIMPLE EXAMPLE

This section presents a simple case study to illustrate the compatibility analysis. In it, the system for the compatibility analysis consists of components C1 and C2. The focus of interest is to determine whether these two components are compatible with each other or not.

The graphical representation of the TICs of the C1 and C2 components is shown in Figures 6 and 7 respectively. The circles in these figures represent different component states. A bold arrow between two states represents a transition from one state to the other. The component method (whose invocation) that causes the transition is denoted in the box along with the direction of the method invocation request. A dashed

Figure 6. TIC for the C1 Component

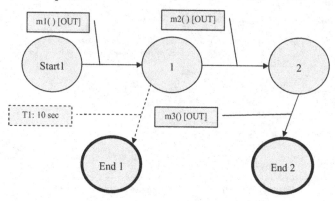

Figure 7. TIC for the C2 Component

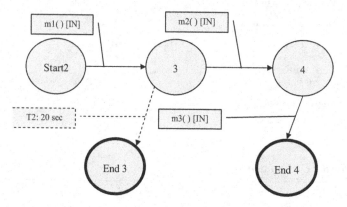

Figure 8. TimeSlice for the C2 Component

```
TimeSlice[Start2, m1] = [0.0,Infinity]$3
TimeSlice[3, m2] = [0.0,20]$4
TimeSlice[4, m3] = [0.0,Infinity]$End4
All other elements are NULL.
```

Figure 9. InteractionTrace for the C1 and C2 Component

```
PARTIAL COMPATIBILTY ANALYSIS
================================

Since InteractionTrace of these two TICs is not null, these two TICs
ARE PARTIALLY COMPATIBLE
The non-null elements of the InteractionTrace are as follows:
InteractionTrace[Start1, Start2, m1] = [0.0,Infinity]$1$3
InteractionTrace[1, 3, m2] = [0.0,10]$2$4
InteractionTrace[2, 4, m3] = [0.0,Infinity]$End2$End4
```

Figure 10. Complete compatibility analysis for the C1 and C2 component

```
COMPLETE COMPATIBILTY ANALYSIS
===============================

Analysis for state "Start1" from first TIC and "Start2" from second
TIC
For message "m1" -
[0.0,Infinity]$1 contains [0.0,Infinity]$3

Analysis for state "1" from first TIC and "3" from second TIC
For message "m2" -
[0.0,20.0]$4 contains [0.0,10.0]$2

Analysis for state "2" from first TIC and "4" from second TIC
For message "m3" -
[0.0, Infinity]$End2 contains [0.0,Infinity]$End4

Since no errors were discovered during anaylsis, these two TICs ARE
COMPLETELY COMPATIBLE
===============================================================
```

arrow represents a temporally constrained transition with associated time value indicated in the box. It is assumed that when a component receives a message, m, it invokes method m( ) of that component.

The computation of the TimeSlice array for the C1 component is as follows. Since the C1 component has five states and four messages, the TimeSlice for C1 component has dimensions of 5 × 4. The TimeSlice array for C1 component is as shown below.

Similarly, as the C2 component has five states and four messages, the TimeSlice for C2 component has dimensions of 5 × 4. The TimeSlice array for C2 component is as shown below.

Partial Compatibility Analysis

The partial compatibility analysis indicates that these two components are partially compatible, that is, there are some interactions that can occur between them. These interactions are listed in the output shown above (essentially the non-null elements of InteractionTrace). This interaction trace indicates which messages can be exchanged between the C1 and C2 and what is the time frame in which these messages can be exchanged. For example, consider the interaction trace element "InteractionTrace[1, 3, m2] = [0.0,10.0]\$2\$4". It indicates that the state 1 from the C1 component and the state 3 from the C2 component can exchange the message m2 in the time slice of [0, 10], that is, 10 seconds after the component enter the 1 and 3 state. If the m2 message is exchanged in this time duration, then the C1 component will move to the 2 state and the C2

component will move to the 4 state. So to conclude, the C1 and C2 components are partially compatible for the given TIC specification.

Complete Compatibility Analysis

The complete compatibility analysis indicates that these two components are completely compatible. The interactions between the two components are listed in the output shown above. It indicates which messages can be exchanged between the C1 and C2 and what is the time frame in which these messages can be exchanged.

CONCLUSION AND FUTURE WORK

This chapter has presented the Temporal Interaction Contracts for software components to describe their interactions and associated time constraints. TIC adds an additional level into the multiple-level contract approach. Along with the matching at other levels, it provides comprehensive criteria for replacing components to achieve better reuse.

Several future extensions to this research work are possible. The formal representation of the temporal interaction contracts is currently done manually. Automatically generating these formal representations would make the task easier. To the present, timing constraints having only fixed value have been considered for analysis. However, TLA (Temporal Logic of

Actions), Lamport (1994), operators could be included in the temporal interaction contracts to expand their expressive power.

REFERENCES

Bastide, R., Sy, O., et al. (1999). Formal specification and prototyping of CORBA systems. *In 13th European Conference on Object-Oriented Programming (ECOOP).* Retrieved June, 2007, from www.springerlink.com/index/YELTFR0GEH3AVNXC.pdf

Beugnard, A., Jezequel, J. M., et al. (1999). Making components contract aware. *Computer, 32*(7), 38-45. Retrieved June, 2007, from http://www.irisa.fr/triskell/publis/1999/Beugnard99.pdf

Canal, C., Pimentel, E. et al. (2001). Extending CORBA interfaces with protocols. *The Computer Journal.* Retrieved June, 2007, from http://congresos.lcc.uma.es/~av/Publicaciones/01/avcompjournal.pdf

Dijkstra, E. W. (1975). Guarded commands, nondeterminacy and formal derivation of programs. *Communications of the ACM, 18*(8), 453-457. Retrieved June, 2007, from http://www.cs.toronto.edu/~chechik/courses05/csc410/readings/dijkstra.pdf

Kumari, A. (2004). *Synchronization and quality of service specifications and matching of software components.* Indianapolis, IUPUI. Unpublished MS Thesis. Retrieved June, 2007, from http://www.cs.iupui.edu/uniFrame/pubs-openaccess/Anjali_Thesis.pdf

Lamport, L. (1994). *Specifying systems: The TLA+ language and tools for hardware and software engineers.* Addison-Wesley, 2002.

McGraw, G. (1999). Software assurance for security. *Computer, 32*(4), 103-105. Retrieved June, 2007, from http://www.cigital.com/papers/download/ieee-computer-secass.pdf

Milner, R. (1993). *The Polyadic pi-Calculus: A tutorial.* Springer-Verlag. Retrieved June, 2007, from www.lfcs.inf.ed.ac.uk/reports/91/ECS-LFCS-91-180/ECS-LFCS-91-180.ps

Musa, J. D. (1999). *Software reliability engineering: More reliable software, faster development and testing.* McGraw-Hill.

Peterson, J. L. (1981). *Petri net theory and the modeling of systems.* Prentice-Hall.

Plasil, F., D. Balek, et al. (1998). SOFA/DCUP: Architecture for component trading and dynamic updating. In *Proceedings Fourth International Conference on Configurable Distributed Systems, 1998.* Retrieved June, 2007, from dsrg.mff.cuni.cz/publications/ICCDS98.pdf

Pryce, N. G. (2000). *Component interaction in distributed systems.* Imperial College of Science, Technology and Medicine, University of London, Department of Computing. PhD Thesis. Retrieved June, 2007, from www.doc.ic.ac.uk/~np2/phd/thesis.pdf

Sturman, D. C. (1996). *Modular specification of interaction policies.* University of Illinois at Urbana-Champaign. PhD Thesis. Retrieved June, 2007, from http://yangtze.cs.uiuc.edu/Theses/UIUCDCS-R-96-1950.pdf

Tilak, O. (2006). *Temporal interaction contracts for components in a distributed system.* Indianapolis, IUPUI. Unpublished MS Thesis.

Zaremski, A. M. & Wing, J. M. (1997). Specification matching of software components. *ACM Transactions on Software Engineering and Methodology, 6,* 333 - 369. Retrieved June, 2007, from www.cs.cmu.edu/~wing/publications/ZaremskiWing97.pdf

KEY TERMS

Component: An encapsulated software piece that has a private state and public behavior as shown by its interface.

Complete Compatibility: A component, as described by its Temporal Interaction Contract (TIC) T1, is said to be completely compatible to another TIC, T2, iff, starting from the initial state, every input message of T1 can be contained by an output message of T2 or every output message of T1 can be contained by an input message of T2.

Contract: A contract is the public interface of the component. Traditionally, a contract indicates the details of the methods a component supports.

Distributed Computing Systems (DCS): A distributed computing system consists of networked processors, each with its own memory, that communicate with each other by sending messages.

Multi-level Contract: The multi-level contracts indicate contracts of a component as different levels, such as, syntax, semantics, synchronization, quality of service and temporal behavior.

Partial Temporal Compatibility: A component, as described by its Temporal Interaction Contract (TIC), T1, is said to be partially compatible to another TIC, T2, iff, some input message of T1 is contained by output messages of T2 or some output message of T1 is contained by input messages of T2.

Temporal Logic of Actions (TLA): TLA is a technique for specifying the behavior of concurrent systems.

Temporal Interaction Contract (TIC): TIC is software component contract which highlights temporal dependencies involved in the execution of a component.

Chapter XXXII
Spatial Authentication Using Cell Phones

Arjan Durresi

Indiana University-Purdue University Indianapolis, USA

ABSTRACT

The latest estimates suggest that there are over two billion cell phone users worldwide. The massive worldwide usage has prompted technological advances which have resulted in more features being packed in the same phone. New dual phones are being built which can connect to both the cellular network and other wireless devices. In this chapter we propose to use the omnipresent cell phones and the secure cellular network for access and location control. Using the cellular network adds to the strength of the authentication process and makes the revocation of access for a user easy. Our scheme also provides spatial control of the entity seeking authentication. In a cell phone based authentication system, our scheme provides location based authentication using two different approaches. One approach uses a trusted hardware sensor placed at a location close to the cell phone to validate the presence of the cell phone. Another approach to obtain the desired spatial control is through the use of GPS. The cellular phones would present the authentication server and the cellular network with the GPS coordinates of its current location using a tamper proof GPS module. This approach also prevents wormhole attacks because the cell phone has to provide the same coordinates to both the authentication server and the cellular network.

INTRODUCTION

Cellular phones are becoming ubiquitous telecommunication devices. These are portable wireless devices and connect to the network through RF communication. Due to their low cost and multitude of features, these phones have been transformed from expensive equipment used for business to a low cost personal item. It is estimated that there are over two billion cell phones worldwide (Cellularonline, 2007). These phones typically have low power transceivers which typically transmit data and voice up to a few miles

where the mobile tower (base station) is located. This base station connects the cellular phone to the backbone telephone network. The mobile phones cannot communicate when they are unable to connect to the base station.

The capabilities of these phones have also increased dramatically over the last few years. In addition to the standard telephone features, the phones also Instant Messaging, MMS, Internet access, and so on. More advanced features like music and video streaming, digital camera, and document scanner are being bundled with the cell phone. These features have transformed the cell phone from a simple phone to a digital Swiss army knife.

More advanced features like Bluetooth, IR have been added to allow the cell phone to connect with other devices. Avaya, Motorola, and Proxim are planning to introduce a new class of mobile phones called *dual phones* (Brewin, 2004; Hochmuth, 2004). These phones will be able to make voice calls over the cellular network and the 802.11a WLAN networks. The advantage of using this phone is that the user can make calls through the WLAN infrastructure when he is able to connect to the WLAN. This would save money because the cell phone user would be able to use the WLAN minutes for free. The companies have also developed the technology to "hand off" calls between the WLAN and cellular network. Cell phones can be developed which are able to connect to both the cellular network and the wireless devices. Such ability could enable them to be used in many applications.

There are many applications in wireless networks where access is granted to a user only when the user is located in certain predefined locations (Hansen & Oleshchuk, 2003; Mavridis, Georgiadis, & Pangalos, 2002; Toye, Sharp, Madhavapeddy, & Scott, 2005). For example, a doctor should be able to access the medical records only when he is located inside the hospital and not in cafeteria. In this scenario the doctor has access to the medical records only when he is located in a safe place like his office and not in a public place like the cafeteria. The server can be certain about the users' location by using a trusted hardware sensor, which is able to determine if the cell phone is in its communication range. Another approach to be certain of the location of the phone is to have a tamper proof GPS module on the SIM card.

In this chapter we assume the cellular infrastructure to be secure. While we believe that security is always in relative terms and a work in progress, cellular networks are much more secure than the other networks like the internet. Vulnerabilities like GSM cloning are being addressed and the GSM are moving away from security by obscurity. 3GPP, which is the next generation of GSM will be using cryptographic primitives which are based out the existing research literature and open to public scrutiny (GSM cloning, 2007). Besides, we believe that cell phones being a multi-billion dollar industry have the resources to provide stronger guarantees for authentication, confidentiality and privacy if such applications are developed.

Dual phones can be used for authentication in many other situations (Escudero-Pascual, 2002). Access to buildings, offices, and labs are controlled by RFID enabled access cards. These access cards work when they are placed close to the RFID reader. The problem with such a scenario is that the user has to have a separate access card for each location. Moreover, the signal coming out of the access card is the same all the time, which makes it vulnerable to duplication. We believe that dual cell phones coupled with the strong cellular network would provide better security than the use of use of cheap RFID based access cards. When one of these phones would come into contact with the access servers and request for authentication, the server sends a random challenge to the phone through the cellular network. This challenge is retransmitted to a secure hardware sensor connected to the hardware server. This approach verifies both the identity and the location of the user. Another approach to verify the location of the user is through the use of GPS. When the cell phone wants to get authenticated it sends the random challenge obtained from the authentication server through the cellular network along with the GPS coordinates. Our scheme is clearly illustrated through Figure 1.

We list some of the advantages of using dual cell phones over the traditional access cards:

- **Ease of use:** A single cell phone can replace all the access cards required by a user. To add a new user, the authentication server has to store the phone number corresponding to every user. In case the cell phone is lost, the base station can revoke the phone. This revokes the user from all the authentication servers.

- **Security:** The security offered by these devices is much stronger than that of the traditional access cards. Unlike the access card, it is much harder to fake the SIM card of a cell phone. Moreover the authentication server provides a new random challenge every time the client requests for access. As a result the challenge is impossible to copy and reuse.

- **Spatial control:** Since the random challenge sent to the phone by the authentication server through the cellular network has to be presented to the authentication server using WLAN or other local radio interface, it makes it very hard for the user to present false location information.

We believe that it would be very hard to duplicate or manipulate the SIM card of a cell phone. As all the information and code required for authentica-

Figure 1. This figure shows the different stages in SAC. In stage 1 authentication is requested. In stage 2 the authentication server verifies the authenticity of the user and sends a random challenge to the user through the cellular infrastructure. In stage 3, the cell infrastructure sends this random challenge to the cell phone. In stages 4 and 5 the cell phone proves to the authentication server that it is indeed seeking authentication and located in an appropriate location.

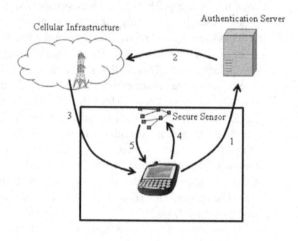

tion would be coded onto the SIM, the difficulty in compromising the SIM card would help in ensuring spatial control. Also, this system would work without any human intervention.

A potential problem for a cellular network-based authentication system is that its working is dependent on the proper functioning of the cellular network. The network could assign a higher priority to such authentication packets and provide more stringent QoS requirements. There are other tradeoffs between security and overhead. We explore these tradeoffs further in the chapter.

The rest of the chapter is organized as follows. Next section provides some of the related work in this area. Then we present our scheme for authentication and spatial control using the cell phones and the cellular network along with the trusted hardware sensor and GPS. We continue with analysis or our scheme, and present our conclusions.

BACKGROUND

Faria and Cheriton (2004) provide an architecture which provides nodes with short term keys to communicate with wireless networks. The architecture provided by them imposes geographical boundaries on the coverage of a wireless network. The central idea of the scheme is to have a large number of access points and implement location based access by requiring the mobile node to be in proximity to many access points. Due to transmission power control, the clients within the communication range of the access points enjoy high SNR levels and are able to get authenticated. The system requires the deployment of a large number of access points. While this may be feasible for a particular location, the overhead of deploying a large number of access points may not be feasible for all locations.

Two-factor authentication requires that a client produce two independent factors based on which a server can verify its authenticity (MacKenzie & Reiter, 2003; Rainbow Technologies, 2001). These two parameters usually are "something that you know" and "something that you have." It has been extensively implemented using Smart Cards and USB Tokens (Rainbow Technologies, 2001). Popular two-factor authentication schemes include the SecurID token by RSA Security and similar products by VeriSign, ActivPack, SafeNet, CRYPTOCard, Rainbow Technologies, and others. These products have a backed server and a token carried by the user. This token generates a random one time password using some pseudo random parameters. This is combined with the password known to the client to create the password dependent on two factors.

Two factor authentication has also been implemented using the cell phones as the second factor. When the user requests for an authentication, the authentication server sends a random passcode to the users' cell phone (Wu, Garfinkel, & Miller, 2004). This combined with the password known to the user makes the one time password required in two factor authentication. This scheme is offered by products such as RSA Mobile.

ASB Bank in New Zealand has implemented a scheme called Netcode Authentication System (Cellularonline, 2007). It uses the cell phone as the token in a two-factor authentication system. When the user wants to perform a transaction, the system sends the user an eight-digit authentication code to the cell phone through a text message. The user of the phone then has to enter this number back into the computer to verify the authenticity of the user. The present scheme can only be used for authentication but cannot be used for spatial-control. We present a scheme in the following section which extends the use of dual cell phones to spatial-control.

OUR SCHEME: SPATIAL AUTHENTICATION USING CELL PHONES (SAC)

Our scheme, Spatial Authentication using Cell phones (SAC) has two parts namely user authentication and spatial control. In the authentication part, the authentication server verifies if the cell phone is genuine or not by sending a message to the cell phone. If the owner of the cell phone is able to reproduce the message sent by the authentication server to the cell phone, then the phone is considered to be genuine. Otherwise the phone is not authenticated.

User Authentication

Once the phone is deemed to be genuine, the authentication server would like to enforce the spatial control. This is useful when the services being provided to the base station are dependent on the location of the cell phone. For example, even though a doctor has access to some health records, he should be allowed to access those records in his office and not in the cafeteria. This problem is non-trivial if the doctor is allowed to access the records through multiple computers at multiple locations. We address this problem by verifying the location of a cell phone using another trusted hardware sensor which is deployed in all the locations at which access is to be granted to the user. We also propose to use GPS to determine the location of a phone.

We now present the different stages of the authentication process:

- **Authentication request:** In this stage the WLAN portion of the dual phone transmits its ID to the authentication server. The phone shares a common ID for both the cellular network and the WLAN.
- **Authentication reply:** Once the authentication server receives a request, it checks if the user corresponding to the ID is authorized. If the user is valid, it generates a random challenge and

sends it to the user through the cellular network. This challenge would reach the cell phone only if it has not been revoked at the base station.

Spatial Authentication

Once the authentication is performed, the authentication server has to check if the cell phone is in the desired location. To detect the presence of the cell phones, we place a hardware sensor in every location where access to the cell phone is allowed. Once the phone receives the random challenge from the authentication server via the base station, the WLAN (or other radio interface) portion of the cell phone sends this random challenge to the hardware sensor which is securely connected to the authentication server. The hardware sensor then verifies the random challenge. If the random challenge sent to the cell phone through the base station matches the challenge sent to the trusted sensor, the user is authenticated and the server is able to establish spatial control because the cell phone is close to one of the trusted hardware sensors. This approach is clearly illustrated in Figure 1.

Another possible approach for a server to establish spatial control is to use GPS (Dana, 1997). In this case we assume that the GPS module is secure and cannot be tampered. When the phone seeks authentication from the cellular network, the cell phone transmits its GPS information to the base station of the cellular infrastructure which sends this information to the Authentication Server. When the cell phone seeks spatial authentication, it sends the GPS coordinates along with the random challenge received from the authentication server. The authentication server matches the GPS values obtained directly and through the GPS. If these values are different, the system then is being subjected to wormhole attack.

This is determined because the location from which the system seeks authentication from the cellular network and the location from which the cell phone seeks spatial authentication from the Authentication Server are different. This use of GPS helps defend the from the wormhole attacks where the attacker tunnels the information from one part of a network to another part. This cheats the Authentication Server into believing that the cell phone is actually located in a location where the service is authorized. This approach is clearly illustrated in Figure 2.

The major advantages of using the trusted hardware sensor is the accuracy and the reliability that it offers. This system is more reliable and consistent

Figure 2. This figure shows the different stages in this scheme when GPS is used. In stage 1 authentication is requested from the cellular infrastructure along with the GPS coordinates. In stage 2 the cell phone requests for spatial authentication from the AS. In stage 3 the cellular infrastructure passes the GPS coordinates to the Authentication Server (AS). If the GPS coordinates from stage 2 and stage 3 match, then in stage 4 the authentication server verifies the authenticity of the user and sends a random challenge to the user through the cellular infrastructure. In stage 5, the cell infrastructure sends this random challenge to the cell phone. In stages 6, the cell phone sends the random challenge and the GPS coordinates to the authentication server.

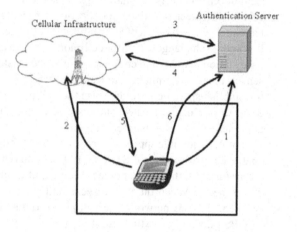

because it does not depend on the vagaries of the GPS system. The disadvantage of this approach is the extra cost and effort required to deploy and maintain the trusted hardware sensors along with the vulnerability to wormhole attacks. Moreover, this approach fixes the number of locations where the cell phone user can get authenticated and prove his location to the authentication server. This approach is unlike the GPS-based approach which avoids the overhead of deploying and managing the trusted hardware sensors. The disadvantage of using the GPS-based approach is the inconsistency in the behavior of GPS. To address the inconsistency in the behavior of GPS many approaches like Differential GPS have been proposed (Farrell & Givargis, 2000). The GPS based scheme could be used to detect the wormhole attacks.

Mobility Management

Once a cell phone gets authenticated and proves its location to the authentication server, it should not be allowed to change its location and move to an inappropriate location. To remove this vulnerability, the proposed scheme should verify the location of the cell phone at regular intervals. In the trusted sensor based scheme, the sensor could verify the existence of the cell phone at the location at regular intervals. In a GPS-based scheme, the authentication server could request for the GPS coordinates of the cell phone at regular intervals. These methods allow the authentication server to continuously establish spatial control over the cell phone.

In our scheme with trusted sensors, once the phone gets authenticated and gets a random challenge from the authentication server, the WLAN portion of the dual phone sends this information to the trusted sensor. This not only authenticates the cell phone to the authentication server but also proves its location. There could be many locations where the cell phone may be authorized to receive service. A malicious user could gain access through the authentication server by replicating the signal sent by the cell phone to the trusted sensor. We present some solutions which can be used to tackle this problem. These solutions offer different degrees of overhead and security.

Multiple logins: If the authentication server receives the same random challenge from multiple locations, the same cell phone is being used login to the system through multiple locations. The authentication server could prevent this attack by storing all the random challenges and comparing them to the challenges presented by different cell phones. This approach would fail when a user gets authenticated by the system and leaves without logging out because it would allow the malicious node to login to the system by faking the random challenge.

To resolve these issues, we propose to use multiple random challenges for one user authentication session. When the hardware sensor requests for a challenge, the cell phone provides one of the several random challenges that it received from the authentication server. This prevents the reuse of the same random challenge and once the cell phone exhausts all the random challenges, it has to reauthenticate itself using the cellular infrastructure.

Figure 3. This figure shows a sample deployment region consisting of 16 valid locations

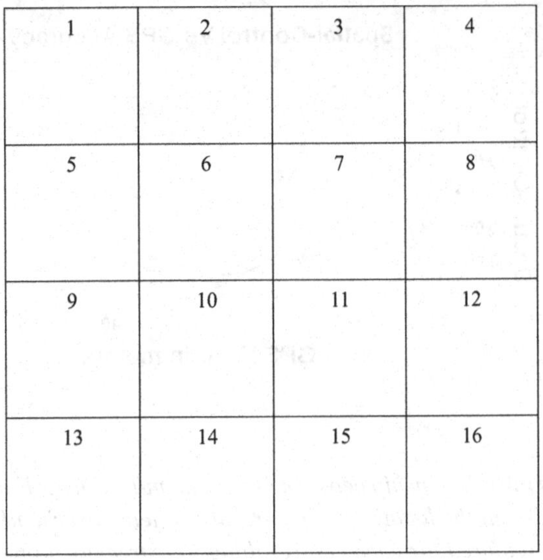

1	2	3	4
5	6	7	8
9	10	11	12
13	14	15	16

Figure 4. This figure shows the tradeoff between frequency of authentication and overhead

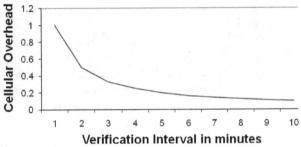

Cellular Overhead Vs Security

Mobility control: Mobility control is an important aspect of this scheme. One approach is to allow an authenticated cell phone mobility across all appropriate locations. A diametrically opposite approach would be to authenticate the cell phone at every location. The latter approach would provide much better security with the overhead of using the cellular infrastructure to authenticate the cell phone. A tradeoff between the two approaches would be to allow access to locations geographically close to the location at which the authentication has been done. This would be a design parameter for the network administrator.

We now present the experimental setup for this scheme. All the 16 locations in Figure 3 are valid for a given cell phone. In the first approach where the cell phone has to get authenticated once for all locations, the cell phone can get authenticated in any location from 1 to 16 and use the services at all locations. In the second case, the user requires authentication at all locations. For example, the user would require authentication through the cellular network to move from cell 2 to cell 3. In the final case, once the user is authenticated in a particular location, he does not have to obtain authentication in the cells which are close to

Figure 5. This figure shows the relation between GPS error and spatial control

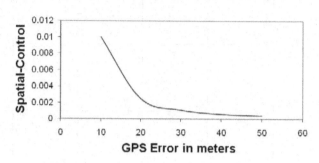

Figure 6. This figure shows the relationship between overhead and security. For single location access one authentication is required to access all the locations which results in least overhead where for multiple location access separate authentication is required for each cell resulting in extremely high overhead. A tradeoff between these two approaches is shown in the mixed location access.

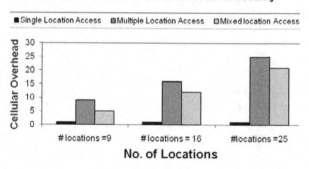

his current cell. For example, if a user is authenticated in cell 1, then he does not have to obtain authentication to get the service from cells 2, 3, 4.

ANALYSIS

In this section we analyze the performance and the tradeoffs involved in the authentication and spatial control. Once the authentication server determines that a given cell phone is genuine and that it is located in the appropriate place, access is granted. Once the access is granted the client should not be in a position to move into an inappropriate location and continue to retain access to the services. To prevent this problem, the location of the device needs to be constantly monitored. The frequency at which the device is monitored presents an interesting tradeoff. If the frequency of monitoring is high, the guarantee that the cell phone is in the appropriate location is high. On the other hand, if the frequency of this monitoring is low, the overhead is low and the probability of the cell phone being in an inappropriate location is high. For this simulation we consider interval of verification in minutes and the overhead is measured in terms of messages per minute using the cellular infrastructure. This is captured in Figure 4.

Although the overhead for the scheme using GPS receivers is low compared to the scheme using a trusted sensor, the varying accuracy of GPS may lead to difficulties in spatial control. The coordinates shown by the receiver may vary from the actual coordinates. The decrease in the accuracy for GPS would result in less spatial control. In Figure 2, we define *spatial control* as the probability of obtaining the exact coordinates of a location from GPS. For example, if the GPS error is 10 units, the probability of the GPS finding the exact location is given by $\pi 1^2/(\pi 10^2)$. For this simulation the GPS accuracy is measured in meters and the spatial control is the probability of the GPS values being accurate. The relation between GPS error and spatial control is clearly shown in Figure 5.

In Figure 6 we show the overhead on the cellular network for different levels of security for mobility management. We consider three cases for the overhead analysis. The first case is Single location access where a cell phone requires authentication only once. The second case is the Multiple Location Access where the cell phone requires authentication at all locations. The third case is the mixed location access where a cell phone is not required to obtain authentication in 4 of its neighboring cells of Figure 3.

CONCLUSION

In wireless communication there are many services which are based on the location of the user. To provide a user with these services, the authentication server not only has to determine the genuineness of the user, but also has to check if the location of the user is appropriate.

In this chapter we presented a scheme which uses cell phones to determine the authenticity of the user and the location. Cell phones are used instead of the tokens for two factor authentication (Wu et al., 2004). When authentication is requested, a random challenge (one time password) is sent to the user through the secure cellular infrastructure. We propose two approaches for determining the location of the user. The first approach uses a secure hardware sensor placed at all locations which are appropriate for the user. This hardware sensor is connected to the authentication server. It verifies the location of the cell phone by connecting to the wireless portion of the dual phone. The second approach uses a tamper proof GPS receiver to determine the location of the user. This is sent to the authentication server directly and through the cellular infrastructure. This approach, unlike the previous one, detects wormhole attacks.

REFERENCES

Brewin, B. (2004). Combo Wi-Fi, cell phone coming soon. *Computerworld*, May 28. Retrieved from http://www.pcworld.com/news/article/0,aid,116334,00.asp

Cellularonline. (2007). http://www.cellular.co.za.

Dana, P. H. (1997). Global positioning system (GPS) time dissemination for real-time applications. *Real-Time Systems*, *12*(1), 9-40.

Escudero-Pascual, A. (2002). Privacy enhanced architecture for location based services in the next generation wireless networks. Proceedings of the *12th IEEE Workshop on Local and Metropolitan Area Networks (LANMAN2002)*, 2002.

Faria, D. B., & Cheriton, D. R. (2004). No long-term secrets: Location-based security in overprovisioned wireless lans. *Proceedings of the Third ACM Workshop on Hot Topics in Networks (HotNets-III), San Diego, USA, November.*

Farrell J., & Givargis, T. (2000). Differential GPS reference station algorithm: Design and analysis. *IEEE Transactions on Control Systems Technology*, *8*(3), 519-531,.

GSM cloning. (2007). http://www.isaac.cs.berkeley.edu/isaac/gsm.html

Hansen, F., & Oleshchuk, V. (2003). Application of role-based access control in wireless healthcare information systems. *Proceedings of Scandinavian Conference in Health Informatics*, pp. 30-33.

Hochmuth, P. (2004). Trio to combine cell and wireless LANs. *Network World*, July, 26. Retrieved from http://www.networkworld.com/news/2004/072604avaya.html

MacKenzie, P., & Reiter, M. K. (2003). Networked cryptographic devices resilient to capture. *International Journal of Information Security, 2*(1), 1-20.

Mavridis, I. K., Georgiadis, C. K., & Pangalos, G. I. (2002). Access-rule certificates for secure distributed healthcare applications over the internet. *Health Informatics Journal, 8*(3), 127-137.

Rainbow Technologies. (2001). *Two-factor authentication? Making sense of all the options.* Technical report. http://whitepapers.zdnet.co.uk/0,1000000651,260015247p,00.htm

Toye, E., Sharp, R., Madhavapeddy, A., & Scott, D. (2005). Using smart phones to access site-specific services. *IEEE Pervasive Computing, 4*(2), 60-66.

Wu, M., Garfinkel, S., & Miller, R. (2004). Secure Web authentication with mobile phones. *MIT Computer Science and Artificial Intelligence Lab.*

KEY TERMS

Authentication: Authentication is the act of establishing or confirming something (or someone) as authentic, that is, that claims made by or about the thing are true.

Bluetooth: Bluetooth is an industrial specification for wireless personal area networks (PANs). Bluetooth provides a way to connect and exchange information between devices such as mobile phones, laptops, PCs, printers, digital cameras, and video game consoles over a secure, globally unlicensed short-range radio frequency.

Global Positioning System (GPS): GPS is a Global Navigation Satellite System. The system uses a constellation of at least 24 medium Earth orbit satellites that transmit precise microwave signals, the system enables a GPS receiver to determine its location, speed/direction, and time.

Global System for Mobile communications (GSM): GSM is the most popular standard for mobile phones in the world.

Infrared (IR): Infrared radiation is electromagnetic radiation of a wavelength longer than that of visible light, but shorter than that of radio waves. The uses of infrared include military, such as: target acquisition, surveillance, homing and tracking and non-military, such as thermal efficiency analysis, remote temperature sensing, short-ranged wireless communication, spectroscopy, and weather forecasting

Location Authentication: Location authentication is the confirmation about the location of the given object.

Radio-frequency identification (RFID): Radio-frequency identification is an automatic identification method, relying on storing and remotely retrieving data using devices called RFID tags or transponders.

Signal-to-noise ratio (SNR): Signal-to-noise ratio is an electrical engineering concept defined as the ratio of a signal power to the noise power corrupting the signal.

Spatial Control: Spatial Control is the probability of obtaining the exact coordinates of a location from GPS.

Subscriber Identity Module (SIM): A Subscriber Identity Module is a removable smart card for mobile cellular telephony devices such as mobile computers and mobile phones. SIM cards securely store the service-subscriber key (IMSI) used to identify a GSM subscriber. The SIM card allows users to change phones by simply removing the SIM card from one mobile phone and inserting it into another mobile phone or broadband telephony device.

Wireless Local Area Network (WLAN): WLAN is a wireless local area network, which is the linking of two or more computers without using wires.

Section IV
Mitigating Security Risks

Chapter XXXIII
Plugging Security Holes in Online Environment

Sushil K. Sharma
Ball State University, USA

Jatinder N.D. Gupta
The University of Alabama at Huntsville, USA

Ajay K. Gupta
Gsecurity, Inc., USA

ABSTRACT

The ability to perform E-Commerce over the Internet has become the driver of the new digital economy. As it has opened up opportunities for businesses and consumers to conduct online transactions on a 24/7 basis, at the same time, it has also opened new opportunities for hackers to exploit the medium for nefarious cyber attacks. This paper discusses various potential security holes that exists in the e-commerce environment and suggests a framework to protect organizations from security breaches.

INTRODUCTION

The Internet, which currently connects more than 300 million computers and 500 million users, is vulnerable to security breaches as indicated in numerous instances in recent times (Internet Users Report, 2007). Online fraud threatens to undermine consumer confidence in online financial services. Beyond simple phishing schemes, significant new threats are posed by spyware, browser hijacking, keystroke logging, and remote administration tools (Shukla & Nah, 2005). The Internet has the capacity to reduce global barriers and is becoming a fast and viable medium for conducting global business. As traditional businesses continue their migration into e-commerce, security will become a central issue to be seriously addressed. Even as organizations are looking at ways to strengthen the security of their networks and services, hackers all around the world are continuously discovering new vulnerabilities and inventing malicious breaches. Organizations who offer e-commerce are quite concerned about security breaches as it lessens the confidence of consumers and businesses in the privacy and integrity of online transaction and therefore their willingness to conduct business online (Araujo & Araujo, 2003). Numerous vulnerability scanners and intrusion detection systems have been developed and implemented but systems still seems to be susceptible to many attacks.

Attacks on computer systems are becoming much more sophisticated—and potentially devastating—than in the even recent past. A variety of security breaches take place in today's world and are often not reported by organizations looking to safeguard their own interests. The Computer Security Institute report (2007) reports that the average annual loss reported by U.S. companies in the 2007 CSI Computer Crime and Security Survey more than doubled, from $168,000 in last year's report to $350,424 in this year's survey (Gordon, Loeb, Lucyshyn, & Richardson, 2006). The 2007 Global Security Survey (2007) for financial institutions by Deloitte indicates that e-commerce security attacks are increasing. GeoTrust, Inc. reports that significant new threats are posed by spyware, browser hijacking, keystroke logging, and remote administration tools for various types of online fraud (GeoTrust Report, 2007). The companies responding to these surveys indicated that information security spending by financial institutions continues to rise. Almost all respondents (98%) indicate increased security budgets, with 11 percent reporting an increase of over 15 percent over 2006. The report indicated that the security budgets increased from 14 percent in 2006 to 36 percent in 2007 (Deloitte Report, 2007). The Federal Financial Institutions Examination Council (FFIEC) also issued new guidance for new multi-factor authentication methods with identity verification best practices and consumer trust components for more effective and reliable means for authenticating end users (GeoTrust Report, 2007).

Despite the increased awareness, the recent frequency of security breaches seems to indicate that many companies have not adequately responded to the issue of data security within their organizations. New regulations and statutes are sure to get some attention, but the pressure to mitigate data security risks certainly increases. Interest in security is increasing and shareholders expect organizations to use proactive security measures to protect their value (Caralli & Wilson, 2004). Customers also expect the organizations with whom they conduct business online also expect a higher level of protection of their personal data. News reports of high-profile attacks on well-known Web sites do have an adverse impact on consumer confidence.

Organizations invest heavily in the latest firewalls, intrusion detection systems and other advanced security technologies, yet losses from security incidents continue to grow each year. As technologies advance, hackers also advance their tools, techniques and methods to break-in to and compromise networks (Dhillon & Torkzadeh, 2006). Up until a few years ago, phishing attacks (phony e-mails designed to entice users to give up personal information) were unheard of. Now they are relatively common and pharming (creating phony Web sites designed to extract personal information) has become one of the latest strategies employed by identity thieves (Gartner Report, 2005). Security experts noted that the legions of infected computers are adding to the number of bot networks controlled by hackers. As such, organizations need to stay abreast of the latest protective measures and services to prevent and immediately respond to and recover from cyber attacks.

It is becoming imperative that networks must have self-defending capabilities to mitigate security threats before they affect operational continuity. Security measures deployed in any system should be commensurate with the risks on the system as well as the value of the system's output and of the data the system holds and/or processes. However, the process to determine which security controls are appropriate and cost effective is quite often a complex and subjective matter (Caralli & Wilson, 2004). Technology is always changing and the need for adequate security over information technology systems is crucial not only to meet regulatory compliance, but to a specific business' needs and the bottom line (Udo, 2001).

Making information available on interconnected networks allows for e-commerce and also creates the possibility for corporate espionage as corporations' business critical and sensitive information is placed on systems that are remotely accessible. This paper identifies possible security holes in an online environment and suggests a framework to prevent organizations from security breaches. The first section of the chapter discusses the various kinds of vulnerabilities at various levels of the E-commerce infrastructure. The next section proposes a comprehensive framework for plugging security holes in an online environment. The paper finally concludes with some directions for future research in this area.

VULNERABILITY IN AN ONLINE ENVIRONMENT

To understand the vulnerabilities that may lead to a security breach, it is worthwhile first to understand the different network components commonly deployed to support e-commerce services in the online environment. With the explosion of the Internet and the advent of e-commerce, global networks need to be accessible, reliable and fast in order to conduct business on a global scale. Business need to consider these network and their underlying components a key strategic and competitive advantage.

Telecommunications form a vital infrastructure for Internet access and hence for e-commerce. Telecommunications and Internet connectivity have now been universally recognized as a key to economic development and social progress. Figure 1 shows security breach vulnerabilities at various network components, which connect business/residential users to Internet resources. The network resources can be present in the local network of the Internet Service Provider (ISP) or on any host in the local, regional, or national networks.

As shown in Figure 1, vulnerabilities can occur at one of the three levels of the e-commerce infrastructure: the server/operating system level, the network architecture level, and the application level.

Server/Operating System Level

It is desirable first to check the vulnerabilities at the server and operating system (OS) since all applications and data that could be of interest to hackers is hosted on these servers and run by the server's operating system. Tackling application compromise at the OS level by kernel-enforced controls is the foremost preposition

since it is more challenging for controls implemented at the kernel to be overridden or subverted from users of the applications. The controls apply to all applications irrespective of the individual application code quality (Dalton & Choo, 2001). The following recommendations should be considered for all servers supporting E-Commerce systems.

- **Disable unused services and ports.** It is important to disable all unused services, including any personal Web servers. Further, all unused ports should be disabled (as well as blocked at the firewall) and a minimum number of open ports should be in use.
- **Delete all sample files and scripts.** All sample files and scripts must be deleted as they often possess well-known and documented vulnerabilities.
- **Remove the Virtual Private Networking Adapter**, unless it is being used to access the server.
- **Unbind the "File and Print Sharing" on any Internet connection device.**
- **Utilize a secure authentication mechanism,** two-factor authentication mechanisms, such as a smart card or a SecurID solution, are recommended. Three factor authentication mechanisms that include a biometric component further increase security.
- **Use a trusted operating system.** An operating system with the least known flaws should be used to support the e-commerce environment. The security of the underlying OS should be

Figure 1. Vulnerabilities in the e-commerce infrastructure

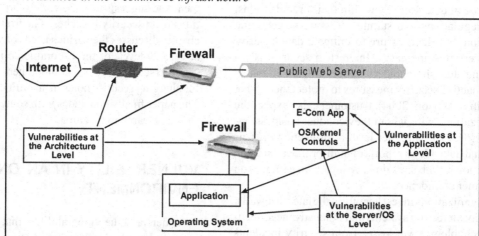

taken into account, just as ease-of-use, cost, and interoperability are considered during the selection process.

- **Maintain the most current patch/service pack level** that will support your application. This does pose a resource burden as a member of the staff must remain vigilant for new patch announcements, receive or download the patch, test the patch's affect on the e-commerce environment in a test network, and then install it into production. However, this is of critical importance. Unpatched and out-dated systems often have well-known and documented vulnerabilities which may be exploited even by modest hackers. This remains a significant problem in today's world. A recent survey conducted by the SANS institute indicates that 50 percent of Domain Name System servers were running vulnerable copies of the popular Berkeley Internet Name Domain (BIND) program (Bort, 2000).

Network Architecture Level

Most Internet-related hacks are traceable to a small number of security holes. Many of them are simply due to lack of effective configuration management (Bort, 2000). The areas of security risk are as follows.

Router configuration: Though routers have been in use for a long time, they are still often not configured to provide optimum security to the network and all too often employ out of date and insecure routing software. A router should be restricted to allow traffic only between legitimate source and destination pairs as shown in Figure 2. Further, routers must be updated as vigilantly as all other computing devices on the network. The router logs documenting connections across the router should be monitored on a regular basis, and at least weekly, to ensure the level of protection provided by the router matches what was expected. Checking router logs is also a key means of knowing who is accessing the network resources.

Firewall configuration: Firewalls must be configured properly to block unwanted and potentially dangerous traffic, such as Internet Control Message Protocol (ICMP) Echo_Request and Echo_Reply packets, also known as pings, that originate outside the network. Depending on the size and topology of the network, a single firewall may not suffice. Each segment of the overall enterprise network may require its own firewall

to monitor, control, and log access, as shown in Figure 3. For example, a different set of rules should govern access to the segments containing the public-facing Web server and the back-end application and database servers that are repositories for sensitive information, such as client stock portfolios or patient history. Also, as with routers, firewall logs should be monitored on a regular basis and at least weekly.

Demilitarized Zone (DMZ) Configuration: A DMZ is a repository of Internet-facing servers (Web, e-mail, FTP, etc.) that generally store public information or information to be accessed by the public. There is generally a less strict authentication scheme for accessing hosts within the DMZ. However, connections between the DMZ and the back-end corporate network must be strictly minimized and carefully monitored—if they are to be allowed at all. Often vulnerabilities in the DMZ allow hackers to compromise the organization's overall network—to which it need not have been connected in the first place.

Anti-Virus Software (AVS) must be installed on all hosts within the enterprise, including all servers. Further, the AVS must be routinely updated, and at least daily, in order to detect and defend against the latest known viruses.

Trusting Relationships between two domains generally allows users in one domain of an enterprise to have rights within another domain. While this allows for convenience, it presents a potentially huge security risk. Trust relationships must be carefully administered and so that the compromise of one segment or domain to immediately lead to others throughout the enterprise. Further, there must be a demonstrable business need for granting access to resources to users of another domain. This also implies that each domain be aware of the user provisioning process of all trusted domains.

Intrusion Detection System (IDS): An integrated network and host based IDS must be deployed that can simultaneously monitor traffic on the network and access to critical servers, including modifications of critical configuration files. The same care must be given to the configuration of the IDS' rule set and signature database as is given to firewall and router configuration. Network based intrusion detection systems (NIDS) monitor traffic passing across their sensor in an effort to identify any traffic which may be representative of

Figure 2. Router - traffic control

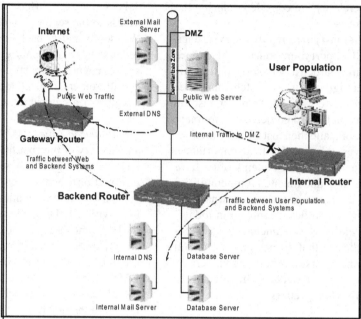

a known attack. Such traffic is often defined by the signature database and rule set. Host based intrusion detection software (HIDS) is installed on critical workstations and servers to monitors network traffic specific to each computer as well as any deviation from normal usage patterns. By performing packet and traffic analysis at the host level, HIDS attempts to solve many of today's hacking problems, including that of the insider threat. Intrusion detection sensors generally communicate with a central management device that can correlate the information gathered and alerts generated from all sensors to provide a comprehensive view of activity across the enterprise (Cavusoglu, Mishra, & Raghunathan, 2005).

Application Level

The application level is often overlooked during the process of securing an e-commerce infrastructure. However, this is a critical area given that user interaction is primarily with the application. Several areas are mentioned that require consideration:

- **Security code review:** A security code review should be performed of all application code. This is to ensure applications themselves do not

allow for a potential intruder to compromise the system. There are numerous areas for potential compromise in both Java and Active X, which are popular languages in which e-commerce applications are written. Some of the items to evaluate for are whether or not input bounds checking or truncation is performed on interactive forms. In addition, it is important to ensure that cookies are properly constructed and handled. It should not be possible to capture and playback an old cookie to re-establish a terminated session or gain access to another user's information.

- **Sample scripts:** All sample scripts should be removed. This is to prevent the exploitation of dangerous and malicious scripts, such as showcode.asp and network.vbs, that have well documented vulnerabilities.

- **Encryption:** Any communication involving sensitive information, especially if it must traverse the Global Information Superhighway, should be encrypted with the strongest encryption allowed by law.

- **Application maintenance:** All applications used should be routinely updated. E-commerce applications can have bugs too. And firms need ensure the level of security is improved, and at least updated, as the feature set is increased.

Figure 3. Firewall: Access control

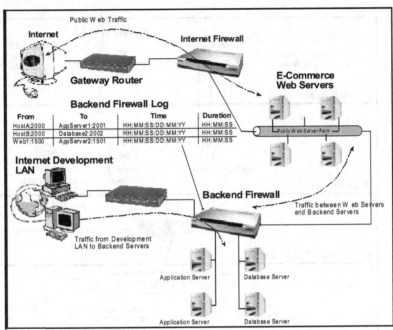

- **Authentication:** This is an issue that should be addressed at every level. An e-commerce environment must have a mechanism by which all users can be securely and reliably authenticated. Two-factor authentication methods that incorporate both a known, secret component and a random string component to the password are recommended. SecurID tokens provide such passwords, which are called one-time passwords as once used, the password will not be again allow access to the secured resource. If a reusable password scheme must be deployed, a password policy must be in place that specifies a minimum password length, preferable seven characters or longer, a password history, minimum and maximum lifetimes, and password composition restrictions (e.g., at least one numeric character, use both upper and lower case characters, use special characters). In addition, biometric devices are currently being researched and considered for deployment.
- **Access control:** There must be a system in place by which individual users can be restricted to view or interact with data and hosts upon which they have access privileges. Further, a mechanism by which the permissions afforded to the

individual can be traced to the person/office who requested and granted those access rights must be included.

A FRAMEWORK FOR PLUGGING SECURITY HOLES

One of the best methods of minimizing the risk of security breaches is to invest in preventive measures rather than solely relying on the find and fix method of addressing security vulnerabilities as they are exploited. There are many preventive software tools available that can be used to monitor and defend against hacks, including, AV software and IDS [6, 7, 9]. In addition, there are many defensive countermeasures that can be taken such as correctly installed firewalls and strict authentication/access control mechanisms. However, this paper suggests that a comprehensive, enterprise-wide framework is required to protect organizations from such security breaches as those shown in Figure 4.

Layered Approach

The TCP/IP Internet protocol that all computers use to connect to the Internet lacks security services.

Figure 4. A layered framework for plugging security holes

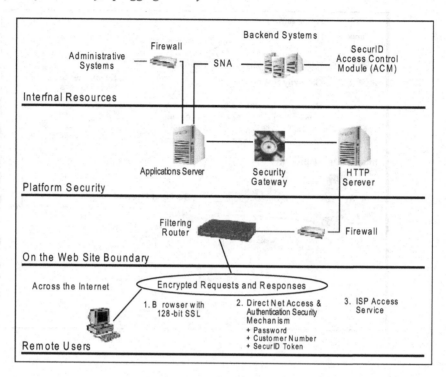

Also no protocol in the entire TCP/IP suite contains any authentication of parties, making it virtually impossible to verify the person or addresses of data packets. However, our framework suggests using layered approach to protect against security breeches. The bottom most layer known as remote user layer is where the customers access the network. The online environments offering e-commerce should ensure that at this layer customers use browsers with 128-bit SSL for their shopping interactions. At this layer authentication and security mechanism is to be ensured using right combination of password, customer number, or SecurID tokens. User identification and authentication typically involves passwords. Smart Card technology can be used for authentication. Smart card contains a small microprocessor that can store 10 to 20 public-key certificates. SecurID smart card generates a new code number every 60 seconds that is unique to that user. Along with smart cards, cryptography can be used to ensure integrity as well as authentication. Secure Socket Layer (SSL) technology provides public key-based authentication, confidentiality and integrity in client-server interactions. The second layer is at the server or merchant end where data is to be scanned against any unauthorized access through filtering

router or configurations of appropriate firewalls. Fire-walls are one of the most effective security measures to ensure authorization of anyone trying to access a system. Packet filtering can authorize access to the systems, which blocks packets that don't meet the security policy guidelines. Firewall could also use the SOCKS approach. SOCKS is a network protocol that can be set up on a server to watch and restrict traffic with other servers. This approach works at the session level to authenticate the network user, control access to the network, and encrypt messages. A third layer could be classified as platform security layer where data is to be protected using security gateway. Security gateway may use strong network based intrusion detection systems (NIDS) that would monitor traffic passing across their sensor in an effort to identify any traffic that may be representative of a known attack. Intrusion detection system utilizes high sensitivity sensors to track electronic traffic passing through network applications and systems, detecting differences in traffic patterns and identifying hacking activities. The fourth layer is of internal resources where backend systems are to be protected through another set of firewalls. Using such a layered approach can isolate the possibility of any security breech since security breeches are

Table 1. Technologies for various controls measures

Controls Measures	Use of Technologies
User ID/Authentication controls	Multi-factor methods/One-Time Passwords/Smart cards/ Biometrix
Authorization controls	Firewalls/Smart cards/Access Control Lists
Integrity controls	PKI/Cryptography – MD5 Hash
Confidentiality controls	PKI/Cryptography – AEC, ECC
Accountability controls	Audit mechanisms, log analysis tools
Disaster Recovery controls	Fail over/Redundant systems, Tape Back-Up/off-site storage.

monitored at each layer. Setting up levels of control in a layered approach is appropriate for proper security. There are a variety of methods that need to be used for not only protecting data but also to restore data in case of any attack. This may require a number of techniques such as encryption, firewalls and disaster recovery software that can operate seamlessly in the background to restore the data. One way is through the use of a Virtual Router Redundancy Protocol. VRRP is a protocol that runs between a pair of devices (such as firewalls) to ensure that one of the firewalls is active at all times (O'Mara, 2001).

Table 1 shows a partial list of the technologies available for various control measures to prevent security breaches. These controls must be deployed in a multi-tiered approach that can be used to protect against vulnerabilities at each level.

Based on our proposed framework and available technologies, we recommend taking the following actions:

- **Establish levels of control** in a layered, or Defense-in-Depth, approach with the use of best of breed or "State of the Art" technologies.
- **Deploy Best of Breed** or "State of the Art" Technologies. Various new security technologies such as digital certificates; trusted (secure) operating systems; new encryption algorithms (e.g., AES); biometrics (e.g., retinal scans, finger prints scans, facial recognition, voice recognition etc.) and security tokens (e.g., smart cards) are available for use in production systems. These need not be resource intensive, though modification of user behavior may be required.
- **Monitor and Analyze Network traffic.** Network monitoring software, such as packet sniffers should be deployed, in addition to an IDS, to

check that traffic is what it claims to be. Further, close analysis of the network traffic, including through examination of router and firewall logs and IDS alerts, can allow for the optimal security posture. This may require a great deal of manual configuration and assessment of the false positives/negatives reported by the IDS in order for the system to effectively identify potential intrusions.

- *Encrypt communication between E-Commerce customers and back-end servers.* This should involve a certificate-based mechanism that allows for the authentication and encrypt traffic to and from the e-commerce servers. For e-commerce infrastructures that involve few parties and high transaction amounts, certificates that authenticate both parties to each other can be considered. In addition, a log of the communication, for non-repudiation purposes, must also exist.
- **Be aware of the potential risks** and inherent need for information security throughout an organization from senior management to staff. This can be achieved through a detailed Security Policies and Procedures document along with a mandatory a Security Awareness and Training program that can educate and communicate the firm's security policies to all employees.
- **Make the end-user aware of the potential risks within e-commerce.** For example, many e-commerce sites allow the user to enter credit card information in a secure (e.g., SSL, HTTPS) page or a normal, unsecured page. Often, when given the choice, end-users still opt for the insecure version. Therefore, the awareness of security issues must be given to all parties in order for the entire e-commerce infrastructure

to be secure. After all, vendors and corporations will be convinced more by consumer demand than any other factor.

FUTURE TRENDS

The e-commerce industry will be the major target for various kinds of online attacks in the future (Tronvig, Thompson, & Gonnella, 2004). Already there has been exponential growth in attacks motivated by economic gains. This is illustrated by an increase in phishing scams and spyware designed to steal confidential information and pass it along to the attackers who can then sell the information for profit to other nefarious parties. The attackers may also exploit known Web application vulnerabilities to an organization's infrastructure and critical information assets in future. Botnet attacks covertly attempt to compromise a machine on a targeted system, allowing an unauthorized user to remotely control the computer, and possible other network resources, for a wide variety of purposes. The number of distinct variants of bots is rising dramatically, increasing by 600 percent over the past six months. Peer-to-peer services (P2P), Internet relay chat (IRC), and network file sharing continue to be popular propagation vectors for worms and other malicious code. Adware is becoming more problematic, making up six of the top 50 malicious code submissions.

Client-side attacks are expected to increase in the near future. The attacks on firewalls, routers, and other security devices protecting users' systems will increase. The experts also expect to see instances of port knocking, a method attackers may use to create direct connections to potential target systems including mobile devices.

Organizations will have to develop new security and audit management systems to combat future security attacks (Gordon, & Loeb, 2006; James, Pirim, Boswell, Reithel, & Barkhi, 2006). Added to the crime problem, privacy issues will also flourish. Whether the improvements come through changes in product liability and related laws or through maturation of the marketplace where security is treated as a basic requirement, the future of security will no longer be up to an organizations' security and audit personnel alone. Rather, the responsibilities for developing security solutions will also through developing more stringent laws and regulations to hold companies liable for information protection or any privacy violations (Boukhonine, Krotov, & Rupert, 2005).

CONCLUSION

E-commerce security is one of the thorniest issues facing the IT community (Marchany & Tront, 2002). There are no simple answers. An effective Internet security solution consists of many elements, including a security policy, well-defined security standards, and careful consideration of which resources to protect. Various kinds of attacks against websites and periodic virus outbreaks such as Nimda and Melissa indicate that in the era of e-commerce and the global Internet landscape, security will be one of the main concerns for both individuals and businesses in future. E-commerce offerings not only provide new opportunities for customers and businesses but also open companies and their customers to security vulnerabilities. This paper identifies various security holes in online environments and suggests a comprehensive framework to defend against these potential vulnerabilities. Any company establishing an e-business presence needs to make Internet security a top priority. High-profile Web attacks can undermine customer confidence, so businesses must address security and service issues in a consistent and proactive manner (Warkentin & Vaughn, 2006).

Organizations should implement a thorough and aggressive security policy that is reflected throughout the business, including firewall configurations, access controls and employee communications (Doherty & Fulford, 2005, 2006). Organizations also need to implement filtering technologies and practices to address the distributed denial-of-service threats and prevent networks from being used as attack agents (Luo, 2006). Steps recommended include reconfiguring routers and firewalls and denying IP-directed broadcasts on perimeter routers. Various security technologies need further development to enhance security, including interoperable digital certificates; secure (trusted) real time operating systems; encryption technology and biometrics (e.g., retinal scans, finger prints, etc.) and security tokens (e.g., smart cards) (Cavusoglu et al., 2005).

REFERENCES

Araujo, I. & Araujo, I. (2003). Developing trust in Internet commerce. *Proceedings of the 2003 Conference of the Centre For Advanced Studies on Collaborative Research*, pp. 1-15.

Bort, J. (2000). The best-kept security secrets. *Network World, 17*(46), 109-114.

Boukhonine, S., Krotov, V., & Rupert, B. (2005). Future security approaches and biometrics. *Communications of the AIS, 16*, 937-966.

Cavusoglu, H., Mishra, B., & Raghunathan, S. (2005). The value of intrusion detection systems in information technology security architecture. *Information Systems Research, 16*(1), 28-46.

Caralli, R. A., & Wilson, W. R. (2004). The challenges of security management. networked systems survivability program, SEI. Retrieved December 22, 2005 from http://www.cert.org/archive/pdf/ESMchallenges.pdf

Computer Security Institute Report (2007). Retrieved from http://www.gocsi.com

Dalton, C. & Choo, T.H. (2001). An operating system approach to securing e-services, Association for Computing Machinery. *Communications of the ACM, 44*(2), 58-64.

Deloitte Report (2007). Global Security Survey 2007- The Shifting Security Paradigm. Retrieved from http://www.deloitte.com/dtt/research/0,1015,cid%253D171332,00.html

Dhillon, G., & Torkzadeh, G. (2006). Value-focused assessment of information system security in organizations. *Information Systems Journal, 16*(3), 293-314.

Doherty, N. F., & Fulford, H. (2005). Do information security policies reduce the incidence of security breaches: An exploratory analysis. *Information Resources Management Journal, 18*(4), 21-39.

Doherty, N. F., & Fulford, H. (2006). Aligning the information security policy with the strategic information systems plan. *Computers and Security, 25*, 55-63.

Gartner Report (2005). Increased phishing and online attacks cause dip in consumer confidence. June 22, Retrieved from http://www.gartner.com/press_releases/asset_129754_11.html

GeoTrust Report (2006). Creating a multi-layered security environment as a means to safer online banking - Meeting the FFIEC Guidance in 2006. Retrieved from http://www.geotrust.com/resources/white_papers/WP_FFIEC_0106s.pdf

Gordon, L., & Loeb, M. (2006). *Managing cyber security resources. A cost-benefit analysis*. New York: McGraw-Hill.

Gordon, L. A., Loeb, M.P. Lucyshyn, W., & Richardson, R. (2006). *2006 CSI/FBI computer crime and security survey*. San Francisco: Computer Security Institute.

Internet Users Report (2007). Retrieved from http://www.internetworldstats.com/stats.htm

James, T., Pirim, T., Boswell, K., Reithel, B., & Barkhi, R. (2006). Determining the intention to use biometric devices: an application and extension of the technology acceptance model. *Journal of Organizational and End User Computing, 18*(3), 1-24.

Luo, X. (2006). A holistic approach for managing spyware. *Information Systems Security, 15*(2), 10-15.

Marchany R.C., & Tront, J.G. (2002) E-commerce security issues. Proceedings of the 35th Hawaii International Conference on System Sciences, pp.2500–2508.

O'Mara, D. (2001). Tiered approach works best for Internet security. *Security, 38*(1), 42-43.

Shukla, S. & Nah, F. F. (2005). Web browsing and spyware intrusion. *Communications of the ACM, 48*(8), 85-90.

Tronvig, M., Thompson, T., & Gonnella, C. (2004). E-commerce security: Risks and countermeasures. Retrieved on December 26, 2006, from http://www.ac.wwu.edu/~tronvim/mis424/Countermeasures.htm

Udo, G.J. (2001). Privacy and security concerns as major barriers for e-commerce: A survey study. *Information Management Computer Security, 9*(4), 165–174.

Wang, Y & Emurian. H. (2005). An overview of online trust. *Computers in Human Behavior, 21*(1), 105-125.

Warkentin, M. & Vaughn, R. (2006). Enterprise information systems assurance and system security: Managerial and technical issues. London: Idea Group Publishing.

KEY TERMS

Defence-in-Depth: Multiple layers of information security measures, a necessary requirement for securely conducting e-commerce. A defence-in-depth strategy often involves the use of hardware devices (e.g., firewalls), software (e.g., intrusion detection systems), process (e.g., audit of user accounts), and user training (e.g., security awareness training).

E-Commerce: Conducting traditional business transactions over an electronic or online medium.

Internet Access: Any mechanism to communicate over the Global Internet; a critical requirement for conducting e-commerce.

Online Environment: The environment used to conduct electronic transactions.

Security Breach: A compromise of the online environment where data and/or transactions are made available or known to unauthorized parties.

Self-Defending Capability: The ability of networks to respond to threats and attempted security breaches in an automated fashion and without human intervention.

Chapter XXXIV
Six Keys to Improving Wireless Security

Erik Graham
General Dynamics C4 Systems, USA

Paul John Steinbart
Arizona State University, USA

ABSTRACT

This chapter presents a step-by-step approach to improving the security of wireless networks. It describes the basic threats to achieving the security objectives of confidentiality, integrity, and availability when using wireless networking. It also explains various countermeasures that can be used to reduce the risks associated with wireless networks. This chapter has two main objectives. The first is to provide managers with practical guidance for improving the security of their organization's wireless networks. The second objective is to summarize the issues and concerns associated with the use of wireless networking so that researchers can identify fruitful areas in need of further investigation.

INTRODUCTION

Organizations implement wireless networking in the hopes of cutting costs and improving productivity. The use of wireless technologies enables network connectivity to be extended faster, and at less cost, than would be associated with having to install additional infrastructure. It can also increase productivity by providing workers with access to computing resources wherever they happen to be working, rather than only from fixed locations thereby potentially improving employee productivity. Wireless networking, however, also poses new and different threats to the confidentiality, integrity, and availability of information resources. Fortunately, with proper planning, organizations can mitigate many of those threats and achieve a reason-

able level of protection to justify the use of wireless networking. This chapter presents a step-by-step approach to guide managers in that process. Keep in mind, however, that wireless technology has evolved dramatically during the past ten years. For example, transmission speeds that used to be measured in kilobits per second now approach 100 megabits per second. This pace of change is likely to continue for the foreseeable future. Nevertheless, many security issues, such as the inherent susceptibility of wireless transmissions to unauthorized interception, will continue to exist and must be addressed by management. Consequently, the discussion in this chapter is necessarily at a high level, with the objective being to concisely summarize the critical issues associated with the use of wireless networks and the corresponding countermeasures for reducing those risks. Readers desiring more detailed technical information about wireless security are referred to the NIST publications SP800-48 (Karygiannis & Owens, 2002) and SP800-97 (Frankel, Eydt, Owens, & Scarfone, 2007). In addition, other chapters in this handbook provide more detailed information about many of the specific countermeasures discussed here (e.g., encryption, firewalls, user authentication, and VPNs).

Our approach focuses on the three basic objectives of information security: preserving the confidentiality, integrity, and availability of information resources. Table 1 shows that wireless networking poses two types of threats to each of those objectives. Confidentiality can be compromised either by intercepting wireless transmissions or by unauthorized access to the network holding sensitive information. The integrity of information can be destroyed by altering it either during transmission or when it is at rest. The availability of information resources can be removed either by disrupting the wireless transmissions or by the loss, theft, or destruction of the wireless networking devices.

Table 1 also lists some of the countermeasures that effectively can mitigate the risks associated with wireless networking. Notice that many of the countermeasures address threats associated with more than one information security objective. Encryption can protect the confidentiality of information both during transmission and at rest. Strong authentication not only protects confidentiality by preventing unauthorized access to sensitive information, but also makes it more difficult to make undetected changes to information. Proper network design and configuration protects confidentiality by making it more difficult to

intercept information and improves availability by making it more difficult to disrupt wireless communications. Thus, managers can significantly improve the security of wireless networking by focusing on these six key items:

1. Encrypt all sensitive information, both during transmission and at rest on mobile devices
2. Employ strong authentication and access controls
3. Proper network design and configuration that focuses on signal emanation and propagation issues
4. Physical security
5. Develop and Monitor Policies
6. User Training and Education

KEY 1: ENCRYPT SENSITIVE DATA

Organizations want to protect the confidentiality of their intellectual property. Marketing plans, ongoing research and development activities, detailed information about product costs, and customer contact information are among the types of information that must be protected from unauthorized disclosure to competitors. In addition, regulations such as the Health Insurance Portability and Accountability Act (HIPAA) and the Gramm-Leach-Bliley Act (GLBA), *require* organizations to take reasonable precautions to protect the privacy of any information entrusted to them by third parties. Failure to adequately safeguard their own intellectual property can result in loss of competitive advantage; failure to comply with regula-

Table 1. Wireless security objectives, threats, and countermeasures

Security Objective	Threats	Countermeasures
Confidentiality	Interception of wireless signals	Encryption Network Design/Configuration
	Unauthorized access	Strong Authentication Encryption Network Design/Configuration Policies and audits
Integrity	Alteration of wireless signals	Strong authentication Encryption
	Alteration of stored data	Strong authentication Encryption
Availability	Disruption of wireless signals	Network Design/Configuration
	Theft of wireless devices	Physical Security

tory requirements can bring fines and, in some cases, imprisonment.

The use of wireless networking makes it much more difficult to preserve the confidentiality of information. In traditional wired networks, attackers must obtain physical access to be able to intercept and eavesdrop on communications. Not so with wireless networking. Because wireless signals travel "through the air" attackers can intercept the messages from miles away (Schneier, 2005), by flying over buildings (Hopper, 2002; Slashdot, 2002), or even by using rockets (Hill, 2006).

This inherent susceptibility of wireless transmissions to interception using tools such as Kismet (http://www.kismetwireless.net) means that the only way to preserve confidentiality in wireless networks is to encrypt all traffic. Encrypting all traffic, rather than just encrypting sensitive data, is preferable because it reduces the risk of sensitive data being exposed through human error (i.e., failing to encrypt sensitive data) or application program or system failure to protect sensitive data. The encryption method, however, must be strong and be properly implemented. The first generation of wireless encryption technologies employed the weak Wired Equivalent Privacy (WEP) protocol. WEP encryption is easily broken because the encryption key is short, it relies on shared secrets, it uses a short (24-bit) initialization vector (IV), the IV is predictable, and it is transmitted in plaintext (Isaac, 2001). These flaws make it possible to "crack" WEP encryption in as little as 10 minutes using tools such as airodump (www.wirelessdefence.org/Contents/Aircrack_airodump.htm), wepcrack (wepcrack.sourceforge.net), weplab (http://sourceforge.net/projects/weplab), KisMac (kismac.de; see also video at http://video.google.com/videoplay?docid=-1021256519470427962 [http://www.ethicalhack.org/videos.php], and Whoppix, now renamed BackTrack (www.remote-exploit.org/index.php/BackTrack; see also the video – Using Whoppix to crack WEP - http://video.google.com/videoplay?docid=-5318506544218229291). In addition, WEP is vulnerable to replay attacks because it is a stateless protocol (Paladugu, Cherukuru, & Pandula, 2001).

The Wi-Fi Association updated WEP to the stronger Wi-Fi Protected Access (WPA) encryption algorithm as a stop-gap solution until the IEEE 802.11i standard was released (Wi-Fi, 2003). WPA is stronger than WEP because it increases the initialization vector (IV) from 24 to 48 bits, which reduces the probability of reusing the same IV. WPA also incorporated a Message Integrity Code (MIC) to verify message integrity; if MIC verification indicates that the message has been tampered with, it automatically generates new encryption keys. Nevertheless, although an improvement over WEP, WPA was still flawed because it relied on the RC4 algorithm. Thus, WPA could be cracked using tools such as Aircrack-ng (aircrack-ng.org/doku.php) and Whax (www.remote-exploit.org/index.php/BackTrack); see also the video—Using Whax to crack WPA—http://www.mirrors.wiretapped.net/security/vulnerability-assessment/aircrack/whax-aircrack-wpa/whax-aircrack-wpa.html).

The IEEE 802.11i standard replaces WEP and the interim WPA with WPA-2, which was developed to overcome the weaknesses inherent in WPA. WPA-2 incorporates two changes that significantly improve security over WPA. First, it replaces the weak RC4 algorithm with AES as the basis for encryption. Second, it uses the Counter-Mode/CBC-MAC Protocol (CCMP) for message integrity. Nevertheless, although WPA-2 appears to provide a reasonable level of protection, the history of problems with wireless encryption techniques suggests the need for caution. Indeed, sites such as Wireless Vulnerabilities and Exploits (http://www.wirelessve.org/) show that there continue to vulnerabilities with wireless technology and its implementation. Organizations wishing to deploy wireless networking should definitely use WPA-2 to preserve confidentiality. However, the most prudent course of action may be to prohibit the sending of extremely sensitive information by wireless altogether, at least until more evidence concerning the long-term effectiveness of WPA-2 is available.

It is also important to encrypt sensitive information while it is at rest. This adds a second layer of protection to preserve confidentiality in the event that an unauthorized user somehow manages to obtain access to stored data, either through accessing the central database or by obtaining possession of a laptop containing sensitive information. The effectiveness of this control, however, depends upon using a strong encryption algorithm and properly managing the encryption and decryption keys.

KEY 2: REQUIRE STRONG AUTHENTICATION

Strong authentication can protect confidentiality by reducing the risk of unauthorized access to sensitive information. It also protects integrity by reducing the risk that information could be altered, either during transmissions or while in storage, without the change being detected. It is important to authenticate both the devices used in wireless networking and the users.

Using 802.1X to Authenticate Wireless Devices

Using the 802.1X protocol to authenticate all wireless devices attempting to connect the organization's internal network can prevent both the installation of unauthorized ("rogue") access points and the ability of unauthorized wireless clients (e.g., visitors' laptops) to connect to the organization's internal network. The use of 802.1X prevents the installation of rogue wireless access points because the access point must first authenticate itself before it is granted an IP address. Without a valid IP address, the wireless access point is useless because clients connecting to it will not be able to access any other network resources. Similarly, the use of 802.1X between the access point and each wireless client restricts unauthorized devices from connecting to network resources without first authenticating themselves.

The 802.1X protocol supports a wide variety of methods called Extensible Authentication Protocols (EAPs) to authenticate devices. The most secure method is EAP-TLS, because both the client and server must use X.509 certificates to mutually authenticate to each other (Kelley, 2003). EAP-TTLS is a less costly alternative that requires only the authentication server to have an X.509 certificate and permits the client to use other types of authentication credentials.

Authenticating Users

Once the *device* has been authenticated via 802.1X the *user* should also be authenticated using a multi-factor authentication method consisting of at least two of the following three basic types of authentication credentials: something you know (e.g., a password or PIN), something you are (i.e., a biometric measure), and something you have (e.g., a token or smart card). User authentication is covered in another chapter of this book, so we will not go into additional detail here.

KEY 3: PROPER NETWORK DESIGN AND CONFIGURATION

Judicious use of signal hiding techniques and proper configuration of network devices can significantly mitigate threats to confidentiality and availability.

Signal Hiding Techniques

Attackers must first identify and locate wireless networks before they can attempt to intercept the transmissions. Thus, organizations should take the following steps to make this more difficult:

1. Assign non-informative names to SSIDs. The service set identifier (SSID) is a code broadcast by a wireless access point that identifies that particular network. Attackers can use a variety of wireless tools like Netstumbler (http://www.netstumbler.com), AirSnarf (http://www.shmoo.com), and Kismet (http://www.kismetwireless.net) to find all SSIDs broadcasting in a given area. There are even Web sites, like www.wigle.net, that list known wireless access points. Therefore, organizations should not use their company name or the function of a particular network (e.g., R&D, Finance, and Payroll) as the SSID in order to avoid drawing undue attention to their networks. Change the default SSID name, too, because failure to do so tells attackers that this network was probably quickly installed with the default (i.e., zero) security settings enabled. A debatable issue is whether to disable broadcasting of the SSID. This does "hide" your network from some of the wireless discovery tools that only listen for access points that broadcast their presence, but will not hide your network from discovery by other tools, such as essid-jack (http://802.11ninja.net), which actively attempt to connect to any wireless networks in the area. Note that disabling SSID broadcasting will create more work for users, who will have to manually connect to the desired network. It may even reduce overall security, because poorly configured wireless clients will attempt to automatically connect with the strongest available SSID, which in this case will be some other network.

2. Reduce signal strength. Wireless signals can travel considerable distances. Reducing signal strength to the level needed to maintain connectivity in the designated areas lessens the ability for attackers to pick up those signals from afar.

3. Locate wireless access points in the interior of buildings. Windows and walls weaken signal strength, thus reducing the effective range over which the signals can be intercepted off site.

4. Use directional antennas for access points. The cheapest antennas are omni-directional, meaning that they broadcast signals 360-degrees. In high-rise office buildings, this means that wireless signals can be picked up on floors above and below the one on which the access point is located. Proper placement of directional antennas can significantly reduce the size of this "leakage" area.

Nevertheless, although these steps can make it more difficult to find a wireless signal, they do not entirely hide the network[1]. Therefore, signal hiding techniques are not an alternative to encryption, but simply provide another layer of defense.

Proper Configuration of Wireless Access Points

It is also important to securely configure wireless access points. Key actions include:

1. Change all default settings, particularly the SSID.
2. If using SNMP to remotely manage the device, replace the default community strings with strong, complex community strings.
3. Use SSH or SSL instead of telnet to remotely manage wireless access points.
4. Use checklists to turn on all desired security features (e.g., encryption) and to disable any unused features. It is particularly important to avoid mistakes such as:
   a. Failing to disable unused protocols such as 802.11a in networks that only use 802.11b and 802.11g.
   b. Failing to disable and remove old SSIDs when establishing new ones.
   c. Failing to correctly route a wireless access point's management traffic or unauthenticated traffic.
5. Regularly patch and update.

Although the above prescriptions seem simple, they are not followed by every organization. One problem is that many organizations use wireless access points from multiple vendors. This makes it difficult to ensure uniformity both in terms of configuration and patch management.

Proper Configuration of Wireless Clients

Wireless clients are vulnerable to compromise like any other device and, therefore, should be securely configured. Secure configuration of end-points is covered in depth in another chapter, so we will not repeat that information here. One particular configuration setting, however, is specific to wireless networking: all wireless clients should be configured to operate only in infrastructure mode. This forces all clients to connect to an access point, which enables the use of 802.1X to require strong authentication.

Proper Network Design to Protect Availability

Wireless networking is vulnerable to disruption either unintentionally, due to radio frequency signals emitted by other nearby devices, or as part of a deliberate denial-of-service (DoS) attack. Proper network design can mitigate both of these threats. Careful site surveys can identify potential offending devices and wireless access points can be located so as to minimize the likelihood of disruptions. Broadcast signal strength can be adjusted and directional antennas used to improve coverage in desired areas. The various signal hiding techniques discussed earlier can be used to make it harder for attackers to locate the organization's wireless networks and attempt to disrupt communications. As with DoS attacks on Web sites, however, deliberate DoS attacks on wireless networks are hard to prevent and defend against. It all comes down to a question of relative power. Whichever signal is stronger, the attacker's or the organization's, is the one that will win.

KEY 4: ENSURE PHYSICAL SECURITY

Physical security is important for both the access points and wireless clients, yet, as with wired networks, it is often overlooked. Unsupervised physical access to wireless access points may permit attackers to change configuration settings to compromise access controls that protect confidentiality and integrity. Or they may simply steal or destroy the access point, thereby impairing availability. Loss or theft of wireless clients, especially laptops, is another serious threat that, unfortunately, is an all too common occurrence.

Such incidents clearly reduce availability and can also compromise confidentiality, if sensitive information is stored unencrypted.

A number of specific actions can reduce the risk of these threats, including:

1. Strong physical access controls are needed to protect wireless access points from tampering, theft, or destruction.
2. Provide users with strong locks to secure laptops and other portable devices. Attackers are becoming more proficient in being able to pick simple locks (Defcon 2006 had a session on lock picking), however, so organizations should purchase high quality locks. It is also necessary to train users to lock their laptops at all times, even when in the office.
3. Configure laptops securely to reduce the risk of unauthorized access to information should the device be lost or stolen. Specific actions should include:
    a. Not displaying the userID of the last person who successfully logged onto device and not having the operating system "remember" a user's password.
    b. Require multi-factor authentication to access any data or programs. Biometric controls, such as a fingerprint reader, are better than the use of smart cards or tokens, because the latter are often inserted in the laptop when it is stolen or lost.
    c. Encryption of all sensitive information stored on the device using a strong algorithm, such as AES.
    d. Installation of "call home" programs that will email the device's location whenever it is connected to the Internet, to assist in recovery. In addition, consider the programming of an "auto-destroy" feature to thoroughly erase any sensitive information on a lost device after a set period of time.

KEY 5: POLICY DEVELOPMENT AND MONITORING

Information security is not only a technical issue, but is first and foremost a management issue. Therefore, in addition to the technical controls already discussed, it is important to establish and enforce sound policies.

In addition, managers need to constantly monitor how new developments and improvements in wireless technologies affect existing security policies.

Develop and Enforce Policies

The risk of unauthorized access increases with the risk of unauthorized wireless access points. Use of 802.1X authentication can effectively mitigate this risk. However, organizations also should develop and enforce a policy prohibiting the installation of unauthorized wireless access points. The policy should clearly specify that only IT staff with security responsibilities are allowed to install wireless access points. Effective enforcement of this policy requires frequent audits of the environment, using many of the same tools used by attackers, to identify and promptly disable any "rogue" wireless access points. Indeed, failure to regularly conduct such wireless audits can create "pseudo-rogue" access points, which were initially approved but subsequently forgotten about. Such pseudo-rogue access points are likely to be overlooked when installing patches and updates, creating a potential weak spot in what might otherwise be a solid defense. Finally, it is also important to appropriately sanction any employees caught violating the organization's wireless policy.

One other important policy-related action concerns logging. It is important to enable logging to create and store a history of corrective actions. Not only does this make it easier to respond to incidents, but the logging data can also satisfy requirements of regulations like Sarbanes-Oxley, by providing information about when a problem was discovered, how long it took to be remedied, and detailed data after the fix to show that the problem has been resolved.

Monitoring New Developments

Wireless technologies, like all IT, are constantly changing. New products create both new opportunities and new risks. New threats are constantly emerging. Managers need to monitor both types of developments so that they are prepared to adjust existing security policies and procedures accordingly.

For example, at Defcon 2006 a new exploit involving an attack based on a vulnerability in wireless device drivers was demonstrated (Cache, 2006). The exploit causes the victim's machine to establish a wireless connection with the attacker. Since the vulnerability exists in the wireless device driver, it bypasses all the security mechanisms and policies implemented at higher layers of the network stack. The exploit works as long as the wireless is enabled on the victim machine, even if it is not in use. Several affected vendors of wireless networking cards released patches to their device drivers to prevent this attack. However, device driver patches are not usually included in automatic patch management programs such as Window Update. Moreover, most IT managers do not want end users modifying device drivers. Therefore, this new threat required specific remediation actions by the IT function. In addition, the fact that the exploit only required that the vulnerable feature be enabled suggests that users may need to be trained to disable such features when not in use.

KEY 6: USER TRAINING

The sixth, and most important, key to improving wireless security involves training and educating users to follow secure practices. Indeed, without proper training, users are likely to take actions that seriously increase the risks associated with wireless networking. As with all aspects of information security, training users to adopt and follow "best practices" for wireless networking needs to be an ongoing process. At a minimum, such training should address the following topics:

1. The rationale underlying the organization's security policies. Users are more likely to cooperate with and follow policies that they understand.
2. Demonstrations of the consequences of not following policies. Showing users how unsafe practices can harm not only the organization, but may also increase risks to themselves (e.g., identity theft) can motivate them to observe safer wireless behaviors.
3. Demonstrations of how to follow safer practices. Users may desire to follow prescribed actions, but many cannot do so without training. In particular, users should be shown:
    a. How to use encryption tools. For example, if using a tool like Windows Encrypting File System, users should be shown why it is important to encrypt an entire folder rather than individual files. They also need to know how to manage encryption and decryption keys to ensure that they will not inadvertently lose access to important files.
    b. How to use multifactor authentication tools properly and how to protect those credentials.
    c. How to safely use public "hot spots," if permitted by security policies. Users should see demonstrations of how easily an attacker can use tools like hotspotter (www.remote-exploit.org/idex.php/Hotspotter_main) to create a fake access point and how to recognize whether a site is legitimate.
    d. How to disable wireless cards when not in use. This would provide protection against newly-discovered vulnerabilities like those involving wireless device drivers. Particular emphasis should be placed on disabling wireless whenever they connect their laptops or other mobile devices to the corporate LAN, as failure to do so creates a potential back-door to the internal network.
    e. How to operate in ad-hoc mode securely. In general, wireless clients should be configured to operate only in infrastructure mode. However, there may be specific situations that warrant allowing users to operate in ad-hoc mode. The 802.11i protocol provides mechanisms for increasing the security of ad-hoc communications by supporting the authentication of all devices trying to form an ad-hoc connection. Showing users what can happen when they allow unauthenticated others to connect to their device in ad-hoc mode will increase their desire to employ the methods made available in the 802.11i protocol to authenticate all peers with whom they wish to connect.

Finally, it is important to budget both time and money for educating and training the IT staff that are responsible for wireless security. New threats are constantly emerging. Failure to stay current and abreast of new developments significantly increases risks.

SUMMARY AND CONCLUSION

Although wireless networking can both increase productivity and cut costs, it also alters an organization's overall computer security risk profile. Confidentiality can be compromised either by intercepting wireless transmissions or by unauthorized access. The integrity of information can be destroyed by altering it either during transmission or when it is at rest. The availability of information resources can be removed either by disrupting the wireless transmissions or by the loss, theft, or destruction of the wireless networking devices. Although it is impossible to totally eliminate all of these risks associated with wireless networking, it is possible to achieve a reasonable level of overall security by implementing a variety of countermeasures. Encryption of data, both during transmission and when at rest on mobile devices, protects confidentiality. Use of strong authentication schemes, such as 802.1X, to authenticate *both* users and devices, reduces threats to integrity. Proper network design and configuration can reduce threats to availability. In addition, adequate physical access controls, the development and enforcement of policies, and user training can all substantially reduce the risks associated with wireless. Implementation of these countermeasures will enable organizations to reap the benefits, and minimize the risks, associated with wireless networking.

REFERENCES

Cache, J. (2006). *Fun with 802.11 Device Drivers by Johnny Cache*. Retrieved from https://www.defcon.org/html/defcon-14/dc-14-speakers.html#Cache

Frankel, S., Eydt, B., Owens, L., & Scarfone, K. (2007). Establishing wireless robust security networks: A guide to IEEE 802.11i, **February.** Retrieved from http://csrc.nist.gov/publications/nistpubs/800-97/SP800-97.pdf

Hill, R. (2006). *WarRocketing—Network stumbling 40 square miles in < 60 seconds*. Presentation at Defcon 14, August 4-6, Las Vegas, NV.

Hopper, D. I. (2002). *Secret Service agents probe wireless networks in Washington*. Retrieved from http://www.securityfocus.com/news/899

Isaac (2001). http://www.isaac.cs.berkeley.edu/isaac/mobicom.pdf. Additional information about WEP insecurities can be found at http://www.isaac.cs.berkeley.edu/isaac/wep-faq.html.

Karygiannis, T., & Owens, L. (2002). *Wireless network security: 802.11, Bluetooth and handheld devices,*

November. Retrieved from http://csrc.nist.gov/publications/nistpubs/800-48/SP800-48.pdf

Kelley, D. (2003). The X factor: 802.1x may be just what you need to stop intruders from accessing your network. *Information Security, 6*(8), 60-69. Also available at http://infosecuritymag.techtarget.com//ss/0,295796,sid6_iss21_art108,00.html

Paladugu, V., Cherukuru, N., & Pandula, S. (2001). *Comparison of security protocols for wireless communications*. Retrieved from http://cnscenter.future.co.kr/resource/hot-topic/wlan/pachpa.pdf

Schneier, B. (2005). http://www.schneier.com/blog/archives/2005/08/wireless_interc.html

Slashdot (2002). *Wardriving from 1500ft up*. Retrieved from http://www.slashdot.org/articles/02/08/18/1239233.shtml

Wi-Fi (2003). *Wi-Fi protected access*. Retrieved from http://www.wi-fi.org/white_papers/whitepaper-042903-wpa/

KEY TERMS

802.1X: An IEEE standard for authentication that can be used in either wireless or wired networks. It improves security by authenticating devices prior to assigning them an IP address, thereby reducing the risk of eavesdropping and other attacks.

Ad-Hoc Mode: A wireless configuration option in which clients communicate directly with one another without having to authenticate to a central access point.

Hot Spots: Publicly-available wireless access points.

Infrastructure Mode: A wireless configuration option in which clients authenticate to a central access point.

Initialization Vector (IV): A string of bits used to pad the initial block of text that is to be encrypted.

Message Integrity Check (MIC): A digital hash used to verify that a message has not been altered.

Rogue Access Points: Unauthorized wireless access points.

SSID: The service set identifier is the code broadcast by a wireless access point to identify itself.

WEP: Wired equivalent privacy, the original method used to encrypt wireless traffic. It is easily cracked and not recommended for use any longer.

WPA: Wi-Fi Protected Access is a "stop-gap" improvement of WEP that was introduced for use pending acceptance of the 802.11i protocol. WPA has been cracked and is not recommended for use any longer.

WPA-2: The wireless encryption method prescribed by 802.11i. It provides much stronger security than either WEP or WPA and is the currently recommended method for encrypting wireless traffic.

ENDNOTE

[1]   It is possible to use metallic window tints, wall paints, and steel or aluminum mesh inside of ceilings, floors, and walls to confine the propagation of wireless signals within a specified area. However, these techniques are normally too expensive or restrictive for widespread use by most organizations.

Chapter XXXV
Human Factors in Information Security and Privacy

Robert W. Proctor
Purdue University, USA

E. Eugene Schultz
High Tower Technologies, USA

Kim-Phuong L. Vu
California State University, USA

ABSTRACT

Many measures that enhance information security and privacy exist. Because these measures involve humans in various ways, their effectiveness depends on the human factor. This chapter reviews basic components of information security and privacy with an emphasis on human factors issues. It provides an overview of empirical investigations that have been conducted regarding the usability of security and privacy measures. These studies show that users have difficulty interacting with complex interfaces and that users' performance can be improved by incorporating human factors principles into the designs. The authors conclude by discussing how human factors analyses can lead to the design of usable systems for information security and privacy assurance.

INTRODUCTION

Human Factors will be critical in resolving issues surrounding privacy, the construction of usable profile interfaces, and many other issues.
Marc Resnick, 2006

Information security and privacy are essential for the functioning of e-commerce and many other Web-based services. Security breaches ("security-related incidents") have become commonplace. A security breach is an event in which a vulnerability is exploited to subvert or bypass security mechanisms. Some of the most frequent types of attacks that occur are Web page defacements, data security compromises, password-guessing attacks, and buffer overflow attacks in which an excessive amount of input is sent to a system or application to cause systems' memory capacity to be exceeded to allow malicious commands to be executed (see Viega, 2005). These incidents often result in considerable disruption and financial loss.

Information security means protecting the confidentiality, integrity and availability of data, applications, systems, and networks, as well ensuring that electronic transactions cannot be falsely repudiated ("non-repudiation"). Confidentiality means protection against unauthorized access to and reading of information, whereas integrity means protection against unauthorized changes in systems, networks, and information. Availability refers to the ability to gain uninterrupted access to systems, networks, and/or information. Non-repudiation denotes providing reasonable proof that the initiator of an electronic transaction was a certain person, even if that person denies having initiated that transaction. Securing a Web site necessitates securing the Web server itself, the application(s) that run on the Web server, data transmitted between the Web server and the client (browser), and the system on which the Web server runs.

Once a system's information is secure, the issue of privacy assurance needs to be addressed. Users should be assured that their personal information will be used in its intended manner and that their preferences regarding use of this information will not be violated. Information privacy refers to protection against unauthorized disclosure of information about individuals. Privacy assurance has become a topic of considerable interest due to numerous highly publicized incidents of personal information being stolen, sold, or otherwise made available to unauthorized parties. Consequently, many organizations hosting Web sites now post privacy policies that are intended to inform users about how their personal information will be stored and used, and organizations may certify that a site's policy adheres to good privacy practices. Also, protocols have been developed for standardizing Web privacy policies in machine-readable form so that client-based applications can automatically determine whether a site's policy conforms to specified needs and preferences.

Human factors plays an important role in information security and privacy, but this role often is overlooked when designing secure systems (Proctor & Vu, 2004; Schultz, 2005). Because ensuring security and privacy relies on the cooperation and performance of end users, system administrators, and other authorized personnel, the maximal benefit of security and privacy measures cannot be achieved unless interactions between all types of users and the systems with which they interact are simple and user-friendly. People will not use security features and functionality if they find them intrusive or non-intuitive. Although user resistance to security- and privacy-related methods and tasks suggests that usability problems abound, too little research examining the relationship between usability and those methods and tasks has been published.

In this chapter, we discuss human factors issues, research, and challenges in both information security and privacy. In the first major section, we examine usability issues associated with each of the major areas of information security. We provide examples of usability problems in security-related tasks, as well as some well-designed interaction sequences. An analysis of each area of information security suggests that usability and security methods are often at least to some degree orthogonal to each other. Solutions discussed include elevating the default level of security in Web servers, offering simple settings that result in groups of related security parameters being set, and making available more security-enhancing reusable software routines and tools that integrate with Web servers and applications. The section concludes with an example focusing on password generation that shows how security can be improved through increased usability.

In the second major section, we consider usability issues associated with information privacy and assurance. We review research on users' privacy concerns and preferences to assess the extent to which such preferences are accommodated by existing Web sites and privacy policies. In addition, users' state of knowledge concerning privacy-related issues and terminology is considered. Finally, we describe studies investigating usability issues associated with implementation of user agents for privacy assurance and protection. We conclude the chapter with the recommendation that human factors be incorporated into the design of future security and privacy technologies.

HUMAN FACTORS ISSUES IN INFORMATION SECURITY

Security-Related Threats and Risks

Many threats and risks to information exist within the systems, files, and databases that store it and networks that transmit it. Major types of security-related risks include:

a. **Denial of service:** Disruption of access to systems, applications, databases, and networks.
b. **Electronic theft and fraud:** These attacks are almost always motivated by the desire to illegally make money.

c. **Malicious code attacks:** Viruses, worms, spyware, and Trojan horse programs (many of which allow backdoor access to compromised systems) are included in this category.

d. **Unauthorized access to computer resources:** These attacks are often referred to as "hacking attacks."

e. **Session hijacking:** In these attacks perpetrators take control of users' network sessions.

f. **Unauthorized utilization of services:** In unauthorized utilization of services attacks perpetrators exploit vulnerabilities in services such as Web or File Transfer Protocol (FTP) services to utilize the services in an undesirable manner.

g. **Unauthorized changes in systems, network devices, or information:** These attacks involve changes in integrity.

h. **Misuse:** Misuse attacks are attacks that violate an organization's information security policy.

i. **Surveillance or reconnaissance attacks:** The purpose of these attacks is to gain knowledge about vulnerabilities in systems, applications, and networks or to map network topologies so that perpetrators can launch attacks that are most likely to work.

j. **Espionage:** Espionage attacks are attacks designed to subvert other organizations or governments.

k. **Hoaxes:** Hoaxes are rumors and other types of false information that are spread.

l. **Social engineering:** Social engineering attacks are attempts to "con" individuals out of something that is of value to perpetrators, such as passwords to systems and/or applications.

Concerns regarding information security have increased greatly in recent years. Electronic theft and fraud in particular have proliferated. Over five years ago, for example, LexisNexis, which gathers and sells personal and financial information pertaining to U.S. consumers to third-party entities such as collection agencies and federal organizations, experienced electronic break-ins to databases that held information of more than 300,000 people within the U.S. (SANS, 2005a). The perpetrators used stolen passwords to illegally access names, addresses, and Social Security Numbers (SSNs). LexisNexis databases were accessed without authorization almost 60 times. Identification (ID) verification services vendor CardSystems Solutions had been obtaining data from the magnetic strips of credit and debit cards and storing it without imple-

menting adequate security safeguards. A break-in into systems that stored this information resulted in more than 260,000 indivdual cases of identity fraud.

"Phishing" attacks are, however, the most common type of electronic theft and fraud attacks. In a phishing attack perpetrators send e-mail messages that appear to be from a bona fide financial institution. Messages typically inform recipients that their accounts or passwords are about to expire and instruct them to click on a URL that superficially appears to be operated by the financial institution whose customers the perpetrators have targeted. If gullible users believe the messages sent to them, they visit the phishers' Web site and enter personal and financial information that the perpetrators use in subsequent identity theft attempts.

Malicious code attacks also comprise a major type of threat. Worms and viruses are becoming less prevalent, but the problem of bots and botnets is growing disproportionately. A bot (short for "robot") is a covert malicious program that is installed in victim systems to accomplish a particular purpose such as launching denial of service attacks or capturing keyboard output such as banking account numbers, personal identification numbers (PINs), and SSNs. Botnets consist of many bots that work in coordination and that are controlled by a single perpetrator or group of perpetrators. A little over three years ago three Dutch citizens were arrested and ultimately convicted of creating a botnet that consisted of approximately one and a half million bots (SANS 2005b). Financial motivation has become the chief reason for writing and installing malicious code in systems. Additionally, many of today's worms and viruses are increasingly being programmed to use instant messaging (IM) to reproduce themselves; others are programmed to infect wireless devices such as BlueTooth and BlackBerry devices as well as smart phones.

Social engineering attacks also pose a growing security-related threat. In one case, perpetrators pretended to be Ford employees in a social engineering attack against Ford Credit Corporation. They were able to deceive Ford Credit employees into revealing an authorization code that allowed them to obtain customer identification data from a database owned by Experian, a credit verification company. Ford Credit then contacted Experian after discovering an unauthorized credit check. Approximately 13,000 individuals were exposed to the risk of identity theft because of this incident.

Figure 1. A sample screen for editing the IIS 6 Metabase

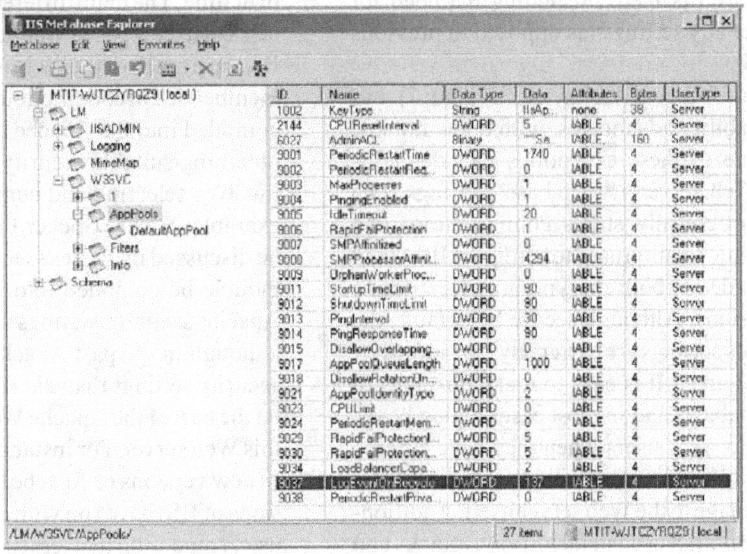

The Relationship between Security and Usability

Human factors challenges in securing Web servers. Web sites consist of a Web server platform such as Microsoft's Internet Information Server (IIS), the Apache Web server, one or more Web applications that run on these platforms, and an operating system such as a Windows operating system, Linux, or Unix. Efforts to secure Web servers thus require securing the Web server platform, the applications that run on it, and the underlying operating system.

The IIS Web server, which runs only on Windows operating systems such as Windows 2000, Windows XP, and Windows Server 2003, leads the way in providing usability in Web server configuration. Installing this Web server is not at all difficult; even individuals who are inexperienced in Web server installation can normally install an IIS Web server quickly. Directory structures, files, executables, and accounts, and other elements needed to build a Web server are provided as the result of installing this Web server. An easy-to-use graphical user interface (GUI) provides few barriers to changing Web server configuration parameters. Furthermore, a generous number of default values in IIS Web servers save substantial installation and configuration time and effort.

From a user perspective, IIS Web servers are generally highly conducive to easy and efficient user interaction, but are IIS Web servers secure? The answer to a large degree depends on the version of IIS. In the case of versions before IIS 6, the answer is "not at all by default." In previous versions, IIS Web services that were enabled by default and configuration parameters were weak from a security viewpoint, resulting in the ability of worms such as the Code Red worm (CERT, 2001) to widely exploit vulnerabilities in IIS Web servers. Code Red, for example, infected tens of thousands of Windows systems that ran the IIS Web server.

Raising the security level of IIS Web servers prior to IIS 6 to an acceptable level necessitated changing a large number of Web server parameters, disabling accounts, removing certain Web access rights, and installing patches for security-related vulnerabilities ("Microsoft hot fixes," see Schultz, 2001). Although the GUI that Microsoft designed for previous versions of this Web server is effective from a human-computer interaction standpoint, the amount of human intervention needed to increase the security of the pre-IIS 6 Web server to a level needed to resist most attacks is quite high (Schultz, 2005).

Microsoft has improved the baseline security level of IIS 6 (and 7) considerably compared to previous versions of this Web server. Security-related default settings are considerably better. For example, by default, only "bare bones" Web server functionality is enabled. Dangerous features such as Front Page

Extensions script mappings used in connection with IIS functions are disabled, precluding the need for users to change any settings (as opposed to previous versions of IIS).

At the same time, however, IIS 6 (and 7) has retained its usability advantages, with a few notable exceptions. One of these exceptions includes editing the IIS 6 Web server's "Metabase" settings. The MetaBase hierarchically stores configuration- and schema-based information used to configure IIS 6 (and 7). It is safeguarded by both encryption and restrictive access permissions. Although secure by default, the Metabase and its settings are extremely non-intuitive, as shown in Figure 1. It is easy to make mistakes in editing this database, and in most cases dialog boxes do not appear to warn users when they have entered values that could result in exploitable vulnerabilities or potential damage to the Web server itself. Additionally, IIS log file output used in identifying attacks and misuse of IIS Web servers is not very conducive to security. This output consists of line after line of rather terse and often non-meaningful entries (see Figure 2), making inspecting the content of each entry tedious and labor intensive. Still, all things considered, IIS 6 (and 7) are good examples of a Web server that blends security and usability nicely.

The Apache Web server, by far the most widely used Web server, has also improved considerably in its security potential and security-related default settings over time. The main difference from IIS is the types of tasks that the Apache Web administrator must perform. Because much of the security functionality of Apache is embedded in code modules that must be selected and compiled into the Apache code, much of the effort in obtaining suitable security levels in this Web server involves selecting and compiling code modules. For example, Secure Socket Layer (SSL) encryption (to be discussed in the next section) requires that the SSL module be compiled into Apache. Like IIS, default Apache security settings have improved over time, although in the past Apache offered stronger default security settings than did IIS, necessitating less effort on the part of the Apache Web administrator to secure this Web server. For instance, by default, older as well as new versions of Apache (in contrast with older versions of IIS) have run with only the privilege level of a user, something that lessens the potential impact if an attacker or malware exploits vulnerabilities; the lower the level of privileges, the less an attacker or malware can potentially do to the Web server.

The main usability hurdle in Apache is the fact that most versions do not offer user interaction through a GUI. Tasks involving security administration thus almost always require entering and editing configuration parameters. For example, the Apache Web server

Figure 2. IIS 6 log output

```
#Software: Microsoft Internet Information Services 6.0
#Version: 1.0
#Date: 2006-05-22 21:51:50
#Fields: date time s-ip cs-method cs-uri-stem cs-uri-query s-port cs-username c-ip cs(User-Agent) sc-status sc-substatus sc-
win32-status
2005-10-22 21:51:49 198.128.4.242 GET /default.html - 80 - 81.152.223.114 Mozilla/
4.0+(compatible;+MSIE+5.5;+Windows+98) 200 0 0
2005-10-22 22:01:55 198.128.4.242 GET /iisstart.htm - 80 - 213.135.235.151 Mozilla/
4.0+(compatible;+MSIE+5.5;+Windows+98) 200 0 0
2005-10-22 22:03:07 198.128.4.242 GET /iisstart.htm - 80 - 68.166.67.7 Mozilla/
4.0+(compatible;+MSIE+5.5;+Windows+98) 200 0 64
2005-10-22 22:11:37 198.128.4.242 GET /iisadmpwd - 80 - 4.65.252.165 Mozilla/
4.0+(compatible;+MSIE+5.5;+Windows+98) 200 0 64
2005-10-22 22:16:46 198.128.4.242 GET /iisstart.htm - 80 - 68.89.177.0 Mozilla/
4.0+(compatible;+MSIE+5.5;+Windows+98) 200 0 0
2005-10-22 22:23:20 198.128.4.242 GET /iisstart.htm - 80 - 131.128.130.185 Mozilla/
4.0+(compatible;+MSIE+5.5;+Windows+98) 200 0 64
2005-10-22 22:24:08 198.128.4.242 GET /default.html - 80 - 68.19.39.135 Mozilla/
4.0+(compatible;+MSIE+5.5;+Windows+98) 200 0 0
2005-10-22 22:34:15 198.128.4.242 GET /default.html - 80 - 63.121.95.34 Mozilla/
4.0+(compatible;+MSIE+5.5;+Windows+98) 200 0 0
2006-05-17 22:34:18 192.168.4.242 POST /samba/smbshr.pl - 443 - 12.168.19.202 Mozilla/
4.0+(compatible;+MSIE+6.0;+Windows+NT+5.0) 404 0 3
```

allows restrictions ("directives") that keep Web users from being able to access certain directories and files and from running programs and services that are dangerous from a security perspective. Although there is nothing particularly difficult about the syntax of "directives," each line of a directive must be formatted in a very specific manner; the slightest format error will cause a directive to not work. Consider, for example, the format of the directive in Figure 3. This directive makes Apache Web users unable to list the contents of a particular directory. Additionally, Apache log output is, as in the case of IIS log output, not formatted very well, making reading and interpreting this output tedious and difficult.

In summary, both IIS 6 (and 7) and the latest versions of Apache (as well as other, less frequently used types of Web servers) now offer a considerable amount of both security and usability. Usability limitations in both types of Web servers exist, but in general these limitations are not sufficiently formidable to create significant barriers in security-related human interaction tasks.

Human factors challenges in writing secure Web applications. Securing Web applications running on servers is a difficult task, and methods of securing Web servers are in general not in alignment with principles of effective human-computer interaction. Although new and improved methods of securing Web applications seem to surface all the time, many if not most Web applications remain vulnerable to attack, to a large degree because organizations and individuals tend to rush Web applications into production without adequately considering security. Additionally, usability hurdles are in general greatest in integrating security into Web applications because few quick and easy methods for securing Web applications exist. Consequently, developing secure Web applications almost always requires carefully constructing Web application code that contains special security-related functionality, such as carefully checking user input to ensure that it does not contain malicious commands or excessive numbers of characters designed to produce memory overflow conditions resulting in

privilege escalation or denial of service. Consider, for example, the following part of a script written in Perl for the purpose of keeping a Web application that requires users to enter their phone numbers from processing malicious and/or non-standard input (see also Schultz, 2005):

$number=~/^[\d-]+{1,12}$/ || die "Non-allowed characters in input [0] ";

The first part ($number=~) states that phone numbers that users enter must conform to certain rules that follow. \d means that numerals comprise the correct input. - means that hyphens between portions of the phone numbers that users enter are also legal. ^[\d-]+ states that any allowed characters (in this particular instance, numerals) are permitted, beginning at the start of every line. {1,12} means the amount of input cannot be less than 1 character, nor can it be more than 12 characters, something that is extremely useful in helping prevent buffer overflow attacks. $ specifies that the string comparison has ended when the end of the line has been reached, something that is instrumental in keeping an attacker from attaching additional, malicious commands or other types of undesirable input after the last character of input. If an entry does not abide by every restriction in this portion of the Perl script, the program aborts, displaying "Non-allowed characters in input."

This is just one of many examples showing how difficult integrating security mechanisms into Web applications can be. Input checking, furthermore, is just one of many security-related mechanisms needed in Web applications. Some of the many other necessary mechanisms include running without elevated privileges wherever possible, rescinding elevated privileges whenever code execution switches from one routine to another, refraining from making dangerous system calls, providing strong user authentication, encrypting session cookies, user credentials, and sensitive information such as credit card numbers, trying to return a minimum of error message information that could facilitate subsequent attacks, avoiding using URLs and

Figure 3. Example of an Apache directive

```
<Directory_path>
Options -Indexes
</Directory>
```

other state and environment variables to keep track of the state of Web transactions, ensuring that all user entry points into the Web application are identified and well-controlled, preventing users from getting access to directories and files to which they are not allowed access by assigning restrictive Web server rather than operating system permissions, and avoiding putting Web content pages on external cache servers (which are generally easy targets for attackers).

A good solution for blending security and usability better in the area of Web applications would be to have commoditized routines that provide security-related functionality and that can be readily integrated into Web application code. This would spare Web application programmers from having to develop their own routines and functions for making Web applications more secure.

Human factors challenges in securing data sent over networks. SSL encrypts data sent over networks when higher levels of confidentiality are needed, such as when personal information is being transferred from one computer to another. SSL, the most frequently used network encryption protocol for Web transmissions, can be used in conjunction with many different application protocols. Any program that uses the TCP (Transmission Control Protocol) network protocol can in fact be modified to use SSL. When a client connects to a Web server, the server usually indicates whether SSL is required for that page. If it is required, the client and the server negotiate to determine the type of encryption their session will use. Generally, the strongest version of the algorithm that the Web server and client support will be chosen. The client and the server then exchange encryption keys. Once the keys have been exchanged, network encryption between the client and the server is set up. Browsers often show that encryption is in place by displaying a padlock icon somewhere at the bottom of the browser. Note that SSL does not provide anything more than confidentiality of transmitted data; it does not protect stored information.

Several years ago, setting up SSL encryption in Web servers required a fairly large number of user interaction steps, some of which were rather difficult for inexperienced Web administrators to perform. The Apache Web server has long been the exception—to enable SSL encryption the Web administrator must compile the mod_ssl module into the Apache code and perform only a few additional task steps. Today's generation of Web servers support enabling and running SSL with a minimum amount of user

interaction. For all practical purposes, the most difficult part of setting up SSL encryption is obtaining a certificate for the server from a certificate provider such as Verisign, the relative ease of which depends largely on each certificate provider's procedures for obtaining certificates. In general, therefore, the area of encrypting Web transmissions over networks is one in which usability and security blend well.

Human factors challenges in securing systems that host Web servers. The last part of Web security to be considered is security in the operating system (e.g., Windows, Linux, Unix, and others) on which Web servers run. Attackers easily can gain unauthorized access to an otherwise secure Web server if one or more vulnerabilities in the operating system on which the Web server runs exist and can be exploited. In general, securing an operating system requires configuring system settings appropriately, keeping the number of services that run to a minimum, ensuring that system directories and files have appropriate permissions and that the superuser (e.g., root in Linux and Unix and Administrator in Windows and Novell systems) owns all of them, assigning superuser privileges only to those who need them to do their jobs, ensuring that patches that eliminate security-related vulnerabilities are installed on a timely basis, enabling a sufficient amount of audit log categories, and carefully and regularly inspecting log output, regularly backing up the system, and other measures. Each operating system also requires that measures specific to that operating system be implemented; a plethora of publicly available guidelines for securing each operating system is available.

Although methods of elevating operating system security are well-known, many operating systems are not secure. A major reason is lack of effort on the part of system administrators, or if there are no system administrators, users themselves. System administrators often know what to do to secure operating systems, but they do not have the time to do what they need to do. In some cases, however, system administrators do not even know what to do. Human interaction tasks in connection with securing operating systems are, unfortunately, generally too complex for users. Vendors such as Microsoft have tried to make the process of securing operating systems easier for both system administrators and users, and they have to some extent succeeded. Built into every recent Windows system, for example, is a feature named "Windows Automatic Updates," which if enabled on any system determines whether any patches are missing. Easy to enable, it will download and install missing patches if so configured. Windows Automatic Updates also has associated liabilities, however, one of which is that faulty patches that damage systems can be downloaded and installed before a system administrator or user can intervene. In general, security is easier to achieve in Windows systems than in Linux and Unix systems; the GUI in Windows systems is a major reason for this difference. Certain human interaction tasks in securing any kind of operating system, Windows included, are, however, unduly difficult. Editing the Windows Registry, a repository of configuration settings, is, for example, unnecessarily difficult. For example, if a Windows system administrator should inadvertently try to add a "Registry key" instead of a "Registry value," about which no warning whatsoever is provided, extremely adverse consequences can potentially result. Setting up IPTables and IPChains, powerful functions that can selective filter and log inbound network traffic to a Linux or Unix system, is also a difficult task because of the intricate and picky syntax required (see Figure 4). In the area of operating system security, therefore, security and usability are to some degree still orthogonal to each other.

Usability studies of passwords as an authentication method. The username-password combination is the most common method of identifying and authenticating users on most Web sites and computer networks. Although there are stronger forms of authentication than passwords, such as fingerprint recognition or token devices, passwords will continue to be used extensively due to their ease of implementation and high user acceptance. Yet, passwords are considered to be weak forms of authentication, in part because users often do not engage in good password security practices. For example, users often generate passwords that contain easy-to-guess information such as their name or birthdate, use the same password for multiple accounts, and write down passwords or share them with other people. Because of the importance of strong passwords to information security, the authors have been conducting research examining usability issues associated with password generation and recall. Our work in this area provides a good illustration of how the usability of alternative security mechanisms can be compared and evaluated, with the goals of improving both the usability and security.

One technique that can be used by system administrators to promote the generation of more crack-resistant passwords is proactive password checking (Bergadano, Crispo, & Ruffo, 1998). With this technique, users are allowed to generate their own passwords, but the passwords must meet certain specified restrictions before the system will accept them. In our initial study, we compared the security and memorability of passwords generated with six restrictions (minimum length of five characters in one experiment and eight in another, must contain an uppercase letter, must contain a lowercase letter, must contain a digit, cannot repeat any character two times in a row, cannot contain a two-letter subset from the username) to ones generated with only the length restriction (Proctor, Lien, Vu, Schultz, & Salvendy, 2002). Users took twice as long to generate acceptable passwords for the six-restriction condition than for the single-restriction condition and made more errors. However, they performed equally well when they were required to login with their username and password after performing a brief distractor task. Although the passwords generated to satisfy six restrictions were not cracked as readily by John the Ripper 1.6, a cracking program, the more important factor was length: eight-character passwords were cracked much less often than five-character passwords.

In Proctor et al.'s (2002) study, users only had to generate a password for one account and were tested only after a short delay. However, most users have multiple accounts for which they must remember passwords over longer periods of time. Therefore, in a follow-up study, we examined the security and memorability of passwords for three and five accounts recalled after a short five-minute delay and again after a longer one-week delay (Vu, Proctor, Bhargav-Spanzel, Tai, Cook, & Schultz, 2007). Users were asked to generate passwords that met seven restrictions (at least six characters; must contain an uppercase letter, a lowercase letter, a special character, a digit; each password must be unique; cannot contain the username for the account or any variant of it). Not too surprisingly, more forgetting occurred when users had to remember passwords for five accounts rather than for only three. Even though the passwords had to satisfy seven restrictions, about half of them were cracked within 12 hours by lc5, a commercially available cracking program.

A final set of experiments examined how mnemonic techniques can be used to improve the memorability and security of the passwords (Vu et al., 2007). In one study, users were asked to generate a sentence and combine the first letters of the words to form a password. In one condition, users were only required to use the first letters, whereas in a second condi-

Figure 4. An example of IPTables syntax

```
iptables -P INPUT DROP
iptables -P FORWARD DROP
iptables -P OUTPUT ACCEPT
# Setup state connection tracking for outbound traffic
iptables -A OUTPUT -m state --state NEW,ESTABLISHED,RELATED -j ACCEPT
# Allow anything on loopback interface
iptables -A INPUT -i lo -m state --state NEW,ESTABLISHED -j ACCEPT
# Allow unfettered communications with a few trusted hosts
iptables -A INPUT -s 128.3.9.x -m state --state NEW,ESTABLISHED -j ACCEPT
iptables -A INPUT -s 128.3.9.y -m state --state NEW,ESTABLISHED -j ACCEPT
# Create a hole for lpd
iptables -A INPUT --dport printer -p TCP -s 128.3.9.0/24 -m state --state NEW, ESTABLISHED -j ACCEPT
# Allow ssh inbound
iptables -A INPUT --dport ssh -p TCP -m state --state \  NEW,ESTABLISHED -j ACCEPT
```

tion they were instructed also to embed digit and symbol characters within the sentence and resulting password. Although the additional requirement to embed a digit and symbol reduced the memorability of the passwords, it increased their strength greatly. lc5 cracked 62 percent of the passwords that did not contain a symbol and digit, but only 2 percent from the group that had the additional restrictions. In both studies, the memorability of passwords was better at the week retention interval than at the five-minute interval. This counterintuitive finding was due to the fact that having to recall the passwords initially after the five-minute interval condition helped participants associate the passwords with the different accounts. When the participants were tested only at the one-week interval, their performance was no better than that of the other participants tested at the five-minute interval and considerably worse than that when those participants were tested again a week later. Unfortunately, immediate re-entry of a password after generating it, as required by many Web sites, was found to be ineffective at improving long-term retention of the password.

HUMAN FACTORS ISSUES IN PRIVACY PROTECTION

Privacy-Related Threats and Risks

Many Web sites in various categories (e.g., financial, pharmaceutical, insurance, retail, travel, technology, gaming) request and collect much information about

users. Some of this information identifies the users (e.g., name, SSN, home address), whereas other information is more general, representing users' preferences and browsing patterns in order to customize the Web experience of the users. Both personally identifiable and non-identifiable information may be of a sensitive nature and can create problems for users if the information is revealed to other parties. For example, something seemingly as innocuous as browsing patterns can reveal much about an individual's personality, interests, and activities. The amount and types of information users have to provide when creating a profile for a Web site varies widely both within and between categories of sites. For example, Proctor, Ali, & Vu (2008) found that six financial institutions requested a mean of 29 pieces of personal information from users. Moreover, the range was 30 pieces of information, with many of the items being unique to one or two of the sites, suggesting that some financial sites were requesting information that was not necessary.

Because of the sensitive nature of personal information, users may not desire to have this information shared with at least some other parties. Although most users indicate that they do not mind providing personally identifiable information to a site when that information is needed to complete a transaction, they do mind if that information is used for marketing purposes or is sold to other parties (Proctor et al., 2008). Users also differ widely in their willingness to provide personal information, with some being very cautious, others being marginally concerned, and the majority being intermediate (Ackerman, Cranor, & Reagle, 1999).

Breaches of privacy of the types described above are likely to lead to identity theft, which can result in the thief ordering merchandise and requesting services in the victim's name. The previous examples of data security breaches also involved violations of privacy. As another example, much coverage was given in 2005 to a breach of privacy involving ChoicePoint, Inc., a provider of identification and credit verification services, in which the personal records of at least 140,000 people were divulged to individuals thought to be involved in criminal activities (CNNMoney.com, 2005). A more recent case that has been highlighted in the media is the burglary of a laptop computer containing names, SSNs, and birthdates of many millions of veterans from the Department of Veteran Affairs (Lemos, 2006). As these examples indicate, an organization's failure to ensure good security and privacy practices could result in the identity theft of thousands or millions of individuals.

In circumstances involving medical and health records, release of private information to unauthorized parties could make it difficult for an individual to receive health or life insurance coverage if certain medical conditions were revealed. Disclosure of personal information may even prevent a person from being employed in certain types of jobs. As with other personal information, breaches of privacy concerning health and medical information have been reported. For example, Kaiser Permanente informed 140 patients that information from their medical records had been posted on a Web site. They blamed this posting on a disgruntled employee, but the employee claimed that she had simply posted information that the company had made available previously on an unsecured Web site (Ostrov, 2005).

The Relationship between Privacy and Usability

Usability of privacy policies. In part because of increased user concern about privacy, the majority of Web sites collecting personal information now post privacy policies (Adkinson, Eisenach, & Lenard, 2002). A privacy policy is a written document intended to provide users with a description of the organization's practices concerning how a user's personal information is collected, stored, and used, as well as the measures taken by the organization to ensure privacy. Because the privacy policy is supposed to provide users with critical facts about the privacy of their personal information, it should describe clearly what information the

site collects, how that information is used, and how it is stored and secured. However, for the most part, privacy policies tend to be long, full of "legalese," and written from the perspective of protecting the organization rather than protecting users (Jensen & Potts, 2004).

As a consequence of their complexity, users seldom read privacy policies. Several studies have shown that the average reading level required for privacy policies is 13 years of education or above. Even when users with this level of education read a policy, they are not able to comprehend all of its content (Jensen & Potts, 2004; Proctor et al., in press). For example, Antón et al. (2004) found that it would take a user all day to analyze certain privacy policies sufficiently to gain a full understanding of their content. Moreover, privacy policies are subject to change, and even if a user analyzed and understood the current policy, he or she would have to re-analyze the policy whenever changes were made. This would be difficult enough if users were notified each time that a change was made, but some organizations do not routinely notify users of changes to their privacy policies (Jensen & Potts, 2004).

Several agencies now have certification programs to verify that a privacy policy incorporates certain principles of good privacy practices, such as describing what personally identifiable information is being collected, the means by which it is being collected, how the information will be used, and whether it will be shared with third parties. Privacy certification seals are provided by the TRUSTe Privacy Program, VeriSign, and BBBOnLine (Better Business Bureau), among others. The seals offer users an easy way to check whether an organization's stated policy adheres to minimal privacy guidelines. Studies have shown that even users who do not know the purpose behind privacy certification seals tend to trust sites that display such seals more than ones that do not (Moores & Dhillon, 2003; Proctor et al., 2008). However, an organization's actual privacy practices may not adhere closely to its stated practices. Although some certification sites allow users to report violations of the certified privacy practices, whether users report violations that they encounter is extremely improbable.

Usability issues in specifying privacy policies and preferences. Recently, there has been an attempt to standardize Web privacy policies in machine-readable form so that they can be checked by privacy-specification applications. The World Wide Web Consortium's (W3C's) Platform for Privacy Preferences (P3P) Project enables websites to encode their data-collection and data-use practices in a machine-readable XML format, known as P3P policies (Cranor, 2002; Cranor & Garfinkle, 2005). The W3C has also designed APPEL (A P3P Preference Exchange Language), which allows users to specify their privacy preferences. Through the use of P3P and APPEL, a user agent (for example, the Privacy Bird® developed by AT&T) can check a Web site's privacy policy against the user's privacy preferences, and automatically determine whether the Web site's data-collection and data-usage practices are consistent with the user's privacy preferences.

Several usability limitations and shortcomings need to be addressed for the P3P goal to be fully realized. One is that users have considerable difficulty setting user agents to appropriately match their privacy preferences. This can be illustrated by an experiment of Proctor, Vu, and Ali (2007) in which users were instructed to set the interface for Privacy Bird to accommodate each of the top 24 privacy concerns indicated by a user survey. It was possible to set Privacy Bird to accommodate only nine of the concerns. For these nine concerns, users configured Privacy Bird appropriately 60 percent of the time. More seriously, for the concerns the Privacy Bird could not accommodate, users thought that they had set the interface appropriately 70 percent of the time, rather than realizing that no configuration of Privacy Bird could address those concerns. Several minor variations in display format, organization, and wording for the specifications interface did not result in significantly better performance.

Another limitation of P3P is that there is no simple translation of verbal privacy-policy statements into P3P language. Thus, the practices specified in the machine-readable policy may not match exactly those specified in the written policy (see, e.g., Raskin, Krachina, & Triezenberg, 2007). Moreover, many privacy policies are written in "natural language," so many of the statements cannot be written in a machine-readable form. Also, the formal language is not able to represent all of the various factors that may influence whether a user would want to provide certain information to a site, and users must think in terms of the policy statements instead of their security. Policy authoring and analysis tools as well as user agents need to be designed based on a comprehensive understanding of the behaviors and preferences of users and existing tools.

CONCLUSION

Because maintaining security and privacy requires complex interactions of many people with computer networks and systems, it should not be surprising that usability is a major factor in determining the success of the measures that are taken. Traditionally, there has been little effort in integrating usability with security and in conducting systematic human factors research on security- and privacy-related issues. Yet, as we have shown in this chapter, examples exist of products (such as the IIS 6 (and 7) Web servers) that are both secure and usable. Moreover, examples of research showing ways that usability and security can be improved together also exist. Thus, although tight security often means low usability, it does not have to in many cases. An interface and protocol that is designed with the human factor in mind will typically produce better end results than one that is not. In agreement with the quote by Resnick (2006) with which we began the chapter, we anticipate that human factors analyses and considerations will play a major role in the development of future systems intended to provide security and protect privacy.

REFERENCES

Ackerman, M. S., Cranor, L. F., & Reagle, J. (1999). Privacy in E-commerce: Examining user scenarios and privacy preferences. *E-commerce 99* (pp. 1-8). New York: ACM.

Adkinson, W. F., Eisenach, J. A., & Lenard, T. M. (2002). *Privacy online: A report on the information practices and policies of commercial Web sites*. Washington. DC: The Progress and Freedom Foundation, Special Report.

Bergadano, F., Crispo, B., & Ruffo, G. (1998). High dictionary compression for proactive password checking. *ACM Transactions on Information and System Security, 1*, 3-25.

CERT (2001). *CERT® Advisory CA-2001-19 "Code Red" Worm Exploiting Buffer Overflow In IIS Indexing Service DLL*. Available at http://www.cert.org/advisories/CA-2001-19.html

CNNMoney.com (2005). *ChoicePoint: More ID theft warnings*. Retrieved on November 12, 2006 from http://money.cnn.com/2005/02/17/technology/personaltech/choicepoint/

Cranor, L. F. (2002). *Web privacy with P3P*. Sebastopol, CA: O'Reilly Media, Inc.

Cranor, L. F., & Garfinkle, S. (2005). *Security and usability.* Sebastopol, CA: O'Reilly Media, Inc.

Jensen, C., & Potts, C. (2004). *Privacy policies as decision-making tools: An evaluation of online privacy notices.* CHI 2004, 6, 471-478.

Krachina, O., Raskin, V., & Triezenberg, K. E. (2007). Reconciling privacy policies and regulations: Ontological semantics perspective. In M. J. Smith & G. Salvendy (Eds.), *Human Interface, Part II, HCII 2007, Lecture Notes in Computer Science 4558* (pp. 730-739). Berlin: Springer-Verlag.

Lemos, R. (2006). *Veterans Affairs warns of massive privacy breach.* SecurityFocus 2006-05-22. Retrieved November 12, 2006 from http://www.securityfocus.com/news/11393

Moores, T. T., & Dhillon, G. (2003). Do privacy seals in e-commerce really work? *Communications of the ACM, 46*(12), 265-271.

Ostrov, B. F. (2005). 140 Kaiser patients' private data put online. *Mercury News, March 11.* Retrieved November 12, 2006 from http://lists.jammed.com/ISN/2005/03/0062.html

Proctor, R. W., Ali, M. M., & Vu, K.-P. L. (2008). Examining usability of Web privacy policies. *International Journal of Human-Communication Interaction.*

Proctor, R. W., Lien, M. C., Vu, K.-P. L., Schultz, E. E., & Salvendy, G. (2002). Improving computer security for authentication of users: Influence of proactive password restrictions. *Behavior Research Methods, Instruments, & Computers, 34,* 163-169.

Proctor, R. W., & Vu, K.-P. L. (2004). Human factors and ergonomics for the Internet. In H. Bidgoli (Ed.), *The Internet encyclopedia* (Vol. 2, pp. 141-149). Hoboken, NJ: John Wiley.

Proctor, R. W., Vu, K.-P. L., & Ali, M. A. (2007). Usability of user agents for privacy-preference specification. In M. J. Smith & G. Salvendy (Eds.) *Human Interface, Part II, HCII 2007, Lecture Notes in Computer Science 4558* (pp. 766-767). Berlin: Springer-Verlag.

Resnick, M. (2006). The future – Human factors and emerging Internet business models. In *Proceedings of the Human Factors and Ergonomics Society 50th Annual Meeting* (pp. 1445-1446). Santa Monica, CA: Human Factors and Ergonomics Society.

SANS (2005a). Consumer data stolen from Seisint databases. *SANS NewsBites, 7*(11), March 16.

SANS (2005b). Dutch police arrest three in Bot scheme. *SANS NewsBites, 7*(43), October 11.

Schultz, E.E. (2001). IIS Web servers: It's time to just be careful. *Information Security Bulletin, 6*(9), 17-22.

Schultz, E.E. (2005). Web security and privacy. In R. W. Proctor & K.-P. L. Vu (Eds.), *Handbook of human factors in Web design* (pp. 613-625). Mahwah, NJ: Lawrence Erlbaum Associates.

Viega, J. (2005). Solutions to many of our security problems already exist, so why are we still so vulnerable? *Queue, June,* 40-50.

Vu, K.-P. L., Proctor, R. W., Bhargav-Spanzel, A., Tai, B.-L., Cook, J., & Schultz, E. E. (2007). Improving password security and memorability to protect personal and organizational information. *International Journal of Human-Computer Studies, 65,* 744-757.

AUTHORS' NOTE

Preparation of this chapter was supported in part by NSF ITR Cyber Trust grant #0430274.

KEY TERMS

Access Control: The process by which system administrators determine who is permitted to gain entry to certain areas of a system or database.

Human Factors: The interdisciplinary field devoted to the investigation of cognitive and physical characteristics of humans that influence their interactions with computers and other machines and systems.

Identification and Authentication: The process by which the system determines whether the user is who he or she claims to be and whether to allow the user access to systems and networks.

Identity Theft: Inappropriately using a person's identifying information, such as social security num-

413

ber or password, to engage in activities under that person's name.

P3P Policy: A privacy policy written in a machine readable format specified by the Platform for Privacy Preferences Project of the World Wide Web Consortium.

Personally Identifiable Information: Information in a computer-based transaction that can be linked directly to the individual user.

Privacy Certification Seal: One of several logos provided by privacy certification companies when an organization's privacy policy satisfies certain good privacy practices. It is posted on the Web site by the organization to assure users that the organization follows good privacy practices.

Privacy Policy: A document that describes the information collected by a Web site and how this information is stored, used, and transferred.

Security/Privacy Breach: A breakdown in the security of a computer system that allows unauthorized persons access to the system and information on it.

Usability: The ease with which a system or interface can be used by a person. Usability studies evaluate alternative designs for products and interfaces to ensure effective transactions.

Chapter XXXVI
Threat Modeling and Secure Software Engineering Process

Wm. Arthur Conklin
University of Houston, USA

ABSTRACT

Software defects lead to security vulnerabilities, which cost businesses millions of dollars each year and threaten the security of both individuals and the nation. Changes to the software engineering process can help to reduce the number of defects, improving the quality of the process. This chapter introduces the concept of threat modeling to include security in the process of developing software. Adding threat modeling to the software development process will improve the quality of the process. The majority of software coding errors are preventable using a process designed to avoid a series of common errors. Increasing the visibility of common errors will enable software engineers to produce code with substantially fewer security errors. Threat modeling provides insight into the risks facing the software at design time, increasing the software engineering team's opportunity to avoid errors during coding.

INTRODUCTION

Software engineering is a relatively new discipline and has grown significantly in the past 30 years. The development of software is a complex task involving many parties working to build a software solution to a particular task. As the level of complexity of the software projects has increased, so has the importance of using a process based model to manage the complexity. With the rise of the Internet, with its inherent connectedness, and the increase in e-commerce, a new threat has emerged, that of e-crime. E-crime is a form of fraud that uses the interconnected nature of the Internet to attack victims. Attacks on software began with simple worms and viruses, and

have now progressed to complicated attacks against Web applications.

Attacks on computer systems are a significant issue for enterprises with Web-facing applications (CSI 2006). The increase in business desire to develop Web-based, customer driven applications has opened the door to even greater exposure to threats and risk. The majority of the security efforts in an enterprise are focused on defending the enterprise against attacks. Software flaws, coupled with the test and patch doctrine, act as a financial burden to both software users and developers. Addressing software flaws in a preventative fashion, before they place the enterprise at risk is highly desired by developers and customers. Preventing and removing vulnerabilities from internally generated applications will significantly strengthen the security posture of an organization and reduce operational costs. Just as the use of software development lifecycle models has reduced the complexity of development, introduction of security into the development lifecycle process will provide a solution to the complexities of securing code.

A very powerful tool that can be used to inject security into any software development lifecycle model is threat modeling. Threat modeling begins acting during the design phase and interacts through testing, helping to build quality into the software. Threat modeling is process agnostic, it can be added to any existing software development process. Threat modeling can act as a comprehensive security communication plan throughout the software development process.

Expertise to achieve the development of a comprehensive threat model and keep the development team apprised of the changing security landscape has led to the need for security experts on the development team. Just as manufacturing needed quality experts to assist in the focus of quality in manufacturing, software production has the same need. In fact, security can be seen to be a lot like quality in manufacturing. Quality in manufacturing has been defined as conformance to requirements, and security can be viewed in the same light.

BACKGROUND

Whether we listen to the news, read the newspaper or online news feeds, or monitor reports from the US CERT, we learn of cyber vulnerabilities and exploitations. These exploits and vulnerabilities are occurring at an alarming rate, costing businesses millions of dollars each year and threatening the security of the nation and of individuals (CSI 2006). Most cyber vulnerabilities can be traced to defects in software that are caused by bad design and poor development practices (Howard & LeBlanc, 2002; Howard, LeBlanc, & Viega, 2005). Defective software is largely the result of poor software engineering techniques that often "add on" security considerations rather than include them from the beginning. Yet the efficacy of bolt-on, after the fact security measures has been called into question (Conklin & Dietrich, 2005).

The Software Engineering Institute (SEI) at Carnegie Mellon University has analyzed programs written by thousands of programmers and concluded that even experienced professionals unintentionally make errors in design and programming. These errors

result occur in the determination of requirements, designing, developing, and testing the software (Davis & Mullaney, 2003). Errors occur in new code and in code corrections, with one defect for every seven to 10 lines of new or changed code being a normal rate. In another benchmark study, analyzing hundreds of software projects, Jones found that released software contains from one to seven defects per thousand lines of new or changed code (Jones, 2000). Regardless of the actual error rate, these errors manifest themselves in the form of vulnerabilities and the need for costly patches.

The cause of errors and defects are known issues. According to a study done by the SEI, over 90 percent of security vulnerabilities are the result of known software defect patterns. This study demonstrated that 10 common defects accounted for about 75 percent of all security vulnerabilities (Davis & Mullaney, 2003). Another study of 45 e-business applications showed that 70 percent of security defects were caused by poor software design (Jacquith, 2002). For the most part, software design and development errors that lead to security breaches include a basic lack of security knowledge, declaration errors, failure to validate input, buffer overflows, and logic errors. The director of research at the Sans Institute observed that all of the conditions listed on the Sans Institute Top 20 Internet Security vulnerabilities are a result of poor coding, testing, and bad software engineering practices (SANS Institute, 2005). All of these defects are preventable. In fact, books have been written about the common causes (Howard et al., 2005). Previous academic research into the subject has examined causes, but has not produced significant reductions in flaws (Baskerville 1993; Wang & Wang 2003).

The cause of the problem has been identified as coming from multiple sources: education of programmers, business practices of software development firms, and application deployment practices of end-users (Bishop & Engle, 2006). This chapter tackles the concept of adding security principles to a software development process, resulting in a secure lifecycle development process (Howard & Lipner, 2006). This chapter proposes an actionable methodology to reduce the number of flaws in software.

Security in software development is a term with different meaning to different people. This chapter examines the concept of applying security related changes to the development process with the overall goal of affecting the output quality. Software quality can be measured using bug counts and normalized in terms of bus per line of code, or bugs per functional module or any other normalizing factor. Quality principles have taught that to manage something, one must measure it. Bugs, or errors in software can be documented, measured and later used in training to prevent repeat mistakes. These measurements are a measure of how accurately the software performs a function and only a function, with no stray or unexpected outcomes. Examples of security features are items such as cryptographic functions, authorization procedures, access control mechanisms, and logging routines. The features are treated exactly like any other functional feature desired in the software, they are not a measure of security associated with the development process. Security in development is not equal to security features or functionality associated with the software.

Tools and Technologies

Security has long been viewed as a combination of people, process and technology. Implementing a secure development process involves the same three items. New tools are needed to assist designers and developers in improving their work product. Inclusion of these new tools in the software development process ensures that they have the desired impact. Training of people, from designers to coders, to testers to program managers is necessary to enact the level of change needed to shift to a new paradigm of secure coding. New tools have been developed to address the problems associated with developing secure code. Threat modeling is a design technique that is effective in illustrating design issues and alternatives early in the development cycle.

Process Enhancements

There are many different models used in software development. From the waterfall model, to the spiral and evolutionary models, to the newer agile methods, each has its supporters. Each of these can be enhanced through the addition of security specific items, resulting in a process more robust to errors, and one that is more capable of producing error free code. The principles behind protecting systems have been known for a long time (Various, 1998), but the main problem has been one of implementation in practice (Howard & Lipner, 2006). Several key process enhancements can be implemented as part of almost any develop-

ment process (Software Engineering Institute, 2006). Management must then manage the new improved process to ensure the changes are effective. Four items that can have a large effect are threat modeling, developer security training, security-based testing, and security reviews. Add executive support through management action and the quality of software can be improved regardless of the specific development process used.

Developer Security Training

Software engineers learn their profession through a combination of schooling and on the job experience. This has produced some very talented software engineers with strong skill sets in a wide array of languages. Software engineering is different than security engineering. In fact, when many software engineers are questioned on security principles, they immediately think of security features, such as cryptography, authentication, access control, and the like. Secure development is about the process to build and deliver all features, and only the desired features without errors or unexpected behaviors. This is a more stringent standard than is followed by most developers. To get developers, from requirements engineers, to designers, to coders, testers, and project managers to embrace new methods of producing code in a manner to control functionality requires awareness and education. This education is different than the typical computer science graduate receives, and is one that changes over time as the threats and standards change.

There are tools that will assist the development team in their quest to produce error free code. Training of the entire development team on them, and how they fit into the development process, is necessary to harness the power of these error reducing tools. Developer training needs vary by experience, role on the development team, type of application being built and current threat levels. Lessons learned from previous projects also add to the items in an effective training program. Regular training, coupled with periodic refresher training events is necessary to achieve the desired level of competency. Just as professional athletes train on a regular basis, so should professionals in software engineering. A solid on-going education program has been credited as one of the key changes that enabled cultural changes at Microsoft and has helped lead to an over 50 percent reduction in bugs in the past three years (Howard & Lipner, 2006).

Threat Modeling

Threat modeling is powerful tool used during the design process of software engineering. The objective of threat modeling is to develop an understanding of the threats to software in the design portion of the development cycle. The earlier in the development cycle that security issues are identified and addressed, the lower the impact on the product cost in terms of resources and time. Studies have illustrated the cost savings associated with early defect removal (McConnell, 2004). Threat modeling begins with the identification of a threat, which is defined as the attacker's objective. By focusing on the objective of the adversary, this frees the design team to use appropriate countermeasures, designed in from the beginning in a proactive mode. This reduces the cost and prevents many potential errors from becoming true vulnerabilities.

A key concept in threat modeling is that of attack surfaces. Software is vulnerable at specific points, such as inputs to functions. The collection of these points acts as a surface and can be measured in a single count. The larger the number of attack surfaces as a result of the design process, the harder the security problem becomes for the development team. Attack surface reduction efforts in the design process can make substantial contributions to the overall software quality. Threat modeling is a relatively new tool, and although it has been described in several references (Howard & LeBlanc, 2002; Swiderski & Snyder, 2004), the latest reference (Howard & Lipner, 2006, Chapter 9) incorporates many changes that streamline and lighten the process without sacrificing effectiveness. A nine-step process is presented to create a threat model. Although the number of steps may seem large, the majority of the steps are not security specific and many are already part of most development processes.

1. Define use case scenarios
2. Enumerate external dependencies
3. Define security assumptions
4. Create external security notes
5. Create a Data Flow Diagram (DFD) for each module
6. Determine threat types
7. Identify threats to the system
8. Determine level of risk
9. Plan mitigations for each identified threat

Use cases are used to document how a system is to be used once deployed. These can also address ele-

ments of security. For a mobile device, the threat of device loss through theft should be documented. The risk associated with the loss of information then should be considered. If the device has sensitive information, then this needs to addressed as part of the design process to ensure confidentiality and integrity are properly supported. Should the device not have sensitive information, this too needs to be documented, if for no other reason than to prevent future modifications from adding sensitive information without addressing the design of security measures.

Software does not operate by itself. Each program has dependencies on other programs, such as the operating system, or a Web server to facilitate its operation. These external dependencies need to be documented. All interactions with the external world are documented and any security assumptions made are documented. Defining and documenting the external dependencies, the security implications and the expectations is very important once modification to the application begin to take place. A clear understanding of trust boundaries and the assumptions across each are essential both in the development and maintenance phases of a project. Documenting this information in the form of an external security note is a method of communicating this important information to other concerned parties, including developers, testers, and ultimately end users.

Data Flow Diagrams (DFDs) have long been used by designers to model data flows in software. DFDs are critical in the threat modeling process, for they represent the software components and trust boundaries. Using a series of DFDs, from the top level context diagram, through detailed breakdowns of complex processes, the movement of data through the design is detailed. Any time data moves from one element to another and the privilege level changes, a trust boundary is defined and analyzed. An anonymous user who submits data to a process running at a higher level of privilege should have the data checked for correctness prior to use. Understanding and documenting where these boundaries exist will help prevent the design of elements where anonymous users directly interact with root level processes via data transfers.

The next step, determining threat types is a more security specific step. Threats can exist in a variety of forms, targeting a variety of security issues. Several taxonomies exist describing security functionality. A common one is CIA, representing confidentiality, integrity, and availability. This taxonomy is not granular enough to benefit the design team. A more granular approach is used in the STRIDE model. STRIDE stands for Spoofing Identity, Tampering, Repudiation, Information Disclosure, Denial of Service and Elevation of Privilege (Howard & Lipner, 2006; Swiderski & Snyder, 2004). The STRIDE categories are used in the next step, Identify Threats to the System. In this section, the DFD information is used together with STRIDE to determine threats for each element in the DFD and the type of threat (STRIDE). For each attack surface identified in the DFD, the elements of STRIDE are used to test for vulnerabilities. Is the specific entry point vulnerable to Spoofing? Is it vulnerable to tampering? And so on, for each element and each entry point. For any identified vulnerability, either the system is redesigned to avoid it, or a control to mitigate the vulnerability is required. This methodical design step will assist in the identification and remediation of errors before they are coded into the system.

Once the design is completely documented with respect to security, the next step is to determine the chance of an attack. Although the future can never be predicted with 100 percent accuracy, a model, DREAD, turns this into a doable endeavor. DREAD stands for Damage potential, Reproducibility, Exploitability, Affected Users, and Discoverability. DREAD is used to determine the specific level of risk associated with each identified vulnerability. This is important whenever resources are limited and prioritization of vulnerability remediation is needed. Several scoring schemes can be used, from simple 1, high, to 4 low or even a 10:1 scale. The scale isn't that important, its use is to compare risks between options.

The last step is the planning of mitigation efforts. For all of the identified vulnerabilities that have a risk assessment that exceeds some set point, the vulnerability is addressed at design time. There are never enough resources to address all of the vulnerabilities so; they are ranked in order of risk and the more serious ones addressed.

The steps of threat modeling act in several ways to improve the software development process. First, the steps of threat modeling are used as part of the design process, increasing the designer's understanding of their design function with respect to security. The data developed as part of threat modeling is also useful to coders, showing them the relationship of entry points and vulnerabilities. Knowing what level of protection is needed for each attack surface enabled coders to build the correct protection elements. Testers can use the threat model information to help design test plans, capitalizing on the previous use case and threat analysis.

Threat Modeling Deliverables

Regardless of the specific software engineering process, the process of threat modeling offers some valuable deliverables to the software engineering team. These deliverables include a set of use cases, a list of external dependencies, a data flow diagram, and a set of failure related plans. The first three items are in place in most development processes. What makes threat modeling unique and valuable is the set of failure related information. This information includes attack surface documentation, a set of security assumptions, external security notes, a list of threats, their risks, and mitigation plans. This security-specific information is designed to communicate to everyone on the team the nature of risks and how they are being dealt with during the design process.

An example is the use of input validation. Input validation failures are a prime culprit in many software failures (Howard et al., 2005; Howard & LeBlanc, 2002). If telling developers to validate input before use was sufficient, then this class of bugs could long ago have been banished. The problem lies in the complex passing of data between modules, some being used, some being passed and in many times multiple teams working on different parts of the same system, each assuming someone else is validating the data. Repeated validation of the same data before each use is also wasteful, impacting performance and raising costs. Proper communication of the flow, the attack points, the attack vectors, and then a designed plan to validate data is the correct answer, and the products of the threat modeling process facilitate this important communication.

Threat model deliverables act as a comprehensive communication plan throughout the development process. The documentation of security assumptions and external security notes inform people throughout the process of the expectations and assumptions that have been made by others. The enumeration of threats, associated risks, attack surfaces, and mitigation plans tell everyone what errors to avoid. This information, used at testing and during security reviews, when coupled with specific examination of previous error patterns will greatly reduce the inclusion of common errors. Numerous sites have listed common errors; the challenge is in incorporating this information at the right point of the development cycle (Howard et al., 2005; OWASP, 2006; SANS Institute, 2005). The threat model, acting as a central communication plan performs this timely communication function well.

Security-Based Testing

Testing is a key element in ensuring that the software meets specifications. Normal testing is done against performance standards, with use cases built to test critical functional requirements. Security-based testing is testing performed to specifically test the software's ability to perform as desired and only as desired. As we saw with threat modeling, we can plan some aspects of the test pattern based on known threats. Threat modeling develops information that can be used to test security issues through out the development process.

During the design phase, the information from threat modeling is used to test potential designs for security issues. Understanding the attack surfaces generated during the design phase, and the potential pathways for exploitation early in the process can give designers time to correct potential flaws before coding begins. Design issues are best tested while in design, not after coding where the cost to change is greatly increased. Testing designs using threat modeling information prior is a critical improvement to the development process.

Once coding commences, threat modeling again provides information that can be used to test coding during development at the unit level. The documentation of risks, attack surfaces, and threats can all be addressed at the unit coding level and reviewed prior to sending the code to formal testing. This security review before the code joins other developer's code will improve each submission to the project. This will again assist in reducing costly rework for failures discovered later in the process.

Formal testing is done against specifications. Previous bugs, common flaws, and the specific requirements for each module all offer opportunities to test. Most testing is designed around functional specifications gathered during the requirements process. The information from threat modeling can provide testers a richer set of specifications used in the test process. This will assist testers in finding flaws before the product ships.

Security Reviews

Software development is a complex issue and one that is best tackled by a team. The issue of developing secure or error free code is complex and a team approach works best in this aspect as well. Each member of the team brings their own expertise to bear on the problems at hand. Designers with design experience, requirements engineers, database designers, and developers each have specific levels of expertise. The addition of a security expert to the team will assist in many places. First and foremost, they can assist in developing a thorough threat model. The threat model is a step of the process where more detail and greater comprehensiveness is desired and useful. Developing the minimal threat model may meet some process check box, but will not assist the development team when it comes to designing and developing secure code.

Security experts have the knowledge on threats, on common error patterns and previous issues that are invaluable in the development of this communication plan. Viewing the output of the threat model as a security communication plan highlights how it can be effectively used throughout the development process. Having security personnel assigned to the design team and working throughout the development process will ensure that the security communication plan is used to greatest effect. Security is not a function that can be added at any specific step of the development process, but one that needs to be considered at every step along the development process. The security experts on the team are not responsible for the level of security in the code, they are responsible for ensuring that the threat modeling information is used throughout the development process. In this manner, each team member can then ensure that their portion of the development process is producing error free code to the best of their ability.

Secure Development Process

The inclusion of threat modeling and security experts with security design reviews throughout the development process has been tried in industry. Microsoft Corporation pioneered this approach in response to security issues in its products. Beginning with executive support from both the company CEO and president, a multi-year effort was undertaken to push security into all of their product lines (Bill Gates Chairman Microsoft Corporation, 2002). A brief glimpse of the early results from Microsoft shows that this is good for at least a 50 percent reduction and probably much more as the process matures through practice (Iacovelli, 2006; Microsoft Corporation, 2006).

FUTURE TRENDS

The future of software engineering lies in the production of quality software, as free from defects as possible. The necessity of security will be one driving force. The economics of software maintenance will be another driving force. Market pressures resulting from these two forces will factor in IT management decisions whether to purchase or build case. Much as the quality movement made positive changes in manufacturing (Dick, 2000; Zantek, Wright, & Plante, 2002), the implementation of secure development based lifecycles will improve the production of software.

Quality software can be produced today, using a wide range of development processes. Whether a traditional waterfall process, a spiral development model, or the newer agile methods are used, security and ultimately quality can be added to the development process. Security and hence the development of quality software is process model agnostic—it will work with any and all development methodologies. What is needed is a focus on the part of the entire development team to include this critical functionality. Threat modeling can act as a centerpiece for the development of the communications needed to bring security into all phases of a development process.

CONCLUSION

The software industry has long since passed the time of ignoring security in its product. The challenge is how to improve the quality of software given the many constraints inherent in a competitive business environment. A simple first step is to add security throughout the existing lifecycle development process. A three-legged stool approach is proposed, with one leg being training, one being new tools (threat modeling), and the last being the inclusion of security experts throughout the process. Just as in the proverbial stool case, the legs must be balanced if one is to achieve any stable outcome.

Continuing education and awareness programs for all members of the development team will help keep skills properly honed. This training needs to be specifically targeted to each domain to permit specific skill sharpening. For training program managers, the impacts on schedules benefits them, where training on vulnerable code patterns benefits coders. Properly implemented, the return in productivity will balance the training cost.

The addition of threat modeling into the process acts as a large comprehensive communication plan and platform. This tool is probably the biggest initial bang for the buck in the security field. After successful implementation of threat modeling, other security tools such as file fuzzing and security pushes can be added. Fully incorporating one tool at a time will limit the disruption and still achieve returns on the security investment.

The last element, the development of security expertise inside the firm is essential. Just as database experts are used for this critical function, and testing experts are needed for testing, security experts are needed to stay abreast of the continually changing security threat landscape. The task of the security expert is to assist all team members in achieving a quality output, one that is free from known security errors.

REFERENCES

Baskerville, R. (1993). Information systems security design methods: Implications for information systems development. *ACM Computing Surveys, 25*(4), 375-414.

Bill Gates Chairman Microsoft Corporation. (2002). Executive e-mail, trustworty computing. Retrieved November 26, 2006 from http://www.microsoft.com/mscorp/execmail/2002/07-18twc.mspx

Bishop, M., & Engle, S. (2006). *The software assurance CBK and university curricula.* Paper presented at the Proceedings of the 10th Colloquium for Information Systems Security Education, University of Maryland, University College, Adelphi, MD, June 5-8.

Conklin, W. A., & Dietrich, G. (2005). *Secure software design principles: A systems approach.* Paper presented at the Proceedings of 2005 Americas Conference on Information Systems, Omaha, NE, August 11-14.

CSI (2006). *11th annual CSI/FBI 2005 computer crime and security survey.* Computer Security Institute.

Davis, N., & Mullaney, J. (2003). *The team software process in practice: A summary of recent results.* Retrieved November 26, 2006 from http://www.sei.cmu.edu/publications/documents/03.reports/03tr014.html

Dick, G. P. M. (2000). ISO 9000 certification benefits, reality or myth? Gavin PM Dick The Authors. *The TQM Magazine, 12*(6), 365-371.

Howard, M., & LeBlanc, D. C. (2002).*Writing secure code* (Second Edition). Redmond, WA: Microsoft Press.

Howard, M., LeBlanc, D., & Viega, J. (2005). *19 deadly sins of software security.* McGraw-Hill Osborne Media.

Howard, M., & Lipner, S. (2006). *The security development lifecycle.* Redmond, WA: Microsoft Press.

Iacovelli, D. (2006). *Patch management challenges and solutions.* Paper presented at the Trustworthy Computing Days, Microsoft Corporation, Redmond WA, April. Retrieved November 26, 2006 from http://download.microsoft.com/download/c/9/8/c98260a1-f82e-409f-b73c-c682c6ae3df8/PatchMngmntChallengesandSolutions-DeanIacovelli.ppt

Jacquith, A. (2002). *The security of applications: Not all are created equal.* @Stake Research. Retrieved March 17, 2003 from http://www.atstake.com/research/reports/acrobat/atstake_app_unequal.pdf

Jones, C. (2000). *Software assessments, benchmarks, and best practices.* Reading, MA: Addison-Wesley.

McConnell, S. (2004). *Code complete* (Second Edition). Redmond, WA: Microsoft Press.

Microsoft Corporation. (2006). *Advancing security progress and commitment.* Paper presented at the Trustworthy Computing Days, Microsoft Corporation, Redmond WA, April. Retrieved November 26, 2006 from http://download.microsoft.com/download/9/4/8/948fa472-45a0-41a3-861b-26c051589370/Security%20Mobilization%20Initiative.ppt

OWASP. (2006). OWASP top ten project. Retrieved November 26, 2006 from http://www.owasp.org/index.php/OWASP_Top_Ten_Project

SANS Institute. (2005). *The twenty most critical Internet security vulnerabilities (Updated) ~ The experts consensus version 6.01.* Retrieved November 26, 2006 from http://www.sans.org/top20/

Software Engineering Institute. (2006). Build security in. Retrieved March 3, 2006 from https://buildsecurityin.us-cert.gov/portal/

Swiderski, F., & Snyder, W. (2004). *Threat modeling.* Microsoft Press.

Various. (1998). *Early computer security papers, Part I.* Retrieved October 30, 2006 from http://csrc.nist.gov/publications/history/index.html

Wang, H., & Wang, C. (2003). Taxonomy of security considerations and software quality. *Communications of the ACM, 46*(6), 75-78.

Zantek, P. F., Wright, G. P., & Plante, R. D. (2002). Process and product improvement in manufacturing systems with correlated stages. *Management Science, 48*(5), 591-606.

KEY TERMS

Attack Surface: The collection of all the input interfaces between a software module and all sources of inputs.

DREAD: A method of analytically assigning values to risk for the sake of comparison in software engineering projects.

Mitigation: Steps taken to address a vulnerability in an attempt to prevent an undesired outcome from occurring.

Risk: Is the probability that something undesired happens combined with the expected loss associated with the event.

Security Review: A team event led by a security expert that is a formal examination of material with respect to meeting security criteria of conforming exactly to requirements and only to the requirements.

STRIDE: A taxonomy of types of attacks that can be manifested against software.

Threat: Any circumstance or event with the potential to cause harm to a software program or the tasks it is designed to perform.

Threat Model: A tool used in software engineering to develop an understanding of the threats to software in the design portion of the development cycle.

Vulnerability: A weakness in software that can be exploited by a threat to cause harm to the process the software is designed to perform.

Chapter XXXVII
Guarding Corporate Data from Social Engineering Attacks

Christopher M. Botelho
Baylor Health, USA

Joseph A. Cazier
Appalachian State University, USA

ABSTRACT

The threat of social engineering attacks is prevalent in today's society. Even with the pervasiveness of mass media's coverage of hackers and security intrusions, the general population is not aware of the possible damage that could occur should they be subjected to a social engineering attack. In order to show the damage caused by these attacks, we will discuss the results of a social engineering attack based on a survey conducted in the downtown area of a large financial center in the United States. The authors make suggestions companies can incorporate into their policies in order to protect their employees, as well as systems from intrusions based on social engineering attacks.

INTRODUCTION

As more and more organizations invest in technology to ease the delivery and dissemination of information, more opportunities are created for security incidents. Before the Internet was a part of everyday life, intruders usually gained access to sensitive data by physically setting foot on a company's premises and breaking into a safe or file cabinet. As a result, companies installed security cameras, door locks, and alarm systems.

Today, corporations still have these devices but must also protect their digital data. Investments in devices, such as intrusion detection/prevention systems to alert them of a security incident; firewalls to protect their internal network; and virtual private networks to ensure individuals connecting from the outside are authorized and have a secure connection are necessary expenses.

Another tool corporations use are organizational controls. These are processes and procedures put in place to control and protect assets, which include physical goods, buildings, money, and even a firm's reputation and image. Of the many types of controls, one of the most fundamental is access control. Access controls restrict access to your business systems to authorized personnel. These controls are key to information security and are one of the ten required domains of study for the certified information systems security professional (CISSP) certification exam (Krutz & Vines, 2001).

One of the most critical types of access control in today's internet-connected world is the use of passwords. We use passwords to access many of our online and company accounts (Zivran & Haga, 1999). Usernames and passwords are the most common form of authentication, but are also the weakest due to human error (Ciampa, 2005). One weakness of passwords is they are difficult to remember, leading people to choose weak passwords they can remember (Cazier & Medlin, 2006) and the tendency of people to reuse their passwords for multiple accounts, making the danger of a weak password greater as it can compromise multiple systems (Ives, Walsh, & Schneider, 2004).

Today, most network and system security devices rely on the username and password to grant access. As such, obtaining this information is the equivalent of hitting the jackpot for a hacker. When a hacker is attempting to break into a system, they want to find the quickest and easiest point of entry. The longer it takes to break into a system, the more information the hacker leaves to get caught in the end. Better security technologies are continually being invented to make it more difficult for an attacker to gain access. As a result, many hackers will rely on social engineering methods, that is, using social skills to obtain information, such as a user's password (Krutz & Vines, 2001), to gain access to a target since in many cases it is a lot easier to exploit a human than a system (Mitnick, 2002). The social engineer utilizes an arsenal of methods, allowing him or her to leverage the emotions of a victim, aiding in an attack. The social engineer can flirt with the victim in an attempt to gain information; make the victim feel guilty so they divulge information they would not have otherwise; or even convince the victim that their job could depend on giving the attacker the requested information (Mitnick, 2002).

With this research, empirical data is presented on the current susceptibility of social engineering attacks on companies. From this information, several suggestions are made for companies to ensure social engineers do not succeed. Recommendations are aimed at preventing potential attacks. Lastly, possible future research aimed at studying social engineering further in different areas is discussed.

BACKGROUND

Each day, numerous employees have access to sensitive data in order to do their job. Generally, they will use a password to access this data. Their password is one of the only things keeping a potential intruder out of their employer's network. In the event their password is compromised, the entire company's infrastructure is at risk. Social engineers use human weaknesses, such as trust and fear, to their advantage to exploit these people and get as much information as possible. With experienced social engineers, the employee will not even know what has happened and will continue their day without so much as a second thought. This creates even more risk, as not only does the social engineer have the employee's password, but he or she also avoids detection and possibly can have free roam of the company's network and systems.

Social engineering is the act of gaining either unauthorized access to a system or sensitive information, such as passwords, through the use of trust and relationship building with those who have access to such information (Damie, 2002). A social engineer uses human psychology to exploit people for his or her own use.

According to Kevin Mitnick, a prominent social engineer, "Savvy technologists have painstakingly developed information-security solutions to minimize the risks connected with the use of computers, yet left unaddressed the most significant vulnerability, the human factor" (Mitnick, 2002, p. 8). In 2005, the FBI conducted a computer crime survey with a sample of 2066 organizations in the U.S. They found that the average cost for the companies that had an incident was $24,000, with a total cost of $31,732,500 for all respondents (FBI, 2006). Based on this information, they estimated a total cost of $67.2 billion per year for security incidents.

Social engineering attacks can take on many methods. Each method uses the same basic four-step cycle in order for the social engineer to be successful. The first step is to gather information about the target and potential weak points (Allen, 2006). The attacker can gather names of people through a company's site, co-workers, or even a phone directory. Since most employees have their name, job title, and whether they will be in the office on their voicemail, an attacker can simply find a day when a specific person is not in the office and imitate them to an unsuspecting employee (Mitnick, 2002). Additionally, most employees who have security badges wear them in public places. This could be during a lunch break, going out after work, or even going out with friends at night and simply forgetting to remove their badge. The attacker could find an area where many employees from the target company congregate and use the information on the badge or from the employee to their advantage. Other methods for the social engineer to gain information are:

- **Call specific personnel.** This generally involves convincing people over the phone into giving them information through persuasion with tools such as fear, imitation, and compassion (Granger, 2001).
- **Dumpster diving.** The social engineer physically goes through a company's garbage to find useful information (Mitnick, 2002). This could lead to a sticky-note with a password on it, or even other sensitive internal documents that a careless employee forgot to shred (Castelluccio, 2002). An example of another useful find is organization charts with names that can enable the social engineer to proceed with another method, such as using the phone, in order to impersonate personnel based on their standing in the company.
- **The Internet.** Not only does it provides anonymity but also allows them to maximize their impact. This method is being used primarily by phishers in an attempt to defraud unsuspecting individuals by getting them to divulge personal financial data. In 2006, the total cost of identity fraud in the US was $56.6 billion. Of this amount, 3 percent was obtained through phishing attacks on home users (Javelin Strategy & Research, 2006).
- **Site visitation.** This method involves the attacker physically going to the target site to carry out their attack. However, the attacker may decide the easiest way to get access to the network is to simply go to the target's site and log in (Mitnick, 2002).

The second step is to develop a relationship with the target individual(s) (Allen, 2006). This is needed in order to build trust with the individual in order to exploit them and continue to use them in the future (Mitnick, 2002). General human nature is to trust others and to receive a sense of satisfaction out of helping others (Dolan, 2004). The social engineer builds this trust in order to exploit it. This can involve simply talking on the phone with the target for a few minutes (Dolan, 2004), or striking up a conversation and exchanging business cards at a bar the target frequently attends (Mitnick, 2002).

The third step is to exploit the trust that has been built with the target by manipulating the target into doing something they would not normally have done (Allen, 2006). The key to this step is to ensure the target does not at any point catch on to what is happening and leaves with a sense of satisfaction. This allows the attacker to continue the trust that has been built up with the target in order to exploit them again in the future (Mitnick, 2002).

The fourth and final step is the execution. Once reached, the target has completed the task requested by the social engineer (Allen, 2006). The goal with this final step is to not only have the desired task completed, but to ensure a continual relationship with the target (Mitnick, 2002).

METHODOLOGY

A survey was created and administered with multiple purposes and multiple sections. Data was gathered to not only establish how many people would disclose their passwords, but also to simulate the type of information a social engineer would attempt to gather, other than a password. The survey was divided into three sections:

The first section of the survey was designed to gather personal non-identifying information, such as a favorite movie, television show, place of birth, or pet. These categories were chosen based on research performed by Medlin, Cazier, and Dave (2006). In their research, they found 19.3 percent of passwords gathered were based on family, 2.1 percent were based on being a fan, 5.7 percent were based on faith, and 1.3 percent were based on places. The survey incorporated as many of these as possible into this section without being overwhelming in order to simulate guessing a password in the event a password was not disclosed.

The second section of the survey was designed to gather information on their employer's information security climate. Through this the researchers are able to show how training and individual awareness relate to success in receiving the individual's password. Since training is considered to be the greatest way of preventing attacks, the researchers felt it was important to include this information to assess if training, and how much, helps prevent these attacks.

The final section was designed primarily to convince the individual that the researchers were doing password research and needed their help. Questions were created based on best password principles, and were designed to show if there was a significant correlation between those who divulged their password and other factors such as password length and composition. Additionally, the section was designed so that in the event a password was not given, the information from the first section and last could be combined to guess the individual's password.

Some personal demographics were also gathered for informative purposes in order to support the research. This was gathered under the context of a drawing for a gift certificate to a local restaurant, and respondents were given a separate sheet of paper with personally identifying information, such as name, address, and phone number, as well as place of employment and email address. The last two pieces of information were especially important in the event of a true social engineering attack. This would give an attacker the company's name, possible login information from the email address, and the password in the event it was filled out.

The survey and demographics were kept separate for two reasons. The first was to protect the respondents as well as the researchers from possible privacy breaches. The second reason was to put them at ease with filling out the survey and to facilitate a greater percentage of respondents disclosing their password by giving the impression the survey was truly anonymous. For ethical reasons, the researchers chose to keep everyone anonymous exactly as promised, however it would have been a simple matter for a social engineer to combine the data.

Sample

In order to assess the current awareness of information security in today's climate, a survey was aimed at corporate employees. However, in order to better represent what a social engineer might be able to do, a survey booth was set up outside the corporate headquarters of several major businesses, rather than have the companies ask their employees to participate. The corporate employees were targeted due to the sensitive information about individuals they are entitled to. Members of this group often have access to social security numbers, account information, healthcare records, or credit information on a daily basis. Additionally, they may have access to the intellectual property of their employer.

The term "corporate employees" is being used as a general category for the random sample of people from the downtown area of a large financial center in the United States. In order to take this sample, the researchers took every step possible to ensure there were no ethics violations and were completely honest with those surveyed. The researchers identified that they were from a university and wore name tags to identify themselves and did exactly what they told people they were doing. A real social engineer would not have this handicap.

A table was set up in the downtown area in front of one of the top five banks in the U.S., with another of the top five only a block away, and an energy company two blocks away. This location was selected due to its centralized nature, as well as the employers it was around. This area has a high concentration of financial institutions, making it a target for not only domestic hackers but terrorists as well. We chose this location to test our attack in an area likely to be more secure than areas with less to protect. This study likely *underestimates* the amount of information the average person is likely to share.

People walking by our table were randomly asked to fill out a survey in exchange for candy and the opportunity to win a free gift card to a restaurant from a drawing. All personal information for the drawing was filled out on a separate piece of paper in order to protect all persons involved, including the researchers.

Table 1. Descriptive statistics

Item	Survey Question	Percent
A	Gave Their Password	52%
B	Password Security Training Offered	56%
C	General Security Training Offered	63%
D	Choose Own Password	89%
E	Password is Alpha-Numeric	91%
F	Password Contains Special Passwords	51%

RESULTS

In all, 53 surveys were completely filled out, with three not being fully filled out (only one side was completed) for a total of 56 surveys. Seventy-four percent of respondents were male. There was no significant difference between males and females in terms of willingness to share their password.

This sample included employees of energy companies, banks, and technology companies. While no identifying information was gathered at any point of filling out the survey, the researchers had the opportunity to mark each survey as well as the demographics slips. Many of the respondents had ID badges, identifying their name, company, and position. It would have been a simple matter to write this info down, or capture it with hidden cameras.

In our sample, 52 percent of respondents shared their password. This was accomplished with very little to no pressure in order to ascertain the true level of ease with which people would give up their passwords. Fifty-six percent work for a company that offers password security training, 63 percent offer general security training. Most people were allowed to choose their own password (89 percent) with 91 percent having both letters and numbers. However, only 51 percent of respondents reported using special characters in their password.

In addition, the average person in our sample accessed a system using a password in the very often range, occasionally changed their password and occasionally too often used the same password on multiple systems. We also measured the last time the users participated in a security training program, with the average person indicating they had participated within the last year. In fact, 63 percent had participated within the last year, with many of those participating more recently.

A test was run to compare whether a password was given to us based on factors found in the survey. We found people who use the same password on more than one system were more likely to share it with us, however security training was found to *not* be a significant factor in whether the password was shared.

Lastly, we ran a test for differences between groups that had training in password security and those that had not. Fortunately those that used passwords the most were also more likely to have received training. Those that had training were more likely to change their passwords frequently and have special characters. However they were not significantly more likely to

not reuse their passwords, have longer passwords, or to incorporate numbers into their passwords. Most importantly, password security training had *no* measurable impact on their willingness to share, or not to share their password with us!

DISCUSSION

This study found that those users who used the same password across multiple systems were more likely to disclose their password. Using a scale of one to five, with one being very often and five being never, the study found that those users who disclosed their password stated they used the same password across multiple systems "often," or an average of a 2.00. On the converse, those who did not disclose their password had an average of 2.60, falling in between "often" and "occasionally." Altogether, 38.5 percent stated they used the same password across multiple systems "very often," and a mere 6.9 percent stated they "never" reused passwords. That those that used the same password on multiple accounts were also the same ones that were more willing to share their password is especially ironic as these people have the most to lose from sharing their password because they can be attacked from multiple angles.

It is also interesting to note that security training was not found to be significant in the sharing of people's passwords. While many would expect this to be the biggest prevention of a social engineering attack, there was no correlation between those who had training and those who did not. Even though a significant correlation was not found, it is important to note that without training, there is no possible way for employees to understand social engineering attacks or even begin to know how to prevent them.

However, even though training did not prevent people from sharing their passwords, those with training did have more secure ones. While this is important, giving your password to a stranger defeats the purpose of having a stronger password. This suggests that security training, while important, perhaps needs to be refocused or expanded to include more on social engineering attacks.

RECOMMENDATIONS

This study finds that employees are way too vulnerable to a social engineering attack. Even though training did not affect the willingness to share the password, it did have some impact on the strength of the password. This shows that if the training program were designed better, it might have a better chance of effecting change. Unfortunately, our other options for improving security are limited. Password strength may be improved through technical means and system requirements. However, people are often the weakest link in the security process. This is a weakness that needs to be addressed.

According to Pramod Damie (2002), "a three-phased approach is helpful in combating social engineering." This three phased approach covers training, policy creation, and testing to ensure the training was understood and policies are being adhered to. Through these processes, an organization can work towards preventing social engineering attacks, and ensuring their infrastructure, employees, and customers are protected.

The first phase of this approach is an elaborate and comprehensive training program. These training programs must cover a wide array of potential vulnerabilities within an organization. In particular, the program must cover the risk of social engineering attacks to the organization, how to spot these attacks, and how to protect against them.

Users must be trained on social engineering attacks and given the knowledge needed to protect the organization as a whole (Dolan, 2004). In a study of user's knowledge of security issues within an organization, it was found that users were "not sufficiently informed about security issues" (Adams & Sasse, 1999, p. 43). The point of the training program must be to eliminate this issue, and ensure all users are informed and well trained.

The second phase is creating policies and procedures in order to protect the organization. These policies must be created with the user, as well as the organization, in mind. The policy outlines the expectations and responsibilities of the employees, as well as the procedures to follow in the event of a breach or attempted attack (Dolan, 2004).

The following outlines areas training programs and policies should include protecting against a social engineering attack:

Password security. At no time should a password ever be shared with anyone. Social engineers will sometimes pose as technical support personnel in order to get the user to disclose information such as username and password (Allen, 2006). The company's

help desk and IS/IT department should never need to ask a user for their password. This allows the employee to be told point blank that no one will ever ask them for their password, and in the event they are asked, they should not give it out. In this study, the perception of anonymity was used as well as the request of college students doing research to exploit individual's human emotions.

Ensure users adhere to a password criteria policy. This policy needs to include factors such as special characters, numbers, letter case, and reuse within the company. The user must know not to reuse passwords, and a system needs to be in place to verify that the user is at least not reusing his or her password on their system. Lastly, dictionary words should not be allowed and again, a system needs to be put in place to ensure the user is not using dictionary words.

Users must understand not to write down their password in any location. In the event a social engineer decides to physically access the company's site, any passwords written down can become a valuable resource. The social engineer needs to only walk past an employee's workspace to gather the information they need to attack the company's infrastructure (Dolan, 2004).

Additionally, two-factor authentication in the form of a token can be used to prevent unauthorized access to the company's system. An asynchronous dynamic password token with a number changing at fixed intervals would significantly decrease the likelihood of an intruder getting into a system, since even if a social engineer gets access to a user's PIN, the password would change each time the specified interval lapses (Krutz & Vines, 2001).

Employee verification. The company must establish policies and procedures for allowing employees to verify people who call them are who they say they are.

For companies with internal caller-ID phones, the system must display their name as well as extension number. The employee must know to verify who they are speaking with and compare it to the display of their phone system. In the event of a discrepancy between the two, the employee should instead rely on an internal directory and inform the caller they need to verify their identity before speaking with them. For companies without an internal caller-id phone system, the end user must know to verify who they are speaking with before disclosing any information. The simplest method is to use an internal directory and the end users tell the caller they will be called back at their extension (Mitnick, 2002). This gives a two-fold protection, since not only does the user call the extension back, establishing the caller was really at that extension, but also by using the directory, the user is guaranteeing they are calling the correct person back (Gragg, 2002).

Physical access. Ensure all employees have an ID badge with a large print of their photo on it. The large photo prevents a social engineer from obtaining a legitimate badge from an employee and relying on having a badge with a smaller picture that cannot be seen.

A determined social engineer may photograph an employee's badge and create their own based off the photograph (Gragg, 2002). With the power of photo editing software, this is a simple task. To combat this, the badge needs to incorporate a form of protection against being counterfeited or have a policy that employees cannot wear their badge off company property. A simple form of counterfeit protection would be a hologram specifically designed for the organization, or printing with ink that can only be seen under a blacklight.

Task all employees with protecting the organization, and inform them they have the right to question anyone, at any time, anywhere. Social engineers sometimes rely on having the appearance of being a person of authority in order to intimidate employees so they will not be questioned (Gragg, 2002). If an employee does not see a badge on an individual in the building, they must stop and ask them to see the badge; otherwise they have to escort them to the front desk.

Sensitive locations, such as the mail room and networking closets, must be secured. The mail room provides a means for an attacker to deliver a forged memo that seems to be internal (Granger, 2002).

Visitor badges must be given to every person who is not an employee, and must be clearly marked as a visitor. Employees should be trained on areas where visitors have to be escorted, as well as areas where a visitor may be without an escort. The employees must have the authority to challenge visitors, and be allowed to report any suspicious behavior to a specific individual (Arthurs, 2001).

Document and media disposal. Employees must be educated on the importance of shredding any and all documents, and ensuring all media that is no longer needed is destroyed. What the employee may view

as safe may actually be the only thing the social engineer needs to attack the organization. Items such as company directories, calendars, planners, and organizational charts can be prized finds for a social engineer (Granger, 2001). This is why all documents must be shredded, regardless of the user's perception of the safety of the contained information.

For documents and media, such as floppy disks and CDs, a licensed disposal company should be used which gives the organization a certificate of destruction and performs the destruction on-site rather than transporting to a separate facility. The company should provide locked trash bins, where all employees would be required to dispose of their documents. They need to be trained to never place documents in a trash can.

General training. Employees must be educated on spotting social engineering attacks, whether through the phone, physically, or spotting someone dumpster diving. They must have specific steps to follow and people to contact to report an incident (Granger, 2002), rather than keeping them private. Many times when an employee falls victim to an attack, they do not tell anyone about it out of fear of ridicule or punishment (Mitnick, 2002). In order to ensure incidents are reported, the employee must feel safe and free from punishment, otherwise they will be more inclined to not report the incident.

The program needs to inform the employee about the organization's policies, as well as the sensitivity of information they give out. This involves personalizing the training to each person and how it applies to them as well as their company (Arthurs, 2001).

Employees must be able to spot and understand emotional social engineering attempts. Frequently, this involves exploiting the employee's natural inclination to help a fellow employee in a time of need (Farber, 2001). Many times this will involve the attacker pretending to have a deadline or other immediate need, and attempts to appeal to the victim's emotions (Mitnick, 2002). The user must understand they have the right to say "no" at any time, and have absolutely no fear of reprimand should the request be legitimate.

The final phase is testing to see whether the training has been understood, and policies are being followed. The testing should be implemented *only* after all employees have been trained. Due to the sensitive nature of social engineering, employees can feel deceived and morale can be hurt from a test (Kabay, 2000).

Once the test has been performed, all employees should meet together to discuss the results of the test without any particular person or department being named (Kabay, 2000). The results of the test can be used to further mold the training program, as well as educating those who participated in the training and creating areas of focus (Coffin, 2003).

All policies and training should have the support of upper management. Employees must understand if they see the CEO of their organization walking down the hallway without his or her badge that they must be challenged without fear of reprimand. Without this, employees may not feel comfortable questioning someone who appears to have authority, and thus may let an intruder roam their premises without any problem. Rather, a reward system should be implemented in the event an employee challenges any member of management. This reinforces that they have the authority and obligation to challenge anyone they see without a badge, further protecting the organization as a whole.

FUTURE RESEARCH

With permission of companies, it would be interesting to put other social engineering methodologies to the test to assess the organizations themselves. Using methods described above, a thorough analysis of multiple organizations could be created and the results compared with other organizations.

An additional area of interest would be how different regions respond to the same type of attack. In 2004, an experiment similar to this one was conducted in the United Kingdom by Claire Sellick, event director for Infosecurity Europe. She found 37 percent of people immediately gave her their password (Kotadia, 2004). This is a much smaller number than the 73 percent, leading to the assumption that different regions can yield different results.

CONCLUSION

The fact that even a single password was gathered shows a distinct need for more training and awareness among users. Having gathered the passwords of 52 percent of those surveyed shows that there is a real threat of social engineering to the corporate environment. A social engineer may need only one username and password in order to gain access to the company's network. After this point, they essentially have free reign, potentially costing the company thousands of dollars per incident (FBI, 2006).

In addition, a stronger emphasis should also be placed on security while students are still in school. Since these are the future employees, they need to have a basic understanding before entering the workforce; otherwise they will become the target of social engineers. They should also feel free to challenge authority if they do not feel comfortable giving out sensitive information. This gives them the ability to enter into a corporate information security training program with a basis of challenging individuals who should not have physical access.

In spite of training, users still voluntarily gave their passwords. These users can end up being the weakest link in a corporate security program, showing a need for a different training strategy since 63 percent of users had participated in a training program within the past year, but 52 percent of those surveyed provided their passwords. The training programs need to have more emphasis on protecting the user's login information, and education on how simple it can be to obtain a password through various social engineering techniques.

Users must be educated in social engineering attacks and have the knowledge to spot and protect against these attacks. They must be given the authority to challenge people they do not believe should have physical access to the company's site. Without the support of management, training programs will fail, and policies will not be followed.

As more and more information becomes digitalized, there needs to be a greater increase in security awareness. This awareness can be the difference between an organization falling victim to a corporate espionage attack, or ensuring their future success.

REFERENCES

Adams, A., & Sasse, M. A. (1999). Users are not the enemy. *Communications of the ACM*, December.

Allen, M. (2006). *Social engineering: A means to violate a computer system.* SANS Reading Room. Retrieved November 3, 2006 from http://www.sans.org/reading_room/whitepapers/engineering/529.php?portal=64b276600d7cb57e57a94e2cf911f2b6

Arthurs, W. (2001). *A proactive defense to social engineering.* SANS Reading Room. Retrieved November 3, 2006 from http://www.sans.org/reading_room/whitepapers/engineering/511.php?portal=64b276600d7cb57e57a94e2cf911f2b6

Ciampa, M. (2005). *Security+ guide to network security fundamentals* (2nd ed.). Boston: Course Technology.

Coffin, B. (2003). *IT takes a thief: Ethical test your defense*. Risk Management. Retrieved October 20, 2006 from http://www.ins.com/WorkArea/showcontent.aspx?id=1311&

Damie, P. (2002). *Social engineering: A tip of the iceberg*. Information Systems Control Journal. Retrieved October 21, 2006 from http://www.isaca.org/Template.cfm?Section=Home&CONTENTID=17032&TEMPLATE=/ContentManagement/ContentDisplay.cfm

Dolan, A. (2004). *Social engineering*. SANS Reading Room. Retrieved November 3, 2006 from http://www.sans.org/reading_room/whitepapers/engineering/1365.php?portal=64b276600d7cb57e57a94e2cf911f2b6

FBI (2006). *2005 computer crime survey*. Retrieved October 30, 2006 from http://mitnicksecurity.com/media0FBI%20Computer%20Crime%20Survey%20Report.pdf

Gragg, D. (2002). *A multi-level defense against social engineering*. SANS Reading Room. Retrieved November 3, 2006 from http://www.sans.org/reading_room/whitepapers/engineering/920.php?portal=64b276600d7cb57e57a94e2cf911f2b6

Granger, S. (2001). *Social engineering fundamentals, Part I: Hacker tactics*. Security Focus. Retrieved October 12, 2006 from http://www.securityfocus.com/infocus/1527

Granger, S. (2002). *Social engineering fundamentals, Part II: Combat strategies*. Security Focus. Retrieved October 12, 2006 from http://www.securityfocus.com/infocus/1533

Ives, B., Walsh, K., & Schneider, H., (2004). The domino effect of password reuse. *Communications of the ACM, 47*(4), 75-78.

Javelin Strategy & Research (2006). *2006 identity fraud survey*. Javelin Strategy & Research. Retrieved November 3, 2006 from http://www.javelinstrategy.com

Kabay, M. E. (2000). *Social engineering simulations*. NetworkWorld. Retrieved November 11, 2006 from http://www.networkworld.com/newsletters/sec/2000/00292157.html

Krutz, R. L., & Vines, R. D. (2001). *The CISSP prep guide*. New York: Wiley Publishing.

Medlin, B. D., Cazier, J. A., & Dave, D. S. (2006). Password security issues on an e-commerce site. In M. Khosrow-Pour (Ed.), *Encyclopedia of e-commerce, e-government, and mobile commerce*. Hershey, PA: Idea Group Reference.

Mitnick, K. (2002). *The art of deception: Controlling the human element of society*. Indianapolis: Wiley Publishing.

Mitnick, K. (2005). *The art of intrusion: The real stories behind the exploits of hackers, intruders, & deceivers*. Indianapolis: Wiley Publishing.

Munir, K. (2004). *New hacking tool: Chocolate*. ZDNet. Retrieved October 13, 2006 from http://news.zdnet.com/2100-1009_22-5195282.html

Zviran, M. & Haga, W. J. (1999). Password security: An empirical study. *Journal of Management Information Systems, 15*(4), 161-185.

KEY TERMS

Authentication: The process of verifying that a person or resource accessing your system is actually how they claim to be.

Access Controls: Controls that restrict access to your business systems to authorized personnel.

Corporate Espionage: The act of covertly obtaining sensitive information on a competing organization. Similar to governments spying on each other, corporations also spy on others.

Dumpster Diving: The act of sifting through discarded items looking for something of value. This can include trash, documents, computer hard drives, or information unintentionally left online.

Hacker: A person trying to break into an information system, either to cause damage, find information or to satisfy their curiosity.

Password: A secret word used to verify a person is authorized to access a system.

Phishing: The art of trying to gain sensitive information through impersonating a legitimate organization and individual interacts with.

Social Engineering: The act of gaining either unauthorized access to a system or sensitive information, such as passwords, through the use of trust and relationship building with those who have access to such information.

Username: The name of a person or object on a system used of identification. Often used with a password for authentication.

Chapter XXXVIII
Data Security for Storage Area Networks

Tom Clark
Brocade Communications, USA

ABSTRACT

Data storage is playing an increasingly visible role in securing application data in the data center. Today virtually all large enterprises and institutions worldwide have implemented networked storage infrastructures to provide high performance input/output (I/O) operations, high availability access, consolidation of storage assets, and data protection and archiving. Storage area networks (SANs) are typically based on Fibre Channel technology and are normally contained within the physical confines of the data center. The security of this physical isolation, however, has proven inadequate to safeguard data from inadvertent or malicious disruption. Both established and emerging Fibre Channel and IP standards are required to secure the storage infrastructure and protect data assets from corruption or misappropriation. This paper provides an overview of storage networking technology and the security mechanisms that have been developed to provide data integrity for data center storage infrastructures.

INTRODUCTION

Security in conventional data communications networks attempts to safeguard data access by implementing both authorization and encryption technologies. Authentication procedures verify that data access between two end points is approved. Encryption ensures that only bona fide senders and receivers will be able to render encrypted data intelligible. Conventional data security techniques are primarily focused on protecting data *in flight*, as it traverses the network from, for example, a server to a workstation. If the data in flight is intercepted, diverted or copied, the security breach may allow unauthorized access to or corruption of sensitive corporate or personal information.

For storage environments, data transactions between servers and storage arrays or tape devices are also vulnerable to in-flight interception. In addition, however, security for storage area networks must provide means to safeguard data *at rest*, that is, after the data is written to disk or tape. This added requirement has generated new security solutions that attempt to protect storage data through its entire cycle of data retrieval and repose. This paper examines the unique characteristics of SANs and security techniques required to safeguard storage assets.

WHY SANs?

Storage area networking is a technology that enables high availability and high performance access between servers and storage devices. First formulated as American National Standards Institute (ANSI) standards in the early 1990s and now widely adopted by all major institutions and enterprises, SANs have displaced earlier storage connections which bound individual storage arrays to individual servers. By placing both servers and storage assets on a dedicated network, it is possible to redirect storage access from one server to another, thus facilitating high availability data access. It also enables administrators to add additional storage capacity without disrupting on-going production.

SAN technology was originally based on the Fibre Channel protocol and transport. Fibre Channel was the first high performance transport to deliver the gigabit speeds required for moving large amounts of storage data. The common analogy differentiating storage networking from conventional LAN and WAN networking is that while LANs and WANs move cars (packets) of data along highway lanes, SANs move freight train loads of data over high performance channels. Today, Fibre Channel SANs can provide 4 Gbps and 10 Gbps performance, while the vast majority of LAN technologies are still implemented at 1 Gbps (Gigabit Ethernet) or 100 Mbps (Fast Ethernet) speeds to workstations, with 10 Gbps links providing the network backbone.

As shown in Figure 1, data center SAN configurations are typically deployed for high availability data access. Each server and storage array is connected to fabric directors or switches for alternate pathing. If an individual link, port or switch fails, servers still have access to their designated storage targets. Fibre Channel directors are designed to provide 99.999 percent availability, or ~ 5.39 minutes of downtime in a given year.

For moderate performance requirements, new IP-based storage network protocols such as iSCSI provide a means to move blocks of storage data over traditional TCP/IP network infrastructures. Given the notorious vulnerability of TCP/IP networks to disruption and latency, however, iSCSI must address the inherent contradiction between the deterministic performance required by storage applications and the indeterministic nature of IP networks. From a security standpoint, iSCSI is the beneficiary of decades of development of IP Security and other IETF standards that provide auxiliary mechanisms to safeguard IP data transport.

Because all applications and data ultimately reside on some form of spinning media, maintaining the high availability and integrity of storage data is fundamental to all IT operations. SANs have generated a wide spectrum of solutions for assuring continuous storage access, including server clustering, failover, point in time data copies, data backup, and disaster recovery. At the same time, SANs have helped reduce operational costs by facilitating consolidation of storage assets (fewer but larger storage arrays) and streamlining backup processes. The end-user value of SAN technology is so clearly established that every major enterprise world-wide is now running its storage data on the basis of a storage area network.

WHERE IS STORAGE SECURITY NEEDED?

Information security has become a top priority for most companies and institutions. According to the Harvard Business Review, computer security breaches cause $17 billion in damages every year. Most of that

Figure 1. A data center SAN provides alternate pathing for high availability

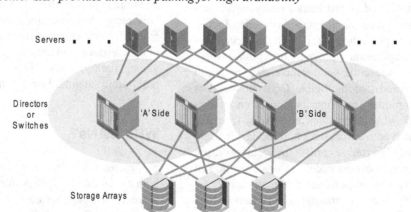